PRINCIPLES OF EXPERT SYSTEMS

INTERNATIONAL COMPUTER SCIENCE SERIES

Consulting editors **A D McGettrick** University of Strathclyde
J van Leeuwen University of Utrecht

SELECTED TITLES IN THE SERIES

POP-11 Programming for Artificial Intelligence *A M Burton and N R Shadbolt*

Logic Programming and Knowledge Engineering *T Amble*

Comparative Programming Languages *L B Wilson and R G Clark*

Clausal Form Logic: An Introduction to the Logic of Computer Reasoning *T Richards*

Software Engineering (3rd Edn) *I Sommerville*

High-Level Languages and their Compilers *D Watson*

Programming in Ada (3rd Edn) *J G P Barnes*

Elements of Functional Programming *C Reade*

Interactive Computer Graphics: Functional, Procedural and Device-Level Methods *P Burger and D Gillies*

Software Development with Modula-2 *D Budgen*

Common Lisp Programming for Artificial Intelligence *T Hasemer and J Domingue*

Program Derivation: The Development of Programs from Specifications *R G Dromey*

Program Design with Modula-2 *S Eisenbach and C Sadler*

Object-Oriented Programming with Simula *B Kirkerud*

Parallel Processing: Principles and Practice *E V Krishnamurthy*

Real-Time Systems and Their Programming Languages *A Burns and A Wellings*

Programming for Artificial Intelligence: Methods, Tools and Applications *W Kreutzer and B J McKenzie*

FORTRAN 77 Programming: With an Introduction to the Fortran 90 Standard (2nd Edn) *T M R Ellis*

The Programming Process: An Introduction Using VDM and Pascal *J T Latham, V J Bush and I D Cottam*

Prolog Programming for Artificial Intelligence (2nd Edn) *I Bratko*

Logic for Computer Science *S Reeves and M Clarke*

Introduction to Expert Systems (2nd Edn) *P Jackson*

Computer Architecture *M De Blasi*

PRINCIPLES OF EXPERT SYSTEMS

PETER LUCAS

Centre for Mathematics and Computer Science, Amsterdam
and Department of Medical Physics and Informatics, University of Amsterdam

LINDA VAN DER GAAG

Centre for Mathematics and Computer Science, Amsterdam
and Department of Computer Science, University of Utrecht

ADDISON-WESLEY
PUBLISHING
COMPANY

Wokingham, England · Reading, Massachusetts · Menlo Park, California · New York
Don Mills, Ontario · Amsterdam · Bonn · Sydney · Singapore
Tokyo · Madrid · San Juan · Milan · Paris · Mexico City · Seoul · Taipei

Cover designed by Crayon Design of Henley-on-Thames
Typeset by Times Graphics, Singapore.
Printed in Great Britain by Mackays of Chatham plc, Chatham, Kent.

First printed 1991.

British Library Cataloguing in Publication Data
Lucas, Peter
Principles of expert systems.
1. Expert systems
I. Title II. Gaag, Linda van der
006.33

ISBN 0–201–41640–9

Library of Congress Cataloging in Publication Data
Lucas, Peter
Principles of expert systems / Peter Lucas and Linda van der Gaag.
p. cm. — (International computer science series)
Includes bibliographical references.
ISBN 0–201–41640–9
1. Expert systems (Computer science) I. Gaag, Linda van der.
II. Title. III. Series.
QA76.76.E95L83 1990
006.3′3—dc20 90–32375
CIP

Foreword

Principles of Expert Systems by Peter Lucas and Linda van der Gaag is a *textbook* on expert systems. In this respect, the book does not distinguish itself from many other, serious textbooks in computer science. It does, however, distinguish itself from many books on expert systems. The book's aim is not to leave the reader dumbfounded by the authors' knowledge of a topic that has aroused wide interest. Neither is the aim to present a bird's-eye view of topical and sometimes modish matters by means of a sloppy review of 'existing' expert systems and their (supposed) applications. Its real aim is to treat in a thorough way the more or less accepted formalisms and methods that place expert systems on a firm footing.

In its first decade, research in artificial intelligence – performed by a relatively small group of researchers – remained restricted to investigations into universal methods for problem solving. In the 1970s, partly due to the advent of cheaper and faster computers with large memory capacity, attention shifted to methods for problem solving in which the focus was not on smart algorithms, but rather on the representation and use of knowledge necessary to solve particular problems. This approach has led to the development of expert systems, programs in which there is a clear distinction between domain-specific knowledge and general knowledge for problem solving. An important stimulant for doing this type of research has been the Japanese initiative aimed at the development of fifth generation computer systems, and the reactions to this initiative by regional and national research programmes in Europe and the United States.

An expert system is meant to embody the expertise of a human expert involved in a particular field, in such a way that non-expert users, looking for advice in that field, have the expert's knowledge at their disposal when questioning the system. An important feature of expert systems is that they are able to explain to the user the line of reasoning which led to the solution of a problem or the desired advice. In many domains the number of available experts is limited, so it may be expensive to consult an expert and experts are not always available. Preserving their knowledge is useful, if only for teaching or training purposes. On the other hand, although they are not always referred to as experts, in every organization there are employees who possess specialized knowledge, obtained as the fruit of long experience, that is often very difficult to transfer from one person to another. Recording this knowledge allows us to use computers in domains where human knowledge, experience, intuition and heuristics are essential. From this, one may not conclude that it is not useful or possible to offer also 'shallow' knowledge, as available in medical, juridical or technical handbooks, to users of expert systems. With these applications it is perhaps more appropriate to speak of knowledge systems or knowledge-based systems than of expert systems. Nor should it be excluded that knowledge in an expert system is based on a scientific theory or on functional or causal models belonging to a particular domain.

Advances in research in expert systems and increasing knowledge derived from experience gained from designing, implementing and using expert systems made it necessary for the authors of this book to choose from the large quantity of topics that can be treated in a textbook. For example, in this book there is no attempt to cover knowledge acquisition, the development of tools for automatic knowledge acquisition, nor the many software engineering aspects of building expert systems. Neither is any attention paid to the use of more fundamental knowledge models (such as causal or functional models) of the problem domain on which an expert system can fall back if it turns out that heuristic reasoning is not sufficient, nor to the automatic conversion of deep, theoretical knowledge to heuristic rules.

Researchers, and those who are otherwise involved in the development of expert systems, set up expectations. It is possible that never before in computer science has so much time been devoted and so much attention been paid to a single topic than during the past years to expert systems. One might think that expert systems have found widespread commercial and non-commercial applications. This hardly is the case. The development of practical expert systems – systems not just of interest to a small group of researchers – turns out to be less straightforward than has sometimes been suggested or has appeared from example programs. Not being able to satisfy the high expectations created may therefore lead to an 'AI winter': the collapse of the confidence that present-day research in artificial intelligence will lead to a widespread use of expert systems in business and industry. Therefore, it should be appreciated that in this book the authors confine themselves to the present-day 'hard core' of their speciality and have not let themselves be tempted to include all sorts of undeniably interesting but not yet proven ideas which one may come across in recent literature. The material presented in this book provides the reader with the knowledge and the insight to read this literature and it gives a useful start for participating in research and development in expert and knowledge-based systems. The reader of this book will be convinced that the principles and techniques discussed here constitute a lasting addition to the already available arsenal of principles and techniques of traditional computer science.

Both authors have gained practical experience in designing and building expert systems. In addition, they have thorough knowledge of the general principles underlying knowledge-based systems. Add their undeniable didactic qualities and we have the right people to write a carefully thought-out textbook on expert systems. Because of its profundity, its consistent style and its balanced choice of subjects this book is a relief from the many superficial books that are presented as introductions to expert systems. It is not always easy reading, but the study of this book will bring a deeper understanding of the principles of expert systems than can be obtained by reading many others. It is up to the reader to benefit from this.

Anton Nijholt
Professor of Computer Science

Twente University of Technology
The Netherlands

Preface

This book is an introductory textbook at undergraduate level, covering the subject of expert systems for students of computer science. The major motive for writing this book was a course on expert systems given by the first author to third and fourth year undergraduate computer science students at the University of Amsterdam for the first time in 1986. Although at that time a large number of books on expert systems was already available, none of these was considered to be suitable for teaching the subject to a computer science audience. The present book was written in an attempt to fill this gap.

The central topics in this book are formalisms for the representation and manipulation of knowledge in the computer: logic, production rules, semantic nets, frames and formalisms for plausible reasoning. The choice for the formalisms discussed in this book has been motivated on the one hand by the requirement that at least the formalisms which nowadays are of fundamental importance to the area of expert systems must be covered, and, on the other hand, that the formalisms which have been in use for considerable time and have laid the foundation of current research into more advanced methods should also be treated. We have in particular paid attention to those formalisms which have been shown to be of practical importance for building expert systems. As a consequence, several other subjects, for example truth maintenance systems and non-standard logics, are not covered or are merely briefly touched upon. These topics have only become a subject of investigation in recent years, and their importance to the area of expert systems was not clear at the time of writing this book. Similarly, in selecting example computer systems for presentation in the book, our selection criterion has been more the way in which such a system illustrates the principles dealt with in the book than recency. Similar observations underlie our leaving out the subject of methodologies for building expert systems; although this is a very active research area, with many competing theories, we feel that none of these is as yet stable enough to justify treatment in a textbook. On the whole, we expect that our choice renders the book less subject to trends in expert system research than if we had for example included an overview of the most recent expert systems, tools, or methodologies.

It is hardly possible to develop an intuition concerning the subjects of knowledge representation and manipulation if these principles are not illustrated by clear and easy to understand examples. We have therefore tried to restrict ourselves as far as possible to one problem area, from which almost all examples have been taken: a very small part of the area of cardiovascular medicine. Although they are not completely serious, our examples are more akin to real-life problems solved by expert systems than the examples usually encountered in literature on knowledge representation. If desirable, however, the chosen problem domain can be supplemented or replaced by any other problem domain.

Most of the principles of expert systems have been worked out in small programs written either in PROLOG or in LISP, or sometimes in both programming languages. These programs are mainly used to illustrate the material treated in the text, and are intended to demonstrate various programming techniques in building expert systems; we have not attempted to make them as efficient as possible, nor have we included extensive user interfaces. We feel that students of artificial intelligence and expert systems should actively master at least one of the programming languages PROLOG and LISP, and also be able to understand programs written in the other language. For those not sufficiently familiar with one or both of these programming languages, two introductory appendices have been included covering enough of them to help the reader to understand the programs discussed in the book. We emphasize that all programs are treated in separate sections; a reader interested only in the principles of expert systems may therefore simply skip these sections.

The book can serve several purposes in teaching a course on expert systems. Experience has taught us that the entire book takes about 25 weeks, two hours a week, of teaching to be covered when supplemented with small student projects. For the typical 16 week course of two hours a week, one may adopt one of the following three frameworks as a point of departure for a course, depending on the audience to whom the subject is taught:

(1) *A course covering both theory and practice of building expert systems.* The lectures may be organized using sections of the book as follows: 1, 2.1, 2.2, 3.1, 3.2.1, 6.1, 3.2.4, 7.1, 4.1, 4.2.1, 4.2.2, 4.2.5, 4.3.1, 5.1, 5.2, 5.3, 5.4, 5.5, 5.6, 6.4, 7.2, 7.3. If some time remains, more of Chapter 2 or Chapter 4 may be covered. In this one-semester 16 week course, none of the LISP or PROLOG programs in the text is treated as part of the lectures; rather, the

students are asked to extend one or two of the programs dealt with in the book in small projects. Several exercises in the text give suggestions for such projects. It may also be a good idea to let the students experiment with an expert system shell by having them build a small knowledge base. The study of OPS5 in Section 7.1 may for example be supplemented by practical lessons using the OPS5 interpreter.

(2) *A course emphasizing practical aspects of building expert systems.* The lectures may be organized using sections of the book as follows: 1, 3.1.1, 3.1.2, 3.1.3, 3.2, 3.3, 6.1, 6.2, 6.3, 7.1, 2.1, 2.2, 4.1.1, 4.1.2, 4.2, 5.1, 5.2, 5.4, 5.5, 6.4, 7.2, 7.3. In this case, as much of logic is treated as is necessary to enable the students to grasp the material in Chapter 4. Chapter 2 may even be skipped if the students are already acquainted on a conceptual level with first-order predicate logic: the technical details of logic do not receive attention in this course. At least some of the programs in the text are treated in the classroom. Furthermore, one of the development methodologies for expert systems described in the recent literature may be briefly discussed in the course. It is advisable to let the students build a knowledge base for a particular problem domain, using one of the PROLOG or LISP programs presented in the book or a commercially available expert system shell.

(3) *A course dealing with the theory of expert systems.* In this course, more emphasis is placed on logic as a knowledge-representation language in expert systems than in courses 1 and 2. The lectures may be organized using sections of the book as follows: 1, 2, 3.1, 3.2, 4.1, 4.2.1, 4.2.2, 4.2.5, 4.2.7, 4.3, 5, 6.1, 7.3. It is advisable to let the students perform some experiments with the programs discussed in Chapter 2, in particular with the LISP program implementing SLD resolution in Sections 2.8 and 2.9. Additional experiments may be carried out using the OTTER resolution-based theorem prover, which can be obtained from the Argonne National Laboratory. This theorem prover may be used to experiment with logic knowledge bases in the same style as the one discussed in Section 2.9.

For the reader mainly interested in the subjects of knowledge representation and automated reasoning, it suffices to read Chapters 1–5, where sections dealing with implementation techniques can be skipped. For those primarily interested in the practical aspects of expert systems, Chapters 1 and 3, Sections 4.2, 5.1, 5.2, 5.3 and 5.4, and Chapters 6 and 7 are of main importance. For a study of the role of logic in expert systems, one may read Chapter 2 and Sections 3.1, 4.1.3, 4.2.1 and 4.2.2, which deal with the relationship of logic to other knowledge-representation formalisms. Those interested in production systems should study Chapters 3 and 6, and Section 7.1. Semantic nets and frame systems are dealt with in Chapter 4 and Sections 7.2 and 7.3. Chapter 5 is a rather comprehensive treatise on methods for plausible reasoning. The dependency between the various sections in the book is given in the dependency graph below.

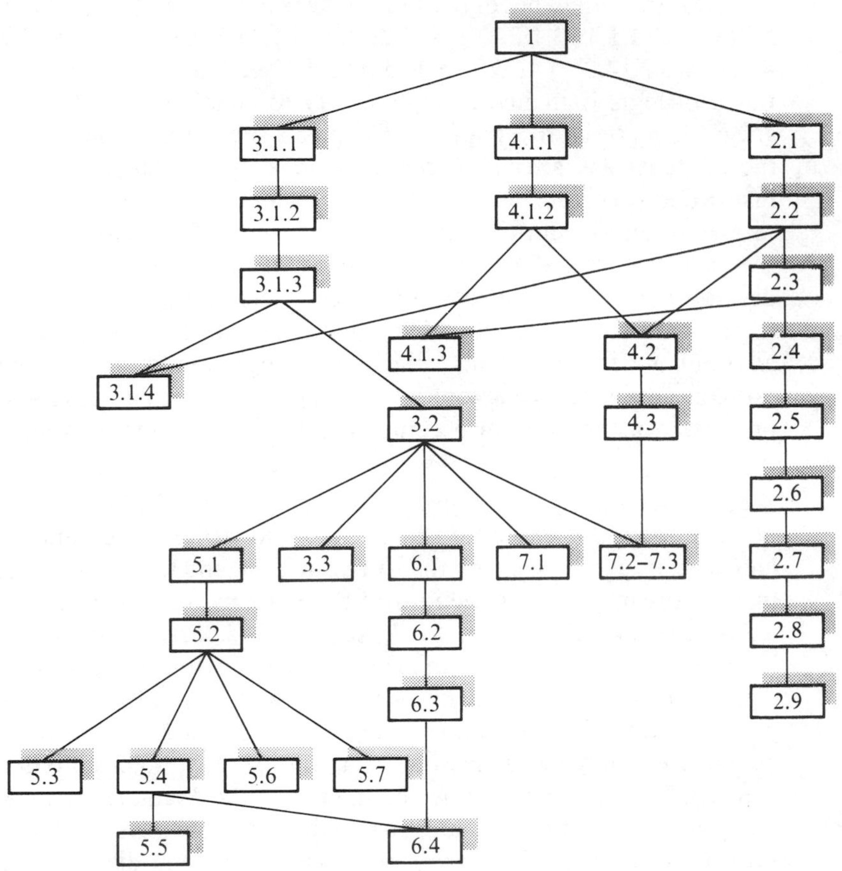

Dependency of sections.

Acknowledgements

We would like to take this opportunity to thank several people who read drafts of the manuscript. We would like to thank the reviewers of Addison-Wesley who suggested several improvements to the original text.

We would especially like to thank Simon Plumtree who displayed so much patience during the evolution of the book.

Peter Lucas and
Linda van der Gaag

Centre for Mathematics and Computer Science
November 1989

Contents

Trademark notice

1 Introduction

During the past decade, interest in the results of *artificial intelligence* research has been growing to an increasing extent. In particular, the area of *knowledge-based systems*, one of the first areas of artificial intelligence to be commercially fruitful, has received a lot of attention. The phrase knowledge-based system is generally employed to indicate information systems in which some symbolic representation of human knowledge is applied, usually in a way resembling human reasoning. Of these knowledge-based systems, expert systems have been the most successful at present. *Expert systems* are systems which are capable of offering solutions to specific problems in a given domain or which are able to give advice, both in a way and at a level comparable to that of experts in the field. Building expert systems for specific application domains has even become a separate subject known as *knowledge engineering*.

The problems in the fields for which expert systems are being developed are those that require considerable human expertise for their solution. Examples of such problem domains are medical diagnosis of disease, financial advice and products design. Most present-day expert systems are capable of dealing only with restricted problem areas. Nevertheless, even in highly restricted domains, expert systems usually need large amounts of knowledge to arrive at a performance comparable to that of human experts in the field.

In this chapter, we review the historical roots of expert systems in the broader field of artificial intelligence, and briefly discuss several classical examples. In addition, the basic principles of expert systems are introduced and related to the subsequent chapters of the book, where these principles are treated in significant depth. The chapter concludes with a description of a problem domain from which almost all examples presented in this book have been selected.

1.1 Expert systems and AI

Although the digital computer was originally designed to be a number processor, even in the early days of its creation there was a small core of researchers engaged in non-numerical applications. The efforts of these researchers eventually led to what has been known since the Dartmouth Summer Seminar in 1956 as artificial intelligence (AI), the area of computer science concerned with systems producing results for which human behaviour would seem necessary.

The early areas of attention in the 1950s were *theorem proving* and *problem solving*. In both fields, the developed computer programs are characterized by being based on complex algorithms which have a general solving capability, independent of a specific problem domain, and which furthermore operate on problems posed in rather simple primitives.

Theorem proving is the field concerned with proving theorems automatically from a given set of axioms by a computer. The theorems and axioms are expressed in logic, and logical inference rules are applied to the given set of axioms in order to prove the theorems. The first program that actually constructed a mathematical proof of a theorem in number theory was developed by M. Davis as early as 1954. Nevertheless, the major breakthrough in theorem proving did not come until halfway through the 1960s. Only after the introduction of an inference rule called resolution did theorem proving become interesting from a practical point of view. Further progress in the field during the 1970s came from the development of several refinements of the original resolution principle.

Researchers in the field of problem solving focused on the development of computer systems with a general capability for solving different types of problems. The best known system is GPS (General Problem Solver), developed by A. Newell, H.A. Simon and J.C. Shaw. A given problem is represented in terms of an initial state, a wished-for final state and a set of transitions to transform states into new states.

Given such a representation by means of states and operators, GPS generates a sequence of transitions that transform the initial state into the given final state when applied in order. GPS has not been very successful. First, representing a non-trivial problem in terms which could be processed by GPS proved to be no easy task. Secondly, GPS turned out to be rather inefficient. Since GPS was a general problem solver, specific knowledge of the problem at hand could not be exploited in choosing a transition on a given state, even if such knowledge indicated that a specific transition would lead to the solution of the problem more efficiently. In each step GPS examined all possible transitions, thus yielding an exponential time complexity. Although the success of GPS as a problem solver has been limited, GPS initiated a significant shift of attention in artificial intelligence research towards more specialized systems. This shift in attention from general problem solvers to specialized systems in which the reasoning process could be monitored using knowledge of the given problem is generally viewed as a breakthrough in artificial intelligence.

For problems arising in practice in many domains, there are no well-defined solutions in the literature. The knowledge an expert in the field has is generally not laid down in clear definitions or unambiguous algorithms, but merely exists in rules of thumb and facts learned by experience, called *heuristics*, so the knowledge incorporated in an expert system is highly domain dependent. The success of expert systems results mainly from their capability for representing heuristic knowledge and techniques, and for making these applicable for computers. Generally, expert systems are able to comment on the solutions and advice they have given, based on the knowledge present in the system. Moreover, expert systems offer the possibility for integrating new knowledge with the knowledge that is already present, in a flexible manner.

1.2 Some examples

The first expert systems were developed as early as the late 1960s. However, it took until the 1970s before the research actually started on a large scale. The early expert systems mostly concerned the field of medical diagnosis. The best-known expert system in medicine, developed in the 1970s, is *MYCIN*. The development of this expert system took place at Stanford University; E.H. Shortliffe, in particular, played an important role in its development. The MYCIN system is able to assist internists in the diagnosis and treatment of a number of infectious diseases, in particular meningitis and bacterial septicaemia. When a patient shows the signs of such an infectious disease, a culture of blood and urine is usually made to determine the bacterial species that causes the infection. Generally, it takes 24–48 hours before the laboratory results become known. In the above-mentioned infectious diseases, however, the physician will have to start treatment before these results are available, because otherwise the disease may progress and actually cause the death of the patient. Given the patient data that are available to the system but which are apt to be incomplete and inexact, MYCIN gives an interim indication of the organisms that are most likely to be the cause of the infection. Given this indication, MYCIN advises the administration of a number of drugs that should control the disease by suppressing the indicated organisms. The interaction of the prescribed drugs with each other and with other drugs the patient already takes, and possible toxic drug reactions are also taken into account. Moreover, MYCIN is able to comment on the diagnosis it has arrived at, and on the prescription of the drugs. The MYCIN system clearly left its mark on the expert systems that have been developed since. Even now, this expert system and its derivatives are sources of ideas concerning the representation and manipulation of medical knowledge. The MYCIN system has also given an important impulse to the development of similar expert systems in fields other than medicine.

The development of the *INTERNIST-I* system started early in the 1970s as well. The system is still being developed by H.E. Pople and J.D. Myers at Pittsburgh University. Later in their research, Pople and Myers renamed the system *CADUCEUS*. One of the objectives of the INTERNIST/CADUCEUS project is the study of models for diagnosing diseases in internal medicine. In internal medicine several hundreds of different diseases are discerned. An internist not only has to bear in mind all the clinical pictures of these diseases during the diagnostic process, but also has to take into account the possible combinations of symptoms and signs that can be caused by the interaction of several diseases present in a patient at the same time. The number of diseases in internal medicine, and the possible combinations of clinical signs and symptoms, is so large that it is not possible to consider them one by one. INTERNIST/CADUCEUS therefore focuses on those diseases that are most likely, given the symptoms, clinical signs, and results of laboratory tests obtained from the patient.

To a growing extent, expert systems are also being developed in technical fields. One of the first systems with which the phrase expert system has been associated is *HEURISTIC DENDRAL*. The DENDRAL project commenced in 1965 at Stanford University. The system was developed by J. Lederberg, an organic chemist (and Nobel prize winner in chemistry), in conjunction with E.A. Feigenbaum and B.G. Buchanan, both well-known research scientists in artificial intelligence. The HEURISTIC DENDRAL system offers assistance in the field of organic chemistry in determining the structural formula of a chemical compound that has been isolated from a given sample. In determining a structural formula, information concerning the chemical formula, such as C_4H_9OH for butanol, and the source the compound has been taken from is used as well as information that has been obtained by subjecting the compound to physical, chemical and spectrometric tests. The method employed is called *generate-and-test*, since the system first generates all plausible molecular structures as hypotheses, which are subsequently tested against the observed data. The original DENDRAL algorithm was developed by J. Lederberg for generating all possible isomers of a chemical compound. HEURISTIC DENDRAL contains a subsystem, the so-called Structure Generator, which implements the DENDRAL algorithm, but in addition incorporates various heuristic constraints on possible structures, thus reducing the number of alternatives to be considered by the remainder of the system. In particular, mass spectrometry is useful for finding the right structural formula. In a mass spectrometer, the compound is bombarded with a beam of electrons in a vacuum, causing the molecule to break up into several smaller charged fragments. These fragments are accelerated within an electrical field, and are deflected in proportion to their mass : charge ratio, using a magnetic field. The fragments that are separated this way cause a pattern called a spectrogram, which is recorded by means of a writing device. Such a spectrogram shows a number of peaks corresponding to the respective mass : charge ratios of the separated fragments. A spectrogram provides significant information about the structure of the original chemical compound. HEURISTIC DENDRAL helps in interpreting the patterns in a spectrogram. To this end, another subsystem of HEURISTIC DENDRAL, called the Predictor, suggests expected mass spectrograms for each molecular structure generated by the Structure Generator. Each expected mass spectrogram is then tested against the mass spectrogram observed using some measure of similarity for comparison; this has been implemented in the last part of the system, the Evaluation Function. Usually, more than one molecular structure matches the pattern found in the spectrogram. Therefore, the system usually produces more than one answer, ordered by the amount of evidence favouring them.

XCON, previously called *R1*, is an expert system able to configure VAX, PDP11 and μVAX computer systems from Digital Equipment Corporation (DEC). DEC offers the customer a wide choice in components when purchasing computer equipment, so that each client can be provided with a custom-made system. Given the customer's order a configuration is made, possibly showing that a specific component has to be replaced by another equivalent component, or that a certain component has to be added in order to arrive at a fully operational system. The problem is not so much that the information is incomplete or inexact but merely that the information is subject to rapid change. Moreover, configuring a computer system requires considerable skill and effort. In the late 1970s, DEC in conjunction with J. McDermott from Carnegie-Mellon University commenced the development of XCON. XCON has been fully operational since 1981. At present, XCON is supplemented with *XSEL*, a system that assists DEC agents in drawing up orders.

The expert systems mentioned above are classics. Inspired by their success, many more expert systems have been constructed since the end of the 1970s. The systems have also led to the construction of various direct derivatives. For example, the MYCIN system has been redesigned to the NEOMYCIN system, in which the various diagnostic tasks are distinguished more explicitly. HEURISTIC DENDRAL has been elaborated further by incorporating improved subsystems for generating and testing plausible molecular structures. Moreover, a system capable of learning heuristics from example has been developed, called METADENDRAL, to ease the transfer of domain knowledge for use in HEURISTIC DENDRAL. In the suggested reading at the end of this chapter, several more recent expert systems are briefly discussed.

1.3 Separating knowledge and inference

In the early years, expert systems were usually written in a high-level programming language. LISP, in particular, was frequently chosen for the implementation language. When using a high-level programming language as an expert system building tool, however, one has to pay a disproportionate amount of attention to the implementational aspects of the system, which have nothing to do with the field to be modelled. Moreover, the expert knowledge of the field and the algorithms for applying this knowledge automatically will be highly interwoven and not easily separated. This led to systems that, once constructed, were practically unadaptable to changing views on the field of concern. Expert knowledge however has a dynamic nature: knowledge and experience are continuously subject to change. Awareness of these properties has led to the view that the explicit separation of the algorithms for applying the highly specialized knowledge from the knowledge itself is highly desirable if not mandatory for developing expert systems. This fundamental insight for the development of present-day expert systems is formulated in the following equation, sometimes called the paradigm of expert system design:

$$\textit{expert system} = \textit{knowledge} + \textit{inference}$$

Consequently, an expert system typically comprises the following two essential components:

- a *knowledge base* capturing the domain-specific knowledge, and
- an *inference engine* consisting of algorithms for manipulating the knowledge represented in the knowledge base.

Nowadays, an expert system is rarely written in a high-level programming language. It is frequently constructed in a special, restricted environment, called an *expert system shell*. An example of such an environment is the well-known *EMYCIN* (Essential MYCIN) system that originated from MYCIN by stripping it of its knowledge concerning infectious disease. Recently, several more general tools for building expert systems, more like special-purpose programming languages, have become available, where again such a separation between knowledge and inference is enforced. These systems will be called *expert system builder tools* in this book.

The domain-specific knowledge is laid down in the knowledge base using a special *knowledge-representation formalism*. In an expert system shell or an expert system builder tool, one or more knowledge-representation formalisms are predefined for encoding the domain knowledge. Furthermore, a corresponding inference engine is present which is capable of manipulating the knowledge represented in such a formalism. In developing an actual expert system only the domain-specific knowledge has to be provided and expressed in the knowledge-representation formalism. Several advantages arise from the fact that a knowledge base can be developed separately from the inference engine; for instance, a knowledge base can be developed and refined stepwise, and errors and inadequacies can easily be remedied without making major changes in the program text necessary. Explicit separation of knowledge and inference has the further advantage that a given knowledge base can be substituted by a knowledge base on another subject, thus producing quite a different expert system.

Developing a specific expert system is done by consulting various *knowledge sources*, such as human experts, textbooks, and databases. Building an expert system is a task requiring highly developed skills; the person performing this task is called the *knowledge engineer*. The process of collecting and structuring knowledge in a problem domain is called *knowledge acquisition*. In particular, if the knowledge is obtained by interviewing domain experts, we speak of *knowledge elicitation*. Part of the work of a knowledge engineer concerns the selection of a suitable knowledge-representation formalism for presenting the domain knowledge to the computer in an encoded form.

We now present a short overview of the subjects which will be dealt with in this book. Representing the knowledge that is to be used in the process of problem solving has for a long time been an underestimated issue in artificial intelligence. Only in the early 1970s was it recognized as an issue of importance and a separate area of research called *knowledge representation* came into being. There are various prerequisites to a knowledge-representation formalism before it may be considered to be suitable for encoding domain knowledge. A suitable knowledge-representation formalism should:

- have sufficient expressive power for encoding the particular domain knowledge;
- possess a clean semantic basis, such that the meaning of the knowledge present in the knowledge base is easy to grasp, especially by the user;
- permit efficient algorithmic interpretation;
- allow for explanation and justification of the solutions obtained by showing why certain questions were asked of the user, and how certain conclusions were drawn.

Part of these conditions concerns the form (*syntax*) of a knowledge-representation formalism; others concern its meaning (*semantics*). Unfortunately, it turns out that there is not a single knowledge-representation formalism which meets all of the requirements mentioned. In particular, the issues of expressive power of a formalism and its efficient interpretation are conflicting. However, as we shall see in the following chapters, by restricting the expressive power of a formalism (in such a way that the domain knowledge can still be represented adequately), we often arrive at a formalism that does indeed permit efficient interpretation.

From the proliferation of ideas that arose in the early years, three knowledge-representation formalisms have emerged which at present still receive a lot of attention:

- *Logic*
- *Production rules*
- *Semantic nets* and *frames*

In the three subsequent chapters, we shall deal with the question of how knowledge can be represented using these respective knowledge-representation formalisms.

Associated with each of the knowledge-representation formalisms are specific methods for handling the represented knowledge. Inferring new information from the available knowledge is called *reasoning* or *inference*. With the availability of the first digital computers, automated reasoning in logic became one of the first subjects of research, yielding results which concerned proving theorems from mathematics. However, in this field, the immanent conflict between the expressiveness of the logic required for representing mathematical problems and its efficient interpretation was soon encountered. Sufficiently efficient algorithms were lacking for applying logic in a broader context. In 1965, though, J.A. Robinson formulated a general inference rule, known as the *resolution principle*, which made automated theorem proving more feasible. This principle served as the basis for the field of logic programming and the programming language PROLOG. In logic programming, logic is used for the representation of the problem to be solved; the logical specification can then be executed by an interpreter based on resolution. Some attempts were made in the 1960s, for example by C.C. Green, to use logic as a knowledge-representation formalism in fields other than mathematics. At that time, these theorem-proving systems were known as *question-answering systems*; they may now be viewed as early logic-based expert systems. In the classical expert systems, however, a choice was made for more specialized and restricted knowledge-representation formalisms for encoding domain knowledge. Consequently, logic has seldom been used directly as a knowledge-representation formalism for building expert systems (although many expert systems have been developed using PROLOG). On the other hand, as we shall see, thinking of the other knowledge-representation formalisms as some special forms of logic often aids in the understanding of their meaning, and makes many of their peculiarities more evident than would otherwise be the case. We therefore feel that a firm basis in logic helps the knowledge engineer to understand building expert systems, even if some other formalism is employed for their actual construction. In Chapter 2 we pay attention to the representation of knowledge in logic and to automated reasoning with logical formulas; it will also be indicated how logic can be used for building an expert system.

Since the late 1960s, considerable effort in artificial intelligence research was spent on developing knowledge-representation formalisms other than logic, resulting in the above-mentioned production rules and frames. For each of these formalisms, special inference methods have been developed which on occasion closely resemble logical inference. Usually, two basic types of inference are discerned. The phrases *top-down inference* and *goal-directed inference* are used to denote the type of inference in which, given some initial goal, subgoals are generated by employing the knowledge in the knowledge base until such subgoals can be reached using the available data. The second type of inference is called *bottom-up inference* or *data-driven inference*. When applying this type of inference, new information is derived from the available data and the knowledge in the knowledge base. This process is repeated until it is no longer possible to derive new information. The distinction between top-down inference and bottom-up inference is most explicitly made in reasoning with production rules, although the two types of reasoning are distinguished in the context of the other knowledge-representation formalisms as well. The production rule formalism and its associated reasoning methods are the topics of Chapter 3.

Chapter 4 is concerned with the third major approach in knowledge representation: semantic nets and frames. These knowledge representation schemes are characterized by a hierarchical structure for storing information. Since semantic nets and frames have several properties in common and the semantic net generally is viewed as the predecessor of the frame formalism, these formalisms are dealt with in one chapter. The method used for the manipulation of knowledge represented in semantic nets and frames is called *inheritance*.

As we have noted before, expert systems are used to solve real-life problems which do not have a predefined solution to be found in the relevant literature. Generally, the knowledge that is explicitly available on the subject is incomplete or uncertain. Nevertheless, a human expert often can arrive at a sound solution to the given problem using such deficient knowledge. Consequently, expert systems research aims at building systems capable of handling incomplete and uncertain information as well as human experts can. Several models for reasoning with uncertainty have been developed. Some of these will be discussed in Chapter 5.

The inference engine of a typical expert system shell is part of a so-called *consultation system*. The consultation system further comprises a *user interface* for interaction with the user, mostly in the form of question-answering sessions. Furthermore, the user of the expert system and the knowledge engineer are provided with a variety of facilities for investigating the contents of the knowledge base and the reasoning behaviour of the system. The *explanation facilities* offer the possibility of asking at any moment during the course of the *consultation* of the knowledge base *how* certain conclusions were arrived at, *why* a specific question is asked, or *why* other conclusions have *not* been drawn. By using the *trace facilities* available in the consultation system, the reasoning behaviour of the system can be followed one inference step at a time during the consultation. It turns out that most of these facilities are often more valuable to the knowledge engineer, who applies them mainly for debugging purposes, than to the final user of the system. Chapter 6 deals with these facilities. Figure 1.1 shows the more or less characteristic architecture of an expert system, built using an expert system shell.

We mentioned before that, in addition to expert system shells, we also have the more powerful expert system builder tools for developing knowledge-based systems, and expert systems in particular. Chapter 7 deals with two well-known tools: OPS5, a special-purpose programming language designed for developing production systems, and LOOPS, a multiparadigm programming environment for expert systems supporting object-oriented programming among other programming paradigms. Chapter 7 also discusses CENTAUR, a dedicated expert system in which several knowledge-representation schemes and reasoning methods are combined.

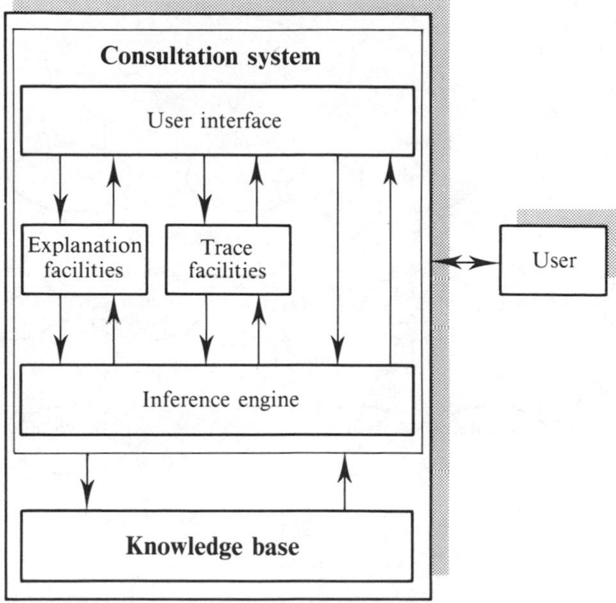

Figure 1.1 Global architecture of an expert system.

This book discusses a number of programs written in LISP and PROLOG to illustrate several implementation techniques for developing an expert system builder tool or shell. For those not familiar with one or both of these languages, Appendix A provides an introduction to PROLOG, and Appendix B introduces LISP.

1.4 A problem domain

In each of the three subsequent chapters, a specific knowledge-representation formalism and its associated inference method will be treated. When discussing these different knowledge-representation formalisms, where possible, examples will be drawn from one medical problem domain: the human cardiovascular system. To this purpose, some aspects of this domain will be introduced here.

The cardiovascular system consists of the heart and a large connected network of blood vessels. The blood vessels are subdivided into three categories: the arteries, the capillaries and the veins. These categories are further subdivided as shown in Figure 1.2. The aorta, the brachial artery and vein, and the ulnar artery are all examples of specific

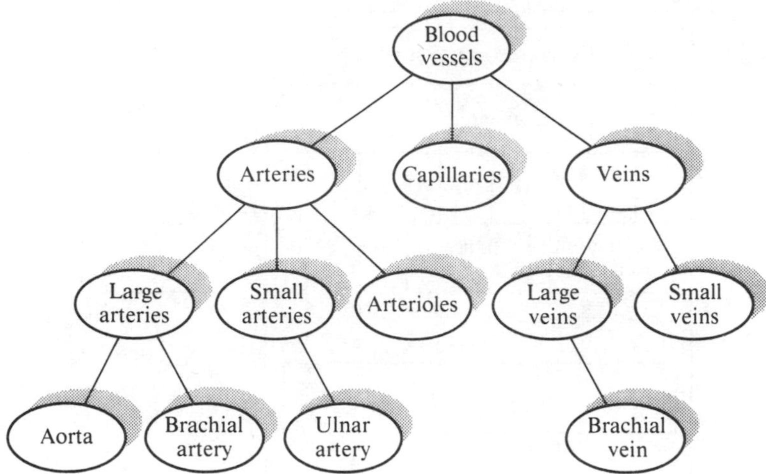

Figure 1.2 Classification of blood vessels.

blood vessels. An artery transfers blood from the heart to the capillaries in the tissues and is distinguished from other vessels by its thick wall containing a thick layer of smooth muscle cells. In most cases, an artery contains blood having a high oxygen level. Contrary to the arteries, veins transfer blood from the capillaries in the tissues back to the heart. They have a relatively thin wall containing fewer muscular fibres than arteries but more fibrous connective tissue. The blood contained in veins is usually oxygen-poor.

The mean blood pressure in arteries is relatively high. For example, the mean blood pressure in the aorta is about 100 mmHg and the mean blood pressure in the ulnar artery is about 90 mmHg. Within the veins a considerably lower blood pressure is maintained. Table 1.1 summarizes some blood pressure values for different portions of the cardiovascular system. Examples of exceptions to the classification of blood vessels just discussed are the pulmonary arteries. These arteries transfer blood from the heart to the lungs and have a thick muscular coat. Because of these characteristics these vessels have been classified as arteries. However, the pulmonary arteries transfer oxygen-poor blood and the mean blood pressure is rather low (13 mmHg), which is, however, still higher than the blood pressure maintained in the pulmonary veins.

Table 1.2 indicates the diameters of blood vessels belonging to various categories. For example the aorta, the largest artery, has a diameter of 2.5 cm. The percentage of the total blood volume contained in the different portions of the vascular system is shown in Table 1.3. The heart contains another 7% of the total blood volume. The way the

Table 1.1 The mean blood pressure for some categories of blood vessels.

Category	*Mean blood pressure (mmHg)*
Arteries	40–100
Large arteries	90–100
Small arteries	80–90
Arterioles	40–80
Veins	<10

cardiovascular system operates is often explained by using the mechanical analogue of a hydraulic system composed of a pump (the heart), a collection of interconnected conduits (the blood vessels), and a container connected to the pump (the pressurization system), which is filled with water (blood).

Table 1.2 Diameters of different blood-vessel categories.

Category	*Diameter*
Large arteries	1–2.5 cm
Small arteries	0.4 cm
Arterioles	30 μm
Large veins	1.5–3 cm
Small veins	0.5 cm

Table 1.3 Percentage of the total blood volume contained in various vessels.

Category	*Percentage of the total blood volume*
Large arteries	11
Small arteries	7
Arterioles	2
Capillaries	9
Large veins	39
Small veins	25

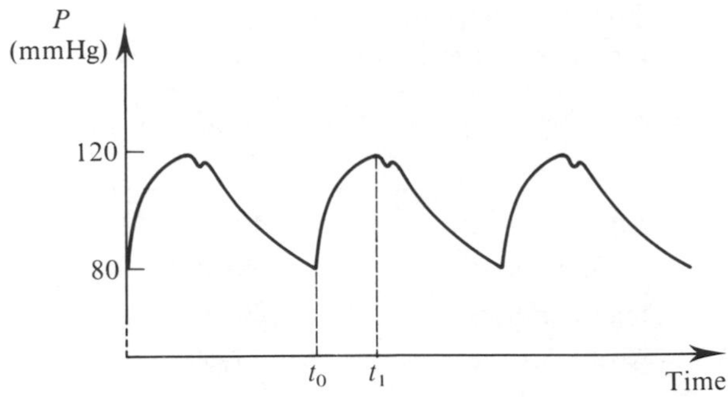

Figure 1.3 Blood pressure contour.

The information presented in the discussion above is generally applicable to any healthy human adult. However, the presence of disease in a person might result in some of the parameters taking a value outside the normal range. For example, in a patient suffering from an arterial stenosis (narrowing), the blood pressure distal (that is, in a direction away from the heart) of the stenosis in the artery is near zero.

The mean blood pressure in a patient is computed from values for the blood pressure over some time interval. If the blood pressure is recorded, a curve similar to that shown in Figure 1.3 is obtained. The blood pressure fluctuates between a maximal pressure, called the systolic level, and a minimal pressure, called the diastolic level. The difference between the systolic and diastolic pressure levels is called the pulse pressure. Suppose that a physician measures the blood pressure in a patient; by using information concerning the time interval during which the blood pressure was measured, the mean blood pressure in the time interval $[t_0,t_1]$ can be calculated using the following formula:

$$\bar{P} = \frac{\int_{t_0}^{t_1} P(t)\,\mathrm{d}t}{t_1 - t_0}$$

where $\bar{P}$ indicates the mean blood pressure, and t_0 and t_1 the points in time at which $P(t)$, the blood pressure, was recorded. In daily practice, only approximate values for the systolic and diastolic pressure are obtained, using an ordinary manometer with an arm cuff.

In addition to the blood pressure, in some patients the cardiac output is determined. The cardiac output is the volume of blood pumped by the heart into the aorta each minute. It may be calculated using the following formula:

$$CO = F \cdot SV$$

where CO is the cardiac output and F the heart rate. SV stands for the stroke volume, that is the volume of blood pumped into the aorta with each heart beat. F and SV can be recorded.

The kind of knowledge concerning the human cardiovascular system presented above is called *deep knowledge*. Deep knowledge entails the detailed structure and function of some system in the domain of discourse. Deep knowledge may be valuable for *diagnostic reasoning*, that is, reasoning aimed at finding the cause of failure of some system. For example, if the blood pressure in a patient is low, we know from the structure and function of the cardiovascular system that the cause may be a failure of the heart to expel enough blood, a failure of the blood vessels to deliver enough resistance to the blood flow, or a volume of the blood too low to fill the system with enough blood. In a patient suffering from some cardiovascular disorder, the symptoms, signs and the data obtained from the tests the patient has been subjected to are usually related to that disorder. On the other hand, the presence of certain symptoms, signs and test results may also be used to diagnose cardiovascular disease. For instance, if a patient experiences a cramp in the leg when walking, which disappears within one or two minutes at rest, a stenosis of one of the arteries in the leg, possibly due to atherosclerosis, is conceivable. This kind of knowledge is often called *shallow knowledge* to distinguish it from deep knowledge. As one can see, no knowledge concerning the structure and function of the cardiovascular system is applied for establishing the diagnosis; instead, the empirical association of a particular kind of muscle cramp and some cardiovascular disease is used as evidence for the diagnosis of arterial stenosis. Many expert systems contain only such shallow knowledge, since this is the kind of knowledge employed in daily practice by field experts for rapidly handling the problems they encounter. However, using deep knowledge frequently leads to a better justification of the solution proposed by the system. Other examples of the application of deep and shallow knowledge will be encountered in the next chapters.

It is not always easy to distinguish sharply between deep and shallow knowledge in a problem domain. Consider the following example from medical diagnosis. If the systolic pressure measured in the patient exceeds 140 mmHg, and on physical examination a diastolic murmur or an enlarged heart is noticed, an aortic regurgitation (leaky aortic valve) may be the cause of symptoms and signs. We see in this example that some, but limited, use is made of the structure and function of the cardiovascular system for diagnosis. The following example from the area of medical diagnosis finishes our description of the problem domain. When a patient is suffering from abdominal pain, and by auscultation a murmur in the abdomen is noticed, and a pulsating mass is felt on examination, an aneurysm (bulge) of the abdominal aorta quite probably causes these signs and symptoms.

Suggested reading

In this chapter the historical development of artificial intelligence was briefly sketched. Examples of textbooks containing a more extensive introduction to the area of artificial intelligence are Bonnet (1985), Winston (1984), Nilsson (1982), and Charniak and McDermott (1986). A more fundamental book on artificial intelligence is Bibel and Jorrand (1986). General introductory textbooks on expert systems are, in addition to this book, Harmon and King (1985), Jackson (1990) and Frost (1986). Luger and Stubblefield (1989) is a general book about artificial intelligence, with some emphasis on expert systems and AI programming languages. In Hayes-Roth *et al.* (1983), the attention is focused on methods for knowledge engineering. A more in-depth study of expert systems may be based on consulting the following papers and books.

The article in which M. Davis describes the implementation of a theorem prover for Presburger's algorithm in number theory can be found in Siekmann and Wrightson (1983a). Question-answering systems are discussed in Green (1969). Chang and Lee (1973) presents a thorough treatment of resolution and discusses a large number of refinements of this principle. The General Problem Solver is discussed in Newell (1963) and Ernst and Newell (1969). In the latter book a number of problems are solved using techniques from GPS.

There is available a large and ever-growing number of books and papers on specific expert systems. Several of the early, and now classic, expert systems in the area of medicine are discussed in Szolovits (1982) and Clancey and Shortliffe (1984). Shortliffe (1976) treats MYCIN in considerable detail. Information about NEOMYCIN can be found in Clancey and Shortliffe (1984). INTERNIST-I is described in Miller *et al.* (1982). QMR is a recent microcomputer-based extension of the INTERNIST knowledge base (Miller *et al.*, 1986; Bankowitz *et al.*, 1989). Except for MYCIN and INTERNIST-I several other expert systems have been developed in the area of medicine: PIP (Pauker *et al.*, 1976) for the diagnosis of renal disorders, PUFF (Aikins *et al.*, 1984) for the interpretation of pulmonary function test results, CASNET (Weiss *et al.*, 1978) for the diagnosis of glaucoma, ABEL (Patil *et al.*, 1982) for the diagnosis of acid–base and electrolyte disorders, VM (Fagan, 1980) for the recording and interpretation of physiological data from patients who need ventilatory assistance after operation, and HEPAR (Lucas *et al.*, 1989) for the diagnosis of liver and biliary disease.

The HEURISTIC DENDRAL system is described in Buchanan *et al.* (1969) and Lindsay *et al.* (1980). METADENDRAL is described in the latter reference and in Buchanan and Feigenbaum (1978). Kraft (1984) discusses XCON. In a large number of areas expert systems have been developed. R1 is discussed in McDermott (1982b). PROSPECTOR (Duda *et al.*, 1979) and DIPMETER ADVISOR (Smith and Baker, 1983) are expert systems in the area of geology, FOSSIL (Brough and Alexander, 1986) is a system meant for the dating of fossils, SPAM (McKeown *et al.*, 1985) is a system for the interpretation of photographs of airport situations, and a system in the area of telecommunication is ACE (Vesonder *et al.*, 1983). RESEDA (Zarri, 1984) is a system that contains biographical data pertaining to French history in the period from 1350 to 1450.

The expert system shell EMYCIN (Essential MYCIN) originated in the MYCIN system. It is discussed in detail in Melle (1979, 1980), Melle *et al.* (1981) and Buchanan and Shortliffe (1984). An interesting non-medical application developed using EMYCIN is SACON (Bennett *et al.*, 1978). The architecture of CENTAUR (Aikins, 1983) has been inspired by practical experience with the MYCIN-like expert system PUFF (Aikins *et al.*, 1984). PUFF and CENTAUR both concern the interpretation of data obtained from pulmonary function tests, in particular spirometry. OPS5 is a programming language for developing production systems. Its use is described in Brownston *et al.* (1985). LOOPS is a programming environment that provides the user with a large number of techniques for the representation of knowledge (Stefik and Bobrow, 1984; Stefik *et al.*, 1986).

An overview of the various formalisms for representing knowledge employed in artificial intelligence is given in Barr and Davidson (1980). In addition, Brachman and Levesque (1985) is a collection of distinguished papers in the area of knowledge representation. In particular, Levesque and Brachman (1985) is an interesting paper, which discusses the relationship between the expressiveness of a knowledge-representation language and the computational complexity of associated inference algorithms.

Information on the anatomy and physiology of the cardiovascular system can be found in Guyton (1976).

EXERCISES

1.1 One of the questions raised in the early days of artificial intelligence was: Can machines think? Nowadays, the question remains the subject of heated debates. This question was most lucidly formulated and treated by A.M. Turing in the paper 'Computing machinery and intelligence' which appeared in *Mind*, **59**, no. 236, 1950. Read the paper by A.M. Turing, and try to think what your answer would be when someone posed that question to you.

1.2 Read the description of GPS in Section 1.1 again. Give a specification of the process of shopping in terms of an initial state, final state and operators, as would be required by GPS.

1.3 An important component of the HEURISTIC DENDRAL system is the Structure Generator subsystem which generates plausible molecular structures. Develop a program in PROLOG or LISP that enumerates all possible structural formulas of a given alkane (that is, a compound having the chemical formula C_nH_{2n+2}) given the chemical formula as input for $n = 1, \ldots, 8$.

1.4 The areas of knowledge engineering and software engineering have much in common. However, there are also some evident distinctions. Which similarities and differences do you see between these fields?

1.5 Give some examples of deep and shallow knowledge from a problem domain you are familiar with.

1.6 Mention some problem areas in which expert systems can be of real help.

Logic and Resolution

One of the earliest formalisms for the representation of knowledge is *logic.* The formalism is characterized by a well-defined syntax and semantics, and provides a number of *inference rules* to manipulate logical formulas on the basis of their form in order to derive new knowledge. Logic has a very long and rich tradition, going back to the ancient Greeks: its roots may be traced to Aristotle. However, it took until the present century before the mathematical foundations of modern logic were laid, among others by T. Skolem, J. Herbrand, K. Gödel and G. Gentzen. The work of these great and influential mathematicians rendered logic firmly established before the area of computer science came into being.

Already from the early 1950s, as soon as the first digital computers became available, research was initiated on using logic for problem solving by means of the computer. This research was undertaken from different points of view. Several researchers were primarily interested in the mechanization of mathematical proofs: the efficient automated generation of such proofs was their main objective. One of them was M. Davis who already in 1954 developed a computer program which was capable of proving several theorems from number theory. The greatest triumph of the program was its proof that the sum of two even numbers is even. Other researchers, however, were more interested in the study of human problem solving, in particular in heuristics. For these researchers, mathematical reasoning served as a point of departure for the study of heuristics, and logic seemed to capture the essence of mathematics; they used logic merely as a convenient language for the formal representation of human reasoning. The classical example of this approach to the area of theorem proving is a program developed by A. Newell, J.C. Shaw and H.A. Simon in 1955, called the *Logic Theory Machine*. This program was capable of proving several theorems from the *Principia Mathematica* of A.N. Whitehead and B. Russell. As early as 1961, J. McCarthy, among others, pointed out that theorem proving could also be used for solving non-mathematical problems. This idea was elaborated by many authors. Well known is the early work on *question-answering systems* by J.R. Slagle and the later work in this field by C.C. Green and B. Raphael.

After some initial success, it soon became apparent that the inference rules known at that time were not as suitable for application in digital computers as had been hoped for. Many AI researchers lost interest in applying logic, and shifted their attention towards the development of other formalisms for a more efficient representation and manipulation of information. The breakthrough came thanks to the development of an efficient and flexible inference rule in 1965, named *resolution*, which allowed applying logic for automated problem solving by the computer, and theorem proving finally gained an established position in artificial intelligence and, more recently, in computer science as a whole.

Logic can directly be used as a knowledge-representation formalism for building expert systems; currently, however, this is done only on a small scale. But, then, the clear semantics of logic makes the formalism eminently suitable as a point of departure for understanding what the other knowledge-representation formalisms are all about. In this chapter, we first discuss the subject of how knowledge can be represented in logic, departing from propositional logic, which although having a rather limited expressiveness is very useful for introducing several important notions. First-order predicate logic, which offers a much richer language for knowledge representation, is treated in Section 2.2. The major part of this chapter however will be devoted to the algorithmic aspects of applying logic in an automated reasoning system, and resolution in particular will be the subject of study.

2.1 Propositional logic

Propositional logic may be viewed as a representation language which allows us to express and reason with statements that are either *true* or *false*. Examples of such statements are:

'The aorta is a large artery'
'10 mmHg > 90 mmHg'

Statements like these are called *propositions* and are usually denoted in propositional logic by upper-case letters. Simple propositions such as P and Q are called *atomic propositions* or *atoms* for short. Atoms can be combined with so-called *logical connectives* to yield *composite propositions*. In the language of propositional logic, we have the following five connectives at our disposal:

negation:	$\neg$	(not)
conjunction:	$\wedge$	(and)
disjunction:	$\vee$	(or)
implication:	$\rightarrow$	(if then)
bi-implication:	$\leftrightarrow$	(if and only if)

For example, when we assume that the propositions G and D have the following meaning

G = 'The aorta is a large artery'
D = 'The aorta has a diameter equal to 2.5 cm'

then the composite proposition

$G \wedge D$

has the meaning:

'The aorta is a large artery *and* the aorta has a diameter equal to 2.5 cm'

However, not all formulas consisting of atoms and connectives are (composite) propositions. To distinguish syntactically correct formulas that do represent propositions from those that do not, the notion of a well-formed formula is introduced in the following definition.

Definition: A *well-formed formula* in propositional logic is an expression having one of the following forms:

(1) An atom is a well-formed formula.

(2) If F is a well-formed formula, then $(\neg F)$ is a well-formed formula.

(3) If F and G are well-formed formulas, then $(F \wedge G)$, $(F \vee G)$, $(F \rightarrow G)$ and $(F \leftrightarrow G)$ are well-formed formulas.

(4) No other formula is well-formed.

EXAMPLE 2.1

Both formulas $(F \wedge (G \rightarrow H))$ and $(F \vee (\neg G))$ are well-formed according to the previous definition, but the formula $(\rightarrow H)$ is not.

In well-formed formulas, parentheses may be omitted as long as no ambiguity can occur; the adopted priority of the connectives is, in decreasing order, as follows:

$$\neg \quad \wedge \quad \vee \quad \rightarrow \quad \leftrightarrow$$

In the following, the term formula is used as an abbreviation when a well-formed formula is meant.

EXAMPLE 2.2

The formula $P \rightarrow Q \wedge R$ is the same as the formula $(P \rightarrow (Q \wedge R))$.

The notion of well-formedness of formulas concerns only the syntax of formulas in propositional logic; it does not express the formulas to be either *true* or *false*. In other words, it tells us nothing with respect to the semantics or meaning of formulas in propositional logic. The truth or falsity of a formula is called its *truth value*. The meaning of a formula in propositional logic is defined by means of a function

$$w\colon PROP \rightarrow \{true, false\}$$

which assigns to each proposition in the set of propositions $PROP$ a truth value either of *true* or *false*. Consequently, the information that the atom P has the truth value *true* is now denoted by $w(P) = true$, and the information that the atom P has the truth value *false* is denoted by $w(P) = false$. Such a function w is called an interpretation function, or an *interpretation* for short, if it satisfies the following properties (we assume F and G to be arbitrary well-formed formulas):

(1) $w(\neg F) = true$ if $w(F) = false$, and $w(\neg F) = false$ if $w(F) = true$.

Table 2.1 The meanings of the connectives.

F	G	$\neg F$	$F \wedge G$	$F \vee G$	$F \rightarrow G$	$F \leftrightarrow G$
true	*true*	*false*	*true*	*true*	*true*	*true*
true	*false*	*false*	*false*	*true*	*false*	*false*
false	*true*	*true*	*false*	*true*	*true*	*false*
false	*false*	*true*	*false*	*false*	*true*	*true*

(2) $w(F \wedge G) = true$ if $w(F) = true$ and $w(G) = true$; otherwise $w(F \wedge G) = false$.

(3) $w(F \vee G) = false$ if $w(F) = false$ and $w(G) = false$; in all other cases, that is, if at least one of the function values $w(F)$ and $w(G)$ equals *true*, we have $w(F \vee G) = true$.

(4) $w(F \rightarrow G) = false$ if $w(F) = true$ and $w(G) = false$; in all other cases we have $w(F \rightarrow G) = true$.

(5) $w(F \leftrightarrow G) = true$ if $w(F) = w(G)$; otherwise $w(F \leftrightarrow G) = false$.

These rules are summarized in Table 2.1. The first two columns in this table list all possible combinations of truth values for the atomic propositions F and G; the remaining columns define the meanings of the respective connectives. If w is an interpretation which assigns to a given formula F the truth value *true*, then w is called a *model* for F.

By repeated applications of the rules listed in Table 2.1, it is possible to express the truth value of an arbitrary formula in terms of the truth values of the atoms the formula is composed of. In a formula containing n different atoms, there are 2^n possible ways of assigning truth values to the atoms in the formula.

EXAMPLE 2.3

Table 2.2 lists all possible combinations of truth values for the atoms in the formula $P \rightarrow (\neg Q \wedge R)$; for each combination, the resulting truth value for this formula is determined. Such a table, where all possible truth values for the atoms in formula F are entered together with the corresponding truth value for the whole formula F, is called a *truth table*.

Definition: A formula is called a *valid* formula if it is *true* under all interpretations. A valid formula is often called a *tautology*. A formula is called *invalid* if it is not valid.

Table 2.2 Truth table for $P \rightarrow (\neg Q \wedge R)$.

P	Q	R	$\neg Q$	$\neg Q \wedge R$	$P \rightarrow (\neg Q \wedge R)$
true	*true*	*true*	*false*	*false*	*false*
true	*true*	*false*	*false*	*false*	*false*
true	*false*	*true*	*true*	*true*	*true*
true	*false*	*false*	*true*	*false*	*false*
false	*true*	*true*	*false*	*false*	*true*
false	*true*	*false*	*false*	*false*	*true*
false	*false*	*true*	*true*	*true*	*true*
false	*false*	*false*	*true*	*false*	*true*

So, a valid formula is *true* regardless of the truth or falsity of its constituent atoms.

EXAMPLE 2.4

The formula $((P \rightarrow Q) \wedge P) \rightarrow Q$ is an example of a valid formula. In Example 2.3 we dealt with an invalid formula.

Definition: A formula is called *unsatisfiable* or *inconsistent* if the formula is *false* under all interpretations. An unsatisfiable formula is also called a *contradiction*. A formula is called *satisfiable* or *consistent* if it is not unsatisfiable.

Note that a formula is valid precisely when its negation is unsatisfiable and vice versa.

EXAMPLE 2.5

The formulas $P \wedge \neg P$ and $(P \rightarrow Q) \wedge (P \wedge \neg Q)$ are both unsatisfiable.

Figure 2.1 depicts the relationships between the notions of valid and invalid, and satisfiable and unsatisfiable formulas.

Definition: Two formulas F and G are called *equivalent*, written as $F \equiv G$, if the truth values of F and G are the same under all possible interpretations.

Two formulas can be shown to be equivalent by demonstrating that their truth tables are identical.

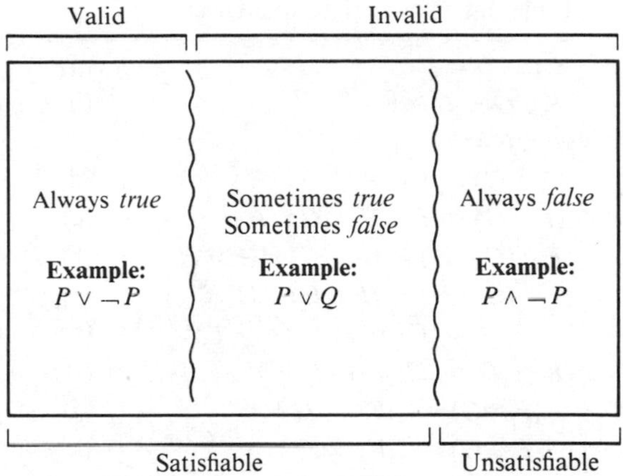

Figure 2.1 Relationship between validity and satisfiability.

EXAMPLE 2.6

Table 2.3 shows that $\neg(P \wedge Q) \equiv \neg P \vee \neg Q$

Using truth tables the logical equivalences listed in Table 2.4 can easily be proved. These equivalences are called *laws of equivalence.* Law (a) is called the *law of double negation*; laws (b) and (c) are called the *commutative laws*; (d) and (e) are the so-called *associative laws*; and (f) and (g) are the *distributive laws.* Laws (j) and (k) are known as the *laws of De Morgan.* These laws are often used to transform a given well-formed formula into a logically equivalent but syntactically different formula.

In the following, a conjunction of formulas is often written as a set of formulas, where the elements of the set are taken as the conjunctive subformulas of the given formula.

Table 2.3 Truth table of $\neg(P \wedge Q)$ and $\neg P \vee \neg Q$.

P	Q	$\neg(P \wedge Q)$	$\neg P \vee \neg Q$
true	*true*	*false*	*false*
true	*false*	*true*	*true*
false	*true*	*true*	*true*
false	*false*	*true*	*true*

Table 2.4 Laws of equivalence.

$\neg(\neg F) \equiv F$	(a)
$F \vee G \equiv G \vee F$	(b)
$F \wedge G \equiv G \wedge F$	(c)
$(F \wedge G) \wedge H \equiv F \wedge (G \wedge H)$	(d)
$(F \vee G) \vee H \equiv F \vee (G \vee H)$	(e)
$F \vee (G \wedge H) \equiv (F \vee G) \wedge (F \vee H)$	(f)
$F \wedge (G \vee H) \equiv (F \wedge G) \vee (F \wedge H)$	(g)
$F \leftrightarrow G \equiv (F \rightarrow G) \wedge (G \rightarrow F)$	(h)
$F \rightarrow G \equiv \neg F \vee G$	(i)
$\neg(F \wedge G) \equiv \neg F \vee \neg G$	(j)
$\neg(F \vee G) \equiv \neg F \wedge \neg G$	(k)

EXAMPLE 2.7

The set $S = \{F \vee G, H\}$ represents the formula $(F \vee G) \wedge H$.

Truth tables can be applied to determine whether or not a given formula follows logically from a given set of formulas. Informally speaking, a formula logically follows from a set of formulas if it is satisfied by all interpretations satisfying the given set of formulas; we say that the formula is a logical consequence of the formulas in the given set. The following is a formal definition of this notion.

Definition: A formula G is said to be a *logical consequence* of the set of formulas $F = \{F_1, \ldots, F_n\}$, $n \geqslant 1$, denoted by $F \models G$, if for each interpretation w for which $w(F_1 \wedge \cdots \wedge F_n) = true$, we have $w(G) = true$.

EXAMPLE 2.8

The formula R is a logical consequence of the set of formulas $\{P \wedge \neg Q, P \rightarrow R\}$. Thus we can write $\{P \wedge \neg Q, P \rightarrow R\} \models R$.

Note that another way of stating that two formulas F and G are logically equivalent, that is, $F \equiv G$, is to say that both $\{F\} \models G$ and $\{G\} \models F$ hold. This tells us that the truth values of F and G are explicitly related to each other, which can also be expressed as $\models (F \leftrightarrow G)$.

Satisfiability, validity, equivalence and logical consequence are *semantic* notions; these properties are generally established using truth tables. However, for deriving logical consequences from a set of formulas, for example, propositional logic also provides other techniques than using truth tables. It is possible to derive logical consequences by *syntactic* operations only. A formula which is derived from a given set of formulas is then guaranteed to be a logical consequence of that set if the syntactic operations employed meet certain conditions. Systems in which such syntactic operations are defined are called (*formal*) *deduction systems*. Various sorts of deduction system are known. An example of a deduction system is an *axiomatic system*, consisting of a formal language, such as the language of propositional logic described above, a set of *inference rules* (the syntactic operations) and a set of *axioms*. In Section 2.4 we shall return to the subject of logical deduction.

2.2 First-order predicate logic

In propositional logic, atoms are the basic constituents of formulas which are either *true* or *false*. A limitation of propositional logic is the impossibility of expressing general statements concerning similar cases. *First-order predicate logic* is more expressive than propositional logic, and such general statements can be specified in its language. Let us first introduce the language of first-order predicate logic. The following symbols are used:

(1) *Predicate symbols*, usually denoted by upper-case letters. Each predicate symbol has associated a natural number n, $n \geqslant 0$, indicating the number of arguments the predicate symbol has; the predicate symbol is called an *n-place* predicate symbol. 0-place or *nullary* predicate symbols are also called (*atomic*) *propositions*. One-place, two-place and three-place predicate symbols are also called *unary*, *binary* and *ternary* predicate symbols, respectively.

(2) *Variables*, usually denoted by lower-case letters from the end of the alphabet, such as x, y, z, possibly indexed with a natural number.

(3) *Function symbols*, usually denoted by lower-case letters from halfway through the alphabet. Each function symbol has an associated natural number n, $n \geqslant 0$, indicating its number of arguments; the function symbol is called *n-place*. Nullary function symbols are usually called *constants*.

(4) The *logical connectives* which have already been discussed in the previous section.

(5) Two *quantifiers*: the *universal quantifier* ∀, and the *existential quantifier* ∃. The quantifiers should be read as follows: if x is a variable, then $\forall x$ means 'for each x' or 'for all x', and $\exists x$ means 'there exists an x'.

(6) A number of *auxiliary symbols* such as parentheses and commas.

Variables and functions in logic are more or less similar to variables and functions in for instance algebra or calculus.

Before we define the notion of an atomic formula in predicate logic, we first introduce the notion of a term.

Definition: A *term* is defined as follows:

(1) A constant is a term.

(2) A variable is a term.

(3) If f is an n-place function symbol, $n \geqslant 1$, and $t_1, \ldots, t_n$ are terms, then $f(t_1, \ldots, t_n)$ is a term.

(4) Nothing else is a term.

So, a term is either a constant, a variable or a function of terms. Recall that a constant may also be viewed as a nullary function symbol. An atomic formula now consists of a predicate symbol and a number of terms to be taken as the arguments of the predicate symbol.

Definition: An *atomic formula*, or *atom* for short, is an expression of the form $P(t_1, \ldots, t_n)$, where P is an n-place predicate symbol, $n \geqslant 0$, and $t_1, \ldots, t_n$ are terms.

EXAMPLE 2.9

If P is a unary predicate symbol and x is a variable, then $P(x)$ is an atom. $Q(f(y), c, g(f(x), z))$ is an atom if Q is a ternary predicate symbol, c is a constant, f a unary function symbol, g a binary function symbol, and x, y and z are variables. For the same predicate symbols P and Q, $P(Q)$ is not an atom, because Q is not a term but a predicate symbol.

Composite formulas can be formed using the five connectives given in Section 2.1, together with the two quantifiers ∀ and ∃ just introduced. As was done for propositional logic, we now define the notion of a well-formed formula in predicate logic. The following definition also introduces the additional notions of free and bound variables.

Definition: A *well-formed formula* in predicate logic, and the set of *free variables* of a well-formed formula, are defined as follows:

(1) An atom is a well-formed formula. The set of free variables of an atomic formula consists of all the variables occurring in the terms in the atom.

(2) Let F be a well-formed formula with an associated set of free variables. Then $(\neg F)$ is a well-formed formula. The set of free variables of $(\neg F)$ equals the set of free variables of F.

(3) Let F and G be well-formed formulas and for each of these formulas let a set of free variables be given. Then $(F \vee G)$, $(F \wedge G)$, $(F \rightarrow G)$ and $(F \leftrightarrow G)$ are well-formed formulas. The set of free variables of each of these last-mentioned formulas is equal to the union of the sets of free variables of F and G.

(4) If F is well-formed formula and x is an element of the set of free variables of F, then both $(\forall xF)$ and $(\exists xF)$ are well-formed formulas. The set of free variables of each of these formulas is equal to the set of free variables of F from which the variable x has been removed. The variable x is said to be *bound* by the quantifier $\forall$ or $\exists$.

(5) Nothing else is a well-formed formula.

Note that we have introduced the notion of a well-formed formula in the preceding definition only from a purely syntactical point of view: nothing has been said about the meaning of such a formula.

Parentheses will be omitted from well-formed formulas as long as ambiguity cannot occur; the quantifiers then have a higher priority than the connectives. The term formula will be used to mean a well-formed formula, unless explicity stated otherwise.

Definition: A well-formed formula is called a *closed formula*, or a *sentence*, if its set of free variables is empty; otherwise it is called an *open formula*.

EXAMPLE 2.10

The set of free variables of the formula $\forall x \exists y(P(x) \rightarrow Q(y,z))$ is equal to $\{z\}$. So only one of the three variables in the formula is a free variable. The formula $\forall x(P(x) \vee R(x))$ has no free variables at all, and thus is an example of a sentence.

In what follows, we shall primarily be concerned with closed formulas.

In the formula $\forall x(A(x) \rightarrow G(x))$ all occurrences of the variable x

in $A(x) \to G(x)$ are governed by the associated universal quantifier; $A(x) \to G(x)$ is called the *scope* of this quantifier.

EXAMPLE 2.11

The scope of the universal quantifier in the formula

$$\forall x\,(P(x) \to \exists y R(x,y))$$

is $P(x) \to \exists y R(x,y)$; the scope of the existential quantifier is the subformula $R(x,y)$.

In propositional logic, the truth value of a formula under a given interpretation is obtained by assigning a truth value either of *true* or *false* to each of its constituent atoms according to this specific interpretation. Defining the semantics of first-order predicate logic is somewhat more involved than in propositional logic. In predicate logic, a structure representing the 'reality' is associated with the *meaningless* set of symbolic formulas; in a structure the objects or elements of the domain of discourse, or domain for short, are enlisted, together with functions and relations defined on the domain.

Definition: A *structure* S is a tuple

$$S = (D, \{\overline{f}_i^n\colon D^n \to D, n \geqslant 1\}, \{\overline{P}_i^m\colon D^m \to \{\mathit{true}, \mathit{false}\}, m \geqslant 0\})$$

having the following components:

(1) a non-empty set of elements D, called the *domain* of S;

(2) a set of n-place *functions* defined on D^n, $\{\overline{f}_i^n\colon D^n \to D, n \geqslant 1\}$;

(3) a non-empty set of mappings, called *predicates*, from D^m to the set of truth values $\{\mathit{true}, \mathit{false}\}$, $\{\overline{P}_i^m\colon D^m \to \{\mathit{true}, \mathit{false}\}, m \geqslant 0\}$.

Now we have to express how a given meaningless formula should be interpreted in a given structure: it is not possible to state anything about the truth value of a formula as long as it has not been prescribed which elements from the structure are to be associated with the elements in the formula.

EXAMPLE 2.12

Consider the formula $A(c)$. We associate the predicate having the intended meaning 'is an artery' with the predicate symbol A. The formula should be *true* if the constant representing the aorta is associated with c; on the other hand, the same formula should be *false* if the constant representing the brachial vein is associated with c. However, if we associate the predicate 'is a vein' with A, the truth values of $A(c)$ for the two constants should be opposite to the ones mentioned before.

In the following definition, we introduce the notion of an assignment, which is a function that assigns elements from the domain of a structure to the variables in a formula.

Definition: An *assignment* (*valuation*) v to a set of formulas F in a given structure S with domain D is a mapping from the set of variables in F to D.

The interpretation of (terms and) formulas in a structure S under an assignment v now consists of the following steps. First, the constants in the formulas are assigned elements from D. Secondly, the variables are replaced by the particular elements from D that have been assigned to them by v. Then, the predicate and function symbols occurring in the formulas are assigned predicates and functions from S. Finally, the truth values of the formulas are determined.

Before the notion of an interpretation is defined more formally, a simple example in which no function symbols occur is given. For the reader who is not interested in the formal aspects of logic, it suffices merely to study this example.

EXAMPLE 2.13

The open formula

$$F = A(x) \rightarrow O(x)$$

contains the unary predicate symbols A and O, and the free variable x. Consider the structure S consisting of the domain

$$D = \{aorta, pulmonary\text{-}artery, brachial\text{-}vein\}$$

and the set of predicates comprising the following elements:

- a unary predicate *Artery*, with the intended meaning 'is an artery', defined by *Artery* (*aorta*) = *true*, *Artery* (*pulmonary-artery*) = *true* and *Artery* (*brachial-vein*) = *false*;
- the unary predicate *Oxygenrich* with the intended meaning 'contains oxygen-rich blood', defined by *Oxygenrich* (*aorta*) = *true*, *Oxygenrich* (*pulmonary-artery*) = *false* and *Oxygenrich* (*brachial-vein*) = *false*.

Let us take for the predicate symbol A the predicate *Artery*, and for the predicate symbol O the predicate *Oxygenrich.* It will be obvious that the atom $A(x)$ is *true* in S under any assignment v for which $Artery(v(x)) = true$; so, for example for the assignment $v(x) = aorta$, we have that $A(x)$ is *true* in S under v. Furthermore, F is *true* in the structure S under the assignment v with $v(x) = aorta$, since $A(x)$ and $O(x)$ are both *true* in S under v. On the other hand, F is *false* in the structure S under the assignment v' with $v'(x) =$ *pulmonary-artery*, because *Artery* (*pulmonary-artery*) = *true* and *Oxygenrich* (*pulmonary-artery*) = *false* in S. Now, consider the closed formula

$$F' = \forall x(A(x) \rightarrow O(x))$$

and again the structure S. It should be obvious that F' is *false* in S.

Definition: An *interpretation* of terms in a structure $S = (D, \{\overline{f_i^n}\}, \{\overline{P_i^m}\})$, under an assignment v, denoted by I_v^S, is defined as follows:

(1) $I_v^S(c_i) = d_i$, $d_i \in D$, where c_i is a constant.

(2) $I_v^S(x_i) = v(x_i)$, where x_i is a variable.

(3) $I_v^S(f_i^n(t_1, \ldots, t_n)) = \overline{f_i^n}\,(I_v^S(t_1), \ldots, I_v^S(t_n))$, where $\overline{f_i^n}$ is a function from S associated with the function symbol f_i^n.

The truth value of a formula in a structure S under an assignment v for a given interpretation I_v^S is obtained as follows:

(1) $I_v^S(P_i^m\,(t_1, \ldots, t_m)) = \overline{P_i^m}(I_v^S(t_1), \ldots, I_v^S(t_m))$, meaning that an atom $P_i^m(t_1, \ldots, t_m)$ is *true* in the structure S under the assignment v for the interpretation I_v^S if $\overline{P_i^m}(I_v^S(t_1), \ldots, I_v^S(t_m))$ is *true*, where $\overline{P_i^m}$ is the predicate from S associated with P_i^m.

(2) If the truth values of the formulas F and G have been determined, the truth values of $\neg F$, $F \wedge G$, $F \vee G$, $F \rightarrow G$ and $F \leftrightarrow G$ are defined by the meanings of the connectives as listed in Table 2.1.

(3) $\exists xF$ is *true* under v if there exists an assignment v' differing from v at most with regard to x, such that F is *true* under v'.

(4) $\forall xF$ is *true* under v if, for each v' differing from v at most with regard to x, F is *true* under v'.

The notions valid, invalid, satisfiable, unsatisfiable, logical consequence, equivalence and model have meanings in predicate logic similar to their

Table 2.5 Laws of equivalence for quantifiers.

$\neg\exists x P(x) \equiv \forall x \neg P(x)$	(a)
$\neg\forall x P(x) \equiv \exists x \neg P(x)$	(b)
$\forall x(P(x) \wedge Q(x)) \equiv \forall x P(x) \wedge \forall x Q(x)$	(c)
$\exists x(P(x) \vee Q(x)) \equiv \exists x P(x) \vee \exists x Q(x)$	(d)
$\forall x P(x) \equiv \forall y P(y)$	(e)
$\exists x P(x) \equiv \exists y P(y)$	(f)

meanings in propositional logic. In addition to the equivalences listed in Table 2.4, predicate logic also has some laws of equivalence for quantifiers, which are given in Table 2.5. Note that the properties

$$\forall x(P(x) \vee Q(x)) \equiv \forall x P(x) \vee \forall x Q(x)$$

and

$$\exists x(P(x) \wedge Q(x)) \equiv \exists x P(x) \wedge \exists x Q(x)$$

do *not* hold.

We conclude this subsection with another example.

EXAMPLE 2.14

We take the unary (meaningless) predicate symbols A, L, W, O and E, and the constants a and p from a given first-order language. Now, consider the following formulas:

(1) $\forall x(A(x) \rightarrow W(x))$
(2) $L(a)$
(3) $\forall x(L(x) \rightarrow A(x))$
(4) $\neg E(a)$
(5) $\forall x((A(x) \wedge \neg E(x)) \rightarrow O(x))$
(6) $L(p)$
(7) $\neg O(p)$
(8) $E(p)$

Consider the structure S in the reality with a domain consisting of the elements *aorta* and *pulmonary-artery*, which are assigned to the constants a and p, respectively. The set of predicates in S comprises the unary predicates *Artery*, *Large*, *Wall*, *Oxygenrich* and *Exception*, which are taken for the predicate symbols A, L, W, O and E, respectively. The structure S and the mentioned interpretation have been carefully chosen to satisfy the above-given closed formulas, for instance by giving the following intended meaning to the predicates:

Artery	=	'is an artery'
Large	=	'is a large artery'
Wall	=	'has a muscular wall'
Oxygenrich	=	'contains oxygen-rich blood'
Exception	=	'is an exception'

In the given structure S, the formula numbered 1 expresses the knowledge that every artery has a muscular wall. The fact that the aorta is an example of a large artery has been stated in formula 2. Formula 3 states that every large artery is an artery, and formula 4 states that the aorta is not an exception to the rule that arteries contain oxygen-rich blood, which has been formalized in logic by means of formula 5. The pulmonary artery is a large artery (formula 6), but contrary to the aorta it does not contain oxygen-rich blood (formula 7) and therefore is an exception to the last-mentioned rule; the fact that the pulmonary artery is an exception is expressed by means of formula 8.

It should be noted that in another structure with another domain and other predicates the formulas given above might have completely different meanings.

2.3 Clausal form of logic

Before turning our attention to reasoning in logic, we introduce in this section a syntactically restricted form of predicate logic, called the *clausal form of logic*, which will play an important role in the remainder of this chapter. This restricted form, however, can be shown to be as expressive as full first-order predicate logic. The clausal form of logic is often employed, in particular in the fields of theorem proving and logic programming.

We start with the definition of some new notions.

Definition: A *literal* is an atom, called a *positive literal*, or a negation of an atom, called a *negative literal*.

Definition: A *clause* is a closed formula of the form

$$\forall x_1 \cdots \forall x_s (L_1 \vee \cdots \vee L_m)$$

where each L_i, $i = 1,\ldots,m$, $m \geq 0$, is a literal, with $L_i \neq L_j$ for each $i \neq j$, and $x_1,\ldots,x_s$, $s \geq 0$, are variables occurring in $L_1 \vee \cdots \vee L_m$. If $m = 0$, the clause is said to be the *empty clause*, denoted by $\square$.

The empty clause $\square$ is interpreted as a formula which is always *false*, in other words, $\square$ is an unsatisfiable formula.

A clause

$$\forall x_1 \cdots \forall x_s(A_1 \vee \cdots \vee A_k \vee \neg B_1 \vee \cdots \vee \neg B_n)$$

where $A_1,\ldots,A_k$, $B_1,\ldots,B_n$ are atoms and $x_1,\ldots,x_s$ are variables, is equivalent to

$$\forall x_1 \cdots \forall x_s(B_1 \wedge \cdots \wedge B_n \rightarrow A_1 \vee \cdots \vee A_k)$$

as a consequence of the laws $\neg F \vee G \equiv F \rightarrow G$ and $\neg F \vee \neg G \equiv \neg(F \wedge G)$, and is often written as

$$A_1,\ldots,A_k \leftarrow B_1,\ldots,B_n$$

The last notation is the more conventional one in logic programming. The commas in $A_1,\ldots,A_k$ each stand for a disjunction, and the commas in $B_1,\ldots,B_n$ indicate a conjunction. $A_1,\ldots,A_k$ are called the *conclusions* of the clause, and $B_1,\ldots,B_n$ the *conditions*.

Each well-formed formula in first-order predicate logic can be translated into a set of clauses, which is viewed as the conjunction of its elements. As we will see, this translation process may slightly alter the meaning of the formulas. We shall illustrate the translation process by means of an example. Before proceeding, we define two normal forms which are required for the translation process.

Definition: A formula F is in *prenex normal form* if F is of the form

$$Q_1x_1 \cdots Q_nx_nM$$

where each Q_i, $i = 1,\ldots,n$, $n \geq 0$, equals one of the two quantifiers $\forall$ and $\exists$, and where M is a formula in which no quantifiers occur. $Q_1x_1 \cdots Q_nx_n$ is called the *prefix* and M is called the *matrix* of the formula F.

Definition: A formula F in prenex normal form is in *conjunctive normal form* if the matrix of F is of the form

$$F_1 \wedge \cdots \wedge F_n$$

where each F_i, $i = 1,\ldots,n$, $n \geq 1$, is a disjunction of literals.

EXAMPLE 2.15

Consider the following three formulas:

$$\forall x(P(x) \vee \exists y Q(x,y))$$

$$\forall x \exists y \forall z((P(x) \wedge Q(x,y)) \vee \neg R(z))$$

$$\forall x \exists y((\neg P(x) \vee Q(x,y)) \wedge (P(y) \vee \neg R(x)))$$

The first formula is not in prenex normal form because of the occurrence of an existential quantifier in the 'inside' of the formula. The other two formulas are both in prenex normal form; moreover, the last formula is also in conjunctive normal form.

The next example illustrates the translation of a well-formed formula into a set of clauses. The translation scheme presented in the example, however, is general and can be applied to any well-formed formula in first-order predicate logic.

EXAMPLE 2.16

Consider the following formula:

$$\forall x(\exists y P(x,y) \vee \neg \exists y(\neg Q(x,y) \rightarrow R(f(x,y))))$$

This formula is transformed in eight steps, first into prenex normal form, subsequently into conjunctive normal form, by applying among others the laws of equivalence listed in the Tables 2.4 and 2.5, and finally into a set of clauses.

Step 1. Eliminate all implication symbols using the equivalence $F \rightarrow G \equiv \neg F \vee G$:

$$\forall x(\exists y P(x,y) \vee \neg \exists y(Q(x,y) \vee R(f(x,y))))$$

Also using $\neg(\neg F) \equiv F$. If a formula contains bi-implication symbols, these can be removed by applying the equivalence $F \leftrightarrow G \equiv (F \rightarrow G) \wedge (G \rightarrow F)$.

Step 2. Diminish the scope of the negation symbols in such a way that each negation symbol governs only a single atom. This can be accomplished by using the equivalences $\neg \forall x F(x) \equiv \exists x \neg F(x)$, $\neg \exists x F(x) \equiv \forall x \neg F(x)$, $\neg(\neg F) \equiv F$, together with the laws of De Morgan:

$$\forall x(\exists y P(x,y) \vee \forall y(\neg Q(x,y) \wedge \neg R(f(x,y))))$$

Step 3. Rename the variables in the formula using the equivalences $\forall xF(x) \equiv \forall yF(y)$ and $\exists xF(x) \equiv \exists yF(y)$, so that each quantifier has its own uniquely named variable:

$$\forall x(\exists yP(x,y) \vee \forall z(\neg Q(x,z) \wedge \neg R(f(x,z))))$$

Formulas differing only in the names of their bound variables are called *variants.*

Step 4. Eliminate all existential quantifiers. For any existentially quantified variable x not lying within the scope of a universal quantifier, all occurrences of x in the formula within the scope of the existential quantifier can be replaced by a new, that is, not previously used, constant symbol c. The particular existential quantifier may then be removed. For instance, the elimination of the existential quantifier in the formula $\exists xP(x)$ yields a formula $P(c)$. However, if an existentially quantified variable y lies within the scope of one or more universal quantifiers with the variables $x_1, \ldots, x_n$, $n \geqslant 1$, the variable y may be functionally dependent on $x_1, \ldots, x_n$. Let this dependency be represented explicitly by means of a new n-place function symbol g such that $g(x_1, \ldots, x_n) = y$. All occurrences of y within the scope of the existential quantifier are then replaced by the function term $g(x_1, \ldots, x_n)$, after which the existential quantifier may be removed. The constants and functions introduced to allow for the elimination of existential quantifiers are called *Skolem functions.*

The existentially quantified variable y in the example lies within the scope of the universal quantifier with the variable x, and is replaced by $g(x)$:

$$\forall x(P(x, g(x)) \vee \forall z(\neg Q(x,z) \wedge \neg R(f(x,z))))$$

Note that by replacing the existentially quantified variables by Skolem functions we lose logical equivalence. Fortunately, it can be shown that a formula F is satisfiable if and only if the formula F', obtained from F by replacing existentially quantified variables in F by Skolem functions, is satisfiable as well. In general, the satisfiability of F and F' will not be based on the same model, since F' contains function symbols not occurring in F. In the following, it will become evident that this property is sufficient for our purposes.

Step 5. Transform the formula into prenex normal form by placing all the universal quantifiers in front of the formula:

$$\forall x \forall z(P(x, g(x)) \vee (\neg Q(x,z) \wedge \neg R(f(x,z))))$$

Note that this is allowed because by step 3 each quantifier applies to a uniquely named variable; this means that the scope of all quantifiers is the entire formula.

Step 6. Bring the matrix into conjunctive normal form using the distributive laws:

$$\forall x \forall z((P(x,g(x)) \vee \neg Q(x,z)) \wedge (P(x,g(x)) \vee \neg R(f(x,z))))$$

Step 7. Select the matrix by disregarding the prefix:

$$(P(x,g(x)) \vee \neg Q(x,z)) \wedge (P(x,g(x)) \vee \neg R(f(x,z)))$$

All variables in the matrix are now implicitly considered to be universally quantified.

Step 8. Translate the matrix into a set of clauses by replacing formulas of the form $F \wedge G$ by a set of clauses $\{F',G'\}$, where F' and G' indicate that F and G are now represented using the notational convention of logic programming:

$$\{P(x,g(x)) \leftarrow Q(x,z),\ P(x,g(x)) \leftarrow R(f(x,z))\}$$

We conclude this subsection with the definition of a special type of clause, a so-called Horn clause, which is a clause containing at most one positive literal.

Definition: A *Horn clause* is a clause having one of the following forms:

(1) $A \leftarrow$
(2) $\leftarrow B_1, \ldots ,B_n,\ n \geqslant 1$
(3) $A \leftarrow B_1, \ldots ,B_n,\ n \geqslant 1$

A is sometimes called the *head* of the clause, and $B_1, \ldots ,B_n$ is sometimes called its *body*. A clause of the form 1 is called a *unit clause*; a clause of form 2 is called a *goal clause*.

Horn clauses are employed in the programming language PROLOG. We will return to Horn clauses in Section 2.7.2.

2.4 Reasoning in logic: inference rules

In Sections 2.1 and 2.2 we described how a meaning could be attached to a meaningless set of logical formulas. This is sometimes called the *declarative semantics* of logic. The declarative semantics offers a means for investigating for example whether or not a given formula is a logical consequence of a set of formulas. However, it is also possible to answer this question without examining the semantic contents of the formulas concerned, by applying so-called *inference rules*. Contrary to truth tables, inference rules are purely syntactic operations which are capable only of modifying the form of the elements of a given set of formulas. Inference rules either add, replace or remove formulas; most inference rules discussed in this book, however, add new formulas to a given set of formulas. In general, an inference rule is given as a schema in which meta-variables occur that may be substituted by arbitrary formulas. An example of such a schema is:

$$\frac{A, A \rightarrow B}{B}$$

The formulas above the line are called the *premises*, and the formula below the line is called the *conclusion* of the inference rule. The above-given inference rule is known as *modus ponens* and, when applied, removes an implication from a formula. Another example of an inference rule, in this case for introducing a logical connective, is the following schema:

$$\frac{A, B}{A \wedge B}$$

Repeated applications of inference rules give rise to what is called a *derivation* or *deduction*. For instance, modus ponens can be applied to draw the conclusion S from the two formulas $P \wedge (Q \vee R)$ and $P \wedge (Q \vee R) \rightarrow S$. It is said that there exists a derivation of the formula S from the set of clauses $\{P \wedge (Q \vee R), P \wedge (Q \vee R) \rightarrow S\}$. This is denoted by:

$$\{P \wedge (Q \vee R), P \wedge (Q \vee R) \rightarrow S\} \vdash S$$

The symbol $\vdash$ is known as the *turnstile*.

EXAMPLE 2.17

Consider the set of formulas $\{P, Q, P \wedge Q \rightarrow S\}$. If the inference rule

$$\frac{A, B}{A \wedge B}$$

is applied to the formulas P and Q, the formula $P \wedge Q$ is derived; the subsequent application of modus ponens to $P \wedge Q$ and $P \wedge Q \rightarrow S$ yields S. So

$$\{P, Q, P \wedge Q \rightarrow S\} \vdash S$$

Now that we have introduced inference rules, it is relevant to investigate how the declarative semantics of a particular class of formulas and its *procedural semantics*, described by means of inference rules, are interrelated. If these two notions are related to each other, we are in the desirable circumstance of being able to assign a meaning to formulas which have been derived using inference rules, simply by our knowledge of the declarative meaning of the original set of formulas. On the other hand, when starting with the known meaning of a set of formulas, it will be possible to derive only formulas which can be related to that meaning. These two properties are known as the soundness and the completeness, respectively, of a collection of inference rules.

More formally, a collection of inference rules is said to be *sound* if and only if for each formula F derived by applying these inference rules on a given set of well-formed formulas S of a particular class (for example clauses), we have that F is a logical consequence of S. This property can be expressed more tersely as follows, using the notations introduced before:

if $S \vdash F$ then $S \models F$

In other words, a collection of inference rules is sound if it preserves truth under the operations of a derivation. This property is of great importance, because only by applying sound inference rules is it possible to assign a meaning to the result of a derivation.

EXAMPLE 2.18

The previously discussed inference rule modus ponens is an example of a sound inference rule. From the given formulas F and $F \rightarrow G$, the formula G can be derived by applying modus ponens, that is, we have $\{F, F \rightarrow G\} \vdash G$. On the other hand, if $F \rightarrow G$ and F are both *true* under a particular interpretation w, then from Table 2.1 we have that G is *true* under w as well. So G is a logical consequence of the two given formulas: $\{F, F \rightarrow G\} \models G$.

The reverse property that, by applying a particular collection of inference rules, each logical consequence F of a given set of formulas S can be derived is called the *completeness* of the collection of inference rules:

if $S \models F$ then $S \vdash F$

EXAMPLE 2.19

The collection of inference rules consisting only of modus ponens is not complete for all well-formed formulas in propositional logic. For example, it is not possible to derive the formula P from $\neg Q$ and $P \lor Q$, although P is a logical consequence of the two formulas. However, by combining modus ponens with other inference rules, it is possible to obtain a complete collection of inference rules.

The important question now arises of whether there exists a mechanical proof procedure, employing a particular sound and complete collection of inference rules, which is capable of determining whether or not a given formula F can be derived from a given set of formulas S. In 1936, A. Church and A.M. Turing showed, independently, that such a general proof procedure does not exist for first-order predicate logic. This property is called the *undecidability* of first-order predicate logic. All known proof procedures are capable of deriving F from S (that is, are able to prove $S \vdash F$) only if F is a logical consequence of S (that is, if $S \models F$); if F is not a logical consequence of S, the proof procedure is not guaranteed to terminate.

However, for propositional logic there do exist proof procedures which always terminate and yield the right answer; for checking whether a given formula is a logical consequence of a certain set of formulas, we can simply apply truth tables. So propositional logic is decidable.

The undecidability of first-order predicate logic has not hindered the progress of the research area of automated theorem proving. The major result of this research has been the development of an efficient and flexible inference rule which is both sound and complete for proving inconsistency, called *resolution*. However, the resolution rule is suitable only for manipulating formulas in clausal form. Hence, to use this inference rule on a set of arbitrary logical formulas in first-order predicate logic, it is necessary to translate each formula into the clausal form of logic by means of the procedure discussed in Section 2.3. The formulation of resolution as a suitable inference rule for automated theorem proving in the clausal form of logic has been mainly due to J.A. Robinson, who departed from earlier work by D. Prawitz. The final working out of resolution in various algorithms, supplemented with specific implementation techniques, has been the work of a large number of researchers. Resolution is the subject of the remainder of this chapter.

2.5 Resolution and propositional logic

We begin this section with a brief, informal sketch of the principles of resolution. Consider a set of formulas S in clausal form. Suppose we are given a formula G, also in clausal form, for which we have to prove that it can be derived from S by applying resolution. Proving $S \vdash G$ is equivalent to proving that the set of clauses W, consisting of the clauses in S supplemented with the negation of the formula G, that is $W = S \cup \{\neg G\}$, is unsatisfiable. Resolution on W now proceeds as follows. First, it is checked whether or not W contains the empty clause $\Box$; if this is the case, W is unsatisfiable and G is a logical consequence of S. If the empty clause $\Box$ is not in W, the resolution rule is applied on a suitable pair of clauses from W, yielding a new clause. Every clause derived this way is added to W, resulting in a new set of clauses on which the same resolution procedure is applied. The entire procedure is repeated until some generated set of clauses has been shown to contain the empty clause $\Box$, indicating unsatisfiability of W, or until all possible new clauses have been derived.

The basic principles of resolution are best illustrated by means of an example from propositional logic. In Section 2.6 we turn our attention to predicate logic.

EXAMPLE 2.20

Consider the following set of clauses:

$$\{C_1 = P \vee R,\ C_2 = \neg P \vee Q\}$$

These clauses contain *complementary* literals, that is, literals having opposite truth values, namely P and $\neg P$. Applying resolution, a new clause C_3 is derived being the disjunction of the original clauses C_1 and C_2 in which the complementary literals have been cancelled out. So, application of resolution yields the clause

$$C_3 = R \vee Q$$

which then is added to the original set of clauses.

The resolution principle is described more precisely in the following definition.

Definition: Consider the two clauses C_1 and C_2 containing the literals L_1 and L_2 respectively, where L_1 and L_2 are complementary. The procedure of *resolution* proceeds as follows:

(1) Delete L_1 from C_1 and L_2 from C_2, yielding the clauses C_1' and C_2'.

(2) Form the disjunction C' of C_1' and C_2'.

(3) Delete (possibly) redundant literals from C', thus obtaining the clause C.

The resulting clause C is called the *resolvent* of C_1 and C_2. The clauses C_1 and C_2 are said to be the *parent clauses* of the resolvent. This most basic form of the resolution inference rule is also known as *binary* resolution since it concerns two clauses.

Resolution has the important property that when two given parent clauses are *true* under a given interpretation, their resolvent is *true* under the same interpretation as well: resolution is a sound inference rule. The following theorem proves that resolution is sound for the case of propositional logic.

Theorem

(*soundness of resolution*) Consider two clauses C_1 and C_2 containing complementary literals. Then, any resolvent C of C_1 and C_2 is a logical consequence of $\{C_1, C_2\}$.

Proof We are given that the two clauses C_1 and C_2 contain complementary literals. So it is possible to write C_1 and C_2 as $C_1 = L \vee C_1'$ and $C_2 = \neg L \vee C_2'$ respectively for some literal L. By definition, a resolvent C is equal to $C_1' \vee C_2'$ from which possibly redundant literals have been removed. Now, suppose that C_1 and C_2 are both *true* under an interpretation w. We then have to prove that C is *true* under the same interpretation w as well. Clearly, either L or $\neg L$ is *false*. Suppose that L is *false* under w then C_1 obviously contains more than one literal, since otherwise C_1 would be *false* under w. It follows that C_1' is *true* under w. Hence, $C_1' \vee C_2'$, and therefore also C, is *true* under w. Similarly, it can be shown that the resolvent is *true* under w if it is assumed that L is *true*. So, if C_1 and C_2 are *true* under w then C is *true* under w as well. Hence, C is a logical consequence of C_1 and C_2.

Resolution is also a complete inference rule. Proving the completeness of resolution is beyond the scope of this book; we therefore confine ourselves to merely stating the property.

EXAMPLE 2.21

In the definition of a clause in Section 2.3, it was mentioned that a clause was not allowed to contain duplicate literals. This condition appears to be a necessary requirement for the completeness of resolution. For example, consider the following set of formulas:

$$S = \{P \vee P, \neg P \vee \neg P\}$$

It will be evident that S is unsatisfiable, since $P \vee P \equiv P$ and $\neg P \vee \neg P \equiv \neg P$. However, if resolution is applied to S then in every step the tautology $P \vee \neg P$ is derived. It is not possible to derive the empty clause $\Box$.

Until now we have used the notion of a derivation only in an intuitive sense. Before giving some more examples, we define the notion of a derivation in a formal way.

Definition: Let S be a set of clauses and let C be a single clause. A *derivation* of C from S, denoted by $S \vdash C$, is a finite sequence of clauses $C_1, C_2, \ldots, C_n$, $n \geqslant 1$, where each C_k is either a clause in S or a resolvent with parent clauses C_i and C_j, $i < k, j < k, i \neq j$, from the sequence, and $C = C_n$. If $C_n = \Box$, then the derivation is called a *refutation* of S, indicating that S is unsatisfiable.

EXAMPLE 2.22

Consider the following set of clauses:

$$S = \{\neg P \vee Q, \neg Q, P\}$$

From $C_1 = \neg P \vee Q$ and $C_2 = \neg Q$ we obtain the resolvent $C_3 = \neg P$. From the clauses C_3 and $C_4 = P$ we derive $C_5 = \Box$. So S is unsatisfiable. The sequence of clauses C_1, C_2, C_3, C_4, C_5 is a refutation of S. Note that it is not the only possible refutation of S. In general, a set S of clauses may have more than one refutation.

Note that by the choice of the empty clause $\Box$ as a formula that is *false* under all interpretations, which is a *semantic* notion, the *proof-theoretical* notion of a refutation has obtained a suitable meaning. A derivation can be depicted in a graph, called a *derivation graph*. In the case of a refutation, the vertices in the derivation graph may be restricted to those clauses and resolvents which directly or indirectly contribute to the refutation. Such a derivation graph has the form of a tree and is usually called a *refutation tree*. The leaves of such a tree are clauses from the original set, and the root of the tree is the empty clause $\Box$. The refutation tree for the derivation discussed in the previous example is shown in Figure 2.2. Note that another refutation of S gives rise to another refutation tree.

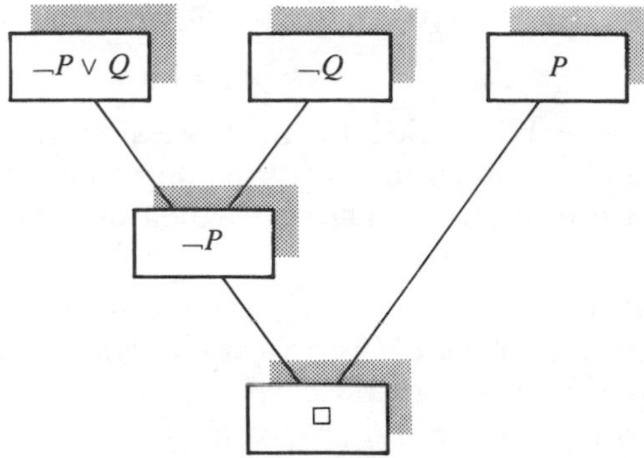

Figure 2.2 A refutation tree.

2.6 Resolution and first-order predicate logic

An important feature of resolution in first-order predicate logic is the manipulation of terms. This has not been dealt with in the previous section, where we had only atomic propositions, connectives and auxiliary symbols as building blocks for propositional formulas. In this section, we therefore first discuss the manipulation of terms before we provide a detailed description of resolution in first-order predicate logic.

2.6.1 Substitution and unification

The substitution of terms for variables in formulas to make these formulas syntactically equal plays a central role in a method known as *unification.* We first introduce the notion of substitution formally and then discuss its role in unification.

Definition: A *substitution* σ is a finite set of the form

$$\{t_1/x_1, \ldots ,t_n/x_n\}$$

where each x_i is a variable and where each t_i is a term not equal to x_i, $i = 1, \ldots ,n$, $n \geqslant 0$; the variables $x_1, \ldots ,x_n$ differ from each other. An element t_i/x_i of a substitution σ is called a *binding* for the variable x_i. If none of the terms t_i in a substitution contains a variable, we have a so-called *ground substitution.* The substitution defined by the empty set is called the *empty substitution*, and is denoted by ε.

Definition: An *expression* is a term, a literal, a conjunction of literals or a disjunction of literals; a *simple expression* is a term or an atom.

A substitution σ can be applied to an expression E, yielding a new expression $E\sigma$ which is similar to E with the difference that the variables in E occurring in σ have been replaced by their associated terms.

Definition: Let $\sigma = \{t_1/x_1, \ldots, t_n/x_n\}$, $n \geqslant 0$, be a substitution and E an expression. Then $E\sigma$ is an expression obtained from E by simultaneously replacing all occurrences of the variables x_i by the terms t_i. $E\sigma$ is called an *instance* of E. If $E\sigma$ does not contain any variables, $E\sigma$ is said to be a *ground instance* of E.

EXAMPLE 2.23

Let $\sigma = \{a/x, w/z\}$ be a substitution and let $E = P(f(x,y),z)$ be an expression. Then $E\sigma$ is obtained by replacing each variable x in E by the constant a and each variable z by the variable w. The result of the substitution is $E\sigma = P(f(a,y),w)$. Note that $E\sigma$ is not a ground instance.

The application of a substitution to a single expression can be extended to a set of expressions, as demonstrated in the following example.

EXAMPLE 2.24

Application of the substitution $\sigma = \{a/x, b/z\}$ to the set of expressions $\{P(x,f(x,z)), Q(x,w)\}$ yields the following set of instances:

$$\{P(x,f(x,z)), Q(x,w)\}\sigma = \{P(a,f(a,b)), Q(a,w)\}$$

The first element of the resulting set of instances is a ground instance; the second is not ground, as it contains the variable w.

Definition: Let $\theta = \{t_1/x_1, \ldots, t_m/x_m\}$ and $\sigma = \{s_1/y_1, \ldots, s_n/y_n\}$, $m \geqslant 1$, $n \geqslant 1$, be substitutions. The *composition* of these substitutions, denoted by $\theta\sigma$, is obtained by removing from the set

$$\{t_1\sigma/x_1, \ldots, t_m\sigma/x_m, s_1/y_1, \ldots, s_n/y_n\}$$

all elements $t_i\sigma/x_i$, for which $x_i = t_i\sigma$, and furthermore all elements s_j/y_j for which $y_j \in \{x_1, \ldots, x_m\}$.

The composition of substitutions is idempotent and associative, that is, for any expression E and for substitutions φ, θ, σ we have $E(\sigma\sigma) = E\sigma$ and $E(\varphi\sigma)\theta = E\varphi(\sigma\theta)$; the operation is not commutative.

Note that the last definition gives us a means of replacing two substitutions by a single one, which is the composition of these substitutions. However, it is not always necessary actually to compute the composition of two subsequent substitutions σ and θ before applying them to an expression E: it can easily be proved that $E(\sigma\theta) = (E\sigma)\theta$. The proof of this property is left to the reader as an exercise (see Exercise 2.11); here, we merely give an example.

EXAMPLE 2.25

Consider the expression $E = Q(x,f(y),g(z,x))$ and the two substitutions $\sigma = \{f(y)/x, z/y\}$ and $\theta = \{a/x, b/y, y/z\}$. We compute the composition $\sigma\theta$ of σ and θ: $\sigma\theta = \{f(b)/x, y/z\}$. Application of the compound substitution $\sigma\theta$ to E yields the instance $E(\sigma\theta) = Q(f(b), f(y), g(y, f(b)))$. We now compare this instance with $(E\sigma)\theta$. We first apply σ to E, resulting in $E\sigma = Q(f(y), f(z), g(z, f(y)))$. Subsequently, we apply θ to $E\sigma$ and obtain the instance $(E\sigma)\theta = Q(f(b), f(y), g(y, f(b)))$. So, for the given expression and substitutions, we have $E(\sigma\theta) = (E\sigma)\theta$.

In propositional logic, a resolvent of two parent clauses containing complementary literals, such as P and $\neg P$, was obtained by taking the disjunction of these clauses after cancelling out such a pair of complementary literals. It was easy to check for complementary literals in this case, because we only had to verify equality of the propositional atoms in the chosen literals and the presence of a negation in exactly one of them. Now, suppose that we want to compare the two literals $\neg P(x)$ and $P(a)$ occurring in two different clauses in first-order predicate logic. These two literals are almost complementary. However, the first literal contains a variable as an argument of its predicate symbol, whereas the second contains a constant. It is here that substitution comes in. Recall that substitution can be applied to make expressions syntactically equal. Moreover, the substitution required to obtain syntactic equality of two given expressions also indicates the difference between the two. If we apply the substitution $\{a/x\}$ to the example above, we obtain syntactic equality of the two atoms $P(x)$ and $P(a)$. So, the two literals $\neg P(x)$ and $P(a)$ become complementary after substitution.

The *unification algorithm* is a general method for comparing expressions; the algorithm computes, if possible, the substitution needed to make the given expressions syntactically equal. Before we discuss the algorithm, we introduce some new notions.

Definition: A substitution σ is called a *unifier* of a given set of expressions $\{E_1, \ldots, E_m\}$ if $E_1\sigma = \cdots = E_m\sigma$, $m \geqslant 2$. A set of expressions is called *unifiable* if it has a unifier.

Definition: A unifier θ of a unifiable set of expressions $E = \{E_1, \ldots, E_m\}$, $m \geqslant 2$, is said to be a *most general unifier* (mgu) if for each unifier σ of E there exists a substitution λ such that $\sigma = \theta\lambda$.

A set of expressions may have more than one most general unifier; however, a most general unifier is unique except for a renaming of the variables.

EXAMPLE 2.26

Consider the set of expressions $\{R(x, f(a, g(y))),\ R(b, f(z, w))\}$. Some possible unifiers of this set are

$$\sigma_1 = \{b/x,\ a/z,\ g(c)/w,\ c/y\}$$

$$\sigma_2 = \{b/x,\ a/z,\ f(a)/y,\ g(f(a))/w\}$$

$$\sigma_3 = \{b/x,\ a/z,\ g(y)/w\}$$

The last unifier is also a most general unifier. By the composition of this unifier with the substitution $\{c/y\}$ we get σ_1; the second unifier is obtained by the composition of σ_3 with $\{f(a)/y\}$.

The unification algorithm, more precisely, is a method for constructing a most general unifier of a finite, non-empty set of expressions. The algorithm considered in this book operates in the following manner. First, the left-most subexpressions in which the given expressions differ is computed. Their difference is placed in a set, called the *disagreement set.* Based on this disagreement set a ('most general') substitution is computed, which is subsequently applied to the given expressions, yielding a partial or total equality. If no such substitution exists, the algorithm terminates with the message that the expressions are not unifiable. Otherwise, the procedure proceeds until each element within each of the expressions has been processed. It can be proved that the algorithm terminates either with a failure message or with a most general unifier of the finite, unifiable set of expressions.

EXAMPLE 2.27

Consider the following set of expressions:

$$S = \{Q(x,f(a),y),\ Q(x,z,c),\ Q(x,f(a),c)\}$$

The left-most subexpression at which the three expressions differ is the second argument of the predicate symbol Q. So the first disagreement set is $\{f(a), z\}$. By means of the substitution $\{f(a)/z\}$ the subexpressions in the second argument position are made equal. The next disagreement set is $\{y, c\}$. By means of the substitution $\{c/y\}$ these subexpressions are also equalized. The final result returned by the unification algorithm is the unifier $\{f(a)/z, c/y\}$ of S. It can easily be seen that this unifier is a most general one.

The following section shows an implementation of the unification algorithm. In Section 2.6.3 we discuss the role of unification in resolution in first-order predicate logic.

2.6.2 Substitution and unification in LISP

The process of substitution as introduced in the previous section can be described in a natural way by means of a recursive algorithm; the substitution algorithm operates on an expression that itself is composed of subexpressions. This idea is the basis of a LISP program that will be discussed below. The program accepts expressions in prefix form, such as `(P (f x (g a)) y)` which stands for the atom $P(f(x,g(a)),y)$. (We will see, however, that the program is a bit more general, and that expressions in infix or postfix form are also accepted.) LISP atoms are used to represent predicate symbols, function symbols, constants and variables.

```
(defun Substitute (s expression)
  (cond ((or (null expression)
             (null s)) expression)
        ((Singleton? expression)
         (let ((binding nil))
           (if (Variable? expression)
               (setq binding (LookUp expression s)))
           (if (null binding)
               expression
               (Term binding))))
        (t (cons (Substitute s (first expression))
                 (Substitute s (rest expression))))))
```

If either the given expression `expression` or the given substitution `s` is empty, the function `Substitute` returns the unmodified expression as its function value. If this is not the case then, by means of the function call (Singleton? expression), it is checked whether or not the expression is a single symbol. Only if the symbol represents a variable, which is determined by means of the call (Variable? expression), is the substitution s examined to find out whether or not it contains a binding for that variable. The actual searching for such a binding is carried out by means of the function LookUp. If a binding for the given variable is found in s, the variable is replaced by its associated term by means of the function call (Term binding). If however no binding is present for it, the variable is returned unmodified. Finally, if the given expression is a compound one, the substitution s is applied recursively to both its first subexpression and its remaining subexpressions. The results of these two recursive function calls are concatenated, thus yielding the required instance of the expression.

The program given above comprises calls to the functions Singleton?, Variable?, LookUp and Term, which will be discussed below. The function Singleton? investigates by means of the call (atom expression) whether or not the expression expression is a LISP atom. As stated above, a LISP atom represents either a predicate symbol, a constant, a function symbol or a variable.

```
(defun Singleton? (expression)
  (atom expression))
```

If the LISP atom expression represents a variable, the function Variable? returns the truth value t. The function Variable? determines whether or not the expression is a variable by checking if its name occurs in a list of reserved variable names:

```
(defun Variable? (expression)
  (member expression '(u v w x y z)))
```

The implementation of the functions Term and LookUp is dependent on the data structures chosen to represent a substitution. In the present program, a substitution is represented by means of an a-list (association list). The following LISP expression gives the general form of a substitution:

$$((t_1 \,.\, x_1) \cdots (t_n \,.\, x_n))$$

The first element of each pair, or binding, in the a-list is a term of the form t_i; the second element is a variable x_i. The function Term enlisted here selects the term of a binding:

```
(defun Term (binding)
  (first binding))
```

To conclude, the function `LookUp` searches for a binding for the variable `var` in the a-list `substitution`:

```
(defun LookUp (var substitution)
  (rassoc var substitution))
```

The actual searching is done using the primitive LISP function `rassoc`; for example, the function call `(rassoc 'x '((a . x) (b . y)))` returns the binding `(a . x)` as a function value.

EXAMPLE 2.28

Consider the substitution `s = ((a . x) ((f y) . z))` and the expression `e = (Q x (g z))`. The function call `(Substitute s e)` yields the result `(Q a (g (f y)))`.

As we have seen above, the substitution algorithm can easily be expressed in the LISP language, providing a definition that looks quite natural. The same can be said of the LISP program that implements the algorithm for computing the composition of two substitutions. The composition algorithm has been implemented by means of the function `Composition`:

```
(defun Composition (r s)
  (append (TermSubst r s)
          (MemberCheck s r)))
```

This function contains calls to two other functions, `TermSubst` and `MemberCheck`, which we now explain. Consider the following two substitutions:

$$r = ((t_1 . x_1) \cdots (t_m . x_m))$$
$$s = ((u_1 . y_1) \cdots (u_n . y_n))$$

By means of the function call `(TermSubst r s)` the substitution `s` will be applied to the terms t_j of `r`, yielding the following result:

$$((t_1 s . x_1) \cdots (t_m s . x_m))$$

From this function `TermSubst`, the function `Substitute`, which has been dealt with above, is called to apply the given substitution `s` to a term which is selected from `r` by means of the function call `(Term binding)`. The last-mentioned function has already been described in the discussion of the function `Substitute`.

The function `TermSubst` is defined as follows:

```
(defun TermSubst (r s)
  (if r
      (let* ((binding (first r))
             (term (Substitute s (Term binding)))
             (var (Variable binding)))
        (if (eq term var)
            (TermSubst (rest r) s)
            (cons (cons term var)
                  (TermSubst (rest r) s))))))
```

The variable in a binding is selected by calling the function `Variable`:

```
(defun Variable (binding)
  (rest binding))
```

Subsequently, in the function `TermSubst` it is checked, by calling the LISP function `eq`, if a (possibly) new binding $(t_i$`s.`$x_i)$ is to be added to the computed composite substitution; the binding is not added if `(eq term var)` returns the truth value `t`. The remaining bindings of the substitution `r` are then processed by means of a recursive call to `TermSubst`. However, if `(eq term var)` returns the value `nil`, the binding resulting from the recursive call to `TermSubst` and the binding just created are concatenated.

After the execution of the function call `(TermSubst r s)` has been completed, the function `MemberCheck` tests which variables y_k of the substitution `s` occur in the set of variables $\{x_1, \ldots, x_m\}$ of the substitution `r`. `MemberCheck` returns a list of bindings from `s`, containing variables not present in the set of variables of the substitution `r`:

```
(defun MemberCheck (v w)
  (if v
      (let ((binding (first v)))
        (if (InsideSubst (Variable binding) w)
            (MemberCheck (rest v) w)
            (cons binding (MemberCheck (rest v) w))))))
```

From `MemberCheck`, the function `InsideSubst` is called. It tests whether or not the variable `var`, selected from a binding from `v` by means of the function call `(Variable binding)`, belongs to the set of variables of the substitution `w`:

```
(defun InsideSubst (var w)
  (if w
      (or (eq var (Variable (first w)))
          (InsideSubst var (rest w)))))
```

To conclude, in the function `Composition`, the results of the function calls to `TermSubst` and `MemberCheck`, both a-lists, are concatenated using the primitive LISP function `append`.

EXAMPLE 2.29

The function call `(Composition '(((f x) . x) (u . z)) '((a . z) (b . x) (z . u)))` returns the value `(((f b) . x) (z . u))`.

Various versions are known of the unification algorithm. The one described in the following LISP program presents the algorithm in a compact, recursive form. As before, expressions entered to the program are supposed to be in prefix form. For example, the expression $P(x,f(a,y))$ should be entered into the program as `(P x (f a y))`.

```
(defun Unify (exp1 exp2)
  (cond ((or (atom exp1) (atom exp2)); exp1 or exp2 is a symbol
         (Disagreement exp1 exp2))
        ; otherwise, both exp1 and exp2 are compound
        (t (let ((subexp1 (first exp1))
                 (remexp1 (rest exp1))
                 (subexp2 (first exp2))
                 (remexp2 (rest exp2))
                 (s1 nil))
             (setq s1 (Unify subexp1 subexp2))
             (if (eq s1 'FAIL) 'FAIL
                 (let ((inst1 (Substitute s1 remexp1))
                       (inst2 (Substitute s1 remexp2))
                       (s2 nil))
                   (setq s2 (Unify inst1 inst2))
                   (if (eq s2 'FAIL) 'FAIL
                       (append s1 s2))))))))
```

The function `Unify` first investigates whether at least one of the expressions `exp1` and `exp2` is an atomic symbol, representing either a constant, a predicate symbol, a function symbol or a variable. If one of these expressions turns out to be an atomic symbol, the function `Disagreement` is invoked to compute the disagreement set. The function `Disagreement` furthermore examines whether it is possible to construct a substitution from the elements in the disagreement set to make the two expressions syntactically equal; if no such substitution exists, the function value `FAIL` is returned. If both expressions `exp1` and `exp2` are compound, the function `Unify` proceeds by first examining the left-most subexpressions `subexp1` and `subexp2` of `exp1` and `exp2` respectively. If unification of `subexp1` and `subexp2` succeeds, yielding the substitution `s1` as its result, then the function `Substitute`, which has been described above, is called to replace the variables occurring in the remaining parts of the expressions, `remexp1` and `remexp2` respectively, by their associated terms from `s1`. Then `Unify` is called recursively to deal with the remaining subexpressions. Note that `remexp1` and `remexp2` are not examined if unification of `subexp1` and `subexp2` fails.

Before we describe the function `Disagreement` in more detail, we illustrate its behaviour by means of an example.

EXAMPLE 2.30

Let `exp1` = `x` and `exp2` = `(f a)`. The function `Disagreement` returns as its value the list `(((f a) . x))`. Note that this list can be used directly for the representation of the necessary substitution to make the expressions `exp1` and `exp2` syntactically equal.

In the function `Disagreement`, it is first examined whether or not the expressions `exp1` and `exp2` are syntactically equal:

```
(defun Disagreement (exp1 exp2)
  (cond ((eq exp1 exp2) nil) ; return nil if both equal
        ((Variable? exp1) (OccurCheck exp1 exp2))
        ((Variable? exp2) (OccurCheck exp2 exp1))
        (t 'FAIL))) ; not unifiable
```

If the expressions are already syntactically equal, then obviously no substitution is required. So in that case the empty substitution, represented in LISP by means of the symbol `nil`, is returned. The function `Variable?` is used to investigate whether one of the given expressions `exp1` and `exp2` is a variable, again by examining a list of valid variable names, just as in the program for substitution. If one of the expressions is a variable, it is necessary to check whether the other expression, now considered as the term in a new binding, contains that variable, since naively adding the binding to the substitution could introduce cyclic dependencies between bindings. This test, called the *occur check*, is performed in the function `Disagreement` by means of a call to the function `OccurCheck`, which is implemented as follows:

```
(defun OccurCheck (var term)
  (if (Inside var term) 'FAIL
      (list (cons term var)))) ; return binding
```

The function `Inside`, called from `OccurCheck`, examines whether or not the variable `var` occurs in the term `term`:

```
(defun Inside (x expression) ; does x occur inside the expression?
  (cond ((null expression) nil)
        ((atom expression) (eq x expression))
        (t (or (Inside x (first expression))
               (Inside x (rest expression))))))
```

EXAMPLE 2.31

Consider the following set of expressions:

$$\{P(x,f(x),y),\ P(g(b),w,z)\}$$

The call `(Unify '(P x (f x) y) '(P (g b) w z))` to the function `Unify` then yields the following result:

```
(((g b) . x) ((f (g b)) . w) (z . y))
```

In studying the function `Unify`, the attentive reader may have noticed that we did not use the function `Composition` for computing the composition of the (partial) substitutions `s1` and `s2`; instead, we simply used the LISP function `append`. This simplification, which is a favourable one from the perspective of efficiency, is allowed in this case, because we explicitly used the earlier mentioned property $E(\sigma\theta) = (E\sigma)\theta$ where E is an expression and σ, θ are substitutions. Immediately after the (partial) substitution `s1` has been computed, all variables in `s1` which occur in the remaining subexpressions `remexp1` and `remexp2` are replaced by their associated terms.

2.6.3 Resolution

Now that we have dealt with the subjects of substitution and unification, we are ready for a discussion of resolution in first-order predicate logic. We start with an informal introduction to the subject by means of an example.

EXAMPLE 2.32

Consider the following set of clauses:

$$\{C_1 = P(x) \vee Q(x),\ C_2 = \neg P(f(y)) \vee R(y)\}$$

As can be seen, the clauses C_1 and C_2 do not contain complementary literals. However, the atoms $P(x)$, occurring in C_1, and $P(f(y))$, occurring in the literal $\neg P(f(y))$ in the clause C_2, are unifiable. For example, if we apply the substitution $\sigma = \{f(a)/x,\ a/y\}$ to $\{C_1, C_2\}$, we obtain the following set of instances:

$$\{C_1\sigma = P(f(a)) \vee Q(f(a)),\ C_2\sigma = \neg P(f(a)) \vee R(a)\}$$

The resulting instances $C_1\sigma$ and $C_2\sigma$ *do* contain complementary literals, namely $P(f(a))$ and $\neg P(f(a))$ respectively. As a consequence, we are now able to find a resolvent of $C_1\sigma$ and $C_2\sigma$, being the clause

$$C_3' = Q(f(a)) \vee R(a)$$

The resolution principle in first-order predicate logic makes use of the unification algorithm for constructing a most general unifier of two suitable atoms; the subsequent application of the resulting substitution to the literals containing the atoms renders them complementary. In the preceding example, the atoms $P(x)$ and $P(f(y))$ have a most general unifier $\theta = \{f(y)/x\}$. The resolvent obtained after applying θ to C_1 and C_2 is

$$C_3 = Q(f(y)) \vee R(y)$$

The clause C_3' from the previous example is an instance of C_3, the so-called *most general clause*: if we apply the substitution $\{a/y\}$ to C_3, we obtain the clause C_3'.

It should be noted that it is necessary to rename different variables having the same name in both parent clauses before applying resolution, since the version of the unification algorithm discussed in the previous section is not capable of distinguishing between equally named variables actually being the same variable, and equally named variables being different variables because of their occurrence in different clauses.

EXAMPLE 2.33

Consider the atoms $Q(x,y)$ and $Q(x,f(y))$ occurring in two different clauses. In this form our unification algorithm reports failure in unifying these atoms (because of the occur check). We rename the variables x and y in $Q(x,f(y))$ to u and v respectively, thus obtaining the atom $Q(u,f(v))$. Now, if we apply the unification algorithm again to compute a most general unifier of $\{Q(u,f(v)), Q(x,y)\}$, it will come up with the (correct) substitution $\sigma = \{u/x, f(v)/y\}$.

We have already mentioned in Section 2.3 that the meaning of a formula is left unchanged by renaming variables. We furthermore recall that formulas differing only in the names of their (bound) variables are called variants.

From the examples presented so far, it should be clear by now that resolution in first-order predicate logic is quite similar to resolution in propositional logic: literals are cancelled out from clauses, thus generating new clauses. From now on, cancelling out a literal L from a clause C will be denoted by $C\backslash L$.

Definition: Consider the parent clauses C_1 and C_2, respectively containing the literals L_1 and L_2. If L_1 and $\neg L_2$ have a most general unifier σ, the clause $(C_1\sigma\backslash L_1\sigma) \vee (C_2\sigma\backslash L_2\sigma)$ is called a *binary resolvent* of C_1 and C_2. Resolution in which each resolvent is a binary resolvent is known as *binary resolution*.

A pair of clauses may have more than one resolvent, since they may contain more than one pair of complementary literals. Moreover, not every resolvent is necessarily a binary resolvent: there are more general ways for obtaining a resolvent. Before giving a more general definition of a resolvent, we introduce the notion of a factor.

Definition: If two or more literals in a clause C have a most general unifier σ, the clause $C\sigma$ is said to be a *factor* of C.

EXAMPLE 2.34

Consider the following clause:

$$C = P(g(x),h(y)) \vee Q(z) \vee P(w,h(a))$$

The literals $P(g(x),h(y))$ and $P(w,h(a))$ in C have a most general unifier $\sigma = \{g(x)/w,\ a/y\}$. So,

$$\begin{aligned} C\sigma &= P(g(x),h(a)) \vee Q(z) \vee P(g(x),h(a)) \\ &= P(g(x),h(a)) \vee Q(z) \end{aligned}$$

is a factor of C. Note that one duplicate literal $P(g(x),h(a))$ has been removed from $C\sigma$.

The generalized form of resolution makes it possible to cancel out more than one literal from one or both of the parent clauses by first computing a factor of one or both of these clauses.

EXAMPLE 2.35

Consider the following set of clauses:

$$\{C_1 = P(x) \vee P(f(y)) \vee R(y),\ C_2 = \neg P(f(a)) \vee \neg R(g(z))\}$$

In the clause C_1 thc two literals $P(x)$ and $P(f(y))$ have a most general unifier $\sigma = \{f(y)/x\}$. If we apply this substitution σ to the clause C_1, one of these literals can be removed:

$$\begin{aligned} (P(x) \vee P(f(y)) \vee R(y))\sigma &= P(f(y)) \vee P(f(y)) \vee R(y) \\ &= P(f(y)) \vee R(y) \end{aligned}$$

The result is a factor of C_1. The literal $P(f(y))$ in $C_1\sigma$ can now be unified with the atom $P(f(a))$ in the literal $\neg P(f(a))$ occurring in C_2, using the substitution $\{a/y\}$. We obtain the resolvent

$$C_3 = R(a) \vee \neg R(g(z))$$

Note that a total of three literals has been removed from C_1 and C_2. The reader can easily verify that there are several other resolvents from the same parent clauses:

- By taking $L_1 = P(x)$ and $L_2 = \neg P(f(a))$ we get the resolvent $P(f(y)) \vee R(y) \vee \neg R(g(z))$
- Taking $L_1 = P(f(y))$ and $L_2 = \neg P(f(a))$ results in the resolvent $P(x) \vee R(a) \vee \neg R(g(z))$
- By taking $L_1 = R(y)$ and $L_2 = \neg R(g(z))$ we obtain $P(x) \vee P(f(g(z))) \vee \neg P(f(a))$

We now give the generalized definition of a resolvent in which the notion of a factor is incorporated.

Definition: A *resolvent* of the parent clauses C_1 and C_2 is one of the following binary resolvents:

(1) a binary resolvent of C_1 and C_2
(2) a binary resolvent of C_1 and a factor of C_2
(3) a binary resolvent of a factor of C_1 and C_2
(4) a binary resolvent of a factor of C_1 and a factor of C_2

The most frequent application of resolution is refutation: the derivation of the empty clause □ from a given set of clauses. The following procedure gives the general outline of this resolution algorithm.

```
procedure Resolution(S)
  clauses ← S;
  while □ ∉ clauses do
    {c_i, c_j} ← SelectResolvable(clauses);
    resolvent ← Resolve(c_i, c_j);
    clauses ← clauses ∪ {resolvent}
  od
end
```

This algorithm is non-deterministic. The selection of parent clauses c_i and c_j can be done in many ways; how it is to be done has not been specified in the algorithm. Several different strategies have been described in the literature, each of them prescribing an unambiguous way of choosing parent clauses from the clause set. Such strategies are called the *control strategies* of resolution or *resolution strategies*. Several of these resolution strategies offer particularly efficient algorithms for making computer-based theorem proving feasible. Some well-known strategies are: *semantic resolution*, which was developed by J.R. Slagle in 1967, *hyperresolution* developed by J.A. Robinson in 1965, and various forms of *linear resolution*, such as *SLD resolution*, in the development of which R.A. Kowalski played an eminent role. At present, SLD resolution in particular is a strategy of major interest, because of its relation to the programming language PROLOG.

2.7 Resolution strategies

Most of the basic principles of resolution have been discussed in the previous section. However, one particular matter, namely the efficiency of the resolution algorithm, has not been dealt with explicitly as yet. It is needless to say that the subject of efficiency is an important one for automated reasoning.

Unfortunately, the general refutation procedure introduced in Section 2.6.3 is quite inefficient, as in many cases it will generate a large number of redundant clauses, that is, clauses not contributing to the derivation of the empty clause.

EXAMPLE 2.36

Consider the following set of clauses:

$$S = \{P, \neg P \vee Q, \neg P \vee \neg Q \vee R, \neg R\}$$

To simplify referring to them, the clauses are numbered as follows:

(1) P
(2) $\neg P \vee Q$
(3) $\neg P \vee \neg Q \vee R$
(4) $\neg R$

If we apply the resolution principle by systematically generating all resolvents, without utilizing a more specific strategy in choosing parent clauses, the following resolvents are successively added to S:

(5) Q (using 1 and 2)
(6) $\neg Q \vee R$ (using 1 and 3)
(7) $\neg P \vee R$ (using 2 and 3)
(8) $\neg P \vee \neg Q$ (using 3 and 4)
(9) R (using 1 and 7)

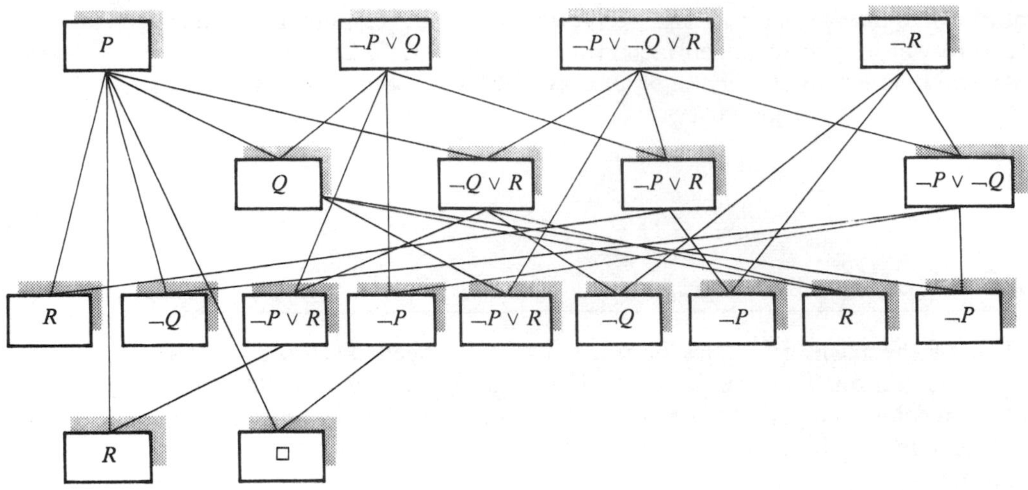

Figure 2.3 Refutation of $\{P, \neg P \vee Q, \neg P \vee \neg Q \vee R, \neg R\}$.

(10) $\neg Q$ (using 1 and 8)
(11) $\neg P \vee R$ (using 2 and 6)
(12) $\neg P$ (using 2 and 8)
(13) $\neg P \vee R$ (using 3 and 5)
(14) $\neg Q$ (using 4 and 6)
(15) $\neg P$ (using 4 and 7)
(16) R (using 5 and 6)
(17) $\neg P$ (using 5 and 8)
(18) R (using 1 and 11)
(19) $\square$ (using 1 and 12)

This derivation of the empty clause $\square$ from S has been depicted in Figure 2.3 by means of a derivation graph. As can be seen, by systematically generating all resolvents in a straightforward manner, 15 of them were obtained, while, for instance, taking the two resolvents

(5′) $\neg P \vee R$ (using 2 and 3)
(6′) R (using 1 and 5′)

would lead directly to the derivation of the empty clause:

(7′) $\square$ (using 4 and 6′)

In the latter refutation, significantly fewer resolvents were generated.

The main goal of applying a resolution strategy is to restrict the number of redundant clauses generated in the process of resolution. This improvement in efficiency is achieved by incorporating particular algorithmic refinements in the resolution principle. Some important resolution strategies will be discussed in the following two sections.

2.7.1 Semantic resolution

Semantic resolution is the name of a class of resolution strategies all having in common that the process of resolution is controlled by the declarative semantics of the clauses to be processed. We will briefly introduce the general idea and present some special forms of semantic resolution informally.

Consider an unsatisfiable set of clauses S. It is possible to divide the set of clauses S into two separate subsets on the basis of a particular interpretation I: the subset S_1 contains the clauses from S which are *false* in I, and the subset S_2 contains the clauses which are *true* in I. Since S is unsatisfiable, no interpretation can ever make all clauses either *true* or *false*. So the clause set S is split into two non-empty subsets. This semantic splitting can be used as the basis for a control strategy in which one of the parent clauses is chosen from S_1, and the other one from S_2. The generated resolvent is added to either S_1 or to S_2, depending on the interpretation I. In the next example, the particulars of this form of resolution are illustrated.

EXAMPLE 2.37

Consider once more the following unsatisfiable set of clauses:

$$S = \{P, \neg P \vee Q, \neg P \vee \neg Q \vee R, \neg R\}$$

Furthermore, consider the interpretation I, defined by

$$I(P) = \mathit{false}$$
$$I(Q) = \mathit{false}$$
$$I(R) = \mathit{false}$$

Using this interpretation, we divide the set S into the following two subsets S_1 and S_2:

$$S_1 = \{P\}$$
$$S_2 = \{\neg P \vee Q, \neg P \vee \neg Q \vee R, \neg R\}$$

The reader can verify that, using the control strategy mentioned above, only the resolvents Q, $\neg Q \vee R$, $\neg P \vee R$, R and $\Box$ will successively be generated.

A further refinement of the described strategy can be obtained by assigning a particular *order* to the literals in the clauses. For example, in propositional logic an ordering is imposed on the propositional symbols occurring in the set of clauses. Resolution is now restricted not only by requiring that the two parent clauses are selected from the different subsets S_1 and S_2 of S (obtained from an interpretation I), but in addition by demanding that the literal from the clause selected from S_1 to be resolved upon is in that clause the highest one according to the ordering imposed.

Another form of semantic resolution is the *set-of-support strategy*. As we mentioned above, resolution is generally applied to prove that a specific clause G is the logical consequence of a satisfiable set of clauses S. Usually such a proof is by refutation, that is, it has the form of a derivation of the empty clause $\square$ from $W = S \cup \{\neg G\}$. The information that the set of clauses S is satisfiable is exploited in the set-of-support strategy to decrease the number of resolvents generated. Obviously, it is not sensible to select both parent clauses from S; since S is satisfiable, the resulting resolvent could never be the empty clause $\square$. In the set-of-support strategy a given set of clauses W is divided into two disjoint sets: the set S being the original satisfiable set of clauses and the set T initially only containing the clauses to be proved. The set T is called the *set of support*. Now, in each resolution step at least one of the parent clauses has to be a member of the set of support. Each resulting resolvent is added to T. It is said that these clauses 'support' the clauses that were to be proved, hence the name 'set of support'. The set-of-support strategy is a powerful control strategy, which prevents the generation of many resolvents not contributing to the actual proof. The strategy is both sound and complete.

EXAMPLE 2.38

Consider the following set of clauses:

$$W = \{P, \neg P \vee Q, \neg P \vee \neg Q \vee R, \neg R\}$$

It can easily be seen that the following subset $S \subset W$ is satisfiable:

$$S = \{P, \neg P \vee Q, \neg P \vee \neg Q \vee R\}$$

(For example, choose an interpretation I such that $I(P) = I(Q) = I(R) = true$.) The remaining clause from W constitutes the set of support $T = \{\neg R\}$; so $S \cup T = W$. For ease of exposition, we again number the clauses in S and T:

(1) P
(2) $\neg P \vee \neg Q \vee R$

(3) $\neg P \vee Q$
(4) $\neg R$

Resolution using the set-of-support strategy successively generates the following resolvents:

(5) $\neg P \vee \neg Q$ (using 2 and 4)
(6) $\neg Q$ (using 1 and 5)
(7) $\neg P$ (using 3 and 5)
(8) $\square$ (using 1 and 7)

Note that this strategy can be considered to be a form of top-down inference; the set of support exploited in this strategy may be viewed as a set of goals.

2.7.2 SLD resolution: a special form of linear resolution

Linear resolution has been named after the structure of the derivation graph created by this class of strategies: in every resolution step the last generated resolvent is taken as a parent clause. The other parent clause is either a clause from the original set of clauses or a resolvent that has been generated before. A special form of linear resolution is *input resolution*. In this strategy, each resolution step, with the exception of the first one, is carried out on the last generated resolvent and a clause from the original set of clauses. The former clauses are called *goal clauses*; the latter clauses are called *input clauses*, thus explaining the name of the strategy. Input resolution is a complete strategy for Horn clauses; for the clausal form of logic in general, however, input resolution is not complete.

A variant of input resolution which currently attracts a great deal of attention is *SLD resolution* for Horn clauses. In this resolution strategy, input resolution is extended with a *selection rule* which determines at every step which literal from the goal clause is selected for resolution. The remainder of this section discusses SLD resolution.

An SLD derivation is defined as follows.

Definition: Let $\{C_i\}$ be a set of Horn clauses of the form

$$C_i = B \leftarrow B_1, \ldots, B_p$$

where $p \geqslant 0$, and let G_0 be a goal clause of the form

$$G_0 = \leftarrow A_1, \ldots, A_q$$

where $q \geqslant 0$. An *SLD derivation* is a finite or infinite sequence $G_0, G_1, \ldots$ of goal clauses, a sequence $C_1, C_2, \ldots$ of variants of input clauses, and a sequence $\theta_1, \theta_2, \ldots$ of most general unifiers, such that each G_{i+1} is derived from $G_i = \leftarrow A_1, \ldots, A_k$ and C_{i+1} using θ_{i+1} if the following conditions hold:

(1) A_j is the atom in the goal clause G_i chosen by the selection rule to be resolved upon.

(2) C_{i+1} is an input clause of the form

$$C_{i+1} = B \leftarrow B_1, \ldots, B_p$$

(in which variables have been renamed, if necessary), such that $A_j\theta_{i+1} = B\theta_{i+1}$, where θ_{i+1} is a most general unifier of A_j and B.

(3) G_{i+1} is the clause

$$G_{i+1} = \leftarrow (A_1, \ldots, A_{j-1}, B_1, \ldots, B_p, A_{j+1}, \ldots, A_k)\theta_{i+1}$$

If for some $n \geqslant 0$, $G_n = \square$, then the derivation is called an *SLD refutation* and the number n is called the *length of the refutation.*

Note that a new goal clause G_{i+1} is the resolvent of the last computed resolvent G_i and (a variant of) an input clause C_{i+1}. Figure 2.4 shows the general form of a derivation tree by SLD resolution. In this figure the sequence of successive goal clauses (resolvents) $G_0, G_1, \ldots$ has been indicated.

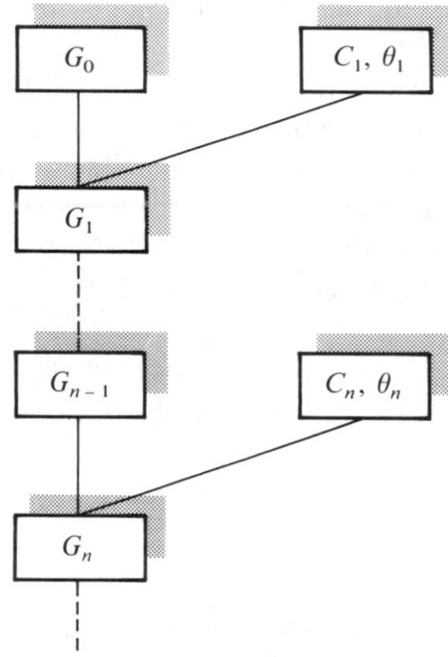

Figure 2.4 Derivation tree of SLD resolution.

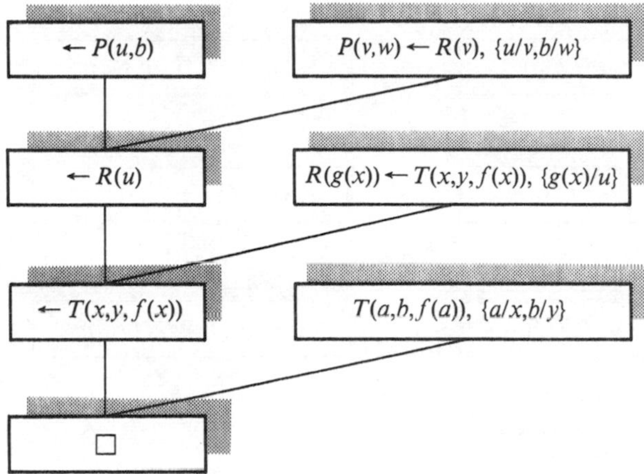

Figure 2.5 An SLD refutation.

EXAMPLE 2.39

Consider the following set of Horn clauses:

$$\{R(g(x)) \leftarrow T(x,y,f(x)),\ T(a,b,f(a)),\ P(v,w) \leftarrow R(v)\}$$

Furthermore, let the following goal clause be given:

$$\leftarrow P(u,b)$$

The clause set obtained by adding the goal clause to the original set of clauses is unsatisfiable. This can be proved using SLD resolution. Figure 2.5 depicts this proof by SLD refutation as a derivation tree.

SLD resolution is both sound and complete for Horn clauses. Furthermore, it is similar to the set-of-support strategy in the sense that it is also a resolution strategy controlled by a set of goals. So SLD resolution is a form of top-down inference as well. In general it is advantageous to restrict applying the resolution principle to clauses satisfying the Horn clause format: various resolution algorithms for propositional Horn clause logic are known to have a worst-case time complexity almost linear in the number of literals. When applying some resolution strategy suitable for the clausal form of logic in general, we always have to face the danger of a combinatorial explosion. Moreover, for systems based on SLD resolution many efficient implementation techniques have been developed by now, one of which will be discussed in the next section. But there definitely are problems for which a resolution strategy applying some form of bottom-up inference turns out to be more efficient than SLD resolution.

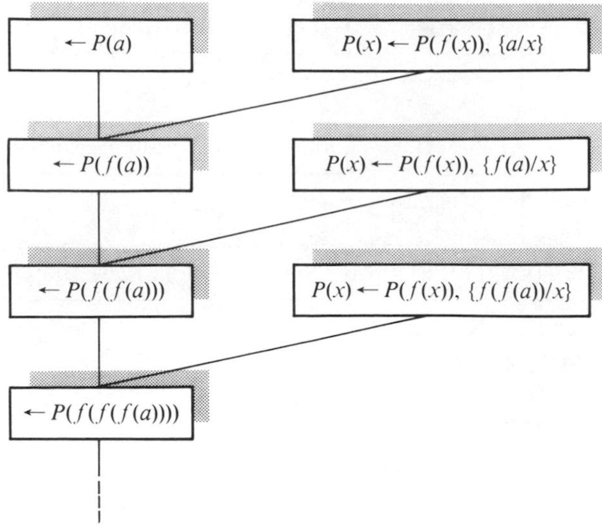

Figure 2.6 Infinite derivation tree by SLD resolution.

Before introducing the notion of a search space for SLD resolution, we give another example.

EXAMPLE 2.40

Consider the following set of Horn clauses:

$$C_1 = P(x) \leftarrow P(f(x))$$
$$C_2 = P(f(f(a))) \leftarrow$$

If these clauses are tried in the order in which they are specified, then for the goal clause $\leftarrow P(a)$ no refutation is found in a finite number of steps, although the resulting set of clauses is obviously unsatisfiable. The corresponding derivation tree is shown in Figure 2.6. However, if the clauses C_1 and C_2 are processed in the reverse order C_2, C_1, a refutation will be found in a finite number of steps; the resulting refutation tree is shown in Figure 2.7.

Now let the search space for SLD resolution for a given goal on a set of clauses be a graph in which every possible SLD derivation is shown. Such a search space is often called an *SLD tree*. The branches of the tree terminating in the empty clause □ are called *success branches*. Branches

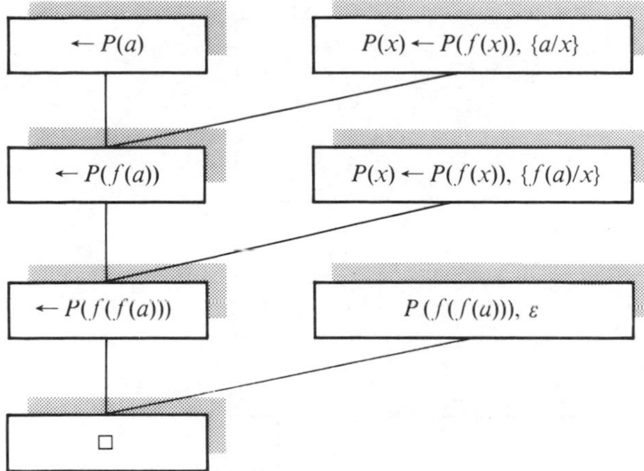

Figure 2.7 Refutation by SLD resolution.

corresponding to infinite derivations are called *infinite branches*, and the branches representing derivations which have not been successful and cannot be pursued any further are called *failure branches*. The *level* of a vertex in an SLD tree is obtained by assigning the number 0 to the root of the tree; the level of each other vertex of the tree is obtained by incrementing the level of its parent vertex by 1. The use of level numbers will be discussed further in the next section.

EXAMPLE 2.41

Figure 2.8 shows the SLD tree corresponding to SLD resolution on the set of clauses from the previous example. The right branch of the tree is a success branch and corresponds to the refutation depicted in Figure 2.7; the left branch is an example of an infinite branch.

It can easily be seen that a specific, fixed order in choosing parent clauses for resolution, such as in the previous example, corresponds to a depth-first search in the search space. Note that such a depth-first search defines an incomplete resolution procedure, whereas a breadth-first search strategy defines a complete one.

Although SLD resolution is both sound and complete for Horn clauses, in practical realizations, for reasons of efficiency, variants of the algorithm are used that are neither sound nor complete. First of all, in

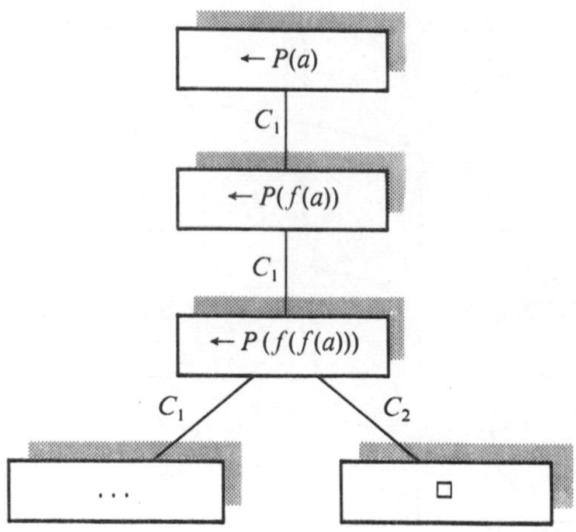

Figure 2.8 An SLD tree.

many implementations the 'expensive' occur check has been left out from the unification algorithm, thus destroying the soundness; the lack of the occur check might lead to circular variable bindings and yield 'resolvents' that are not logical consequences of the set of clauses. Furthermore, often the original clauses are tried in some specific order, such as for example the order in which the clauses have been specified; the next input clause is only examined after the previous one has been fully explored. As a consequence, the algorithm might not be able to find a proof of a given theorem; because of an inappropriate choice of the order in which the clauses are processed, an infinite derivation tree can be created. In this way, completeness of SLD resolution will be lost.

We have mentioned before that SLD resolution is of major interest because of its relation with the programming language PROLOG. In PROLOG, the control strategy employed is roughly an implementation of SLD resolution; the variant used, however, is neither sound nor complete. In most (standard) PROLOG systems, the selection rule picks the left-most atom from a goal for resolution. A depth-first strategy for searching the SLD tree is used; most PROLOG systems try the clauses in the order in which they have been specified. Furthermore, in PROLOG systems, for efficiency reasons, the occur check has been left out of the implementation.

The Horn clause subset of logic is not as expressive as the full clausal form of logic is. As is shown in the following example, this might lead to problems when translating the logical formulas into the Horn clause subset. We next show what solution PROLOG offers to this problem.

EXAMPLE 2.42

In Section 2.2 we defined the following predicates with their associated intended meaning:

Artery	=	'is an artery'
Large	=	'is a large artery'
Wall	=	'has a muscular wall'
Oxygenrich	=	'contains oxygen-rich blood'
Exception	=	'is an exception'

The formula $\forall x(Artery(x) \rightarrow Wall(x))$ represents the knowledge that every artery has a muscular wall. This formula is logically equivalent to $\forall x(\neg Artery(x) \vee Wall(x))$ and results in the following PROLOG clause:

```
wall(X) :- artery(X).
```

The knowledge that the aorta is an artery is represented in PROLOG by a single fact:

```
artery(aorta).
```

The implication

$$\forall x((Artery(x) \wedge \neg Exception(x)) \rightarrow Oxygenrich(x))$$

states that almost every artery contains oxygen-rich blood, except for instance the pulmonary artery, which contains oxygen-poor blood. This formula is equivalent to

$$\forall x(\neg(Artery(x) \wedge \neg Exception(x)) \vee Oxygenrich(x))$$

and to the formula

$$\forall x(\neg Artery(x) \vee Exception(x) \vee Oxygenrich(x))$$

in disjunctive normal form. Unfortunately, it is not possible to translate this formula directly into PROLOG representation, because the clause contains two positive literals instead of at most one.

However, it is possible to represent the knowledge expressed by the clause in PROLOG by means of the rather special programming trick offered by the standard predicate `not`, which will be discussed below. The PROLOG clause we arrive at is the following:

```
oxygenrich(X) :-
      artery(X),
      not(exception(X)).
```

Note that in the analogous example in Section 2.2 it was necessary to specify that the aorta is not an exception to the general rule that arteries contain oxygen-rich blood. In fact, for a correct behaviour of a proof procedure it was necessary to specify for each artery explicitly whether or not it is an exception to the rule. In most applications, however, it is unreasonable to expect users explicitly to express all negative information relevant to the employed proof procedure. This problem can be handled by considering a ground literal $\neg P$ proved if an attempt to prove P using SLD resolution has not succeeded. So, in the particular case of the example, it is assumed that the goal clause `not(exception(aorta))` is proved.

The inference rule that a negative literal is assumed proved when the attempt to prove the complementary literal has failed is called *negation as failure*. Negation as failure is similar to the so-called *closed-world assumption,* which is quite common in database applications. In PROLOG, an even stronger assumption, known as negation as *finite* failure, is made by taking $\neg P$ as proved only if proving P using SLD resolution has failed in a finite number of steps. The PROLOG predicate `not` is the implementation of this negation as finite failure and therefore should not be taken as the ordinary negation: it is an extra-logical feature of PROLOG.

2.8 Implementation of SLD resolution

The publication of the resolution principle in literature in 1965 was not followed immediately by its application in practical problem solving, which was partly due to the inefficiency of the original algorithm. Further research, aimed at making resolution more suitable for automated theorem proving on a computer, was directed towards the development of control strategies, several of which were mentioned in the previous section, and towards developing better techniques for implementation. A particularly important implementation technique, known as *structure sharing*, was developed in 1972 by R.S. Boyer and J.S. Moore; it remedied part of the efficiency problems. The basic idea of this method is to store and manipulate only a set of variable bindings and pointers to parts of the original clauses, instead of adding the complete data representation of a resolvent to the data representation of a set of clauses. So the atoms in the goal clauses are represented only once, namely in the original clauses. This improves the space complexity of the program considerably. Any resolvent can be reconstructed, just by using the created bindings and the pointers to the original set of Horn clauses.

The variable bindings created during resolution are stored in a data structure which is called an environment.

Definition: An *environment of bindings* ω, or for short an *environment*, is a set of the following form:

$$\omega = \{\langle n_1,t_1\rangle/\langle m_1,x_1\rangle, \ldots ,\langle n_p,t_p\rangle/\langle m_p,x_p\rangle\}$$

where $p \geqslant 0$. The elements $\langle n_i,t_i\rangle/\langle m_i,x_i\rangle$ are called *bindings*. The elements $\langle n_i,t_i\rangle$, called *terms*, are renamed terms t_i and elements of the form $\langle m_i,x_i\rangle$, called *variables*, are renamed variables x_i; t_i and x_i are taken from the original set of clauses. In a term $\langle n_i,t_i\rangle$ and a variable $\langle m_i,x_i\rangle$, n_i and m_i are natural numbers, indicating the level of the derivation at which the particular term or variable has been introduced during resolution. The numbers n_i and m_i are called *level numbers*; t_i and x_i are said to be *names*.

EXAMPLE 2.43

Consider the following goal clause:

(1) $\leftarrow P(x,b)$

and the following ordered collection of Horn clauses:

(2) $P(x,z) \leftarrow Q(x,y), P(y,z)$
(3) $P(x,x) \leftarrow$
(4) $Q(a,b) \leftarrow$

An application of 'ordinary' SLD resolution yields the following resolvents, all of which are added to the given input set of Horn clauses:

(5) $\leftarrow Q(x,y), P(y,b)$ (using 1 and 2)
(6) $\leftarrow P(b,b)$ (using 4 and 5)

Now, if we proceed with goal clause 6, there are two possible derivations between which we have to choose. The first one containing the resolvent

(7) $\leftarrow Q(b,y), P(y,b)$ (via 2 and 6)

is not successful, because it is not possible to derive the empty clause from this goal clause; in fact, it is not even possible to pursue resolution from clause 7. The second, alternative derivation, obtained by proceeding with the clauses 3 and 6 as parents, leads immediately to the derivation of the empty clause:

(7′) $\square$

We now repeat the two derivations just described to illustrate the role the environment of bindings plays in structure sharing.

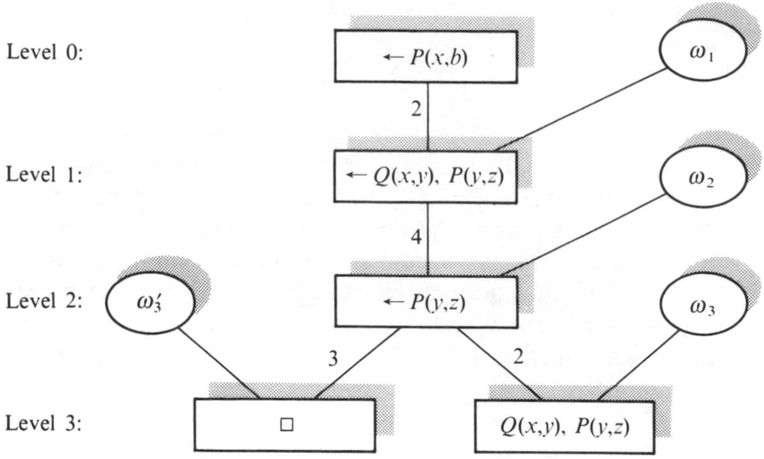

Figure 2.9 SLD tree for structure sharing.

In Figure 2.9 both derivations have been depicted by means of an SLD tree. For each of the two derivations an environment of bindings is built. The atoms occurring in each goal clause originate from the original clauses 1–4. Note that these atoms have not been modified by unification. Next to each goal clause, the bindings of the variables in the particular clause created during resolution have been specified. Let us reconsider the resolvents that are generated:

(5) $\leftarrow Q(x,y), P(y,z)$ (using 1 and 2) and the environment

$$\omega_1 = \{\langle 1,x\rangle/\langle 0,x\rangle, \langle 0,b\rangle/\langle 1,z\rangle\}$$

The binding $\langle 1,x\rangle/\langle 0,x\rangle$ contains the variable $\langle 0,x\rangle$ having the name x at level 0. This variable originates from goal clause 1, the root of the tree. The term in this binding, $\langle 1,x\rangle$, comes from clause 2; it is bound to the variable $\langle 0,x\rangle$ in the first resolution step, through unification of the body of clause 1 and the head of clause 2. Note that the different variables both named x in the clauses 1 and 2, have been renamed by means of level numbers. Similarly, the binding $\langle 0,b\rangle/\langle 1,z\rangle$ indicates that in the first resolution step the variable named z in clause 2 is bound to the constant named b occurring in goal clause 1.

(6) $\leftarrow P(y,z)$ (using 4 and 5 with ω_1) and the environment

$$\omega_2 = \{\langle 1,x\rangle/\langle 0,x\rangle, \langle 0,b\rangle/\langle 1,z\rangle, \langle 2,a\rangle/\langle 1,x\rangle, \langle 2,b\rangle/\langle 1,y\rangle\}$$

Note that ω_1 is contained in ω_2.

(7) $\leftarrow Q(x,y),\ P(y,z)$ (using 2 and 6 with ω_2) and the environment

$$\omega_3 = \{\langle 1,x\rangle/\langle 0,x\rangle,\ \langle 0,b\rangle/\langle 1,z\rangle,\ \langle 2,a\rangle/\langle 1,x\rangle,\ \langle 2,b\rangle/\langle 1,y\rangle,\ \langle 1,y\rangle/\langle 3,x\rangle,\ \langle 1,z\rangle/\langle 3,z\rangle\}$$

(7′) □ (using 3 and 6 with ω_2) and the environment

$$\omega_3' = \{\langle 1,x\rangle/\langle 0,x\rangle,\ \langle 0,b\rangle/\langle 1,z\rangle,\ \langle 2,a\rangle/\langle 1,x\rangle,\ \langle 2,b\rangle/\langle 1,y\rangle,\ \langle 2,b\rangle/\langle 3,x\rangle\}$$

Both environments ω_3 and ω_3' evolve from resolution with clause 6. However, it is not possible to proceed with resolution using clause 7. The environment ω_3' is an alternative extension of ω_2, which, contrary to the other derivation, *does* lead to the derivation of the empty clause □. In this successful derivation, the binding $\langle 2,b\rangle/\langle 3,x\rangle$ is created by resolving the goal $\leftarrow P(y,z)$ with clause 3, $P(x,x)$, in the environment ω_2. Although the variable $\langle 1,z\rangle$ in $\leftarrow P(y,z)$ is bound to the term $\langle 0,b\rangle$ in the environment, and the second argument of $P(x,x)$, the variable $\langle 3,x\rangle$, is already bound to the term $\langle 2,b\rangle$, these variables are unifiable; it is assumed that constants with equal names are equal, independent of their level numbers. Now, to find for example the binding for the variable named x in goal clause 1 after resolution, first the environment ω_3' is searched for the term associated with the variable $\langle 0,x\rangle$, which is $\langle 1,x\rangle$. Subsequently, the binding for the variable $\langle 1,x\rangle$ is looked up. The term bound to this variable is $\langle 2,a\rangle$. We conclude that the variable $\langle 0,x\rangle$ has obtained the binding $\langle 2,a\rangle$, that is, the constant with name a. This binding has been created in two resolution steps.

It is not strictly necessary to use level numbers for the renaming of variables; every method that systematically renames variables in clauses is adequate. However, in the case of SLD resolution, the application of level numbers offers a simple and elegant technique. Furthermore, applying an environment of bindings in the resolution process turns out to be especially useful in logic programming, as here the bindings created by resolution are viewed as the relevant input and output of a deductive computation.

After these introductory remarks concerning structure sharing in resolution, we will proceed by discussing how to implement SLD resolution in the LISP language. Structure sharing will be one of the principal aspects of the program to be developed. In what follows, the set of Horn clauses is taken to be *ordered* according to the specification of its elements. We begin our discussion with the LISP implementations of several important data structures used within the program, respectively for the representation of Horn clauses, for the representation of goals and subgoals in the derivation, and for the representation of the environment of bindings.

Each Horn clause is represented as a list of sublists representing atoms in prefix form. The first element of the list representation of a clause corresponds to the *head* of the clause; the remaining elements of the list constitute its *body*.

EXAMPLE 2.44

In the list `((P x z) (Q x y) (P y z))`, the first element `(P x z)` represents the head of the Horn clause $P(x,z) \leftarrow Q(x,y), P(y,z)$; `(Q x y)` and `(P y z)` together form its body.

A set of Horn clauses is represented in LISP using a list, and is entered to the program by means of the global variable `*clause-set*`.

EXAMPLE 2.45

Consider the following ordered set of Horn clauses once more:

$$P(x,z) \leftarrow Q(x,y), P(y,z)$$
$$P(x,x) \leftarrow$$
$$Q(a,b) \leftarrow$$

This set is entered into LISP as follows:

```
(setq *clause-set*
      '(((P x z) (Q x y) (P y z))
        ((P x x))
        ((Q a b))))
```

The goals and subgoals generated during a derivation are represented in a list of sublists, in which each sublist contains the subgoals originating from a single clause. Such a list of goals has the following form:

$$((G_{1,1} \cdots G_{1,p}) \cdots (G_{n,1} \cdots G_{n,q}))$$

where each goal or subgoal $G_{i,j}$ is represented in prefix form. Later on we will see that our resolution program adds new subgoals, represented as lists of atoms, in front of the given list of goals.

EXAMPLE 2.46

Consider the following list of goals which contains one goal clause consisting of two atoms:

```
( ((P a x) (Q x b)) )
```

From the foregoing discussion it should be evident that this list corresponds with the goal clause $\leftarrow P(a,x), Q(x,b)$. Now, suppose that the following clause is one of the input clauses:

```
((P x y) (Q x z) (P z y))
```

Then applying resolution leads to the creation of the following new list of goals:

```
( ((Q x z) (P z y)) ((Q x b)) )
```

and to a new environment. Note that the subgoal `(P a x)` has disappeared from the list of goals.

In each step during a derivation, an atom is selected from the list of goals for unification with the head of an input clause. Note that this is the selection rule mentioned in Section 2.7. In the program, this atom is obtained by means of a call to the function `FirstGoal` which can be viewed as the implementation of the selection rule:

```
(defun FirstGoal (x)
  (caar x))
```

`FirstGoal` always selects the first atom of the first sublist of goals. The selected atom is subsequently removed from this sublist by the function `ButFirst`:

```
(defun ButFirst (x)
  (cons (cdar x) (rest x)))
```

If only one atom is present in the first sublist, the function `ButFirst` replaces the whole sublist by the empty list. In the other case, the selected atom will just be removed from the first sublist. In the latter case, a new call to the function `FirstGoal` will yield the next goal atom of this sublist.

The selection and deletion of atoms from the goal list is employed as part of SLD resolution. After selecting an atom, the algorithm investigates whether the selected atom is unifiable with the head of one of the clauses kept in the variable `*clause-set*`. The bindings created by unification are added to the environment of bindings already constructed. For the purpose of renaming variables before unification is carried out, both the selected atom and the head of the clause which is being processed are supplemented with a level number. The atoms then have the following representation:

$(n\ a)$

where n is a level number and a is an atom.

The environment of bindings is represented in the program by means of the following LISP data structure, being an a-list:

$(((n_1\ t_1) . (m_1\ x_1)) \cdots ((n_p\ t_p) . (m_p\ x_p)))$

Furthermore, special functions are provided for searching the environment and for adding new bindings to it. The function `LookUp` is used for looking up the binding for a given variable in the environment `environment`:

```
(defun LookUp (x environment)
  (cond ((null x) nil)
        ((Variable? x)
         (let ((binding (LookUp (GetBinding x environment)
                                environment)))
           (cond ((null binding) x)
                 (t binding))))
        (t x)))
```

If the first argument of the function call is not a variable but instead is the empty list, then `LookUp` yields the empty list. If the argument is neither the empty list nor a variable, the function returns the argument unmodified. The last situation occurs in the case of a constant, a predicate symbol or a function term. If `x` is a variable, however, the function `GetBinding` is called for retrieving the binding the variable possibly already has in the environment `environment`. It should be noted that the term of the binding returned by `GetBinding` may in turn be a bound variable. In this case, the function `LookUp` is called recursively to search the environment further until a binding is found which is either a constant, a function term or an unbound variable.

The function `GetBinding`

```
(defun GetBinding (var environment)
  (first (rassoc var environment :test #'equal)))
```

expects for its first argument a variable represented as $(n\ x)$. Looking up a binding for a variable in the environment `environment` is done by means of the primitive function `rassoc`. (The specification `:test #'equal` in the function call specifies that in comparing the first argument of `rassoc` with the cdr of each successive association in the second argument, the function `equal` will be used instead of the usual function `eq`. This specification is necessary in this case, because we utilize a list instead of a symbol as a key in the search; contrary to the function `equal`, the function `eq` does not examine its arguments on structural equality.)

A new binding is added to the environment by means of the function `AddBinding`. This function returns the extended environment as its function value:

```
(defun AddBinding (var term environment)
  (cons (cons term var) environment))
```

We have now discussed the most important data structures with their associated functions. It is time to turn our attention to the implementation of the resolution algorithm.

EXAMPLE 2.47

Consider the following set of Horn clauses once more:

$$P(x,z) \leftarrow Q(x,y), P(y,z)$$
$$P(x,x) \leftarrow$$
$$Q(a,b) \leftarrow$$

and suppose that the goal clause $\leftarrow P(x,b)$ is added to this set. The interface to the SLD resolution program provided for the user is by means of the function `Prove`, which has to be called with a goal clause as an argument. For instance, the function call

```
(Prove '((P x b)))
```

tries to refute the goal clause $\leftarrow P(x,b)$ from the clauses in the variable `*clause-set*`.

To start the resolution process, the function `Prove` calls the function `Resolution`; this function constitutes the actual kernel of the program.

```
(defun Prove (goals)
  (Resolution (list goals) '(0) 1 nil))
```

The first argument in the function call to `Resolution` is a list of goals. Note that the function `list` is applied to construct a list of lists containing goals; this data structure for representing goals is as discussed above. The second argument is a list of level numbers. Each subsequent level number in the list corresponds to a sublist of goals. The list of level numbers is initialized with a list which contains only the level number 0, being the level of the root of the SLD tree. The third argument specifies the level at which resolution might take place in the next step. Finally, the fourth argument is the environment of bindings. Obviously, at the start of the resolution process, there are no bindings present; it therefore is initialized with the empty environment. The main function `Resolution` defining the top-level of the interpreter is as follows:

```
(defun Resolution (goals level-list level environment)
  (cond ((null goals) environment)
        ((null (first goals))
         (Resolution (rest goals)
                     (rest level-list)
                     level
                     environment))
        (t (let ((goal-atom (list (first level-list)
                                  (FirstGoal goals)))
                 (rest-goals (ButFirst goals)))
             (ResolveUnit goal-atom
                          rest-goals
                          level-list
                          level
                          environment)))))
```

In the function `Resolution` it is first investigated whether the list of goals is empty. In that case, the environment which has been constructed so far and which is kept in the parameter `environment` is returned. If the first sublist of goals is empty, which is investigated by means of the form `(null (first goals))`, `Resolution` is recursively invoked to process the remaining goals. Since each level number corresponds to a sublist of goals, and since the first sublist is empty in this case, we also remove the first level number from the list of level numbers by means of the form `(rest level-list)`. However, if the list of goals is neither empty nor has an empty list as its first sublist, the first atom, that is goal, in the list is selected by means of the function `FirstGoal`, supplemented with a level number, and finally assigned to the variable `goal-atom`. Moreover, the selected atom is removed from the list of goals by means of the function `ButFirst`. The result of this function call is assigned to the variable `rest-goals`. Finally, by calling the function `ResolveUnit`, a resolution step is carried out with the selected atom.

The function `ResolveUnit` examines whether the selected atom, `goal`, is unifiable with one of the heads of the clauses from the variable `*clause-set*`. An applicable clause in `*clause-set*` is found by traversing the set of clauses by means of an iterative `do` form. Using the function `Unify`, which will be discussed shortly, it is investigated whether or not the head of a specific clause and the atom `goal` are unifiable. When this atom and the head of the clause are not unifiable, the value `FAIL` is returned by

Unify. In the other case, the possibly extended environment will be returned as a function value. If unification has succeeded, the function Resolution is called again recursively. In the argument list of this recursive call, the body of the selected clause is inserted at the front of the goal list; note that this imposes a depth-first search strategy. Furthermore, the level number that was already reserved for the body of the clause is added to the front of the list level-list, and the current level number is incremented by 1 for the next derivation step.

```
(defun ResolveUnit (goal
                    rest-goals
                    level-list
                    level
                    environment)
  (do ((clause (first *clause-set*)
               (first rest-clauses))
       (rest-clauses (rest *clause-set*)
                     (rest rest-clauses))
       (result 'FAIL)
       (env2 nil))
      ((or (null clause)
           (not (eq result 'FAIL))) result)
    (let ((head (first clause))
          (body (rest clause)))
      (setq env2 (Unify goal
                        (list level head)
                        environment))
      (unless (eq env2 'FAIL)
        (setq result (Resolution (cons body rest-goals)
                                 (cons level level-list)
                                 (1+ level)
                                 env2))))))
```

The function Unify is quite similar to the unification algorithm described in Section 2.6.2. However, here we utilize an environment of bindings in computing a most general unifier of a set of expressions, instead of substituting terms for variables right away in the given expressions at every step. A further distinction is that in the present program the expressions to be unified are supplemented with a level number. Other differences between the two programs will become evident as we proceed with the discussion.

Upon entering the body of the function Unify, the function LookUp is called twice for looking up possible bindings for the expressions x and y. The function LookUp has been discussed above. If both x and y are bound, they are examined on equality by means of the call (equal x y). When one of the arguments is still unbound, the test yields the truth value nil, because then we certainly have different level numbers supplied with the variables, although their names may be equal. If at least one of the arguments x and y is a variable, or if we have found a binding having a variable as its associated term, a new binding is added to the environment by means of a call to the function Addbinding. Note that, contrary to the unification algorithm discussed in Section 2.6.2, the occur check has been left out, so it is possible to create cyclic bindings, thus losing soundness. If one of x and y is a compound expression, Unify is called recursively to examine the first subexpressions and successively the remainders of the expressions if the first partial unification has succeeded.

```
(defun Unify (x y environment)
  (let ((x (LookUp x environment))
        (y (LookUp y environment)))
    (cond ((equal x y) environment)
          ((Variable? x) (AddBinding x y environment))
          ((Variable? y) (AddBinding y x environment))
          ((or (Constant? x)
               (Constant? y))
           (if (eq (Name x)
                   (Name y)) environment
               'FAIL))
          (t (setq environment
                   (Unify (FirstExpr x) (FirstExpr y) environment))
             (if (eq environment 'FAIL) 'FAIL
                 (Unify (RestExpr x)
                        (RestExpr y) environment))))))
```

As can be seen, the function Unify calls several simple functions, such as functions for verifying whether the argument of a function call is a variable or a constant symbol, and functions that split expressions into two separate components. Every symbol is supplemented with a level number. For selecting the name of the symbol the function Name is applied, which is defined as:

```
(defun Name (x)
  (cadr x))
```

The function Variable? investigates whether or not its argument is a variable:

```
(defun Variable? (x)
  (member (Name x) '(u v w x y z)))
```

After extracting the name of the variable from x, the name is checked to see whether or not it occurs in a list of predefined variable names. By means of the function `Constant?` it is investigated whether `x` is a predicate symbol, a function symbol, or a constant:

```
(defun Constant? (x)
  (atom (Name x)))
```

The function `FirstExpr` selects by means of the function call `(first x)` the level number of an expression `x`. This level number and the result of the call `(caadr x)`, yielding the first subexpression of `x`, are concatenated using the primitive function `list`:

```
(defun FirstExpr (x)
  (list (first x) (caadr x)))
```

Finally, the function `Unify` uses the function `RestExpr` which differs from `FirstExpr` only by selecting the remaining subexpressions instead of the first subexpression. The remaining subexpressions are supplemented with the level number and returned as the function value of `RestExpr`:

```
(defun RestExpr (x)
  (list (first x) (cdadr x)))
```

We have now finished the description of the LISP program that implements SLD resolution. By means of the following example we illustrate how the program may be used.

EXAMPLE 2.48

After evaluation of the assignment

```
(setq *clause-set*
      '(((P x z) (Q x y) (P y z))
        ((P x x))
        ((Q a b))))
```

the function call

```
(Prove '((P x b) (P a a)))
```

returns the following environment as its function value:

```
(((0 a) 4 x)
 ((2 b) 3 x)
 ((2 b) 1 y)
 ((2 a) 1 x)
 ((0 b) 1 z)
 ((1 x) 0 x))
```

It should be evident that, after refutation, the variable `x` in the given goal clause is bound to the constant `a` from level 2.

2.9 Applying logic for building expert systems

In the preceding sections, much space has been devoted to the many technical details of knowledge representation and automated reasoning using logic. In the present section, we shall indicate how logic can actually be used for building a logic-based expert system.

In the foregoing, we have seen that propositional logic offers rather limited expressiveness, which in fact is too limited for most real-life applications. First-order predicate logic offers much more expressive power, but that alone does not yet render the formalism suitable for building expert systems. There are some problems. Any automated reasoning method for full first-order logic is doomed to have a worst-case time complexity at least as bad as that of checking satisfiability in propositional logic, which is known to be NP-complete. (This means that no-one has been able to come up with a better deterministic algorithm than an exponentially time-bounded one, although it has not been proved that better ones do not exist.) Furthermore, we know that first-order predicate logic is undecidable, so it is not even certain that an algorithm for checking satisfiability will actually terminate. Fortunately, the circumstances are not always as bad as that. A worst-case characterization seldom gives a realistic indication of the time an algorithm will generally spend on solving an arbitrary problem. Moreover, several suitable syntactic restrictions on first-order formulas have been formulated from which a substantial improvement in the time complexity of the algorithm is obtained; the Horn clause format is one such restriction.

Since syntactic restrictions are acceptable only as far as permitted by the problem domain, we will reconsider the area of cardiovascular disease introduced in Chapter 1 and use it as the problem domain for our logic-based expert system. Of course, only a very small part of that domain can be dealt with here. The SLD resolution program developed in Section 2.8 will be taken as the point of departure for the inference engine of the system. This program will turn out to be too simple to be applicable for our purposes. However, we will show that, by adding a small number of features the program can indeed be used for consulting a logic knowledge base.

Consider again the problem area of cardiovascular disease as introduced in Chapter 1. To formalize some of the knowledge from this problem area, we introduce several predicate symbols, function symbols and so on; these symbols should be interpreted as having the meaning that would be intuitively expected. First of all, we would like to define the notion of a 'cardiovascular disease'. This notion may be formalized by the following logical implication:

$$\forall x((Disorder(x,heart) \vee Disorder(x,bloodvessels)) \rightarrow \\ DiseaseNature(x,cardiovascular))$$

The four specific cardiovascular diseases mentioned in Section 1.4 can now be represented as follows:

$$Disorder(abdominal\text{-}aneurysm, bloodvessels)$$
$$Disorder(aortic\text{-}regurgitation, heart)$$
$$Disorder(arterial\text{-}stenosis, bloodvessels)$$
$$Disorder(atherosclerosis, bloodvessels)$$

This small set of definitions of some of the basic notions used in the domain of cardiovascular disease is now extended with a collection of logical implications, expressing the diagnostic knowledge described in Section 1.4:

$$\forall x((Symptom(x, abdominal\text{-}pain) \wedge Sign(x, abdominal\text{-}murmur) \wedge Sign(x, pulsating\text{-}mass)) \rightarrow SuffersFrom(x, abdominal\text{-}aneurysm))$$

$$\forall x((Symptom(x, leg\text{-}cramp)) \wedge Present(leg\text{-}cramp, walking) \wedge Absent(leg\text{-}cramp, rest)) \rightarrow SuffersFrom(x, arterial\text{-}stenosis))$$

$$\forall x((SuffersFrom(x, arterial\text{-}stenosis) \wedge age(x) > 50) \rightarrow SuffersFrom(x, atherosclerosis))$$

$$\forall x((systolic\text{-}pressure(x) > 140 \wedge (Sign(x, diastolic\text{-}murmur) \vee Sign(x, enlarged\text{-}heart))) \rightarrow SuffersFrom(x, aortic\text{-}regurgitation))$$

Note that we have used function symbols such as *age* to express unique properties of individuals in the domain of discourse and predicate symbols, such as *Sign*, to state properties which are not necessarily unique. In addition, note that these implications contain an atom in which a special binary predicate symbol is used in infix notation, instead of in the usual prefix notation: the predicate $>$. In general, we allow for the *equality predicate* $=$ and the *ordering predicates* $<$ and $>$. These predicates are usually specified in infix position, since this is normal mathematical practice. Both the equality and the ordering predicates have a special meaning, which is described by means of a collection of axioms. We will return to this subject below.

To show how this tiny knowledge base can be applied in a medical diagnostic setting, let us consider a small number of patient cases. Table 2.6 lists all the relevant information concerning two of our patients.

Table 2.6 Two patient cases.

Name	*Sex*	*Age*	*Symptoms*	*Signs*	*Systolic/ diastolic pressure*
Ann	Female	12	Fever	Diastolic murmur	150/60
John	Male	60	Abdominal pain	Abdominal murmur	130/90
				Pulsating mass	

This information may be specified in first-order predicate logic as a set of (positive) literals as follows:

$name(patient) = Ann$
$sex(Ann) = female$
$age(Ann) = 12$
$Symptom(Ann, fever)$
$Sign(Ann, diastolic\text{-}murmur)$
$systolic\text{-}pressure(Ann) = 150$
$diastolic\text{-}pressure(Ann) = 60$

$name(patient) = John$
$sex(John) = male$
$age(John) = 60$
$Symptom(John, abdominal\text{-}pain)$
$Sign(John, abdominal\text{-}murmur)$
$Sign(John, pulsating\text{-}mass)$
$systolic\text{-}pressure(John) = 130$
$diastolic\text{-}pressure(John) = 90$

This completes the specification of our small knowledge base.

We have already mentioned that the equality and ordering predicates have special meanings. These will now be discussed in some detail. The meaning of the equality predicate is defined by means of the following four axioms:

E_1 (*reflexivity*): $\forall x(x = x)$

E_2 (*symmetry*): $\forall x \forall y(x = y \rightarrow y = x)$

E_3 (*transitivity*): $\forall x \forall y \forall z(x = y \wedge y = z \rightarrow x = z)$

E_4 (*substitutivity*): $\forall x_1 \cdots \forall x_n \forall y_1 \cdots \forall y_n((x_1 = y_1 \wedge \cdots \wedge x_n = y_n) \rightarrow f(x_1, \ldots, x_n) = f(y_1, \ldots, y_n))$, and $\forall x_1 \cdots \forall x_n \forall y_1 \cdots \forall y_n((x_1 = y_1 \wedge \cdots \wedge x_n = y_n \wedge P(x_1, \ldots, x_n)) \rightarrow P(y_1, \ldots, y_n))$

Axiom E_1 states that each term in the domain of discourse is equal to itself. Axiom E_2 expresses that the order of the arguments of the equality predicate is irrelevant. Axiom E_3 furthermore states that two terms which are equal to some common term are equal to each other. Note that axiom E_1 follows from the axioms E_2 and E_3; nevertheless, it is usually mentioned explicitly. The three axioms E_1, E_2 and E_3 together imply that equality is an *equivalence relation*. Addition of axiom E_4 renders it a *congruence relation*. The first part of axiom E_4 states that equality is preserved under the application of a function; the second part expresses that equal terms may be substituted for each other in formulas.

EXAMPLE 2.49

Consider the following set of clauses S:

$$S = \{\neg P(f(x),y) \vee Q(x,x),\ P(f(a),a),\ a = b\}$$

Suppose that, in addition, we have the equality axioms. If we add the clause $\neg Q(b,b)$ to S, the resulting set of clauses will be unsatisfiable. This can easily be seen informally as follows. We have $P(f(a),a) \equiv P(f(b),a)$ using the given clause $a = b$ and the equality axiom E_4. Now, we replace the atom $P(f(a),a)$ by the equivalent atom $P(f(b),a)$ and apply binary resolution.

The explicit addition of the equality axioms to the other formulas in a knowledge base suffices for rendering equality available for use in an expert system. However, it is well known that proving theorems in the presence of the equality axioms can be very inefficient, since many redundant clauses may be generated using resolution. Again, several refinements of the (extended) resolution principle have been developed to overcome the inefficiency problem. For dealing with equality, the resolution principle has for example been extended with an extra inference rule: *paramodulation*. Informally speaking, the principle of paramodulation is the following. If clause C contains a term t and if we have a clause $t = s$, then derive a clause by substituting s for a single occurrence of t in C. Therefore, in practical realizations, equality is often present only implicitly in the knowledge base, that is, it is used as a 'built-in' predicate.

In many real-life applications, a universally quantified variable ranges over a finite domain $D = \{c_i \mid i = 1, \ldots, n,\ n \geqslant 0\}$. The following property is usually satisfied:

$$\forall x(x = c_1 \vee x = c_2 \vee \cdots \vee x = c_n) \text{ with } c_i \neq c_j \text{ if } i \neq j$$

These properties are known as the *domain closure* and the *unique name assumption*; from the last assumption we have that objects with different names are different.

EXAMPLE 2.50

Consider the following set of clauses S:

$$S = \{\neg P(x) \vee x = a\}$$

We suppose that the equality axioms as well as the unique name assumption hold. Now, if we add the clause $P(b)$ to S, we obtain an inconsistency, since the derivable clause $b = a$ contradicts the unique name assumption.

The ordering predicates $<$ and $>$ define a *total order* on the set of real numbers. They express the usual, mathematical 'less than' and 'greater than' binary relations between real numbers. Their meaning is defined by means of the following axioms:

O_1 (*irreflexivity*): $\forall x \neg(x < x)$
O_2 (*antisymmetry*): $\forall x \forall y (x < y \rightarrow \neg(y < x))$
O_3 (*transitivity*): $\forall x \forall y \forall z ((x < y \wedge y < z) \rightarrow x < z)$
O_4 (*trichonomy law*): $\forall x \forall y (x < y \vee x = y \vee x > y)$

Axiom O_1 states that no term is less than itself. Axiom O_2 states that reversing the order of the arguments of the predicate $<$ reverses the meaning. Axiom O_3 furthermore states that if a term is less than some other term, and this term is less than a third term, then the first term is less than the third one as well. Note that axiom O_2 follows from O_1 and O_3. Axioms O_1, O_2 and O_3 concern the ordering predicate $<$. The axioms for the ordering predicate $>$ are similar to these; we may just substitute $>$ for $<$ to obtain them. Axiom O_4 states that a given term is either less than, equal to or greater than another given term. Again, in practical realizations, these axioms are not usually added explicitly to the knowledge base, but are assumed to be present implicitly as 'built-in' predicates.

We would now like to use the program for SLD resolution developed in the preceding section for consulting the knowledge base to determine the disorders the given patients are likely to be suffering from. To begin with, it is noted that all formulas can be translated directly into Horn clause format. In extending the program, we impose some restrictions on the use of the equality and ordering predicates in Horn clauses:

- Only the equality predicate $=$ and user-defined predicates are allowed in the conclusion of a Horn clause.
- The second arguments of the equality and ordering predicates are either variables or (numeric) constants; function terms are not

allowed as the second argument of an equality and ordering predicate.

In addition, it is assumed that a knowledge base is consistent before adding the goal clause.

As we have pointed out in the previous section, one of the difficulties with the LISP program for SLD resolution is that it is neither sound nor complete. However, the program can easily be extended to obtain a program which is both sound and complete; in the following, it is assumed that the program has been modified accordingly. The extension is left to the reader as an exercise (see Exercise 2.15). The implementation of the equality and ordering predicates deserves some special attention. We will not add the axioms for these predicates explicitly to our knowledge base. We have chosen an approach in which atoms specifying an equality or an ordering predicate will be treated as *evaluable expressions* if both arguments are numeric constants or properly bound to numeric constants. First of all we have to adapt the unification algorithm for handling evaluable goals. We modify the function `ResolveUnit` discussed in the preceding section by replacing the call to the function `Unify` by a call to the function `Match`, to which the same arguments as before will be passed:

```
(defun Match (goal head environment)
  (cond ((Evaluable? goal environment)
         (EvalAtom goal head environment))
        ((and (OrderPred? goal)
              (EqualityPred? head))
         (let ((new-env (Unify (LevelFirstArg goal)
                               (LevelFirstArg head)
                               environment)))
           (if (eq new-env 'FAIL)
               new-env
               (EvalAtom goal head new-env))))
        (t (Unify goal head environment))))
```

In the function `Match`, the given goal atom is first examined to determine whether it is an evaluable expression, that is, it is investigated to see whether it contains an equality or ordering predicate, and, if so, has arguments which are numbers or are properly bound to numeric constants. This is done by means of the function `Evaluable`:

```
(defun Evaluable? (atom environment)
  (and (or (OrderPred? atom) (EqualityPred? atom))
       (NumericInstance? atom environment)))
```

The functions `OrderPred?` and `EqualityPred?` test whether the predicate of atom is either an ordering or an equality predicate, respectively:

```
(defun OrderPred? (atom)
  (member (Predicate atom) '(< <= > >=)))

(defun EqualityPred? (atom)
  (member (Predicate atom) '( = != )))
```

The function Predicate for selecting the predicate of an atom is defined by:

```
(defun Predicate (atom)
  (first (Name atom)))
```

The function Evaluable? furthermore checks whether both arguments of an atom with a binary predicate symbol are numeric constants or variables bound to numeric constants by means of the function NumericInstance?. This function calls the function LookUp to search for variable bindings in the given environment:

```
(defun NumericInstance? (atom environment)
  (let ((arg1 (LookUp (LevelFirstArg atom) environment))
        (arg2 (LookUp (LevelSecondArg atom) environment)))
    (and (numberp (Name arg1)) (numberp (Name arg2)))))
```

The functions LevelFirstArg and LevelSecondArg yield the first and second arguments, respectively, of the equality or ordering predicate, supplemented with the level number of the original atom atom:

```
(defun LevelFirstArg (atom)
  (list (first atom) (FirstArg atom)))

(defun LevelSecondArg (atom)
  (list (first atom) (SecondArg atom)))
```

The functions FirstArg and SecondArg are defined as follows:

```
(defun FirstArg (atom)
  (cadr (Name atom)))

(defun SecondArg (atom)
  (caddr (Name atom)))
```

If a goal has been shown to be an evaluable expression, the function EvalAtom is called from Match. This function evaluates the given atom by first substituting the bindings for the variables, if these are present, and subsequently passing the resulting instance to the LISP interpreter for evaluation by means of a call to the built-in function `eval`. The function `EvalAtom` is also called from `Match` if we have a goal atom containing an ordering predicate and a head of a clause containing the equality predicate. We then apply the predicate in the goal atom on the second argument of the head and the second argument of the given goal:

```
(defun EvalAtom (goal head environment)
  (let ((goal (Instantiate goal environment))
        (head (Instantiate head environment)))
    (cond ((NumericInstance? goal environment)
           (if (eval (Name goal)) environment
               'FAIL))
          (t (if (and (numberp (SecondArg goal))
                      (numberp (SecondArg head))
                      (funcall (Predicate goal)
                               (SecondArg head)
                               (SecondArg goal)))
                 environment
                 'FAIL)))))
```

The process of substituting the bindings of the variables for the variables in a given atom is done by the function `Instantiate`:

```
(defun Instantiate (atom environment)
  (let ((arg1 (LookUp (LevelFirstArg atom) environment))
        (arg2 (LookUp (LevelSecondArg atom) environment)))
    (list (first atom) (list (Predicate atom)
                             (Name arg1) (Name arg2)))))
```

This completes our description of some extensions to the SLD resolution program. Let us now study an example of how the program can be applied for consulting a logic-based expert system.

EXAMPLE 2.51

Consider again the partial formalization of the domain of cardiovascular disease presented at the beginning of this section. To start with, the given formulas have to be translated into the clausal form of logic. The resulting clauses must then be translated into the LISP representation of Horn clauses, as discussed in the previous section. The resulting list of clauses is assigned to the variable `*clause-set*`. The following knowledge base is obtained:

```
(setq *clause-set*
  '(
  ; DATA FOR John
    ((= (name patient) John))
    ((= (age John) 60))
    ((= (sex John) male))
    ((Symptom John abdominal-pain))
    ((= (systolic-pressure John) 130))
    ((= (diastolic-pressure John) 90))
    ((Sign John abdominal-murmur))
    ((Sign John pulsating-mass))

  ; DATA FOR Ann
    ((= (name patient) Ann))
    ((= (age Ann) 12))
    ((= (sex Ann) female))
    ((Sign Ann diastolic-murmur))
    ((= (systolic-pressure Ann) 150))
    ((= (diastolic-pressure Ann) 60))
    ((Symptom Ann fever))

  ; KNOWLEDGE BASE
    ((DiseaseNature x cardiovascular) (Disorder x heart))
    ((DiseaseNature x cardiovascular) (Disorder x bloodvessels))
    ((Disorder aortic-regurgitation heart))
    ((Disorder abdominal-aneurysm bloodvessels))
    ((Disorder atherosclerosis bloodvessels))
    ((Disorder arterial-stenosis bloodvessels))

    ((SuffersFrom x aortic-regurgitation)
     (> (systolic-pressure x) 140)
     (Sign x diastolic-murmur))
    ((SuffersFrom x aortic-regurgitation)
     (> (systolic-pressure x) 140)
     (Sign x enlarged-heart))
    ((SuffersFrom x abdominal-aneurysm)
     (Symptom x abdominal-pain)
     (Sign x abdominal-murmur)
     (Sign x pulsating-mass))
    ((SuffersFrom x arterial-stenosis)
     (Symptom x legg-cramp)
     (Present legg-cramp walking)
     (Absent legg-cramp rest))
    ((SuffersFrom x artherosclerosis)
     (SuffersFrom x arterial-stenosis)
     (> (age x) 50))))
```

We may now consult the knowledge base, by using the function `Prove` discussed in the previous section. For example, to find out whether or not Ann is suffering from some disease, and if she does what the nature of her disease is, we may enter the following query:

```
>(Prove '((SuffersFrom Ann x) (DiseaseNature x y))))

(((4 cardiovascular) 0 y) ((1 aortic-regurgitation) 4 x)
 ((1 aortic-regurgitation) 0 x) ((0 Ann) 1 x))
```

The result tells us that Ann is suffering from aortic regurgitation, since the variable `x` at level 0 is bound to the constant `aortic-regurgitation`. This appears to be a cardiovascular disease, since the variable `y` at level 0 is bound to the constant `cardiovascular`.

The user interface of the program is rather crude; it is left as an exercise to the reader to make the interaction to the program more enjoyable from a user's point of view (see Exercise 2.16).

2.10 Logic as a representation formalism

Compared with other knowledge representation formalisms in artificial intelligence, logic has the great advantage of having a clear syntax and semantics. A logical deductive system in principle offers a set of inference rules, which is sound and complete: each formula derived using such a set of inference rules has a meaning that is unique in terms of the meaning of the formulas it was derived from. So logic offers a starting point for studying the foundations of knowledge representation and manipulation.

First-order logic in its pure form, however, has hardly ever been used as a knowledge representation formalism in expert systems. This is partly due to the difficulty of expressing domain knowledge in logical formulas. When in a specific problem domain the knowledge is not available in a form 'close' to logic, a lot of energy has to be invested into converting expert knowledge to logical formulas, and in this process valuable information is often lost. Moreover, the type of logic that has been dealt with in this chapter, which is sometimes called *standard logic*, is not suitable for encoding all types of knowledge. For example, reasoning about time and reasoning about reasoning strategies to be followed, often called meta-inference, cannot be represented directly in first-order predicate logic. Moreover, in standard logic it is not possible to handle incomplete and uncertain information, or to deal adequately with exceptional cases to general rules. Currently, however, a lot of research is being carried out concerning *non-standard logics* for expressing such concepts in a formal way. It seems likely that logic will achieve a more prominent place in future generation expert systems.

Suggested reading

For a mathematical introduction to logic and logical deduction the reader is referred to Enderton (1972) and Van Dalen (1983).

The computer program for theorem proving developed by M. Davis is described in Davis (1957). Newell *et al.* (1957) presents the Logic Theory Machine. These papers were reprinted in two highly interesting books edited by Siekmann and Wrightson (1983a, b) containing classic papers on theorem proving. Early papers on the use of theorem-proving techniques in question-answering systems are Slagle (1965) and Green and Raphael (1968). The original article by J.A. Robinson in which the resolution principle was first introduced is Robinson (1965).

Wos *et al.* (1984) gives an introductory overview of various resolution strategies, and describes several interesting applications. Other books on resolution and resolution strategies are Chang and Lee (1973), Loveland (1978) and Robinson (1979). Gallier (1987) follows an approach to resolution different from that of the four books mentioned above; it treats resolution as a special Gentzen proof system. Kowalski (1979) is a readable account of using Horn clause logic for the representation and manipulation of knowledge. Lloyd (1987) discusses the declarative semantics of Horn clause logic by means of Herbrand models and a fixed point operator, and also the operational semantics of SLD resolution. Boyer and Moore (1972) is the original paper concerning structure sharing. Nilsson (1984) offers a description of a LISP implementation of an interpreter that more closely resembles a PROLOG interpreter than the program discussed in this book. A recent efficient implementation of a resolution-based theorem prover, which is available from Argonne National Laboratory, is OTTER (McCune, 1989). The system is highly recommended to those interested in experimenting with theorem proving.

Books introducing a logic-based approach to artificial intelligence are Thayse (1988) and Genesereth and Nilsson (1987). To conclude with, Smets *et al.* (1988) presents an overview of non-standard logics.

EXERCISES

2.1 Consider the interpretation v: *PROP* $\rightarrow$ {*true*, *false*} in propositional logic, which is defined by $v(P) =$ *false*, $v(Q) =$ *true* and $v(R) =$ *true*. What is the truth value of the formula $((\neg P) \wedge Q) \vee (P \rightarrow (Q \vee R))$ given this interpretation v?

2.2 Determine whether each of the following formulas in propositional logic is valid, invalid, satisfiable or unsatisfiable using truth tables:

(a) $P \vee (Q \rightarrow \neg P)$
(b) $P \vee (\neg P \wedge Q \wedge R)$
(c) $P \rightarrow \neg P$
(d) $(P \wedge \neg Q) \wedge (\neg P \vee Q)$
(e) $(P \rightarrow Q) \rightarrow (Q \rightarrow P)$

2.3 Suppose that $F_1, \ldots, F_n$, $n \geqslant 1$, and G are formulas in propositional logic, such that the formula G is a logical consequence of $\{F_1, \ldots, F_n\}$. Construct the truth table of the implication $F_1 \wedge \cdots \wedge F_n \rightarrow G$. What do you call such a formula?

2.4 Prove the following statements using the laws of equivalence for propositional logic:

(a) $P \rightarrow Q \equiv \neg P \rightarrow \neg Q$
(b) $P \rightarrow (Q \rightarrow R) \equiv (P \wedge Q) \rightarrow R$
(c) $(P \wedge \neg Q) \rightarrow R \equiv (P \wedge \neg R) \rightarrow Q$
(d) $P \vee (\neg Q \vee R) \equiv (\neg P \wedge Q) \rightarrow R$

2.5 Prove that the proposition $((P \rightarrow Q) \rightarrow P) \rightarrow P$, known as *Peirce's law*, is a tautology, using the laws of equivalence in propositional logic and the property that, for any propositions π and φ, the formula $\pi \vee \neg\pi \vee \varphi$ is a tautology.

2.6 In each of the following cases, we restrict ourselves to a form of propositional logic offering only a limited set of logical connectives. Prove by means of the laws of equivalence that every formula in full propositional logic can be translated into a formula containing only the given connectives:

(a) the connectives $\neg$ and $\vee$,
(b) the connective $|$ which is known as the *Sheffer stroke*; its meaning is defined by the truth table given in Table 2.7.

Table 2.7 Sheffer stroke.

F	G	$F \mid G$
true	*true*	*false*
true	*false*	*true*
false	*true*	*true*
false	*false*	*true*

2.7 Consider the formula $\forall x(P(x) \vee Q(y))$ in first-order predicate logic. Suppose that the structure

$$S = (\{2,3\}, \varnothing, \{A: \{2,3\} \rightarrow \{true, false\}, B: \{2,3\} \rightarrow \{true, false\}\})$$

is given. The predicates A and B are associated with the predicate symbols P and Q, respectively. Now define the predicates A and B and a valuation v in such a way that the given formula is satisfied in the given structure S and valuation v.

2.8 Consider the following statements. If the statement is correct, prove its correctness using the laws of equivalence; if it is not correct, give a counterexample.

(a) $\forall x P(x) \equiv \neg \exists x \neg P(x)$
(b) $\forall x \exists y P(x,y) \equiv \forall y \exists x P(x,y)$
(c) $\exists x(P(x) \rightarrow Q(x)) \equiv \forall x P(x) \rightarrow \exists x Q(x)$
(d) $\forall x(P(x) \vee Q(x)) \equiv \forall x P(x) \vee \forall x Q(x)$

2.9 Transform the following formulas into the clausal form of logic:

(a) $\forall x \forall y \exists z(P(z,y) \wedge (\neg P(x,z) \rightarrow Q(x,y)))$
(b) $\exists x(P(x) \rightarrow Q(x)) \wedge \forall x(Q(x) \rightarrow R(x)) \wedge P(a)$
(c) $\forall x(\exists y(P(y) \wedge R(x,y)) \rightarrow \exists y(Q(y) \wedge R(x,y)))$

2.10 For each of the following sets of clauses determine whether or not it is satisfiable. If a given set is unsatisfiable, give a refutation of the set using binary resolution; otherwise give an interpretation satisfying it:

(a) $\{\neg P \vee Q, P \vee \neg R, \neg Q, \neg R\}$
(b) $\{\neg P \vee Q \vee R, \neg Q \vee S, P \vee S, \neg R, \neg S\}$
(c) $\{P \vee Q, \neg P \vee Q, P \vee \neg Q, \neg P \vee \neg Q\}$
(d) $\{P \vee \neg Q, Q \vee R \vee \neg P, Q \vee P, \neg P\}$

2.11 Let E be an expression and let σ and θ be substitutions. Prove that $E(\sigma\theta) = (E\sigma)\theta$.

2.12 For each of the following sets of expressions, determine whether or not it is unifiable. If a given set is unifiable, compute a most general unifier:

(a) $\{P(a,x,f(x)), P(x,y,x)\}$
(b) $\{P(x,f(y),y), P(w,z,g(a,b))\}$
(c) $\{P(x,z,y), P(x,z,x), P(a,x,x)\}$
(d) $\{P(z,f(x),b), P(x,f(a),b), P(g(x),f(a),y)\}$

2.13 Use binary resolution to show that each of the following sets of clauses is unsatisfiable:

(a) $\{P(x,y) \vee Q(a,f(y)) \vee P(a,g,(z)), \neg P(a,g(x)) \vee Q(a,f(g(b))), \neg Q(x,y)\}$
(b) $\{append(nil,x,x), append(cons(x,y), z, cons(x,u)) \vee \neg append(y,z,u), \neg append(cons(1,cons(2,nil)),cons(3,nil),x)\}$
(c) $\{R(x,x), R(x,y) \vee \neg R(y,x), R(x,y) \vee \neg R(x,z) \vee \neg R(z,y), R(a,b), \neg R(b,a)\}$

Note that the first three clauses in (c) define an equivalence relation.

2.14 Consider the set of clauses $\{\neg P, P \vee Q, \neg Q, R\}$. We employ the set-of-support resolution strategy. Why do we not achieve a refutation if we set the set of support initially to the clause R?

2.15 Section 2.8 discusses an implementation of SLD resolution in COMMON LISP. This implementation follows the strategy of the variant of SLD resolution employed in PROLOG in the sense that the strategy is incomplete because of its using depth-first search for finding a refutation, and in addition is not sound because of the absence of the occur check in the unification algorithm. Modify this program in such a way that the resulting resolution algorithm will be both sound and complete.

Hints. Use breadth-first search instead of depth-first search. The occur check can be incorporated into the unification algorithm in a similar fashion to that discussed in Section 2.6.2, but now we have to pass the environment of bindings to the function `OccurCheck` as a third argument. Try also to develop a program where *bounded depth-first search* is employed in addition to the occur check. This means including in the program in Section 2.8 the definition `(defconstant *level-bound*` <number>`)` of a constant `*level-bound*`. As the parameter `level` is incremented by one at each next recursive call to `Resolution`, the parameter is checked to see whether it has surpassed the preset maximal level number `*level-bound*`. If this is the case the function returns failure. An alternative solution will then be looked for. Note that bounded depth-first search does not yield full completeness. Experiment with the value assigned to `*level-bound*`.

2.16 Develop a logic knowledge base for a problem domain you are familiar with. Use the program discussed in Section 2.9 after extending it with a more user-friendly interface, together with the knowledge base for answering certain questions concerning the problem domain.

3 Production Rules and Inference

In the early 1970s, A. Newell and H.A. Simon introduced the notion of a *production system* as a psychological model of human behaviour. In this model, part of human knowledge is represented in separate units called *productions* or *production rules*. These units contain information concerning actions a person has to take on perceiving certain stimuli from the environment. Such actions may affect a person's view of environmental reality, on the one hand because previous assumptions may have to be revised, and on the other hand because new phenomena may have to be explained. The model of Newell and Simon closely resembles the two-process theory of memory in cognitive psychology, where two different mechanisms for the storage of incoming sensory information are distinguished: the short-term memory and the long-term memory. Short-term memory contains only a limited amount of rapidly decaying information. It corresponds to the part of a production system in which input and derived data are kept. Long-term memory is for permanent storage of information, and corresponds to the rule base of a production system in which the production rules are specified. The production-rule formalism has been employed by many other researchers in addition to Newell and Simon. Most of them, however, view the production-rule formalism merely as a formal language for expressing certain types of knowledge. The formalism has for example been used in the HEURISTIC DENDRAL system for predicting the molecular structure of compounds, as discussed in Chapter 1. Part of the knowledge necessary for the purpose of this system has been encoded by means of production rules. The greatest success of the formalism, however, came with the building of the MYCIN and EMYCIN systems, in which the suitability of production rules for building diagnostic expert systems was convincingly shown. Another successful system, more directly employing the work of Newell and Simon, is OPS5, which will be discussed in Chapter 7.

Many current expert systems use the production-rule formalism as a knowledge representation scheme. Practical experience with production rules has proved this formalism to be particularly suitable in solving classification problems in which the available knowledge takes the form of rules of thumb. In other types of application, such as design and planning, production rules have also been applied with success. The suitability of the production system approach for building certain types of expert system depends not only on the production-rule formalism itself, but also on the type of inference method employed for rule-based reasoning.

In this chapter, we look closely at a number of important notions from production systems. Section 3.1 discusses the various schemes for representing the knowledge a production system offers. We proceed by discussing the two basic reasoning methods for systems with production rules in Section 3.2. To conclude, Section 3.3 discusses a technique for enlarging the expressive power of the production-rule formalism.

3.1 Knowledge representation in a production system

A production system offers a number of formalisms for representing expert knowledge. The most important of these, of course, is the production-rule formalism, in which the actual problem-solving knowledge is expressed. The entire set of production rules in a production system is called its *rule base*. In addition to the production-rule formalism, a production system provides a means for defining the objects referred to in the production rules, called the *domain declaration* in this book. The rule base and the domain declaration together constitute the *knowledge base* of the production system. These and other schemes for representing knowledge will be discussed in detail in the subsequent sections.

3.1.1 Variables and facts

During a consultation of the knowledge base of a production system, information is constantly being added, removed or modified as a result of the application of production rules, in the light of data entered by the user, or as a result of querying some database. The facts that become known to the system during a consultation are stored in a so-called *fact set*, also known as the *global database* or *working memory* of the system.

Factual information can be represented in a number of ways. One simple way is to represent facts by means of *variables* which can take either a single constant or a set of constants as a value. Note that the set of all variables defined in a production system, together with their possible values, presents a picture of the information which is relevant in the field modelled in the system.

In general, two types of variables are discerned:

- *single-valued variables*, that is, variables which can take at most one constant value at a time, and
- *multi-valued variables*, that is, variables which can take a set of constants for a value.

Single-valued variables are used to represent information which in the case under consideration is unique; multi-valued variables are used for representing a collection of interrelated facts.

EXAMPLE 3.1

In a medical expert system, a variable with the name *complaint* may be used for storing information about the complaints of a certain patient. This variable has to be multi-valued, because a patient may have more than one complaint at the same time. An example of a single-valued variable is the *sex* of the patient.

Properties of variables, such as whether they are single- or multi-valued, and usually also information concerning the values a variable is allowed to take, are all described in the domain declaration of a knowledge base. The following definition provides a formal description of such a domain declaration.

Definition: Let τ denote a non-empty set of constants, called a *type*. A *typed variable declaration* is an expression of one of the following forms:

(1) $x^s : \tau$, where x^s is a single-valued variable
(2) $x^m : 2^\tau$, where x^m is a multi-valued variable

Untyped variable declarations are expressions of the form x^s in the single-valued case, or x^m in the multi-valued case. A set D of variable declarations for all variables occurring in the knowledge base is called the *domain declaration* of the knowledge base.

Examples of types are the set of integer numbers, denoted by ***int***, the set of real numbers, denoted by ***real***, and finite sets of constants such as {*fever*, *jaundice*, *headache*}. Note that a domain declaration is similar to a variable declaration part in, for instance, Pascal. It restricts the values a variable may take.

A variable together with the value(s) it has adopted during a consultation is called a fact.

Definition: A *fact* is a statement having one of the following forms:

(1) $x^s = c$, where $c \in \tau$ if x^s is a single-valued variable declared as $x^s : \tau$

(2) $x^m = C$, where $C \subseteq \tau$ if x^m is a multi-valued variable declared as $x^m : 2^\tau$

A fact set has the following form:

$$\{x_1^s = c_1, \ldots, x_p^s = c_p,\ x_1^m = C_1, \ldots, x_q^m = C_q\}$$

where c_i are constants and C_j are sets of constants. A variable may occur only once in a fact set.

EXAMPLE 3.2

Consider the following domain declaration:

$$\begin{aligned} D = \{&sex : \{female, male\}, \\ &age : \textbf{\textit{int}}, \\ &complaint : 2^{\{fever, abdominal\text{-}pain, headache\}}, \\ &disorder : 2^{\{aortic\text{-}aneurysm, arterial\text{-}stenosis\}}\} \end{aligned}$$

of a knowledge base of a medical expert system. The following facts are typical elements of a fact set after a specific consultation:

$$\begin{aligned} &sex = male \\ &age = 27 \\ &complaint = \{fever, abdominal\text{-}pain\} \\ &disorder = \{aortic\text{-}aneurysm\} \end{aligned}$$

The statement $x^s = unknown$ (or $x^m = unknown$) is used to indicate that the variable x^s (or x^m, respectively) has not been assigned an actual value; x^s (or x^m) is then called *unknown*. The constant *unknown* has a special meaning: it expresses that the inference engine has not been able to derive one or more values for the variable. Since its meaning goes beyond (that is, *meta*) the contents of the fact set and the knowledge base, the constant *unknown* is called a *meta-constant*.

It must be emphasized that a fact set is not a part of a knowledge base, but is instead a separate component of the system. A fact set comprises information which is specific for a particular consultation, whereas a knowledge base contains only *declarations* of variables and therefore does not specify consultation-dependent values. In the following sections, we will frequently assume that suitable variable declarations are present in the domain declaration of a knowledge base without explicitly referring to them.

3.1.2 Conditions and conclusions

At the beginning of this chapter, we mentioned that production rules are used for representing problem-solving knowledge from a specific problem domain. The major part of this type of knowledge takes the form of *heuristic rules* or rules of thumb, which, as we shall see, are the informal, real-life analogies of production rules. In a heuristic rule, several conditions and conclusions are interrelated, as follows:

if
  certain *conditions* are fulfilled
then
  certain *conclusions* may be drawn.

EXAMPLE 3.3

An example of a heuristic rule, taken from the domain of medical diagnosis in cardiovascular disease, is the following:

if
  the patient suffers from abdominal pain, and
  an abdominal murmur is perceived by auscultation, and
  a pulsating mass is felt in the abdomen
then
  the patient has an aortic aneurysm

In the process of knowledge engineering, such heuristic rules have to be transformed into their formal counterparts, that is, into production rules.

A production rule, just like a heuristic rule, consists of a number of conditions and conclusions. In a production rule, which unlike a heuristic rule is a formal statement, the conditions and conclusions comprise the following elements:

- Symbolic and numerical constant values
- Variables
- Predicates and actions

An important part of the translation process therefore concerns the identification of the variables and constants that are relevant in the heuristic rules.

EXAMPLE 3.4

Consider the preceding heuristic rule once more. In the first condition a variable *complaint* may be identified, the second condition concerns the findings by *auscultation*, the third concerns the findings from physical examination by *palpation*, and, finally, the conclusion concerns the patient's *disorder*. The following constant values may be introduced to represent the information further contained in the heuristic rule: *abdominal-pain*, *abdominal-murmur*, *pulsating-mass* and *aortic-aneurysm*.

Several syntactic forms have been devised for the representation of production rules. In this book we employ the syntax described in the following definition.

Definition: A *production rule* is a statement having the following form:

```
<production rule>  ::=  if <antecedent> then <consequent> fi
<antecedent>       ::=  <disjunction> {and <disjunction>}*
<disjunction>      ::=  <condition> {or <condition>}*
<consequent>       ::=  <conclusion> {also <conclusion>}*
<condition>        ::=  <predicate> (<variable>, <constant>)
<conclusion>       ::=  <action> (<variable>, <constant>)
<predicate>        ::=  same | notsame | greaterthan | · · ·
<action>           ::=  add | remove | · · ·
```

In the production-rule formalism it is assumed that the ***or*** operator has a higher precedence than the ***and*** operator. Note that the nesting of conjunctions and disjunctions is limited; this is typical for production systems.

A condition is built from a *predicate* and two associated arguments: a variable and a constant. By means of its predicate, a condition expresses a comparison between the specified constant value and the actual value(s) the specified variable has adopted. In the context of production systems, a predicate is a function which upon evaluation returns either the truth value *true* or the value *false*. The way predicates are evaluated is illustrated by means of the following example.

EXAMPLE 3.5

Let F be the following fact set:

$$F = \{age = 50,\ complaint = \{abdominal\text{-}pain, fever\}\}$$

where *age* is a single-valued variable and *complaint* is a multi-valued one. Now consider the following condition:

same(*complaint*,*abdominal-pain*)

Upon evaluation, the predicate *same* returns the truth value *true* if *abdominal-pain* is one of the constants in the set of constants adopted by the multi-valued variable *complaint*; otherwise, the value *false* is returned. So, in the present example, the evaluation of the condition will return the value *true*. In the case of a single-valued variable, *same* tests whether or not the constant specified as its second argument is equal to the constant which the variable mentioned as its first argument has adopted. Given the present fact set, the condition

same(*age*,40)

therefore yields the value *false* upon evaluation.

A conclusion is built from an *action* and two associated arguments. An action can be considered to operate on a variable. The most frequently applied action is *add*, which adds the constant specified as its second argument to the value set of the multi-valued variable mentioned in its first argument; in case of a single-valued variable, the action *add* assigns the constant value from its second argument to the specified variable.

EXAMPLE 3.6

Consider the fact set F:

$$F = \{disorder = \{atherosclerosis\},\ sex = male,\ age = 76\}$$

in which *disorder* is the only multi-valued variable. The action *add* in the conclusion

add(*disorder*,*aortic-aneurysm*)

adds the constant *aortic-aneurysm* to the set of constant values the variable *disorder* has already adopted. So, after evaluation of this conclusion, we have obtained the following fact set F':

$$F' = \{disorder = \{atherosclerosis, aortic\text{-}aneurysm\}, sex = male, age = 76\}$$

A production rule is built from such conditions and conclusions.

EXAMPLE 3.7

The heuristic rule informally introduced above can now be translated into the production-rule formalism, for example as follows:

if
  same(*complaint*,*abdominal-pain*) ***and***
  same(*auscultation*,*abdominal-murmur*) ***and***
  same(*palpation*,*pulsating-mass*)
then
  add(*disorder*,*aortic-aneurysm*)
fi

EXAMPLE 3.8

In the informal heuristic rule:

if
  the systolic pressure exceeds 140 mmHg, and
  the pulse pressure exceeds 50 mmHg, and
  upon examination a diastolic murmur is perceived, or
  an enlarged heart is observed
then
  the patient suffers from an aortic regurgitation

the first two conditions concern the variables *systolic-pressure* and *pulse-pressure*, respectively. If the patient is suffering from an aortic regurgitation, either a diastolic murmur may be perceived by auscultation, or an enlarged heart is observed by percussion. It suffices to observe one of these signs, together with the other evidence mentioned in the rule, to conclude that the patient has an aortic regurgitation. The variables that can be distinguished in the last two constituent conditions are *auscultation* and *percussion*, respectively. Finally, the conclusion states the *disorder* the patient is likely to be suffering from if the mentioned conditions are *true*. This heuristic rule may now be expressed in the production-rule formalism as follows:

if
greaterthan(*systolic-pressure*,140) ***and***
greaterthan(*pulse-pressure*,50) ***and***
same(*auscultation*,*diastolic-murmur*) ***or***
same(*percussion*,*enlarged-heart*)
then
add(*disorder*,*aortic-regurgitation*)
fi

To conclude, the following example discusses a production rule comprising more than one conclusion.

EXAMPLE 3.9

The following heuristic rule:

if
the patient experiences a pain in the calf when walking, which disappears gradually in rest
then
a stenosis of one of the arteries in the leg, possibly due to atherosclerosis, is conceivable

may be expressed in the production-rule formalism as follows:

if
same(*complaint*,*calf-pain*) ***and***
same(*presence*,*walking*) ***and***
same(*absence*,*rest*)
then
add(*cause*,*arterial-stenosis*) ***also***
add(*disorder*,*atherosclerosis*)
fi

The only action we have considered up to now is the action *add*. If this action is the only one specified in the consequent of a production rule, the rule closely resembles a logical implication, in which the conditions of the rule appear on the left of the implication symbol and the conclusions are specified to the right of it. This interpretation, however,

Table 3.1 Some predicates and actions, and their meaning.

Example	*Semantics for single-valued variables*	*Semantics for multi-valued variables*
same(*x*,*c*)	$x^s = c$	$c \in x^m$
notsame(*x*,*c*)	$x^s \neq c$ and $x^s \neq \mathit{unknown}$	$c \notin x^m$ and $x^m \neq \mathit{unknown}$
lessthan(*x*,*c*)	$x^s < c$	–
greaterthan(*x*,*c*)	$x^s > c$	–
known(*x*)	$x^s \neq \mathit{unknown}$	$x^m \neq \mathit{unknown}$
notknown(*x*)	$x^s = \mathit{unknown}$	$x^m = \mathit{unknown}$
add(*x*,*c*)	$x^s \leftarrow c$	$x^m \leftarrow x^m \cup \{c\}$
remove(*x*,*c*)	$x^s \leftarrow \mathit{unknown}$	if $x^m = \{c\}$ then $x^m \leftarrow \mathit{unknown}$ else $x^m \leftarrow x^m \setminus \{c\}$

is no longer valid when actions other than *add* have been specified in the consequent of a rule. Consider, for example, the action *remove*, which upon execution cancels the assignment of a specific constant to a single-valued variable or deletes a constant from the set of constants of a multi-valued variable. A production rule in which this action has been specified cannot possibly be viewed as a logical implication. More about the correspondence between the production-rule formalism and logic will be said in Section 3.1.4.

In Table 3.1 the semantics of some frequently used predicates and actions are described. Note that numerical predicates such as *greaterthan* always take a single-valued variable as an argument. From the special meaning of the constant *unknown* as discussed in the preceding section, we have that the predicates *known* and *notknown* mentioned in the table have a special meaning as well: they express knowledge concerning the derivability of values for variables, which again goes beyond the contents of the fact set and the rule base of a production system. We call such predicates *meta-predicates*; note that these meta-predicates take only one argument. In Section 3.2.1 we will turn again to the meanings of the predicates and the effects the different actions have on a fact set.

3.1.3 Object–attribute–value tuples

The production-rule formalism introduced in Section 3.1.2 does not provide a means for specifying formal relationships between the variables of concern. In many problem domains to be modelled, however, one can often discern separate subdomains, or *objects*, which are interrelated in some way. Each subdomain is then described by a number of properties or *attributes* which are specific for that subdomain. The idea is illustrated in the following example.

EXAMPLE 3.10

In the heuristic rule from Example 3.9, a description is given of the pain a patient is suffering from. Pain is usually described by several criteria which are specific to the notion of pain. We may now view *pain* as a separate object, and the *site* of the pain and the *character* of the pain as attributes belonging to that object.

In production systems, objects are often used to explicitly group the properties which are mentioned in the heuristic rules. The objects themselves are often even further exploited for directing the inference process. If we extend the production-rule formalism to include the specification of an object, predicates and actions have to be changed from binary, in the previous case of variable–value pairs, to ternary operators. We call a tuple consisting of an object, an attribute and a constant value an *object–attribute–value tuple*, or *o–a–v triple*. The following simple extension to the original syntax definition of production rules is thus obtained:

<condition> ::= <predicate> (<object>, <attribute>, <value>)
<conclusion> ::= <action> (<object>, <attribute>, <value>)

Note that an object–attribute pair always explicitly indicates that the mentioned attribute belongs to the specified object. The object–attribute pairs in an object–attribute–value tuple just act like the variables discussed in the foregoing sections. The attributes of an object are declared as being either *single-valued* or *multi-valued*, in a way resembling the declaration of variables. In the following discussion, we shall write $o.a^s$ to denote the single-valued attribute a^s belonging to the object o; we use $o.a^m$ for the multi-valued case.

EXAMPLE 3.11

The following production rule:

> ***if***
> *same*(*patient*,*complaint*,*calf-pain*) ***and***
> *same*(*pain*,*presence*,*walking*) ***and***
> *same*(*pain*,*absence*,*rest*)
> ***then***
> *add*(*pain*,*cause*,*arterial-stenosis*) ***also***
> *add*(*patient*,*disorder*,*atherosclerosis*)
> ***fi***

concerns the objects *patient* and *pain*. Attributes of the object *pain* referred to in the rule are *presence*, *absence* and *cause*. The attributes of the object *patient* referred to are *complaint* and *disorder*.

The extension of the definitions of predicates and actions with the specification of an object enables us to express relationships between objects and their attributes. However, it is still not possible explicitly to express relationships between objects among themselves in a natural way. Yet it may be desirable in an expert system to have this type of information available as well. Therefore, in addition to the rule base, often an *object schema* is present in an expert system; this is usually added to the domain declaration of a knowledge base. An object schema defines the interrelationships between the objects, and the relationships between the objects and their associated attributes. Figure 3.1 shows a portion of the object schema of a system comprising information concerning the human cardiovascular system. An object is represented by an ellipse. A solid line is used to represent a relationship between two objects. In Figure 3.1 the object *pain* is called a *subobject* of the object *patient*. A dashed line indicates a relationship between an object and an associated attribute. An object schema is frequently used for storing meta-information, for example directives to the inference engine to handle certain attributes in a special way.

3.1.4 Production rules and first-order predicate logic

In the preceding sections, we have informally discussed the meanings of predicates and actions in a production system. In general, we can say that the semantics of production rules in a production system is described in terms of a specific inference method for applying the rules. The only available semantics for a production system is therefore procedural in

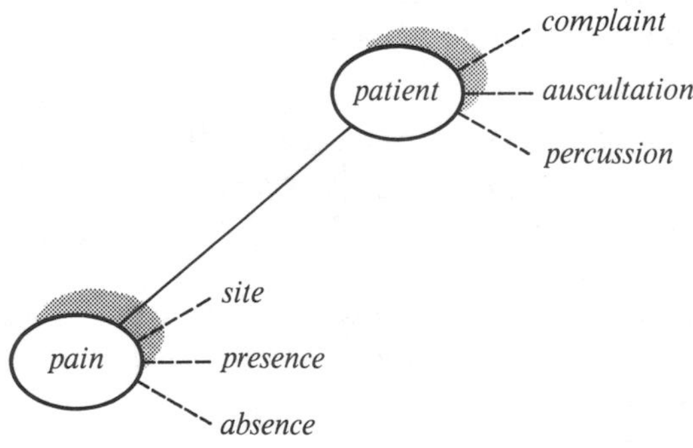

Figure 3.1 An object schema.

nature. This is contrary to first-order logic which, as we have seen in Chapter 2, also has a neat declarative semantics. There is, however, a strong relationship between the production-rule formalism and the formalism of first-order logic, as we already briefly touched on in Section 3.1.1. In most rule bases, at least part of the production rules can be translated into first-order predicate logic in a straightforward and natural way. This is fortunate, as it enables a rule base to be developed without precise knowledge of the working of the inference engine; the declarative readings of the corresponding logical formulas can thus be exploited.

Let us start by looking at the correspondence between conditions and conclusions in production rules on the one hand and literals in first-order logic on the other. Without loss of generality, we can assume that the production system makes use of object–attribute–value tuples. As we discussed above, the predicates *same* and *notsame* test whether the specified attribute of some object has or has not, respectively, the specified constant as a value or in its set of values. Again, we distinguish between multi-valued and single-valued attributes. A multi-valued attribute may be viewed as a relation A defined on the cartesian product of a set of objects and a set of constants, that is, $A \subseteq O \times V$, where O is the set of objects, and V is the set of constant values. Recall that, in first-order predicate logic, predicate symbols may be employed for representing such relations. Conditions of the form $same(o,a^m,v)$ and $notsame(o,a^m,v)$, containing a multi-valued attribute, may therefore be translated into first-order logic in the literals $a(o,v)$ and $\neg a(o,v)$, respectively. In the single-valued case, we have to take into account that the attribute may adopt at most one value at a time. Single-valuedness is best expressed in first-order logic by using function symbols. Single-valued attributes may be viewed as functions a from the set of objects O to the set of values V, that is, $a: O \rightarrow V$. Note that, for expressing the meaning of the predicate *same*, we have the equality predicate $=$ at our disposal. The following translation is now straightforward: the condition $same(o,a^s,v)$ is translated into the literal $a(o) = v$, and the condition $notsame(o,a^s,v)$ is translated into $\neg a(o) = v$. Many other predicates used in production rules can be translated in much the same way. Table 3.2 summarizes some of these translations. Note that the semantics of first-order logic implies that the unit clause $a(o,v)$ in the presence of the unit clause $\neg a(o,v)$ leads to an inconsistency. In addition, the unit clauses $a(o) = v$ and $a(o) = w$, where $v \neq w$, are inconsistent in the presence of the equality axioms. As can be seen from Table 3.2, the action *add* is treated in the same way as the predicate *same*; this reflects the transition from a procedural to a declarative semantics. The meta-predicates *known* and *notknown* are not included in Table 3.2, because it is not possible to express meta-information in standard first-order logic. A similar remark can be made concerning the action *remove*. Special non-standard logics have been developed providing such meta-predicates and non-monotonic

Table 3.2 Translation of conditions and actions into first-order logic.

Example	*Logic representation for single-valued attributes*	*Logic representation for multi-valued attributes*
same(*o*,*a*,*v*)	$a(o) = v$	$a(o,v)$
notsame(*o*,*a*,*v*)	$\neg a(o) = v$	$\neg a(o,v)$
equal(*o*,*a*,*v*)	$a(o) = v$	—
lessthan(*o*,*a*,*v*)	$a(o) < v$	—
greaterthan(*o*,*a*,*v*)	$a(o) > v$	—
add(*o*,*a*,*v*)	$a(o) = v$	$a(o,v)$

actions. The subject of non-standard logic, however, goes beyond the scope of this book.

Further translation of a production rule into a logical formula is now straightforward. The general translation scheme is as follows:

$$
\begin{array}{ll}
\textbf{\textit{if}} & \\
\quad c_{1,1} \textbf{\textit{ or }} c_{1,2} \textbf{\textit{ or }} \cdots \textbf{\textit{ or }} c_{1,m} \textbf{\textit{ and}} & ((c'_{1,1} \vee c'_{1,2} \vee \cdots \vee c'_{1,m}) \wedge \\
\quad \vdots & \vdots \\
\quad c_{n,1} \textbf{\textit{ or }} c_{n,2} \textbf{\textit{ or }} \cdots \textbf{\textit{ or }} c_{n,p} & \Rightarrow (c'_{n,1} \vee c'_{n,2} \vee \cdots \vee c'_{n,p})) \\
\textbf{\textit{then}} & \rightarrow \\
\quad a_1 \textbf{\textit{ also }} a_2 \textbf{\textit{ also }} \cdots \textbf{\textit{ also }} a_q & (a'_1 \wedge a'_2 \wedge \cdots \wedge a'_q) \\
\textbf{\textit{fi}} &
\end{array}
$$

where conditions $c_{i,j}$ and actions a_k are translated into literals $c'_{i,j}$ and a'_k, respectively, as prescribed by Table 3.2. From the table it can readily be seen that the kind of production rules we have looked at are translated into *ground* logical implications.

The following example illustrates the translation scheme.

EXAMPLE 3.12

Consider the following production rule:

if
  greaterthan(*blood*,*systolic-pressure*,140) ***and***
  greaterthan(*blood*,*pulse-pressure*,50) ***and***
  same(*patient*,*auscultation*,*diastolic-murmur*) ***or***
  same(*patient*,*percussion*,*enlarged-heart*)
then
  add(*patient*,*disorder*,*aortic-regurgitation*)
fi

Translation of this rule into first-order logic yields the following implication:

$$(\textit{systolic-pressure}(\textit{blood}) > 140 \wedge \textit{pulse-pressure}(\textit{blood}) > 50 \wedge (\textit{auscultation}(\textit{patient},\textit{diastolic-murmur}) \vee \textit{percussion}(\textit{patient},\textit{enlarged-heart}))) \rightarrow \textit{disorder}(\textit{patient},\textit{aortic-regurgitation})$$

The formalism of first-order logic is in certain ways more flexible than the production-rule formalism is. For instance, it is not restricted to the use of *o–a–v* triples only; it allows us, for example, to specify the literal

$$\textit{systolic-pressure}(\textit{patient},\textit{blood}) > 140$$

instead of the first literal in the implication shown above. This literal is more in correspondence with the intended meaning of the original heuristic rule.

To conclude, the fact set of a production system may be translated into the logic formalism in much the same way as the rule base is. A fact $o.a^s = v$ concerning a single-valued attribute a^s is translated into a unit clause $a(o) = v$. Recall that in the presence of the equality axioms single-valuedness is guaranteed. Now consider the multi-valued case. A fact concerning a multi-valued attribute a^m is translated into a set of unit clauses $a(o,v_i)$ for each v_i in the set of constant values that a^m has adopted. However, it is not sufficient only to add these positive clauses: it is typical for production systems that values of multi-valued attributes not explicitly entered into the fact set are taken implicitly by the system as being not true. This behaviour has been copied from human problem solving. For example, a physician usually records in a patient report only the symptoms and signs that have actually been observed in the patient; all information not explicitly recorded for the specific patient is implicitly assumed to be negative. This aspect of problem solving is reflected in the meaning of the *notsame* predicate. Note that this way of dealing with negations is quite different from the meaning of a negative literal in first-order logic, which holds only in a model in which it has actually been satisfied. For a correct meaning of the *notsame* predicate therefore we have to add explicitly unit clauses $\neg a(o,v_i)$ for the remaining constants v_i occurring in the type τ of a^m, as at least one positive unit clause $a(o,v_j)$, $j \neq i$, occurs in the fact set (in the case of an untyped attribute, we add unit clauses $\neg a(o,v_i)$ for the remaining constants v_i mentioned in the rule base). The explicit addition of negative unit clauses is called *negation by absence*. It is a special case of the closed world assumption mentioned in Chapter 2.

EXAMPLE 3.13

Consider the following domain declaration:

$$D = \{disorder^m : 2^{\{aortic\text{-}regurgitation,\ atherosclerosis\}},\ age^s: \textbf{\textit{int}}\}$$

and the fact set $F = \{disorder^m = \{atherosclerosis\},\ age^s = 70\}$. We obtain the following translation into first-order logic:

$disorder(patient, atherosclerosis)$
$\neg disorder(patient, aortic\text{-}regurgitation)$
$age(patient) = 70$

3.2 Inference in a production system

Several inference methods have been devised for dealing with production rules. An inference method in a production system explicitly exploits the difference between facts and rules; it operates on the fact set, which can be looked upon as the global working memory for the production rules. Note that, in logic, such an explicit separation between facts (unit clauses) and rules (implications) generally is not made, although it should be noted that several inference methods, such as SLD resolution, make use of a similar distinction.

Roughly speaking, an inference method selects and subsequently applies production rules from a rule base. In applying the selected production rules, it executes the actions specified in their conclusions. Execution of such actions may cause facts to be added to, to be modified in, or to be deleted from the fact set. In this chapter we discuss the addition and deletion of facts; a discussion of the modification of facts as a result of executing actions will be postponed until Chapter 7, where we shall discuss the language OPS5. Figure 3.2 shows the general idea of inference in a production system. The manipulation of production rules and facts is depicted in the figure by means of arrows.

The distinction between the two basic forms of inference mentioned in Chapter 1 is essential when considering production systems; they yield entirely different reasoning strategies. Before discussing the two basic inference methods, top-down and bottom-up inference, in detail, we introduce them informally with the help of a simplified example, in which we abstract from the syntactical structure of conditions, conclusions and facts. To simplify matters further, we suppose that all conditions of the form *c* succeed upon evaluation in the presence of the fact *c*. Now, consider Table 3.3.

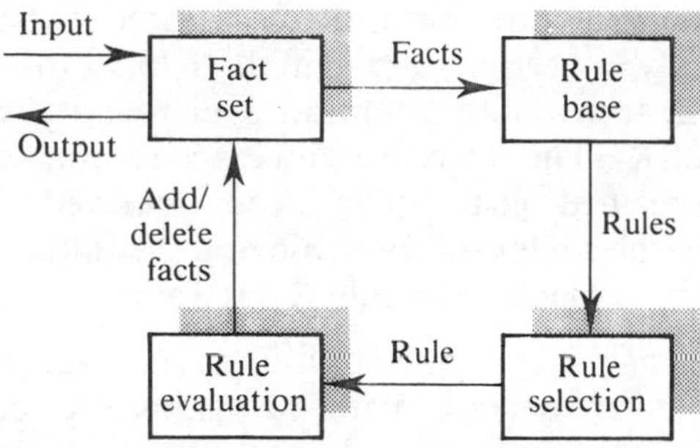

Figure 3.2 Global architecture of a production system.

- *Top-down inference* starts with a statement of one or more *goals* to be achieved. In our example, we have just the single goal g. A goal may match with a conclusion of one or more production rules present in the rule base. All production rules thus matching with a certain goal are selected for application. In the present case, the only rule selected is R_1. Each one of the selected production rules is subsequently applied by first considering the conditions of the rule as the new subgoals to be achieved. Roughly speaking, if there are facts present in the fact set which match with these new subgoals, these subgoals are taken as been achieved; subgoals for which no matching facts can be found are matched against the conclusions of the production rules from the rule base. Again, matching production rules are selected for application. In our example, we have from rule R_1 the new subgoal b, which in turn causes the selection of production rule R_3. This process is repeated recursively. Note that, in top-down inference, production rules are applied in a backward manner. When all the subgoals, that is, the conditions of a selected production rule, have been achieved, the actions in the conclusions of the rule are executed, possibly causing

Table 3.3 Production system before and after execution.

State	*Component*	*Top-down inference*	*Bottom-up inference*
Initial	*Goal*	g	—
	Facts	$\{a\}$	$\{a\}$
	Rules	R_1: ***if*** b ***then*** g ***fi***	R_1: ***if*** b ***then*** g ***fi***
		R_2: ***if*** g ***then*** c ***fi***	R_2: ***if*** g ***then*** c ***fi***
		R_3: ***if*** a ***then*** b ***fi***	R_3: ***if*** a ***then*** b ***fi***
Final	*Facts'*	$\{a,b,g\}$	$\{a,b,c,g\}$

changes in the fact set. Since subgoal a of the selected production rule R_3 matches with fact a, the condition of the rule is fulfilled. Subsequently, its action is executed, yielding the new fact b. This new fact in turn fulfils condition b of rule R_1, which led to the selection of R_3. The inference process is terminated as soon as the initially specified goals have been achieved. Note that only production rules relevant for achieving the initially given goals are applied. This explains why rule R_2 in Table 3.3 has not been used.

- *Bottom-up inference* starts with a fact set, in our example $\{a\}$. The facts in the fact set are matched against the conditions of the production rules from the rule base. If for a specific production rule all conditions are fulfilled, then it is selected for application. The rule is applied by executing the actions mentioned in its conclusions. So, in our example, rule R_3 will be applied first. The application of the selected production rules is likely to result in changes in the fact set, thus enabling other production rules to be applicable. In the present case, after the application of rule R_3, we have obtained the new fact set $\{a,b\}$, which results in the rule R_1 now being applicable. The fact g added to the fact set as a result of executing the action of rule R_1, results in the subsequent application of R_2. We therefore conclude that the final fact set is equal to $\{a,b,c,g\}$. The inference process is terminated as soon as all applicable production rules have been processed.

Note the difference in the resulting fact sets in Table 3.3 obtained from applying top-down and bottom-up inference, respectively. As a consequence of their different inference behaviour, top-down and bottom-up inference are suitable for developing different kinds of expert systems. Top-down inference is often used in inference engines of diagnostic expert systems in which the inference process is controlled by a specific goal and a small amount of data. Bottom-up inference is most suitable for applications in which the interpretation of a vast amount of data is important, and in which there are no preset goals. In the following section, we first address top-down inference and its implementation in detail, before discussing bottom-up inference in Section 3.2.4.

3.2.1 Top-down inference and production rules

As we discussed before, top-down inference is usually incorporated in diagnostic expert systems. If it employs the variable–value representation, such a system tries to derive facts concerning one or more preset goal variables. In a typical medical diagnostic expert system, for example, one could think of a multi-valued variable *diagnosis*, for which we want to establish for a specific patient the set of values (that is, the possible disorders). So, in general, top-down inference starts with a set of *goals*

$\{G_1,G_2,\ldots,G_m\}$, $m \geqslant 1$, essentially being goal variables. For this purpose, in the domain-declaration part of a knowledge base, the variable declarations are extended to include a specification of whether or not they are goals. In the following discussion, we shall use x_g^s to denote a single-valued goal variable and x_g^m to denote a multi-valued goal variable. The subset of all facts concerning the goal variables in the fact set after applying the inference algorithm is called a *solution*.

The top-down inference algorithm used in this book for establishing the goals G_i from the initial set of goals informally amounts to the following. Suppose that we are given a fixed rule base $\{R_1,R_2,\ldots,R_n\}$, $n \geqslant 1$, of production rules R_i. For deriving values for a multi-valued variable, the inference engine will try to apply production rules as long as there are production rules available which can extend the set of constants for a goal variable by adding new ones to it. In the single-valued case, the inference engine proceeds until a single value has been derived for the variable, and then it terminates. If the system has not been able to derive values for the variable from the rule base, for instance because applicable production rules are absent, then on some occasion it will turn to the user and ask for additional information. For this purpose a distinction is made between variables for which values may be asked from the user, which are called *askable variables*, and variables which may not be asked. The askability of a variable is again denoted in the domain declaration of the variables, this time by means of a subscript a, so we have x_a^m for askable multi-valued variables and x_a^s for askable single-valued ones.

EXAMPLE 3.14

In a medical expert system intended for diagnosing a patient's disorder, it is undesirable to ask the user to specify the patient's disorder when the system has not been able to attain a diagnosis. Therefore, the variable *disorder* should not be askable. On the other hand, *complaint* and *sex* are typical examples of askable variables; these can usually not be derived using the production rules.

It will be evident that goal variables should never be askable.

The entire process of deriving values for a variable by applying the production rules, and possibly asking the user for values for it, is called *tracing* the variable. In what follows, we abstract from the distinction between single- and multi-valued variables in the description of the top-down inference algorithm, since the basic structure of the algorithm is the same for both types of variable. The algorithm for tracing a variable pictured above is described by the following procedure:

```
procedure TraceValues(variable)
  Infer(variable);
  if not established(variable) and askable(variable) then
    Ask(variable)
  fi
end
```

The function call established(variable) is used to examine whether or not a value for the variable variable has been obtained from the rule base by means of the procedure call Infer(variable); askable(variable) is used to determine whether the variable concerned is askable.

For deriving values for a variable from the rule base, called *inferring* the variable, the procedure Infer is invoked. In the procedure Infer, a subset $\{R_{i_1}, R_{i_2}, \ldots, R_{i_k}\}$ of the production rules is selected; a rule R_j will be selected if the name of the given variable occurs in one of the conclusions of the rule, in other words, if the given variable and the variable in the conclusion *match*. The thus selected rules are then *applied*. The procedure for selecting production rules and subsequently applying them is as follows:

```
procedure Infer(variable)
  Select(rule-base, variable, selected-rules);
  foreach rule in selected-rules do
    Apply(rule)
  od
end
```

The actual selection of the relevant production rules from the rule base is described in the following procedure:

```
procedure Select(rule-base, variable, selected-rules)
  selected-rules ← ∅;
  foreach rule in rule-base do
    matched ← false;
    foreach concl in consequent(rule) with not matched do
      pattern ← variable(concl);
      if Match(variable, pattern) then
        selected-rules ← selected-rules ∪ {rule};
        matched ← true
      fi
    od
  od
end
```

The set of selected production rules is called the *conflict set*. In the foreach statement in the Infer procedure this conflict set is traversed: the rules from this set are applied one by one by means of a call to the procedure Apply, which will be described shortly. Note that this way the rules are applied exhaustively, that is, all rules concluding on the variable being traced are applied.

Neither the order in which the production rules from the conflict set are applied nor the order in which the conditions and the conclusions of the rules are evaluated is fixed as yet. If the order in applying the selected rules has not been fixed, we speak of *non-determinism of the first kind*. The evaluation order of the conditions and the conclusions in a rule not being fixed is called *non-determinism of the second kind*. Non-determinism of the first kind is resolved by using a so-called *conflict-resolution strategy*, which imposes some order on the rules from the conflict set. The simplest conflict-resolution strategy is, of course, just to apply the production rules in the order in which they have been selected from the rule base (which is then viewed as a sequence of production rules instead of as a set). More sophisticated conflict-resolution strategies order the conflict set using some context-sensitive criterion. An example of such a strategy is ordering the rules according to the number of conditions not yet fulfilled; in this way, solutions which are close to the information already available to the system generally prevail over more remote solutions. From the user's point of view, a system provided with a context-sensitive conflict-resolution strategy behaves much more intelligently, because likely solutions are explored before unlikely ones. Non-determinism of the second kind is usually handled by evaluating the conditions and conclusions of a selected production rule in the order of their appearance. However, more sophisticated techniques are also possible. Sophisticated conflict-resolution strategies and evaluation ordering methods are seldom used in expert systems using top-down inference, because the goal-directed nature of top-down inference is itself an 'intelligent' control strategy, rendering additional ones less necessary. As a consequence, most systems employing top-down inference use the simplest strategies in solving the two types of non-determinism, that is, they apply production rules, and evaluate conditions and conclusions in the order of their specification. This particular strategy will be called *backward chaining*.

The application of a selected production rule commences with the evaluation of its conditions. If upon evaluation at least one of the disjunctions of conditions is found to be *false*, the rule is said to *fail*. If, on the other hand, all disjunctions of conditions evaluate to be *true*, the rule is said to *succeed*. The application of a production rule is described in the following procedure:

```
procedure Apply(rule)
  EvalConditions(rule);
  if not failed(rule) then
    EvalConclusions(rule)
  fi
end
```

The procedure Apply first evaluates the condition part of the rule by calling EvalConditions. If this evaluation ends in success, it evaluates the conclusions of the rule by means of EvalConclusions.

Let us take a closer look at the procedure EvalConditions, which checks whether all conditions in the antecedent of the production rule yield the truth value *true* on evaluation. Beginning with the first condition, the procedure traces the variable occurring in the condition by means of a recursive call to TraceValues. Subsequently, the test specified by means of the predicate in the condition is executed. In the EvalConditions procedure presented below, we have assumed, for simplicity's sake, that the antecedent of a production rule only comprises a conjunction of conditions.

```
procedure EvalConditions(rule)
  foreach condition in antecedent(rule) do
    var ← variable(condition);
    TraceValues(var); { indirect recursion }
    ExecPredicate(condition);
    if condition failed then
      return
    fi
  od
end
```

It should be noted that there are many ways to optimize the last procedure, several of which will be discussed below. The ExecPredicate procedure executes the test denoted by the predicate which has been specified in the condition under consideration. It compares the value the mentioned variable has with the constant specified in its second argument (if any). This test yields either the truth value *true* or the truth value *false*. We have already seen an example of the execution of such a predicate in the preceding section.

If all conditions of the production rule have been evaluated and have yielded the value *true*, the rule succeeds and its conclusions are subsequently evaluated. The evaluation of the conclusion part of a successful production rule merely comprises the execution of the actions specified in its conclusions:

```
procedure EvalConclusions(rule)
  foreach conclusion in consequent(rule) do
    ExecAction(conclusion)
  od
end
```

We have mentioned before that executing the action *add* results in the assignment of a constant value to a single-valued variable, or in the addition of a constant value to the set of values of a multi-valued variable. In Section 3.1.2, we also briefly discussed the action *remove.* Execution of this action results in deleting the specified constant value from the fact concerning the variable. Execution of this action can therefore disrupt the monotonicity of the reasoning process, thus rendering it difficult to reconstruct the inference steps which have been carried out. Furthermore, it is quite conceivable that the action is executed on a variable which has not been traced as yet, in which case the continuation of the inference is undefined. Therefore, in many expert systems, particularly those systems employing backward chaining, this action is not allowed.

It may happen that a certain variable is specified in one of the conditions as well as in one of the conclusions of a production rule. Such a rule is called a *self-referencing production rule.* When applying a self-referencing rule during a top-down inference process as discussed above, the rule may occasion infinite recursion. For the moment, therefore, we do not allow self-referencing rules in a rule base. We shall return to these rules below in discussing some optimizations of the inference algorithm.

The procedures discussed above together constitute the entire top-down inference algorithm. The following example demonstrates the behaviour of a system employing this form of inference.

EXAMPLE 3.15

Let $D = \{x_a^m, y^m, z_a^m, v_g^m, w_{a}^s\}$ be the domain declaration of a knowledge base. As can be seen, all variables except y and v are askable; v is the only goal variable. Suppose that initially we have the following fact set:

$$F = \{w = 5\}$$

Now consider the following production rules:

R_1: ***if*** *same*(x,a) ***and*** *same*(x,b) ***then*** *add*(z,f) ***fi***
R_2: ***if*** *same*(x,b) ***then*** *add*(z,g) ***fi***

R_3: ***if*** *same*(x,d) ***and*** *greaterthan*$(w,0)$ ***then*** *add*(z,e) ***fi***
R_4: ***if*** *same*(x,c) ***and*** *lessthan*$(w,30)$ ***then*** *add*(v,h) ***fi***
R_5: ***if*** *same*(y,d) ***and*** *lessthan*$(w,10)$ ***then*** *add*(v,i) ***fi***
R_6: ***if*** *known*(x) ***and*** *notsame*(z,e) ***then*** *add*(y,d) ***fi***

The backward-chaining algorithm starts with the selection of the two production rules R_4 and R_5, as the goal variable v appears in their respective conclusions. The production rule R_4 will be the first one to be applied. Because there are no production rules concluding on the variable x occurring in the first condition of rule R_4, the user is asked to enter values for x. We suppose that the user answers by entering $x = \{c\}$. Evaluation of the first condition therefore yields the truth value *true*. It follows that R_4 succeeds, since the evaluation of the second condition, *lessthan*$(w,30)$, yields the value *true* as well. The evaluation of the conclusion of the rule results in the addition of the fact $v = \{h\}$ to the fact set. Next, rule R_5 is applied. The first condition of this rule mentions the variable y. Since the variable y occurs in the conclusion of rule R_6, this rule is the next to be applied in order to obtain a value for y. The first condition of R_6 upon evaluation yields the truth value *true*. Evaluation of the second condition of rule R_6 ultimately results in a request to the user to supply values for the variable z, because the production rules R_1, R_2 and R_3 fail to infer values for it. When the user, for instance, provides the answer $z = \{i,j\}$, rule R_6 will succeed and the fact $y = \{d\}$ will be added to the fact set. We recall that rule R_6 was invoked during the evaluation of the first condition of rule R_5. From the new fact $y = \{d\}$ we have that the first condition of rule R_5 yields the truth value *true* upon evaluation. Since the second condition is fulfilled as well, the action specified in the conclusion of the rule is executed; the value i is inserted into the fact concerning the variable v. We conclude that the following fact set F' has been obtained:

$$F' = \{x = \{c\},\ y = \{d\},\ z = \{i,j\},\ v = \{h,i\},\ w = 5\}$$

So, the solution arrived at is $\{v = \{h,i\}\}$.

An analysis of the *search space* generated by top-down inference can be instructive when developing optimizations of the algorithm. The search space of the top-down inference algorithm discussed above is largely determined by the initial set of goals and the rule base, and has the form of a tree. We start the analysis by taking the backward-chaining strategy as a starting-point, and shall introduce several refinements to that algorithm. By means of the following example, we demonstrate how the search space is structured.

EXAMPLE 3.16

Let $D = \{x_a^m, y^m, z_g^s, u_a^m, v^m, w_a^m\}$ be the domain declaration of a production system. Note that the single-valued variable z is the only goal variable. The fact set initially is empty. Consider the following set of production rules:

R_1: ***if*** *same*(*w*,*a*) ***and*** *same*(*x*,*b*) ***then*** *add*(*v*,*c*) ***fi***

R_2: ***if*** *same*(*w*,*d*) ***and*** *same*(*v*,*c*) ***then*** *add*(*y*,*e*) ***fi***

R_3: ***if*** *same*(*v*,*c*) ***then*** *add*(*z*,*k*) ***fi***

R_4: ***if*** *same*(*x*,*j*) ***and*** *same*(*y*,*e*) ***then*** *add*(*z*,*h*) ***fi***

R_5: ***if*** *same*(*u*,*f*) ***and*** *same*(*x*,*g*) ***then*** *add*(*z*,*i*) ***fi***

The inference engine starts with the construction of the conflict set: $\{R_3, R_4, R_5\}$. The rule R_3 is the first to be applied. The variable v mentioned in the first condition of rule R_3 occurs in the conclusion of rule R_1. This is the only rule in the new conflict set. So rule R_1 is the next rule to be evaluated. Suppose that rule R_1 fails; as a consequence, no value will be inferred for v. The reader can easily verify that given this set of production rules the variables w, x and u will be asked from the user. The search space generated from the set of goals and the rules using backward chaining takes the form of a tree, as shown in Figure 3.3. The label *Infer* indicates that the variable is inferred from the rule base; *Ask* indicates that the variable is asked from the user. Now note that the mere presence of a fact concerning a specific variable in the fact set does not guarantee that the variable has actually been traced by exhaustively

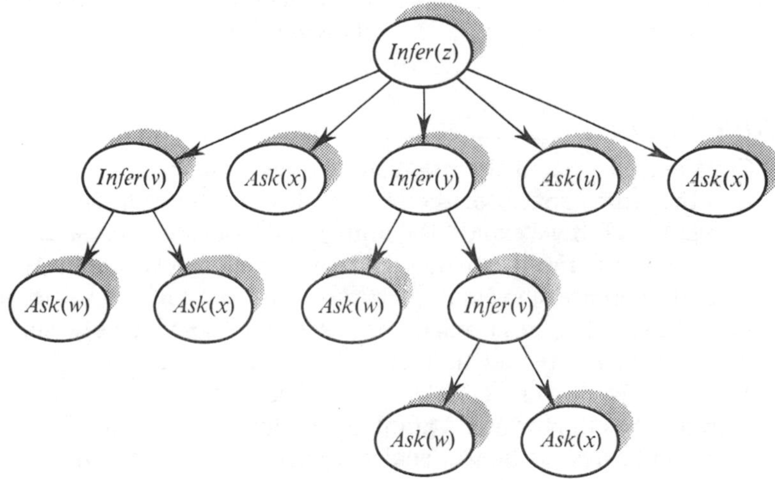

Figure 3.3 A search space generated using backward chaining.

applying the production rules; the fact may have been entered into the fact set as a side-effect of the application of a production rule having more than one conclusion when tracing another variable. Therefore the figure shows that the variable v has to be traced twice, even if a fact concerning v already occurs in the fact set. Furthermore, it indicates that several variables have to be asked from the user more than once.

In Example 3.16, we showed that the process of tracing a specific variable may be repeated unnecessarily; it will be evident that optimization is required here. We therefore introduce the notion of a 'traced' variable. A variable is marked as *traced* as soon as the process of tracing the variable has been performed, independent of whether it has yielded a value for the variable or not. We now modify the TraceValues procedure as follows:

```
procedure TraceValues(variable)
  Infer(variable);
  if not established(variable) and askable(variable) then
    Ask(variable)
  fi;
  traced(variable) ← true
end
```

This procedure was invoked from the EvalConditions procedure, which is now modified in such a way that the TraceValues procedure is invoked for a given variable only if the variable has not yet been marked as traced. This simple refinement has a dramatic effect on the structure of the search space, as is shown in the following example.

EXAMPLE 3.17

Consider once again the production rules from Example 3.16 and also the search space for the set of goals and the rule base shown in Figure 3.3. If we exploit the refinement discussed here and mark a variable as traced as soon as it has been traced exhaustively, several inference steps and questions to the user will have become superfluous. The resulting search space is considerably smaller than the one depicted in Figure 3.3, because now it suffices to represent each vertex only once. The resulting search space therefore has the form of a graph; it is depicted in Figure 3.4. Note that it indicates the dependencies between the variables during the inference.

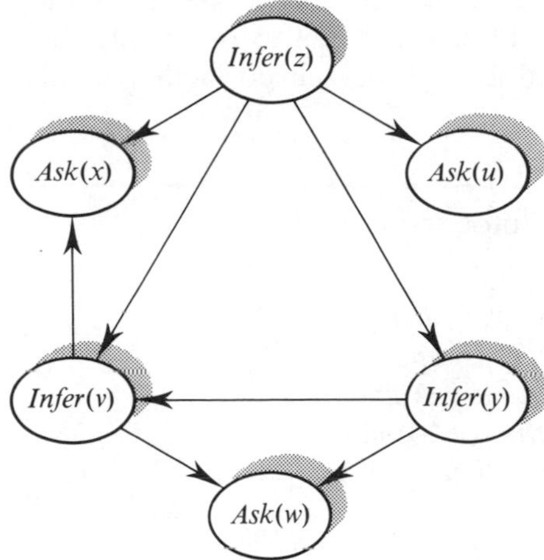

Figure 3.4 A search graph for backward chaining.

If a production rule contains two or more conclusions concerning different variables, the rule may be applied more than once by the top-down inference algorithm. However, if we assume that production rules do not contain actions removing or modifying facts, it suffices to apply such a production rule only once: applying such a rule a second time cannot result in the addition of new facts to the fact set. To prevent a rule from being applied more than once, each rule will be marked as having been *used* as soon as the inference algorithm applies it.

```
procedure Infer(variable)
  Select(rule-base, variable, selected-rules);
  foreach rule in selected-rules with not used(rule) do
    used(rule) ← true;
    Apply(rule)
  od
end
```

Moreover, marking a production rule before it is actually applied has the further advantage of preventing infinite recursion with self-referencing rules.

Here we have introduced two refinements of the basic backward-chaining (and top-down) algorithm: the marking of a variable after its examination by the inference engine as 'traced', and the marking of a production rule as 'used' upon its application. The last refinement we will discuss is the *look-ahead facility*. This facility, by pruning the search space in an effective way, can under certain circumstances yield a remarkable increase in efficiency. The general structure of the search space, however, is not changed. Let us first study the following example illustrating the need for the look-ahead facility.

EXAMPLE 3.18

Consider the production rule:

> ***if***
> *same*(x,a) ***and***
> *same*(y,b) ***and***
> *notsame*(z,c) ***and***
> *lessthan*(v,40) ***and***
> *greaterthan*(w,90)
> ***then***
> *add*(u,6)
> ***fi***

in which v and w are the only single-valued variables. Now, suppose that the fact $v = 80$ is present in the fact set. This single fact provides us with enough information to deduce that this rule will certainly fail because of its fourth condition. However, the backward-chaining algorithm as introduced above will detect the failure only when at least one (and possibly all three) of the variables x, y and z from the first three conditions has been traced.

The look-ahead facility now amounts to examining all conditions from a selected production rule before it is actually applied. If a condition is encountered which has already failed using the information from the fact set, the entire production rule will fail; the inference engine proceeds with the next rule. A possible algorithm for the look-ahead facility is as follows:

```
function LookAhead(rule)

  foreach condition in antecedent(rule) do
    var ← variable(condition);
    if traced(var) then
      ExecPredicate(condition);
      if condition failed then
        return(false)
      fi
    fi
  od;
  return(true)
end
```

Note that in the look-ahead facility only conditions specifying a traced variable are examined; it just skips the other conditions. If the look ahead returns the value *true*, the top-down inference algorithm continues as usual. This function LookAhead is called from the procedure Infer just before calling Apply. The procedure Apply is then invoked only if LookAhead has succeeded.

In the following, the most important procedure and function calls are shown, indicating the level at which they are introduced in the top-down inference algorithm:

```
TraceValues
  Infer
    Select
    LookAhead
      ExecPredicate
    Apply
      EvalConditions
        TraceValues
        ExecPredicate
      EvalConclusions
        ExecAction
  Ask
```

This shows once more the indirect recursive call to the procedure TraceValues from EvalConditions.

Note that only relatively slight modifications of the discussed algorithm are needed to extend it to an object–attribute–value representation. We have only to add a procedure for tracing the *goal attributes* of an object, a notion similar to the notion of a goal variable:

```
procedure Activate(object)

  foreach attr in attributes(object) do
    if goal(attr) then
      TraceValues(object, attr)
    fi
  od
end
```

The other procedures need only slight alteration by adding the object as an extra argument to the procedures, and by taking for a variable an attribute of the given object.

3.2.2 Top-down inference in PROLOG

Sections 3.2.2 and 3.2.3 are concerned with implementing top-down inference along the lines set out above. In this section, the implementation language will be PROLOG; in Section 3.2.3 we shall demonstrate how to realize top-down inference in LISP.

Adhering to the basic formalisms for knowledge representation in a production system, the PROLOG representation of a knowledge base consists of a domain declaration section and a rule base, both stored as a file of Horn clauses. The PROLOG program discussed here makes use of the variable–value representation, in which, for reasons of simplicity, single-valued and multi-valued variables are not explicitly distinguished. Moreover, not all optimizations dealt with in the preceding section are elaborated in the program. The remaining ones are left as an exercise to the reader (see Exercise 3.5).

In the present implementation, the domain declaration specifies explicitly only the questions to be posed to the user. These questions are represented in Horn clauses having the following general form:

```
prompt(<variable-name>) :-
    write(<string>).
```

The presence of such a prompt for a variable indicates that the variable is askable; the absence of a prompt indicates that the variable should not be asked from the user.

EXAMPLE 3.19 ______________________________

Consider the following clause:

```
prompt(complaint) :-
    write('Enter the complaints of the patient.').
```

This clause defines the system's question concerning the variable *complaint*. Note that a production-system variable is represented in PROLOG as a constant.

Furthermore, it is assumed that initially there is only a single goal variable. However, it is a relatively straightforward task to extend the program in such a way that it is also able to deal with a set of goals.

In the program, production-system facts are represented as PROLOG facts concerning a relation `fact` having two arguments.

EXAMPLE 3.20

A fact of the form

$$age = 27$$

is represented in the PROLOG program as

```
fact(age,27).
```

Notice once more that a production-system variable is not a variable in terms of the implementation language, but a constant.

A fact concerning a multi-valued variable is represented in as many unit clauses as there are values specified for the variable.

EXAMPLE 3.21

Consider the following fact:

$$disorder = \{aortic\text{-}aneurysm,\ aortic\text{-}regurgitation\}$$

It is represented in the following two clauses:

```
fact(disorder,aortic_aneurysm).
fact(disorder,aortic_regurgitation).
```

The fact set is kept in the PROLOG database.

Production rules may be represented in PROLOG in quite a natural way. When we compare the Horn clause formalism with the formalism of production rules, they appear to have various properties in common. A production rule having a conjunction of conditions in the antecedent and a single conclusion in its consequent can be translated directly into a Horn clause of the following form:

```
<action>(<variable>,<constant>) :-
  <predicate_1>(<variable_1>,<constant_1>),
        .
        .
        .
  <predicate_n>(<variable_n>,<constant_n>).
```

The only syntactic changes necessary arise from adaptation to the PROLOG conventions. Note that, in the Horn clause representation of a production rule, the conclusion is mentioned before the conditions.

EXAMPLE 3.22

Consider the following production rule:

> ***if***
> *same*(*complaint*,*abdominal-pain*) ***and***
> *same*(*auscultation*,*murmur*) ***and***
> *same*(*palpation*,*pulsating-mass*)
> ***then***
> *add*(*disorder*,*aortic-aneurysm*)
> ***fi***

This rule is translated into the following Horn clause:

```
add(disorder,aortic_aneurysm) :-
    same(complaint,abdominal_pain),
    same(auscultation,murmur),
    same(palpation,pulsating_mass).
```

For the representation of the logical ***or*** between two conditions, we simply use the PROLOG 'or' operator, that is, the symbol ';'.

EXAMPLE 3.23

The production rule

> ***if***
> *greaterthan*(*systolic-pressure*,140) ***and***
> *greaterthan*(*pulse-pressure*,50) ***and***
> *same*(*auscultation*,*diastolic-murmur*) ***or***
> *same*(*percussion*,*enlarged-heart*)
> ***then***
> *add*(*disorder*,*aortic-regurgitation*)
> ***fi***

is represented in PROLOG as follows:

```
add(disorder,aortic_regurgitation) :-
    greaterthan(systolic_pressure,140),
    greaterthan(pulse_pressure,50),
    (same(auscultation,diastolic_murmur);
     same(percussion,enlarged_heart)).
```

Recall that production rules may have more than one conclusion. However, the Horn clause formalism permits only a single conclusion per clause. For the representation of a production rule having more than one conclusion, we create as many Horn clauses as there are conclusions in the rule. The antecedents of the Horn clauses created for a specific rule are all the same.

EXAMPLE 3.24

Consider the following production rule:

> ***if***
> *same*(*complaint*,*calf-pain*) ***and***
> *same*(*presence*,*walking*) ***and***
> *same*(*absence*,*rest*)
> ***then***
> *add*(*cause*,*arterial-stenosis*) ***also***
> *add*(*disorder*,*atherosclerosis*)
> ***fi***

This rule is represented by means of the following two PROLOG clauses:

```
add(cause,arterial_stenosis) :-
     same(complaint,calf_pain),
     same(presence,walking),
     same(absence,rest).
add(disorder,atherosclerosis) :-
     same(complaint,calf_pain),
     same(presence,walking),
     same(absence,rest).
```

It should be remarked that the representation of production rules discussed here is only one of many possible ways for representing rules in PROLOG.

The explicit separation of a knowledge base and the inference engine generally sought after in expert system shells is readily realized in PROLOG: the basic principles of this language as a practical realization of logic programming closely fit the paradigm of expert systems stated in Chapter 1. Roughly speaking, the knowledge base of a production system is entered into the PROLOG database and the PROLOG interpreter is taken to constitute the inference engine. However, although the backtracking algorithm employed by the PROLOG interpreter may be viewed as a possible realization of top-down inference, it is not possible to exploit the PROLOG interpreter directly as a top-down inference engine. For this purpose, we have to add some special features to it; for example, for managing the fact set, for tracing of variables and for querying the user. Furthermore, the predicates and actions used in production rules have to be defined and added to the predefined system predicates. We will now describe how the PROLOG interpreter can be extended to a production-rule inference engine.

The first extension to the PROLOG interpreter we discuss is the procedure for tracing a variable. Recall that, in tracing a variable, first all production rules relevant for the variable are selected from the rule base. The selected production rules are subsequently applied one by one by first evaluating their conditions. Before executing the predicate of a specific condition, it is first checked whether the mentioned variable has been marked as traced. If the variable has not yet been traced, the inference engine generates a new subgoal, which is essentially the variable to be inferred from the rule base. If no information can be inferred concerning the given variable, the system turns to the user with a request for information. This process is described by means of the following two PROLOG clauses:

```
trace_values(Variable) :-
     fact(Variable,_),!.
trace_values(Variable) :-
     infer(Variable),
     ask(Variable).
```

The first clause investigates whether there are any facts concerning the variable `Variable` present in the fact set. Note that this test now suffices for determining whether or not the variable has already been traced. First of all, we have only single-conclusion production rules, so that facts cannot be entered into the fact set merely as a side-effect. Furthermore, we shall see that, if inspecting the knowledge base and querying the user have not yielded values for the variable, a special fact indicating that the particular variable is *unknown* is added explicitly to the fact set. We shall return to the latter observation when discussing the procedure `ask`. If the first `trace_values` clause succeeds, the second clause will not be executed, thus preventing needless examination of the rule base. If no fact concerning `Variable` occurs in the fact set, the call `fact(Variable,_)` in the first clause fails, and the second clause will be interpreted.

The two `infer` clauses

```
infer(Variable) :-
     select_rule(Variable),
     fail.
infer(_).
```

describe the process of selecting and subsequently applying the relevant production rules from the rule base. The selection and application of a single rule is accomplished by means of the procedure `select_rule`; the built-in predicate `fail` forces backtracking to select all relevant production rules.

```
select_rule(Variable) :-
     add(Variable,Value),
     asserta(fact(Variable,Value)).
```

The select_rule procedure contains a call add(Variable,Value) for selecting one production rule from the rule base. Note that the entire selection process is executed by the PROLOG interpreter. This call matches with a conclusion of a production rule having the instantiated variable Variable at the first argument position of the predicate add. If a match is found, the conditions of the selected production rule are evaluated in the specified order; the evaluation of a selected rule is entirely done by the PROLOG interpreter. So the evaluation algorithm described in the previous section in the procedure Apply is already present in PROLOG itself. If the selected rule succeeds upon evaluation, the variable Value will have been instantiated to the constant specified in the conclusion of the rule. The fact inferred from the rule is then added to the fact set kept in the PROLOG database using the built-in predicate asserta.

After the variable has been inferred by means of the infer procedure called from trace_values, the procedure ask is executed:

```
ask(Variable) :-
     fact(Variable,_),!.
ask(Variable) :-
     prompt(Variable),
     read(Values),
     add_facts(Variable,Values),!,
     nl.
ask(Variable) :-
     asserta(fact(Variable,unknown)).
```

The first clause in the procedure ask investigates by means of fact(Variable,_) whether or not facts have been inferred for the variable Variable from the rule base. If there are no facts present in the fact set for the particular variable, the first ask clause fails and the second clause is interpreted, possibly prompting the user to enter information by means of the message printed on the screen by prompt(Variable). The input from the user is subsequently read in using the built-in predicate read and entered into the fact set by means of a call to the procedure add_facts. If no prompt has been specified in the knowledge base for the particular variable, indicating that it is not askable, the second clause fails. The third clause is then interpreted, which sets the value of the variable to *unknown*.

The user has to enter his or her answer as a list of constants, as is shown in the following example. The user interface is rather crude and should be further elaborated for a more serious application.

EXAMPLE 3.25

Suppose that the following prompt appears on the screen during a consultation:

```
Enter the complaints of the patient.
```

This query indicates that the system has not been able to derive values for the variable *complaint* from the rule base. The user now is requested to enter relevant values. If we assume that the patient for which the system is being consulted is suffering from abdominal pain and fever, the user has to enter this information in the following way:

```
[abdominal_pain,fever].
```

Note the terminating dot.

The user's input is entered into the fact set by means of the `add_facts` procedure called from the second `ask` clause. This procedure merely adds each constant from the list of constants as a fact to the fact set:

```
add_facts(_,[]) :- !.
add_facts(Variable,[Value|Rest]) :-
    asserta(fact(Variable,Value)),
    add_facts(Variable,Rest).
```

We still have to discuss the PROLOG definitions of the predicates allowed in the conditions of production rules. We refer to these predicates as *system predicates*, to distinguish them from the built-in predicates provided by PROLOG itself. The most frequently used predicate, *same*, is described by means of the following PROLOG clause:

```
same(Variable,Value) :-
    trace_values(Variable),!,
    fact(Variable,Value).
```

As can be seen from the first condition of this clause, the process of tracing a variable is executed independent of the constant specified in the condition. Only after a variable has been traced is it checked whether or not the specified value has been found for the variable. If the particular constant does not occur in the fact set as a value for the variable, the call to `same` fails. Note that the cut prevents a second call to `trace_values`.

The system predicates *greaterthan* and *lessthan* may be implemented in PROLOG as follows. Recall that numerical variables are always single-valued:

```
greaterthan(Variable,Value) :-
     values_known(Variable,Knownvalue),!,
     Knownvalue > Value.

lessthan(Variable,Value) :-
     values_known(Variable,Knownvalue),!,
     Knownvalue < Value.

values_known(Variable,Knownvalue) :-
     trace_values(Variable),!,
     fact(Variable,Knownvalue),
     not(Knownvalue = unknown).
```

Again, note the indirect recursive call to `trace_values`.

To conclude, the clause

```
consultation(Goal_variable) :-
     trace_values(Goal_variable),!,
     output(Goal_variable),
     nl.
```

starts the consultation by means of a call to `trace_values` for the goal variable to which `Goal_variable` is instantiated; it prints the results on the screen. It is left as an exercise for the reader to develop the relevant `output` clauses. Before starting the consultation, both the knowledge base and the above-given extension onto the PROLOG interpreter must have been loaded into the PROLOG database.

EXAMPLE 3.26

Consider the following tiny knowledge base, consisting of only two production rules:

```
% DOMAIN DECLARATION

prompt(complaint) :-
     write('Enter complaints of patient.'),
     nl.
prompt(presence) :-
     write('When is the pain present?'),
     nl.
prompt(absence) :-
     write('When does the pain disappear?'),
     nl.
prompt(age) :-
     write('Enter age of the patient.'),
     nl.
prompt(smokes) :-
     write('Does the patient smoke?'),
     nl.
```

```
% RULE BASE

add(diagnosis,arterial_stenosis) :-
     same(disorder,atherosclerosis),
     same(complaint,calf_pain),
     same(presence,walking),
     same(absence,rest).

add(disorder,atherosclerosis) :-
     greaterthan(age,60),
     same(smokes,yes).
```

Application of the PROLOG program developed above yields the following consultation:

```
| ?- consultation(diagnosis).

Enter age of the patient.
|: [70].

Does the patient smoke?
|: [yes].

Enter complaints of patient.
|: [calf_pain].

When is the pain present?
|: [walking].

When does the pain disappear?
|: [rest].

The diagnosis is: arterial_stenosis
```

3.2.3 Top-down inference in LISP

In the present section, we shall develop an implementation of the top-down inference algorithm in the programming language LISP. We start with a description of the representation of variable declarations and production rules in LISP, and then proceed with a discussion of the basic inference algorithm. In developing the inference engine, we exploit the LISP interpreter to a large extent by adding only a small number of extra features to it, just as we have done in the PROLOG implementation.

The knowledge base of the LISP system consists of a collection of variable declarations and production rules. A variable declaration has the following form:

```
(def <variable-name>
  (prompt <string>)
  (class <trace-class>))
```

The keyword `def` is followed by the variable name. If following the keyword `prompt` a question to the user is specified, the variable is askable. The empty prompt `nil` indicates that the variable should never be asked from the user. A variable declaration furthermore contains a so-called *trace class* which tells us whether or not the variable is a goal. If the keyword `goal` is filled in after the keyword `class`, the variable is a goal; `nil` indicates that it is not a goal. Again, for ease of exposition, single-valued and multi-valued variables are not explicitly distinguished in this program. Moreover, some of the optimizations we discussed in Section 3.2.1 have not been incorporated, but instead are left as an exercise for the reader (see Exercises 3.5 and 3.6).

EXAMPLE 3.27

Let *complaint* be an askable variable. Using the syntax of a variable declaration given above, we obtain the following specification:

```
(def complaint
  (prompt "Enter the complaints of the patient.")
  (class nil))
```

For the goal variable *diagnosis*, we obtain the following specification:

```
(def diagnosis
  (prompt nil)
  (class goal))
```

Production rules are explicitly distinguished from variable declarations by means of the keyword `rule`. The syntax used in the LISP program for representing production rules closely resembles the representation defined in the first section of this chapter, as is shown in Example 3.28.

EXAMPLE 3.28

Consider the following production rule:

if
same(*complaint*,*abdominal-pain*) ***and***
same(*auscultation*,*abdominal-murmur*) ***and***
same(*palpation*,*pulsating-mass*)
then
add(*disorder*,*aortic-aneurysm*)
fi

This rule is represented in LISP by means of the following expression:

```
(rule
  (and (same complaint abdominal-pain)
       (same auscultation abdominal-murmur)
       (same palpation pulsating-mass))
  (add disorder aortic-aneurysm))
```

Recall that a production rule may also contain a disjunction of conditions. The following LISP expression represents such a rule:

```
(rule
 (and (greaterthan systolic-pressure 140)
      (greaterthan pulse-pressure 50)
      (or (same auscultation diastolic-murmur)
          (same percussion enlarged-heart)))
 (add disorder aortic-regurgitation))
```

A knowledge base has to be read in and parsed by the LISP program before it can be consulted. The function `ConsultationSystem` shown below therefore first prompts the user to enter the name of the file in which the knowledge base is kept, and then calls the function `Parse` for analysing the knowledge base:

```
(defun ConsultationSystem ( )
  (terpri)
  (princ "Name of the knowledge base: ")
  (let ((knowledge-base (open (read-line))))
    (setq *var-decls* nil
          *rule-base* nil)
    (Parse knowledge-base)
    (close knowledge-base)
    (Consultation *var-decls*)))
```

After the knowledge base has been parsed, all variables declared in the domain declaration will have been stored in the global variable `*var-decls*`, and the set of production rules will have been stored in the global variable `*rule-base*`. Note that, since in COMMON LISP all variables by default have a lexical scope, it is necessary to declare them as special to render them globally accessible. This is achieved by means of the following declarations:

```
(defvar *var-decls*)
(defvar *rule-base*)
```

In parsing the knowledge base, the recursive function `Parse` examines the first element of each expression `expr` read in to determine whether it is a keyword of a variable declaration or of a production rule:

```
(defun Parse (knowledge-base)
  (let ((expr (ReadExpression knowledge-base)))
    (cond ((eq expr 'eof) nil)
          (t (case (first expr)
               (def  (ParseDecl (rest expr)))
               (rule (ParseRule (rest expr)))
               (otherwise (error "Unknown keyword: ~A" (first expr))))
             (Parse knowledge-base)))))
```

If a variable declaration is encountered, the function `ParseDecl` is called; if the expression read in represents a production rule, `Parse` calls the function `ParseRule`. Note that a variable declaration or production rule is stripped from its keyword before it is passed on to the appropriate function. If the expression does not represent a variable declaration or a production rule, it is an illegal expression.

An expression is read from file by means of a call to the function `ReadExpression`, which returns the function value `eof` after all expressions from the knowledge base have been read in:

```
(defun ReadExpression (stream)
  (read stream nil 'eof))
```

Note that, as soon as `ReadExpression` has returned the function value `eof`, the function `Parse` terminates.

The function `ParseDecl` called from `Parse` translates a variable declaration into a LISP symbol with a property list:

```
(defun ParseDecl (expr)
  (let ((variable (first expr))
        (spec (rest expr)))
    (setf (get variable 'prompt) (Prompt spec)
          (get variable 'class) (Class spec)
          (get variable 'traced) nil) ; not traced
    (set variable nil) ; value is unknown by default
    (setq *var-decls* (append *var-decls*
                              (list variable)))))
```

The name of the variable is selected from the given expression by means of the function call `(first expr)`. Its prompt and trace class are extracted from the remainder of the declaration and translated into properties of a LISP symbol having the same name as the variable. The

LISP functions setf and get are used for initializing the properties prompt, class and traced of the symbol. The property traced is given the value nil to indicate that the variable is initially untraced. Furthermore, the value of the variable is set to nil, using the function set, to indicate that the variable has no value at the beginning of a consultation of the knowledge base. The name of the variable is subsequently added to the list of variable declarations in *var-decls*.

The selection of the prompt and the trace class belonging to a variable is accomplished by means of the following functions Prompt and Class:

```
(defun Prompt (spec)
  (cadr (assoc 'prompt spec)))

(defun Class (spec)
  (cadr (assoc 'class spec)))
```

In various places in the program we shall need functions for accessing the property values in the property list of a given symbol. For each property a corresponding function is defined:

```
(defun Goal? (var)
  (eq (get var 'class) 'goal))

(defun Traced? (var)
  (get var 'traced))

(defun GetPrompt (var)
  (get var 'prompt))
```

These functions allow us in the program to abstract from the particular data structures used for representing the features of a variable.

The last function to be discussed with respect to a variable declaration is the function SetTraced. Upon evaluation, this function assigns the value t to the property traced of the specified variable:

```
(defun SetTraced (var)
  (setf (get var 'traced) t))
```

Recall that, if a production rule is read in, the function ParseRule is called from Parse. This function is similar in concept to the function ParseDecl: it adds an expression representing a production rule to the global variable *rule-base*:

```
(defun ParseRule (expr)
  (setq *rule-base* (cons expr *rule-base*)))
```

We now define several functions for selecting relevant production rules from a given rule base, and for evaluating a selected rule. The functions `FirstRule` and `RestRule` yield the first rule of the rule base and the remaining rules after removal of the first one, respectively:

```
(defun FirstRule (rule-base)
  (first rule-base))

(defun RestRules (rule-base)
  (rest rule-base))
```

The functions `Antecedent` and `Consequent` return the part of a given production rule indicated by their respective function names:

```
(defun Antecedent (rule)
  (first rule))

(defun Consequent (rule)
  (rest rule))
```

For selecting parts of a consequent of a production rule, the functions `FirstConclusion` and `RestConclusions` are provided. They yield the first conclusion and the remaining ones, respectively:

```
(defun FirstConclusion (conseq)
  (first conseq))

 (defun RestConclusions (conseq)
   (rest conseq))
```

Finally, the function `Var` is provided for selecting the name of a variable from a condition or conclusion:

```
(defun Var (assertion)
  (second assertion))
```

This concludes the description of the auxiliary functions used in the program. We have now arrived at its kernel. Recall that, after the variable declarations and production rules have been read in and processed, the function `Consultation` is called from the function `ConsultationSystem` for the actual consultation of the knowledge base:

```
(defun Consultation (var-decls)
  (TraceGoals var-decls)
  (PrintGoals var-decls))
```

The function `Consultation` traces the goal variables occurring in `var-decls` one by one by means of the function `TraceGoals`. After all goal variables have been traced, the values established for them are printed on the screen by means of the function `PrintGoals`:

```
(defun PrintGoals (var-decls)
  (cond ((null var-decls) nil)
        ((Goal? (first var-decls))
         (let ((var (first var-decls)))
           (terpri)
           (print var)
           (princ (eval var)))
         (PrintGoals (rest var-decls)))
        (t (PrintGoals (rest var-decls)))))
```

The tracing of a goal variable is implemented by the function `TraceGoals`. For each variable occurring in `var-decls` it is checked whether or not it is a goal; if it is, the function `TraceValues` is called for actually tracing it. The remaining goal variables are selected and traced by means of a recursive call to `TraceGoals`:

```
(defun TraceGoals (var-decls)
  (if var-decls
      (let ((variable (first var-decls)))
        (if (Goal? variable) ; is it a goal variable?
            (TraceValues variable))
        (TraceGoals (rest var-decls)))))
```

The function `TraceValues`, which is used for actually tracing a variable, is implemented as described in Section 3.2.1. It first tries to infer values for the variable from the rule base. If the application of the production rules has not been successful, the user is prompted to enter values for the variable:

```
(defun TraceValues (variable)
  (if (not (Infer variable))
      (Ask variable))
  (SetTraced variable))
```

Deriving one or more constant values for a variable using the production rules from the rule base is done by means of the function `Infer`. This function first selects all relevant production rules and then applies them one by one by calling `ApplyRule`:

```
(defun Infer (variable)
  (dolist (rule (Select variable *rule-base* nil)
                (eval variable))
    (ApplyRule rule)))
```

The function value returned by `Infer` is a list of the constants which have been derived for the variable after all applicable production rules have been applied. This value is obtained from the evaluation of the form `(eval variable)`.

Note that in `TraceValues` the function `Ask` is called for a variable only if `Infer` has yielded the function value `nil`; that is, only if no values have been inferred for the variable from the rule base. After the call to `Infer`, and possibly also after the call to `Ask`, has been evaluated, the variable has been traced, since all possible ways to obtain values have been tried. So the variable is marked as traced by means of a call to the function `SetTraced`.

The function `Infer` employs the recursive function `Select` for selecting applicable production rules from the rule base. In `Select`, each production rule is examined on its relevance to the variable being traced by means of a call to `Occurs`, which checks whether one of its conclusions contains the given variable. If the variable occurs in one of the conclusions, the production rule is added to the conflict set. The conflict set is kept in the parameter `selected`:

```
(defun Select (variable rules selected)
  (cond ((null rules) selected)
        (t (let ((rule (FirstRule rules)))
             (if (Occurs variable (Consequent rule))
                 (Select variable (RestRules rules)
                         (cons rule selected))
                 (Select variable (RestRules rules) selected))))))
```

The function `Select` returns the conflict set as its function value.

The function `Occurs`, which is called from `Select`, examines the conclusions of the consequent of a rule one by one until a conclusion has been found in which `var` occurs, or until all conclusions have been examined:

```
(defun Occurs (var conseq)
  (cond ((null conseq) nil)
        (t (if (eq (Var (FirstConclusion conseq)) var)
               t
               (Occurs var (RestConclusions conseq))))))
```

Recall that, in the function `Infer`, each rule from the conflict set is applied by means of a call to the function `ApplyRule`. The function `ApplyRule` applies a selected production rule by first evaluating its conditions by means of `EvalConditions?`. If evaluation of the antecedent of the rule has returned the truth value `t`, its conclusions are evaluated by means of the function `EvalConclusions`:

```
(defun ApplyRule (rule)
  (if (EvalConditions? (Antecedent rule))
      (EvalConclusions (Consequent rule))))
```

Most of the actual evaluation of a production rule is carried out by the standard interpreter provided by LISP. For example, within the following function `EvalConditions?`, the entire antecedent of a production rule is passed on to the LISP interpreter for evaluation:

```
(defun EvalConditions? (antecedent)
  (eval antecedent))
```

When discussing the representation of production rules by means of LISP expressions, we have mentioned that the consequent of a production rule is represented as a list of subexpressions each representing a conclusion. In `EvalConclusions`, the conclusions of a rule are evaluated by calling the standard LISP function `mapc` for the entire consequent:

```
(defun EvalConclusions (consequent)
  (mapc #'eval consequent))
```

Note that in this way the function `eval` is applied to each conclusion.

As we have mentioned before, most of the evaluation of a production rule is left to the LISP interpreter. However, to be able to exploit the LISP interpreter in this way, the standard evaluation rules adhered to in LISP have to be modified for predicates and actions. The LISP interpreter, for example, evaluates the arguments of a function call before passing them on. However, for predicates and actions we do not want to pass the values of the arguments but the arguments themselves, that is, without evaluation. LISP offers a solution to this problem in the form of macros: contrary to function calls the arguments of a macro call are not evaluated beforehand.

The macro `Same` now defines the predicate *same*. It checks whether the constant specified in the condition being evaluated occurs in the list of constants the variable has as a value. If the constant occurs in the value set, the truth value `t` is returned:

```
(defmacro Same (variable value)
  '(Compare #'member ',variable ',value))
```

The macro `NotSame` is almost complementary to `Same`; however, it has to reckon with the case that the variable is *unknown*. We recall that a variable is *unknown* if it has been traced and nevertheless has the value `nil`. To determine whether or not the variable is *unknown*, `NotSame` first calls the macro `Known`:

```
(defmacro NotSame (variable value)
  '(and (Known ,variable)
        (not (Same ,variable ,value))))
```

The macro `Known` yields the truth value `t` if the variable passed as an argument has a value different from `nil`, in other words, if the variable is *known*:

```
(defmacro Known (variable)
  '(not (Compare #'eq ',variable nil)))
```

The following macros implement the various system predicates for numerical variables:

```
(defmacro LessThan (variable value)
  '(Compare #'> ',variable ,value))
(defmacro Equals (variable value)
  '(Compare #'= ',variable ,value))
(defmacro GreaterThan (variable value)
  '(Compare #'< ',variable ,value))
```

From all macros defined so far, the function `Compare` is called. This function specifies the indirect recursive call to `TraceValues` for tracing values for a yet untraced variable, as has been discussed in Section 3.2.1:

```
(defun Compare (operator variable value)
  (cond ((Traced? variable)
         (if (or (eval variable) ; variable has a value?
                 (eq operator #'eq))
             (funcall operator value (eval variable))))
        (t (TraceValues variable)
           (Compare operator variable value))))
```

Finally, the action *add* is defined. Upon evaluation, it adds the specified constant to the list of constants for a given variable:

```
(defmacro Add (variable value)
  '(set ',variable (cons ',value ,variable))))
```

It should be noted that, in this implementation, numerical variables are not allowed in the conclusions of a production rule.

We still have to discuss one function, namely the function `Ask`, which is called from `TraceValues`. Recall that this function is invoked only if the inference engine has not been able to derive values from the rule base by means of the function `Infer`. The function `Ask` prompts the user to enter values for the variable. Input should be entered as a list of one or more LISP atoms. By means of `(unknown)` the user may indicate that the values of the variable are *unknown*:

```
(defun Ask (variable)
  (when (GetPrompt variable)
    (terpri)
    (princ (GetPrompt variable))
    (terpri)
    (princ "-> ")
    (let ((response (read)))
      (unless (eq (first response) 'UNKNOWN)
        (if (numberp (first response))
            (set variable (first response))
            (set variable response))))))
```

The entire program has now been discussed. As the reader may have noticed, the program is not as efficient as it could be. For example, applicable production rules for a given variable are selected by scanning the entire rule base. A more efficient search method will be required when the rule base contains more than a hundred or so production rules. The implementation, however, can be improved without much effort by attaching to each variable in `*var-decls*` a list of pointers to those production rules having the variable in one of their conclusions; in this case, there is no longer any need for scanning the entire rule base. This improvement is left to the reader as an exercise (see Exercise 3.6). We finish this section with a sample program run.

EXAMPLE 3.29

Consider the following LISP version of the tiny knowledge base from Example 3.26:

```
; DOMAIN DECLARATION

(def complaint
  (prompt "Enter complaints of patient.")
  (class nil))

(def presence
  (prompt "When is the pain present?")
  (class nil))

(def absence
  (prompt "When does the pain disappear?")
  (class nil))

(def age
  (prompt "Enter age of patient.")
  (class nil))

(def smokes
  (prompt "Does the patient smoke?")
  (class nil))

(def diagnosis
  (prompt nil)
  (class goal))

(def disorder
  (prompt nil)
  (class nil))
```

```
; RULE BASE

(rule
  (and (same disorder atherosclerosis)
       (same complaint calf-pain)
       (same presence walking)
       (same absence rest))
  (add diagnosis arterial-stenosis))

(rule
  (and (greaterthan age 60)
       (same smokes yes))
  (add disorder atherosclerosis))
```

When applying the LISP program for top-down inference, we obtain the following transcript of a consultation:

```
Name of the knowledge base: example

Enter age of patient.
-> (70)

Does the patient smoke?
-> (yes)

Enter complaints of patient.
-> (calf-pain)

When is the pain present?
-> (walking)

When does the pain disappear?
-> (rest)

diagnosis(arterial-stenosis)
```

3.2.4 Bottom-up inference and production rules

Broadly speaking, bottom-up inference with production rules differs from top-down inference only by being controlled by the fact set instead of by goals and subgoals. As in top-down inference, each time a set of relevant production rules is selected from a rule base; the resulting set of applicable production rules is again called the conflict set. Recall that, in top-down inference, only production rules having a particular (sub)goal variable in one of their conclusions were included in the conflict set. In bottom-up inference, however, a production rule is entered into the conflict set if its conditions are fulfilled using the information from the given fact set. In applying the rules from the conflict set, there is also a difference between the two forms of inference. In top-down inference all production rules from the conflict set are applied exhaustively. In bottom-up inference, however, generally only one of them is applied.

This difference arises from the action *remove* being applied frequently in production systems employing bottom-up inference, in contrast with top-down inference systems. It will be evident that the evaluation of this action may have as an effect that certain conditions, which were true before evaluation of the action took place, no longer hold after its evaluation. As a consequence, the other rules in the conflict set have to be reconsidered, because some may specify conditions that fail upon evaluation using the altered fact set. Furthermore, the changes in the fact set may render other rules successful, which should then be added to the conflict set. Therefore, after applying a single rule from a specific conflict set, a new conflict set is selected. In practice, however, many of the rules previously present in the conflict set will appear again in the new conflict set in the next inference step. The entire process is repeated again and again, until some predefined termination criterion is met; a frequently employed criterion is the emptiness of the set of applicable rules. The inference is started just by the presence of initial facts in the fact set. The general approach of bottom-up inference in a production system is described in the following procedure:

```
procedure Infer(rule-base, fact-set)

  rules ← Select(rule-base, fact-set);
  while rules ≠ ∅ do
    rule ← ResolveConflicts(rules);
    Apply(rule);
    rules ← Select(rule-base, fact-set)
  od
end
```

The function Select is applied for selecting the applicable production rules from the rule base. The function ResolveConflicts subsequently chooses from the resulting conflict set a single rule for application; this function implements a conflict-resolution strategy, several of which will be discussed below. The selected production rule is then applied by means of a call to the procedure Apply. In bottom-up inference, the procedure Apply just evaluates the actions of the conclusions specified in the consequent of the rule.

The selection of the relevant production rules from the rule base is described in the following function Select. Again, for ease of exposition, we have assumed that the antecedent of a production rule comprises only a conjunction of conditions. The procedure EvalCondition evaluates a single condition of a production rule. It returns failure if the variable mentioned in the condition does not occur in the fact set, or if the specified predicate on evaluation yields the truth value *false*; otherwise the procedure returns success.

```
function Select(rule-base, fact-set)
  selected-rules ← ∅;
  foreach rule in rule-base do
    failed ← false;
    foreach cond in antecedent(rule) with not failed do
      EvalCondition(cond, fact-set, failed)
    od;
    if not failed then
      selected-rules ← selected-rules ∪ {rule}
    fi
  od;
  return(selected-rules)
end
```

Note that this evaluation differs from the evaluation described for top-down inference, because here the evaluation of a condition does not lead to the generation of a new subgoal.

The basic bottom-up inference algorithm is very simple. However, much more is still to be said about incorporating control strategies into the basic bottom-up inference scheme. Neither the order in which the rule base is traversed nor the order in which the conditions and conclusions of a selected rule are evaluated has been fixed in the function Select. As in Section 3.2.1, we again call the non-fixed order in which production rules are selected and applied non-determinism of the first kind, and the non-fixed order in which conditions and conclusions are evaluated non-determinism of the second kind. Non-determinism of the first kind is again resolved by means of a conflict-resolution strategy. These strategies are much more often applied in systems with bottom-up inference than in systems using top-down inference. If rules, and conditions and conclusions of rules, are evaluated in the order in which they have been specified we speak of *forward chaining*; this is the simplest possible form of conflict resolution. So, in forward chaining, the first successful production rule encountered will be selected for application. Note that the choice of the order in which the conditions of the rules from the rule base are evaluated in bottom-up inference has no effect on the resulting behaviour of the system. Only the order in which the rules are applied, and the order in which the conclusions of the rules are evaluated, are of importance.

Many conflict-resolution strategies have been developed for bottom-up inference; here we only discuss three more of them in addition to forward chaining. The main reason for augmenting the basic inference algorithm with a conflict-resolution strategy which is more sophisticated than simple forward chaining is to obtain a more context-sensitive and problem-directed reasoning behaviour, that is, to control the inference better. Since bottom-up inference lacks the 'intelligent' goal-directed nature of top-down inference, conflict-resolution strategies are evidently much more important in bottom-up inference than in top-down inference. Possible conflict resolution strategies differing from forward chaining are:

- conflict resolution by *prioritization*, which for selecting a rule for application uses priorities of the production rules which have been indicated explicitly by the knowledge engineer;
- conflict resolution by *specificity*, which causes the system to prefer more strongly stated production rules over weaker ones;
- conflict resolution by *recency*, which uses the most recently derived facts in selecting a production rule for application, thus causing the system to pursue a single line of reasoning.

Conflict resolution by production rule prioritization has the same advantages as forward chaining; it is easy to implement and use, while being effective in many applications. However, an obvious disadvantage of this strategy is the burden it places on the knowledge engineer who has to impose an ordering on the production rules from the rule base explicitly.

Conflict resolution by specificity is based on some measure of specificity for production rules, such as the number of tests specified in the conditions of the rules. A production rule R_1 is considered to be more specific than a production rule R_2 if R_1 contains at least the same conditions as R_2.

EXAMPLE 3.30

Consider the following two production rules:

```
R1: if
        same(auscultation,diastolic-murmur)
    then
        add(disorder,cardiac-disorder)
    fi

R2: if
        greaterthan(systolic-pressure,140) and
        same(auscultation,diastolic-murmur) and
        same(percussion,enlarged-heart)
    then
        add(disorder,aortic-regurgitation)
    fi
```

Production rule R_2 is more specific than production rule R_1 because it contains the condition from R_1 as well as some additional conditions. Furthermore, the conclusion of R_2 is more specific than the one from R_1. It will be obvious that success of R_2 will yield a stronger result than success of rule R_1. A specificity strategy will therefore choose R_2 from the conflict set $\{R_1,R_2\}$ for application.

The use of a specificity strategy increases the extensibility of the rule base: a rule base can easily be enlarged by adding new, more specific rules to it without our having to worry too much about older rules, because more specific production rules will prevail over more general ones. Note that most humans exhibit a similar behaviour. For example, a person encountering a friend in the street will not be inclined to think that this other person is a mammal, but will instead think of the person by name, just applying the most specific knowledge available.

The last conflict-resolution strategy we will discuss, the recency strategy, is undoubtedly the most complicated of the ones we have mentioned. This conflict-resolution strategy requires that each fact in the fact set is supplemented with a time tag, a unique number indicating the 'time' the fact was derived. In the following definition, the notion of a fact is redefined for the case of bottom-up inference using the recency strategy. We will deal only with single-valued variables; the extension to multi-valued ones is straightforward.

Definition: A *fact* is an expression of the following form:

$$t\colon x^s = c$$

where $t \in \mathbb{N}$ is a *time tag* which uniquely identifies the fact, x^s is a single-valued variable, and c is a constant. A *fact set* has the following form:

$$\{t_1\colon x_1^s = c_1, \ldots, t_n\colon x_m^s = c_m\}$$

Constants and variables may now occur more than once in the fact set. However, a time-tag–variable pair is unique. Each fact added to the fact set as a result of applying a production rule is assigned a new time tag $t + 1$ where t is the last assigned one.

EXAMPLE 3.31

Consider the following fact set:

$$\{1\colon x = a, 2\colon x = b, 3\colon y = c, 4\colon z = d\}$$

The variable x occurs twice among these facts, with different time tags. This should be interpreted as follows: at time 1 the variable x

has taken the value a, and at time 2 it has obtained the value b. Therefore, x has two values, one at time 1 and another one at time 2.

There are various ways in which time tags may be interpreted in the representation of facts. Time tags for example may be taken to monitor progress in time of some parameter.

EXAMPLE 3.32

Consider the following fact set:

$$\{1: temp = 36.2,\ 2: temp = 37,\ 3: temp = 38\}$$

Here, time tags are used to indicate the change in body temperature of some person with time; each time tag for example indicates a day.

Recall that here we introduced time tags to enable conflict resolution by recency; this is the main usage of time tags. After the applicable production rules have been selected from the rule base, it is possible to order the resulting conflict set using the time tags associated with individual facts from the fact set. Each rule in the conflict set is associated with a sequence of time tags, where each time tag originates from a fact matching with a condition of the specific rule. These time tags are then sorted in decreasing order. Each sequence of time tags thus obtained is padded with as many zeros as required to make all sequences of equal length. This way, the production rules in the conflict set may be compared with each other.

EXAMPLE 3.33

Consider the following fact set:

$$\{1: x = a,\ 2: x = b,\ 3: y = c,\ 4: z = d,\ 5: w = e,\ 6: z = f\}$$

Now, suppose that the conflict set consists of the following three production rules:

R_1: ***if*** *same*(z,f) ***then*** *add*(x,e) ***fi***
R_2: ***if*** *same*(x,b) ***and*** *same*(z,d) ***then*** *add*(y,f) ***fi***
R_3: ***if*** *same*(x,s) ***and*** *same*(y,c) ***and*** *same*(w,e) ***then*** *add*(x,d) ***fi***

Rule R_3 has the largest number of conditions, namely three. So with each rule we associate a sequence of time tags having length three:

R_1: 6 0 0
R_2: 4 2 0
R_3: 5 3 1

The production rules in the conflict set are now ordered according to the lexicographical order of their associated sequences of time tags; in the ordering, a rule R_1 precedes a rule R_2 if the sequence of time tags associated with R_1, read from left to right, is larger than the one associated with rule R_2. The order relation between members of the conflict set is denoted by the symbol $\geqslant$. The relation $\geqslant$ is a total ordering, and has therefore the following four properties:

(1) *Reflexivity:* For each production rule R we have $R \geqslant R$.
(2) *Transitivity:* For each three production rules R_1, R_2, and R_3, satisfying $R_1 \geqslant R_2$ and $R_2 \geqslant R_3$, we have that $R_1 \geqslant R_3$.
(3) *Antisymmetry:* For each pair of rules satisfying $R_1 \geqslant R_2$ and $R_2 \geqslant R_1$, we have that $R_1 = R_2$.
(4) *Totality:* For each pair of production rules R_1 and R_2, we have either $R_1 \geqslant R_2$ or $R_2 \geqslant R_1$.

EXAMPLE 3.34

Consider the following sequences of time tags, associated with four production rules R_1, R_2, R_3 and R_4, respectively:

R_1: 6 0 0
R_2: 4 3 2
R_3: 5 3 1
R_4: 6 1 0

For these rules we have that $R_4 \geqslant R_1 \geqslant R_3 \geqslant R_2$.

This ordering of the rules from a conflict set enables us to give an algorithm for conflict resolution based on recency; it is described in the following function ResolveConflicts. The function Max-Time-tag-Subset called from ResolveConflicts selects from the conflict set rules the rules with the highest time tag. If the resulting set r contains more than one element, then, after the earlier examined time tags have been skipped, the function ResolveConflicts is called recursively for this set r. Note that, contrary to what has been described before, the conflict set is not ordered entirely before it is examined; each time, only a subset of the rules relevant for conflict resolution is selected. The presented algorithm does not always yield a single production rule, since it is possible to have two or more (different) production rules, having the same sequence of time tags. In this case, on arbitrary grounds the first specified production rule is returned as a result.

```
function ResolveConflicts(rules)
  if rules = ∅ then return (∅)
  else
    r ← Max-Time-tag-Subset(rules);
    if r is singleton then return(r)
    else
      result ← ResolveConflicts(r)
    fi;
    if result = ∅ then return(first(r))
    else
      return(result)
    fi
  fi
end
```

As has been discussed above, a variable specified in a condition of a production rule may have more than one occurrence in the fact set, although with different time tags. As a consequence, a condition may match with more than one fact. So a production rule may be applied more than once, using different facts.

EXAMPLE 3.35

Consider the following fact set:

$$F = \{1\colon x = a\}$$

and the rule base consisting of the following two production rules:

R_1: ***if*** *same*(x,a) ***then*** *add*(y,b) ***fi***
R_2: ***if*** *same*(y,b) ***then*** *add*(y,b) ***fi***

Then, the application of rule R_1 in the first inference step results in the following modified fact set:

$$F' = \{1\colon x = a,\ 2\colon y = b\}$$

Subsequent application of rule R_2 yields the following fact set:

$$F'' = \{1\colon x = a,\ 2\colon y = b,\ 3\colon y = b\}$$

Rule R_2 can now be applied again. In fact, the inference will not terminate; rule R_2 will be applied forever.

In Example 3.35, we have shown that a production rule may be applied more than once, using different facts. It is therefore necessary to specify in the conflict set all possible *applications* of a rule, instead of the rule itself. For this purpose, we introduce the notion of a rule instance.

> **Definition:** Let F be a fact set, and R a production rule. Let $M \subseteq F$ be a subset of facts, such that each element $f \in M$ matches with a condition of R, and each condition of the production rule R matches with an element from M. Then the pair (R,M) is called a *rule instance.*

In other words, a rule instance consists of a production rule and the facts matching with its conditions. It will be evident that, although production rules may be applied several times, it is undesirable that rule instances are applied more than once. Note that the conflict set should now be taken as a set of rule instances.

The basic algorithm for bottom-up inference discussed above has to be altered for dealing with such rule instances. Recall that, so far, we have treated four procedures which together constitute the bottom-up inference algorithm:

- the procedure Infer, which described the global inference process;
- the function Select, which was used for the selection of applicable rules from the rule base;
- the function ResolveConflicts, which specified the conflict-resolution method;
- the procedure Apply, which applied the selected production rule.

First, reconsider the procedure Infer. Here, we have to record the rule instances which have been applied, to prevent rule instances from being applied more than once:

```
procedure Infer(fact-set, rule-base)
  applied-instances ← ∅;
  instances ← Select(rule-base, applied-instances, fact-set);
  while instances ≠ ∅ do
    instance ← ResolveConflicts(instances);
    Apply(instance);
    applied-instances ← applied-instances ∪ {instance};
    instances ← Select(rule-base, applied-instances, fact-set)
  od
end
```

The function Select now has to generate rule instances from the production rules in the rule base instead of the production rules themselves:

```
function Select(rule-base, applied, fact-set)

  selected-instances ← ∅;
  foreach rule in rule-base do
    failed ← false;
    rule-instances ← {(rule, ∅)};
    foreach cond in antecedent(rule) with not failed do
      ModifyInstances(cond, rule-instances, fact-set, failed)
    od;
    if not failed then
      selected-instances ← selected-instances ∪
                           (rule-instances \ applied)
    fi
  od;
  return(selected-instances)
end
```

Note that the second argument of Select now contains a set of rule instances. The procedure ModifyInstances called from Select evaluates a given condition cond using the fact set. Each different matching fact gives rise to the creation of a new rule instance. Of course, if a condition fails, no rule instance will be created. Because the rule instances are built recursively, evaluation of subsequent conditions of a production rule may lead to discarding rule instances under construction from the set rule-instances:

```
procedure ModifyInstances(condition, rule-instances, fact-set,
                          failed)

  relevant-facts ← EvalCondition(condition, fact-set);
  failed ← relevant-facts = ∅;
  new-instances ← ∅;
  if not failed then
    foreach fact in relevant-facts do
      foreach rule-inst in rule-instances do
        new-instances ← new-instances ∪ Add(rule-inst, fact)
      od
    od
  fi;
  rule-instances ← new-instances
end
```

After the conflict set has been created, the next step in Infer is to select a single rule instance from it by conflict resolution. This is achieved by means of the procedure ResolveConflicts, which has already been discussed. Finally, the procedure Apply is called to evaluate the conclusions of the selected rule instance. Recall that evaluation of the action *add* adds a new fact to the fact set, which is assigned a new time tag. Evaluation of the action *remove* deletes a fact from the fact set; the fact to be deleted is selected either by explicitly referring to its time tag, or simply by matching.

We conclude this section with an example.

EXAMPLE 3.36

Consider the following fact set F:

$$F = \{1\text{: } x = a,\ 2\text{: } x = b,\ 3\text{: } y = 4\}$$

Furthermore, let us have the following set of production rules:

R_1: ***if*** *same*(*x*,*a*) ***and*** *same*(*x*,*b*) ***then*** *add*(*z*,*e*) ***fi***
R_2: ***if*** *same*(*z*,*e*) ***and*** *same*(*w*,*g*) ***then*** *add*(*z*,*f*) ***fi***
R_3: ***if*** *lessthan*(*y*,10) ***and*** *same*(*x*,*a*) ***or*** *same*(*x*,*b*) ***then*** *add*(*w*,*g*) ***fi***

The given fact set F gives rise to the creation of the following rule instances, together constituting the conflict set:

$(R_1, \{1\text{: } x = a,\ 2\text{: } x = b\})$
$(R_3, \{3\text{: } y = 4,\ 1\text{: } x = a\})$
$(R_3, \{3\text{: } y = 4,\ 2\text{: } x = b\})$

Note that two rule instances of R_3 have been created. Using the recency conflict-resolution strategy, the second instance of R_3 is selected for evaluation, because the time tag of its second matching fact is larger than the time tag of the second matching fact of the first instance of R_3. Evaluation of the instance $(R_3, \{3\text{: } y = 4,\ 2\text{: } x = b\})$ causes the fact 4: $w = g$ to be added to the fact set, resulting in:

$$F' = \{1\text{: } x = a,\ 2\text{: } x = b,\ 3\text{: } y = 4,\ 4\text{: } w = g\}$$

The inference is now repeated; the instance $(R_3, \{3\text{: } y = 4, 2\text{: } x = b\})$ however is no longer selected for application.

The algorithm discussed in this section provides a more or less complete description of the bottom-up inference method. However, an inference engine implementing this algorithm will be quite inefficient, because at every inference step all instances are created all over again. A first step towards improving the efficiency of the algorithm is to save the instances between two consecutive inference steps. Such an algorithm exists.

It is called the *rete algorithm*, and has been developed by C.L. Forgy as part of the system OPS5. We shall return to this rete algorithm and OPS5 in Chapter 7.

3.3 Pattern recognition and production rules

Various means for representing knowledge in a production system have been discussed in the preceding sections, such as using variable–value pairs and object–attribute–value tuples in facts and production rules. In this section, we introduce a more expressive means for representing facts in the fact set, and conditions and conclusions in production rules. Instead of a single variable–value pair or an object–attribute–value tuple, conditions and conclusions may now contain an arbitrary number of variables and constants. In the following discussion, such a collection of variables and constants will be called a *pattern*. An important operation in a production system incorporating such pattern representations is *(pattern) matching*, that is, informally speaking, to make a pattern in a production rule and a fact syntactically equal by binding variables to constants. Matching closely resembles the process of unification discussed in Chapter 2. We will first introduce some terminology with respect to patterns, facts and matching, and then proceed with patterns in production rules.

3.3.1 Patterns, facts and matching

The following definition introduces the kind of patterns which will be dealt with in this section.

> **Definition:** A *pattern* is a finite, ordered sequence of elements of the following form:
>
> $$(e_1 \cdots e_n)$$
>
> where each element e_i, $i = 1, \ldots, n$, $n \geq 1$, is a constant or a variable. An element e_i in a pattern is called a *pattern element*. A variable in a pattern will be called a *pattern variable*.

Pattern variables will be distinguished from other pattern elements by having names starting with a question mark or an exclamation mark. In the following, a variable having a name starting with a question mark will denote a *single-valued pattern variable*: a variable having a name starting with an exclamation mark denotes a *multi-valued pattern variable*.

EXAMPLE 3.37

The names

?*a*, ?*patient*, !*xy*, ?, !

are all legal names of pattern variables.

The syntax of a fact is similar to that of a pattern; however, a fact does not contain any variables.

Definition: A *fact* is a finite, ordered sequence of elements of the following form:

$$(f_1 \cdots f_n)$$

where each element f_i, $i = 1, \ldots, n$, $n \geqslant 1$, is a constant.

It will be evident that patterns and facts share the same basic structure, thus making it possible to examine them on equality.

The pattern variables occurring in a pattern may be replaced by one or more constants depending on the type of the variable; for a single-valued pattern variable only a single constant may be filled in, whereas for a multi-valued pattern variable we may fill in a sequence of constants. A constant or a sequence of constants which is filled in for a variable is called a *binding* for the variable. The replacement of a variable by its binding is called a *substitution*. If a single-valued variable ?x is bound to the constant d, this will be denoted by ?$x = d$; if a variable !y is bound to a sequence of constants $(c_1 \cdots c_n)$, the binding for !y is denoted by !$y = (c_1 \cdots c_n)$.

Definition: Let P be a pattern and F be a fact. It is said that the pattern P and the fact F *match* if there exists a binding for the variables occurring in P such that, after substitution of the variables by their respective bindings, P and F are syntactically equal.

Variables having a name which just is a question mark or an exclamation mark are special by being allowed to be bound to any constant, or any sequence of constants, respectively; however, they do not preserve their bindings. These variables are called *don't-care variables*. Note the analogy with the don't-care variable in PROLOG.

EXAMPLE 3.38

Consider the following pattern P and fact F:

P: (? ? a b)

F: (a d a b)

It is readily seen that the given pattern and fact match, since the don't-care variable ? matches with the first element a as well as with the second element d in F. If the don't-care variable is replaced by an ordinary single-valued variable ?x, which preserves its binding, the new pattern P and the fact F do not match:

P: (?x ?x a b)

F: (a d a b)

It is not possible to find a binding for ?x making P and F syntactically equal; the first possible binding ?$x = a$, obtained from the first element position, renders the pattern and the fact different in the second element position, whereas the other possible binding ?$x = d$ obtained from the second element position causes a difference in the first element position.

The following example illustrates the use of multi-valued pattern variables.

EXAMPLE 3.39

Consider the following pattern P and fact F:

P: (?x ? a ? !x a !x)
F: (g b a c c d a c d)

Note that ?x and !x indicate different variables. It will be evident that the pattern P and the fact F match for the bindings ?$x = g$ and !$x = (c\ d)$.

3.3.2 Patterns and production rules

In the present section we shall briefly discuss how pattern matching may be employed as part of the inference in a production system. We now take production rules to have conditions and conclusions specifying patterns. Note that this goes beyond the use of variable–value pairs and object–attribute–value tuples. A variable–value pair may be represented by a pattern consisting of two constants, and an object–attribute–value tuple may be represented by a pattern consisting of three constants; the production rules introduced in this section are therefore more general than rules employing variable–value or object–attribute–value representations, because these may be viewed as special cases of a pattern representation. As a consequence, the present rule formalism has more expressive power than those discussed in the preceding sections.

Here it is assumed that conditions and conclusions in rules adhere to the following syntax:

<condition> ::= <predicate> (<pattern>)
<predicate> ::= *same* | *notsame* | *lessthan* | $\cdots$
<conclusion> ::= <action> (<pattern>)
<action> ::= *add* | *remove* | *write* | $\cdots$

where <pattern> is a pattern as defined in Section 3.3.1. We have defined three predicates. The predicate *same* compares a given pattern with the facts in the fact set. If the pattern matches with at least one fact, the predicate returns the truth value *true*. The behaviour of the predicate *notsame* is again complementary to that of the predicate *same*. The predicate *lessthan* may only be applied to a pattern in which all variables have been bound to constants before the predicate is being evaluated; the predicate *lessthan* then investigates whether the obtained sequence of numbers is strictly increasing.

We have also defined three actions. The action *add* adds a new fact to the fact set; if the pattern in a conclusion contains variables, these should all be bound to constants or sequences of constants before the action *add* is executed.

EXAMPLE 3.40

Consider the following fact set, containing just a single fact:

$F = \{(person\ name\ John\ age\ 10)\}$

and the following production rule:

if
same(*person name* ?*x age* ?*y*) ***and***
greaterthan(?*y* 9) ***and***
lessthan(?*y* 20)
then
add(?*x is a teenager*)
fi

Upon application, this rule adds the fact (*John is a teenager*) to the fact set.

The action *remove* deletes a fact from the fact set which matches with the pattern in the conclusion in which it has been specified. The action *write* prints the values of the successive elements of its pattern to the screen. For both actions, all variables should be bound to constants before execution.

We conclude this section with a simple example demonstrating the use of the production-rule formalism containing patterns in conditions and conclusions.

EXAMPLE 3.41

Consider the following fact set:

$F = \{(list\ a\ b\ f\ g\ h), (element\ g)\}$

The first fact represents a list containing five elements; the second fact represents a single element. By means of production rules we can check whether the single element *g* represented in the second fact occurs among the elements of the list represented in the first fact. Now, consider the following three production rules:

R_1: ***if***
  same(*list ?x !y*) ***and***
  notsame(*element ?x*)
then
  remove(*list ?x !y*) ***also***
  add(*list !y*)
fi

R_2: ***if***
  same(*list ?x*) ***or***
  same(*list ?x !*) ***and***
  same(*element ?x*)
then
  write(*?x belongs to the list*)
fi

R_3: ***if***
  same(*list ?x*) ***and***
  notsame(*element ?x*)
then
  write(*The element ?x does not belong to the list*)
fi

The first condition in rule R_1, *same*(*list ?x !y*), investigates whether there exists a fact in the fact set having as its first element the constant *list*, and at least two additional constants. If this is the case, the variable ?x will be bound to the second constant of the matching fact; the variable !y will be bound to the sequence of its remaining constants. The second condition of R_1 checks whether or not the fact set contains a fact having as its first element the constant *element* and as its second element a constant equal to the binding obtained for ?x. If so, the rule fails; otherwise a new fact is added to the fact set, having as its first element the constant *list*, followed by the collection of constants the pattern variable !y has been bound to. As long as the fact set does not contain a fact which binds ?x to the constant g and as long as the fact set contains *list* facts containing at least two more constants following the constant *list*, rule R_1 will succeed. The second rule investigates whether the fact set contains a pattern in which the first element following the constant *list* equals g. Note that, as a consequence of the disjunction in the condition part of the rule, all facts containing one or more constants following the constant *list* are examined. The last rule handles the situation that the only constant in the *list* fact is not equal to g. It is readily seen that, given the present fact set and rule base, production rule R_2 will succeed in finding the element g in the fact (*list a b f g h*).

As we have argued, the production-rule formalism in which conditions and conclusions may contain arbitrary patterns is more expressive than the formalisms in which only variable–value pairs or object–attribute–value tuples are allowed. The problem described in Example 3.41 cannot be formulated in as compact a way using the simpler representation formalisms. In Chapter 7 we shall return to using patterns in production rules in relation with OPS5.

3.3.3 Implementation of pattern matching in LISP

In this section we present an implementation of a pattern-matching algorithm in LISP. The algorithm we shall develop closely resembles the unification algorithm as discussed in Section 2.8. However, there are some important differences between unification and pattern matching which justify treatment of the pattern-matching algorithm. In the first place, whereas unification is a symmetrical operation in which expressions to be unified may be interchanged without effect, pattern matching is asymmetrical. The asymmetrical nature of matching may be exploited for efficiency purposes. In the second place, in pattern matching various kinds of variables are usually distinguished and explicitly treated in a different way.

The pattern-matching algorithm is described by the function `Match` given below, which compares a pattern and a fact in a given environment of variable bindings. It is supposed that the pattern as well as the fact is represented as a list of symbols; for example, the list `(?x !y one)` is a pattern containing the variables `?x` and `!y`, and the constant `one`. The environment of variable bindings has been implemented using an a-list, where each element contains as its first element the name of a variable and as its remaining element(s) the constant(s) to which the variable has been bound.

```
(defun Match (pattern fact environment)
  (cond ((and (null pattern) (null fact)) environment)
        ((or (null pattern) (null fact)) 'FAIL)
        (t (let ((fp (first pattern))
                 (rp (rest pattern))
                 (ff (first fact))
                 (rf (rest fact)))
             (case (Type fp)
               (const (if (eq fp ff)
                          (Match rp rf environment)
                          'FAIL))
               (?-dcv (Match rp rf environment))
               (!-dcv (let ((result (Match rp rf environment)))
                        (if (eq result 'FAIL)
                            (Match pattern rf environment)
                            result)))
               (?-var (let ((new-env (Bind? fp ff environment)))
                        (if (eq new-env 'FAIL) 'FAIL
                            (Match rp rf new-env))))
               (!-var (let ((binding (LookUp fp environment)))
                        (if (null binding)
                            (Bind! fp rp fact environment)
                            (Match (Replace binding pattern)
                                   fact environment)))))))))
```

The function `Match` first investigates whether `pattern` and `fact` are both empty. In this case, the environment of variable bindings `environment` is returned. If only one of the arguments `pattern` and `fact` is empty, it is evidently not possible to find a match, and the value `FAIL` is returned. In all other cases, the elements of `pattern` and `fact` will be examined recursively given the environment of bindings.

For this purpose, the type of the first element of the pattern is obtained by means of the function call `(Type fp)`. Five different types are distinguished; a pattern element is either a constant (`const`), a single-valued don't-care variable (?-dcv), a multi-valued don't-care variable (!-dcv), a single-valued variable (?-var), or a multi-valued variable (!-var). For each possible type an entry has been included in the case form indicating how to proceed with the matching process. If the first element of the pattern, fp, is a constant, then pattern and fact match if fp and the first element of the fact, ff, represent the same constant, and if the remainder of the pattern, rp, and the remainder of the fact, rf, match. The latter condition is investigated by means of a recursive call to the function Match. If fp is a single-valued don't-care variable, then pattern and fact match in the environment environment if rp and rf match in that same environment. Note that in this case it suffices to compare rp and rf in the same environment, since a single-valued don't-care variable matches with any constant without adding a variable binding to the environment. If fp is a single-valued variable, the function Bind? is called. This function either yields a new environment in which a binding for the single-valued variable has been added, or returns the function value FAIL, indicating that the constant found for the variable in the environment of bindings does not match with the constant ff in the given fact. If the first element in pattern turns out to be a multi-valued don't-care variable, Bind? investigates whether rp and rf match in the given environment of bindings. If this match fails, the original pattern is passed along to a recursive call to Match in an attempt to extend the 'binding' for the don't care variable. To conclude, if fp is an ordinary multi-valued variable, the function LookUp is invoked to find out whether the variable already occurs in environment. If a binding has been found in environment, the variable in pattern is replaced by its binding. This is accomplished by means of a call to Replace. Subsequently, the function Match is called for this modified pattern and once more for the entire fact. If on the other hand the variable is still unbound, the function Bind! determines for which binding for the variable a match results for the remaining elements of pattern and fact.

Let us give an example before we discuss the functions called from Match.

EXAMPLE 3.42

Consider the following pattern P and the fact F:

P: (?x ? b !x a !x)
F: (d a b c b a c b)

The function call (Match '(?x ? b !x a !x) '(d a b c b a c b) nil) binds the parameters in Match to the corresponding arguments. The first element in pattern is a single-valued variable ?x. The part of the case form following the entry ?-var applies to this type of variable:

```
(let ((new-env (Bind? fp ff environment)))
  (if (eq new-env 'FAIL) 'FAIL
      (Match rp rf new-env)))
```

As a result of a call to Bind?, the variable ?x will be bound to the first element d of the fact fact. This binding is subsequently added to the environment of variable bindings; the variable new-env is therefore bound to the a-list ((?x d)). The function Match is then called recursively for processing the remainder of the pattern, (? b !x a !x), and the remainder of the fact, (a b c b a c b), given this new environment of variable bindings. The next element in the pattern is a single-valued don't-care variable which will match with any constant without extending the environment. Hence, the function Match is recursively called for the remainder of the pattern, (b !x a !x), the remainder of the fact, (b c b a c b), and the old environment ((?x d)). The next element in the pattern is the constant b, which is equal to the next element in the given fact. So, the then part of the following if form will be executed for the remainder of the pattern, (!x a !x), the remainder of the fact, (c b a c b), and the environment ((?x d)):

```
(if (eq fp ff)
    (Match rp rf environment)
    'FAIL)
```

The next element encountered in the pattern is the multi-valued variable !x, which is processed by the entry in the case form following the symbol !-var:

```
(let ((binding (LookUp fp environment)))
  (if (null binding)
      (Bind! fp rp fact environment)
      (Match (Replace binding pattern)
             fact environment)))
```

The environment does not yet contain a binding for !x. A new binding is created by means of a call to Bind!. In Bind!, the first attempt is to add the binding (!x c) to the environment of bindings. It is then investigated whether the pattern (!x a !x) matches with the fact (c b a c b) in this new environment. This match fails, and the binding for !x is extended with the next element b from the fact. It is then checked whether the pattern (!x a !x) matches with the fact (c b a c b) in the new environment ((!x c b) (?x d)). This last match will succeed, and the function `Match` yields the environment `((!x c b) (?x d))` as a result.

This section is concluded with a discussion of the remaining functions. Recall that the function `Type` determines whether a pattern element is a single-valued don't-care variable, a single-valued variable, a multi-valued don't-care variable, a multi-valued variable, or a constant:

```
(defun Type (x)
  (let* ((name (symbol-name x))
         (indicator (char name 0)))
    (cond ((char= indicator #\?)
           (if (= (length name) 1)
               '?-dcv
               '?-var))
          ((char= indicator #\!)
           (if (= (length name) 1)
               '!-dcv
               '!-var))
          (t 'const))))
```

The call `(char name 0)` selects the first character of the name of `x`. It then depends on the particular character obtained and the length of the name, which type is returned.

The function `Bind?` first examines whether there already exists a binding for the single-valued variable `var` in the given environment of variable bindings `env`. To this end, it calls the function `LookUp`, which either returns the binding or returns `nil` if no binding is present:

```
(defun Bind? (var data env)
  (let ((binding (LookUp var env)))
    (if (null binding)
        (cons (list var data) env) ; no binding in environment
        (if (eq binding data)
            env ; binding equal to data
            'FAIL)))) ; not equal, return failure
```

If `LookUp` has returned a binding, `Bind?` checks whether this binding for `var` equals the constant in `data`. In case of equality the environment `env` is returned unaltered, otherwise the function returns the value `FAIL`. If on the other hand `LookUp` has returned the value `nil`, indicating that no binding for the variable was present in the environment `env`, the new binding `(var data)` will be added to it.

The function Bind! adds a binding for the multi-valued variable to the environment:

```
(defun Bind! (var rpattern fact env)
  (if (null fact) 'FAIL
      (let* ((ff (first fact))
             (rf (rest fact))
             (new-env1 (Add var ff env))
             (new-env2 (Match rpattern rf new-env1)))
        (if (eq new-env2 'FAIL)
            (Bind! var rpattern rf new-env1)
            new-env2))))
```

The extended environment new-env1, which is returned by the function Add, is passed as an argument to the function Match. If this call yields the value FAIL, the function Bind! investigates whether a match can be produced for the pattern rpattern and the fact rf, that is, the original fact after removal of the first element. Note that this first element is already part of the binding for the multi-valued variable var in the environment.

The function Add adds a new binding for a variable to the environment of variable bindings env, or extends an already existing binding by means of the built-in function rplacd:

```
(defun Add (var data env)
  (let ((binding (assoc var env)))
    (cond ((null  binding) (cons (list var data) env))
          (t (rplacd binding
                     (append (rest binding) (list data)))
             env))))
```

The function LookUp has already been mentioned several times. This function searches for bindings for both single-valued and multi-valued variables in the environment of variable bindings. Since the environment has been implemented using an a-list, the built-in function assoc serves well for this purpose:

```
(defun LookUp (key a-list)
  (rest (assoc key a-list)))
```

Finally, the function Replace is defined for replacing a multi-valued variable in a pattern by its associated binding:

```
(defun Replace (binding pattern)
  (append binding (rest pattern)))
```

An interesting question is how this pattern-matching algorithm can be integrated in for example bottom-up inference. The following example illustrates its use. The actual implementation is left to the reader (see Exercise 3.11).

EXAMPLE 3.43

Consider the example from the preceding section once more. The following fact set was given:

$$F = \{(person\ name\ John\ age\ 10)\}$$

and the following single production rule:

if
same(*person name* ?*x age* ?*y*) ***and***
greaterthan(?*y* 9) ***and***
lessthan(?*y* 20)
then
add(?*x is a teenager*)
fi

The forward-chaining algorithm first evaluates the first condition of the rule given the fact set. As part of the evaluation of the first condition, the pattern (*person name* ?*x age* ?*y*) is matched against the fact set, yielding the environment ((?*y* 10) (?*x John*)). The predicate *same* returns the truth value *true* on evaluation. Subsequently, the second and third conditions are evaluated in this new environment of variable bindings ((?*y* 10) (?*x John*)). These will succeed as well. The evaluation of the conclusion of the rule will take the computed environment into account. It results in the addition of the fact (*John is a teenager*) to the fact set.

3.4 Production rules as a representation formalism

In this chapter we have discussed several forms of knowledge representation and inference used in production systems. Various attempts in the past in using production rules for building expert systems have proved the production system approach to be a flexible one, and suitable for many problem areas. In fact, many of the expert systems mentioned in Chapter 1 are examples of rule-based systems. In addition, several large expert systems have been and still are being developed using the techniques discussed in this chapter. However, some disadvantages and restrictions of the formalism have also been recognized:

- Descriptive knowledge cannot be represented in the formalism in a natural way. An example of descriptive knowledge has been given in Chapter 1 where we described the cardiovascular system. We shall see in Chapter 4 that the frame formalism is much more suitable for representing this type of knowledge.
- The different types of knowledge encountered in a problem area, such as problem-dependent knowledge, problem-independent knowledge, and knowledge used for exerting control on the inference process (often called meta-knowledge) have to be expressed using the same formalism and therefore cannot be distinguished explicitly.
- The production rule formalism has a strong operational flavour. As a consequence, some knowledge of the underlying execution model of the inference engine is required to represent a problem domain adequately in a knowledge base. Compare this situation with the one in logic, where no knowledge concerning inference is required for specifying a correct knowledge base; familiarity with the declarative semantics of logic suffices in this case.
- A more involved application generally leads to a large rule base, which is difficult to develop and maintain. So, for developing large applications, the necessity of partitioning a large rule base into smaller modules arises. However, the production rule formalism offers no direct means for explicitly indicating and exploiting such a modularization.

Some of these problems may be solved by combining production rules with some other formalism, such as for example a frame formalism, or with other programming paradigms such as object-oriented programming. Chapter 7 discusses several solutions that have been proposed and incorporated in actual systems.

Suggested reading

The work of Newell and Simon on human problem solving is described in Newell and Simon (1972). In Newell (1973) the formalism of production rules is presented from the perspective of a psychological model of human behaviour. Waterman and Hayes-Roth (1978) reviews some of the principles of production systems, which in this book are called *pattern-directed inference systems*. In Buchanan and Duda (1983) the two basic forms of inference, that is top-down and bottom-up inference, are discussed. A typical system based on top-down inference is EMYCIN (van Melle, 1980). OPS5 and CLIPS are typical examples of systems employing bottom-up inference (Forgy, 1981; Giarrantano, 1989). Brownston *et al.* (1985) discusses the kind of forward chaining employed in OPS5. In EMYCIN and OPS5 object–attribute–value tuples are used for representing facts. The representation of knowledge in object–attribute–value tuples in production rules is discussed in Buchanan and Shortliffe (1984) in relation to the EMYCIN system. In CLIPS, patterns are used (Giarrantano, 1989). Sauers (1988) describes the application of control strategies in production systems.

Bratko (1986), and Sterling and Shapiro (1986) present alternative techniques for implementing a rule-based expert system in PROLOG. In Winston and Horn (1989) a LISP program based on production rules and forward chaining is discussed, which uses streams for the representation of facts; Luger and Stubblefield (1989) contains an implementation of backward chaining also using streams.

EXERCISES

3.1 Consider a knowledge base containing the following domain declaration:

$$D = \{x_a^s, y^s, z_a^s, w_g^m\}$$

and the following rule base:

$\{R_1$: ***if*** *lessthan*$(z,20)$ ***and*** *notknown*(y) ***then*** *add*(w,b) ***fi***,
R_2: ***if*** *same*(x,c) ***and*** *known*(y) ***then*** *add*(w,d) ***fi***,
R_3: ***if*** *notsame*(x,b) ***and*** *greaterthan*$(z,100)$ ***then*** *add*(y,f) ***fi***$\}$

The variables x_a^s, y^s and z_a^s are single-valued, and the variable w_g^m is multi-valued. As can be seen, w_g^m is a goal variable, and the variables x_a^s and z_a^s are askable. Furthermore, let the following fact set be given:

$$F = \{x = c,\ z = 5\}$$

(a) Determine the fact set F' which results from applying backward chaining to this set of production rules. Which production rules have succeeded, and which ones have failed?

(b) Suppose that the following self-referencing production rule is added to the three rules listed above:

R_4: ***if*** *notknown*(y) ***then*** *add*(y,A) ***fi***

Again we employ backward chaining, starting with the same initial fact set F as given above. Which fact set F'' do we now obtain?

3.2 Has the choice of the conflict-resolution strategy employed in top-down inference with the look-ahead facility any effect on the values inferred for a multi-valued goal variable? Explain your answer. Now answer the same question for an arbitrary (subgoal) variable.

3.3 A production rule can be translated into a collection of PROLOG clauses by generating one clause for each conclusion of the rule. This translation has been discussed in detail in Section 3.2.2. Recall that the resulting clauses all have a different conclusion and the same condition part. What is the advantage of this translation scheme compared with translating a rule into a single PROLOG fact, expressing a relation between the condition part and the conclusion part of the rule?

3.4 Reconsider the PROLOG program for top-down inference developed in Section 3.2.2 and the LISP program in Section 3.2.3. In these programs we have only made limited use of the domain declaration as defined in Section 3.1.

(a) In both programs no distinction is made between single-valued and multi-valued variables. Extend one of the programs in such a way that single-valued and multi-valued variables are distinguished and handled in a semantically satisfactory way.

(b) The domain declarations employed in the programs do not comprise type declarations for the variables. Extend either the presented PROLOG program or the LISP program in such a way that a domain declaration may include a specification of the datatype for a variable. Note that this type information may be used to inform the user which values may be entered for a variable.

3.5 In Section 3.2.1 we have discussed several ways of optimizing the top-down inference algorithm. Not all these optimizations have been incorporated in the implementations of the algorithm in PROLOG and LISP.

(a) Extend one of these implementations with the notion of a *used* production rule.

(b) Implement the look-ahead facility in one of the programs.

3.6 Improve the LISP program discussed in Section 3.2.3 by incorporating an indexing method for direct access to production rules concluding on a particular variable.

Hint. Add to each production rule definition a unique rule name, and extend the variable declarations by specifying for each variable the names of the rules in which the variable appears in the conclusion part. An example of such a variable declaration is:

```
(define diagnosis
  (prompt nil)
  (class goal)
  (rules rule1 rule2 rule5 rule7))
```

Assign pointer references to the rules during the parsing phase. The resulting implementation is quite typical for efficient LISP programs, and applies methods taken from imperative programming languages such as C.

3.7 Consider the following knowledge base, containing the domain declaration

$$D = \{x^s, y^s, z^s, u^s\}$$

and the rule base:

$\{R_1$: ***if*** *same*(x,a) ***and*** *known*(y) ***then*** *add*(y,b) ***fi***,
R_2: ***if*** *same*(x,c) ***and*** *lessthan*(z,15) ***then*** *add*(u,d) ***fi***,
R_3: ***if*** *same*(y,b) ***and*** *lessthan*(z,5) ***then*** *add*(u,f) ***fi***$\}$

Furthermore, consider the following fact set:

$$F = \{1\colon x = a,\ 2\colon y = b,\ 3\colon z = 10,\ 4\colon x = c\}$$

Bottom-up inference is employed to derive new facts from the given rule base and the facts present in the fact set.

(a) Give all rule instances created by matching the initial fact set F and the rule base given above. This set of instances is the conflict set.

(b) Order the conflict set obtained in (a), using conflict resolution by recency. Which one of the rule instances will then be selected for application?

(c) Give the fact set that results after evaluation of the rule instance chosen in (b). Will the inference eventually terminate? Explain your answer by giving the successive changes that take place in the fact set.

3.8 Consider the following knowledge base, containing the domain declaration

$$D = \{x^s, y^s, z^s\}$$

and the rule base:

$\{R_1$: ***if*** *same*(x,a) ***and*** *equal*(y,10) ***then*** *add*(z,b) ***fi***,
R_2: ***if*** *same*(z,c) ***and*** *lessthan*(y,20) ***then*** *add*(x,a) ***fi***$\}$

Furthermore, consider the following fact set:

$$F = \{1\colon x = A,\ 2\colon z = C,\ 3\colon y = 10,\ 4\colon z = C\}$$

Bottom-up inference is employed for inferring new facts from the given rule base and the fact set.

(a) Which rule instances will be created in the first inference step, and which one of these will be selected for application if we apply conflict resolution by recency? Give the new fact set obtained after evaluation of the chosen rule instance. Will the inference eventually terminate?

(b) Suppose that we add the following production rule to the ones shown above, before consulting the knowledge base:

R_3: ***if*** *same*(z,b) ***then*** *add*(z,c) ***fi***

We start with the same initial fact set F as in (a). Give the fact set that eventually results. Will the inference terminate? Explain your answer by comparing the results with those of (a).

3.9 Develop data structures and an algorithm for bottom-up inference such that the selection of production rules for the conflict set is optimized.

3.10 Recall that two types of non-determinism are distinguished in production systems because of the need to specify the order in which applicable rules are selected from the rule base and the order in which conditions and conclusions are evaluated. If we take a particular conflict-resolution strategy in bottom-up inference, which choice(s) for resolving non-determinism do(es) influence the behaviour of the system?

3.11 In Section 3.3 we have discussed the role of pattern matching in production systems. Develop a LISP program for bottom-up inference along the lines sketched, applying the pattern-matching algorithm given in Section 3.3.3 as part of the entire program.

4 Frames and Inheritance

Representing knowledge in graph-like structures has a rich tradition in philosophy and psychology. At the end of the nineteenth century, the philosopher C.S. Peirce used a graph-like notation for the representation of logical sentences. This approach to representing human knowledge has been further pursued since by many researchers, yielding explicit psychological models of human memory and intellectual behaviour. In particular the area of natural language processing has contributed much to the research on the representation of information in graph-like structures, there called *semantic nets* or *associative nets*; in fact, the earliest use of graph-based representations in computers was for machine translation. In the early 1960s, R. Quillian for example used the semantic net formalism for representing meanings of English words in terms of associative links to other words, yielding a dictionary-like representation; he developed a program for finding relationships between words by traversing the net. Through this work, R. Quillian has given a major impetus to the research on graph-based representations and their use in AI systems; he is generally credited with the development of the semantic net in its original form.

For handling more complicated problem domains and for dealing with more sophisticated forms of inference, the semantic net formalism as devised by R. Quillian soon proved to be too limited. Much of the later work on semantic nets has therefore been directed towards more structured formalisms, again mostly for natural language processing. Semantic nets have seldom been used for building expert systems. Nevertheless, we shall briefly discuss some characteristics of the formalism, since the semantic net is often viewed as a precursor of the frame formalism, which is much more frequently applied within expert systems.

The basic idea underlying the notion of frames has already been posed at the beginning of this century by the psychologist O. Selz. He considered human problem solving as the process of filling in the gaps of partially completed descriptions. The present notion of frames was introduced in the mid-1970s by M. Minsky for exerting semantic control in a pattern-recognition application. Since its introduction, however, the frame formalism has been employed in several other kinds of knowledge-based systems as well. The general idea of a frame-based system is that all knowledge concerning individuals or classes of individuals, including their interrelationships, is stored in a complex entity of representation called a *frame*. Instead of the term frame, the terms *unit*, *object* and *concept* are also often used in literature. A set of frames representing the knowledge in a domain of interest is organized hierarchically in what is called a *taxonomy*. Such a taxonomy forms the basis of a method of automated reasoning called *inheritance*. The frame formalism and its associated inheritance are the primary topics of this chapter. To prepare for a thorough treatment of these subjects, we shall first discuss the semantic net formalism briefly in Section 4.1.

4.1 Semantic nets

A *semantic net* is usually depicted as a labelled directed graph, consisting of vertices and labelled arcs between vertices; such a graph is sometimes further restricted by the requirement to be acyclic. Several disciplines have influenced the original idea of a semantic net as it was introduced in the 1960s; each discipline has brought its own interpretation of the vertices and arcs, and each discipline has adapted the notion of the semantic net in certain ways to arrive at a more structured formalism suitable for its own purposes. As a consequence, there is hardly any consensus as to what a semantic net is, nor is there any consensus as to what meaning should be ascribed to the basic elements of such a semantic net. Since the semantic net formalism is seldom used in expert systems, we will introduce it in a simple form, just to give the reader an idea about what graph-based representations are like.

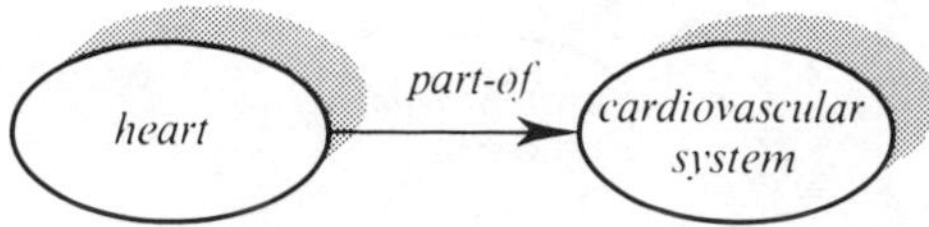

Figure 4.1 A graphical representation of a semantic net.

4.1.1 Vertices and labelled arcs

We have mentioned before that a semantic net is usually depicted as a labelled, directed graph. Each vertex in the graphical representation of a semantic net is taken to represent a *concept*. The arcs of the graph represent binary relations between concepts. The following informal examples show how knowledge is represented in a semantic net.

EXAMPLE 4.1

Consider the following statement concerning the human body:

'The heart is part of the cardiovascular system'

This statement comprises two concepts: the concept 'heart' and the concept 'cardiovascular system'. These concepts are related in the sense that the first concept, the 'heart', forms an anatomical part of the second concept, the 'cardiovascular system'. This knowledge is represented by means of the graph shown in Figure 4.1. The concepts are depicted by ellipses, labelled *heart* and *cardiovascular system*; the relation between the concepts is represented by means of an arc labelled *part-of*.

EXAMPLE 4.2

In the semantic net depicted in Figure 4.2, two different kinds of relations are used in representing information concerning the cardiovascular system of the human body: the 'part-of' relation and the 'is-a' relation.

In this example we encounter the is-a relation. This is quite a common relation between concepts. It reflects the two different senses in which a concept can be used; in this book, the term concept is used to denote either an *individual object* or a *class of objects*. The is-a relation may be used as follows:

- To express that a class of objects is a subclass of another class of objects, such as in the statement

  'A large artery is an artery'

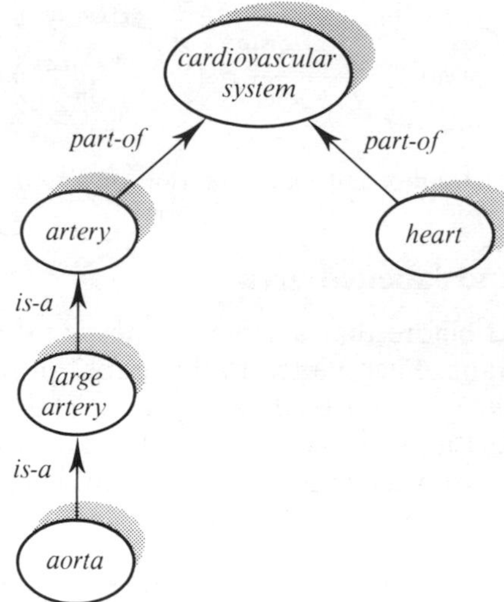

Figure 4.2 Some information concerning the cardiovascular system in a semantic net.

This statement is depicted in a semantic net as follows:

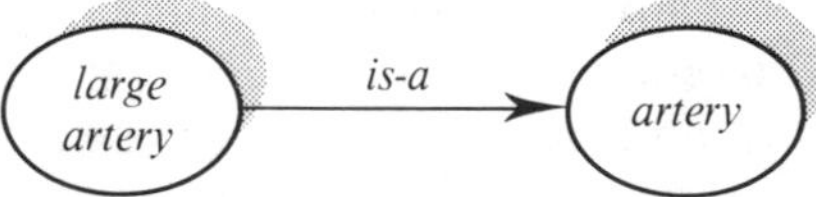

In this case, the is-a part of the statement defines a *set inclusion relation.*

- To express that a specific object is a member of a certain class of objects, such as in the statement

  'The aorta is a large artery'

  This statement is depicted as follows:

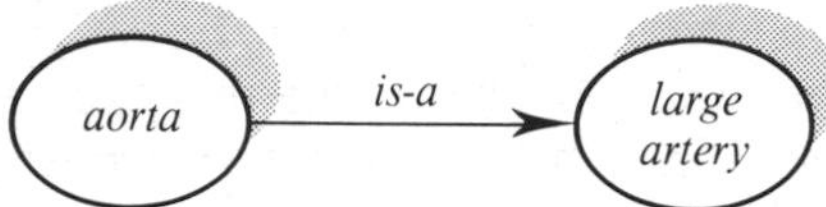

Here, the is-a part of the statement defines a *membership relation* between an element and a set of elements.

In the early semantic net formalism, no explicit distinction was made between these different uses of the is-a relation, called the *is-a link* in

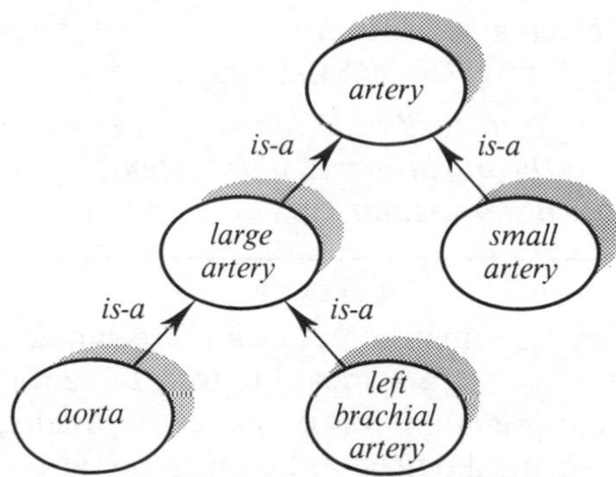

Figure 4.3 Counting specific objects.

semantic net terminology; individual objects and classes of objects were handled identically. The following example illustrates that this may lead to problems.

EXAMPLE 4.3

In Figure 4.3 some information concerning the arteries of the cardiovascular system is represented. Consider a knowledge-based system comprising the information as shown. Suppose that we ask this system on how many specific arteries information is available. If we assume that the system 'knows' that information on individual objects is contained in the leaves of the net, the system will answer 3: the *aorta*, the *left brachial artery*, and the *small artery*. The system is not able to distinguish between the *small artery* representing a class of objects, and the individual objects *aorta* and *left brachial artery*.

This example gives us a valid reason for distinguishing between different types of is-a link. From now on, we distinguish between the *subset-of link* and the *member-of link*.

Before proceeding, we define the notion of a semantic net more formally.

Definition: A *semantic net* S is a labelled graph $S = (V(S), A(S), \lambda)$ where $V(S)$ is the set of *vertices* of S and $A(S) \subseteq V(S) \times V(S)$ is the set of *arcs* of S; λ is the *labelling function* $\lambda : A(S) \rightarrow L(S)$ associated with S where $L(S)$ is the set of *arc labels*.

EXAMPLE 4.4

Consider the semantic net from Figure 4.1 once more. This net is defined by $S = (V(S), A(S), \lambda)$ where

$$V(S) = \{heart, cardiovascular\text{-}system\}$$
$$A(S) = \{(heart, cardiovascular\text{-}system)\}$$
$$\lambda(heart, cardiovascular\text{-}system) = part\text{-}of$$

Here we have defined a semantic net as a mere syntactical object; it has no meaning as yet. To assign a meaning to a semantic net, we have to define a proper interpretation for it. Note the analogy with a logical formula being a syntactical object and its interpretation (see Sections 2.1 and 2.2).

We start by giving an example of a possible interpretation for the subset-of link. We assign to the relation defined by the subset-of links the meaning of the usual set inclusion relation $\subseteq$. The relation $\subseteq$ has the following properties:

(1) *Reflexivity:* For each X, we have $X \subseteq X$.

(2) *Antisymmetry:* For each X, Y, if $X \subseteq Y$ and $Y \subseteq X$, then $X = Y$.

(3) *Transitivity:* For each X, Y, Z, if $X \subseteq Y$ and $Y \subseteq Z$, then $X \subseteq Z$.

Any binary relation having these properties is called a *partial order*. With each vertex $x \in V(S)$ taking part in a subset-of link – note that from this observation we have that the vertex represents a class of objects – we associate a set of elements $I(x)$ from a (semantic) domain of discourse D, that is, $I(x) \subseteq D$. We may now interpret $\lambda(x,y) = subset\text{-}of$ as $I(x) \subseteq I(y)$. From the reflexivity of the set inclusion relation we have that we may add to or delete from a semantic net arcs of the form (x,x) for which $\lambda(x,x) = subset\text{-}of$:

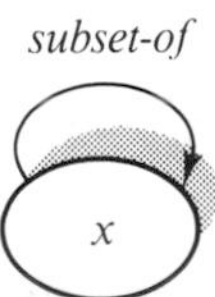

This is called a *trivial cycle*; in the sequel, such trivial cycles will not be shown explicitly. From the transitivity of the set inclusion relation it furthermore follows that, if we have $\lambda(x,y) = subset\text{-}of$ and $\lambda(y,z) = subset\text{-}of$ in a specific net, we may add $\lambda(x,z) = subset\text{-}of$ to the net without changing its meaning. The two nets

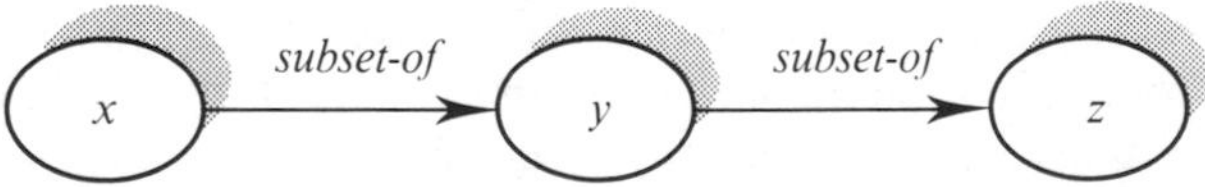

and

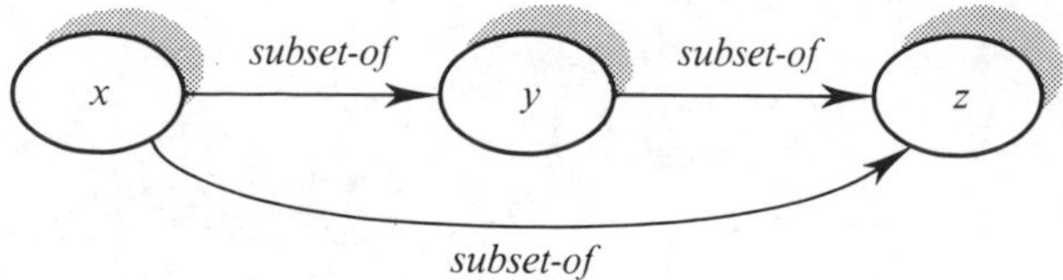

therefore express the same information.

Similar to the interpretation of the subset-of link, vertices $u \in V(S)$ taking part in the left-hand side of a member-of link – from which we have that u represents an individual object – have associated an element $I(u)$ from the domain D, that is, $I(u) \in D$. The relation defined by the member-of links is now assigned the meaning of the usual membership relation $\in$; that is, we interpret $\lambda(u,v) = \textit{member-of}$ as $I(u) \in I(v)$.

It will be evident that for a semantic net to have a neat semantics we have to define a proper interpretation for each type of link used in the net. Especially if no restrictions have been imposed on the types of links, this will be a cumbersome endeavour. It is no wonder therefore that, since the introduction of the semantic net idea, researchers have sought after more restricted special-purpose net formalisms. Here, we will not pursue the subject of the declarative semantics of a semantic net any further.

4.1.2 Inheritance

The subset-of and member-of links of a semantic net may be exploited to derive new information from it, that is, they may be used as the basis for an inference engine. We illustrate the use of these links in reasoning with the help of an example.

EXAMPLE 4.5

Consider the semantic net shown in Figure 4.4. Among others, the following two statements are represented in the net:

'A large artery is an artery'
'An artery is a blood vessel'

From these two statements we may derive the statement

'A large artery is a blood vessel'

exploiting the transitivity of the relation defined by the subset-of links. Furthermore, the statement

'The aorta is an artery'

can be derived from the net using the semantics of both the member-of and subset-of link.

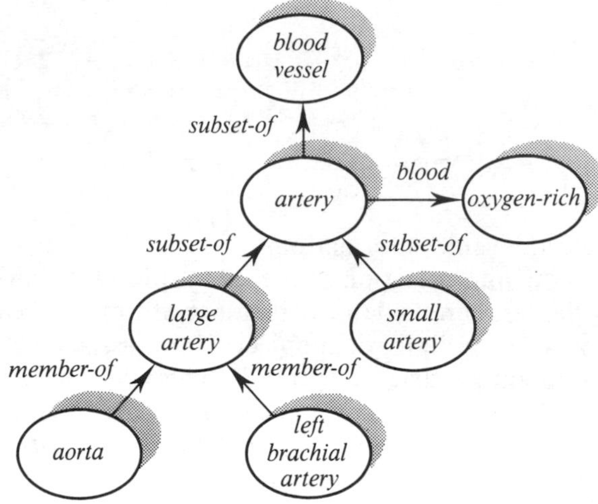

Figure 4.4 Inheritance.

Exploiting the semantics of the member-of and subset-of links in the manner discussed informally in the preceding example forms the basis of a reasoning mechanism called (*property*) *inheritance*; a concept *inherits* the properties of the concepts 'higher' in the net through these member-of and subset-of links. The general idea is demonstrated in the following example.

EXAMPLE 4.6

Consider the semantic net shown in Figure 4.4 once more. Using property inheritance, we may derive from it the following statement:

'The aorta contains oxygen-rich blood'

The concept 'aorta' has inherited the property 'contains oxygen-rich blood' from the concept 'artery' which is found higher in the net.

In Section 4.3 we shall discuss the principle of inheritance more formally.

The semantic net is a natural formalism for expressing knowledge in which the basic concepts are organized in a hierarchical manner. Several problems, however, arise from the rigidity of the principle of inheritance as introduced above. We give two examples to illustrate some of these problems.

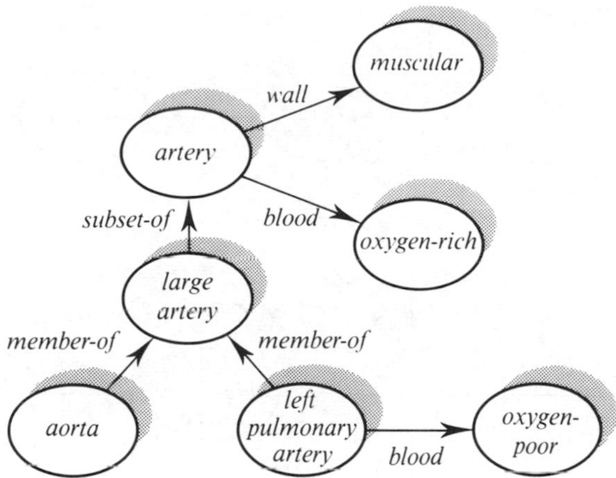

Figure 4.5 An exception to a general property.

EXAMPLE 4.7

Consider Figure 4.5, which shows some information concerning the arteries. Among other information, it has been specified that arteries in general have muscular walls and transport oxygen-rich blood. An exception to the latter property of arteries is for example the left pulmonary artery which is an artery containing oxygen-poor blood.

Using the member-of and subset-of links shown in the net the aorta inherits the properties of the arteries; the aorta has a muscular wall and transports oxygen-rich blood. Using a similar argument, the left pulmonary artery inherits these two properties as well. The left pulmonary artery, however, transports oxygen-poor blood! So the property that arteries transport oxygen-rich blood should not be inherited by the left pulmonary artery. When employing the principle of inheritance discussed so far, the inheritance of this property cannot be prevented. A possible solution to this problem is to store the information that an artery contains oxygen-rich blood explicitly with each artery for which this property holds. This is shown in Figure 4.6. A major drawback of this solution is that the general property has been lost.

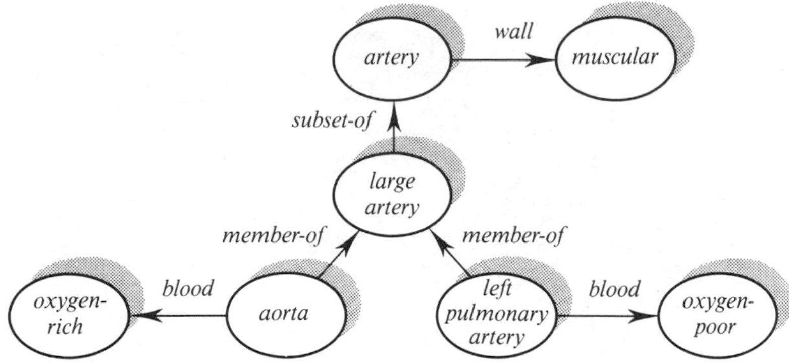

Figure 4.6 Loss of a general property.

EXAMPLE 4.8

In the foregoing examples we have discussed properties which are relevant to individual objects. In the semantic net shown in Figure 4.7 some information has been stored that is relevant to a class of objects as a whole and not to the individuals belonging to it. For example, in the net we have represented the information that the large arteries together contain approximately 11% of all the blood the human body contains. This information is relevant only to the class as a whole and not to a single large artery, so this property should not be inherited by the aorta and the left brachial artery. Furthermore, the information that all arteries together contain 20% of the total blood volume should not be inherited by the class of the small arteries; the latter class contains only 7% of the total blood volume. Again, inheritance cannot be prevented.

It has been mentioned that the semantic net formalism has undergone many changes since its introduction. The resulting formalisms on the one hand are more restricted; only a limited number of predefined link-types is allowed, each having a clear semantics. On the other hand, many new features have been added to the formalism. In particular the principle of inheritance has been revised to make inheritance of properties more flexible. Furthermore, some facilities for representing procedural knowledge have been added to the semantic net. Many of these extensions bear a close resemblance to features of frames. Therefore, we shall not discuss these features in relation to semantic nets here, but only in relation to the frame formalism in Section 4.2.

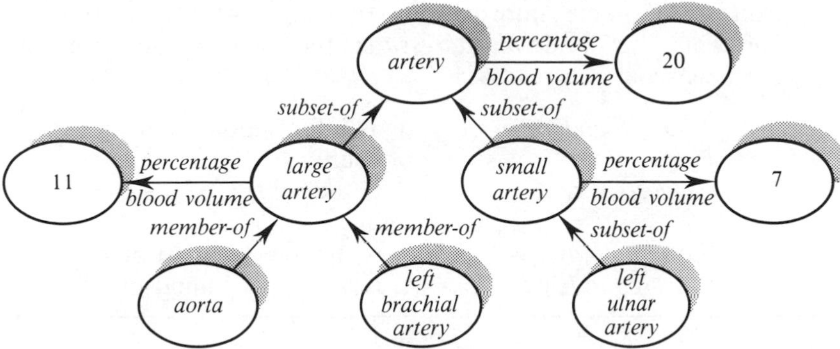

Figure 4.7 Inheritance of properties relevant to a class as a whole.

4.1.3 The extended semantic net

Before we turn our attention to knowledge representation in frames, we conclude this section with a discussion of an interesting type of semantic net: the *extended semantic net*. The extended semantic net was developed by A. Deliyanni and R.A. Kowalski as an alternative representation formalism for the clausal form of logic with a restriction to binary predicate symbols. It should be noted that the restriction to binary predicates is not an essential one: any atom containing an n-place predicate symbol can be replaced by a conjunction of atoms involving binary predicates only. If $n > 2$, $n + 1$ new predicates are needed to represent the original information; if $n = 1$, only a single new predicate is required.

EXAMPLE 4.9

Consider the three-place predicate symbol *Bloodpressure*, which is intended to have the following meaning:

Bloodpressure(x,y,z) = 'the mean blood pressure in x lies between y mmHg and z mmHg'

The clause

Bloodpressure(*artery*,40,80) ←

for example, can be replaced by the following four clauses:

Info(*fact*,*bloodpressure*) ←
Subject(*fact*,*artery*) ←
Lowerbound(*fact*,40) ←
Upperbound(*fact*,80) ←

in which only binary predicate symbols have been used to express the same information. We have introduced the new constants *fact* and *bloodpressure*; the new binary predicate symbols should be read as:

Info(*w*,*bloodpressure*)	=	'*w* is information about blood pressure'
Subject(*w*,*x*)	=	'*x* is the subject of the information *w*'
Lowerbound(*w*,*y*)	=	'*y* is the lower bound of *w*'
Upperbound(*w*,*z*)	=	'*z* is the upper bound of *w*'

EXAMPLE 4.10

Consider the unary predicate symbol *Artery* with the following intended meaning:

Artery(*x*) = '*x* is an artery'

The clause

Artery(*aorta*) ←

may be replaced by the clause

Isa(*aorta*,*artery*) ←

We have mentioned before that the extended semantic net provides an alternative syntax for the clausal form of logic; the arguments to the predicate symbols occurring in a set of clauses are taken as the vertices, and the binary predicate symbols themselves are taken as the labels of the arcs of a directed graph. The direction of the arc expresses the order of the arguments to the predicate symbol. The conclusions and conditions of a clause are represented by different types of arcs; conditions are denoted by solid arcs and conclusions are indicated by dashed arcs.

EXAMPLE 4.11

The extended semantic net shown in Figure 4.8 represents the clause

Wall(*x*,*muscular*) ← *Isa*(*x*,*artery*)

A particular constant may occur in more than one clause. If we represent all occurrences of a constant by means of a single vertex, it is not always

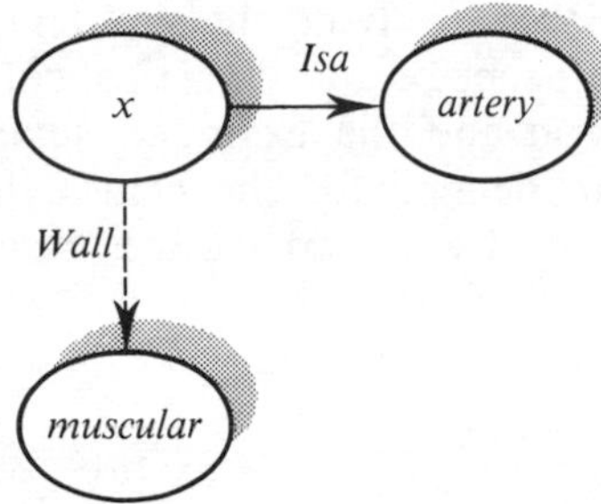

Figure 4.8 The extended semantic net for the clause
Wall(x,muscular) ← Isa(x,artery).

apparent in the representation discussed above to which clauses a particular vertex belongs. This is why an extended semantic net representing a set of clauses is divided into a number of subnets, each representing a single clause.

EXAMPLE 4.12

The following set of clauses

{*Wall*(*x*,*muscular*) ← *Isa*(*x*,*artery*),
Isa(*y*,*artery*) ← *Isa*(*y*,*large-artery*)}

has been represented in Figure 4.9. The net is partitioned into two subnets; for each clause from the given clause set we have one corresponding subnet.

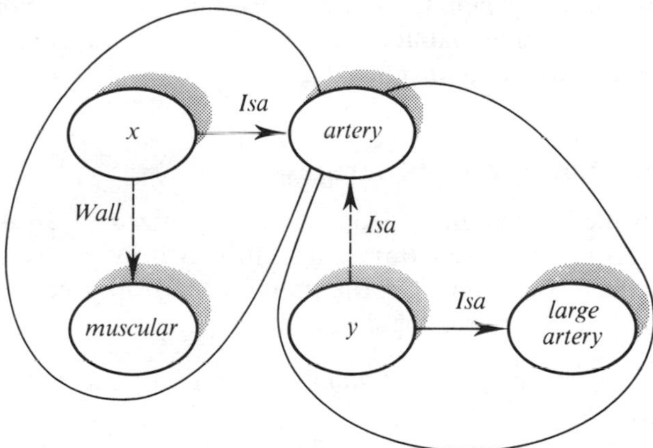

Figure 4.9 Partition of an extended semantic net into subnets.

Note that, if a similar situation arises concerning a variable, we can simply rename the variables to avoid the problem.

A pleasant consequence of the syntactical correspondence between the clausal form of logic and the extended semantic net is that the inference rules that are defined for the clausal form of logic can be applied for manipulation of arcs and vertices in an extended semantic net.

4.2 Frames and single inheritance

In a frame-based system all knowledge relevant to a concept is stored in a complex entity of representation called a *frame*. Frames provide a formalism for explicitly grouping all knowledge concerning the properties of individual objects or classes of objects. Within a frame, part of the properties is specified as reference information to other, more general frames. This reference information is represented by means of is-a links which are quite similar in concept to the is-a links in a semantic net. This way, the knowledge in a domain of interest is organized hierarchically in what is called a *frame hierarchy* or *frame taxonomy* (*taxonomy* for short). A taxonomy is often depicted graphically as a directed, acyclic graph, bearing a close resemblance to a semantic net. However, in the graph representation of a frame taxonomy, only the is-a links are shown (as for the semantic net, trivial cycles are not shown in the graph because they do not represent additional information); the knowledge concerning an individual object or a class of objects itself is part of the internal structure of the vertices of the graph. In contrast with the semantic net, in a frame representation different components are distinguished, all having a special status allowing them to be treated explicitly as such. For example, the is-a links in a frame taxonomy are represented and treated in a way different from other components.

4.2.1 Tree-like frame taxonomies

As has been mentioned above, frames are organized in a taxonomy in which the vertices represent frames and in which every arc denotes an is-a link between two frames. In the frame formalism used in this book, two types of frames are distinguished:

- *class frames*, or *generic frames*, which represent knowledge concerning classes of objects;
- *instance frames*, which represent knowledge concerning individual objects.

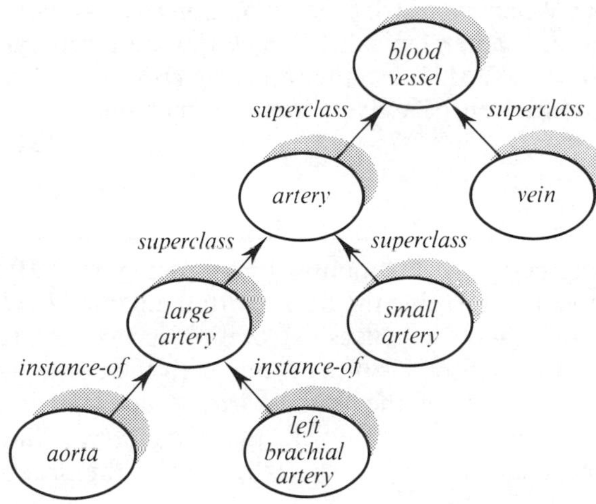

Figure 4.10 A tree-like taxonomy.

Class frames have much in common with the record data type as, for example, provided in the Pascal programming language, and instances are similar to filled-in record variables.

Since there are two types of frames, we also distinguish two types of is-a link by means of which a frame indicates its relative position in the frame taxonomy:

- an *instance-of link*, which is an is-a link between an instance frame and a class frame;
- a *superclass link*, which is an is-a link between two class frames, defining a partial order on the set of class frames in a frame taxonomy.

These is-a links are similar in meaning to the member-of and subset-of links, respectively, distinguished for semantic nets in the previous section. Their formal meaning will be discussed below.

In the present section, we consider frame taxonomies that can be represented as trees. Section 4.3 discusses the more general graph-like taxonomies. An example of a tree-like taxonomy is shown in Figure 4.10. In this figure, a frame is represented as an ellipse; the internal structure of a frame is not shown. In a tree-like frame taxonomy capturing knowledge concerning a given domain, the root of the tree represents the most general description of the domain; the other frames represent descriptions of concepts that are more specific. The descendants of a certain frame in the taxonomy are therefore often called *specializations* of that frame. The ancestors of a frame in the taxonomy are called its *generalizations*. When we restrict the discussion to classes of objects only, specializations are generally called *subclasses* and generalizations are called *superclasses*. We shall use the terms *superframe* and *subframes* for the parent and children of a given frame, respectively.

EXAMPLE 4.13

Consider the frame taxonomy shown in Figure 4.10 once more. The vertex representing the frame with the name *blood vessel* is the father (and therefore ancestor) of the vertices representing the frames *artery* and *vein*. So the frame with the name *blood vessel* is the generalization of the frames *artery* and *vein*; it is equally a generalization of the frame with the name *aorta*. The frame with the name *small artery* is a specialization of the *artery* frame.

A frame representing an individual object cannot be specialized any further. Therefore, in a tree-like frame taxonomy an instance is always a leaf of the tree.

EXAMPLE 4.14

Consider Figure 4.10 once more. The frames with the names *aorta* and *left brachial artery* cannot be specialized any further, since these frames represent individual objects and are therefore instances. Except for the vertices representing these two frames, the tree has another two leaves: the frames *small artery* and *vein*. These two frames are generic; the descriptions given in these frames may be further specialized. Note that although an instance is always a leaf of the tree, not every leaf is an instance.

We shall now turn our attention to the internal structure of a frame. We assume that each frame in a taxonomy has a unique name. The information specific to the concept represented by a frame is laid down in so-called *attributes* or *slots*, so attributes offer a means for representing the properties of individual objects or classes of objects. In the following definition, we shall present a syntax of a language for the representation of frames; from then on we shall be able to be more precise in discussing frames and their formal meaning.

Definition: A *frame* is a statement having the following form:

<frame> ::= <class> | <instance>

<class> ::= ***class*** <class-name> ***is***
superclass <super-spec>;
<class-attributes>
end

<instance> ::= ***instance*** <instance-name> ***is***
instance-of <super-spec>;
<instance-attributes>
end

<super-spec> ::= <class-name> | ***nil***

<class-attributes> ::= <declaration> {; <declaration> }* |
<empty>

<instance-attributes> ::= <attribute-value-pair>
{; <attribute-value-pair> }* |
<empty>

<declaration> ::= <attribute-type-pair> |
<attribute-value-pair>

<attribute-type-pair> ::= <attribute-name> : <type>

<attribute-value-pair> ::= <attribute-name> = <value>

<type> ::= ***int*** | ***real*** | ***string*** | <set> |
<class-name>

<value> ::= <elementary-constant> |
<instance-name>

<empty> ::=

A <super-spec> equal to the special symbol ***nil*** is used to indicate that the frame concerned is the root of the tree-like taxonomy. As a type, a <set> consists of elementary constants and instance names, separated by commas and enclosed in curly brackets. An elementary constant is either a real or integer constant, or a string of non-blank characters, that is, an instance of one of the predefined (or standard) classes ***real***, ***int*** and ***string***. The <instance-name> value of an attribute refers to a uniquely defined instance in the taxonomy.

For the moment we assume that an attribute–type or attribute–value pair for an attribute occurs only once in a frame taxonomy. Later on we shall drop this restriction. In the preceding definition, we have stated for ease of exposition that a class frame is the root of a tree-like taxonomy if it has a super-specification equal to ***nil***, where it is actually a subclass of the most general class ***nil***. This more accurate interpretation of the symbol ***nil***, however, is important only in frame taxonomies in which more than one most general class frame not equal to ***nil*** occurs; if we did not consider ***nil*** as the most general class, the graph representation of such taxonomy would be a forest of trees instead of just a tree.

As can be seen in the preceding definition, the definition of an instance frame is composed of the specification of the class to which the instance belongs followed by a collection of attribute–value pairs. Together they give a description of an individual concept in the domain of discourse. Let us give an example of such an instance.

EXAMPLE 4.15

We consider the left brachial artery, which is one of the arteries in the human body. It is known that the left brachial artery has an approximate diameter of 0.4 cm, that it is located in the upper arm, and that it contains oxygen-rich blood. All this information is captured by the following instance frame:

instance *left-brachial-artery* ***is***
  instance-of *artery*;
  diameter = 0.4;
  location = *arm*;
  blood = *oxygen-rich*
end

We have used the attributes *diameter*, *location* and *blood* for the representation of the mentioned properties of the individual concept 'left brachial artery'. Note that all three attributes have been assigned actual values. The values 0.4 and *oxygen-rich* are assumed to be elementary constants. The value *arm* of the attribute *location* is an instance of the class frame *limb*:

instance *arm* ***is***
  instance-of *limb*;
  position = *superior*
end

The value *superior* is an elementary constant.

The information specified in the attribute parts of instance frames has to accord with the following rules. All attributes occurring in the instances of a class frame must have been declared in the attribute part of that class frame or in one of its generalizations; the values which have been filled in for the attributes in the instance must be of the appropriate attribute type as defined by the classes in the taxonomy. Note that these rules provide part of the meaning of the instance-of link.

EXAMPLE 4.16

Consider the instance *left-brachial-artery* from Example 4.15 once more. The class to which *left-brachial-artery* belongs is defined as follows:

> ***class*** *artery* ***is***
>   ***superclass*** *blood-vessel*;
>   *location* : {*arm*,*head*,*leg*,*trunk*}
> ***end***

This class frame provides a type declaration for the attribute *location*. It indicates that the *location* attribute is allowed to take a value only from the set {*arm*, *head*, *leg*, *trunk*}. Note that the value *arm* given for the *location* attribute in the *left-brachial-artery* instance is indeed of the correct type; not all attributes occurring in the instance have been declared in the class frame *artery*, so the *diameter* and *blood* attributes must have been declared in some of the generalizations of the *artery* class. In Example 4.15 we have mentioned that the instance frame *arm* belongs to the class *limb*. This class frame, for example, is defined as follows:

> ***class*** *limb* ***is***
>   ***superclass nil***;
>   *position* : {*inferior*, *superior*}
> ***end***

From the superclass specification ***nil*** we have that this class is the root of a tree-like taxonomy.

In the preceding example, the class frames we considered had attribute–type pairs only in their declaration part. However, the syntax definition indicates that attribute–value pairs are also allowed in the declaration part of a class frame. The following example illustrates this idea.

EXAMPLE 4.17

Consider the previous examples once more. Since most arteries contain oxygen-rich blood, there is no purpose in repeating this information for all individual arteries separately. In this case, it appears to be convenient to fix the value *oxygen-rich* for the attribute *blood* in advance in the class frame *artery*. We then obtain the following alternative definition for the *artery* frame:

```
class artery is
  superclass blood-vessel;
  location : {arm, head, leg, trunk};
  blood = oxygen-rich
end
```

The instance frame *left-brachial-artery* may now be simplified to

```
instance left-brachial-artery is
  instance-of artery;
  diameter = 0.4;
  location = arm
end
```

without affecting the intended meaning.

Although only informally, we have now fully described the meaning of the instance-of link. We now turn our attention to the superclass link. Recall that we have distinguished two different types of attribute information in a frame taxonomy: information about attribute types and information about attribute values. Accordingly, in assigning a meaning to the superclass link, we have to distinguish between these different types of attribute information. First of all, the superclass link defines a partial order on the class frames in a taxonomy and may be applied for reasoning about attribute values in much the same way as we have seen for semantic nets. Secondly, however, the superclass link may be viewed as defining a relation which restricts the semantic contents of the frame taxonomy as we have shown in the preceding example. This is essentially a higher-order relation. These two different ways of interpreting the superclass link are best treated separately. We shall therefore first study the meaning of attribute values in a tree-like taxonomy and show how it is possible to reason about such attribute values. From now on, we shall, for ease of exposition, completely disregard the fact that classes may contain type information until Section 4.2.7 in which we shall return to attribute types.

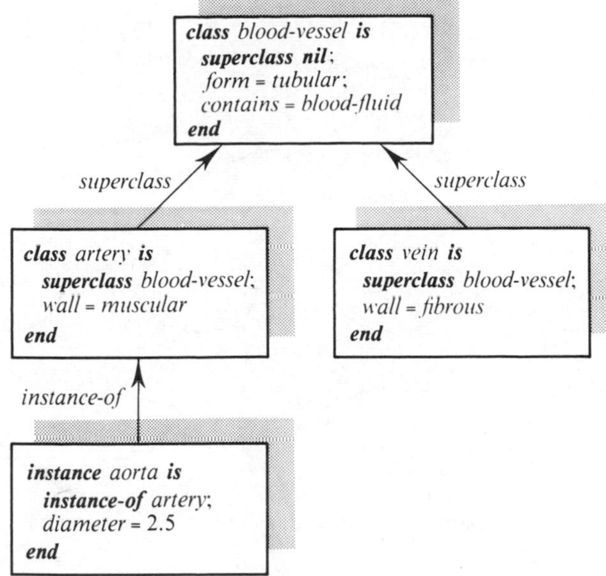

Figure 4.11 A tree-like taxonomy showing the internal frame structure.

We have mentioned before that the semantic net formalism we have briefly discussed in Section 4.1 may be viewed as a precursor of the frame formalism. We take a closer look at the relationship between the two formalisms. This relationship can be examined more readily if we depict a frame taxonomy in a graph as we have done with the semantic net. The following example shows the general idea.

EXAMPLE 4.18

Figure 4.11 shows four frames in a tree-like taxonomy. The frames are represented as boxes; the internal structure of each of the frames is depicted. The arcs in the graph represent the instance-of and superclass links between the frames. Note that the frames themselves already indicate their position in the taxonomy explicitly; the graphical representation of the taxonomy therefore contains redundant information. From a graph representing a frame taxonomy we can easily derive an equivalent semantic net. Figure 4.12 shows the semantic net equivalent to the taxonomy depicted in Figure 4.11. Note that, although the corresponding semantic net essentially comprises the same information as the original frame taxonomy, the apparent modularity of the taxonomy has been lost.

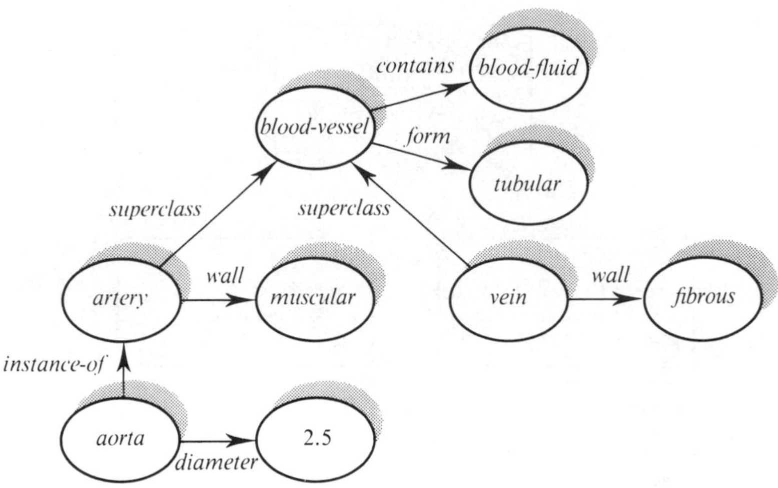

Figure 4.12 The semantic net corresponding to the taxonomy shown in Figure 4.11.

Based on the frame formalism defined above we shall discuss the meaning that can be associated with the frame formalism. The discussion takes the following example for a starting point.

EXAMPLE 4.19

Suppose that we want to represent in a frame the following information concerning the vascular system: the aorta is an artery having a diameter of 2.5 cm. Using our frame formalism, this information may be represented as follows:

> ***instance*** *aorta* ***is***
>   ***instance-of*** *artery*;
>   *diameter* = 2.5
> ***end***

The information that an artery is a blood vessel having a muscular wall is represented in the following class frame:

> ***class*** *artery* ***is***
>   ***superclass*** *blood-vessel*;
>   *wall* = *muscular*
> ***end***

To conclude, the following class frame shows that a blood vessel is tubular in form and contains blood:

> ***class*** *blood-vessel* ***is***
>   ***superclass nil***;
>   *form* = *tubular*;
>   *contains* = *blood-fluid*
> ***end***

The last frame furthermore indicates that the *blood-vessel* frame is the root of the taxonomy concerned.

The information that is specified in a frame taxonomy can also be expressed in first-order predicate logic, roughly by complying with the following directions:

- take the names of the instances as constants;
- take the names of the class frames as unary predicate symbols;
- translate an instance-of link into a predicate symbol having a constant for an argument;
- translate a superclass link into a logical implication;
- take the attribute names as unary function symbols, and
- translate an attribute–value pair into an equality between a function term and a constant.

EXAMPLE 4.20

Assuming a suitable interpretation, the following formulas represent the same information as the frames in Example 4.19 do:

$$artery(aorta)$$
$$diameter(aorta) = 2.5$$

$$\forall x(artery(x) \rightarrow blood\text{-}vessel(x))$$
$$\forall x(artery(x) \rightarrow wall(x) = muscular)$$

$$\forall x(blood\text{-}vessel(x) \rightarrow form(x) = tubular)$$
$$\forall x(blood\text{-}vessel(x) \rightarrow contains(x) = blood\text{-}fluid)$$

The semantics of first-order predicate logic may now be exploited to define a semantics for the frame formalism. Under the assumption that each attribute occurs only once in the taxonomy, we may ascribe a meaning based on first-order predicate logic to the set of frames of this taxonomy using the following general translation scheme:

class C ***is***		
superclass S;		$\forall x(C(x) \rightarrow S(x))$
$a_1 = b_1$;	$\Rightarrow$	$\forall x(C(x) \rightarrow a_1(x) = b_1)$
$\vdots$		$\vdots$
$a_n = b_n$		$\forall x(C(x) \rightarrow a_n(x) = b_n)$
end		

instance I ***is***		
instance-of C;		$C(I)$
$a_1 = b_1$;	$\Rightarrow$	$a_1(I) = b_1$
$\vdots$		$\vdots$
$a_n = b_n$		$a_n(I) = b_n$
end		

Under the same assumption we have that there always exists an interpretation I of the logical formulas thus obtained, which is a model. In the next section where we shall study the case in which the restriction that an attribute–value pair for an attribute occurs only once in a taxonomy has been dropped we shall see that the existence of such an interpretation is not guaranteed.

We conclude this section with a discussion of the inference method associated with the frame formalism. We start by examining the derivations that can be made from the corresponding logical formulas by means of a sound and complete collection of inference rules.

EXAMPLE 4.21

Consider the formulas given in the previous example once more. From the formulas

$$artery(aorta)$$
$$\forall x(artery(x) \rightarrow wall(x) = muscular)$$

we can derive the formula

$$wall(aorta) = muscular$$

using modus ponens. Similarly, from the set of formulas in Example 4.20 the following formula can be derived:

$$blood\text{-}vessel(aorta)$$

On examining these derivations closely, we see that the information holding for arteries in general is explicitly said to hold for the aorta in particular; since we know that the aorta is an artery, the aorta *inherits* this information from the arteries. Similarly, the aorta inherits the information specific to blood vessels.

In this example we have demonstrated the reasoning behaviour with logical formulas representing the information stored in a given frame taxonomy. This reasoning behaviour is modelled in an inference method for frames called *single inheritance*. In case of a tree-like taxonomy, we speak of *single* inheritance to stress the fact that each frame has at most one superframe. In contrast, the inference method associated with more general, graph-like taxonomies is called *multiple* inheritance; we shall discuss multiple inheritance in Section 4.3. Informally speaking, in single inheritance all information that holds for a particular frame is determined by traversing the taxonomy from the frame itself to the root of the taxonomy, that is, the most general frame, and successively collecting the attributes that are found in the encountered frames with their associated values. This may be viewed roughly as exploiting the transitivity property of the superclass relation. This procedure terminates as soon as the information in the root of the taxonomy has been processed. The function shown below describes this recursive inference procedure:

```
function Inherit(frame, attribute-value-pairs)
  if frame = nil then
    return(attribute-value-pairs)
  end;
  attribute-value-pairs ← attribute-value-pairs ∪
                          AttributePart(frame);
  return(Inherit(Superframe(frame), attribute-value-pairs))
end
```

The parameters **frame** and **attribute-value-pairs** take as values a frame name and a collection of attribute–value pairs, respectively. If the parameter frame equals **nil**, then either the taxonomy is empty or the root of the taxonomy has been reached; in both cases all attribute–value pairs holding for the frame concerned have been collected in the second argument attribute-value-pairs. If the parameter frame differs from the value **nil**, then all attribute–value pairs specified in the frame frame are extracted from it using the function AttributePart, and added to attribute-value-pairs. The information holding for the superframe of the given frame frame is subsequently determined by means of a recursive call to the Inherit function.

EXAMPLE 4.22

Consider Figure 4.11 again. In the instance frame with the name *aorta* the attribute–value pair

diameter = 2.5

has been specified. Using the Inherit function described in the foregoing, the instance inherits the attribute–value pair

wall = *muscular*

from its superframe *artery*. From the superframe *blood-vessel* of the frame *artery*, the instance inherits the following two attribute–value pairs:

contains = *blood-fluid*
form = *tubular*

4.2.2 Exceptions

In the previous section we have introduced a semantics for the frame formalism based on first-order predicate logic. To this end, we assumed that attributes occurred only once in a frame taxonomy. This assumption, however, renders the frame formalism too inflexible for coping with practical applications. In this section we therefore abandon this rather restrictive assumption and investigate the problems that arise from doing so; we will assume, however, that in a given frame an attribute can take only one value at a time. Allowing attributes to occur more than once in a frame taxonomy increases the expressive power of the formalism; it has become possible to state *exceptions* to information that holds in general but for some special cases. The following example shows the way an exception may be represented. It furthermore discusses the consequence of the introduction of exceptions into the formalism with respect to its semantics.

EXAMPLE 4.23

We have said in the preceding section that most arteries contain oxygen-rich blood. The following class frame captures this knowledge:

class *artery* ***is***
  superclass *blood-vessel*;
  blood = *oxygen-rich*
end

However, it is known that the left and right pulmonary arteries are exceptions to this property of arteries; the pulmonary arteries have almost all the properties that arteries have but, unlike arteries in general, they transport oxygen-poor blood. Restricting the discussion to the left pulmonary artery only, this information has been specified in the following instance frame:

> ***instance*** *left-pulmonary-artery* ***is***
>   ***instance-of*** *artery*;
>   *blood* = *oxygen-poor*
> ***end***

We have now expressed that the value *oxygen-poor* of the attribute *blood* is an exception to the value *oxygen-rich* of the attribute *blood* that has been specified in the superframe *artery* of the instance; informally speaking, the 'general' value has been surpassed. Note that the attribute *blood* is no longer unique in the taxonomy.

Applying the general translation scheme for converting these two frames into formulas in first-order predicate logic, we obtain the following set of formulas:

$$artery(left\text{-}pulmonary\text{-}artery)$$
$$blood(left\text{-}pulmonary\text{-}artery) = oxygen\text{-}poor$$

$$\forall x(artery(x) \rightarrow blood\text{-}vessel(x))$$
$$\forall x(artery(x) \rightarrow blood(x) = oxygen\text{-}rich)$$

This set of logical formulas is inconsistent, since we can derive the following logical consequences:

$$blood(left\text{-}pulmonary\text{-}artery) = oxygen\text{-}poor$$
$$blood(left\text{-}pulmonary\text{-}artery) = oxygen\text{-}rich$$

The inconsistency now follows from the equality axioms (which are assumed to be implicitly present); we have also assumed that the unique name assumption holds, that is, symbols (function symbols, predicate symbols and constants) with different names are assumed to be different. Now observe that in any model for the logical formulas shown above the constants *oxygen-rich* and *oxygen-poor* have to be equal. This, however, contradicts the unique name assumption.

In the foregoing example we have demonstrated that in the frame formalism exceptions can be represented by locally surpassing attribute values. Furthermore, it has been shown that if we allow multiple occurrences of attributes the translation of the frame formalism into first-order predicate logic may render an inconsistent set of formulas; it is not possible fully to capture the notion of exceptions by standard first-order predicate logic. The meaning of the frame formalism allowing for exceptions, however, can be described using a non-standard logic, such as for example the non-monotonic logic developed by D. McDermott and J. Doyle, or by the default logic developed by R. Reiter. We do not enter into these theories in detail; we merely give a sketch of their respective general idea.

We first consider the *non-monotonic logic* of McDermott and Doyle. In non-monotonic logic, first-order predicate logic is extended with a special *modal operator* M. The truth of a formula $M(f(x) = c)$ now means that the formula $f(x) = c$ is *possibly* true; in other words, it is not possible to derive from the given set of formulas, formulas $f(x) = d$ with $d \neq c$. In our example, the formula *blood*(*left-pulmonary-artery*) = *oxygen-poor* must be true in all models for our set of logical formulas. It is therefore undesirable that the formula *blood*(*left-pulmonary-artery*) = *oxygen-rich* can be derived, as this would lead to an inconsistency. Using the modal operator M we can block the derivation of the latter formula. The new formulas representing the given information are now as follows:

artey(*left-pulmonary-artery*)
blood(*left-pulmonary-artery*) = *oxygen-poor*

$\forall x(artery(x) \rightarrow blood\text{-}vessel(x))$
$\forall x(artery(x) \wedge M(blood(x) = oxygen\text{-}rich) \rightarrow$
$\quad blood(x) = oxygen\text{-}rich)$

Informally speaking, these formulas state that for a constant e the formula *blood*(e) = *oxygen-rich* can only be derived if no other formula *blood*(e) = c with $c \neq$ *oxygen-rich* can be derived. So, the formula *blood* (*left-pulmonary-artery*) = *oxygen-rich* is no longer a logical consequence of the above-given set of formulas.

The *default logic* developed by R. Reiter equally provides a way of handling exceptions, but from a different perspective than non-monotonic logic does. In default logic, special inference rules, called *defaults*, are added to first-order predicate logic. The translation of the frame formalism into default logic now yields a set of logical formulas and a set of defaults. In the present case, we obtain the following set of logical formulas:

artery(*left-pulmonary-artery*)
blood(*left-pulmonary-artery*) = *oxygen-poor*

$\forall x(artery(x) \rightarrow blood\text{-}vessel(x))$

and the following default:

$$\frac{artery(x) : blood(x) = oxygen\text{-}rich}{blood(x) = oxygen\text{-}rich}$$

A default consists of a *prerequisite*, in our case the formula $artery(x)$, and a set of so-called *justifications*, here just the formula $blood(x) = oxygen\text{-}rich$; these are specified above the line. It furthermore contains a *consequent*, here $blood(x) = oxygen\text{-}rich$, specified below the line. In this example, the default expresses that given the satisfiability of the prerequisite $artery(x)$ for some x in the domain and given that there are no formulas which contradict the justification $blood(x) = oxygen\text{-}rich$, then the consequent $blood(x) = oxygen\text{-}rich$ may be derived. So, in the present case, $blood(left\text{-}pulmonary\text{-}artery) = oxygen\text{-}rich$ cannot be derived. This is precisely what we wanted to achieve.

We conclude this section by introducing an inheritance procedure that respects the intuitive meaning of a frame formalism allowing for exceptions. It is obvious that the inheritance procedure described in the previous section cannot be applied when attributes occur more than once in a taxonomy; this procedure might come up with conflicting information. However, only a minor modification of the procedure suffices to let it cope with exceptions. The general idea of the alteration of the inheritance procedure is as follows. Just before an attribute–value pair is added to the set of collected attribute–value pairs, it is examined whether the attribute name concerned already occurs in this set; in that case, the attribute value has been surpassed by an exception somewhere lower in the taxonomy. An attribute–value pair is then added to the set of collected attribute values only if the attribute name is not already present in this set. The following function describes the altered inheritance procedure more formally:

```
function Inherit(frame, attribute-value-pairs)
  if frame = nil then
    return(attribute-value-pairs)
  end;
  pairs ← AttributePart(frame);
  attribute-value-pairs ← attribute-value-pairs ∪
      NewAttributes(pairs, attribute-value-pairs);
  return(Inherit(Superframe(frame), attribute-value-pairs))
end
```

The function NewAttributes is used to delete from pairs those attribute–value pairs of which the attribute name already occurs in attribute-value-pairs.

The intuitive idea of this new inheritance function is that the value which holds for an attribute is given in the frame itself or in the nearest frame higher in the taxonomy providing a value for the attribute.

4.2.3 Single inheritance in PROLOG

In the previous section, we have described an algorithm for single inheritance with exceptions. Implementing this algorithm is a relatively straightforward task. We shall discuss two implementations of it. In this section, we shall develop a PROLOG program for inheritance; in Section 4.2.4 the same will be done using the LISP programming language.

Before we discuss our implementation of inheritance with exceptions in PROLOG, we have to consider the representation of frames in the Horn clause formalism. Two types of frames have been distinguished above: instance frames and class frames. In the PROLOG representation we have to distinguish between the two types explicitly. For this purpose, we introduce the predicates `instance` and `class`. The three-place predicate `instance` is used for representing an instance frame:

```
instance(<instance-name>,
         instance_of = <superframe>,
         <attributes>).
```

The first argument to `instance`, <instance-name>, specifies the name of the instance frame. In the second argument, the instance-of link of the frame is specified by means of the term `instance_of = <superframe>` in which <superframe> denotes the name of the superclass to which the instance belongs. The third argument, <attributes>, contains a list of terms of the form <attribute-name> = <attribute-value>.

EXAMPLE 4.24

Consider the following instance frame. It describes part of the characteristics of the left pulmonary artery:

instance *left-pulmonary-artery* ***is***
  instance-of *artery*;
  blood = *oxygen-poor*
end

This instance is represented in a Horn clause as follows:

```
instance(left_pulmonary_artery,
         instance_of = artery,
         [blood = oxygen_poor]).
```

A class frame is represented in a Horn clause in much the same way as an instance is:

class(<class-name>,superclass = <superframe>,<attributes>).

If the class frame with the name <class-name> is the root of the represented tree-like taxonomy, the second argument in the Horn clause representation of the frame specifies the term `superclass = nil`.

EXAMPLE 4.25

Consider the following formal description of the class of arteries:

> ***class*** *artery* ***is***
> ***superclass*** *blood-vessel*;
> *wall* = *muscular*;
> *blood* = *oxygen-rich*
> ***end***

This class frame is represented in PROLOG as follows:

```
class(artery,
      superclass = blood_vessel,
      [wall = muscular,blood = oxygen-rich]).
```

The following Prolog clause describes the class of blood vessels:

```
class(blood_vessel,
      superclass = nil,
      [contains = blood_fluid,structure = tubular]).
```

Now suppose that the PROLOG database contains a set of Horn clauses representing a frame taxonomy. The following procedure `query_taxonomy` then allows for querying this taxonomy:

```
query_taxonomy(Frame) :-
     inherit(Frame,Attributes),
     print_info(Frame,Attributes).
query_taxonomy(_) :-
     nl,
     write('The specified frame is not present in the taxonomy').
```

The user can pose a query to the taxonomy by means of a call to `query_taxonomy` in which the variable `Frame` must be instantiated to the frame of interest. The procedure `inherit` called from `query_taxonomy` takes care of the actual inheritance of all properties that hold for the frame of concern. The print_info procedure just prints the derived information onto the screen; the implementation of this procedure will not be shown here and is left to the reader.

The algorithm for single inheritance with exceptions can be specified in PROLOG quite tersely; our implementation comprises six Horn clauses only. The following three clauses of the procedure inherit together govern the process of inheritance in a tree-like taxonomy. Note that, in the call to the procedure inherit from query_taxonomy, the variable Frame has been instantiated to a frame name. The variable Attributes is initially uninstantiated; it will be used for collecting the attribute–value pairs that hold for the given frame.

```
inherit(Frame,Attributes) :-
     class(Frame,superclass = nil,Attributes).
inherit(Frame,Attribute_list) :-
     class(Frame,superclass = Superframe,Attributes),
     inherit(Superframe,Superattributes),
     new_attributes(Attributes,Superattributes,Attribute_list).
inherit(Frame,Attribute_list) :-
     instance(Frame,instance_of = Superframe,Attributes),
     inherit(Superframe,Superattributes),
     new_attributes(Attributes,Superattributes,Attribute_list).
```

The first inherit clause states the termination criterion of the recursion; the inheritance process is terminated as soon as the root of the taxonomy has been reached. Note that the termination condition is tested by means of a call to class in which the term superclass = nil has been specified as a second argument. If the root of the tree has been reached, then, as a result of the match found for the class call, the variable Attributes will have been instantiated to the list of attribute–value pairs present in the root frame. However, if the root of the taxonomy has not been reached as yet, the first inherit clause fails and the PROLOG interpreter tries to find a match with the second one. In this second inherit clause, the list of attribute–value pairs of the frame that is being investigated is extracted from it, again by means of a call to class; subsequently the list of all attribute–value pairs inherited by the superframe Superframe of the current frame is determined through a recursive call to inherit. The two lists thus obtained then are concatenated by means of a call to the new_attributes procedure in which exceptions are handled properly if necessary. The third inherit clause deals with instances instead of with classes. This clause has been specified as the last of the three inherit clauses for reasons of efficiency; since the third clause will only be used at most once in a specific inheritance process, many needless invocations of this clause are prevented by specifying this clause as the last one.

The three clauses given below give shape to the procedure `new_attributes`. This procedure takes three arguments. In the call to the `new_attributes` procedure from `inherit`, the second argument is instantiated to the list of all attribute–value pairs inherited by the superframe of the current frame, while the first argument is the list of attribute–value pairs specified in the frame itself. Initially, the third argument is uninstantiated; after the execution of `new_attributes` it will have been instantiated to the list of all attribute–value pairs that hold for the given frame.

```
new_attributes(Attributes,[],Attributes).
new_attributes(Attributes,[X = Value|Rest],
                          [X = Value|Rest_attributes]) :-
    not(member(X = _,Attributes)),
    new_attributes(Attributes,Rest,Rest_attributes).
new_attributes(Attributes,[_|Rest],Attribute_list) :-
    new_attributes(Attributes,Rest,Attribute_list).
```

The approach to handling exceptions employed in `new_attributes` is as follows. For each attribute–value pair in the second argument, whether it concerns an attribute for which some information is already present in the list of attribute–value pairs in the first argument is determined. The occurrence of the attribute name in that list indicates that another attribute–value pair concerning the same attribute has been specified lower in the taxonomy, that is, that an exception has been specified for the attribute. In that case, the new attribute–value pair will not be added to the list of all attribute–value pairs applicable to the frame. This process is described in a recursive manner. In studying the `new_attributes` procedure the reader should bear in mind that this procedure is called from `inherit` after the recursive call to itself, that is, after all information higher in the taxonomy has been collected. The first `new_attributes` clause states the termination criterion of the recursion; as soon as all elements in the second argument have been examined, the attribute–value pairs from the frame itself are added to the list of inherited information collected in the third argument. The second clause tests whether the first attribute–value pair of the list in its second argument specifies an attribute name that occurs in the list of attribute–value pairs from the frame itself, that is, in its first argument. If the attribute is not present in that list in the first argument, no exception has been specified for it and the attribute–value pair concerned is added to the third argument in the head of the clause. If on the other hand the attribute specified in the attribute–value pair under consideration is present in the list of attribute–value pairs from the frame itself, then the second clause fails; that specific attribute–value pair is subsequently disregarded in favour of the exception by means of the third `new_attributes` clause.

EXAMPLE 4.26

Consider once more the frames described in Horn clauses from Examples 4.24 and 4.25. Suppose that we enter the following query:

```
?- query_taxonomy(left_pulmonary_artery).
```

The PROLOG interpreter then returns the following answer:

```
left_pulmonary_artery
     [contains = blood_fluid,
      structure = tubular,
      wall = muscular,
      blood = oxygen_poor]
```

4.2.4 Single inheritance in LISP

In this section we shall examine an implementation of single inheritance in the LISP programming language. First of all, we have to discuss a representation for frames in terms of LISP expressions. The syntax of our LISP representation of frames is very close to the one defined in Section 4.2.2; the general idea is demonstrated in the following example.

EXAMPLE 4.27

Consider once more the class of arteries. The information that an artery is a blood vessel which contains blood that is oxygen-rich and flows from the heart to the tissues, and which furthermore has a muscular wall, is represented in the following LISP expression:

```
(CLASS artery
  (SUPERCLASS blood-vessel)
  (wall . muscular)
  (blood . oxygen-rich)
  (blood-flow . away-from-heart))
```

The class frame with the name `blood-vessel` specifies the information that blood vessels are tubular structures filled with blood:

```
(CLASS blood-vessel
  (SUPERCLASS nil)
  (contains . blood-fluid)
  (structure . tubular))
```

In this class definition, it is indicated by means of the subexpression `(SUPERCLASS nil)` that the `blood-vessel` class frame is the root of the tree-like taxonomy. Analogously, we represent the information that the left pulmonary artery is an artery containing oxygen-poor blood in the following expression:

```
(INSTANCE left-pulmonary-artery
  (INSTANCE-OF artery)
  (blood . oxygen-poor))
```

The keyword `INSTANCE` is used to indicate that the expression concerned defines an instance frame. Note that the attribute value `oxygen-poor` specified for the `blood` attribute in the instance `left-pulmonary-artery` is an exception to the attribute value for the same attribute specified in the `artery` class. Together, these frames will serve as an input example to our program.

The expressions representing the frames of a given taxonomy will have to be read in by the program at the beginning of a consultation and translated into internal data structures. We shall see that, in this process, each frame results in a fill-in for the following structure:

```
(defstruct (frame)
  (name nil)
  (type nil)
  (superframe nil)
  (attributes nil))
```

After the structure has been filled in, the field `name` contains the frame name, the field with the name `type` specifies the type of the frame, which is either `class` or `instance`, and the `superframe` field contains a reference to the superframe of the represented frame or `nil` if the frame is the root of the taxonomy. The field with the name `attributes` then contains the attribute part of the given frame. The attribute part is a list of pairs consisting of an attribute name and a value. Such a pair is represented internally by means of a fill-in for the following structure:

```
(defstruct (attribute)
  (name nil)
  (value nil))
```

The following recursive function `ParseFrames` parses the frame expressions which are stored in the file `in-stream`, and translates them into appropriate fill-ins for the structures described above:

```
(defun ParseFrames (in-stream taxonomy)
  (let ((frame (ReadExpression in-stream)))
    (cond ((eq frame 'eof) taxonomy)
          (t (ParseFrames in-stream
               (cons (ConstructFrame frame) taxonomy))))))
```

The frame expressions are read in by means of the function `ReadExpression`. This function has already been dealt with in Section 3.2.3 concerning the implementation of top-down inference; we shall not repeat its definition here. One by one the read-in expressions are bound to the local variable `frame` and subsequently translated into a structure by means of a call to the function `ConstructFrame`. The result of this function call is concatenated with the list of previously created frame structures in `taxonomy`. As soon as all frames have been parsed, the variable `frame` is bound to the symbol `eof` and the test `(eq frame 'eof)` returns the truth value `t`. The function `ParseFrames` then yields the value of the parameter `taxonomy` as its function value.

In the process of translating the frame expressions into LISP structures several functions are employed. We will discuss these functions in detail before we show the `ConstructFrame` function. The function `Type` is used for selecting the type of a frame. Recall that a frame is either of type `class` or of type `instance`:

```
(defun Type (frame)
  (first frame))
```

Similarly, the function `Name` selects the frame name from a given frame expression:

```
(defun Name (frame)
  (second frame))
```

For selecting from a frame expression the reference to the superframe of the frame concerned, the function `Superframe` is used:

```
(defun Superframe (frame)
  (let ((frm-rest (cddr frame)))
    (or (cadr (assoc 'superclass frm-rest))
        (cadr (assoc 'instance-of frm-rest)))))
```

Finally, the function `SelectAttributes` governs the translation of the attribute part of a frame into appropriate attribute structures:

```
(defun SelectAttributes (frame)
  (ConstructAttributes (cdddr frame)))
```

The last function calls the recursive function `ConstructAttributes` for creating the necessary attribute structures:

```
(defun ConstructAttributes (attr-list)
  (cond ((null attr-list) nil)
        (t (let ((attribute (first attr-list))
                 (rest-attr (rest attr-list)))
             (cons (make-attribute :name (first attribute)
                                   :value (second attribute))
                   (ConstructAttributes rest-attr))))))
```

The function make-attribute creates the proper attribute structure for a given attribute–value pair. The created structure is subsequently added to the beginning of the list of attribute structures processed earlier by means of the primitive function cons.

The functions described above are invoked from the function ConstructFrame; recall that this function is applied for the creation of an entire frame data structure.

```
(defun ConstructFrame (frame)
  (set (Name frame)
    (make-frame :name (Name frame)
                :type (Type frame)
                :superframe (Superframe frame)
                :attributes (SelectAttributes frame))))
```

Note that the set form is applied for creating an association between the frame name and the data structure in which the frame is stored internally.

The function Consultation shown below is the top-level function of the program:

```
(defun Consultation ( )
  (terpri)
  (princ "Name of the frame taxonomy: ")
  (let ((file (open (read-line))))
    (QueryTaxonomy (ParseFrames file nil))
    (close file)))
```

The function Consultation calls the function PraseFrames dealt with above for creating the frame taxonomy. Subsequently, the user is given the opportunity to query the taxonomy. The call to the function QueryTaxonomy allows for queries to be entered. This function prints a prompt and then reads the query entered by the user:

```
(defun QueryTaxonomy (taxonomy)
  (print 'query=>)
  (let ((query (read)))
    (cond ((eq query 'exit) (print 'bye))
          (t (GetAnswer query taxonomy)
             (QueryTaxonomy taxonomy)))))
```

A query consists of either a particular frame name or the keyword exit which is made available to the user for immediately quitting the consultation. Now consider the case in which the user has specified a frame name. The function GetAnswer is called with the query specified by the user substituted for the parameter query and the created frame taxonomy substituted for the parameter taxonomy. This function looks up all attribute–value pairs which hold for the frame with the given name.

To this end, the function GetAnswer recursively searches the list of frames in taxonomy until a frame having a name equal to the specified one has been found:

```
(defun GetAnswer (query taxonomy)
  (let ((frame (first taxonomy)))
    (cond ((null frame) (princ "Frame not present."))
          (t (if (Match query frame)
                 (pprint (Inherit nil frame))
                 (GetAnswer query (rest taxonomy)))))))
```

Each frame in taxonomy is compared with the query entered by the user by means of the function Match:

```
(defun Match (query frame)
  (eq query (frame-name frame)))
```

As soon as a match has been found, in GetAnswer the function Inherit is called. This function implements the actual inheritance algorithm. After the execution of Inherit has been finished, the gathered attribute–value pairs are printed to the screen by means of the primitive function pprint. The user is then offered the opportunity of entering a new query.

As has been mentioned before, the actual algorithm for single inheritance is implemented by the function Inherit. Informally speaking, this function just traverses the is-a links in the taxonomy; recall that an is-a link is specified in the superframe field of a frame structure.

```
(defun Inherit (attrs frame)
  (let ((collected-attr (NewAttributes attrs
                                       (frame-attributes frame)))
        (superframe (frame-superframe frame)))
    (cond ((null superframe) collected-attr)
          (t (Inherit collected-attr
                      (symbol-value superframe))))))
```

The cond form investigates whether the name of the superframe of the given frame equals nil. If this test succeeds, the inheritance process has reached the root of the tree-like taxonomy; the process then terminates and returns with the value of collected-attr, that is, with the list of collected attribute–value pairs. In the other case, the process continues by recursively collecting attribute–value pairs for the given frame.

The function NewAttributes called from Inherit investigates whether or not the attribute–value pairs that have been found in the frame frame should be added to the list of previously collected attribute–value pairs. To this end, NewAttributes examines the new attribute–value pairs one by one by recursively traversing the list `frame-attr`:

```
(defun NewAttributes (old-attr frame-attr)
  (let ((attribute (first frame-attr)))
    (cond ((null attribute) old-attr)
          (t (if (MemberOf attribute old-attr)
                 (NewAttributes old-attr (rest frame-attr))
                 (NewAttributes (cons (AttrValuePair attribute)
                                      old-attr)
                                (rest frame-attr)))))))
```

For each attribute–value pair in `frame-attr`, the function `MemberOf` determines whether or not the attribute name specified in the pair already occurs in the list of attribute–value pairs `old-attr`. If the attribute name occurs in `old-attr`, the attribute–value pair being investigated is disregarded and the function `NewAttributes` is called recursively for the remaining attribute–value pairs. However, if the attribute name does not yet occur in `old-attr`, the pair is added as a dotted pair to the beginning of the list of inherited attribute–value pairs.

Within the function `MemberOf` the primitive function `assoc` is used for checking whether an attribute name occurs in a given list of attribute–value pairs:

```
(defun MemberOf (attribute a-list)
  (assoc (attribute-name attribute) a-list))
```

The function `AttrValuePair` which is equally called from `NewAttributes` returns a dotted pair of which the first element is an attribute name and the second element is the associated value:

```
(defun AttrValuePair (attribute)
  (cons (attribute-name attribute)
        (attribute-value attribute)))
```

We finish this section by giving an example of the use of the program discussed.

EXAMPLE 4.28

Consider once more the frame expressions in Example 4.27. We suppose that these frame expressions are contained in the file named `vessels`. A possible consultation of this tiny knowledge base is as follows:

```
> (Consultation)
Name of frame taxonomy: vessels
query=> left-pulmonary-artery
```

```
((structure . tubular)
 (contains . blood-fluid)
 (blood-flow . away-from-heart)
 (wall . muscular)
 (blood . oxygen-poor))
query => artery
((structure . tubular)
 (contains . blood-fluid)
 (blood-flow . away-from-heart)
 (blood . oxygen-rich)
 (wall . muscular))
query => exit
bye
```

4.2.5 Inheritance and attribute facets

In our treatment of inheritance of attribute values in the preceding sections, the way in which these values were obtained could not be specified. In many practical applications, however, it may be important to know whether an attribute value for a given instance has been obtained by inheritance or has been explicitly specified in some way. In the latter case, the user is likely to have more confidence in the accuracy of the value than in the former case where the value has only been stated for an entire class of instances. Furthermore, it often is desirable to be able to compute attribute values based on the values of some other attributes which have been obtained during a consultation. The frame formalism discussed in the preceding sections is not able to cope with such situations. It is not surprising therefore that most frame formalisms employed in systems which are actually used in practical applications offer special language constructs, called *facets*, for the purpose of handling the situations mentioned above. In this section, we shall discuss some of the facets that are most frequently met in literature.

A facet may be viewed as a property associated with an attribute. The most common facet is the *value facet* referring to the actual value of the attribute. The value stored in a value facet of an attribute is assumed to have been established with absolute certainty. Since it is often difficult to specify with certainty in advance the values that attributes of instances of a class will adopt, the initial values for class attributes are often specified in *default facets*. These default values may be overridden as the consultation proceeds. Note that our algorithm for single inheritance with exceptions already exhibits this behaviour; the difference, however, is that when facets are used an inherited default attribute value is still marked as being a default value. In general, it depends on the characteristics of the problem area which part of the attribute values will be specified in a default facet and which part is specified in a value facet.

The values specified in the default facets of attributes in a frame taxonomy together offer a typical picture of the domain of discourse.

The third facet we discuss is the *demon facet*, or *demon* for short. A demon is a procedure that will be invoked at a particular time during the manipulation of the frame in which it has been specified. The condition under which a demon is activated depends on the type of the demon. An *if-needed demon* is activated the moment an attribute value is needed but not yet known for the attribute it is attached to. An *if-added demon* is activated the moment a value is entered into the value facet of the attribute concerned. An *if-removed demon* is invoked the moment a value is removed from the value facet of the attribute it is attached to. This way of integrating procedural and declarative knowledge is called *procedural attachment*. The frame formalism gains enormously in expressive power by the incorporation of demons. Using demons and attribute values, for example, it is possible to represent local state changes due to computation; the state of the computation at a certain moment during a consultation is described by the values the attributes have at that moment.

So far, we have discussed inheritance as the only method for frame manipulation. It will be evident, however, that inheritance alone does not provide a full inference engine; inheritance accounts for only a small portion of the inference engine of most frame-based systems. In many systems, demons are used to influence the overall control exerted in manipulating the frame taxonomy; an if-added demon, for instance, may be used to direct the control to a particular frame as a side-effect. However, great care must be taken in applying such techniques; when such side-effects are applied very often, the behaviour of the system will become difficult to fathom. This, however, is not true for every use of demons. An if-needed demon, for instance, can be an algorithm for asking the user for further information or for calculating a value, for example in handling time-dependent information.

EXAMPLE 4.29

Consider a real-time expert system for controlling some ongoing process which has the possibility to read off several gauges indicating the status of this process. The activation of an if-needed demon may result in reading off some of the gauges as soon as information concerning the status of the process is required.

To conclude this informal introduction to demons, we observe that frames are often used as a means of partitioning a given set of production rules. Each frame then has command of a certain partition of the set of rules. In a frame taxonomy supporting this idea, a demon is used to initiate the consultation of such a partition. An example of such a use of demons will be discussed in Chapter 7 in connection with the CENTAUR system, the development of which has been based on some of the principles discussed here. In the same chapter LOOPS will be treated. LOOPS is an environment for object-oriented programming in which frames are considered as being autonomous objects that are able to communicate with each other by means of demons (then called *methods*). Besides the three general facets discussed above it is of course possible to define several domain-dependent facets for a given application where appropriate.

With reference to the foregoing discussion, the following definition states a simple, implementation-oriented formalism for frames allowing for facets to be attached to attributes; once more we have refrained from type information.

Definition: A frame is an expression of the following form:

<frame> ::= <class> | <instance>

<class> ::= ***class*** <class-name> ***is***
  superclass <super-spec>;
  <attributes>
end

<instance> ::= ***instance*** <instance-name> ***is***
  instance-of <super-spec>;
  <attributes>
end

<super-spec> ::= <class-name> | ***nil***

<attributes> ::= <attribute-facet-pair>
{; <attribute-facet-pair>}* |
  <empty>

<attribute-facet-pair> ::= <attribute-name> =
  (<facet>{,<facet>}*)

<facet> ::= <facet-name> <value> |
  demon <demon-type>
  <demon-call>

<facet-name> ::= ***value*** | ***default***

<demon-type> ::= ***if-needed*** | ***if-added*** |
  if-removed

<value> ::= <elementary-constant> |
  <instance-name>

<empty> ::=

Again, a class specification equal to the special symbol ***nil*** is used to indicate that the frame concerned is the root of the tree-like taxonomy.

EXAMPLE 4.30

The frame shown below describes the class of arteries, which is a subclass of the class of blood-vessels:

class *artery* ***is***
  superclass *blood-vessel*;
  wall = (***value*** *muscular*);
  blood = (***default*** *oxygen-rich*);
  blood-pressure = (***default*** 20);
  blood-flow = (***default*** 4);
  resistance = (***demon if-needed***
        R(*blood-pressure*,*blood-flow*))
end

The frame has five attributes. For the attribute with the name *wall* a value facet has been specified, because we are absolutely certain that all arteries have a muscular wall. For the three attributes with default facets things are different. We already know that not all arteries contain oxygen-rich blood, hence the default facet for the *blood* attribute. The attribute *blood-pressure* represents the difference in blood pressure between the pressure at the beginning and at the end of an artery. The value specified for this attribute and the value for the *blood-flow* attribute are average values for middle-sized arteries. Evidently, such knowledge is best represented in default facets. Finally, we have one attribute, the *resistance* attribute, for which an if-needed demon has been specified for calculating a value on request. The demon call *R*(*blood-pressure*,*blood-flow*) represents the call to the procedure *R* for computing the resistance to the blood flow in the given artery using the formula

$$resistance = \frac{blood\text{-}pressure}{blood\text{-}flow}$$

The values of the attributes *blood-pressure* and *blood-flow* are passed to the procedure.

Since we now allow for various facets to be attached to attributes, it has become necessary to incorporate information concerning the order in which such facets are considered in our algorithm for single inheritance. Basically, there are two types of inheritance of attributes with facets, differing only in the order in which the facets are dealt with:

- *N-inheritance*
- *Z-inheritance*

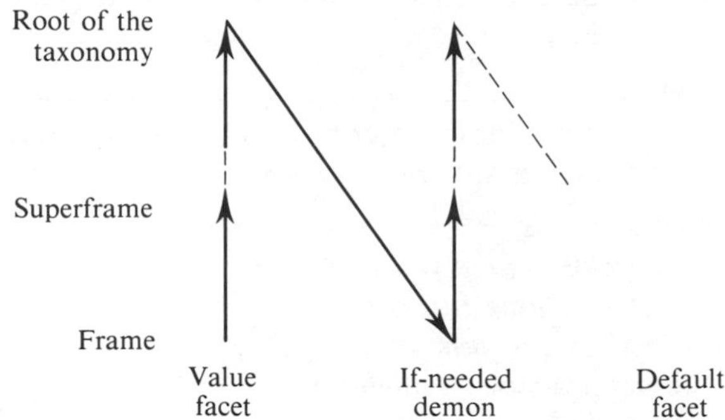

Figure 4.13 *N*-inheritance.

These types of inheritance owe their respective names to the way the taxonomy is traversed.

The intuition underlying *N*-inheritance is that any value in a value facet appearing in a frame or in one of its generalizations is closer to the real value than any value obtained from a default facet or from invoking a demon. As usual, of all the values of an attribute stored in value facets in the various frames in the frame taxonomy the most specific one will be inherited by the frame of concern. The basic idea underlying the use of *Z*-inheritance is that any specific attribute value appearing in a frame, whether obtained from a value facet, from invoking a demon or from a default facet, is more reliable than any more general attribute value no matter in which facet it has been specified; however, within a given frame, values specified in a value facet are preferred over those computed by a demon or provided by a default facet.

The procedures for *N*- and *Z*-inheritance can now be described informally as follows. Applying *N*-inheritance, an attribute value is determined by first examining the value facet of the frame concerned. If no value facet has been specified, the value facet attached to the corresponding attribute in the superframe of the frame is examined. This process is repeated until, in a frame higher in the taxonomy, a value facet has been found or the root of the taxonomy has been reached. If the process has not yielded an attribute value as yet, control is returned to the frame of interest, and the process is repeated for the if-needed demons. Finally, if this process has still not yielded an attribute value, the default facets will be examined in a similar way. Figure 4.13 depicts the behaviour of *N*-inheritance graphically. Applying *Z*-inheritance, an attribute value is determined by successively examining the value facet, the if-needed demon and the default facet of the frame concerned before the frames higher in the taxonomy are considered. Figure 4.14 shows the behaviour of *Z*-inheritance.

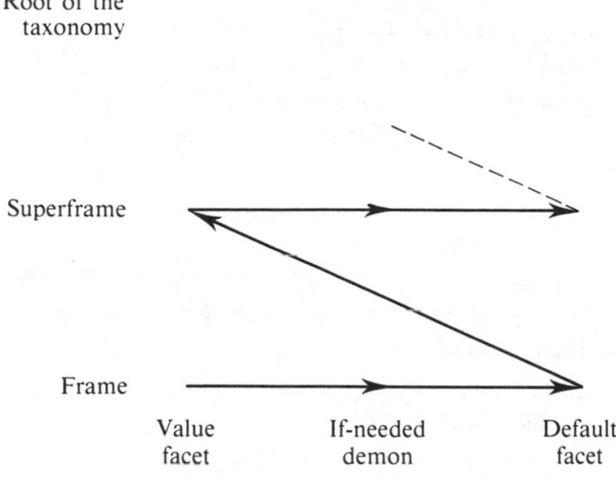

Figure 4.14 *Z*-inheritance.

4.2.6 *Z*-inheritance in PROLOG

In this section we shall develop a simple PROLOG program that implements *Z*-inheritance. The representation of frames used in this section closely resembles the Horn clause representation for frames chosen in Section 4.2.3. However, in this section we extend our representation to allow for facets of attributes. Recall the following Horn clause description of a class frame:

```
class(<class-name>,superclass = <superframe>,<attributes>).
```

The predicate `class` has the same meaning as before, just as the first two arguments of `class` do. However, the third argument <attributes>, which is again supposed to contain a list of attributes, now differs from the previous representation by allowing for facets to be attached to the specified attributes. The following example illustrates the chosen representation.

EXAMPLE 4.31

Consider the following class frame which gives a description of the class of arteries, where *R*(*blood-pressure*,*blood-flow*) is a demon call for computing the resistance to the blood flow in the given artery just as discussed in Example 4.30.

> ***class*** *artery* ***is***
>   ***superclass*** *blood-vessel*;
>   *wall* = (***value*** *muscular*);
>   *blood* = (***default*** *oxygen-rich*);
>   *resistance* = (***demon if-needed***
>   *R*(*blood-pressure*,*blood-flow*))
> ***end***

Note that, unlike in Example 4.30, we have not specified the attributes *blood-pressure* and *blood-flow* in this class. These attributes therefore have to be specified in all instances of the class separately. The class frame shown above is represented in a Horn clause as follows:

```
class(artery,
      superclass = blood_vessel,
      [wall = (value,muscular),
       blood = (default,oxygen_rich),
       resistance = (if_needed,r(blood_pressure,blood_flow))]).
```

The Horn clause representation for instances discussed in Section 4.2.3 is extended in a similar way to allow for facets.

We now turn our attention to a possible implementation of *Z*-inheritance with exceptions in PROLOG. The program is developed along the same lines as the program in Section 4.2.3. The main procedure of the program is the `inherit` procedure, which upon invocation starts a search process for a value for the specified attribute:

```
inherit(Frame,Attribute) :-
     get_facet(Frame,Attribute,Value,Frame),
     print_value(Frames,Attribute,Value).
inherit(_,_) :-
     nl,
     write('No value has been found for the specified attribute.').
```

In a call to `inherit`, the variables `Frame` and `Attribute` have to be instantiated to a frame name and an attribute name, respectively. The procedure `get_facet` called from `inherit` takes care of the actual inheritance. The `print_value` procedure just prints the value found for the specified attribute to the screen; the implementation of this output procedure is left to the reader.

The actual searching for a value for the attribute of concern is done by the recursive procedure `get_facet`. This procedure is called from `inherit` with an extra fourth argument. We shall see that this fourth argument is needed in case one of the superframes of the given frame specifies a demon for the attribute of concern which requires for its proper execution a number of attribute values from the frame that started the inference.

```
get_facet(Frame,Attribute,Value,_) :-
    get_attributes(Frame,List_of_attributes),
    search(Attribute,List_of_attributes,Value,value).
get_facet(Frame,Attribute,Value,Parameter_frame) :-
    get_attributes(Frame,List_of_attributes),
    search(Attribute,List_of_attributes,Demon,if_needed),
    Demon =.. [X|L],!,
    get_actual_values(Parameter_frame,L,Value_list),
    Parameter_demon =.. [X,Value|Value_list],
    call(Parameter_demon).
get_facet(Frame,Attribute,Value,_) :-
    get_attributes(Frame,List_of_attributes),
    search(Attribute,List_of_attributes,Value,default).
get_facet(Frame,Attribute,Value,Parameter_frame) :-
    get_superframe(Frame,Superframe),
    get_facet(Superframe,Attribute,Value,Parameter_frame).
```

The first `get_facet` clause investigates whether the frame `Frame` contains a value facet for the attribute `Attribute`. For this purpose, the list of attributes is selected from the frame by means of `get_attributes`; this list is traversed by means of the procedure `search`. Both procedures will be described shortly. Here we only note that the last argument to the call to `search` indicates by means of the keyword `value` that this procedure only has to examine the value facet. If in the frame `Frame` a value facet is found for the attribute, the variable `Value` will be instantiated to the value specified in that facet. If the frame `Frame` does not contain a value facet for the attribute `Attribute`, the first `get_facet` clause fails and the second one is tried. This second clause investigates whether the frame concerned contains an if-needed demon for the specified attribute. If indeed a demon is present for the attribute, then the demon is executed in the context of the frame for which the `inherit` procedure was invoked initially. Note that the name of that frame is specified in the fourth argument of the clause. The correct demon call is created in the third, fourth and fifth condition of the clause. The demon is actually executed by means of the built-in predicate `call`. The third `get_facet` clause has a meaning similar to that of the first clause with the only difference that it deals with the default instead of with the value facet. If these three clauses fail to return a value for the given attribute `Attribute`, the fourth `get_facet` clause is executed. The superframe of the frame `Frame` is determined by means of the `get_superframe` procedure. The procedure `get_facet` is then called recursively for that superframe. Note that the fourth argument of `get_facet` is passed unchanged: the variable `Parameter_frame` is still instantiated to the initially specified frame.

We now consider the procedure `get_actual_values` which is called from the second `get_facet` clause. First, however, we take a closer look at the creation of the proper demon call. After execution of `Demon =.. [X|L]` we have that X is instantiated to the name of the procedure to be invoked, and furthermore that L is instantiated to a list of the attributes of which the values have to be passed to the procedure with the name X. The procedure get_actual_values now finds the values of the attributes named in L by means of a recursive call to inherit for each of them, beginning with the frame that started the computation:

```
get_actual_values(_,[],[]).
get_actual_values(Frame,[Attribute|L],[Value|Value_list]) :-
     inherit(Frame,Attribute,Value,Frame),!,
     get_actual_values(Frame,L,Value_list).
```

From the get_facet procedure three more procedures are invoked. The procedure get_superframe finds the superframe of a given frame in the taxonomy:

```
get_superframe(Frame,Superframe) :-
     class(Frame,superclass = Superframe,_),!,
     not(Superframe = nil).
get_superframe(Frame,Superframe) :-
     instance(Frame,instance_of = Superframe,_),!,
     not(Superframe = nil).
```

The first get_superframe clause finds the superframe of a class frame; the second clause does the same for an instance frame. Note that a call to get_superframe fails if the root of the taxonomy has been reached.

The procedure get_attributes selects the list of attributes from a given frame:

```
get_attributes(Frame,List_of_attributes) :-
     class(Frame,_,List_of_attributes),!.
get_attributes(Frame,List_of_attributes) :-
     instance(Frame,_,List_of_attributes),!.
```

The procedure search still remains to be discussed. It merely traverses a given list of attributes with associated facets. This procedure takes four arguments. The first argument passed to search from the inherit procedure is instantiated to an attribute name, the second argument contains a list of attributes with facets, and the fourth argument indicates the facet type to be looked for. The third argument is initially uninstantiated.

```
search(_,[],_,_) :- !,fail.
search(Attribute,[Attribute = (Facet,Value)|_],Value,Facet) :- !.
search(Attribute,[_|Rest],Value,Facet) :-
     search(Attribute,Rest,Value,Facet).
```

The first and second search clause together define the termination criterion for the recursion. If the list of attributes is empty, then apparently no appropriate value is found for the given attribute. In this case, the call to search fails. The second clause describes the situation in which the attribute Attribute occurs in the head of the list of attributes with the indicated facet. The variable Value is then instantiated to the attribute value found in the facet. The third clause specifies the recursive call to search for the remainder of the attribute list.

EXAMPLE 4.32

Consider the following frame taxonomy represented in PROLOG clauses:

```
class(artery,
      superclass = blood_vessel,
      [wall = (value,muscular),
       blood = (default,oxygen_rich),
       resistance = (if_needed,r(blood_pressure,blood_flow))]).

instance(left_brachial_artery,
         instance_of = artery,
         [blood_pressure = (value 4),
          blood_flow = (value 20)]).

r(Value,Pressure,Flow) :- Value is Pressure / Flow.
```

The value for the attribute resistance is now obtained from the following query:

```
?- inherit(left_brachial_artery,resistance).
```

The PROLOG interpreter returns with:

```
resistance = 0.20
```

4.2.7 Subtyping in tree-like taxonomies

In Section 4.2.1 we introduced a syntax for a frame formalism which allowed for declarations of attribute types. Until now we have disregarded such type information. In this section, however, we shall consider type information and discuss the properties of the relation defined by the superclass links now viewed as a relation between attribute types. In discussing this relation in the context of type information, it is more common to speak of the *supertype relation*, or conversely of the *subtype relation*; exploiting the subtype relation is known as *subtyping*. In this section, we study subtyping in tree-like frame taxonomies in which attribute–type pairs for a particular attribute may occur more than once.

It will be evident that it is desirable to have type information available in a frame taxonomy; attribute types may be exploited for checking entered values to see that they are of the proper type. This way, an 'unexpected' attribute value can be detected as soon as it is entered into the attribute concerned; in this case, the attribute value is considered to be erroneous.

EXAMPLE 4.33

Consider a frame taxonomy representing information concerning the human cardiovascular system. We assume that the class frame with the name *artery* has an attribute *mean-blood-pressure* that describes the mean blood pressure in mmHg in the arteries in a normal, healthy human being. In the arteries the mean blood pressure ranges from 30 to 100 mmHg. This information may be stored as type information for the *mean-blood-pressure* attribute. When in a patient a mean blood pressure of 10 mmHg is found for a specific artery, say the ulnar artery, this is an unexpected value and probably some action has to be taken. The specification of an attribute type can be further specialized, that is, narrowed down, as the frame it is specified in is further specialized. Suppose for example that the *artery* class has three specializations: the *large-artery*, the *small-artery* and the *arteriole* class. In the class representing the large arteries, the information for the *mean-blood-pressure* attribute is further specialized to the range 90–100 mmHg, in the *small-artery* class to the range 60–90 mmHg and in the *arteriole* class to 30–60 mmHg.

The following example is a more formal example in which we have specified some type information in the manner prescribed by the frame formalism.

EXAMPLE 4.34

Consider again the class of blood vessels. The following class representation shows some attribute types for this class of objects:

> ***class*** *blood-vessel* ***is***
>   ***superclass nil***;
>   *blood* : {*oxygen-rich*,*oxygen-poor*};
>   *wall* : {*muscular*,*fibrous*,*mixed*}
> ***end***

The class of arteries is a subclass of the class of blood vessels. It is represented in the following class frame:

> ***class*** *artery* ***is***
> ***superclass*** *blood-vessel*;
> *wall* : {*muscular,mixed*};
> *wall-thickness* : ***real***
> ***end***

Every attribute type specified in the class frame with the name *blood-vessel* is now taken to apply to the class *artery* as well, as long as it has not been further specialized in the *artery* class itself. Note that both classes contain a type declaration for the attribute with the name *wall*. The type declaration included in the *blood-vessel* class is more general than the one in the *artery* class.

From these two examples, we may conclude that subtyping involves the relationship between attributes occurring in the classes as well as the relationship between the types of those attributes. Before going into more detail, we will first introduce some new notions that will be used in formalizing subtyping in a tree-like frame taxonomy. We shall see that it is convenient to have some representation of the set of attribute names that are of concern to a specific class. Since an attribute type may itself be a class, it does not suffice simply to list the attribute names actually occurring in a class. Therefore, we associate with a class a set of so-called attribute sequences.

Definition: Let A be the set of all attribute names occurring in a frame taxonomy. An *attribute sequence a* is a string of the form $a_1: \cdots :a_n$, where $a_i \in A$, $i = 1, \ldots, n$, $n \geq 0$, that is, an attribute sequence is composed of elements from A separated by colons. The attribute sequence comprising no elements at all, that is, for which $n = 0$, is called the *empty attribute sequence* and is denoted by ε. From now on, we shall use A^* to denote the (infinite) set of all attribute sequences constructed from A.

Note that we have not imposed any restriction on for example the order in which attribute names are allowed to occur in an attribute sequence.

With every class frame in a frame taxonomy we now associate a subset of the set of all attribute sequences.

Definition: Let A^* be a set of attribute sequences associated with a frame taxonomy as defined above. Let y be a class frame in the taxonomy. With y we associate the set $D(y) \subseteq A^*$, called the *domain* for y, defined by:

(1) $\varepsilon \in D(y)$.

(2) For every attribute name a specified in y, we have that $a \in D(y)$.

(3) For every attribute with the name a of type w specified in y, $D(y)$ contains the attribute sequences $a : b$ for all elements $b \in D(w)$.

(4) The set $D(z)$ of attribute sequences associated with the superframe z of y is a subset of $D(y)$.

EXAMPLE 4.35

Consider the following class frame with the name *blood-vessel*:

> ***class*** *blood-vessel* ***is***
>   ***superclass nil***;
>   *volume* : *cubic-measure*
> ***end***

This frame specifies an attribute *volume* providing information concerning the blood volume for the specializations of the class. The type *cubic-measure* of this attribute is a class frame itself. This class is defined as follows:

> ***class*** *cubic-measure* ***is***
>   ***superclass nil***;
>   *size* : ***real***;
>   *unit* : $\{mm^3, cm^3, dm^3, m^3\}$
> ***end***

The set of attribute names in the taxonomy consisting of these two frames is equal to $A = \{volume, size, unit\}$. The set of attribute sequences associated with the class frame *blood-vessel* is the set $D(blood\text{-}vessel) = \{\varepsilon, volume, volume : size, volume : unit\}$; the domain for the *cubic-measure* class is the set $D(cubic\text{-}measure) = \{\varepsilon, size, unit\}$.

In the following definition we introduce the notion of a type function for computing the types of the attribute sequences associated with a given frame.

Definition: Let A^* be the set of attribute sequences in a frame taxonomy. Let K be the set of class names in that frame taxonomy (including the standard classes and the most general class ***nil***). For each class $y_i \in K$, let $D(y_i) \subseteq A^*$ be the set of attribute sequences associated with y_i as in the preceding definition. Now, for each $y_i \in K$, we define a *type function* τ_i: $A^* \rightarrow K$ as follow:

(1) For the empty attribute sequence ε, we have that $\tau_i(\varepsilon) = y_i$.
(2) For each attribute sequence $a \equiv a_1: \cdots : a_n \in D(y_i)$, $n \geqslant 1$, we have that $\tau_i(a) = t$ where t is the type of the attribute with the name a_n.
(3) For each $a \in A^* \setminus D(y_i)$, we have $\tau_i(a) =$ ***nil***.

EXAMPLE 4.36

Consider the frame taxonomy consisting of the two class frames from the previous example. The set K of classes in this taxonomy equals

$$K = \{\textbf{\textit{nil}}, \textit{blood-vessel}, \textit{cubic-measure}, \textbf{\textit{real}}, \{mm^3, cm^3, dm^3, m^3\}\}$$

Let $D(\textit{blood-vessel})$ be the set of attribute sequences associated with the *blood-vessel* class as in the previous example. For this class, the type function τ_1: $A^* \rightarrow K$ is defined by

$\tau_1(\varepsilon) = \textit{blood-vessel}$
$\tau_1(\textit{volume}) = \textit{cubic-measure}$
$\tau_1(\textit{volume} : \textit{size}) = \textbf{\textit{real}}$
$\tau_1(\textit{volume} : \textit{unit}) = \{mm^3, cm^3, dm^3, m^3\}$
$\tau_1(a) = \textbf{\textit{nil}}$ for all $a \in A^* \setminus D(\textit{blood-vessel})$

Let $D(\textit{cubic-measure})$ be the domain for the class frame *cubic-measure*. For this class, the type function τ_2: $A^* \rightarrow K$ is defined as follows:

$\tau_2(\varepsilon) = \textit{cubic-measure}$
$\tau_2(\textit{size}) = \textbf{\textit{real}}$
$\tau_2(\textit{unit}) = \{mm^3, cm^3, dm^3, m^3\}$
$\tau_2(a) = \textbf{\textit{nil}}$ for all $a \in A^* \setminus D(\textit{cubic-measure})$

We are now ready to consider a type semantics for the superclass links in a taxonomy and to introduce the notion of a subtype.

Definition: Let y_1 and y_2 be two class frames in a tree-like frame taxonomy. Let A^* be the set of attribute sequences in the taxonomy. Furthermore, let $D(y_i)$ be the set of attribute sequences associated with the class frame y_i, $i = 1,2$. Now, let τ_i be the type function associated with y_i. We say that y_1 is a *subtype* of y_2, denoted by $y_1 \leqslant y_2$, if the following two properties hold:

(1) $D(y_2) \subseteq D(y_1)$.

(2) For each attribute sequence $a \in A^*$, we have that $\tau_1(a) \leqslant \tau_2(a)$.

We say that a taxonomy is *correctly typed* if the superclass links in the taxonomy satisfy the properties of the relation $\leqslant$ from the previous definition. Note that we now have that the meaning of the subtype relation can be described in terms of set inclusion $\subseteq$. We associate with each type t a subset $I(t)$ of elements from a domain of discourse U such that, if for two types t_1 and t_2 we have that $t_1 \leqslant t_2$, then we have that the property $I(t_1) \subseteq I(t_2)$ holds.

EXAMPLE 4.37

Consider Example 4.34 once more. We have that the *blood-vessel* class is a superframe of the *artery* class. The set of attribute sequences associated with the *blood-vessel* class is equal to the set

$$D(\textit{blood-vessel}) = \{\varepsilon, \textit{blood}, \textit{wall}\}$$

The domain for the *artery* class is equal to

$$D(\textit{artery}) = \{\varepsilon, \textit{blood}, \textit{wall}, \textit{wall-thickness}\}$$

So the first condition in the preceding definition is satisfied since we have that $D(\textit{blood-vessel}) \subseteq D(\textit{artery})$. The type function τ_1: $A^* \to K$ associated with the class *artery* is defined by:

$\tau_1(\varepsilon) = \textit{artery}$
$\tau_1(\textit{blood}) = \{\textit{oxygen-rich}, \textit{oxygen-poor}\}$
$\tau_1(\textit{wall}) = \{\textit{muscular}, \textit{mixed}\}$
$\tau_1(a) =$ ***nil*** for all $a \in A^* \setminus D(\textit{artery})$

The type function τ_2: $A^* \to K$ associated with the class *blood-vessel* is defined by:

$\tau_2(\varepsilon) = \textit{blood-vessel}$
$\tau_2(\textit{blood}) = \{\textit{oxygen-rich}, \textit{oxygen-poor}\}$
$\tau_2(\textit{wall}) = \{\textit{muscular}, \textit{fibrous}, \textit{mixed}\}$
$\tau_2(a) =$ ***nil*** for each $a \in A^* \setminus D(\textit{blood-vessel})$

The reader can easily verify that $\tau_1(a) \leqslant \tau_2(a)$ for each $a \in A^*$. We conclude that the frame taxonomy is correctly typed.

4.3 Frames and multiple inheritance

So far, we have dealt only with tree-like frame taxonomies and single inheritance. In this section, we introduce more general frame taxonomies. The frame formalism that has been defined in Section 4.2.1 is extended by admitting in class frames more than one class name in the superclass link field; in this way, it is possible for a class to have more than one superclass. The graphical representation of such a taxonomy then takes the form of a general directed graph instead of a tree. In the following, we shall restrict the discussion to acyclic directed graphs, because trivial cycles obtained from the reflexivity property of the subclass relation, which are the only cycles that can be constructed when the superclass relation is viewed as a partial order, will not be explicitly indicated. The inheritance algorithm associated with graph-like frame taxonomies is known as *multiple* inheritance. In discussing multiple inheritance, we assume that more than one value for an attribute may have been specified in a frame taxonomy, that is, we allow for exceptions; we speak of *multiple inheritance with exceptions*. However, we shall restrict the discussion to value facets of attributes only. Note that the theory developed in this section should hold for tree-like frame taxonomies and general graph-like taxonomies alike, since the former are just a special case of the latter.

4.3.1 Multiple inheritance of attribute values

Multiple inheritance differs from single inheritance mainly in the way it handles attributes occurring more than once in a taxonomy with different values. As in Section 4.2.2, we shall call such attribute values *exceptions*. Recall that, when exceptions have been specified, conflicting information may be derived due to the inheritance of mutually exclusive values. In Section 4.2.2, however, we have seen that the problem of handling exceptions is easily solved in the case of single inheritance in a tree-like taxonomy; inheritance is taken as the process for finding a value for an attribute that starts with a given vertex in the tree, which moves along the branches of the tree towards the root and stops as soon as a value for the attribute of concern has been obtained. This algorithm always finds at most one attribute value. Unfortunately, the problem is much more complicated in the case of multiple inheritance in a general graph-like taxonomy. The algorithm for multiple inheritance in graph-like taxonomies in which exceptions occur will have to incorporate a method for explicitly deciding which value of an attribute obtained from different superframes is to be preferred. The main part of this section will be devoted to the development of such an algorithm for multiple inheritance with exceptions.

To start with, some new notions and notational conventions are introduced, including a more compact notation for the representation of frame information which has a stronger mathematical flavour than the implementation-oriented syntax introduced in the preceding section. From now on, $K = \{y_1, y_2, \ldots, y_n\}$, $n \geqslant 0$, will denote a fixed set of class frames, and $I = \{x_1, x_2, \ldots, x_m\}$, $m \geqslant 0$, will denote a fixed set of instance frames; the sets I and K are disjoint. The set of frames F is equal to $I \cup K$.

In a frame taxonomy, the superclass links are viewed as members of a relation between class frames. In the following definition we indicate that this relation may be viewed as a partial order.

Definition: Let K denote the fixed set of class frames. The *subclass relation* $\leqslant$ is a binary relation on K, that is $\leqslant \subseteq K \times K$, that defines a partial order on the set K. For a pair $(x,y) \in \leqslant$, denoted by $x \leqslant y$, it is said that *x is a subclass of y*.

Recall that, since the subclass relation $\leqslant$ defines a partial order on the set of class frames K, it satisfies the properties mentioned in Section 4.1.1.

The instance-of links are viewed as members of a relation between the set of instance frames I and the set of class frame K. We assume that an instance belongs to exactly one class. The instance-of links are therefore best formalized by means of a function.

Definition: Let I denote the fixed set of instance frames and K the fixed set of classes. The *instance-of function* $\ll$ is a mapping from I to K, that is, $\ll: I \rightarrow K$. In what follows, we shall denote $\ll(x) = y$ by $x \ll y$; we say that *x is an instance of y*.

The subclass relation and the instance-of function introduced in these two definitions describe only reference information. The following definition introduces another relation meant to arrive at a full language for the specification of frame information.

Definition: Let F be the set of frames such that $F = I \cup K$, where I is the set of instance frames in F, and K the set of class frames in F. Let A be a fixed set of attribute names and let C be a fixed set of constants. Then, a triple $(x,a,c) \in F \times A \times C$, denoted by $x[a = c]$, is called an *attribute–value specification.* An *attribute–value relation* Θ is a ternary relation on F, A and C, that is, $\Theta \subseteq F \times A \times C$.

In the previous definition we have explicitly specified a set of constants C. Note, however, that this set of constants may be identified with the set of instances I, as we have done in the preceding sections. An attribute–value specification $x[a = c]$ expresses that in the frame x the attribute a has the constant value c. The notions introduced in the foregoing definitions are now used formally to define a frame taxonomy.

Definition: Let I be the set of instances and K the set of classes. Furthermore, let A be the set of attribute names and C the set of constants. I, K and A are disjoint. Now, let N be the quadruple $N = (I,K,A,C)$. Furthermore, let the relations $\leqslant$ and Θ, and the function $\ll$ be defined as above. Then, a *taxonomy* T is a quadruple $T = (N,\Theta,\ll,\leqslant)$.

We now give an example of the frame formalism we have just defined and its relation with the frame formalism introduced in Section 4.2.1.

EXAMPLE 4.38

Consider the information specified in the following three classes represented in the frame formalism from Section 4.2.1:

```
class blood-vessel is
  superclass nil;
  contains = blood-fluid
end

class artery is
  superclass blood-vessel;
  blood = oxygen-rich;
  wall = muscular
end

class vein is
  superclass blood-vessel;
  wall = fibrous
end
```

```
instance aorta is
  instance-of artery;
  diameter = 2.5
end
```

In the specified taxonomy, we have that $I = \{aorta\}$ is the set of instance frames and that $K = \{artery, vein, blood\text{-}vessel\}$ is the set of classes. Furthermore, we have that $A = \{contains, blood, wall, diameter\}$, and $C = \{blood\text{-}fluid, oxygen\text{-}rich, muscular, fibrous, 2.5\}$. We have the following set of attribute–value specifications:

$$\begin{aligned}\Theta = \{&blood\text{-}vessel[contains = blood\text{-}fluid],\\ &artery[blood = oxygen\text{-}rich],\\ &artery[wall = muscular],\\ &vein[wall = fibrous],\\ &aorta[diameter = 2.5]\}\end{aligned}$$

The function $\ll$ and the relation $\leq$ are defined by

$$\begin{aligned}&aorta \ll artery\\ &artery \leq blood\text{-}vessel\\ &vein \leq blood\text{-}vessel\end{aligned}$$

Now, $T = (N,\Theta,\ll,\leq)$ is the taxonomy shown above, this time represented using our new formalism.

Just as before, a taxonomy $T = (N,\Theta,\ll,\leq)$ can be represented graphically by means of an acyclic directed graph in which the vertices represent the frames in I and K, and the arcs represent the relation $\leq$ and the function $\ll$. A vertex is assumed to have an internal structure representing the collection of attribute–value specifications associated with the frame by the relation Θ. In the graphical representation, an attribute–value specification is depicted next to the vertex it belongs to; only the attribute and constant of an attribute–value specification are shown. We indicate the relation $\leq$ by means of a solid arrow; and the function $\ll$ will be depicted by means of a dashed arrow. In the graphical representation of a taxonomy, arcs expressing the reflexivity and transitivity of the subclass relation will be left out in most cases. Figure 4.15 shows the taxonomy from Example 4.38. The omission of the arcs representing reflexivity has no effect on the inheritance of attribute values, and is therefore permitted. However, leaving out arcs representing the transitivity property of the subclass relation is one of the causes of problems concerning the inheritance of mutually exclusive attribute values, since this may alter the meaning of a taxonomy. Most of the remainder of this

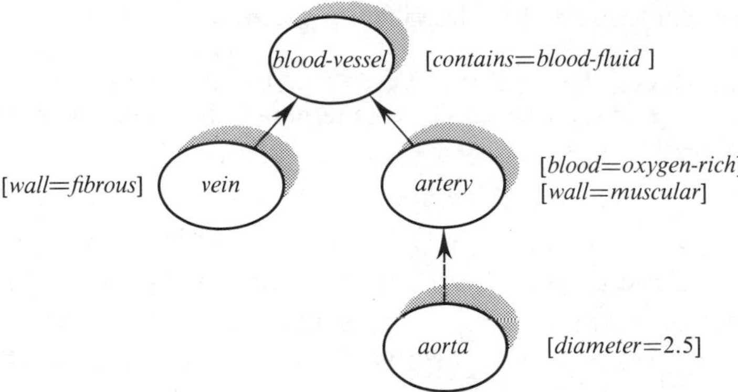

Figure 4.15 A taxonomy consisting of three classes and one instance.

section is therefore devoted to an investigation of the consequences of this decision.

The relation $\leqslant$ defined above is now taken as the basis for reasoning with frames. We shall define so-called inheritance chains for the representation of the reasoning process that may take place in a frame taxonomy. These chains will constitute our principal device for dealing with exceptions in multiple inheritance. In the following two definitions the syntactic form of such inheritance chains and a procedure for their construction is presented. We shall first consider inheritance of attribute values for classes only; later on we turn to inheritance of attribute values for instances.

> **Definition:** Let $T = (N,\Theta,\ll,\leqslant)$ be a taxonomy having the usual meaning, where $N = (I,K,A,C)$. An *inheritance chain* in T is an expression having one of the following forms:
>
> $y_1 \leqslant \cdots \leqslant y_n$
> $y_1 \leqslant \cdots \leqslant y_n[a = c]$
>
> where $y_i \in K$, $i = 1,\ldots,n$, $n \geqslant 1$, are class frames, and $y_n[a = c] \in \Theta$ is an attribute–value specification.

Note that attribute–value specifications are allowed only in isolation, or at the end of an inheritance chain. Furthermore, we observe that inheritance chains of the form $y_1 \leqslant \cdots \leqslant y_n$ are just another way of characterizing the subclass relation, obtained from its satisfying the properties of reflexivity and transitivity. Although we allow inheritance chains in which the reflexivity of the subclass relation $\leqslant$ is exploited, we shall not show such chains in our examples because they do not contribute to the notions we want to illustrate.

The set of all possible inheritance chains in a given frame taxonomy is constructed as described in the next definition.

Definition: Let $T = (N, \Theta, \ll, \leqslant)$ be a taxonomy where $N = (I, K, A, C)$. The set Ω_T of inheritance chains in T is defined as follows:

(1) For each $y \in K$, we have $y \in \Omega_T$.

(2) For each $y[a = c] \in \Theta$ where $y \in K$, we have $y[a = c] \in \Omega_T$.

(3) For each pair $(y_1, y_2) \in \leqslant$, we have $y_1 \leqslant y_2 \in \Omega_T$.

(4) For each $y_1 \leqslant \cdots \leqslant y_k \in \Omega_T$ and $y_k \leqslant \cdots \leqslant y_n \in \Omega_T$, $1 \leqslant k \leqslant n$, $n \geqslant 1$, where $y_i \in K$, $i = 1, \ldots, n$, we have that $y_1 \leqslant \cdots \leqslant y_n \in \Omega_T$.

(5) For each $y_1 \leqslant \cdots \leqslant y_n \in \Omega_T$ and $y_n[a = c] \in \Omega_T$, where $y_i \in K$, $i = 1, \ldots, n$, $n \geqslant 1$, we have that $y_1 \leqslant \cdots \leqslant y_n[a = c] \in \Omega_T$.

EXAMPLE 4.39

Consider the taxonomy $T = (N, \Theta, \ll, \leqslant)$ in which

$I = \{aorta\}$
$K = \{large\text{-}artery, artery, blood\text{-}vessel\}$
$\Theta = \{aorta[diameter = 2.5], artery[wall = muscular],$
$large\text{-}artery[mean\text{-}pressure = 100],$
$blood\text{-}vessel[contains = blood\text{-}fluid]\}$

The function $\ll$ is defined by *aorta* $\ll$ *large-artery*, and the relation $\leqslant$ is defined by *large-artery* $\leqslant$ *artery* and *artery* $\leqslant$ *blood-vessel*. Recall that inheritance chains in which the reflexivity of the subclass relation $\leqslant$ is used will not be shown; they look like the following example:

artery $\leqslant$ *artery* $\leqslant$ *artery*

Now, the set of inheritance chains Ω_T consists of the following elements:

artery
large-artery
blood-vessel
artery[*wall* = *muscular*]
large-artery[*mean-pressure* = 100]
blood-vessel[*contains* = *blood-fluid*]
large-artery $\leqslant$ *artery*
large-artery $\leqslant$ *artery*[*wall* = *muscular*]
large-artery $\leqslant$ *artery* $\leqslant$ *blood-vessel*

large-artery $\leqslant$ *artery* $\leqslant$ *blood-vessel*[*contains* = *blood-fluid*]·
artery $\leqslant$ *blood-vessel*
artery $\leqslant$ *blood-vessel*[*contains* = *blood-fluid*]

Inheritance chains are viewed as descriptions of which attribute–value specifications may *possibly* be inherited by the frames in the taxonomy. It will be evident that in multiple inheritance with exceptions certain combinations of attribute–value specifications when actually inherited represent contradictory information. Under suitable conditions, however, certain inheritance chains may be cancelled from the set of all inheritance chains in the taxonomy, thus preventing the occurrence of a contradiction. Before discussing this idea in further detail, we will introduce the notion of the conclusion of an inheritance chain, which is an explicit means for establishing which attribute–value specification may be inherited from the chain.

Definition: Let $T = (N,\Theta,\ll,\leqslant)$ be a taxonomy where $N = (I,K,A,C)$. Let Ω_T be the set of inheritance chains in T. The *conclusion* $c(\omega)$ of an inheritance chain $\omega \in \Omega_T$ is defined as follows:

(1) For each $\omega \equiv y_1 \leqslant \cdots \leqslant y_n[a = c]$, $n \geqslant 1$, we have that $c(\omega) = y_1[a = c]$.

(2) For all other ω, we have that $c(\omega)$ is not defined.

The *conclusion set* $C(\Omega_T)$ of Ω_T is defined as the set of conclusions of all elements from Ω_T, that is, $C(\Omega_T) = \{c(\omega) \mid \omega \in \Omega_T\}$.

When the attribute–value specification $z[a = c]$ is obtained as the conclusion of an inheritance chain, we say that the value c of the attribute a has been *inherited* by z.

EXAMPE 4.40

Consider again the set Ω_T of inheritance chains from the preceding example. The conclusion set $C(\Omega_T)$ of Ω_T then consists of the following attribute–value specifications:

large-artery[*mean-pressure* = 100]
large-artery[*wall* = *muscular*]
large-artery[*contains* = *blood-fluid*]
artery[*wall* = *muscular*]
artery[*contains* = *blood-fluid*]
blood-vessel[*contains* = *blood-fluid*]

The conclusion set $C(\Omega_T)$ of a given set of inheritance chains Ω_T may contain attribute–value specifications which differ only in their specified constant. We have already encountered the notion of exception and its related problems in Section 4.2.2. In the following example, we restate the problem in terms of inheritance chains.

EXAMPLE 4.41

In the foregoing, it has frequently been pointed out that the left and right pulmonary arteries have much in common with arteries except that they contain oxygen-poor instead of oxygen-rich blood. Now, consider the set Ω of inheritance chains containing, among others, the following two chains:

$$pulmonary\text{-}artery[blood = oxygen\text{-}poor]$$
$$pulmonary\text{-}artery \leqslant artery[blood = oxygen\text{-}rich]$$

The conclusion set constructed from Ω contains at least the following two attribute–value specifications:

$$pulmonary\text{-}artery[blood = oxygen\text{-}poor]$$
$$pulmonary\text{-}artery[blood = oxygen\text{-}rich]$$

Clearly, if a sensible meaning is to be associated with the frame formalism, only one of these conclusions should be satisfied.

We call a conclusion set $C(\Omega_T)$ inconsistent if it contains contradictory information such as in this example. In the following definition the notions of consistency and inconsistency of a conclusion set are defined more formally.

Definition: Let $T = (N,\Theta,\ll,\leqslant)$ be a taxonomy where $N = (I,K,A,C)$. Let Ω_T be the set of inheritance chains in T. Furthermore, let $C(\Omega_T)$ be the conclusion set of Ω_T. The conclusion set $C(\Omega_T)$ is called *inconsistent* if it contains attribute–value specifications $y[a = c_1]$ and $y[a = c_2]$, $c_1, c_2 \in C$, such that $c_1 \neq c_2$. Otherwise, the conclusion set $C(\Omega_T)$ is said to be *consistent*.

Inconsistency of the conclusion set of a taxonomy indicates that inheritance in the taxonomy is not defined uniquely; only if the conclusion set is consistent do the instances of the taxonomy inherit unambiguous information from the classes they belong to. We now consider inheritance of attribute values for instances in more detail. Informally speaking, the attribute–value specifications that hold for an instance of a specific class frame are the attribute–value specifications explicitly specified in the instance itself supplemented with the attribute–value specifications holding for the class it belongs to that do not contradict the attribute–value specifications from the instance. This is defined more formally below.

Definition: Let $T = (N, \Theta, \ll, \leq)$ be a taxonomy where $N = (I, K, A, C)$. Let Ω_T be the set of inheritance chains in T and let $C(\Omega_T)$ be the conclusion set of Ω_T. For each instance frame $x \in I$, the set $e_C(x)$ is defined by $e_C(x) = \{x[a = c] \mid x[a = c] \in \Theta\}$ $\cup$ $\{x[a = c] \mid x \ll y,\ y[a = c] \in C(\Omega_T)$ and for all $d \neq c$, $x[a = d] \notin \Theta\}$ if $C(\Omega_T)$ is consistent; $e_C(x)$ is undefined otherwise. The *extension* of Ω_T, denoted by $E_C(\Omega_T)$, is defined by

$$E_C(\Omega_T) = \bigcup_{x \in I} e_C(x)$$

if $C(\Omega_T)$ is consistent; $E_C(\Omega_T)$ is undefined otherwise.

EXAMPLE 4.42

Consider the taxonomy T from the first example of this section once more. Let Ω_T be the set of inheritance chains in T and let $C(\Omega_T)$ be the conclusion set of Ω_T. The extension of Ω_T is equal to the following set of attribute–value specifications:

$$\begin{aligned} E_C(\Omega_T) = \{&aorta[contains = blood\text{-}fluid], \\ &aorta[mean\text{-}pressure = 100], \\ &aorta[wall = muscular], \\ &aorta[diameter = 2.5]\}. \end{aligned}$$

A taxonomy that is inconsistent in the sense of its having an inconsistent conclusion set can sometimes be made consistent by cancelling some of the inheritance chains from the set of inheritance chains in the taxonomy by using knowledge concerning the hierarchical ordering of the frames. As a consequence, certain conclusions are cancelled from the conclusion set of the taxonomy as well, thereby preventing the occurrence of some contradictory attribute values. Note that in this way non-monotonic reasoning is introduced within the frame formalism.

For cancelling inheritance chains, we shall exploit the notion of an intermediary, which is introduced in the following definition.

Definition: Let $T = (N, \Theta, \ll, \leq)$ be a taxonomy where $N = (I, K, A, C)$. Let Ω_T be the set of inheritance chains in T. A class $y \in K$ is called an *intermediary* to an inheritance chain

$y_1 \leq \cdots \leq y_n \in \Omega_T$, $y_i \in K$, $i = 1, \ldots, n$, $n \geq 1$, if one of the following conditions is satisfied:

(1) We have $y = y_i$ for some i, $1 \leq i \leq n$.

(2) There exists a chain

$$y_1 \leq \cdots \leq y_p \leq z_1 \leq \cdots \leq z_m \leq y_q \in \Omega_T$$

for some p, q, $1 \leq p < q \leq n$, where $z_j \neq y_i$, $i = 1, \ldots, n$, $z_j \in K$, $j = 1, \ldots, m$, $m \geq 1$, such that $y = z_k$, for some k, $1 \leq k \leq m$.

EXAMPLE 4.43

Consider the taxonomy $T = (N, \Theta, \ll, \leq)$, where $I = \varnothing$, $K = \{$*blood-vessel, artery, oxygen-poor-artery, pulmonary-artery*$\}$, Θ is empty, and the relation $\leq$ is defined by

pulmonary-artery $\leq$ *oxygen-poor-artery*
pulmonary-artery $\leq$ *artery*
artery $\leq$ *blood-vessel*
oxygen-poor-artery $\leq$ *artery*

The graphical representation of the taxonomy is shown in Figure 4.16. The set of inheritance chains in T contains, among others, the following two chains:

pulmonary-artery $\leq$ *artery* $\leq$ *blood-vessel*
pulmonary-artery $\leq$ *oxygen-poor-artery* $\leq$ *artery*

It will be evident that the class *oxygen-poor-artery* is an intermediary to both chains.

Figure 4.16 is useful for gaining some intuitive feeling concerning the notion of an intermediary.

We shall see that intermediaries may be applied for solving part of the problem of multiple inheritance with exceptions. Take a closer look at the figure. It seems as if the arc between the vertices *pulmonary-artery* and *artery*, an arc resulting from the transitivity property of the subclass relation, is redundant, since all attribute–value specifications from the classes *artery* and *blood-vessel* can be inherited by *pulmonary-artery* via the vertex *oxygen-poor-artery*. Therefore, the removal of this arc from the taxonomy should not have any influence on the result of multiple inheritance. Whether or not this is true is, of course, dependent on our formalization of multiple inheritance. Therefore, let us investigate by means of an example whether the notion of a conclusion set defined above provides a suitable means for dealing with exceptions.

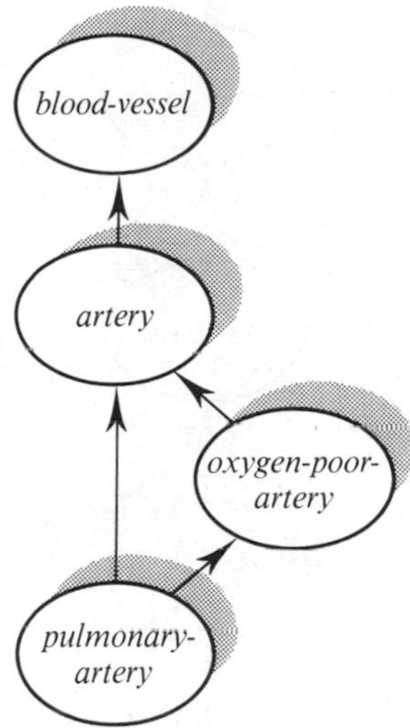

Figure 4.16 A taxonomy with an intermediary.

EXAMPLE 4.44

Consider Figure 4.16 once more. Figure 4.17 shows the taxonomy from Figure 4.16 after removal of the seemingly redundant arc. Now, suppose that the following attribute–value specifications are given:

oxygen-poor-artery[*blood* = *oxygen-poor*]
artery[*blood* = *oxygen-rich*]

Furthermore, suppose that no attribute–value specifications have been given for *pulmonary-artery*. In the taxonomy shown in Figure 4.17, the frame *pulmonary-artery* inherits only the value *oxygen-poor* for the attribute *blood*; note that this is a consequence of the way exceptions are handled in tree-like taxonomies. However, in Figure 4.16 the frame *pulmonary-artery* inherits both values *oxygen-poor* and *oxygen-rich* for the attribute *blood*, leading to an inconsistent conclusion set. The conclusion set of the taxonomy in Figure 4.16 therefore differs from the one obtained for the taxonomy shown in Figure 4.17, using the algorithm for single inheritance with exceptions discussed in Section 4.2.2 in the last case.

It turns out that a conclusion set only reveals the presence of exceptions in a taxonomy. We shall see that the notion of an intermediary is more

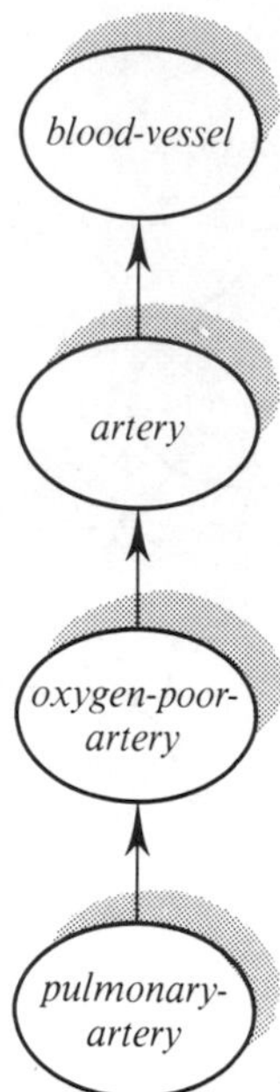

Figure 4.17 The taxonomy after removal of the redundant arc.

useful in dealing with exceptions in multiple inheritance. In Figure 4.16 we have that the class *oxygen-poor-artery* lies in between the classes *pulmonary-artery* and *artery*, and is an intermediary to the inheritance chains in which the class *pulmonary-artery* and either or both the classes *artery* and *oxygen-poor-artery* occur. As we have suggested before, by means of intermediaries some of the inheritance chains may be cancelled, producing a different set of conclusions of the taxonomy. Such cancellation of inheritance chains is called *preclusion* and is defined more formally below.

Definition: Let $T = (N,\Theta,\ll,\leqslant)$ be a taxonomy where $N = (I,K,A,C)$. Let Ω_T be the set of inheritance chains in T. A chain $y_{i_1} \leqslant \cdots \leqslant y_{i_n}[a = c_1] \in \Omega_T$, where $n \geqslant 1$, is said to *preclude* a chain $y_{j_1} \leqslant \cdots \leqslant y_{j_m}[a = c_2] \in \Omega_T$, $i_1 = j_1$ where $m \geqslant 1$, $j_m \neq i_n$, and c_1, $c_2 \in C$ with $c_1 \neq c_2$, if y_{i_n} is an intermediary to $y_{j_1} \leqslant \cdots \leqslant y_{j_m}$.

EXAMPLE 4.45

Consider the set Ω_T of inheritance chains consisting of the following elements:

ω_1: *pulmonary-artery* $\leqslant$ *oxygen-poor-artery*
ω_2: *pulmonary-artery* $\leqslant$ *artery*
ω_3: *pulmonary-artery* $\leqslant$ *oxygen-poor-artery* $\leqslant$ *artery*
ω_4: *pulmonary-artery* $\leqslant$
oxygen-poor-artery [*blood* = *oxygen-poor*]
ω_5: *pulmonary-artery* $\leqslant$ *artery*[*blood* = *oxygen-rich*]
ω_6: *pulmonary-artery* $\leqslant$ *artery* $\leqslant$
artery[*blood* = *oxygen-rich*]

The reader can easily verify that the inheritance chain ω_4 precludes both chains ω_5 and ω_6 since *oxygen-poor-artery* is an intermediary to the chains ω_2 and ω_3.

The notion of preclusion is used for introducing a new type of conclusion set of a set of inheritance chains.

Definition: Let $T = (N,\Theta,\ll,\leqslant)$ be a taxonomy. Let Ω_T be the set of inheritance chains in T. An inheritance chain $\omega \in \Omega_T$ is said to be *inheritable* if there exists no other inheritance chain $\omega' \in \Omega_T$ which precludes ω. The set of conclusions of all inheritable chains $\omega \in \Omega_T$ is called the *inheritable conclusion set* of Ω_T and is denoted by $H(\Omega_T)$.

From now on we take the notions of consistency and inconsistency defined for a conclusion set to apply to inheritable conclusion sets as well. We will give some (more abstract) examples.

EXAMPLE 4.46

Consider the taxonomy $T = (N,\Theta,\ll,\leqslant)$ where $I = \{x\}$ is the set of instances and $K = \{y_1, y_2, y_3\}$ is the set of classes; furthermore, Θ is defined by

$$\Theta = \{x[a_1 = c_1], y_1[a_2 = c_2], y_2[a_3 = c_3], y_3[a_3 = c_4]\}$$

Herein a_1, a_2 and a_3 are distinct attribute names and c_1, c_2, c_3 and c_4 are different constants. In addition, the relation $\leqslant$ is defined by $y_1 \leqslant y_2$, $y_1 \leqslant y_3$ and $y_2 \leqslant y_3$; the function $\ll$ is defined by $x \ll y_1$. This taxonomy is depicted in Figure 4.18.

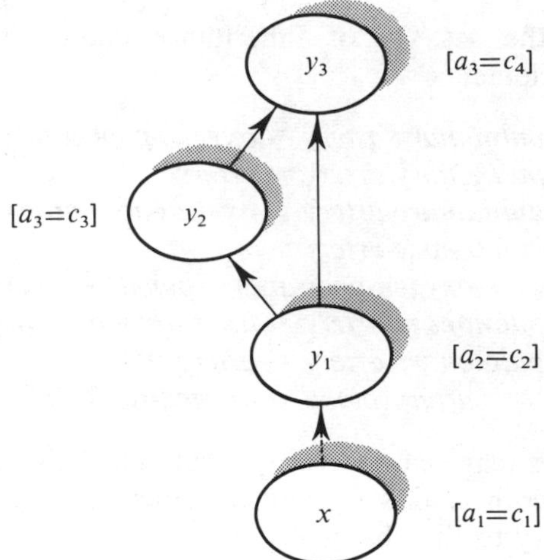

Figure 4.18 A taxonomy having a consistent inheritable conclusion set.

The set of inheritance chains Ω_T consists of the following elements:

(1) y_1
(2) y_2
(3) y_3
(4) $y_1[a_2 = c_2]$
(5) $y_2[a_3 = c_3]$
(6) $y_3[a_3 = c_4]$
(7) $y_1 \leqslant y_2$
(8) $y_1 \leqslant y_3$
(9) $y_2 \leqslant y_3$
(10) $y_1 \leqslant y_2 \leqslant y_3$
(11) $y_1 \leqslant y_2[a_3 = c_3]$
(12) $y_1 \leqslant y_3[a_3 = c_4]$
(13) $y_2 \leqslant y_3[a_3 = c_4]$
(14) $y_1 \leqslant y_2 \leqslant y_3[a_3 = c_4]$

The conclusion set of Ω_T is equal to $C(\Omega_T) = \{y_1[a_2 = c_2], y_1[a_3 = c_3], y_1[a_3 = c_4], y_2[a_3 = c_3], y_2[a_3 = c_4], y_3[a_3 = c_4]\}$. Note that $C(\Omega_T)$ is inconsistent.

Consider the set Ω_T once more. We will investigate which attribute–value specifications are in the inheritable conclusion set. As stated in the previous definition, an inheritance chain $\omega \in \Omega_T$ is inheritable if it is not precluded by any other chain from Ω_T. Since only a chain ending in an attribute–value specification can be precluded by another chain also ending in an attribute–value specification, examination of chains of such a form will suffice, so we will consider the following inheritance chains:

(4) $y_1[a_2 = c_2]$
(5) $y_2[a_3 = c_3]$
(6) $y_3[a_3 = c_4]$
(11) $y_1 \leqslant y_2[a_3 = c_3]$
(12) $y_1 \leqslant y_3[a_3 = c_4]$
(13) $y_2 \leqslant y_3[a_3 = c_4]$
(14) $y_1 \leqslant y_2 \leqslant y_3[a_3 = c_4]$

Chain 12 is precluded by chain 11 because y_2 is an intermediary to $y_1 \leqslant y_3$. Furthermore, inheritance chain 13 is precluded by chain 5. The reader may verify that chain 14 is precluded by chain 5 as well. The inheritable conclusion set $H(\Omega_T)$ of Ω_T is therefore equal to $H(\Omega_T) = \{y_1[a_2 = c_2], y_1[a_3 = c_3], y_2[a_3 = c_3], y_3[a_3 = c_4]\}$. We conclude that the inheritable conclusion set is consistent.

The next example will show that even if we apply preclusion it is still possible to obtain an inheritable conclusion set specifying contradictory information.

EXAMPLE 4.47

Consider the taxonomy $T = (N,\Theta,\ll,\leqslant)$ where the set I is empty, and $K = \{y_1, y_2, y_3, y_4\}$. The attribute–value relation Θ is defined by $\Theta = \{y_2[a = c_1], y_3[a = c_2]\}$ where a is an attribute, and c_1 and c_2 are distinct constants. Furthermore, the relation $\leqslant$ is defined by the following elements:

$y_1 \leqslant y_2$
$y_1 \leqslant y_3$
$y_2 \leqslant y_4$
$y_3 \leqslant y_4$

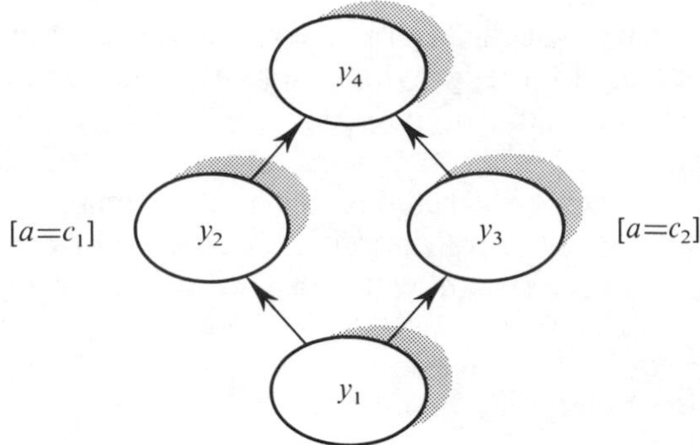

Figure 4.19 A taxonomy having an inconsistent inheritable conclusion set.

This taxonomy is depicted graphically in Figure 4.19. The inheritable conclusion set of the set of inheritance chains in this taxonomy is equal to $H(\Omega_T) = \{y_1[a = c_1],\ y_1[a = c_2],\ y_2[a = c_1],\ y_3[a = c_2]\}$. Note that $H(\Omega_T)$ is inconsistent.

From this example we have that the application of multiple inheritance using preclusion may still lead to the derivation of contradictory information. From now on, such a taxonomy will be called inconsistent.

Definition: Let $T = (N,\Theta,\ll,\leqslant)$ be a taxonomy, and let Ω_T be the set of inheritance chains in T. Furthermore, let $H(\Omega_T)$ be the inheritable conclusion set obtained from Ω_T. The taxonomy T is said to be *consistent* if $H(\Omega_T)$ is consistent; otherwise T is said to be *inconsistent.*

We conclude this section by introducing the refined notion of an inheritable extension of a set of inheritance chains.

Definition: Let $T = (N,\Theta,\ll,\leqslant)$ be a taxonomy. Let Ω_T be the set of inheritance chains in T and let $H(\Omega_T)$ be the inheritable conclusion set of Ω_T. For each instance frame $x \in I$, the set $e_H(x)$ is defined by $e_H(x) = \{x[a = c] \mid x[a = c] \in \Theta\} \cup \{x[a = c] \mid x \ll y,\ y[a = c] \in H(\Omega_T)$ and for all $d \neq c,\ x[a = d] \notin \Theta\}$ if $H(\Omega_T)$ is consistent; $e_H(x)$ is undefined otherwise. The *inheritable extension* of Ω_T, denoted by $E_H(\Omega_T)$, is defined by

$$E_H(\Omega_T) = \bigcup_{x \in I} e_H(x)$$

if $H(\Omega_T)$ is consistent; $E_H(\Omega_T)$ is undefined otherwise.

EXAMPLE 4.48

Consider the taxonomy T from Example 4.46 once more. The inheritable extension of Ω_T equals $E_H(\Omega_T) = \{x[a_1 = c_1], x[a_2 = c_2], x[a_3 = c_3]\}$.

4.3.2 Subtyping in graph-like taxonomies

In Section 4.2.7 we discussed the subject of subtyping in tree-like frame taxonomies. In this section, we extend the theory developed there to graph-like taxonomies. Recall that the subtype relation $\leqslant$ defines a partial order on a set of types. Before we treat subtyping in graph-like taxonomies in more detail, we will review some properties of partially ordered sets.

> **Definition:** Let $S = \{t_1,t_2, \ldots ,t_n\}$, $n \geqslant 1$, be a set on which we have a partial order $\leqslant$. An *upper bound* to a subset $X \subseteq S$ is an element $v \in S$ such that for each $x \in X$ we have that $x \leqslant v$; the *least upper bound* to X is an upper bound u for which we have that $u \leqslant v$ for each upper bound v to X. Similarly, a *lower bound* to a subset $X \subseteq S$ is an element $m \in S$ such that for each $x \in X$ we have that $m \leqslant x$; the *greatest lower bound* to X is a lower bound l for which we have that $m \leqslant l$ for each lower bound m to X.

There may be more than one lower or upper bound to a subset of a partially ordered set, or even none at all. However, if lower and upper bounds do exist, then the least upper bound and the greatest lower bound are unique.

EXAMPLE 4.49

Consider the following set

$$S = \{\{1\}, \{1,2\}, \{1,2,3\}, \{1,2,3,4\}, \{2,3\}, \{2,3,4\}\}$$

having elements which are also sets; on S we have the partial order induced by the set inclusion relation between its elements. We consider the subset $X = \{\{1,2,3\}, \{1,2,3,4\}\}$ of S. It will be evident that $\{1\}$, $\{1,2\}$, $\{1,2,3\}$ and $\{2,3\}$ are lower bounds to X since these sets are subsets of all elements of X. The greatest lower bound is equal to $\{1,2,3\}$; every other lower bound is a subset of this lower bound. In this example, we have only one upper bound, namely the set $\{1,2,3,4\}$; each element of X is a subset of this upper bound. Note that this upper bound is therefore the least upper bound to X at the same time.

In Section 4.2.7 we have seen that type information in a correctly typed tree-like taxonomy may be considered to be a set of types which is ordered partially by the subtype relation $\leqslant$. For correctly typed graph-like taxonomies an even stronger property has to hold; in such taxonomies, the type information has to constitute a type lattice.

> **Definition:** A *type lattice* S is a set of types with a partial order $\leqslant$ such that for every two types $t_1, t_2 \in S$ there exist in S a least upper bound and a greatest lower bound. The greatest lower bound of t_1 and t_2 is denoted by $t_1 \wedge t_2$ and is usually called the *meet* of t_1 and t_2. Furthermore, the least upper bound of t_1 and t_2 is denoted by $t_1 \vee t_2$ and is usually called the *join* of t_1 and t_2. The *universal upper bound* of S, denoted by $\top$, is an element of S such that for each type $t \in S$ we have that $t \leqslant \top$. The *universal lower bound* of S, denoted by $\bot$, is an element of S such that for each type $t \in S$ we have that $\bot \leqslant t$.

We will give an example of a type lattice.

EXAMPLE 4.50

Consider the graphical representation of a type lattice shown in Figure 4.20. This type lattice contains the type *vessel* having the type *blood-vessel* as a specialization. The *blood-vessel* type itself is considered to be subdivided into the types *vein* and *artery*. The type lattice also specifies a kind of blood vessel, called *AV-anastomosis*, being a subtype of both the *vein* and *artery* type. Furthermore, the type lattice contains the type *blood*, which describes the characteristics of blood. Two kinds of blood are distinguished – oxygen-rich blood and oxygen-poor blood – having different characteristics (think for example of the range of the typical oxygen pressure in oxygen-rich and oxygen-poor blood, and of the colour of the blood which is typically darker in oxygen-poor than in oxygen-rich blood). The type *mixed-blood* describes blood having characteristics lying between those of oxygen-poor and oxygen-rich blood. Now, note that from the type lattice we have $\textit{vein} \vee \textit{artery} = \textit{blood-vessel}$, in other words, the type *blood-vessel* is the meet of the types *vein* and *artery*. Note that the type *vessel* is an upper bound to the *vein* and *artery* types, but not the least one. Furthermore, the join of the types *vein and artery* is equal to the type *AV-anastomosis*, that is, we have $\textit{vein} \wedge \textit{artery} = \textit{AV-anastomosis}$.

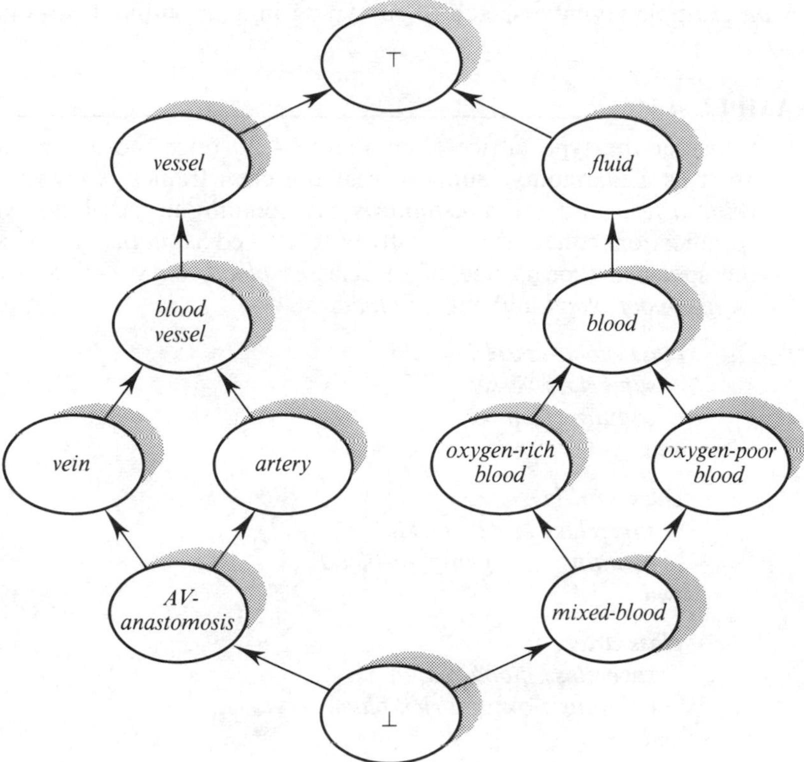

Figure 4.20 A type lattice.

Now recall from Section 4.2.7 that, in a correctly typed tree-like taxonomy, the relation defined by the superclass links in the taxonomy coincides with the partial order $\leqslant$ on the set of types specified by it. Similarly, we have that we may view a graph-like taxonomy as a type lattice (including the predefined classes), and vice versa. Furthermore, recall the definitions of the notions of attribute sequence, domain and type function, presented in Section 4.2.7. We now take these notions to apply to graph-like taxonomies.

In Section 4.2.7 we interpreted types as sets. Here, we do likewise. Consider two types t_1 and t_2. We associate with these types the sets $I(t_1)$ and $I(t_2)$, respectively, where $I(t_i) \subseteq U$, $i = 1,2$, for some domain of discourse U. As we have mentioned before, in a graph-like frame taxonomy having the form of a lattice there exists a meet and a join for every pair of types. The set associated with the meet $t_1 \wedge t_2$ now has to satisfy the property $I(t_1 \wedge t_2) = I(t_1) \cap I(t_2)$; the set associated with the join $t_1 \vee t_2$ has to satisfy $I(t_1 \vee t_2) = I(t_1) \cup I(t_2)$. We conclude this section with an example giving a sketch of subtyping in a graph-like taxonomy.

EXAMPLE 4.51

Consider the type lattice from Figure 4.20 once more; we look on it as a taxonomy. Suppose that the class frames *blood-vessel*, *vein*, *artery* and *AV-anastomosis* all contain an attribute–type specification concerning an attribute named *contains*, in which the specified type is one of the classes *blood*, *oxygen-rich-blood*, *oxygen-poor-blood* and *mixed-blood*:

```
class blood-vessel is
  superclass vessel;
  contains : blood
end

class vein is
  superclass blood-vessel;
  contains : oxygen-poor-blood
end

class artery is
  superclass blood-vessel;
  contains : oxygen-rich-blood
end

class AV-anastomosis is
  superclass {artery,vein};
  contains : mixed-blood
end
```

Furthermore, the classes *blood*, *oxygen-rich-blood*, *oxygen-poor-blood* and *mixed-blood* specify a single attribute named *colour*:

```
class blood is
  superclass nil;
  colour : {blue,dark-red,red,bright-red}
end

class oxygen-rich-blood is
  superclass blood;
  colour : {dark-red,red,bright-red}
end

class oxygen-poor-blood is
  superclass blood;
  colour : {blue,dark-red,red}
end
```

```
class mixed-blood is
  superclass {oxygen-rich-blood,oxygen-poor-blood};
  colour : {dark-red,red}
end
```

In this example, the set of attributes A in the frame taxonomy is equal to $A = \{contains, colour\}$. Let A^* be the set of attribute sequences. We now have eight domains to consider; they are denoted by D_1 to D_8 for the classes in the order shown above. The domains for the first four classes are all equal to $\{\varepsilon, contains, contains : colour\}$. The domains D_5 to D_8 for the classes starting with the class *blood* are equal to $\{\varepsilon, colour\}$. The reader can easily verify that the properties required for these domains for subtyping hold. For simplicity's sake we will consider only the type functions associated with the first four classes. The type functions associated with the classes *blood-vessel*, *vein*, *artery* and *AV-anastomosis* are denoted by τ_1 to τ_4, respectively. Recall from Section 4.2.7 that we have to verify that for all $a \in A^*$ we have:

$$\tau_2(a) \leqslant \tau_1(a)$$
$$\tau_3(a) \leqslant \tau_1(a)$$
$$\tau_4(a) \leqslant \tau_2(a)$$
$$\tau_4(a) \leqslant \tau_3(a)$$

We will discuss only some of these properties in detail. To start we note that the type for the attribute *contains* in the class *blood-vessel* equals the join of the types *oxygen-rich-blood* and *oxygen-rich-blood* given for the classes *artery* and *vein*, respectively. Furthermore, the meet of the types *oxygen-poor-blood* and *oxygen-rich-blood* for the attribute *contains* in the classes *vein* and *artery* respectively is equal to *mixed-blood*. It will be evident that we have the following properties:

$$\tau_3(contains) \leqslant \tau_1(contains)$$
$$\tau_2(contains) \leqslant \tau_1(contains)$$
$$\tau_4(contains) \leqslant \tau_3(contains)$$
$$\tau_4(contains) \leqslant \tau_2(contains)$$

Furthermore, note that we not only have that $blood\text{-}vessel = vein \vee artery$, but in addition that

$$\tau_1(contains) = \tau_2(contains) \vee \tau_3(contains)$$

since $blood = oxygen\text{-}poor\text{-}blood \vee oxygen\text{-}rich\text{-}blood$, that is, the subtyping of classes is extended from the classes to the attributes of the classes. Similarly, we have that

$$\tau_4(contains) = \tau_2(contains) \wedge \tau_3(contains)$$

Furthermore, we have that

$$\begin{aligned}\tau_4(contains : colour) &\leqslant \tau_3(contains : colour)\\ \tau_4(contains : colour) &\leqslant \tau_2(contains : colour)\\ \tau_4(contains : colour) &= \tau_2(contains : colour) \wedge\\ &\quad\ \tau_3(contains : colour)\end{aligned}$$

Checking the remaining properties is straightforward and is left to the reader (see Exercise 4.13). We conclude that the taxonomy is correctly typed.

4.4 Frames as a representation formalism

Frames (and semantic nets) provide a knowledge-representation formalism in which hierarchically structured knowledge can be specified in a natural way. Especially for the representation of knowledge of a descriptive nature, such as the knowledge concerning the cardiovascular system used in the examples in this chapter, the frame formalism appears to be highly suitable. The advantage of frames when compared, for example, with Horn clauses or production rules lies in the ease with which distinct types of knowledge can be distinguished and handled as such, and in the fact that an explicit hierarchical organization of knowledge is obtained.

In this chapter the only means of knowledge manipulation discussed was the method of inheritance. We must stress once more that this knowledge-manipulation scheme in itself is not sufficient as an inference engine for all applications; it often turns out to be necessary to develop a more elaborate inference engine for the manipulation of frames in which inheritance is only part of a collection of knowledge-manipulation methods. In Chapter 7 we shall discuss some examples of such inference engines.

For many non-trivial applications it will be necessary to use a rich frame formalism, for example including procedural components. We have suggested before that an often employed hybrid knowledge-representation scheme is that of frames containing demons for invoking small sets of production rules. Instead of integrating frames with production rules, one could also think of a more declarative extension to the frame formalism, for example by Horn clauses in combination with SLD resolution. In this way a hybrid system is obtained that still has a clear declarative semantics. Most present frame-based systems are more like programming languages than like languages for knowledge representation. A major disadvantage of many of these systems is the loss of a neat declarative semantics. Furthermore, working with these systems often requires a lot from the knowledge engineer, who may have to resort to a store of programming tricks.

Suggested reading

For the work of C.S. Peirce the reader is referred to Burks (1960). The original paper in which the notion of a semantic net was introduced is Quillian (1968). The views of O. Selz on human problem solving are presented in Selz (1922). Sowa (1984) is an interesting book on using graph-like structures for representing knowledge. The book also contains an excellent summary of philosophical, linguistic and psychological views on human cognition. Brachman (1983) offers an extensive discussion of the is-a link and its possible meaning. Findler (1979) describes various extensions to the original semantic net idea. KL-ONE is one of several systems in which the notion of a semantic net is further elaborated (Brachman and Schmolze, 1985); it incorporates a number of ideas which were not part of the original formalism. The extended semantic net is treated in Deliyanni and Kowalski (1979).

Frames were introduced in Minsky (1975). Fikes and Kehler (1985) gives an introduction to frame-based systems using the programming environment KEE as an example. Two other well-known frame-based systems, CENTAUR and LOOPS, will be discussed in Chapter 7.

Non-monotonic logic is discussed in two papers, McDermott and Doyle (1980) and McDermott (1982a). A clear paper on default logic is Reiter (1980). Touretzky (1986) and Froidevaux and Kayser (1988) give a mathematical treatment of inheritance with exceptions. Note that our approach to handling exceptions in frame taxonomies is only one of many possible varieties. Touretzky *et al.* (1987) discusses various other views on inheritance and exceptions in semantic nets. Lucas (1989) gives a more elaborate mathematical treatment of multiple inheritance with exceptions in frame systems than this book; the report also discusses various algorithms for multiple inheritance. Our approach to subtyping has been inspired by Aït-Kaci and Nasr (1986), which discusses an interesting algorithm for multiple inheritance for a typed PROLOG-like language, incorporated into the unification algorithm.

EXERCISES

4.1 Use the semantic net formalism to represent information concerning a problem domain you are familiar with. Try to define a neat semantics for the types of links you have used. What information can you derive from the net by property inheritance?

4.2 Write a LISP program that implements property inheritance in semantic nets. The program should be able to find for a specific object all properties that can be derived for it.

4.3 Consider the following three frames:

class *computer-program* ***is***
  superclass nil
end

class *expert-system* ***is***
  superclass *computer-program*;
  synonym = *knowledge-system*;
  contains = *expert-knowledge*
end

instance *mycin* ***is***
  instance-of *expert-system*;
  implementer = *Shortliffe*
end

(a) Translate the knowledge specified in the three frames shown above into standard first-order predicate logic with equality.

(b) Suppose that the following frame

instance *internist-I* ***is***
  instance-of *expert-system*;
  contains = *medical-knowledge*;
  implementer = *Pople*
end

is added to the three frames given above. Discuss the problem that arises if we translate all four frames into standard first-order predicate logic with equality. Give a possible solution to the problem.

4.4 Consider the following two frames:

class *automobile* ***is***
  superclass nil;
  wheels = 4;
  seats = 4
end

instance *Rolls-Royce* ***is***
  instance-of *automobile*;
  max-velocity = enough
end

Translate the knowledge specified in these two frames into a semantic net representation.

4.5 Consider the algorithm for single inheritance with exceptions in a tree-like taxonomy discussed in Section 4.2.2 once more. Extend this algorithm in a straightforward manner to render it applicable to graph-like taxonomies. Show by means of an example that your algorithm may produce results that are incorrect from a semantic point of view.

4.6 Develop an algorithm for N-inheritance and implement your algorithm in PROLOG or LISP.

4.7 Represent a problem domain you are familiar with using the frame formalism introduced in Section 4.2.5. Experiment with the PROLOG program for Z-inheritance discussed in Section 4.2.6 and the LISP or PROLOG program for N-inheritance developed in Exercise 4.6 and study their differences in behaviour.

4.8 Develop a LISP or PROLOG program for determining whether or not a given tree-like taxonomy is correctly typed.

4.9 Extend the LISP program discussed in Section 4.2.4 in such a way that it offers an interface to the SLD resolution program discussed in the Sections 2.8 and 2.9. The resulting program should be able to handle a demon call to the SLD resolution program by taking a demon call as a goal clause.

4.10 Consider the frame taxonomy $T = (N,\Theta,\ll,\leqslant)$ where $N = (I,K,A,C)$. We have that $K = \{x,y,z\}$ is the set of classes, $I = \{w\}$ is the set of instances and $\Theta = \{x[a = 1], y[b = 2], z[b = 4]\}$ is the set of attribute–value specifications. The relation $\leqslant$ and the function $\ll$ are defined by:

$$x \leqslant y$$
$$z \leqslant x$$
$$z \leqslant y$$
$$w \ll z$$

First, determine the set Ω_T of inheritance chains in T. Subsequently, compute the conclusion set and inheritable conclusion set of Ω_T. Is the taxonomy T consistent? If so, what is the inheritable extension of Ω_T?

4.11 Consider the following taxonomy $T = (N,\Theta,\ll,\leqslant)$ where $N = (I,K,A,C)$. We have that $K = \{u, x, y, z\}$ is the set of classes, $I = \{w\}$ is the set of instances and $\Theta = \{u[a = 1], x[b = 2], y[c = 10], z[c = 20]\}$. The relation $\leqslant$ and the function $\lessdot$ are defined as follows:

$$\begin{aligned} x &\leqslant y \\ y &\leqslant z \\ u &\leqslant x \\ u &\leqslant y \\ w &\lessdot u \end{aligned}$$

Answer the same questions as in Exercise 4.10.

4.12 Read Touretzky *et al.* (1987), which discusses several possible intuitions underlying the definition of multiple inheritance with exceptions. Explain which view on inheritance appeals to you most.

4.13 Study Example 4.51. Specify the type functions associated with the classes *blood, oxygen-rich-blood, oxygen-poor-blood* and *mixed-blood.* Check that the properties of these functions for subtyping are satisfied.

5 Reasoning with Uncertainty

In the early 1960s, researchers in applied logic assumed that theorem provers were powerful and general enough to solve practical, real-life problems. In particular, the introduction of the resolution principle by J.A. Robinson led to this conviction. By and by however it became apparent that the appropriateness of mathematical logic for solving practical problems was highly overrated. One of the complications with real-life situations is that the facts and experience necessary for solving the problems are often typified by a degree of uncertainty; moreover, often the available information is imprecise and insufficient for solving the problems. Yet human experts are able to form judgements and take decisions from uncertain, incomplete and contradictory information. To be useful in an environment in which only such imprecise knowledge is available, an expert system has to capture and exploit not only the highly specialized expert knowledge, but the uncertainties that go with the represented pieces of information as well. This observation has led to the introduction of models for handling uncertain information in expert systems. Research into the representation and manipulation of uncertainty has grown into a major research area called *inexact reasoning* or *plausible reasoning*.

Probability theory is one of the oldest mathematical theories concerning uncertainty, so it is no wonder that in the early 1970s this formal theory was chosen as the first point of departure for the development of models for handling uncertain information in rule-based expert systems. It was soon discovered that this theory could not be applied in such a context in a straightforward manner; in Section 5.2 we shall discuss some of the problems encountered in a straightforward application of probability theory. Research then centred for a short period of time around the development of modifications of probability theory that should overcome the problems encountered and that could be applied efficiently in a rule-based environment. Several models were proposed, but none of these presented a mathematically well-founded solution to these problems. This observation justifies the phrase *quasi-probabilistic models* to denote all models developed in the 1970s for rule-based systems. In this chapter, two quasi-probabilistic models will be discussed in some detail:

- the *subjective Bayesian method*, which was developed for application in the expert system PROSPECTOR;
- the *certainty factor model*, which was designed by E.H. Shortliffe and B.G. Buchanan for the purpose of dealing with uncertain information in MYCIN.

The treatment of these models will not only comprise a discussion of their basic notions but will also include an outline of their application in a rule-based expert system. In preparation for this, Section 5.1 shows which components should be present in a model for handling uncertainty in such an expert system.

The incorrectness of the quasi-probabilistic models from a mathematical point of view and an analysis of the problems the researchers were confronted with led to a world-wide discussion concerning the appropriateness of probability theory for handling uncertain information in a knowledge-based context. This discussion has yielded on the one hand other points of departure, that is, other (more or less) mathematical foundations for models for handling uncertainty, and on the other hand new, less naive applications of probability theory. In Section 5.6 we shall present an introduction to the *Dempster–Shafer theory*, which has largely been inspired by probability theory and may be considered an extension of it. We conclude this chapter with a discussion of two so-called *network models* which have resulted from a more recent probabilistic trend in plausible reasoning in which graphical representations of problem domains are employed.

5.1 Production rules, inference and uncertainty

In Chapter 3 we saw that in a rule-based expert system the specialized domain knowledge an expert has is modelled in production rules having the following form:

if *e* ***then*** *h* ***fi***

The left-hand side e of such a rule is a combination of atomic conditions which are interrelated by means of the (logical) operators ***and*** and ***or***. In the following discussion such a combination of conditions will be called a (*piece of*) *evidence*. The right-hand side h of a production rule in general is a conjunction of conclusions. In this chapter we assume production rules to have just one conclusion. Note that this restriction is not an essential one from a logical point of view. Henceforth, an atomic conclusion will be called a *hypothesis*. Furthermore, we will abstract from actions and predicates, and from variables and values, or objects, attributes and values; conditions and conclusions will be taken to be indivisible primitives. A production rule now has the following meaning: if evidence e has been observed, then the hypothesis h is confirmed as being true.

In this section we take top-down inference as the method for applying production rules, and more specifically we use backward chaining as described in Chapter 3. The application of production rules as it takes place in top-down inference may be represented graphically in an *inference network*. We introduce the notion of an inference network by means of an example.

EXAMPLE 5.1

Consider the following production rules:

R_1: ***if*** *a* ***and*** (*b* ***or*** *c*) ***then*** *h* ***fi***
R_2: ***if*** *d* ***and*** *f* ***then*** *b* ***fi***
R_3: ***if*** *f* ***or*** *g* ***then*** *h* ***fi***
R_4: ***if*** *a* ***then*** *d* ***fi***

In the following, the goal for consulting a specific rule base will be called the *goal hypothesis*. We suppose that h is the goal hypothesis for consulting the set of production rules shown above. The first production rules that are selected for evaluation are the rules R_1 and R_3. Of these, rule R_1 is evaluated first. The piece of evidence a mentioned in the left-hand side of the rule now becomes the current goal hypothesis. Since none of the production rules concludes on a, the user is requested to supply further information on a. We shall assume that the user confirms a as being true. Subsequently, b becomes the new goal hypothesis. Since rule R_2 concludes on the hypothesis b, this rule is now selected for evaluation. The first piece of evidence mentioned in rule R_2 is d; the truth of d will be derived from rule R_4. The success of rule R_4 is depicted as follows:

In the evaluation of rule R_2 it remains to be examined whether or not the piece of evidence f has been observed. We assume that, on a request for further information, the user confirms the truth of f. So rule R_2 succeeds; the success of rule R_2 is shown by:

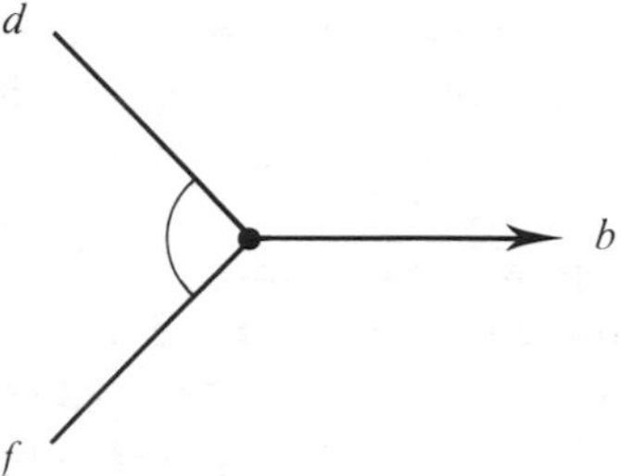

Success of rule R_3 is depicted as follows:

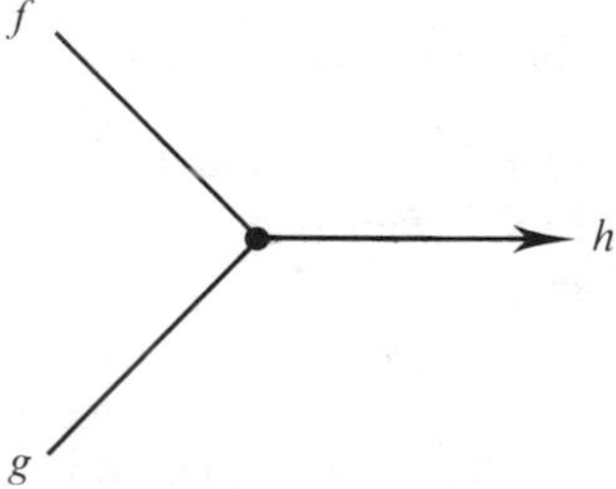

These three figures are the basic building blocks for constructing an inference network from a given set of production rules and a given goal hypothesis. The inference network resulting from a consultation of the four production rules of this example with h as the goal hypothesis is shown in Figure 5.1.

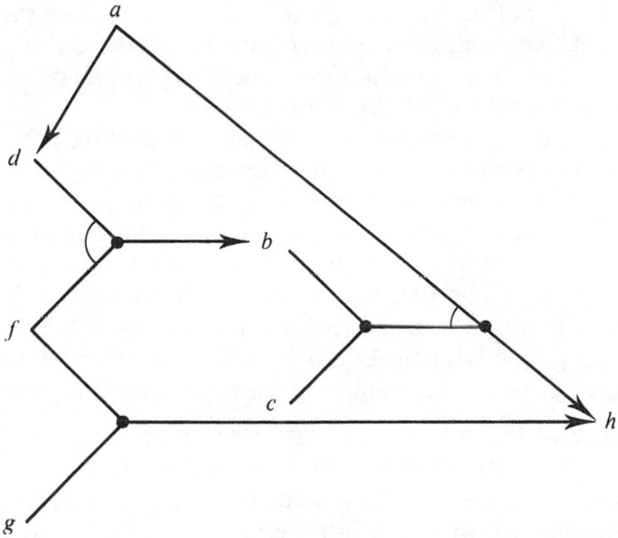

Figure 5.1 An inference network.

Up to now a production rule ***if*** *e* ***then*** *h* ***fi*** has been interpreted as stating: if evidence *e* has been observed, the hypothesis *h* is confirmed as being true. In practice, however, a hypothesis is seldom confirmed to absolute certainty by the observation of a certain piece of evidence. Therefore, the notion of a production rule is extended by allowing for a *measure of uncertainty*; a measure of uncertainty is associated with the hypothesis *h* of the production rule ***if*** *e* ***then*** *h* ***fi***, indicating the degree to which *h* is confirmed by the observation of *e*.

EXAMPLE 5.2

The measure of uncertainty *x* being associated with the hypothesis *h* in the rule ***if*** e_1 ***and*** e_2 ***then*** *h* ***fi*** is denoted by:

if e_1 ***and*** e_2 ***then*** h_x ***fi***

In an inference network an associated measure of uncertainty is shown next to the arrow in the graphical representation of the rule. So success of this production rule is represented in an inference network as follows:

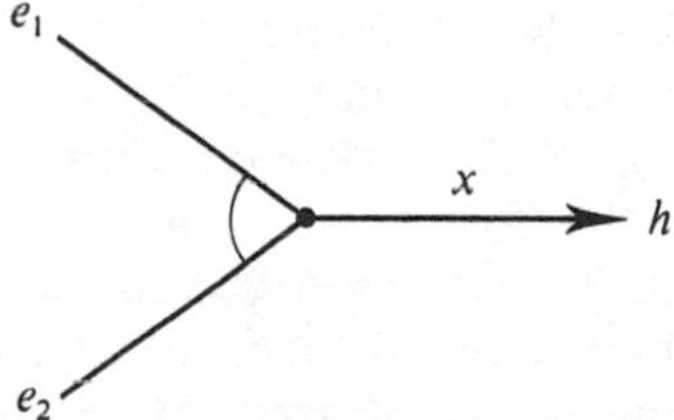

A model for handling uncertain information therefore provides the knowledge engineer with a means for representing the uncertainties that go with the pieces of information the expert has specified, so the model provides a means for *knowledge representation*.

The purpose of employing a model for dealing with uncertain information is to associate a measure of uncertainty with each conclusion the system arrives at. Such a measure of uncertainty is dependent on the measures of uncertainty associated with the conclusions of the production rules used in deriving the final conclusion and the measures of uncertainty the user has specified with the information supplied to the system. For this purpose, a model for handling uncertainty provides a means for reasoning with uncertainty, that is, it provides an *inference method*. Such an inference method consists of several components:

- Because of the way production rules of the form ***if*** e ***then*** h_y ***fi*** are applied during top-down inference, the truth of the evidence e (that is, whether or not e has actually been observed) cannot always be established with absolute certainty; e may itself have been confirmed to some degree by the application of other production rules. In this case, e acts as an intermediate hypothesis which in turn is used as evidence for the confirmation of another hypothesis. The following inference network depicts the situation in which the hypothesis e has been confirmed to the degree x on account of some prior evidence e':

  Note that the left half of this figure shows a *compressed* inference network whereas the right half represents a single production rule. Recall that the measure of uncertainty y associated with the hypothesis h in the rule ***if*** e ***then*** h_y ***fi*** indicates the degree to which h is confirmed by the *actual observation*, that is, the absolute truth of e. It will be evident that, in the situation shown above, we cannot simply associate the measure of uncertainty y with the hypothesis h. The actual measure of uncertainty to be associated with h depends on y as well as on x, the measure of uncertainty associated with the evidence e used in confirming h; the uncertainty of e has to be *propagated* to h. A model for handling uncertainty provides a function for computing the actual measure of uncertainty to be associated with h on account of all prior evidence. In the following, such a function will be called the *combination function for (propagating) uncertain evidence*; the function will be denoted by f_{prop}. The inference network shown above can now be compressed to:

$$e' \xrightarrow{f_{prop}(x,y)} h$$

where e' denotes *all* prior evidence (now including e).

- The evidence e in a production rule ***if*** e ***then*** h_z ***fi*** in general is a combination of atomic conditions which are interrelated by means of the operators ***and*** and ***or***. For instance, the production rule may have the form ***if*** e_1 ***and*** e_2 ***then*** h_z ***fi*** as depicted in the inference network below. Each of the constituent pieces of evidence of e may have been derived with an associated measure of uncertainty. The inference network, for example, shows that e_1 and e_2 are confirmed to the degrees x and y, respectively, on account of the prior evidence e':

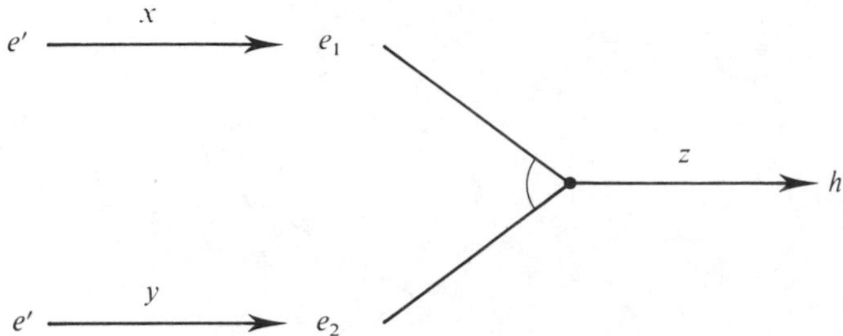

To be able to apply the combination function for propagating uncertain evidence, a measure of uncertainty for e has to be computed from the measures of uncertainty that have been associated separately with the constituent pieces of evidence of e. For this purpose, a model for handling uncertainty provides two functions which will be called the *combination functions for composite hypotheses*; they will be denoted by f_{and} and f_{or}. The inference network shown above may now be compressed to:

$$e' \xrightarrow{f_{and}(x,y)} e_1 \textbf{ and } e_2$$

- The occurrence of different production rules ***if*** e_i ***then*** h ***fi*** (that is, rules with different left-hand sides e_i) concluding on the same hypothesis h in the rule base indicates that the hypothesis h may be confirmed and/or disconfirmed along different lines of reasoning. The following inference network, for example, shows the two production rules ***if*** e_1 ***then*** h_{x_2} ***fi*** and ***if*** e_2 ***then*** h_{y_2} ***fi*** concluding on the hypothesis h, the first of which uses the prior evidence e_1' in (dis)confirming h and the second of which uses the prior evidence e_2':

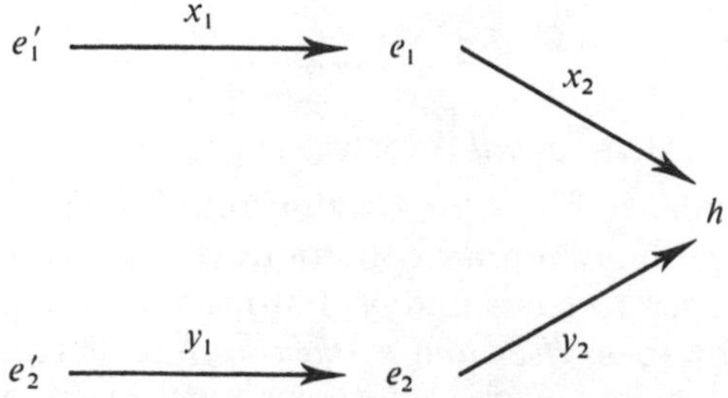

The combination function for propagating uncertain evidence is applied to compute two *partial* measures of uncertainty x and y for h such that:

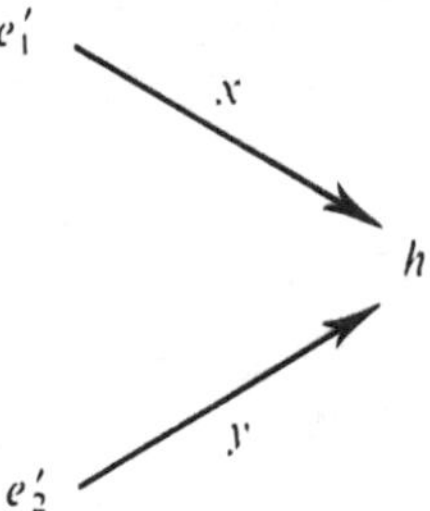

The total or *net* measure of uncertainty to be associated with h depends on the partial measures of uncertainty that have been computed for h from the two different lines of reasoning. A model for handling uncertain information therefore provides a function for computing the net measure of uncertainty for h in the inference network shown above. Such a function will be called the *combination function for co-concluding production rules*; it will be denoted by f_{co}:

$$e' = e'_1 \ \mathbf{co} \ e'_2 \xrightarrow{f_{co}(x,y)} h$$

To summarize, we have introduced four combination functions:

- The function for propagating uncertain evidence: f_{prop}
- The functions for composite hypotheses: f_{and} and f_{or}
- The function for co-concluding production rules: f_{co}

It will be evident that a model for handling uncertainty in a rule-based expert system has to provide fill-ins for these combination functions.

5.2 Probability theory

Probability theory is one of the earliest methods for associating with a statement a measure of uncertainty concerning its truth. In this section several notions from probability theory are introduced briefly before we discuss the problems encountered in applying this theory in a rule-based expert system in a straightforward manner.

5.2.1 The probability function

The notions that play a central role in probability theory have been developed for the description of experiments. In empirical research a more or less standard procedure is to perform a certain experiment repeatedly under essentially the same conditions. Each performance yields an *outcome* which cannot be predicted with certainty in advance. For many types of experiment, however, one is able to describe the set of all *possible* outcomes. The non-empty set of all possible outcomes of such an experiment is called its *sample space*; it is generally denoted by Ω. We shall be concerned here only with experiments having a countable sample space.

EXAMPLE 5.3

Consider the experiment of throwing a die. The outcome of the experiment is the number of spots up on the die. The sample space of this experiment therefore consists of six elements: $\Omega = \{1,2,3,4,5,6\}$.

A subset e of the sample space Ω of a certain experiment is called an *event*. If on performance of the experiment the outcome is in e, it is said that the event e has occurred. When the event e has not occurred, we use the notation $\bar{e}$, called the *complement* of e. Note that we have $\bar{e} = \Omega \backslash e$. The event that occurs if and only if both events e_1 and e_2 occur is called the *intersection* of e_1 and e_2, and will be denoted by $e_1 \cap e_2$. The intersection of n events e_i will be denoted by

$$\bigcap_{i=1}^{n} e_i$$

The event occurring if at least one of e_1 and e_2 occurs is called the *union* of e_1 and e_2, and will be denoted by $e_1 \cup e_2$. The union of n events e_i will be denoted by

$$\bigcup_{i=1}^{n} e_i$$

EXAMPLE 5.4

Consider the experiment of throwing a die and its associated sample space Ω once more. The subset $e_1 = \{2,4,6\}$ of Ω represents the event that an even number of spots has come up. The subset $e_2 = \bar{e}_1 = \Omega \backslash e_1 = \{1,3,5\}$ represents the event that an odd number of spots has come up. The events e_1 and e_2 cannot occur simultaneously; if event e_1 occurs, that is, if an even number of spots has come up, it is not possible that in the same throw an odd number of spots has come up. So the event $e_1 \cap e_2$ cannot occur. Note that the event $e_1 \cup e_2$ occurs in every performance of the experiment. The subset $e_3 = \{3,6\}$ represents the event that the number of spots that has come up is a multiple of three. Note that the events e_1 and e_3 have occurred simultaneously in case six spots are shown on the die; in that case the event $e_1 \cap e_3$ has occurred.

Definition: The events $e_1, \ldots, e_n \subseteq \Omega$, $n \geqslant 1$, are called *mutually exclusive* or *disjoint events* if $e_i \cap e_j = \varnothing$, $i \neq j$, $1 \leqslant i, j \leqslant n$.

We assume that an experiment yields an outcome independent of the outcomes of prior performances of the experiment. Now suppose that a particular experiment has been performed N times. If throughout these N performances an event e has occurred n times, the ratio n/N is called the *relative frequency* of the occurrence of event e in N performances of the experiment. As N increases, the relative frequency of the occurrence of the event e tends to stabilize about a certain value; this value is called the *probability* that the outcome of the experiment is in e, or the probability of event e, for short.

In general, the notions of a probability and a probability function are defined axiomatically.

Definition: Let Ω be the sample space of an experiment. If a number $P(e)$ is associated with each subset $e \subseteq \Omega$, such that

(1) $P(e) \geqslant 0$

(2) $P(\Omega) = 1$

(3) $P(\bigcup_{i=1}^{n} e_i) = \sum_{i=1}^{n} P(e_i)$, if $e_i, i = 1, \ldots, n$, $n \geqslant 1$, are mutually exclusive events

then the function P is called a *probability function* on the sample space Ω. For each subset $e \subseteq \Omega$, the number $P(e)$ is called the *probability* that event e will occur.

Note that a probability function P on a sample space Ω is a function $P\colon 2^{\Omega} \to [0,1]$.

EXAMPLE 5.5

Consider the experiment of throwing a die once more, and its associated sample space $\Omega = \{1,2,3,4,5,6\}$. The function P such that $P(\{1\}) = P(\{2\}) = \cdots = P(\{6\}) = \frac{1}{6}$ is a probability function on Ω. Since the sets $\{2\}$, $\{4\}$ and $\{6\}$ are disjoint, we have according to the third axiom of the preceding definition that $P(\{2,4,6\}) = \frac{1}{2}$; the probability of an even number of spots coming up on the die equals $\frac{1}{2}$.

Theorem

Let Ω be the sample space of an experiment and P a probability function on Ω. Then, for each event $e \subseteq \Omega$, we have

$$P(\bar{e}) = 1 - P(e)$$

Proof We have $\Omega = e \cup \bar{e}$. Furthermore, $e \cap \bar{e} = \varnothing$ holds since e and $\bar{e}$ are mutually exclusive events. From axioms 2 and 3 of the preceding definition we have that $P(\Omega) = P(e \cup \bar{e}) = P(e) + P(\bar{e}) = 1$.

5.2.2 Conditional probabilities and Bayes' theorem

We consider the case in which probability theory is applied in a medical diagnostic expert system. A user might like to know, for example, the probability of the event that a specific patient has a certain disease. For many diseases, the prior probability of the disease occurring in a certain population is known. In the case of a specific patient, however, information concerning the patient's symptoms and medical history is available, which might be useful in determining the probability of the presence of the disease.

In some cases, therefore, we are interested only in those outcomes which are in a given non-empty subset e of the entire sample space, which represents the pieces of evidence concerning the final outcome that are known in advance. Let h be the event we are interested in, that is, the hypothesis. Given that the evidence e has been observed, we are now interested in the degree to which this information influences $P(h)$, the prior probability of the hypothesis h. The probability of h given e is introduced in the following definition.

Definition: Let Ω be the sample space of a certain experiment and let P be a probability function on Ω. For each $h, e \subseteq \Omega$ with $P(e) > 0$, the *conditional probability* of h given e, denoted by $P(h \mid e)$, is defined as

$$P(h \mid e) = \frac{P(h \cap e)}{P(e)}$$

A conditional probability $P(h \mid e)$ is often called a *posterior* probability.

The conditional probabilities given a fixed event $e \subseteq \Omega$, with $P(e) > 0$, again define a probability function on Ω since the three axioms of a probability function are satisfied:

(1) $P(h \mid e) = \dfrac{P(h \cap e)}{P(e)} \geqslant 0$, since $P(h \cap e) \geqslant 0$ and $P(e) > 0$

(2) $P(\Omega \mid e) = \dfrac{P(\Omega \cap e)}{P(e)} = \dfrac{P(e)}{P(e)} = 1$

(3) $P(\bigcup_{i=1}^{n} h_i \mid e) = \dfrac{P((\bigcup_{i=1}^{n} h_i) \cap e)}{P(e)} = \dfrac{P(\bigcup_{i=1}^{n} (h_i \cap e))}{P(e)}$

$$= \frac{\sum_{i=1}^{n} P(h_i \cap e)}{P(e)} = \sum_{i=1}^{n} \frac{P(h_i \cap e)}{P(e)} = \sum_{i=1}^{n} P(h_i \mid e)$$

for mutually exclusive events h_i, $i = 1, \ldots, n$, $n \geqslant 1$.

This probability function is called the *conditional probability function given e*.

In real-life practice, the probabilities $P(h \mid e)$ cannot always be found in the literature or obtained from statistical analysis. The conditional probabilities $P(e \mid h)$, however, often are easier to come by; in medical textbooks, for example, a disease is described in terms of the signs likely to be found in a typical patient suffering from the disease. The following theorem now provides us with a method for computing the conditional probability $P(h \mid e)$ from the probabilities $P(e)$, $P(h)$ and $P(e \mid h)$; the theorem may therefore be used to reverse the 'direction' of probabilities.

Theorem (*Bayes' theorem*)

Let P be a probability function on a sample space Ω. For each h, $e \subseteq \Omega$ such that $P(e) > 0$ and $P(h) > 0$, we have:

$$P(h \mid e) = \frac{P(e \mid h)P(h)}{P(e)}$$

Proof The conditional probability of h given e is defined as

$$P(h \mid e) = \frac{P(h \cap e)}{P(e)}$$

Furthermore, we have

$$P(e \mid h) = \frac{P(e \cap h)}{P(h)}$$

So,

$$P(e \mid h)P(h) = P(h \mid e)P(e) = P(h \cap e)$$

The property stated in the theorem follows from these observations.

EXAMPLE 5.6

Consider the problem domain of medical diagnosis. Let h denote the hypothesis that a patient is suffering from liver cirrhosis; furthermore, let e denote the evidence that the patient has jaundice. In this case, the prior probability of liver cirrhosis, that is, $P(\textit{liver-cirrhosis})$, is known; it is the relative frequency of the disease in a particular population. If the prior probability of the occurrence of jaundice in the same population, that is, $P(\textit{jaundice})$, is likewise available and if the probability that a patient suffering from liver cirrhosis has jaundice, that is, the conditional probability $P(\textit{jaundice} \mid \textit{liver-cirrhosis})$, is known, we can compute the probability that a patient showing signs of jaundice suffers from liver cirrhosis, that is, using Bayes' theorem we can compute the conditional probability $P(\textit{liver-cirrhosis} \mid \textit{jaundice})$. It will be evident that this probability is of importance in medical diagnosis.

To conclude, we define the notions of independence and conditional independence. Intuitively speaking, it seems natural to call an event h independent of an event e if $P(h \mid e) = P(h)$: the prior probability of event h is not influenced by the knowledge that event e has occurred. However, this intuitive definition of the notion of independence is not symmetrical in h and e; furthermore, the notion is defined this way only when $P(e) > 0$. By using the definition of conditional probability and by considering the case for n events, we come to the following definition.

Definition: The events $e_1, \ldots, e_n \subseteq \Omega$ are (*mutually*) *independent* if

$$P(e_{i_1} \cap \cdots \cap e_{i_k}) = P(e_{i_1}) \cdot \cdots \cdot P(e_{i_k})$$

for each subset $\{i_1, \ldots, i_k\} \subseteq \{1, \ldots, n\}$, $1 \leqslant k \leqslant n$, $n \geqslant 1$. The events $e_1, \ldots, e_n$ are *conditionally independent* given an event $h \subseteq \Omega$ if

$$P(e_{i_1} \cap \cdots \cap e_{i_k} \mid h) = P(e_i \mid h) \cdot \cdots \cdot P(e_{i_k} \mid h)$$

for each subset $\{i_1, \ldots, i_k\} \subseteq \{1, \ldots, n\}$.

Note that, if the events h and e are independent and if $P(e) > 0$, we have that the earlier mentioned, intuitively more appealing notion of independence

$$P(h \mid e) = \frac{P(h \cap e)}{P(e)} = \frac{P(h)P(e)}{P(e)} = P(h)$$

is satisfied.

5.2.3 Application in rule-based expert systems

We have mentioned in the introduction that probability theory was chosen as the first point of departure in the pioneering work on automated reasoning under uncertainty. During the 1960s several research efforts on probabilistic reasoning were undertaken. The systems constructed in this period of time were primarily for (medical) diagnosis. Although these systems did not exhibit any intelligent reasoning behaviour, they may now be viewed as the precursors of the diagnostic expert systems developed in the 1970s.

Let us take a closer look at the task of diagnosis. Let $H = \{h_1, \ldots, h_n\}$ be a set of n possible hypotheses, and let $E = \{e_1, \ldots, e_m\}$ be a set of pieces of evidence which may be observed. For ease of exposition, we assume that each of the hypotheses is either *true* or *false* for a given case; equally, we assume that each of the pieces of evidence is either *true* (that is, it is actually observed in the given case) or *false*. The diagnostic task is now to find a set of hypotheses $h \subseteq H$, called the (differential) *diagnosis*, which most likely accounts for the set of observed evidence $e \subseteq E$. If we have observed a set of pieces of evidence $e \subseteq E$, we can simply compute the conditional probability $P(h \mid e)$ for each subset $h \subseteq H$ and select the set h' with the highest probability. We have mentioned before that since, for real-life applications, the conditional probabilities $P(e \mid h)$ are often easier to come by than the conditional probabilities $P(h \mid e)$, generally Bayes' theorem is used for computing $P(h \mid e)$. It will be evident that the task of diagnosis in this form is computationally complex; since a diagnosis may comprise more than one hypothesis out of n possible ones, the number of diagnoses to be investigated, that is, the number of probabilities to be computed, equals 2^n. A simplifying assumption generally made in the systems for probabilistic reasoning developed in the 1960s is that the hypotheses in H are mutually exclusive and collectively exhaustive. With this assumption, we have to consider only the n singleton hypotheses $h_i \in H$ as separate possible diagnoses. Bayes' theorem can easily be reformulated to deal with this case.

> ***Theorem*** (*Bayes' theorem*)
> Let P be a probability function on a sample space Ω. Let $h_i \subseteq \Omega$, $i = 1, \ldots, n$, $n \geqslant 1$, be mutually exclusive hypotheses with $P(h_i) > 0$, such that $\bigcup_{i=1}^{n} h_i = \Omega$ (that is, they are collectively exhaustive). Furthermore, let $e \subseteq \Omega$ such that $P(e) > 0$. Then the following property holds:
>
> $$P(h_i \mid e) = \frac{P(e \mid h_i)P(h_i)}{\sum_{j=1}^{n} P(e \mid h_j)P(h_j)}$$

Proof Since $h_1, \ldots, h_n$ are mutually exclusive and collectively exhaustive, we have that $P(e)$ can be written as

$$P(e) = P\left(\left(\bigcup_{i=1}^{n} h_i\right) \cap e\right) = P\left(\bigcup_{i=1}^{n} (h_i \cap e)\right)$$

$$= \sum_{i=1}^{n} P(h_i \cap e) = \sum_{i=1}^{n} P(e \mid h_i)P(h_i)$$

Substitution of this result in the form of Bayes' theorem given in Section 5.2.2 yields the property stated in the theorem.

For a successful application of Bayes' theorem in the form mentioned in the previous theorem, several conditional and prior probabilities are required. For example, conditional probabilities $P(e \mid h_i)$ for every combination of pieces of evidence $e \subseteq E$ have to be available; note that, in general, these conditional probabilities $P(e \mid h_i)$ cannot be computed from their 'component' conditional probabilities $P(e_j \mid h_i)$, $e_j \in e$. It will be evident that exponentially many probabilities have to be known beforehand. Because it is hardly likely that for practical applications all these probabilities can be obtained from for example statistical analysis, a second simplifying assumption was generally made in the systems developed in the 1960s; it was assumed that the pieces of evidence $e_j \in E$ are conditionally independent given any hypothesis $h_i \in H$. Under this assumption Bayes' theorem reduces to the following form.

> ***Theorem*** (*Bayes' theorem*)
> Let P be a probability function on a sample space Ω. Let $h_i \subseteq \Omega$, $i = 1, \ldots, n$, $n \geqslant 1$, be mutually exclusive and collectively

exhaustive hypotheses as in the previous theorem. Furthermore, let $e_{j_1}, \ldots, e_{j_k} \subseteq \Omega, 1 \leqslant k \leqslant m$, $m \geqslant 1$, be pieces of evidence such that they are conditionally independent given any hypothesis h_i. Then the following property holds:

$$P(h_i \mid e_{j_1} \cap \cdots \cap e_{j_k}) = \frac{P(e_{j_1} \mid h_i) \cdots P(e_{j_k} \mid h_i) P(h_i)}{\sum_{l=1}^{n} P(e_{j_1} \mid h_l) \cdots P(e_{j_k} \mid h_l) P(h_l)}$$

Proof The theorem follows immediately from the preceding theorem and the definition of conditional independence.

It will be evident that with the two assumptions mentioned above only $m \cdot n$ conditional probabilities and $n - 1$ prior probabilities suffice for a successful use of Bayes' theorem.

The pioneering systems for probabilistic reasoning constructed in the 1960s, which basically employed the last-mentioned form of Bayes' theorem, were rather small-scale; they were devised for clear-cut problem domains with only a small number of hypotheses and restricted evidence. For these small systems, all probabilities necessary for applying Bayes' theorem were acquired from a statistical analysis of the data of several hundred sample cases. Now recall that in deriving this form of Bayes' theorem several assumptions were made:

- The hypotheses $h_1, \ldots, h_n$, $n \geqslant 1$, are mutually exclusive.
- Furthermore, the hypotheses $h_1, \ldots, h_n$ are collectively exhaustive, that is, $\bigcup_{i=1}^{n} h_i = \Omega$.
- The pieces of evidence $e_1, \ldots, e_m$, $m \geqslant 1$, are conditionally independent given any hypothesis h_i, $1 \leqslant i \leqslant n$.

These conditions, which have to be satisfied for a correct use of Bayes' theorem, are generally not met in practice. But, in spite of these (over-)simplifying assumptions underlying the systems from the 1960s, they performed considerably well. Nevertheless, interest in this approach to reasoning with uncertainty faded in the early 1970s. One of the reasons for this decline in interest is that the method informally sketched above is feasible only for highly restricted problem domains. For larger domains or domains in which the above-mentioned simplifying assumptions are seriously violated, the method will inevitably become demanding, either computationally or from the point of view of obtaining the necessary probabilities. Often a large number of conditional and prior probabilities is needed, thus requiring enormous amounts of experimental data.

At this stage, the first diagnostic rule-based expert systems began to emerge from the early artificial intelligence research efforts. As a consequence of their ability to concentrate only on those hypotheses which are suggested by the evidence, these systems were capable in principle of dealing with larger and more complex problem domains than the early probabilistic systems were. At least, they were so from a computational point of view; the problem that a large number of probabilities was required still remained. In many practical applications, the experimental data necessary for computing all probabilities required simply were not available. In devising a probabilistic reasoning component to be incorporated in a rule-based system, the artificial intelligence researchers therefore had to depart from *subjective probabilities* which had been assessed by human experts in the field. Human experts, however, are often uncertain and uncomfortable about the probabilities they are providing. The difficulty of assessing probabilities is well known as a result of research on human decision making and judgement under uncertainty. We will not discuss this issue any further, but merely observe that domain experts generally are unable fully and correctly to specify a probability function on the problem domain. In a rule-based context, an expert is now typically asked to associate probabilities only with the production rules he or she has provided.

Recall that the production rule formalism is defined in terms of expressions more or less resembling logical formulas, whereas the notion of a probability function has been related to sets. Therefore, we have to have a mapping that transforms logical propositions into sets and that preserves probability, for then we have that the probability of an event is equivalent to the probability of the truth of the proposition asserting the occurrence of the event. A more or less standard translation of sets into logical formulas is the following: if Ω is a sample space, then we define for each event $e \subseteq \Omega$ a predicate e' such that $e'(x) = true$ if and only if $x \in e$. The intersection of two events then corresponds with the conjunction of two corresponding propositions; the union of two events translates into the disjunction of the corresponding propositions. In probabilistic computations, we will adhere to the set notation; when discussing production-rule related subjects, we will often use a logical convention.

With each production rule ***if*** *e* ***then*** *h* ***fi*** an expert now associates a conditional probability $P(h \mid e)$ indicating the influence of the observation of evidence e on the prior probability $P(h)$ of the hypothesis h:

$$e \xrightarrow{P(h \mid e)} h$$

The last-mentioned form of Bayes' theorem now provides us with a method for computing the probability of a certain hypothesis when several pieces of evidence have been observed. Bayes' theorem can therefore be taken as the combination function for co-concluding production rules when probability theory is viewed as a method for handling uncertainty as discussed in Section 5.1. Consider the following inference network:

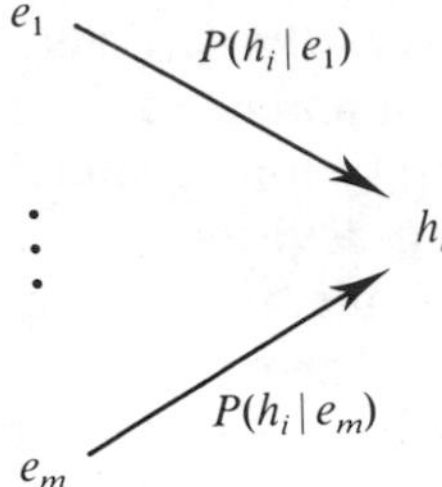

Using Bayes' theorem we can compute the combined influence of the pieces of evidence $e_1, \ldots, e_m$ on the prior probability of the hypothesis h_i such that:

$$\bigcap_{j=1}^{m} e_j \xrightarrow{P(h_i \mid \bigcap_{j=1}^{m} e_j)} h_i$$

(Note that some additional prior probabilities have to be known to the system.)

In a rule-based expert system, the production rules are used for pruning the search space of possible diagnoses; in this pruning process, heuristic as well as probabilistic criteria are employed. It is therefore necessary to compute the probabilities of all intermediate results derived using the production rules. However, these probabilities generally cannot be computed from the probabilities associated with the rules only; probability theory does not provide an explicit combination function for propagating uncertain evidence nor does it provide combination functions for composite hypotheses in terms of the available probabilities. We have suggested before that the quasi-probabilistic models do offer explicit combination functions. From the previous observation it will be evident that these functions cannot accord with the axioms of probability theory. Therefore, they can only be viewed as approximation functions rendering the models to some extent insensitive to the lack of a fully specified probability function and erroneous probability assessments.

5.3 The subjective Bayesian method

In Section 5.2 we have highlighted some of the problems encountered when applying probability theory in a rule-based expert system.

R.O. Duda, P.E. Hart and N.J. Nilsson have recognized these problems and have developed a new method for handling uncertainty in PROSPECTOR, an expert system for assisting non-expert field geologists in exploring sites; part of the knowledge incorporated in PROSPECTOR is represented in production rules. The model of Duda, Hart and Nilsson is based on probability theory but provides solutions to the problems mentioned in the previous section.

5.3.1 The likelihood ratios

As has been mentioned before, the subjective Bayesian method is a modification of probability theory. However, the model uses the notion of 'odds' instead of the related notion of probability.

> **Definition:** Let P be a probability function on a sample space Ω. Furthermore, let $h \subseteq \Omega$ such that $P(h) < 1$. The *prior odds* of the event h, denoted by $O(h)$, are defined as follows:

$$O(h) = \frac{P(h)}{1 - P(h)}$$

Note that conversely

$$P(h) = \frac{O(h)}{1 + O(h)}$$

In probability theory the notion of conditional or posterior probability is used. The subjective Bayesian method uses the related notion of posterior odds.

> **Definition:** Let P be a probability function on a sample space Ω. Let $h, e \subseteq \Omega$ such that $P(e) > 0$ and $P(h \mid e) < 1$. The *posterior odds* of a hypothesis h given evidence e, denoted by $O(h \mid e)$, are defined as follows:

$$O(h \mid e) = \frac{P(h \mid e)}{1 - P(h \mid e)}$$

We now introduce two more notions: the positive and negative likelihood ratios.

> **Definition:** Let P be a probability function on a sample space Ω. Furthermore, let $h, e \subseteq \Omega$ such that $0 < P(h) < 1$ and $P(e \mid \bar{h}) > 0$.

The (*positive*) *likelihood ratio* λ, given h and e, is defined by

$$\lambda = \frac{P(e \mid h)}{P(e \mid \bar{h})}$$

The likelihood ratio λ is often called the *level of sufficiency*; it represents the degree to which the observation of evidence e influences the prior probability of hypothesis h. A likelihood ratio $\lambda > 1$ indicates that the observation of e tends to confirm the hypothesis h; a likelihood ratio $\lambda < 1$ indicates that the hypothesis $\bar{h}$ is confirmed to some degree by the observation of e, or in other words that the observation of e tends to disconfirm h. If $\lambda = 1$, the observation of e does not influence the prior confidence in h.

Definition: Let P be a probability function on a sample space Ω. Let $h, e \subseteq \Omega$ be such that $0 < P(h) < 1$ and $P(e \mid \bar{h}) < 1$. The (*negative*) *likelihood ratio* $\bar{\lambda}$, given h and e, is defined by

$$\bar{\lambda} = \frac{1 - P(e \mid h)}{1 - P(e \mid \bar{h})}$$

The negative likelihood ratio $\bar{\lambda}$ is often called the *level of necessity*. A comparison of the likelihood ratios λ and $\bar{\lambda}$ shows that from $\lambda > 1$ it follows that $\bar{\lambda} < 1$, and vice versa; furthermore we have $\lambda = 1$ if and only if $\bar{\lambda} = 1$.

When applying the subjective Bayesian method in a production system, a positive likelihood ratio λ and a negative likelihood ratio $\bar{\lambda}$ have to be associated with each production rule ***if*** *e* ***then*** *h* ***fi***:

$$e \xrightarrow{\lambda,\ \bar{\lambda}} h$$

Furthermore, the prior probabilities $P(h)$ as well as $P(e)$ have to be known to the system. Note that this information is not sufficient for uniquely defining a probability function on the sample space; the expert has provided probabilities for only a few events, the ones mentioned in the specified production rules.

In the following section, in some cases the conditional probabilities $P(h \mid e)$ and $P(h \mid \bar{e})$ will be preferred to λ and $\bar{\lambda}$. We then assume that these conditional probabilities are associated with each production rule. We note that the probabilities $P(h \mid e)$ and $P(h \mid \bar{e})$ can be computed uniquely from λ, $\bar{\lambda}$, $P(h)$ and $P(e)$. The reader may for example verify that the following property holds:

$$P(e \mid h) = \lambda \cdot \frac{1 - \bar{\lambda}}{\lambda - \bar{\lambda}}$$

Bayes' theorem can subsequently be applied to compute the probability $P(h \mid e)$.

5.3.2 The combination functions

Recall that a model for dealing with uncertainty provides means for representing and reasoning with uncertainty. The purpose of applying such a model is to compute a measure of uncertainty for each goal hypothesis. If a probability function on the domain were known, the probabilities of these goal hypotheses could simply be calculated from the probability function. However, as we have argued before, such a probability function is virtually never available in practical applications. The required probabilities are therefore approximated from the ones that are actually known to the system.

In a rule-based expert system using top-down inference, several intermediate hypotheses are confirmed or disconfirmed to some degree. We have seen before that these uncertain hypotheses may in turn be used as pieces of evidence in other production rules. In Section 5.1 a combination function for propagating such uncertain evidence has been introduced: the function f_{prop}. Recall that probability theory does not provide an explicit fill-in for this function f_{prop} in terms of the probabilities known to the system. The subjective Bayesian method, however, does provide such a combination function.

Suppose that the intermediate hypothesis e is used as evidence in confirming hypothesis h by applying the production rule ***if** e **then** h **fi***. We suppose that the intermediate hypothesis e has been confirmed by the observation of some prior evidence e', and that for e the posterior probability $P(e \mid e')$ has been computed.

$$e' \xrightarrow{\quad P(e \mid e') \quad} e \xrightarrow{\quad P(h \mid e),\, P(h \mid \bar{e}) \quad} h$$

After application of the rule, we are interested in the probability $P(h \mid e')$ such that

$$e' \xrightarrow{\quad P(h \mid e') \quad} h$$

Note that in general the probability $P(h \mid e')$ will not have been assessed by the expert and cannot be computed from the probability function P since P has not been fully specified. Therefore, it has to be approximated. In general, we have

$$\begin{aligned}
P(h \mid e') &= P(h \cap e \mid e') + P(h \cap \bar{e} \mid e') \\
&= \frac{P(h \cap e \cap e')}{P(e')} \cdot \frac{P(e \cap e')}{P(e \cap e')} + \frac{P(h \cap \bar{e} \cap e')}{P(e')} \cdot \frac{P(\bar{e} \cap e')}{P(\bar{e} \cap e')} \\
&= \frac{P(h \cap e \cap e')}{P(e \cap e')} \cdot \frac{P(e \cap e')}{P(e')} + \frac{P(h \cap \bar{e} \cap e')}{P(\bar{e} \cap e')} \cdot \frac{P(\bar{e} \cap e')}{P(e')} \\
&= P(h \mid e \cap e')P(e \mid e') + P(h \mid \bar{e} \cap e')P(\bar{e} \mid e')
\end{aligned}$$

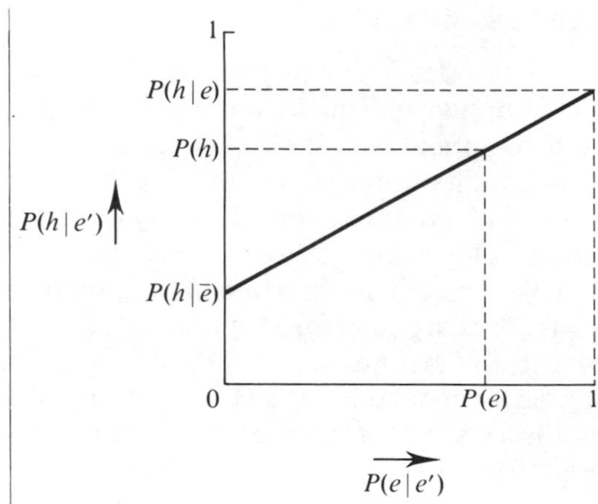

Figure 5.2 $P(h \mid e')$ as a linear interpolation function in $P(e \mid e')$.

We assume that, if we know e to be absolutely true (or false), the observations e' relevant to e do not provide any *further* information on the hypothesis h. This assumption can be taken into account in the formula given above as follows:

$$\begin{aligned} P(h \mid e') &= P(h \mid e)P(e \mid e') + P(h \mid \bar{e})P(\bar{e} \mid e') \\ &= (P(h \mid e) - P(h \mid \bar{e})) \cdot P(e \mid e') + P(h \mid \bar{e}) \end{aligned}$$

We have that $P(h \mid e')$ is a linear interpolation function in $P(e \mid e')$ (since the function has the form $f(x) = ax + b$). Figure 5.2 depicts such an interpolation function for the situation of the production rule ***if*** *e* ***then*** *h* ***fi***. This interpolation function has two extreme values; for $P(e \mid e') = 0$ we have the extreme value $P(h \mid e') = P(h \mid \bar{e})$, and for $P(e \mid e') = 1$ we have the extreme value $P(h \mid e') = P(h \mid e)$. For any $P(e \mid e')$ between 0 and 1 the corresponding value for $P(h \mid e')$ can be read from the figure. For instance, if evidence e' has been observed confirming e, that is, if $P(e \mid e') > P(e)$, we find that the probability of h increases from applying the production rule ***if*** *e* ***then*** *h* ***fi***: $P(h \mid e') > P(e)$. Note that this effect is exactly what is meant by the rule. In the special case where $P(e \mid e') = P(e)$, we have

$$P(h \mid e') = P(h \mid e)P(e) + P(h \mid \bar{e})P(\bar{e}) = P(h)$$

In principle, this interpolation function offers an explicit computation rule for propagating uncertain evidence. Duda, Hart and Nilsson however have observed that when an expert is asked to assess for each rule ***if*** *e* ***then*** *h* ***fi*** the four probabilities $P(h)$, $P(e)$, $P(h \mid e)$ and $P(h \mid \bar{e})$, the

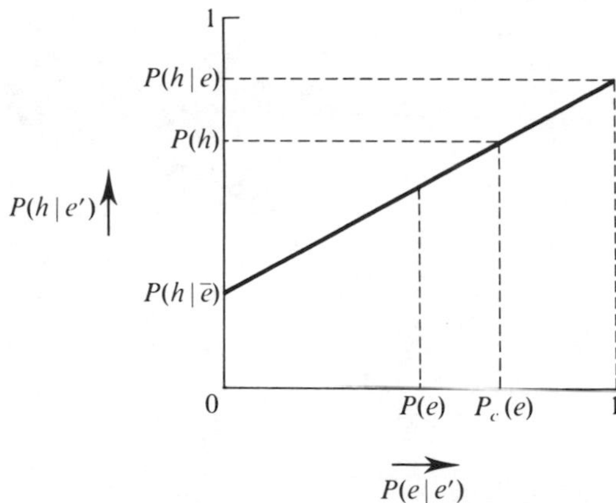

Figure 5.3 Inconsistent prior probabilities $P(h)$ and $P(e)$.

specified values are likely to be *inconsistent*, in the sense that there is not an underlying actual probability function. More specifically, the relation between $P(h)$ and $P(e)$ as shown in Figure 5.2 will be violated. Such an inconsistency may lead to problems. Consider Figure 5.3. The assessed probabilities $P(h)$, $P(e)$, $P(h \mid e)$ and $P(h \mid \bar{e})$ shown in the figure are inconsistent; the consistent value for $P(e \mid e')$ corresponding with $P(h)$ is indicated as $P_c(e)$. Now suppose that evidence e' has been observed confirming e to a degree $P(e \mid e')$ such that $P(e) < P(e \mid e') < P_c(e)$. From Figure 5.3 we have that $P(h \mid e') < P(h)$. The production rule ***if** e **then** h **fi*** however was meant to express that confirmation of e leads to confirmation of h; because of the inconsistency the reverse has been achieved! A natural solution to this problem would be to reassess $P(e)$ by choosing $P(e) = P_c(e)$ (or, where the assessment of $P(h)$ is less certain than the assessment of $P(e)$, to reassess $P(h)$ by choosing a consistent value for $P(h)$). The hypotheses h and e, however, may occur in several places in a given set of production rules and each reassessment affects all these occurrences. Reassessing prior probabilities therefore is not a feasible solution to the problem we have discussed.

Duda, Hart and Nilsson have developed several methods for employing inconsistently specified probabilities, one of which has been implemented as the function for propagating uncertain evidence in PROSPECTOR. The basic idea of the method that has been chosen for implementation is shown in Figure 5.4. The original interpolation function is split in two separate interpolation functions on the intervals $[0,P(e)]$ and $(P(e),1]$, respectively, to enforce the property $P(h \mid e') = P(h)$ if $P(e \mid e') = P(e)$. Note that the closer the function value for $P(e)$ is to the value for $P(e)$ from the original interpolation function, the better the initial assessments of $P(e)$ and $P(h)$ are. The resulting interpolation function is defined as follows:

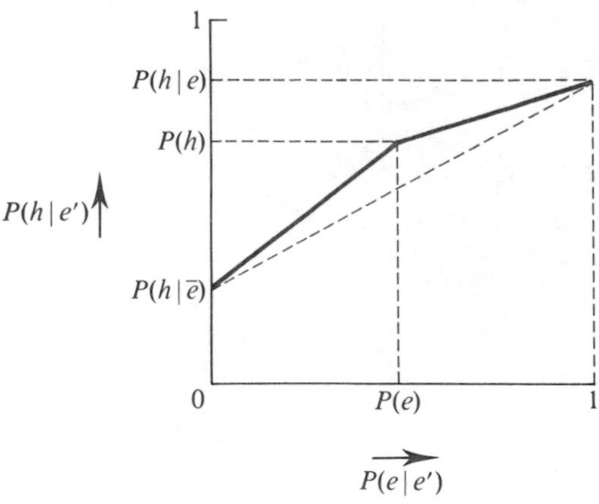

Figure 5.4 A consistent interpolation function.

$$P(h \mid e') = \begin{cases} P(h \mid \bar{e}) + \dfrac{P(h) - P(h \mid \bar{e})}{P(e)} \cdot P(e \mid e') & \text{if } 0 \leqslant P(e \mid e') \leqslant P(e) \\[2ex] P(h) + \dfrac{P(h \mid e) - P(h)}{1 - P(e)} \cdot (P(e \mid e') - P(e)) & \text{if } P(e) < P(e \mid e') \leqslant 1 \end{cases}$$

Recall that the conditional probabilities $P(h \mid e)$ and $P(h \mid \bar{e})$ used in this function are obtained from the likelihood ratios λ and $\bar{\lambda}$ provided by the expert.

We have mentioned before that with each production rule ***if*** *e* ***then*** *h* ***fi*** the two likelihood ratios λ and $\bar{\lambda}$ have been associated; λ stands for the influence of the observation of evidence e on the prior probability of the hypothesis h, and $\bar{\lambda}$ indicates the degree to which observation of $\bar{e}$ changes the probability of h. The ratios λ and $\bar{\lambda}$ can be viewed as the bounds of an interval containing a value indicating the degree to which evidence e, which has been (dis)confirmed to some degree by some prior evidence e', really influences the prior probability of h. This value is called the effective likelihood ratio, and will be denoted by λ'. The ratio λ' is computed from the value $P(h \mid e')$ according to the following definition.

Definition: Let P be a probability function on a sample space Ω, and let O be the corresponding odds as defined before. Furthermore, let $h, e' \subseteq \Omega$. The *effective likelihood ratio* λ', given h and e', is defined as follows:

$$\lambda' = \frac{O(h \mid e')}{O(h)}$$

The effective likelihood ratio λ' lies between λ and $\bar{\lambda}$. λ' will be closer to λ if e has been confirmed to some degree by the observation of the evidence e'; conversely, λ' will be closer to $\bar{\lambda}$ if e has been disconfirmed to some degree by the prior evidence e'.

Until now we have considered only production rules ***if*** *e* ***then*** *h* ***fi*** in which e is an atomic piece of evidence. We have seen above that the condition part of a production rule may be a combination of atomic pieces of evidence which are interrelated by means of the logical operators ***and*** and ***or***. The following inference network, for example, depicts the evidence e_1 ***or*** e_2; the constituting pieces of evidence have been obtained from prior observations e':

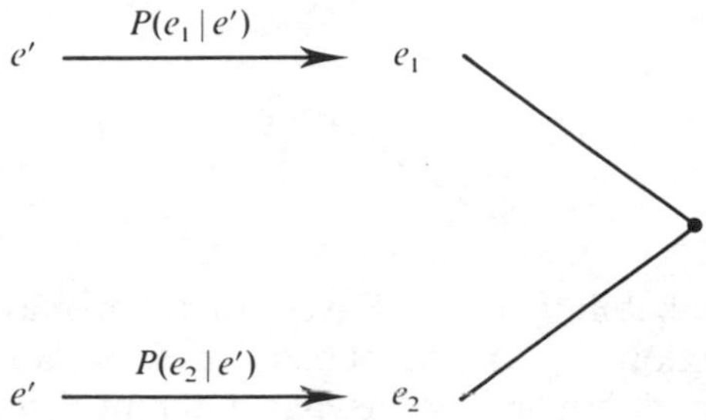

To be able to propagate the uncertainty of the composite evidence e_1 ***or*** e_2, we have to know the probability $P(e_1 \textbf{ or } e_2 \mid e')$ such that:

$$e' \xrightarrow{P(e_1 \textbf{ or } e_2 \mid e')} e_1 \textbf{ or } e_2$$

Note that the exact probability cannot be computed from the probabilities $P(e_1 \mid e')$ and $P(e_2 \mid e')$ of the separate components. Again, we have to approximate the required probability using a combination function.

Let evidence e be composed of a number of atomic pieces of evidence e_i, $i = 1, \ldots, n$, $n \geqslant 2$, which are interrelated by means of ***and*** and ***or***. In PROSPECTOR, the probability $P(e \mid e')$ of e given the prior observations e' is approximated from the separate probabilities $P(e_i \mid e')$ of the constituting pieces of evidence e_i in e by recursively applying the following two functions:

$$P(e_1 \textbf{ and } e_2 \mid e') = \min\{P(e_1 \mid e'), P(e_2 \mid e')\}$$

$$P(e_1 \textbf{ or } e_2 \mid e') = \max\{P(e_1 \mid e'), P(e_2 \mid e')\}$$

These functions therefore fulfil the role of the combination functions for composite hypotheses, that is, of f_{and} and f_{or}, respectively. Note that the order in which the constituting pieces of evidence have been specified does not influence the resulting probability of a composite hypothesis.

The combination function which still remains to be discussed is the function for co-concluding production rules ***if*** e_i ***then*** h ***fi***, that is, we still have to discuss the function f_{co}. If the pieces of evidence e_i specified in a number of co-concluding production rules have been obtained from prior observations e_i', respectively, then the uncertainty of these pieces of evidence e_i given e_i' can be propagated to h in the manner described above. For two co-concluding production rules, the resulting inference network is the following:

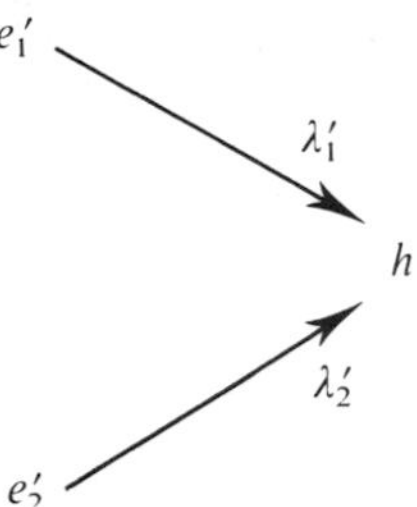

Recall that in probability theory Bayes' theorem may be used as the combination function f_{co}. In the subjective Bayesian method, Bayes' theorem is also used, but in a somewhat different form in terms of the odds.

> ***Theorem***
>
> Let P be a probability function on a sample space Ω, and let O be the corresponding odds as defined above. Let $h, e \subseteq \Omega$. Furthermore, let the likelihood ratio λ be defined as above. Then, the following property holds:
>
> $$O(h \mid e) = \lambda \cdot O(h)$$

Proof From Bayes' theorem we have

$$P(h \mid e) = \frac{P(e \mid h)P(h)}{P(e)}$$

For the complement of h we have, again from Bayes' theorem,

$$P(\bar{h} \mid e) = \frac{P(e \mid \bar{h})\,P(\bar{h})}{P(e)}$$

Dividing the first equation by the second one results in the following equation:

$$\frac{P(h \mid e)}{P(\bar{h} \mid e)} = \frac{P(e \mid h)P(h)}{P(e \mid \bar{h})P(\bar{h})}$$

from which we have

$$\frac{P(h \mid e)}{1 - P(h \mid e)} = \frac{P(e \mid h)}{P(e \mid \bar{h})} \cdot \frac{P(h)}{1 - P(h)}$$

From this observation it follows that $O(h \mid e) = \lambda \cdot O(h)$.

This alternative form of Bayes' theorem is called the *odds-likelihood form* of the theorem.

The theorem stated above concerns the situation where evidence e has been obtained with absolute certainty. Where e has definitely not occurred, that is, where $\bar{e}$ has been observed with absolute certainty, we obtain a similar formula.

Theorem

Let P be a probability function on a sample space Ω, and let O be the corresponding odds as defined above. Let h, $e \subseteq \Omega$. Furthermore, let the negative likelihood ratio $\bar{\lambda}$ be defined as above. Then the following property holds:

$$O(h \mid \bar{e}) = \bar{\lambda} \cdot O(h)$$

The above theorems apply to the case of a single production rule. In the situation where several production rules ***if*** e_i ***then*** h ***fi*** conclude on the same hypothesis h, the results from these production rules have to be combined into a single measure of uncertainty for h. Again, we first consider the case where all pieces of evidence e_i have been obtained with absolute certainty. It should be evident that by assuming that the pieces of evidence e_i are conditionally independent given h we have that the following property holds:

$$O\left(h \,\middle|\, \bigcap_{i=1}^{n} e_i\right) = \left[\prod_{i=1}^{n} \lambda_i\right] O(h)$$

where

$$\lambda_i = \frac{P(e_i \mid h)}{P(e_i \mid \bar{h})}$$

Similarly, for the case where all pieces of evidence $\bar{e}_i$ have been obtained with absolute certainty, we have:

$$O\left(h \,\middle|\, \bigcap_{i=1}^{n} \bar{e}_i\right) = \left[\prod_{i=1}^{n} \bar{\lambda}_i\right] O(h)$$

We have argued before that in general the pieces of evidence e_i (or $\bar{e}_i$ respectively) will not have been obtained with absolute certainty, but with a probability $P(e_i \mid e'_i)$ given some prior observations e'_i. From the probabilities $P(e_i \mid e'_i)$ the posterior odds $O(h \mid e'_i)$ are obtained from applying the combination function for propagating uncertain evidence. From these posterior odds we then compute the effective likelihood ratios λ'_i. Again under the assumption that the pieces of evidence e'_i are conditionally independent given h we obtain:

$$O\left(h \,\middle|\, \bigcap_{i=1}^{n} e'_i\right) = \left[\prod_{i=1}^{n} \lambda'_i\right] O(h)$$

Since multiplication is commutative and associative, we have that the order in which the co-concluding production rules are applied will be irrelevant for the resulting uncertainty for h. This finishes our discussion of the subjective Bayesian method.

5.4 The certainty factor model

The certainty factor model has been developed by E.H. Shortliffe and B.G. Buchanan for the purpose of introducing the notion of uncertainty in the MYCIN system. The development of the model was motivated, just as the subjective Bayesian method was, by the problems encountered in applying probability theory in production systems in a straightforward manner. We have suggested before that the model is unfounded from a theoretical point of view. Nevertheless, the model has since its introduction enjoyed widespread use in rule-based expert systems built after MYCIN: the model has been used, and is still being used, in a large number of rule-based expert systems. Even though it is not well-founded, in practice it seems to behave satisfactorily. The relative success of the model can be further accounted for by its computational simplicity. Following the treatment of the model in this section, Section 5.5 discusses an implementation of the model in PROLOG.

5.4.1 The measures of belief and disbelief

In Section 5.1 it has been argued that when modelling knowledge in production rules of the form ***if*** e ***then*** h_x ***fi***, a measure of uncertainty x

is associated with the hypothesis h expressing the degree to which the observation of evidence e influences the confidence in h. In developing the certainty factor model Shortliffe and Buchanan have chosen two basic measures of uncertainty: the *measure of belief* expressing the degree to which an observed piece of evidence increases the belief in a certain hypothesis, and the *measure of disbelief* expressing the degree to which an observed piece of evidence decreases the belief in a hypothesis. Although both measures are probability based, they model a notion of uncertainty conceptually different from probabilities. According to Shortliffe and Buchanan the need for new notions of uncertainty arose from their observation that an expert was often unwilling to accept the logical implications of probabilistic statements, such as: if $P(h \mid e) = x$, then $P(\bar{h} \mid e) = 1 - x$. They state that an expert would claim that 'evidence e in favour of hypothesis h should not be construed as evidence against the hypothesis as well'. The reason that the logical implication concerning $P(\bar{h} \mid e)$ may seem counterintuitive is explained by J. Pearl as follows. The phrase 'evidence e in favour of hypothesis h' is interpreted as stating an *increase* in the probability of the hypothesis from $P(h)$ to $P(h \mid e)$, with $P(h \mid e) > P(h)$; $P(h \mid e)$ is viewed relative to $P(h)$. On the other hand, in the argument of Shortliffe and Buchanan $P(\bar{h} \mid e)$ seems to be taken as an absolute probability irrespective of the prior $P(\bar{h})$. This somehow conveys the false idea that $P(\bar{h})$ increases by some positive factor. However, if for example $P(\bar{h}) = 0.9$ and $P(\bar{h} \mid e) = 0.5$, no expert will construe this considerable decrease in the probability of $\bar{h}$ as supporting the negation of h!

Shortliffe and Buchanan concluded from their observation that the number attached by an expert to a production rule is not a probability, but a measure of belief or disbelief in the hypothesis concerned.

Definition: Let P be a probability function defined on a sample space Ω, and let $h, e \subseteq \Omega$ such that $P(e) > 0$. The *measure of (increased) belief* MB is a function MB: $2^{\Omega} \times 2^{\Omega} \to [0,1]$, such that

$$\text{MB}(h,e) = \begin{cases} 1 & \text{if } P(h) = 1 \\ \max\left\{0, \dfrac{P(h \mid e) - P(h)}{1 - P(h)}\right\} & \text{otherwise} \end{cases}$$

The *measure of (increased) disbelief* MD is a function MD: $2^{\Omega} \times 2^{\Omega} \to [0,1]$, such that

$$\text{MD}(h,e) = \begin{cases} 1 & \text{if } P(h) = 0 \\ \max\left\{0, \dfrac{P(h) - P(h \mid e)}{P(h)}\right\} & \text{otherwise} \end{cases}$$

The measure of belief can be accounted for intuitively as follows. Let us depict the prior probability of the hypothesis h, that is $P(h)$, on a scale from 0 to 1:

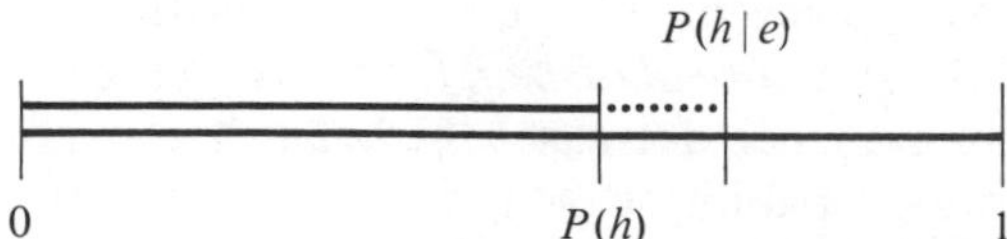

The maximum amount of belief that can still be added to the prior belief in h equals $1 - P(h)$. If a piece of evidence e is observed confirming h, that is, such that $P(h \mid e) > P(h)$, this observation results in adding the amount of belief $P(h \mid e) - P(h)$ to the prior belief in h. The belief in h has therefore been increased to the degree

$$\frac{P(h \mid e) - P(h)}{1 - P(h)}$$

The measure of disbelief can be accounted for similarly.

From the previous definition, it can readily be seen that for a given hypothesis h and a given piece of evidence e only one of the functions MB and MD attains a function value greater than zero. If $\text{MB}(h,e) > 0$, we have either $P(h \mid e) - P(h) > 0$ or $P(h) = 1$. If $P(h \mid e) - P(h) > 0$ we have $P(h) - P(h \mid e) < 0$ and consequently $\text{MD}(h,e) = 0$. Where $P(h) = 1$, we have $P(h \mid e) = 1$, hence $P(h) - P(h \mid e) = 0$ and $\text{MD}(h,e) = 0$. Similarly, it can be shown that $\text{MB}(h,e) = 0$ if $\text{MD}(h,e) > 0$. This corresponds explicitly with the idea that a particular piece of evidence may not be used both for and against a hypothesis. For evidence e neither confirming nor disconfirming the hypothesis h, that is, evidence e for which $P(h \mid e) = P(h)$ holds, we have $\text{MB}(h,e) = \text{MD}(h,e) = 0$.

We now associate a measure of belief $\text{MB}(h,e)$ and a measure of disbelief $\text{MD}(h,e)$ with a hypothesis h in a production rule ***if*** e ***then*** h ***fi***, as follows:

$$e \xrightarrow{\text{MB}(h,e),\ \text{MD}(h,e)} h$$

In this rule, the numbers $\text{MB}(h,e)$ and $\text{MD}(h,e)$ have the following meaning. An $\text{MB}(h,e) > 0$ (and hence $\text{MD}(h,e) = 0$) means that the observation of evidence e increases the confidence in h. $\text{MB}(h,e) = 1$ means that the hypothesis h has been fully confirmed by e. An $\text{MD}(h,e) > 0$ (and hence $\text{MB}(h,e) = 0$) indicates that the observation of e tends to disconfirm the hypothesis h. Note that the measures of belief and disbelief MB and MD are generally specified by the domain expert only for a selection of the arguments in their domain. If a probability function on the domain were known, the other function values of MB and MD could be computed using the respective definitions of these functions. However, we have argued before that such a probability function is virtually never known in practical applications. Similar to the subjective Bayesian method, the certainty factor model therefore offers a number of combination functions for approximating the function values of MB and MD that were not specified beforehand by the expert.

5.4.2 The combination functions

As we have seen before, when applying production rules various intermediate results are derived with a certain measure of uncertainty, which in turn are used as evidence in other production rules. The combination function which will be considered first is the one for propagating such uncertainty in evidence. Suppose that an intermediate result e has been obtained from earlier evidence e' with a measure of belief $\text{MB}(e,e')$ and a measure of disbelief $\text{MD}(e,e')$. This e is subsequently used as evidence in the production rule ***if*** *e* ***then*** *h* ***fi***:

$$e' \xrightarrow{\text{MB}(e,e'),\ \text{MD}(e,e')} e \xrightarrow{\text{MB}(h,e),\ \text{MD}(h,e)} h$$

Note once more that the left half shows a compressed network whereas the right half represents a single production rule. After applying the rule, we are interested in the measure of belief $\text{MB}(h,e')$ and the measure of disbelief $\text{MD}(h,e')$ such that:

$$e' \xrightarrow{\text{MB}(h,e'),\ \text{MD}(h,e')} h$$

The following combination functions prescribe that the measure of belief of e given e' will be used as a scaling factor for the measures of belief and disbelief associated with the production rule:

$$\text{MB}(h,e') = \text{MB}(h,e) \cdot \text{MB}(e,e')$$
$$\text{MD}(h,e') = \text{MD}(h,e) \cdot \text{MB}(e,e')$$

Here, $\text{MB}(h,e)$ is the measure of belief to be assigned to the hypothesis h if the piece of evidence e has been fully confirmed; it is the measure of belief associated with h in the production rule ***if*** *e* ***then*** *h* ***fi***. The meaning of $\text{MD}(h,e)$ is analogous. Note that the production rule does not contribute to the belief nor to the disbelief in h if e has been disconfirmed to some extent by evidence e', in other words if the condition e has failed. The certainty factor model in this respect differs conceptually from the subjective Bayesian method.

The condition part of a production rule generally consists of a number of constituent pieces of evidence which are interrelated by means of the operators ***and*** and ***or***. For example, the following inference network represents the composite evidence e_1 ***and*** e_2 where the constituent pieces of evidence e_1 and e_2 have been derived from some prior evidence e':

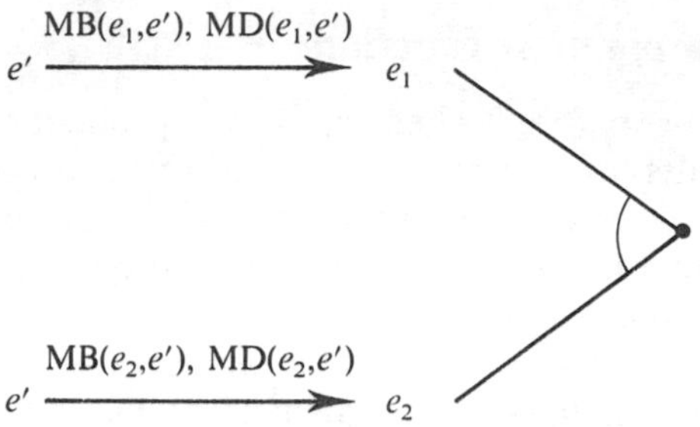

The certainty factor model comprises a number of combination functions for computing the measure of belief and the measure of disbelief for certain combinations of pieces of evidence. These combination functions are similar to the corresponding functions in the subjective Bayesian method:

$$\text{MB}(e_1 \textbf{ and } e_2,e') = \min\{\text{MB}(e_1,e'),\text{MB}(e_2,e')\}$$
$$\text{MB}(e_1 \textbf{ or } e_2,e') = \max\{\text{MB}(e_1,e'),\text{MB}(e_2,e')\}$$

$$\text{MD}(e_1 \textbf{ and } e_2,e') = \max\{\text{MD}(e_1,e'),\text{MD}(e_2,e')\}$$
$$\text{MD}(e_1 \textbf{ or } e_2,e') = \min\{\text{MD}(e_1,e'),\text{MD}(e_2,e')\}$$

The combination functions given above are commutative and associative in the first argument, so the order in which two constituent pieces of evidence in the condition part of a production rule have been specified has no influence on the resulting measures of belief and disbelief.

Until now, a production rule has been considered in isolation from the other production rules in a rule base. It is however possible that more than one production rule ***if*** e_i ***then*** h ***fi*** concludes on the same hypothesis h. Each of these different rules results in a separate measure of belief and disbelief for the same hypothesis h. We suppose that the pieces of evidence e_i specified in the co-concluding production rules have been derived from prior evidence e'_i. The uncertainty of the pieces of evidence e_i may be propagated to h in the manner described earlier in this section.

For two co-concluding production rules the inference network looks as follows:

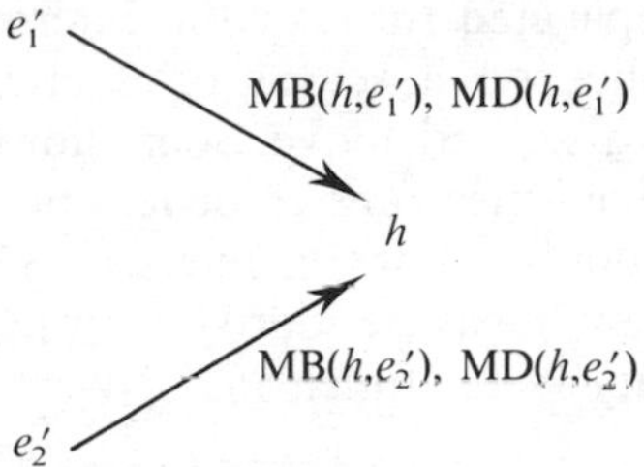

These partial measures of belief and disbelief each contribute to the total belief and disbelief in h. The combination functions for co-concluding production rules combine these partial measures of belief and disbelief to obtain the total belief and disbelief in h:

$$\mathrm{MB}(h,e'_1 \textbf{ co } e'_2) = \begin{cases} 0 & \text{if } \mathrm{MD}(h,e'_1 \textbf{ co } e'_2) = 1 \\ \mathrm{MB}(h,e'_1) + \mathrm{MB}(h,e'_2)(1 - \mathrm{MB}(h,e'_1)) & \text{otherwise} \end{cases}$$

$$\mathrm{MD}(h,e'_1 \textbf{ co } e'_2) = \begin{cases} 0 & \text{if } \mathrm{MB}(h,e'_1 \textbf{ co } e'_2) = 1 \\ \mathrm{MD}(h,e'_1) + \mathrm{MD}(h,e'_2)(1 - \mathrm{MD}(h,e'_1)) & \text{otherwise} \end{cases}$$

These combination functions are commutative and associative in the second argument, so the order in which the production rules are applied has no effect on the final result.

It should be remarked that the formulas given by Shortliffe and Buchanan as shown above suggest a number of properties of the measures of belief and disbelief which do not hold in general. For instance, it is possible that the measure of belief in h as well as the measure of disbelief in h given prior evidence e' are greater than zero after applying the combination functions for co-concluding production rules, which is contradictory to the original definitions of the functions MB and MD. Only in a small number of special cases under rigorous conditions concerning the interrelationships between the pieces of evidence and the hypotheses do the properties suggested in the formulas hold. In general, however, the combination functions are not correct with respect to the probabilistic foundation of the model.

5.4.3 The certainty factor function

In the original formulation of the certainty factor model, computation took place in terms of the measures of belief and disbelief; the uncertainties were propagated through the inference network obtained from top-down inference on a set of production rules by using the combination functions discussed above. Soon, however, the need arose to express the finally derived measures of belief and disbelief for a certain hypothesis in a single number. For this purpose, Shortliffe and Buchanan have introduced a new measure derived from the two basic ones mentioned: the certainty factor function.

> **Definition:** Let Ω be a sample space, and let $h, e \subseteq \Omega$. Let MB and MD be defined as in Section 5.4.1. The *certainty factor function* CF is a function $\mathrm{CF}: 2^{\Omega} \times 2^{\Omega} \rightarrow [-1,1]$, such that:
>
> $$\mathrm{CF}(h,e) = \frac{\mathrm{MB}(h,e) - \mathrm{MD}(h,e)}{1 - \min\{\mathrm{MB}(h,e),\mathrm{MD}(h,e)\}}$$

The 'scaling factor' $1 - \min\{\mathrm{MB}(h,e),\mathrm{MD}(h,e)\}$ has been incorporated into the model for pragmatic reasons. This scaling factor has no influence on the certainty factor when considering only one piece of evidence, since then we have $1 - \min\{\mathrm{MB}(h,e),\mathrm{MD}(h,e)\} = 1$. However, when we consider more than one piece of evidence or more than one hypothesis, this is not always the case as has been mentioned before.

Note that, for given h and e, a certainty factor is a number between -1 and $+1$; this is contrary to the measures of belief and disbelief, each lying in the closed interval $[0,1]$. It can easily be seen from the definition given above that a negative certainty factor indicates that the hypothesis is disconfirmed by the evidence and that a positive certainty factor indicates that the hypothesis is confirmed by the evidence. A certainty factor equal to zero indicates that the evidence does not influence belief in the hypothesis.

In present implementations of the certainty factor model, the measures of belief and disbelief are no longer used in the computation; only the certainty factor is applied instead of the measure of belief and disbelief MB(h,e) and MD(h,e). With each production rule ***if*** *e* ***then*** *h* ***fi*** now is associated a certainty factor CF(h,e):

$$e \xrightarrow{\mathrm{CF}(h,e)} h$$

For manipulating these certainty factors, Shortliffe and Buchanan have defined new combination functions expressed in terms of certainty factors only. A small calculation effort suffices to prove that these combination functions can be derived from the corresponding ones for the measures of belief and disbelief.

The combination function for propagating uncertain evidence is the following:

$$\mathrm{CF}(h,e') = \mathrm{CF}(h,e) \cdot \max\{0,\mathrm{CF}(e,e')\}$$

Here, $\mathrm{CF}(h,e)$ is the certainty factor associated with the hypothesis h by the production rule ***if*** *e* ***then*** *h* ***fi*** if the evidence e has been observed with absolute certainty; $\mathrm{CF}(e,e')$ indicates the actual confidence in e based on some prior evidence e'.

The function for combining two certainty factors $\mathrm{CF}(e_1,e')$ and $\mathrm{CF}(e_2,e')$ of two constituting pieces of evidence e_1 and e_2 to obtain a certainty factor for the conjunction e_1 ***and*** e_2 of these pieces of evidence is:

$$\mathrm{CF}(e_1 \textbf{ and } e_2,e') = \min\{\mathrm{CF}(e_1,e'),\mathrm{CF}(e_2,e')\}$$

For the disjunction of these pieces of evidence, we have:

$$\mathrm{CF}(e_1 \textbf{ or } e_2,e') = \max\{\mathrm{CF}(e_1,e'),\mathrm{CF}(e_2,e')\}$$

Finally, the combination function for combining two certainty factors $\mathrm{CF}(h,e_1')$ and $\mathrm{CF}(h,e_2')$ which have been derived from two co-concluding production rules ***if*** e_i ***then*** *h* ***fi***, $i = 1,2$, is as follows:

$$\mathrm{CF}(h,e_1' \textbf{ co } e_2')$$

$$= \begin{cases} \mathrm{CF}(h,e_1') + \mathrm{CF}(h,e_2')(1-\mathrm{CF}(h,e_1')) & \text{if } \mathrm{CF}(h,e_i') > 0,\ i = 1,2 \\ \dfrac{\mathrm{CF}(h,e_1')+\mathrm{CF}(h,e_2')}{1 - \min\{|\mathrm{CF}(h,e_1')|,|\mathrm{CF}(h,e_2')|\}} & \text{if } -1 < \mathrm{CF}(h,e_1')\cdot\mathrm{CF}(h,e_2') \leqslant 0 \\ \mathrm{CF}(h,e_1') + \mathrm{CF}(h,e_2')(1+\mathrm{CF}(h,e_1')) & \text{if } \mathrm{CF}(h,e_i') < 0,\ i = 1,2 \end{cases}$$

The following example demonstrates how these combination functions for certainty factors can be applied.

EXAMPLE 5.7

Consider the following five production rules:

R_1: ***if*** *a* ***and*** (*b* ***or*** *c*) ***then*** $h_{0.80}$ ***fi***

R_2: ***if*** *d* ***and*** *f* ***then*** $b_{0.60}$ ***fi***

R_3: ***if*** *f* ***or*** *g* ***then*** $h_{0.40}$ ***fi***

R_4: ***if*** *a* ***then*** $d_{0.75}$ ***fi***

R_5: ***if*** *i* ***then*** $g_{0.30}$ ***fi***

The expert has associated with the conclusion h of rule R_1 the certainty factor CF(h,a ***and*** (b ***or*** c)) = 0.80, with the conclusion b of rule R_2 the certainty factor CF(b,d ***and*** f) = 0.60, and so on. We suppose that h is the goal hypothesis. When applying backward chaining, the user will be asked to provide further information on a, c, f and i. We assume that, using the prior knowledge e', the user associates the following certainty factors with his answers:

$$\begin{aligned}
\mathrm{CF}(a,e') &= 1.00\\
\mathrm{CF}(c,e') &= 0.50\\
\mathrm{CF}(f,e') &= 0.70\\
\mathrm{CF}(i,e') &= -0.40
\end{aligned}$$

Using backward chaining, R_1 will be the first rule selected for application. Note that this rule will eventually yield a partial certainty factor for h. It will be evident that we cannot simply associate the certainty factor 0.80 with h after application of R_1; this number indicates the certainty of h only in the case of absolute certainty of a ***and*** (b ***or*** c). Recall that, for computing the actual certainty of h from this rule, we have first to compute the actual certainty of a ***and*** (b ***or*** c) and then to propagate it to h using the combination function for uncertain evidence. However, the actual certainty of a ***and*** (b ***or*** c) is not known; we have to compute it from the separate certainty factors for a, b and c using the combination functions for composite hypotheses. The actual certainty factors of a and c are known; the user has specified the certainty factors 1.00 and 0.50 for these pieces of evidence. For b, however, we still have to compute a certainty factor. We select the production rule R_2 for doing so. The combination function for uncertain evidence now prescribes that we have to multiply the certainty factor 0.60 for b mentioned in the rule by the actual certainty factor of the evidence d ***and*** f. Again, we have to obtain separate certainty factors for d and f. The user has associated the certainty factor 0.70 with f; by applying rule R_4 we find for d the certainty factor $1.00 \cdot 0.75 = 0.75$. Using the combination function for composite hypotheses we arrive at the following certainty factor for d ***and*** f (we use e'_1 to denote all evidence used in this particular reasoning chain):

$$\mathrm{CF}(d\ \textbf{\textit{and}}\ f,e'_1) = \min\{\mathrm{CF}(d,e'_1),\mathrm{CF}(f,e'_1)\} = 0.70$$

Subsequently, the combination function for uncertain evidence is applied to compute the actual certainty factor for b:

$$\begin{aligned}\mathrm{CF}(b,e'_1) &= \mathrm{CF}(b,d\ \textbf{\textit{and}}\ f)\cdot\max\{0,\mathrm{CF}(d\ \textbf{\textit{and}}\ f,e'_1)\}\\ &= 0.60\cdot 0.70 = 0.42\end{aligned}$$

Recall that we had to compute certainty factors for a, b and c separately in order to be able to compute a certainty factor for the composite evidence a ***and*** (b ***or*** c). All the required certainty factors are now available. We apply the combination function for a disjunction of hypotheses to compute:

$$\mathrm{CF}(b\ \textbf{\textit{or}}\ c,e'_1) = \max\{\mathrm{CF}(b,e'_1),\mathrm{CF}(c,e'_1)\} = 0.50$$

and, subsequently, the combination function for a conjunction of hypotheses to compute:

$$\mathrm{CF}(a\ \textbf{\textit{and}}\ (b\ \textbf{\textit{or}}\ c),e'_1) = \min\{\mathrm{CF}(a,e'_1),\mathrm{CF}(b\ \textbf{\textit{or}}\ c,e'_1)\} = 0.50$$

From the production rule R_1 we therefore obtain the following (partial) certainty factor for h:

$$\begin{aligned}\mathrm{CF}(h,e'_1) &= \mathrm{CF}(h,a\ \textbf{\textit{and}}\ (b\ \textbf{\textit{or}}\ c))\cdot\max\{0,\mathrm{CF}(a\ \textbf{\textit{and}}\ (b\ \textbf{\textit{or}}\ c),e'_1)\}\\ &= 0.80\cdot 0.50 = 0.40\end{aligned}$$

Similarly, from the other production rule concluding on h, that is, rule R_3, the following certainty factor is obtained:

$$\begin{aligned}\mathrm{CF}(h,e'_2) &= \mathrm{CF}(h,f\ \textbf{\textit{or}}\ g)\cdot\max\{0,\mathrm{CF}(f\ \textbf{\textit{or}}\ g,e'_2)\}\\ &= 0.40\cdot 0.70 = 0.28\end{aligned}$$

In the course of this computation a certainty factor equal to zero is associated with g due to $\mathrm{CF}(i,e') = -0.40$. The net certainty factor for h is computed from the two partial ones by applying the combination function for co-concluding production rules:

$$\begin{aligned}\mathrm{CF}(h,e'_1\ \textbf{\textit{co}}\ e'_2) &= \mathrm{CF}(h,e'_1) + \mathrm{CF}(h,e'_2)\cdot(1-\mathrm{CF}(h,e'_1))\\ &= 0.40 + 0.28\cdot 0.60 = 0.568\end{aligned}$$

Note that this net certainty factor is greater than each of the certainty factors for h separately.

5.5 The certainty factor model in PROLOG

Because of its simplicity, the certainty factor model has been employed in many rule-based expert systems as a means for representing and reasoning with uncertainty. In this section we shall see that the model is easy to implement; we shall discuss an implementation of the model in the PROLOG language. The point of departure for this program will be the top-down inference program as discussed in Chapter 3. In the preceding sections dealing with the certainty factor model no explicit distinction was made between facts and production rules, and no attention was paid to the way in which the predicates and actions in the conditions and conclusions of a production rule deal with certainty factors. In the next section, we shall concentrate on these two issues before discussing the actual implementation of the model in Section 5.5.2.

5.5.1 Certainty factors in facts and rules

In an expert system using production rules as a knowledge-representation formalism, a distinction is made between facts and production rules. In Chapter 3 we have introduced notational conventions for the representation of facts and production rules. Now recall that, when employing the certainty factor model, each conclusion of each production rule is assigned a certainty factor. To this end, we extend the syntax of a production rule. In the following definition, this extended formalism is introduced.

Definition: A *production rule* is an expression of the following form:

<production-rule>	::=	***if*** <antecedent> ***then*** <consequent> ***fi***
<antecedent>	::=	<disjunction> {***and*** <disjunction>}*
<disjunction>	::=	<condition> {***or*** <condition>}*
<consequent>	::=	<conclusion> ***with*** <cf>
<condition>	::=	<predicate> (<object>,<attribute>, <constant>)
<conclusion>	::=	<action> (<object>,<attribute>, <constant>)
<predicate>	::=	*same* | *greaterthan* | ···
<action>	::=	*add*
<cf>	::=	*cf* = <real with range [−1,1]>

In the previous definition we have restricted ourselves to production rules containing precisely one conclusion in their consequent; furthermore, only the action *add* has been specified. In addition, note that we have chosen for a representation in object–attribute–value tuples instead of the variable–value representation.

EXAMPLE 5.8

Consider the following production rule:

if
same(*patient,complaint,abdominal-pain*) ***and***
same(*patient,auscultation,murmur*) ***and***
same(*patient,palpation,pulsating-mass*)
then
add(*patient,disorder,aortic-aneurysm*) ***with*** $cf = 0.8$
fi

In this rule, three pieces of evidence have been specified: the patient suffers from abdominal pain, upon auscultation a murmur is perceived, and upon palpation a pulsating mass is felt. If these three pieces of evidence have been observed in a particular patient, the hypothesis that the patient has an aortic aneurysm will be confirmed to a degree 0.8 in the range of −1 to +1.

In Chapter 3 we have seen that facts are derived from applying the production rules; recall that a fact is considered to be an object–attribute pair with the value(s) the attribute has adopted. It will be evident that, if we employ the certainty factor model, values may be derived which have not necessarily been established with absolute certainty. During the inference, therefore, each value is assigned an appropriate certainty factor. For this purpose, the representation formalism for facts introduced in Chapter 3 has to be extended with the notion of a certainty factor as well.

Definition: A *fact* is an expression of one of the following forms:

(1) $o.a^s = c_{cf}$, where o is an object, a^s is a single-valued attribute, c is a constant, and cf is a certainty factor in the closed interval $[-1,1]$, or

(2) $o.a^m = \{c^i_{cf_i} \mid i \geqslant 1\}$, where a^m is a multi-valued attribute, c^i a constant, and cf_i is a certainty factor.

EXAMPLE 5.9

Consider the production rule from the preceding example once more. If all three pieces of evidence mentioned in the condition part of the rule have been observed with absolute certainty, then by applying the production rule the hypothesis that the patient suffers from an aortic aneurysm will be confirmed with a certainty factor equal to 0.8. Application of this rule therefore results in the fact (we assume here that the attribute *disorder* is single-valued):

$$patient.disorder = aortic\text{-}aneurysm_{\ 0.8}$$

In Chapter 3 we stated that a predicate in a condition of a production rule specifies a comparison of the actual value(s) the attribute mentioned in the condition has obtained with the constant specified in the condition. Recall that such a predicate yields one of the truth values *true* or *false*. Now, when applying the certainty factor model we not only have to consider the values the attribute has adopted, but we also have to take into account the certainty factors associated with these values. Most system predicates therefore also test whether the certainty factor associated with the attribute value of interest lies within a certain range.

EXAMPLE 5.10

In the condition:

same(*patient*,*complaint*,*abdominal-pain*)

the predicate *same* compares the constant *abdominal-pain* with the actual complaints of the patient. Only if the attribute value *abdominal-pain* has been found for the attribute *complaint* of the object *patient* with a certainty factor greater than 0.2 does evaluation of the condition yield the truth value *true*. For example, if the fact set contains the fact:

$$patient.complaint = \{abdominal\text{-}pain_{\ 0.15}\}$$

then evaluation of the above condition yields the truth value *false*. However, should the fact set contain the following fact:

$$patient.complaint = \{abdominal\text{-}pain_{\ 0.8}\}$$

then evaluation of the mentioned condition would yield the value *true*. The 0.2 threshold employed by the predicate *same* was chosen by Shortliffe and Buchanan to prevent MYCIN from pursuing hypotheses for which there was only limited, insufficient evidence.

Table 5.1 Behaviour of some predicates with respect to certainty factors.

Predicate name	*Returns* true *if* $(o.a,v)$ *satisfies*	*Returned certainty factor*
same (o,a,v)	$cf(o.a,v) > 0.2$	$cf(o,a,v)$
notsame (o,a,v)	$cf(o.a,v) \leq 0.2$	1
known (o,a,v)	$\exists v\,[cf(o.a,v)] > 0.2$	1
notknown (o,a,v)	$\forall v\,[cf(o.a,v)] \leq 0.2$	1

A predicate not only returns a truth value, but in case of success it returns a certainty factor for the particular piece of evidence as well; the predicate *same* for example just returns the certainty factor found in the fact set for the attribute value concerned.

EXAMPLE 5.11

Consider once more the condition:

same(patient,complaint,abdominal-pain)

and the fact set:

$$patient.complaint = \{abdominal\text{-}pain_{\ 0.8}\}$$

Evaluation of the condition not only yields the value *true* but a certainty factor as well; in this case the certainty factor 0.8 is returned.

Table 5.1 summarizes the behaviour of a number of frequently used predicates. In this table $(o.a,v)$ denotes the object–attribute–value tuple specified in the condition; $cf(o.a,v)$ denotes the certainty factor for the value v in the fact concerning the object–attribute pair $o.a$. The last line in the table should now be read as follows: upon evaluation the condition *notknown*$(o.a,v)$ yields the truth value *true* if all attribute values in the fact concerning the object–attribute pair $o.a$ have a certainty factor less than or equal to 0.2. In that case, the predicate returns the certainty factor 1.

5.5.2 Implementation of the certainty factor model

In this section, the certainty factor model for reasoning with uncertainty is integrated into the PROLOG implementation of top-down inference, as discussed in Section 3.2.2.

The first thing we have to do is to extend the representation of a production rule in a Horn clause with the notion of a certainty factor. To start with, we restrict ourselves to production rules having only conjunctions in their condition part; we shall deal with disjunctions later on in this section.

EXAMPLE 5.12

We recall from Section 3.2.2 that a production rule is represented in a Horn clause of the following form:

```
add(patient,disorder,aortic_aneurysm) :-
    same(patient,complaint,abdominal_pain),
    same(patient,auscultation,murmur),
    same(patient,palpation,pulsating_mass).
```

Recall that the representation of a production rule in a Horn clause illustrated in Example 5.12 has the advantage that the production rule itself may be looked on as a procedure for its own evaluation; the actual evaluation is performed by the PROLOG interpreter. In accord with this idea, the production rule could also take care of computing the appropriate certainty factor to be associated with the fact which is derived by the rule when evaluation of its conditions has succeeded. However, we have mentioned before that a major objective in designing knowledge-based systems is to keep knowledge and inference explicitly separated from each other. Therefore, we have chosen an approach in which the computation takes place outside the production rules in the inference engine.

For computing the appropriate certainty factor for a fact which is derived from a successful production rule, it is not enough to have only the certainty factor specified in the conclusion of the rule available. It will be evident from the discussion in the previous sections that the certainty factors resulting from the evaluation of the conditions of the rule have to be known as well. Since we apply the PROLOG interpreter for the evaluation of a production rule and PROLOG does not support global variables, it is necessary to pass the certainty factors obtained from the evaluation of the conditions of a production rule to its conclusion explicitly. In the PROLOG representation of a production rule we therefore augment each condition with an extra argument, which is used as an output parameter to be instantiated to the certainty factor resulting from evaluation of that condition. The conclusion of a production rule is equally augmented with an extra argument. This extra argument is a term `cf(CFrule,CFlist)` in which `CFrule` is the certainty factor associated with the conclusion of the rule, and `CFlist` is a list of variables which will be instantiated to the certainty factors obtained from the conditions.

EXAMPLE 5.13

The following Horn clause once more shows the production rule from Example 5.12, but this time certainty factors have been included in the manner discussed above:

```
add(patient,disorder,aortic_aneurysm,cf(0.8,[CF1,CF2,CF3])) :-
    same(patient,complaint,abdominal_pain,CF1),
    same(patient,auscultation,murmur,CF2),
    same(patient,palpation,pulsating_mass,CF3).
```

When the predicate *same* returns the truth value *true*, the evaluation of the first condition of this rule leads to instantiation of the variable `CF1` to a certainty factor (we return to this shortly). A similar remark can be made with respect to the second and third condition. The resulting certainty factors are then collected in the second argument of the term `cf(0.8,[CF1,CF2,CF3])` in the conclusion of the clause. The specified number 0.8 is the certainty factor associated by the expert with the conclusion of the rule.

It will be evident that, after the evaluation of the rule has been completed, the term `cf(CFrule,CFlist)` in the conclusion of the rule contains all ingredients necessary for applying the combination functions for composite hypotheses and the combination function for uncertain evidence.

EXAMPLE 5.14

Reconsider the production rule from Example 5.13. Suppose that evaluation of the rule led to instantiation of the variable `CF1` to the value 0.5, of `CF2` to the value 0.7, and of `CF3` to 0.9. The fourth argument in the conclusion of the rule is therefore instantiated to the term `cf(0.8,[0.5,0.7,0.9])`. The evidence mentioned in the condition part of the rule consists of three distinct pieces of evidence. We now have to compute a certainty factor for the composite evidence before the uncertainty can be propagated to the hypothesis specified in the conclusion of the rule. The inference engine can find the information which is necessary for doing so in the fourth argument of the conclusion of the rule; using the combination function for composite hypotheses it determines the minimum of the certainty factors which resulted from evaluation of the separate conditions, in the present example $\min\{0.5, 0.7, 0.9\} = 0.5$. Then it applies the combination function for propagating uncertain evidence; the certainty factor associated with the conclusion of the rule is multiplied by the certainty factor of the composite evidence. The inference engine can also find the certainty factor of the rule in the fourth argument of the conclusion of the rule. In this example, the computation yields $0.8 \cdot 0.5 = 0.4$. This number is the certainty factor for the fact derived from the applied rule.

Extending the PROLOG implementation of the top-down inference engine with the certainty factor model only requires some minor alterations and additions. In Chapter 3 we have described that, in the process of tracing an object–attribute pair, first it is checked whether or not the pair has already been traced before. If the object–attribute pair has not been traced as yet, the inference engine tries to infer values for it by selecting and applying relevant production rules. If applying rules has failed to yield values for the object–attribute pair, the user is requested to provide further information. Since this process is not affected by the incorporation of the certainty factor model, the basic Horn clauses remain unaltered:

```
trace_values(Object,Attribute) :-
     fact(Object,Attribute,_,_),!.
trace_values(Object,Attribute) :-
     infer(Object,Attribute),!,
     ask(Object,Attribute).

infer(Object,Attribute) :-
     select_rule(Object,Attribute),
     fail.
infer(_,_).
```

The clause responsible for the selection and evaluation of a production rule is modified to deal with certainty factors as follows:

```
select_rule(Object,Attribute) :-
     add(Object,Attribute,Value,Cffunction),
     compute(Object,Attribute,Value,Cffunction).
```

By means of `add(Object,Attribute,Value,Cffunction)`, `select_rule` selects and evaluates a single production rule. Recall that, after the evaluation of the selected rule has been completed, the variable `Cffunction` will have been instantiated to a term of the form `cf(CFrule,CFlist)`. Following the selection and evaluation of a rule, `select_rule` calls the procedure `compute`. This procedure takes care of computing the appropriate certainty factor to be associated with the newly derived fact and then adds it with the computed certainty factor to the fact set:

```
compute(Object,Attribute,Value,cf(CFrule,CFlist)) :-
    composite_hypotheses(CFlist,CFmin),
    uncertain_evidence(CFrule,CFmin,CF),
    co_concluding_rules(Object,Attribute,Value,CF,CFfact),!,
    asserta(fact(Object,Attribute,Value,CFfact)).
```

Using the combination function for composite hypotheses first a certainty factor is computed for the composite evidence in the rule. This combination function simply takes the minimum of the certainty factors of the constituting pieces of evidence in the condition part of the rule, and is described in the following clause:

```
composite_hypotheses(CFlist,CFmin) :-
    minimum(CFlist,CFmin).
```

The computed certainty factor `CFmin` for the composite evidence is subsequently propagated to the hypothesis in the conclusion of the rule by means of the combination function for uncertain evidence that multiplies `Cfmin` by the certainty factor associated with the conclusion of the rule:

```
uncertain_evidence(CFrule,CFmin,CF) :-
    maximum([0,CFmin],CFcond),
    CF is CFcond * CFrule.
```

`CF` is the certainty factor that will be attached to the specified attribute value solely on account of this rule. Now recall that other rules which conclude the same attribute value may have been applied before. The certainty factors yielded by applying such co-concluding production rules have to be combined into one net certainty factor. In the procedure `compute` therefore the procedure `co_concluding_rules` is called. This procedure implements the combination function for co-concluding production rules:

```
co_concluding_rules(Object,Attribute,Value,CFnew,CFfact) :-
    retract(fact(Object,Attribute,Value,CFold)),!,
    case(CFnew,CFold,CFfact).
co_concluding_rules(_,_,_,CF,CF).
```

The first clause of `co_concluding_rules` investigates by means of the call `retract(fact(Object,Attribute,Value,CFold))` whether or not the specified object–attribute–value tuple occurs in the fact set. If such a fact is not present, the match with the first clause fails. In this case, the just evaluated rule was the first to draw a conclusion concerning the given tuple. The certainty factor computed from this rule for the attribute value is therefore the certainty factor to be associated with the newly derived fact. This certainty factor will be attached to the fact by means of the second clause of `co_concluding_rules`. On the other hand, if the call `retract(fact(Object,Attribute,Value,CFold))` in the `co_concluding_rules` clause succeeds, this specific object–attribute–value tuple has already been derived before from applying at least one other rule. The combination function for co-concluding production rules now has to be applied for computing the net certainty factor. We repeat the combination function for co-concluding rules here, using a somewhat different notation:

$$\mathrm{CF}\mathit{fact} = \begin{cases} \mathrm{CF}\mathit{old} + \mathrm{CF}\mathit{new} - \mathrm{CF}\mathit{old} \cdot \mathrm{CF}\mathit{new} & \text{if } \mathrm{CF}\mathit{old} > 0 \text{ and } \mathrm{CF}\mathit{new} > 0 \\ \dfrac{\mathrm{CF}\mathit{old} + \mathrm{CF}\mathit{new}}{1 - \min\{|\mathrm{CF}\mathit{old}|, |\mathrm{CF}\mathit{new}|\}} & \text{if } -1 < \mathrm{CF}\mathit{old} \cdot \mathrm{CF}\mathit{new} \leqslant 0 \\ \mathrm{CF}\mathit{old} + \mathrm{CF}\mathit{new} + \mathrm{CF}\mathit{old} \cdot \mathrm{CF}\mathit{new} & \text{if } \mathrm{CF}\mathit{old} < 0 \text{ and } \mathrm{CF}\mathit{new} < 0 \end{cases}$$

CF*new* is the certainty factor for the object–attribute–value tuple yielded by the last applied production rule; CF*old* is the certainty factor associated with the attribute value on account of previously applied production rules. To conclude, CF*fact* is the net certainty factor that will be associated with the attribute value by the combination function. In the following three Horn clauses, the three cases discerned can easily be distinguished:

```
case(CFnew,CFold,CFfact) :-
     CFnew > 0,
     CFold > 0,!,
     CFfact is CFold + CFnew - CFold * CFnew.
case(CFnew,CFold,CFfact) :-
     CFnew < 0,
     CFold < 0,!,
     CFfact is CFold + CFnew + CFold * CFnew.
case(CFnew,CFold,CFfact) :-
     Numerator is CFnew + CFold,
     (CFnew >= 0, AbsCFnew is CFnew;
      AbsCFnew is -CFnew),
     (CFold >= 0, AbsCFold is CFold;
      AbsCFold is -CFold),
     minimum([AbsCFnew,AbsCFold],Min),
     Denominator is 1 - Min,
     (Denominator > 0,
      CFfact is Numerator/Denominator;
      nl,
      write('Contradictory information found!'),
      nl,!,
      fail).
```

In Section 5.5.1 we mentioned that most system predicates take the certainty factor of an attribute value found in the fact set into account. The predicate *same*, for example, tests whether the value of the certainty factor of the specified attribute value is greater than 0.2. So the definitions of the system predicates have to be extended to include a test on certainty factors. The clause defining the predicate *same* is extended in the following way:

```
same(Object,Attribute,Value,CF) :-
     trace_values(Object,Attribute),!,
     fact(Object,Attribute,Value,CF),!,
     CF > 0.2.
```

Until now we have considered only production rules having no disjunctions in their condition part. Recall that in Chapter 3 we simply used the PROLOG ';' for representing the logical ***or***. Due to the introduction of certainty factors we can no longer use ';' for doing so. The PROLOG interpreter evaluates conditions connected by means of ';' from left to right until one of the conditions has been fulfilled. Then the evaluation stops, that is, the remaining conditions will not be examined. When employing the certainty factor model, however, in case of a disjunction, *all* conditions in the disjunction must be examined, since the combination function for composite hypothesis has to return the maximum of the certainty factors yielded by the conditions which are part of the disjunction. (There is one exception not dealt with here; where a condition yields a certainty factor equal to one the remaining conditions may be skipped.) Therefore, we introduce for the representation of the logical ***or*** a new system predicate `or` having two arguments. The first argument is a list of the conditions which are connected by the ***or*** operator; the second argument is a variable which will be instantiated to the certainty factor yielded by the combination function for composite hypotheses for the entire disjunction. This certainty factor is inserted at the fourth argument of the conclusion of the rule just like the certainty factors of the other conditions are.

EXAMPLE 5.15

An example of a production rule containing the predicate `or` is the following:

```
add(patient,disorder,aortic_regurgitation,cf(0.7,[CF1,CF2,CF3])) :-
     greaterthan(patient,systolic_pressure,'140mmHg',CF1),
     greaterthan(patient,pulse_pressure,'50mmHg',CF2),
     or([same(patient,auscultation,diastolic_murmur,_),
         same(patient,palpation,enlarged_heart,_)],CF3).
```

Note that a disjunction of two pieces of evidence is treated as being a single piece of evidence.

The predicate or is defined by the following Horn clause:

```
or(Conditions,Cf) :-
    or_conditions(Conditions,List_of_cf),!,
    not(List_of_cf = []),
    maximum(List_of_cf,Cf).
```

The conditions in the list `Conditions` are evaluated by means of `or_conditions(Conditions,List_of_cf)`. We shall see in `or_conditions` that if the evaluation of a condition yields the truth value *true*, the corresponding certainty factor is added to the list `List_of_cf`. If this list turns out to be non-empty after evaluation of all conditions from `Conditions` then at least one of them has been satisfied. The combination function for composite hypotheses subsequently selects the maximal certainty factor occurring in the list. If, on the other hand, the list is empty, the entire condition fails.

In the following procedure:

```
or_conditions([],[]) :- !.
or_conditions([Condition|Restconditions],[Cf|List_of_cf]) :-
    call(Condition),
    arg(4,Condition,Cf),!,
    or_conditions(Restconditions,List_of_cf).
or_conditions([Condition|Restconditions],List_of_cf) :-
    or_conditions(Restconditions,List_of_cf).
```

the separate conditions specified in the list `Conditions` are evaluated one by one by recursively calling `or_conditions`. The first clause represents the termination criterion for the recursion specified. The second clause evaluates the first condition in the list of conditions by means of the predefined predicate `call`. If the condition is satisfied, the certainty factor resulting from the evaluation is added to the list of certainty factors. Subsequently, `or_conditions` is called recursively for the remainder of the disjunction. If on the other hand the condition fails, it is simply skipped by means of the third `or_conditions` clause. So a condition that fails upon evaluation does not contribute to the list of certainty factors `List_of_cf`. This recursive evaluation process is repeated until all conditions from the disjunction have been examined.

5.6 The Dempster–Shafer theory

In the 1960s, A. Dempster laid the foundation for a new mathematical theory of uncertainty; in the 1970s, this theory was extended by G. Shafer to what is now known as the *Dempster–Shafer theory*. This theory may be viewed as a generalization of probability theory. Contrary to the subjective Bayesian method and the certainty factor model, Dempster–Shafer theory has not been especially developed for reasoning with uncertainty in expert systems. Only at the beginning of the 1980s did it become apparent that the theory might be suitable for such a purpose. However, the theory cannot be applied in an expert system without modification. For application in a rule-based system, for example, several combination functions are lacking. Moreover, the theory in its original form has an exponential computational complexity. For rendering it useful in the context of expert systems, therefore, several modifications of the theory have been proposed. In Sections 5.6.1 and 5.6.2 the main principles of the theory are discussed. Section 5.6.3 briefly touches on a possible adaptation of the theory for application in a production system.

5.6.1 The probability assignment

We have mentioned above that the Dempster–Shafer theory may be viewed as a generalization of probability theory. The development of the theory has been motivated by the observation that probability theory is not able to distinguish between *uncertainty* and *ignorance* owing to incompleteness of information. Recall that, in probability theory, probabilities have to be associated with individual atomic hypotheses. Only if these probabilities are known are we able to compute other probabilities of interest. In the Dempster–Shafer theory, however, it is possible to associate measures of uncertainty with sets of hypotheses, interpreted as disjunctions, instead of with the individual hypotheses only, and nevertheless to be able to make statements concerning the uncertainty of other sets of hypotheses. Note that, in this way, the theory is able to distinguish between uncertainty and ignorance.

EXAMPLE 5.16

Consider a house officers' practice where a patient consults his physician for chest pain radiating to the arms and neck; the pain does not disappear during rest. In this simplified example we assume that there are only four possible disorders to be considered as a diagnosis: the patient is either suffering from a heart attack, pericarditis, pulmonary embolism, or an aortic dissection. Heart attack and pericarditis are disorders of the heart; pulmonary embolism and aortic dissection are disorders of the blood vessels. Now suppose that we have certain clues indicating that the patient has a disorder of the heart; the strength of our belief is expressed in the number 0.4. In the Dempster–Shafer theory this number is assigned to the set

> {*heart-attack,pericarditis*}, viewed as the composite hypothesis *heart-attack* ***or*** *pericarditis*; there is no number associated with the individual hypotheses, because more specific information indicating that one of these two hypotheses is the cause of the complaints is not available. Note that in probability theory the number 0.4 would have to be distributed over the individual hypotheses (without more information, each of the two hypotheses would be assigned the number 0.2). In that case, the false impression would be given of more information than is actually present.

The strategy followed in the Dempster–Shafer theory for dealing with uncertainty roughly amounts to starting with an initial set of hypotheses, then for each piece of evidence associating a measure of uncertainty with certain subsets of the original set of hypotheses until measures of uncertainty may be associated with all possible subsets on account of the combined evidence. The initial set of all hypotheses in the problem domain is called the *frame of discernment*. In such a frame of discernment the individual hypotheses are assumed to be disjoint. The impact of a piece of evidence on the confidence or belief in certain subsets of a given frame of discernment is described by means of a function which is defined below.

> **Definition:** Let Θ be a frame of discernment. If with each subset $x \subseteq \Theta$ a number $m(x)$ is associated such that:
>
> (1) $m(x) \geqslant 0$
>
> (2) $m(\varnothing) = 0$
>
> (3) $\sum_{x \subseteq \Theta} m(x) = 1$
>
> then m is called a *basic probability assignment* on Θ. For each subset $x \subseteq \Theta$, the number $m(x)$ is called the *basic probability number* of x.

We must define another two notions.

> **Definition:** Let Θ be a frame of discernment and let m be a basic probability assignment on Θ. A set $x \subseteq \Theta$ is called a *focal element* in m if $m(x) > 0$. The *core* of m, denoted by $\kappa(m)$, is the set of all focal elements in m.

Note the similarity between a basic probability assignment and a probability function. A probability function associates with each element in Θ a number from the interval [0,1] such that the sum of these numbers equals 1; a basic probability assignment associates with each element in 2^Θ a number in the interval [0,1] such that once more the sum of the numbers equal 1.

EXAMPLE 5.17

Consider the preceding medical example once more. In this example, the frame of discernment is the set $\Theta = \{$*heart-attack, pericarditis,pulmonary-embolism,aortic-dissection*$\}$. Note that each basic probability assignment on Θ assigns basic probability numbers to $2^4 = 16$ sets (including the empty set). If for a specific patient there is no evidence pointing at a certain diagnosis in particular, the basic probability number 1 is assigned to the entire frame of discernment:

$$m_0(x) = \begin{cases} 1 & \text{if } x = \Theta \\ 0 & \text{otherwise} \end{cases}$$

Note that each proper subset of the frame of discernment gets assigned the number 0. The core of m_0 is equal to $\{\Theta\}$. Now suppose that some evidence has become available that points to the composite hypothesis *heart-attack* ***or*** *pericarditis* with some certainty. Then the subset {*heart-attack,pericarditis*} will be assigned a basic probability number, for example 0.4. Because of lack of further information, the remaining certainty 0.6 is assigned to the entire frame of discernment:

$$m_1(x) = \begin{cases} 0.6 & \text{if } x = \Theta \\ 0.4 & \text{if } x = \{\textit{heart-attack,pericarditis}\} \\ 0 & \text{otherwise} \end{cases}$$

The set {*heart-attack,pericarditis*} is an element of the core of m_1. Now suppose that we have furthermore obtained some evidence against the hypothesis that our patient is suffering from pericarditis. This information can be considered as support for the hypothesis that the patient is *not* suffering from pericarditis. This latter hypothesis is equivalent to the composite hypothesis *heart-attack* ***or*** *pulmonary-embolism* ***or*** *aortic-dissection*. In consequence of this evidence, we therefore assign a basic probability number, for example 0.7, to the set {*heart-attack,pulmonary-embolism,aortic-dissection*}:

$$m_2(x) = \begin{cases} 0.3 & \text{if } x = \Theta \\ 0.7 & \text{if } x = \{\textit{heart-attack, pulmonary-embolism,} \\ & \qquad\quad \textit{aortic-dissection}\} \\ 0 & \text{otherwise} \end{cases}$$

A probability number $m(x)$ expresses the confidence or belief assigned to precisely the set x; it does not express any belief in subsets of x. It will be evident, however, that the total confidence in x is not only dependent on the confidence in x itself, but also on the confidence assigned to subsets of x. For a given basic probability assignment, we now define a new function describing the cumulative belief in a set of hypotheses.

> **Definition:** Let Θ be a frame of discernment, and let m be a basic probability assignment on Θ. Then the *belief function* (or *credibility function*) corresponding with m is the function Bel: $2^\Theta \rightarrow [0,1]$ defined by
>
> $$\mathrm{Bel}(x) = \sum_{y \subseteq x} m(y)$$
>
> for each $x \subseteq \Theta$.

Several properties of this belief function can easily be proved:

(1) $\mathrm{Bel}(\Theta) = 1$ since $\sum_{y \subseteq \Theta} m(y) = 1$.

(2) For each $x \subseteq \Theta$ containing exactly one element, we have that $\mathrm{Bel}(x) = m(x)$.

(3) For each $x \subseteq \Theta$, we have $\mathrm{Bel}(x) + \mathrm{Bel}(\bar{x}) \leqslant 1$, since

$$\mathrm{Bel}(\Theta) = \mathrm{Bel}(x \cup \bar{x}) = \mathrm{Bel}(x) + \mathrm{Bel}(\bar{x}) + \sum_{\substack{x \cap y \neq \varnothing \\ \bar{x} \cap y \neq \varnothing}} m(y) = 1$$

We furthermore have the inequality $\mathrm{Bel}(x) + \mathrm{Bel}(y) \leqslant \mathrm{Bel}(x \cup y)$ for each $x, y \in \Theta$.

We define some special belief functions. In Example 5.17, we have demonstrated how complete ignorance may be expressed. Recall that a basic probability assignment describing lack of evidence had the following form:

$$m(x) = \begin{cases} 1 & \text{if } x = \Theta \\ 0 & \text{otherwise} \end{cases}$$

The belief function corresponding to such an assignment has been given a special name.

> **Definition:** Let Θ be a frame of discernment and let m be a basic probability assignment such that $\kappa(m) = \{\Theta\}$. The belief function corresponding to m is called a *vacuous belief function*.

The following definition concerns belief functions corresponding with basic probability assignments of the form

$$m(x) = \begin{cases} 1 - c_1 & \text{if } x = \Theta \\ c_1 & \text{if } x = A \\ 0 & \text{otherwise} \end{cases}$$

where $A \subset \Theta$, and $0 < c_1 < 1$ is a constant.

Definition: Let Θ be a frame of discernment and let m be a basic probability assignment such that $\kappa(m) = \{A, \Theta\}$ for a certain $A \subset \Theta$. The belief function corresponding to m is called a *simple support function.*

A belief function provides for each set x only a lower bound to the 'actual' belief in x. It is also possible that belief has been assigned to a set y such that $x \subseteq y$. Therefore, in addition to the belief function the Dempster–Shafer theory defines another function corresponding with a basic probability assignment.

Definition: Let Θ be a frame of discernment and let m be a basic probability assignment on Θ. Then the *plausibility function* corresponding to m is the function $\text{Pl}: 2^{\Theta} \rightarrow [0,1]$ defined by

$$\text{Pl}(x) = \sum_{x \cap y \neq \varnothing} m(y)$$

for each $x \subseteq \Theta$.

A function value $\text{Pl}(x)$ indicates the total confidence *not* assigned to $\bar{x}$, so $\text{Pl}(x)$ provides an upper bound to the 'real' confidence in x. It can easily be shown that, for a given basic probability assignment m, the property

$$\text{Pl}(x) = 1 - \text{Bel}(\bar{x})$$

for each $x \subseteq \Theta$, holds for the belief function Bel and the plausibility function Pl corresponding to m. The difference $\text{Pl}(x) - \text{Bel}(x)$ indicates the confidence in the sets y for which $x \subseteq y$ and therefore expresses the uncertainty with respect to x.

Definition: Let Θ be a frame of discernment and let m be a basic probability assignment on Θ. Let Bel be the belief function corresponding to m, and let Pl be the plausibility function corresponding to m. For each $x \subseteq \Theta$, the closed interval $[\text{Bel}(x), \text{Pl}(x)]$ is called the *belief interval* of x.

EXAMPLE 5.18

Let Θ be a frame of discernment, and let $x \subseteq \Theta$. Now, consider a basic probability assignment m on Θ and its corresponding functions Bel and Pl.

- If $[\text{Bel}(x),\text{Pl}(x)] = [0,1]$, then no information concerning x is available.
- If $[\text{Bel}(x),\text{Pl}(x)] = [1,1]$, then x has been completely confirmed by m.
- If $[\text{Bel}(x),\text{Pl}(x)] = [0.3,1]$, then there is some evidence in favour of the hypothesis x.
- If $[\text{Bel}(x),\text{Pl}(x)] = [0.15,0.75]$, then we have evidence in favour as well as against x.

If we have $\text{Pl}(x) - \text{Bel}(x) = 0$ for each $x \subseteq \Theta$, we are back to conventional probability theory. In such a case, the belief function is called a Bayesian belief function. This notion is defined more formally in the following definition.

Definition: Let Θ be a frame of discernment and let m be a basic probability assignment such that the core of m consists only of singleton sets. The belief function corresponding to m is called a *Bayesian belief function.*

5.6.2 Dempster's rule of combination

The Dempster–Shafer theory provides a function for computing from two pieces of evidence and their associated basic probability assignment a new basic probability assignment describing the combined influence of these pieces of evidence. This function is known as *Dempster's rule of combination.* The remainder of this section is devoted to an example of the use of this function. First, however, it is defined formally in the following definition.

Definition (*Dempster's rule of combination*): Let Θ be a frame of discernment, and let m_1 and m_2 be basic probability assignments on Θ. Then, $m_1 \oplus m_2$ is a function $m_1 \oplus m_2\colon 2^{\Theta} \rightarrow [0,1]$ such that

(1) $m_1 \oplus m_2(\varnothing) = 0$, and

(2) $$m_1 \oplus m_2(x) = \frac{\sum_{y \cap z = x} m_1(y) \cdot m_2(z)}{\sum_{y \cap z \neq \varnothing} m_1(y) \cdot m_2(z)} \quad \text{for all } x \neq \varnothing$$

$\text{Bel}_1 \oplus \text{Bel}_2$ is the function $\text{Bel}_1 \oplus \text{Bel}_2\colon 2^\Theta \rightarrow [0,1]$ defined by

$$\text{Bel}_1 \oplus \text{Bel}_2(x) = \sum_{y \subseteq x} m_1 \oplus m_2(y)$$

The usage of Dempster's rule of combination will now be illustrated by means of an example.

EXAMPLE 5.19

Consider once more the frame of discernment $\Theta = \{$*heart-attack,pericarditis,pulmonary-embolism,aortic-dissection*$\}$. Furthermore, consider the basic probability assignment m_1 obtained from the evidence that a given patient suffers from a heart attack or pericarditis, and the basic probability assignment m_2 obtained from the evidence that the patient does not suffer from pericarditis. These functions are shown below:

$$m_1(x) = \begin{cases} 0.6 & \text{if } x = \Theta \\ 0.4 & \text{if } x = \{\textit{heart-attack,pericarditis}\} \\ 0 & \text{otherwise} \end{cases}$$

$$m_2(x) = \begin{cases} 0.3 & \text{if } x = \Theta \\ 0.7 & \text{if } x = \{\textit{heart-attack,pulmonary-embolism,} \\ & \qquad \textit{aortic-dissection}\} \\ 0 & \text{otherwise} \end{cases}$$

From applying Dempster's rule of combination, we obtain a new basic probability assignment $m_1 \oplus m_2$, describing the combined effect of m_1 and m_2. The basic principle of this rule is demonstrated in Figure 5.5; such a figure is called an *intersection tableau.* In front of each row of the intersection tableau a subset of the frame of discernment and the basic probability number assigned to it by the basic probability assignment m_1 are specified. The figure shows only those subsets having a basic probability number not equal to zero. Above the columns of the intersection tableau all subsets of Θ are specified again, but this time with their basic probability numbers according to m_2. The crossing of a row and a column now contains the intersection of the sets associated with the row and column concerned, and specifies the product of the two basic probability numbers associated with these sets. So, at the crossing of the row corresponding with the set $\{$*heart-attack, pericarditis*$\}$ having the basic probability number 0.4, and the column corresponding with the set $\{$*heart-attack,pulmonary-embolism,aortic-dissection*$\}$ with the basic probability number 0.7, we find the set $\{$*heart-attack*$\}$ with the number 0.28.

m_2 / m_1	...	{*heart-attack*, *pulmonary-embolism*, *aortic-dissection*} (0.7)	...	Θ (0.3)
...				
{*heart-attack*, *pericarditis*} (0.4)		{*heart-attack*} (0.28)		{*heart-attack*, *pericarditis*} (0.12)
...				
Θ (0.6)		{*heart-attack*, *pulmonary-embolism*, *aortic-dissection*} (0.42)		Θ (0.18)

Figure 5.5 Intersection tableau for m_1 and m_2.

Now observe that the set {*heart-attack*} is also present at other places in the tableau since there are various possibilities for choosing two sets $x,y \subseteq \Theta$ such that $x \cap y = \{\textit{heart-attack}\}$. Dempster's rule of combination now sums all basic probability numbers assigned to the set {*heart-attack*}. The result of this computation (possibly after normalization to 1; we shall return to this shortly) is the basic probability number assigned by $m_1 \oplus m_2$ to that specific set. The intersection tableau in Figure 5.5 shows all sets having a probability number not equal to zero. So we have obtained the following probability assignment:

$$m_1 \oplus m_2(x) = \begin{cases} 0.18 & \text{if } x = \Theta \\ 0.28 & \text{if } x = \{\textit{heart-attack}\} \\ 0.12 & \text{if } x = \{\textit{heart-attack,pericarditis}\} \\ 0.42 & \text{if } x = \{\textit{heart-attack}, \\ & \quad \textit{pulmonary-embolism}, \\ & \quad \textit{aortic-dissection}\} \\ 0 & \text{otherwise} \end{cases}$$

However, in computing the combination of the two basic probability assignments, as demonstrated above, we may encounter a problem.

Consider m_1 once more and the basic probability assignment m_3 defined by

$$m_3(x) = \begin{cases} 0.5 & \text{if } x = \Theta \\ 0.5 & \text{if } x = \{\textit{pulmonary-embolism}\} \\ 0 & \text{otherwise} \end{cases}$$

Figure 5.6 shows an intersection tableau which has been constructed using the same procedure as before. However, in this *erroneous* intersection tableau a basic probability assignment greater than zero has been assigned to the empty set; we have that $m_1 \oplus m_3(\varnothing) = 0.2$. So the function $m_1 \oplus m_3$ is not a basic probability assignment, since it does not satisfy the axiom $m_1 \oplus m_3(\varnothing) = 0$. Dempster's rule of combination now simply sets $m_1 \oplus m_3(\varnothing) = 0$. As a consequence, the second axiom is violated; we now have that

$$\sum_{x \subseteq \Theta} m_1 \oplus m_3(x)$$

is less than instead of equal to 1. To remedy this problem, Dempster's rule of combination divides the remaining numbers by the scaling factor

$$\sum_{x \cap y \neq \varnothing} m_1(x) \cdot m_3(y)$$

in this example the factor 0.8. The correct intersection tableau for m_1 and m_3 is depicted in Figure 5.7.

5.6.3 Application in rule-based expert systems

In the preceding subsections, we have paid some attention to the principal notions of the Dempster–Shafer theory. These principles have been dealt with separately from application in rule-based expert systems because the theory in its original form is not directly applicable as a model for plausible reasoning in this context. However, in the early 1980s, research was initiated to elaborate the model further to render it suitable for application in an expert system. We have mentioned before that the basic problems preventing the use of the model in rule-based systems are its computational complexity and the lack of several combination functions. In this book, we shall not discuss the complexity

m_3 / m_1	...	{*pulmonary-embolism*} (0.5)	...	Θ (0.5)
...				
{*heart-attack, pericarditis*} (0.4)		$\varnothing$ (0.2)		{*heart-attack, pericarditis*} (0.2)
...				
Θ (0.6)		{*pulmonary-embolism*} (0.3)		Θ (0.3)

Figure 5.6 An *erroneous* intersection tableau for m_1 and m_3.

m_3 / m_1	...	{*pulmonary-embolism*} (0.5)	...	Θ (0.5)
...				
{*heart-attack, pericarditis*} (0.4)		$\varnothing$ (0)		{*heart-attack, pericarditis*} (0.25)
...				
Θ (0.6)		{*pulmonary-embolism*} (0.375)		Θ (0.375)

Figure 5.7 The *correct* intersection tableau for m_1 and m_3.

problem. With respect to the second problem, various *ad hoc* solutions have been proposed, none of which is really satisfactory. One of these *ad hoc* solutions will be briefly discussed to illustrate the problems encountered in providing for the missing combination functions. The simple approach sketched here has been developed by M. Ishizuka for the expert system SPERIL.

We consider a production rule ***if*** e_1 ***then*** h ***fi***. The Dempster–Shafer theory does not prescribe explicitly which information should be associated with the hypothesis h of this production rule. It is straightforward, however, to associate a basic probability assignment with the rule. If the rule ***if*** e_1 ***then*** h ***fi*** is meant to express that the hypothesis h is confirmed with certainty c_1 if the evidence e_1 has been observed with absolute certainty, then a basic probability assignment m_{e_1} such that

$$m_{e_1}(x) = \begin{cases} 1 - c_1 & \text{if } x = \Theta \\ c_1 & \text{if } x = h \\ 0 & \text{otherwise} \end{cases}$$

is associated with the hypothesis of the rule. Note that the corresponding belief function Bel_{e_1} is a simple support function. So, we have

$$e_1 \xrightarrow{\quad m_{e_1} \quad} h$$

Recall from Section 5.1 that plausible reasoning in a rule-based system requires the presence of a number of combination functions: a combination function for propagating uncertain evidence, a combination function for co-concluding production rules, and two combination functions for composite hypotheses. In the Dempster–Shafer theory in its original form, only the combination function for co-concluding production rules is available; we shall see that Dempster's rule of combination may be viewed as such. Consider again the production rule ***if*** e_1 ***then*** h ***fi*** given above and its associated functions m_{e_1} and Bel_{e_1}. Furthermore, suppose that we have a second rule ***if*** e_2 ***then*** h ***fi*** also concerning the hypothesis h, with the following associated basic probability assignment:

$$m_{e_2}(x) = \begin{cases} 1 - c_2 & \text{if } x = \Theta \\ c_2 & \text{if } x = h \\ 0 & \text{otherwise} \end{cases}$$

This situation is shown in the following inference network:

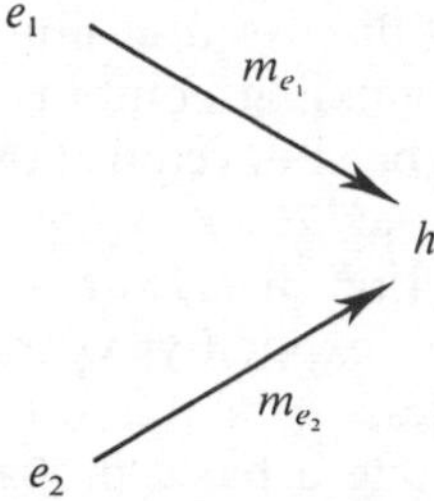

If we assume that e_1 and e_2 have been observed with complete certainty, then the basic probability assignment that will be associated with h based on e_1 and e_2 is equal to $m_{e_1} \oplus m_{e_2}$. The other three combination functions are unfortunately lacking in the Dempster–Shafer theory.

M. Ishizuka has augmented the Dempster–Shafer theory by providing combination functions for use in his system SPERIL. We first consider the combination function for propagating uncertain evidence. Suppose that we are given a production rule ***if*** *e* ***then*** *h* ***fi*** with which a basic probability assignment m_e has been associated. We have seen in Section 5.1 that the evidence e is not always established with complete certainty since e itself may have been derived from applying other production rules. For example, e may have been confirmed with a measure of uncertainty $\text{Bel}_{e'}(e)$ on account of some prior evidence e':

$$e' \xrightarrow{\text{Bel}_{e'}(e)} e \xrightarrow{m_e} h$$

In this situation we are interested in $\text{Bel}_{e'}(h)$, the actual measure of uncertainty of h after application of the production rule shown above. This $\text{Bel}_{e'}(h)$ may be obtained from $m_{e'}(h)$ which is computed as follows:

$$m_{e'}(h) = m_e(h) \cdot \text{Bel}_{e'}(e)$$

Note that this provides us with a combination function for uncertain evidence. The following functions are employed in SPERIL as combination functions for composite hypotheses:

$$\begin{aligned} \text{Bel}_{e'}(e_1 \textbf{\textit{ and }} e_2) &= \min\{\text{Bel}_{e'}(e_1), \text{Bel}_{e'}(e_2)\} \\ \text{Bel}_{e'}(e_1 \textbf{\textit{ or }} e_2) &= \max\{\text{Bel}_{e'}(e_1), \text{Bel}_{e'}(e_2)\} \end{aligned}$$

The approach to applying Dempster–Shafer theory in a rule-based setting as sketched in this section is simple, but hardly satisfying. We have mentioned before that in the recent literature several other approaches have been proposed, none of which is really satisfactory. We chose to discuss Ishizuka's method merely because of its simplicity and its obvious similarity to the quasi-probabilistic models treated earlier in this chapter.

5.7 Network models

In the mid-1980s, a new trend in probabilistic reasoning with uncertainty in knowledge-based systems became discernible, taking a graphical representation of knowledge as a point of departure. We use the phrase *network models* to denote this type of model. In the preceding sections, we have concentrated primarily on models for plausible reasoning that were developed especially for expert systems using production rules for knowledge representation. In contrast, network models build on another knowledge-representation formalism: the so-called *belief network.* Informally speaking, a belief network is a graphical representation of a problem domain consisting of the statistical variables discerned in the domain and their probabilistic interrelationships. The relationships between the statistical variables are quantified by means of 'local' probabilities together defining a total probability function on the variables. The phrase *causal graph* is also used to denote the same formalism; statisticians often use the phrase *recursive model* to denote similar graphical representations of a problem domain. This section presents a brief introduction to network models. In Section 5.7.1 we shall discuss the way knowledge is represented in a belief network. Sections 5.7.3 and 5.7.4 discuss two approaches to reasoning with such a network.

5.7.1 Knowledge representation in a belief network

We have mentioned above that belief networks provide a formalism for representing a problem domain. A belief network comprises two parts: a *qualitative representation* of the problem domain and an associated *quantitative representation.* The qualitative part takes the form of an acyclic directed graph $G = (V(G),A(G))$ where $V(G) = \{V_1, \ldots, V_n\}$, $n \geqslant 1$, is a finite set of vertices and $A(G)$ is a finite set of arcs (V_i,V_j), V_i, $V_j \in V(G)$. Each vertex V_i in $V(G)$ represents a statistical variable which in general can take one of a set of values. In the following discussion, however, we shall assume for simplicity's sake that the statistical variables can take only one of the truth values *true* and *false.* We take an arc $(V_i,V_j) \in A(G)$ to represent a direct 'influential' or 'causal' relationship between the variables V_i and V_j: the arc (V_i,V_j) is interpreted as stating that 'V_i directly influences V_j'. Absence of an arc between two vertices means that the corresponding variables do not influence each other directly. In general, such a directed graph has to be configured by a domain expert from human judgement; hence the phrase *belief* network.

The following is an example of such a qualitative representation of a problem domain.

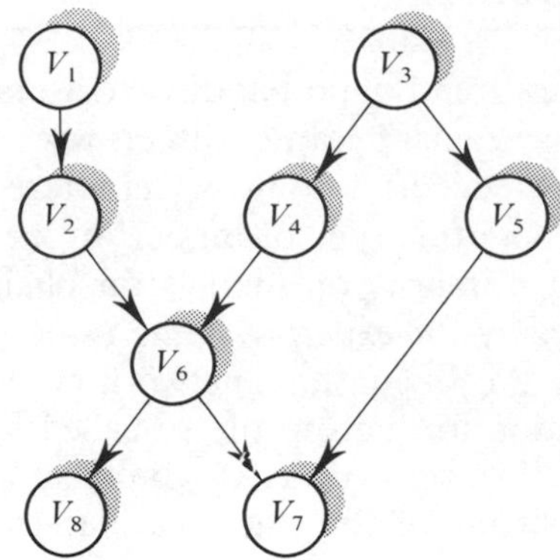

Figure 5.8 The acyclic directed graph of a belief network.

EXAMPLE 5.20

Consider the following qualitative medical information:

> Shortness of breath (V_7) may be due to tuberculosis (V_2), lung cancer (V_4) or bronchitis (V_5), or more than one of them. A recent visit to Asia (V_1) increases the chance of tuberculosis, while smoking (V_3) is known to be a risk factor for both lung cancer and bronchitis. The results of a single chest radiograph (V_8) do not discriminate between lung cancer and tuberculosis (V_6), and neither does the presence or absence of shortness of breath.

In this information, we may discern several statistical variables; with each variable we have associated a name V_i. The information has been represented in the acyclic directed graph G shown in Figure 5.8. Each vertex in G represents one of the statistical variables, and the arcs in G represent the causal relationships between the variables. The arc between the vertices V_3 and V_4 for example represents the information that smoking may cause lung cancer. Note that, although the graph depicts only direct causal relationships, we can read indirect influences from it. For example, the graph shows that V_3 influences V_7 indirectly through V_4, V_5 and V_6; smoking may cause lung cancer and bronchitis, and these may in turn cause shortness of breath. However, as soon as V_4, V_5 and V_6 are known, V_3 itself does not provide any further information concerning V_7.

The qualitative representation of the problem domain is now interpreted as the representation of all probabilistic dependency and independency relationships between the statistical variables discerned. With the graph, a domain expert associates a numerical assessment of the 'strengths' of the represented relationships in terms of a probability function P on the sample space defined by the statistical variables. Before discussing this in further detail, we introduce the notions of predecessor and successor.

> **Definition:** Let $G = (V(G), A(G))$ be a directed graph. Vertex $V_j \in V(G)$ is called a *successor* of vertex $V_i \in V(G)$ if there is an arc $(V_i, V_j) \in A(G)$; alternatively, vertex V_i is called a *predecessor* of vertex V_j. A vertex V_k is a *neighbour* of V_i if V_k is either a successor or a predecessor of V_i.

Now, for each vertex in the graphical part of a belief network, a set of (conditional) probabilities describing the influence of the values of the predecessors of the vertex on the values of the vertex itself is specified. We shall illustrate the idea with the help of our example shortly.

We introduce some new notions and notational conventions. From now on, the variable V_i taking the truth value *true* will be denoted by v_i; the probability that the variable V_i has the value *true* will then be denoted by $P(v_i)$. We use $\neg v_i$ to denote that $V_i = false$; the probability that $V_i = false$ is then denoted by $P(\neg v_i)$. Now, let $V(G) = \{V_1, \ldots, V_n\}$, $n \geqslant 1$, again be the set of all statistical variables discerned in the problem domain. We consider a subset $V \subseteq V(G)$ with $m \geqslant 1$ elements. A conjunction of length m in which for each $V_i \in V$ either v_i or $\neg v_i$ occurs is called a *configuration* of V. The conjunction $v_1 \wedge \neg v_2 \wedge v_3$ is an example of a configuration of the set $V = \{V_1, V_2, V_3\}$. The conjunction of length m in which each $V_i \in V$ is named only, that is, specified without its value, is called the *configuration template* of V. For example, the configuration template of $V = \{V_1, V_2, V_3\}$ is $V_1 \wedge V_2 \wedge V_3$. Note that we can obtain the configuration $v_1 \wedge \neg v_2 \wedge v_3$ from the template $V_1 \wedge V_2 \wedge V_3$ by filling in v_1, $\neg v_2$ and v_3 for the variables V_1, V_2 and V_3, respectively. In fact, every possible configuration of a set V can be obtained from its template by filling in proper values for the variables occurring in the template.

We return to the quantitative part of a belief network. With each variable, that is, with each vertex $V_i \in V(G)$ in the qualitative part of the belief network, a domain expert associates conditional probabilities $P(v_i \mid c)$ for all configurations c of the set of predecessors of V_i in the graph. Note that for a vertex with m incoming arcs, 2^m probabilities have to be assessed; for a vertex V_i with zero predecessors, only one probability has to be specified, namely the prior probability $P(v_i)$.

EXAMPLE 5.21

Consider the medical information from the previous example and its graphical representation in Figure 5.8 once more. For example, with the vertex V_3 the domain expert associates the prior probability that a patient smokes. For the vertex V_4 two conditional probabilities have to be specified: the probability that a patient has lung cancer given the information that he smokes, that is, the probability $P(v_4 \mid v_3)$, and the probability that a non-smoker gets lung cancer, that is, the probability $P(v_4 \mid \neg v_3)$. Corresponding with the graph, a domain expert therefore has to assess the following 18 probabilities:

$P(v_1)$
$P(v_2 \mid v_1)$ and $P(v_2 \mid \neg v_1)$
$P(v_3)$
$P(v_4 \mid v_3)$ and $P(v_4 \mid \neg v_3)$
$P(v_5 \mid v_3)$ and $P(v_5 \mid \neg v_3)$
$P(v_6 \mid v_2 \wedge v_4)$, $P(v_6 \mid v_2 \wedge \neg v_4)$, $P(v_6 \mid \neg v_2 \wedge v_4)$ and $P(v_6 \mid \neg v_2 \wedge \neg v_4)$
$P(v_7 \mid v_5 \wedge v_6)$, $P(v_7 \mid v_5 \wedge \neg v_6)$, $P(v_7 \mid \neg v_5 \wedge v_6)$ and $P(v_7 \mid \neg v_5 \wedge \neg v_6)$
$P(v_8 \mid v_6)$ and $P(v_8 \mid \neg v_6)$

Note that from these probabilities we can uniquely compute the 'complementary' probabilities; for example, we have that $P(\neg v_7 \mid v_5 \wedge v_6) = 1 - P(v_7 \mid v_5 \wedge v_6)$.

We observe that a probability function P on a sample space defined by n statistical variables $V_1, \ldots, V_n$, $n \geqslant 1$, is completely described by the probabilities $P(c)$ for all configurations c of $V(G) = \{V_1, \ldots, V_n\}$. The reader can easily verify that from these probabilities any other probability may be computed using the axioms mentioned in Section 5.2.1. In the following, therefore, we will frequently use the template $P(V_1 \wedge \cdots \wedge V_n)$ to denote a probability function. Note that from this template we can obtain the probabilities $P(c)$ for all configurations c of $V(G)$, from which we can compute any probability of interest. Since there are 2^n different configurations c of $V(G)$, in theory 2^n probabilities $P(c)$ are necessary for defining a probability function. In a belief network, however, often far fewer probabilities suffice for doing so; an important property is that, under the assumption that the graphical part of a belief network represents all independency relationships between the statistical variables discerned, the probabilities associated with the graph provide enough information to define a unique probability function on the domain of concern. To be more precise, we have

$$P(V_1 \wedge \cdots \wedge V_n) = \prod_{i=1,\ldots,n} P(V_i \mid C_{\rho(V_i)})$$

where $C_{\rho(V_i)}$ is the configuration template of the set $\rho(V_i)$ of predecessors of V_i. Note that the probability of any configuration of $V(G)$ can be obtained by filling in proper values for the statistical variables V_1 up to V_n inclusive and then computing the resulting product on the right-hand side from the initially assessed probabilities. We now look at our example again.

EXAMPLE 5.22

Consider the previous examples once more. We have that

$$P(V_1 \wedge \cdots \wedge V_8) = P(V_8 \mid V_6) \cdot P(V_7 \mid V_5 \wedge V_6) \cdot P(V_6 \mid V_2 \wedge V_4) \cdot P(V_5 \mid V_3) \cdot P(V_4 \mid V_3) \cdot P(V_3) \cdot P(V_2 \mid V_1) \cdot P(V_1)$$

Note that in this example only 18 probabilities suffice for specifying a probability function on our problem domain with eight variables.

In a belief network, the quantitative representation of the problem domain comprises only probabilities that involve a vertex and its predecessors in the qualitative part of the network. Note that the representation of uncertainty in such local factors closely resembles the approach followed in the quasi-probabilistic models in which uncertainty is represented in factors that are local to the production rules constituting the qualitative representation of the domain.

5.7.2 Evidence propagation in a belief network

In Section 5.7.1 we introduced the notion of a belief network as a means for representing a problem domain. Such a belief network may be used for reasoning with uncertainty, for example for interpreting pieces of evidence that become available during a consultation. For making probabilistic statements concerning the statistical variables discerned in the problem domain, we have to associate two methods with a belief network:

- a method for computing probabilities of interest from the belief network;
- a method for processing evidence, that is, a method for entering evidence into the network and subsequently computing the conditional probability function given this evidence. This process is generally called *evidence propagation*.

In the relevant literature, the emphasis lies on methods for evidence propagation; in this chapter we do likewise.

Recall that the probabilities associated with the graphical part of a belief network uniquely define a probability function on the sample space defined by the statistical variables discerned in the problem domain. The impact of a value of a specific variable becoming known on each of the other variables, that is, the conditional probability function given the evidence, can therefore be computed from these initially assessed local probabilities. The resulting conditional probability function is often called the *updated probability function.* Calculation of a conditional probability from the initially given probabilities in a straightforward manner will generally not be restricted to computations which are local in terms of the graphical part of the belief network. Furthermore, the computational complexity of such an approach is exponential in the number of variables; the method will become prohibitive for larger networks. In the literature, therefore, several less naive schemes for updating a probability function as evidence becomes available have been proposed. Although all methods build on the same notion of a belief network, they differ considerably in concept and in computational complexity. All schemes proposed for evidence propagation however have two important characteristics in common:

- For propagating evidence, the graphical part of a belief network is exploited more or less directly as a computational architecture.
- After a piece of evidence has been processed, a belief network again results. Note that this property renders the notion of a belief network invariant under evidence propagation and therefore allows for recursive application of the method for processing evidence.

In the following two sections, we shall discuss different methods for evidence propagation. In Section 5.7.3, we shall discuss the method presented by J.H. Kim and J. Pearl. In this method, computing the updated probability function after a piece of evidence has become available essentially entails each statistical variable (that is, each vertex in the graphical part of the belief network) updating the probability function locally from messages it receives from its neighbours in the graph, that is, from its predecessors as well as its successors, and then in turn sending new, updated messages to them. S.L. Lauritzen and D.J. Spiegelhalter have presented another, elegant method for evidence propagation. They have observed that calculating the updated probability function after a piece of evidence has become available will generally entail going against the initially assessed 'directed' conditional probabilities. They concluded that the directed graphical representation of a belief network is not suitable as an architecture for propagating evidence directly. This observation, among others, motivated an initial transformation of the belief network into an undirected graphical and probabilistic representation of the problem domain. We shall see in Section 5.7.4, where this method will be discussed in some detail, that this new representation allows for an efficient method for evidence propagation in

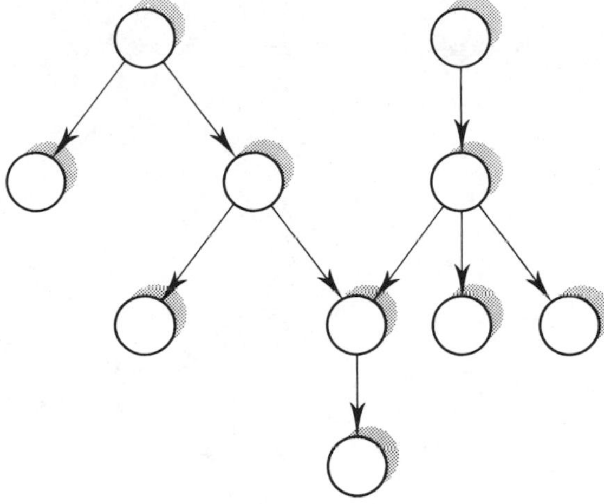

Figure 5.9 A causal polytree.

which the computations to be performed are local to small sets of variables.

5.7.3 The network model of Kim and Pearl

One of the earliest methods for reasoning with a belief network was proposed by J.H. Kim and J. Pearl. Their method is defined for a restricted type of belief network only. It is therefore not as general as the method of Lauritzen and Spiegelhalter which will be discussed in Section 5.7.4.

The method of Kim and Pearl is applicable to belief networks in which the graphical part is a so-called causal polytree. A *causal polytree* is an acyclic directed graph in which at most one path exists between any two vertices. Figure 5.9 shows such a causal polytree; note that the graph shown in Figure 5.8 is not a causal polytree because there exist two different paths from the vertex V_3 to the vertex V_7. For evidence propagation in their restricted type of belief network, Kim and Pearl exploit this topological property of a causal polytree. Observe that from this property we have that, by deleting an arbitrary arc from a causal polytree, it falls apart into two separate components. In a causal polytree G, therefore, we can identify, for a vertex V_i with m neighbours, m subgraphs of G each containing a neighbour of V_i such that after removal of V_i from G there does not exist a path from one such subgraph to another one. The subgraphs corresponding with the predecessors of the vertex will be called the *upper graphs* of V_i; the subgraphs corresponding

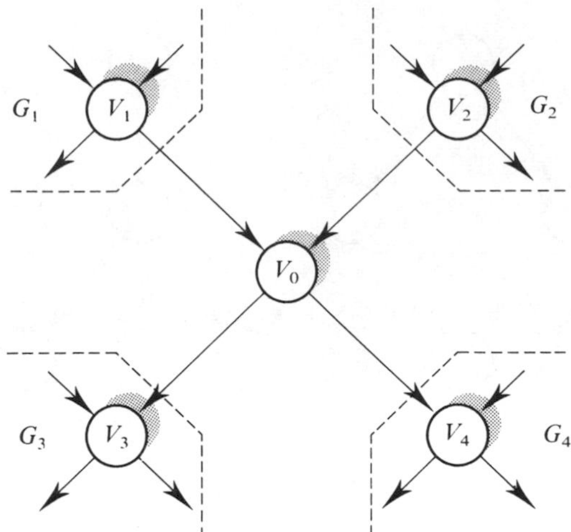

Figure 5.10 A part of a causal polytree.

with the successors of V_i will be called the *lower graphs* of V_i. The following example illustrates the idea. From now on, we shall restrict the discussion to this example; the reader may verify, however, that it can easily be extended to apply to more general causal polytrees.

EXAMPLE 5.23

Figure 5.10 shows a part of a causal polytree G. The vertex V_0 has the four neighbours V_1, V_2, V_3 and V_4. V_0 has two predecessors and therefore two upper graphs, which are denoted by G_1 and G_2, respectively; V_0 has also two lower graphs, denoted by G_3 and G_4. Note that there do not exist any paths between these subgraphs G_1, G_2, G_3 and G_4 other than through V_0.

So far, we have only looked at the graphical part of a belief network. Recall that associated with the causal polytree we have a quantitative representation of the problem domain concerned; for each vertex, a set of local probabilities has been specified.

Let us suppose that evidence has become available that one of the statistical variables in the problem domain has adopted a specific value. This piece of evidence has to be entered into the belief network in some way, and subsequently its effect on all other variables has to be computed to arrive at the updated probability function. The method for propagating evidence associated with this type of belief network will be discussed shortly. First, however, we consider how probabilities of interest may be computed from the network. In doing so, we use an object-oriented style of discussion and view the causal polytree of the belief network as a *computational architecture*. The vertices of the polytree are viewed as *autonomous objects* which hold some *private data* and are able to perform some computations. Recall that a set of local probabilities is associated with each vertex; these probabilities constitute the private data the object holds. The arcs of the causal polytree are taken as *communication channels*: the vertices are able to communicate only with their direct neighbours.

Now suppose that we are interested in the probabilities of the values of the variable V_0 after some evidence has been processed. It will be evident that, in terms of the graphical part of the belief network, these probabilities cannot be computed from the private data the vertex holds; they are dependent on the information from its upper and lower graphs as well. We shall see, however, that the neighbours of V_0 are able to provide V_0 with all information necessary for computing the probabilitics of its values locally.

We shall now introduce one more notational convention. After several pieces of evidence have been entered into the network and processed, some of the statistical variables have been *instantiated* with a value and some have not. Now, consider the configuration template $C_{V(G)} = V_1 \wedge \cdots \wedge V_n$ of the vertex set $V(G) = \{V_1, \ldots, V_n\}$, $n \geqslant 1$, in such a situation: we have that in the template some variables have been filled in. We shall use the notation $\tilde{c}_{V(G)}$ to denote the instantiated part of the template. If, for example, we have the configuration template $C = V_1 \wedge V_2 \wedge V_3$ and we know that the variable V_2 has adopted the value *true* and that the variable V_3 has the value *false*, and we do not know as yet the value of V_1, then $\tilde{c} = v_2 \wedge \neg v_3$.

We return to our example.

EXAMPLE 5.24

Consider the causal polytree from Figure 5.10 once more. We are interested in the probabilities of the values of the variable V_0. It can be proved, using Bayes' theorem and the independency relationships shown in the polytree, that these probabilities may be computed according to the following formula:

$$\begin{aligned}
P(V_0 \mid \tilde{c}_{V(G)}) = \alpha \cdot P(\tilde{c}_{V(G_3)} \mid V_0) \cdot P(\tilde{c}_{V(G_4)} \mid V_0) \\
\cdot [P(V_0 \mid v_1 \wedge v_2) \cdot P(v_1 \mid \tilde{c}_{V(G_1)}) \cdot P(v_2 \mid \tilde{c}_{V(G_2)}) \\
+ P(V_0 \mid \neg v_1 \wedge v_2) \cdot P(\neg v_1 \mid \tilde{c}_{V(G_1)}) \cdot P(v_2 \mid \tilde{c}_{V(G_2)}) \\
+ P(V_0 \mid v_1 \wedge \neg v_2) \cdot P(v_1 \mid \tilde{c}_{V(G_1)}) \cdot P(\neg v_2 \mid \tilde{c}_{V(G_2)}) \\
+ P(V_0 \mid \neg v_1 \wedge \neg v_2) \cdot P(\neg v_1 \mid \tilde{c}_{V(G_1)}) \cdot P(\neg v_2 \mid \tilde{c}_{V(G_2)})]
\end{aligned}$$

where α is normalization factor chosen to guarantee that $P(v_0 \mid \tilde{c}_{V(G)}) = 1 - P(\neg v_0 \mid \tilde{c}_{V(G)})$. Let us take a closer look at this formula. Note that the probabilities $P(v_0 \mid v_1 \wedge v_2)$, $P(v_0 \mid \neg v_1 \wedge v_2)$, $P(v_0 \mid v_1 \wedge \neg v_2)$ and $P(v_0 \mid \neg v_1 \wedge \neg v_2)$ necessary for computing the updated probabilities of the values of V_0 have been associated with V_0 initially: V_0 holds these probabilities as private data. So if V_0 were to obtain the probabilities $P(\tilde{c}_{V(G_i)} \mid v_0)$ and $P(\tilde{c}_{V(G_i)} \mid \neg v_0)$ from its successors V_i, and the probabilities $P(v_j \mid \tilde{c}_{V(G_j)})$ and $P(\neg v_j \mid (\tilde{c}_{V(G_j)})$ from each of its predecessors V_j, then V_0 would be able to compute locally the probabilities of its values.

In the previous example we have seen that the vertex V_0 has to receive some specific probabilities from its successors and predecessors before it is able to compute locally the probabilities of its own values. The vertex V_0 has to receive from each of its successors a so-called *diagnostic evidence parameter*; the diagnostic evidence parameter that the successor V_i sends to V_0 is a function λ_{V_i} defined by $\lambda_{V_i}(v_0) = P(\tilde{c}_{V(G_i)} \mid v_0)$ and $\lambda_{V_i}(\neg v_0) = P(\tilde{c}_{V(G_i)} \mid \neg v_0)$. The vertex V_0 furthermore has to receive from each of its predecessors a *causal evidence parameter*; the causal evidence parameter that the predecessor V_j sends to V_0 is a function π_{V_0} defined by $\pi_{V_0}(v_j) = P(v_j \mid \tilde{c}_{V(G_j)})$ and $\pi_{V_0}(\neg v_j) = P(\neg v_j \mid \tilde{c}_{V(G_j)})$. These evidence parameters may be viewed as being associated with the arcs of the causal polytree; Figure 5.11 shows the parameters associated with the causal polytree from Figure 5.10. Note that the π and λ parameters may be viewed as *messages* sent between objects.

Until now we have not addressed the question of how a vertex computes the evidence parameters to be sent to its neighbours. We therefore turn our attention now to evidence propagation. Suppose that evidence becomes available that a certain variable $V_i \in V(G)$ has adopted a certain value, say *true*. Informally speaking, the following happens. This evidence forces that variable V_i to update its private data; it will be evident that the updated probabilities for the values of V_i are $P(v_i) = 1$ and $P(\neg v_i) = 0$, respectively. From its local knowledge about the updated probability function, V_i then computes the proper π and λ parameters to be sent to its neighbours. These neighbours are subsequently forced to update their local knowledge about the probability function and to send new parameters to their neighbours in turn. This way evidence, once entered, is spread through the entire belief network.

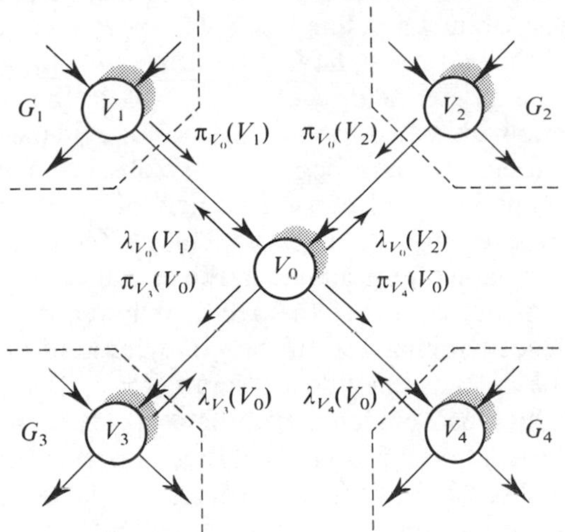

Figure 5.11 The π and λ parameters associated with the causal polytree.

EXAMPLE 5.25

Consider the causal polytree from Figure 5.11 once more. The vertex V_0 computes the following causal evidence parameter to be sent to its successor V_3:

$$\begin{aligned}\pi_{V_3}(V_0) = \alpha \cdot \lambda_{V_4}(V_0) \cdot [&P(V_0 \mid v_1 \wedge v_2) \cdot \pi_{V_0}(v_1) \cdot \pi_{V_0}(v_2) \\ &+ P(V_0 \mid \neg v_1 \wedge v_2) \cdot \pi_{V_0}(\neg v_1) \cdot \pi_{V_0}(v_2) \\ &+ P(V_0 \mid v_1 \wedge \neg v_2) \cdot \pi_{V_0}(v_1) \cdot \pi_{V_0}(\neg v_2) \\ &+ P(V_0 \mid \neg v_1 \wedge \neg v_2) \cdot \pi_{V_0}(\neg v_1) \cdot \pi_{V_0}(\neg v_2)]\end{aligned}$$

where α is again a normalization factor. In computing this causal evidence parameter, V_0 uses its private data and the information it obtains from its neighbours V_1, V_2 and V_4. Note that, if owing to some new evidence for example the information $\lambda_{V_4}(V_0)$ has changed, then this change is propagated from V_4 through V_0 to V_3.

The vertex V_0 furthermore computes the following diagnostic evidence parameter to be sent to its predecessor V_1:

$$\begin{aligned}\lambda v_0(V_1) = \alpha \cdot \lambda_{V_3}(v_0) \cdot \lambda_{V_4}(v_0) \cdot [&P(v_0 \mid V_1 \wedge v_2) \cdot \pi_{V_0}(v_2) \\ &+ P(v_0 \mid V_1 \wedge \neg v_2) \cdot \pi_{V_0}(\neg v_2)] \\ + \alpha \cdot \lambda_{V_3}(\neg v_0) \cdot \lambda_{V_4}(\neg v_0) \cdot [&P(\neg v_0 \mid V_1 \wedge v_2) \cdot \pi_{V_0}(v_2) \\ &+ P(\neg v_0 \mid V_1 \wedge \neg v_2) \cdot \pi_{V_0}(\neg v_2)]\end{aligned}$$

where α once more is a normalization factor.

We add to this example that the vertices V_i having no predecessors send a causal evidence parameter defined by $\pi_{V_j}(V_i) = P(V_i)$ to their successors V_j; furthermore, the vertices V_i having no successors initially send a diagnostic evidence parameter defined by $\lambda_{V_i}(V_j) = 1$ to their successors V_j.

We have now discussed the way a piece of evidence, once entered, is propagated through the causal polytree. We observe that any change in the probability function in response to a new piece of evidence spreads through the polytree in a single pass. This statement can readily be verified by observing that any change in the causal evidence parameter π associated with a specific arc of the causal polytree does not affect the diagnostic evidence parameter λ on the same arc (and vice versa), since in computing the diagnostic evidence parameter $\lambda_{V_k}(V_0)$ associated with the arc (V_0, V_k) the causal evidence parameter $\pi_{V_k}(V_0)$ associated with the same arc is not used. So, in a causal polytree, a perturbation is absorbed without reflection at the 'boundary' vertices, that is, vertices with either one outgoing or one incoming arc.

It remains to be discussed how a piece of evidence may be entered into the network. This is done rather elegantly; if evidence has become available that the variable V_i has the value *true* (or *false*, alternatively), then a dummy successor W of V_i is temporarily added to the polytree sending a diagnostic parameter $\lambda_W(V_i)$ to V_i such that $\lambda_W(v_i) = 1$ and $\lambda_W(\neg v)_i = 0$ (or vice versa if the value *false* has been observed).

5.7.4 The network model of Lauritzen and Spiegelhalter

In Section 5.7.3 we have seen that propagating a piece of evidence concerning a specific statistical variable to the other variables in the graphical part of a belief network will generally involve going against the directions of the arcs. This observation, among others, motivated S.L. Lauritzen and D.J. Spiegelhalter to transform an initially assessed belief network into an equivalent undirected graphical and probabilistic representation of the problem domain. Their scheme for evidence propagation is defined on this new representation. The scheme has been inspired to a large extent by the existing statistical theory of *graphical models* (probabilistic models that can be represented by an undirected graph). In this theory, the class of so-called decomposable graphs has proved to be an important subclass of graphs. Before we define the notion of a decomposable graph, we introduce several other notions.

Definition: Let $G = (V(G), E(G))$ be an undirected graph where $E(G)$ is a finite set of edges $(V_i, V_j), V_i, V_j \in V(G)$. A *cycle* is a path of length at least one from V_0 to $V_0, V_0 \in V(G)$. A cycle is *elementary* if all its vertices are distinct. A *chord* of an elementary cycle $V_0, V_1, \ldots, V_k = V_0$ is an edge (V_i, V_j), $i = (j \pm 1) \bmod (k + 1)$.

We now are ready to define the notion of a decomposable graph.

> **Definition:** An undirected graph is *decomposable* if all elementary cycles of length $k \geqslant 4$ have a chord.

It can be shown that a probability function on such a graph may be expressed in terms of local probability functions, called *marginal* probability functions, on small sets of variables. We shall see that a representation of the problem domain in a decomposable graph and an associated representation of the probability function then allows for an efficient scheme for evidence propagation, in which the computations to be performed are local to these small sets of variables.

To exploit the theory of graphical models fully, Lauritzen and Spiegelhalter propose a transformation of the initially assessed belief network in which the graphical representation of the belief network is transformed into a decomposable graph, and in which from the probabilistic part of the network a new representation of the probability function associated with the resulting decomposable graph is obtained. The resulting representation of the problem domain is a new type of belief network, which will henceforth be called a *decomposable belief network*. We shall describe such a transformation of the initially assessed belief network into a decomposable belief network only informally.

The transformation of the original acyclic directed graph G into a decomposable graph involves three steps:

(1) Add arcs to G in such a way that no vertex in $V(G)$ has non-adjacent predecessors.

(2) Subsequently, drop the directions of the arcs.

(3) Finally, cut short each elementary cycle of length four or more by adding a chord.

It will be evident that the resulting graph is decomposable. Note that the result obtained is not unique.

EXAMPLE 5.26

Consider the belief network from Example 5.20 once more. The transformation of the graphical part of this belief network into a decomposable graph is demonstrated in Figure 5.12. We consider the transformation steps in further detail. First of all, we have to add new arcs to the graph such that no vertex has non-adjacent predecessors. Now observe that in Figure 5.8 the vertex V_6 has two predecessors: the vertices V_2 and V_4. Since there does not exist an arc between V_2 and V_4, we have that the predecessors of V_6 are non-adjacent. We therefore add an

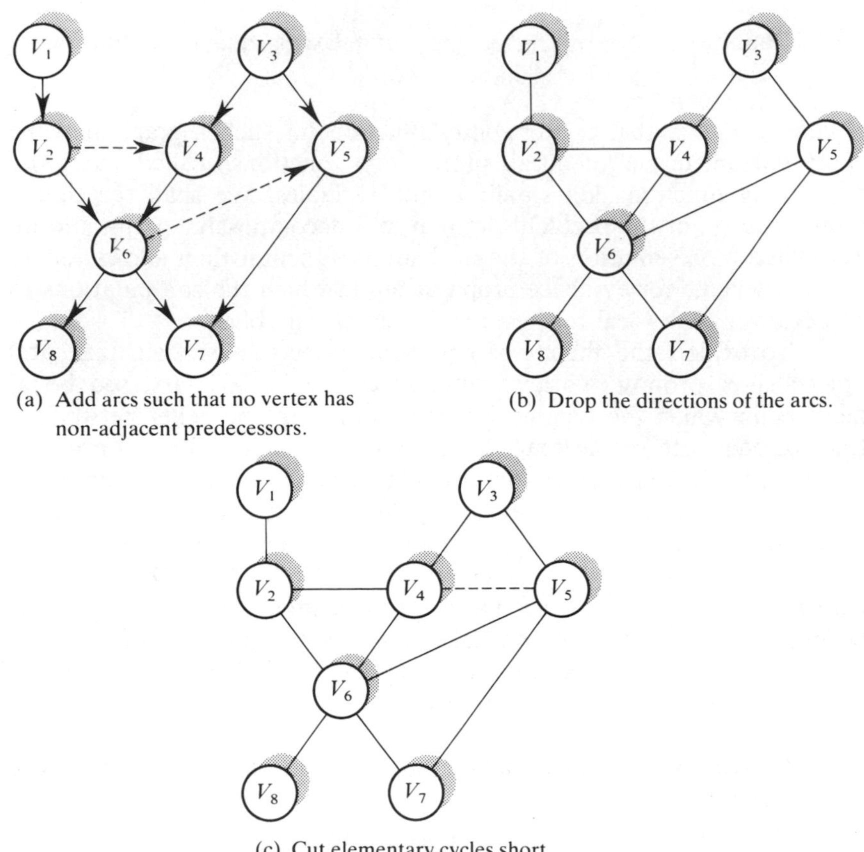

(a) Add arcs such that no vertex has non-adjacent predecessors.

(b) Drop the directions of the arcs.

(c) Cut elementary cycles short.

Figure 5.12 Construction of the decomposable graph.

arc between V_2 and V_4. Note that we also have to add an arc between the vertices V_5 and V_6. Since we will drop all directions in the second transformation step, the directions of the added arcs are irrelevant. From subsequently dropping the directions of the arcs, we obtain an undirected graph. The resulting graph, however, is still not decomposable, because it has an elementary cycle of length 4 without any shortcut: V_3, V_4, V_6, V_5, V_3. We cut this cycle short by adding an edge between the vertices V_4 and V_5. Note that addition of an edge between V_3 and V_6 would have yielded a decomposable graph as well.

We have now obtained an undirected graphical representation of the problem domain. An 'undirected' representation of the probability function is associated with this undirected graph. We confine ourselves to a discussion of this new representation, without describing how it is actually obtained from the initially assessed probabilities. It should however be evident that the new representation can be obtained from the original one, since the initial probabilities define a unique probability function.

We shall see that the probability function can be expressed in terms of marginal probability functions on the cliques of the decomposable graph. We define the notion of a clique.

Definition: Let $G = (V(G), E(G))$ be an undirected graph. A *clique* of G is a subgraph $H = (V(H), E(H))$ of G such that for any two distinct vertices $V_i, V_j \in V(H)$ we have that $(V_i, V_j) \in E(H)$. H is called a *maximal clique* of G if there does not exist a clique H' of G differing from H such that H is a subgraph of H'.

In the following, we shall take the word clique to mean a maximal clique.

EXAMPLE 5.27

Consider the decomposable graph from Figure 5.12 once more. The reader can easily verify that this graph contains six cliques.

To arrive at the new representation of the probability function, we obtain an ordering of the vertices and of the cliques of the decomposable graph. Its vertices are ordered as follows:

(1) Assign to an arbitrary vertex the number 1.

(2) Subsequently, number the remaining vertices in increasing order such that the next number is assigned to the vertex having a largest set of previously numbered neighbours.

We say that the ordering has been obtained from a *maximum cardinality search*. After the vertices of the decomposable graph have been ordered, the cliques of the graph are numbered in the order of their highest numbered vertex.

EXAMPLE 5.28

Consider the decomposable graph $G = (V(G), E(G))$ as shown in Figure 5.12 once more. The vertices of G are ordered using maximum cardinality search. An example of such an ordering is shown in Figure 5.13. The six cliques of the graph are subsequently numbered in the order of their highest numbered vertex. Let Cl_i be the clique assigned number $i, i = 1, \ldots, 6$. Then we have obtained the following ordering (for ease of exposition we identify a clique with its vertex set):

$$\begin{aligned}
\text{Cl}_1 &= \{V_1, V_2\} \\
\text{Cl}_2 &= \{V_2, V_4, V_6\} \\
\text{Cl}_3 &= \{V_4, V_5, V_6\} \\
\text{Cl}_4 &= \{V_3, V_4, V_5\} \\
\text{Cl}_5 &= \{V_5, V_6, V_7\} \\
\text{Cl}_6 &= \{V_6, V_8\}
\end{aligned}$$

Let us consider the ordering $\text{Cl}_1, \ldots, \text{Cl}_m, m \geqslant 1$, of the cliques of a decomposable graph G in further detail. Let $V(\text{Cl}_i)$ denote the vertex set of clique Cl_i, $i = 1, \ldots, m$. The ordering now has the following important property: for all $i \geqslant 2$ there is a $j < i$ such that $V(\text{Cl}_i) \cap (V(\text{Cl}_1) \cup \cdots \cup V(\text{Cl}_{i-1})) \subset V(\text{Cl}_j)$. In other words, the vertices clique has in common with the lower numbered cliques are all contained in one such clique. This property is known as the *running intersection property*. This property now enables us to write the probability function on the decomposable graph as the product of the marginal probability functions on its cliques divided by a product of the marginal probability functions on the clique intersections:

$$P(C_{V(G)}) = \prod_{i=1,\ldots,m} \frac{P(C_{V(\text{Cl}_i)})}{P(C_{S_i})}$$

where S_i is the set of vertices Cl_i has in common with the lower numbered cliques (with $S_1 = 0$).

EXAMPLE 5.29

Consider the decomposable graph G shown in Figure 5.13 once more. The probability function on G may be expressed as

$$\begin{aligned}
&P(V_1 \wedge \cdots \wedge V_8) \\
&\quad = P(V_1 \wedge V_2) \cdot \frac{P(V_2 \wedge V_4 \wedge V_6)}{P(V_2)} \cdot \frac{P(V_4 \wedge V_5 \wedge V_6)}{P(V_4 \wedge V_6)} \\
&\quad \cdot \frac{P(V_3 \wedge V_4 \wedge V_5)}{P(V_4 \wedge V_5)} \cdot \frac{P(V_5 \wedge V_6 \wedge V_7)}{P(V_5 \wedge V_6)} \cdot \frac{P(V_6 \wedge V_8)}{P(V_6)}
\end{aligned}$$

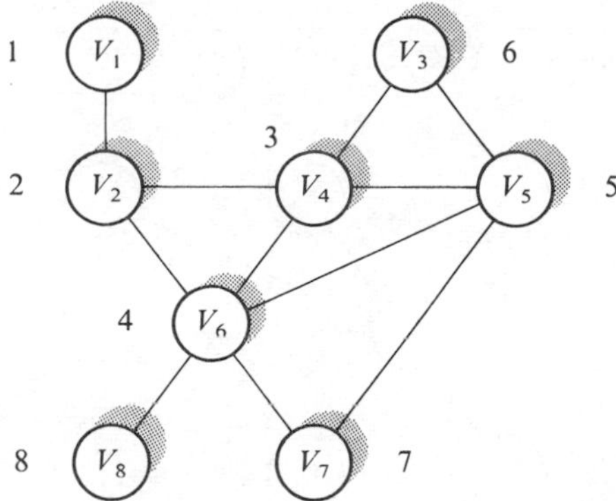

Figure 5.13 An ordering of the vertices obtained from a maximum cardinality search.

The initially assessed belief network has now been transformed into a decomposable belief network. The scheme for evidence propagation proposed by Spiegelhalter and Lauritzen operates on this decomposable belief network. We emphasize that for a specific problem domain the transformation has to be performed only once; each consultation of the system proceeds from the obtained decomposable belief network.

Recall that for making probabilistic statements concerning the statistical variables discerned in a problem domain we have to associate with a decomposable belief network a method for computing probabilities of interest from it and a method for propagating evidence through it. As far as computing probabilities from a decomposable belief network is concerned, it will be evident that any probability which involves only variables occurring in one clique can simply be computed locally from the marginal probability function on that clique.

The method for evidence propagation is less straightforward. Suppose that evidence becomes available that the statistical variable V has adopted a certain value, say v. For ease of exposition, we assume that the variable V occurs in one clique of the decomposable graph only. Informally speaking, propagation of this evidence amounts to the following. The vertices and the cliques of the decomposable graph are ordered anew, this time starting with the instantiated vertex. The ordering of the cliques then is taken as the order in which the evidence is propagated through the cliques. For each subsequent clique, the updated marginal probability function is computed locally using the computation scheme shown below; we use P to denote the initially given probability function and P^* to denote the new probability function after updating. For the first clique in the ordering we simply compute:

$$P^*(C_{V(\mathrm{Cl}_1)}) = P(C_{V(\mathrm{Cl}_1)} \mid v)$$

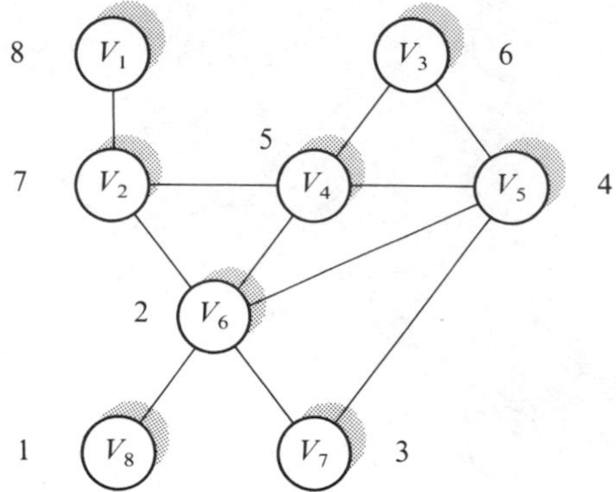

Figure 5.14 An ordering of the vertices starting with V_8.

For the remaining cliques, we compute the updated marginal probability function using:

$$\begin{aligned}P^*(C_{V(\mathrm{Cl}_i)}) &= P(C_{V(\mathrm{Cl}_i)} \mid v) \\ &= P(C_{V(\mathrm{Cl}_i)\setminus S_i} \mid C_{S_i} \wedge v) \cdot P(C_{S_i} \mid v) \\ &= P(C_{V(\mathrm{Cl}_i)\setminus S_i} \mid C_{S_i}) \cdot P^*(C_{S_i}) \\ &= P(C_{V(\mathrm{Cl}_i)}) \cdot \frac{P^*(C_{S_i})}{P(C_{S_i})}\end{aligned}$$

where S_i is once more the set of vertices Cl_i has in common with the lower numbered cliques. So an updated marginal probability function is obtained by multiplying the 'old' marginal probability function with the quotient of the 'new' and the 'old' marginal probability function on the appropriate clique intersection.

Look once more at our example.

EXAMPLE 5.30

Consider the decomposable graph from Figure 5.12 and its associated probability function once more. Suppose that we obtain the evidence that the variable V_8 has the value *true*. Using maximum cardinality search, we renumber the vertices of the graph starting with the vertex V_8. Figure 5.14 shows an example of such an ordering. From this new ordering of the vertices we obtain an ordering of the six cliques of the graph (once more, we identify a clique with its vertex set):

$Cl_1 = \{V_6, V_8\}$
$Cl_2 = \{V_5, V_6, V_7\}$
$Cl_3 = \{V_4, V_5, V_6\}$
$Cl_4 = \{V_3, V_4, V_5\}$
$Cl_5 = \{V_2, V_4, V_6\}$
$Cl_6 = \{V_1, V_2\}$

The impact of the evidence on the first clique is

$$P^*(V_4) = P(V_4 \mid V_8)$$

For the second clique we find:

$$P^*(V_5 \wedge V_6 \wedge V_7) = P(V_5 \wedge V_6 \wedge V_7) \cdot \frac{P^*(V_6)}{P(V_6)}$$

For the remaining cliques we obtain similar results.

After the marginal probability functions have been updated locally, the instantiated vertex is removed from the graph, and the updated marginal probability functions are taken as the marginal probability functions on the cliques of the remaining graph. The process may now simply be repeated for a new piece of evidence.

Suggested reading

For some of the early research efforts on probabilistic reasoning undertaken during the 1960s, the reader is referred to Gorry and Barnett (1968) and De Dombal *et al.* (1972); Szolovits and Pauker (1978) provides an extensive discussion of the problems encountered in these early systems.

The notions of an inference network and the four combination functions for plausible reasoning in rule-based systems are discussed in further detail in Van der Gaag (1989). The PROSPECTOR system is described in Duda *et al.* (1979); Reboh (1981) also treats PROSPECTOR and briefly discusses the application of the subjective Bayesian method. Duda *et al.* (1976) contains a more extensive treatment of this quasi-probabilistic model.

The certainty factor model is discussed in detail in Shortliffe and Buchanan (1975) and Buchanan and Shortliffe (1984). The latter describes the certainty factor model in a rather informal and imprecise way; a more rigorous treatment of the model is given in Van der Gaag (1988).

The foundations of the Dempster–Shafer theory have been laid by A. Dempster (1967); G. Shafer further elaborated the theory to its present form (Shafer, 1976). Buchanan and Shortliffe (1984) also contains an introduction to the Dempster–Shafer theory. The contribution of J. Gordon and E.H. Shortliffe (1984) is very readable; based on earlier research, Gordon and Shortliffe propose a model for applying Dempster–Shafer theory in rule-based expert systems. W.F. Eddy and G.P. Pei (1986) suggest another way of using the Dempster–Shafer theory. The technique employed by M. Ishizuka, which has been described in Section 5.6.3, is presented in Ishizuka (1983).

The methods mentioned above have also been dealt with in Black and Eddy (1985) and Lecot (1986). In the latter report, implementation of the various methods in PROLOG receives much attention.

Excellent introductions to network models are Pearl (1988) and Neapolitan (1990). The original paper introducing the model proposed by J.H. Kim and J. Pearl is Kim and Pearl (1983). An implementation of this model for a non-trivial application is treated in Jensen *et al.* (1987). Lauritzen and Spiegelhalter (1987) introduces the model of S.L. Lauritzen and D.J. Spiegelhalter; the example used in Section 5.7.4 has been borrowed from this paper. Van der Gaag (1990) addresses the problem of having only a partially quantified belief network.

In this book, we have discussed only some probability-based models for plausible reasoning. Another major trend in plausible reasoning is based on *fuzzy set theory* and *fuzzy logic*, see for example Zadeh (1975, 1983); the name of L.A. Zadeh is intimately connected with this trend. Moreover, not only numerical methods have been developed in the past, but also a small number of *qualitative methods*, for example the *model of endorsements* developed by P.R. Cohen (1985). For a wide range of alternative approaches, the reader is referred to Kanal and Lemmer (1986), Lemmer and Kanal (1988) and Kanal *et al.* (1989).

EXERCISES

5.1 The subjective Bayesian method uses a linear interpolation function as a combination function for propagating uncertain evidence. Recall that this interpolation function consists of two distinct linear functions, each defined on half of the domain of the combination function. Instead of the function employed in PROSPECTOR as discussed in Section 5.3.2, we could use for example the function shown in the following figure.

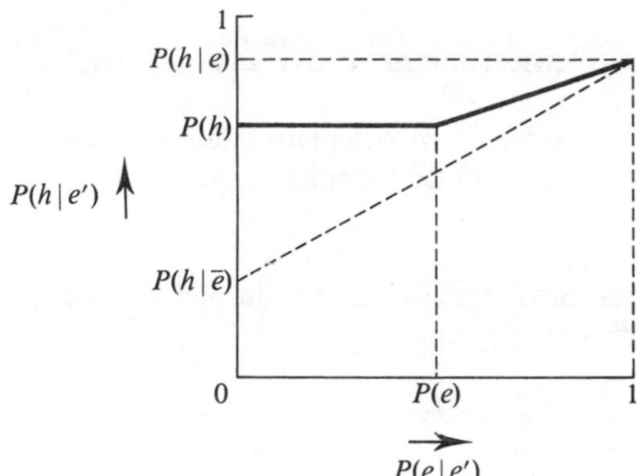

Describe the effect of applying the production rule ***if*** e ***then*** h ***fi*** on the prior probability of h if this function is used as the combination function for uncertain evidence.

5.2 Prove by means of counterexamples that the combination functions for composite evidence in the subjective Bayesian method are not correct when viewed from the perspective of probability theory.

5.3 Write a PROLOG or LISP program implementing the subjective Bayesian method. You can start from the program for top-down inference discussed in Chapter 3.

5.4 A particular rule-based system employs the certainty factor model for modelling the uncertainty that goes with the problem domain of concern. Let the following three production rules be given (only the names of the attributes in the conditions and conclusions are shown):

if b ***or*** c ***then*** $f_{0.3}$ ***fi***

if f ***and*** g ***then*** $a_{0.8}$ ***fi***

if d ***or*** e ***then*** $a_{0.2}$ ***fi***

Furthermore, suppose that the attributes b, c, d, e and g have been established with the certainty factors 0.2, 0.5, 0.3, 0.6 and 0.7, respectively. The attribute a is the goal attribute of top-down inference. Give the inference network resulting from top-down inference with these facts and production rules. Compute the certainty factor which results for the attribute a.

5.5 Consider the following frame of discernment: $\Theta = \{a,b,c\}$. Let the basic probability assignment m be defined by $m(\{a\}) = 0.3$, $m(\{a,b\}) = 0.4$,

$m(\{a,b,c\}) = 0.2$, $m(\{a,c\}) = 0.1$; the remaining basic probability numbers all equal 0. Compute $\text{Bel}(\{a,c\})$.

5.6 Let Θ be a frame of discernment. Prove that, for each $x \subseteq \Theta$, $\text{Pl}(x) \geqslant \text{Bel}(x)$.

5.7 Let $\Theta = \{a,b,c,d\}$ be a frame of discernment. Give an example of a basic probability assignment on Θ that defines a probability function on Θ at the same time.

5.8 Consider the frame of discernment $\Theta = \{a,b,c\}$ and the following two basic probability assignments m_1 and m_2:

$$m_1(x) = \begin{cases} 0.3 & \text{if } x = \Theta \\ 0.6 & \text{if } x = \{a,c\} \\ 0.1 & \text{if } x = \{b,c\} \\ 0 & \text{otherwise} \end{cases}$$

$$m_2(x) = \begin{cases} 0.8 & \text{if } x = \Theta \\ 0.2 & \text{if } x = \{b\} \\ 0 & \text{otherwise} \end{cases}$$

Construct the intersection tableau for the function $m_1 \oplus m_2$ using Dempster's rule of combination.

5.9 Consider the frame of discernment $\Theta = \{a,b,c\}$ and the following basic probability assignments m_1 and m_2:

$$m_1(x) = \begin{cases} 0.3 & \text{if } x = \Theta \\ 0.6 & \text{if } x = \{a,c\} \\ 0.1 & \text{if } x = \{a,b\} \\ 0 & \text{otherwise} \end{cases}$$

$$m_2(x) = \begin{cases} 0.8 & \text{if } x = \Theta \\ 0.2 & \text{if } x = \{a\} \\ 0 & \text{otherwise} \end{cases}$$

Why is it not necessary in this case to normalize? Compute the value of $\text{Bel}_1 \oplus \text{Bel}_2(\{a\})$.

5.10 Consider the following medical information (borrowed from Cooper (1984)):

> Metastatic cancer is a possible cause of a brain tumour, and is also an explanation for increased total serum calcium. In turn, either of these could explain a patient falling into a coma. Severe headache is also possibly associated with a brain tumour.

Suppose that we use a belief network to represent this information. Give the graphical part of the belief network. Which probabilities have to be associated with the graph?

5.11 Consider the causal polytree from Figure 5.9 and an associated set of probabilities. Suppose that we apply the method of J.H. Kim and J. Pearl for evidence propagation. Find out how evidence spreads through the network if entered in one of the vertices.

5.12 Consider the belief network obtained in Exercise 5.10 once more. Transform this belief network into a decomposable belief network as described in Section 5.7.4.

(a) Give the resulting decomposable graph. Which cliques do you discern?

(b) Givc the new representation of the original probability function.

(c) What happens if we obtain the evidence that a specific patient is suffering from severe headaches?

6 Tools for Knowledge and Inference Inspection

In Chapters 2–5 we have presented the basic principles of expert systems. The representation and manipulation of knowledge were the central themes in these chapters, and we have discussed several programs implementing these principles. In each of these programs, the interaction between the user and the computer program has been kept as simple as possible. For example, in Chapter 3 two programs for top-down inference were discussed, in which the interaction was completely controlled by the program asking for input from the user. Furthermore, in Chapter 4 we paid attention to a number of programs implementing single inheritance, where the user was allowed to pose only simple questions to the knowledge base for retrieving information. It will be evident that several disadvantages arise from these restricted forms of interaction between user and computer. For example, in the case of an object–attribute–value representation in a rule-based expert system it is mandatory for the system to be able to inform the user about the values that may be entered for a particular attribute. Entering other values than those occurring in the production rules in most cases will be senseless. Moreover, only with stringent input handling will the system be able to detect incorrect input data, for example due to alternative spelling or to typing errors. Of course, simple checking of the user's input is only the very beginning of the development of a practical expert system environment; both the end user and the knowledge engineer need tools to enable them to inspect the knowledge base, for example to determine which and to what extent subjects in the domain have been covered by the system, and for exploring the reasoning process of the system during an actual consultation. In fact, such facilities are quite characteristic for expert systems and constitute one of the main differences between conventional software systems and expert systems; expert systems used in practice normally have one or more of the facilities sketched.

In this chapter we concentrate on several simple means offering the end user and the knowledge engineer insight into the overall structure of an expert system's knowledge base and inference strategy employed. In Sections 6.1–6.3 we discuss facilities for obtaining information about the behaviour of the inference engine. In Section 6.4 we discuss a facility that provides a global high-level view of a knowledge base. The knowledge-representation formalism and associated inference method used to illustrate the principles in this chapter are the production-rule formalism employing object–attribute–value tuples, and top-down inference. However, facilities similar to the ones dealt with in this chapter can be developed for other knowledge-representation formalisms as well.

6.1 User interface and explanation

One of the main challenges in the development of user interfaces to expert systems is to provide both the end user and the knowledge engineer with means for applying the knowledge in the system in different ways. For example, the same medical knowledge base may be consulted by a physician to solve a medical diagnostic problem, or it may be browsed to determine which findings are typical in a given disease, or it may even be used to instruct a medical student by explaining why the disease she or he suspects in a patient does or does not fit the patient data available. It will be evident that such different ways of exploiting a knowledge base require different user interfaces.

There are various possible dialogue forms for the interaction between a computer program and the user. Where the initiative of the interaction is always on the side of the user, one speaks of a *user-initiated dialogue*. It is also possible that the initiative of the dialogue is taken by the computer, prompting the user to enter data; this dialogue form is called a *computer-initiated dialogue*. Most current expert systems have a dialogue form lying somewhere in between these two extremes; the initiative of the dialogue is switched between the user and the machine in an alternating fashion. An expert system incorporating such a dialogue form is called a system supporting a *mixed-initiative dialogue*. Expert systems primarily developed for the inexperienced user usually take the initiative of the dialogue by posing questions for input to the user. On the other hand, systems mainly developed for use by the experienced user generally leave the initiative of the dialogue to the user. Hence, the way an expert system interacts with the user should depend on the experience the user has both with computers and the problem domain concerned. Expert systems capable of adapting their behaviour to the user are said to apply a *user model*. The application of user models in expert systems is a subject of ongoing research.

An aspect of the dialogue between user and program that is generally considered important in expert systems is the explanation to a user of the reasoning steps undertaken by the system during a specific consultation. A clear and understandable explanation can be a valuable means for *justifying* the recommendations of the expert system, for indicating its limitations to the user, and for *instructing* users about the problem domain covered by the system. Furthermore, it is indispensable for *debugging* a knowledge base in the process of its development. Designing an expert system that is able to provide understandable and helpful explanations involves issues such as the level of detail of the information presented to the user, the structuring of the information presented, and the distinction between various types of knowledge, such as shallow and deep knowledge, or declarative and strategic procedural knowledge. An example of an experimental program that is able to justify its line of reasoning to some extent is XPLAIN, developed by W.R. Swartout. This system makes use of the structure of the problem domain covered by the expert system to guide the explanation of the problem-solving activity that is being undertaken. The difficulty of developing expert systems providing explanatory support to a wide variety of users arises from the fact that explanation is a very complicated form of human communication which is not well understood. Most conventional expert systems therefore provide a form of explanation limited to a description of the reasoning steps that were undertaken in confirming or rejecting the members of the set of hypotheses considered. They are not capable of providing a justification of their line of reasoning, nor are they able to adapt their behaviour to the user's experience in the problem domain.

Apart from the problems mentioned above, which have a psychological flavour, some additional issues arise from the technical requirements for tools for inspecting the contents of the knowledge base and the behaviour of the inference engine of an expert system. Obviously, these tools should possess different characteristics depending on whether they are applied to support the end user or the knowledge engineer; the end user is mainly interested in the problem domain itself, while the knowledge engineer is primarily concerned with the representation of the domain. Most of the remainder of this chapter is devoted to the development of a number of such tools. We shall deal mainly with expert systems supporting a mixed-initiative dialogue. The development of software tools to support a user-initiated dialogue is left as an exercise (see Exercise 6.4).

We consider an expert system that poses questions to the user, which may be answered directly by typing an appropriate string of symbols; however, the user is also given the opportunity to postpone answering the question by entering a command to first retrieve some information from the knowledge base. Commands may be entered by the user only after the system has posed a question, or possibly at the end of a consultation, but not at any other time. Moreover, the user is not allowed to exert any control on the inferential behaviour of the system by means of these commands, so the initiative of the dialogue between system and user is quite strongly balanced towards the system. For the purpose of explaining its behaviour, the system records the inference during a consultation in an inference search space. Now let us review some of the facilities for knowledge and inference inspection which expert systems normally possess. A facility that is quite valuable for the knowledge engineer for obtaining a detailed description of the reasoning behaviour of the expert system is the *trace facility*. This facility makes it possible to visualize all inference steps undertaken, at various levels of detail. The level of detail can usually be adjusted to the need. This facility is strongly related to the trace facilities offered by programming languages, such as in the programming environments for the languages LISP and PROLOG. Facilities offering the user the possibility to inspect selective parts of the inference are called *explanation facilities*, although, as we have argued above, they provide only a very limited form of explanation. The following three forms of explanation of the inference process are usually distinguished:

- The *why facility* offers the user the possibility to examine why a certain question is being asked. The facility shows which production rules are currently being applied by the inference engine, and which subgoal led to posing the question. It is also possible to visualize all production rules and subgoals which indirectly led to the question, by successive activation of this facility. In the end, the why facility will display the goal that initially started the inference process.
- The *how facility* offers a means for investigating how a particular attribute has been traced, that is, which production rules have been applied for deriving its values and whether or not a question concerning the attribute has been posed to the user.
- The *why-not facility* is complementary to the how facility. It offers a means for determining during a specific consultation why a particular value has *not* been derived. The expert system visualizes the production rules having that object–attribute–value tuple in their conclusion which have not been applied as yet, or have been applied but failed.

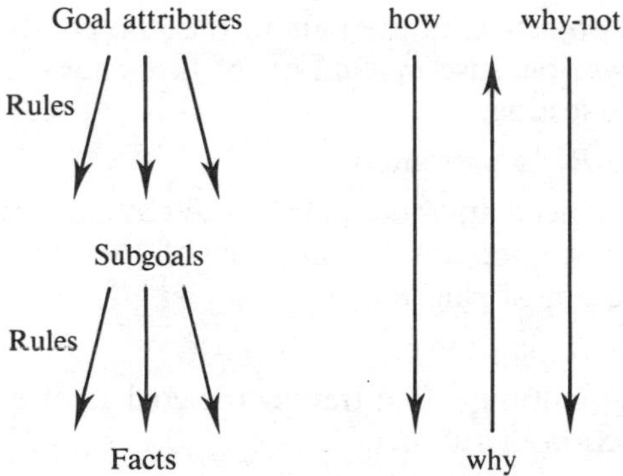

Figure 6.1 Explanation facilities.

Each one of the types of explanation mentioned above uses information present in the rule base, in the fact set, and also information concerning the inference search space which has been recorded during the consultation. Figure 6.1 shows in a schematic way how information concerning the inference search space is employed by the various forms of explanation.

The following example demonstrates the use of the explanation facilities discussed above.

EXAMPLE 6.1

Consider the following three production rules:

R_1: ***if*** *lessthan*(*object*,*a*,10) ***then*** *add*(*object*,*b*,*D*) ***fi***

R_2: ***if*** *same*(*object*,*c*,*A*) ***and*** *same*(*object*,*b*,*E*) ***then*** *add*(*object*,*d*,*H*) ***fi***

R_3: ***if*** *same*(*object*,*c*,*B*) ***and*** *notsame*(*object*,*b*,*E*) ***then*** *add*(*object*,*d*,*G*) ***fi***

The attribute a is single-valued; all other attributes are multi-valued. We assume that the attribute d is the goal attribute of the consultation. Let $F = \{object.c = \{B\}\}$ be the initial fact set. Now, when top-down inference is applied, the user is asked to enter values for the attribute a. If the user wants to know which inference steps led to the question, the why facility may be invoked. This facility will display some information taken from the top-down inference search space:

- The object–attribute pair in the first condition of rule R_1 is shown, because evaluation of this condition directly led to the question.
- Rule R_1 is presented.
- The object–attribute pair in the second condition of rule R_3 is shown, because evaluation of this condition led to the selection of rule R_1.
- Rule R_3 is shown.
- It is mentioned that tracing the goal attribute d has led to the selection of rule R_3.

If the user enters the value 5 as a response to the original question, the final fact set after termination of the inference process will be as follows:

$$F' = \{object.a = 5,\ object.b = \{D\},\ object.c = \{B\},\ object.d = \{G\}\}$$

Application of the how facility for the object–attribute pair *object.d* yields the following information:

- Rule R_3, which has been used for deriving the value G for the object–attribute pair *object.d*, is displayed.
- The fact *object.c* = $\{B\}$, which resulted in the success of the first condition in rule R_3, is shown.
- For a similar reason, the fact *object.b* = $\{D\}$ is shown.
- Rule R_1 is shown, because it has been applied for inferring the fact *object.b* = $\{D\}$.
- The fact *object.a* = 5 is shown; this fact resulted in the success of the first condition in rule R_1. Moreover, it is mentioned that this fact has been entered by the user.

By means of the why-not facility we can for example figure out why the value H is not part of the set of values for the goal attribute d. The following information will then be presented:

- Rule R_2 will be shown, because the given object–attribute–value tuple occurs in the conclusion of this rule.
- The fact *object.c* = $\{B\}$ is subsequently shown as an explanation for the failure of rule R_2.

The explanation facilities treated above often apply some stylized form of natural language for displaying information. Such a facility is called a *quasi-natural language interface.* In such an interface, usually only a rather straightforward mechanical translation of the original representation of facts and production rules into natural language is undertaken. Predicates, objects, attributes and values have associated short phrases, which will be joined together using simple grammar rules for producing a complete sentence describing the contents of a rule. The following example illustrates the usage of such a quasi-natural language interface.

EXAMPLE 6.2

Consider the following condition in a given production rule:

same(patient,complaint,fever)

Suppose that the auxiliary verb '*is*' has been associated with the predicate *same*, for example by including the following specification in the domain declaration of the knowledge base:

trans(same) = '*is*'

Similarly, the following specifications have been included:

trans(patient) = '*the patient*'
trans(complaint) = '*the complaint*'
trans(fever) = '*fever*'

Now suppose that our explanation facilities apply the following grammar rule:

trans(<predicate>(<object>,<attribute>,<constant>)) →
trans(<attribute>) '*of*' *trans*(<object>)
trans(<predicate>) *trans*(<constant>)

If this grammar rule is applied to translate the condition above, the following sentence will be presented to the user:

the complaint of the patient is fever

6.2 A user interface in PROLOG

In Chapter 3, we discussed a PROLOG program for top-down inference. In this section, we shall extend this program with two of the three explanation facilities introduced in Section 6.1, namely the how and the why-not facilities. Contrary to the program dealt with in Section 3.2.2, however, facts will be represented here by means of object–attribute–value tuples instead of by variable–value pairs. Furthermore, for ease of exposition we shall not allow disjunctive conditions in the antecedents of production rules.

We shall see that, for extending our program with a more elaborate user interface, the representations of facts and production rules as Horn clauses need to be slightly changed. It will be necessary that production rules in a rule base each have a unique (possibly mnemonic) name or number. In the Horn clause representation of a production rule, the conclusion is therefore extended with an extra argument for specifying the name or number of the rule.

EXAMPLE 6.3

Consider the following Horn clause:

```
add(patient,diagnosis,atherosclerosis,diag_1) :-
    same(patient,complaint,leg_cramps),
    same(pain,present,walking),
    same(pain,absent,rest).
```

As can be seen, the production rule represented in the clause has been assigned the name `diag_1`.

Facts are supplied with an extra argument as well. This argument is used for storing information on how the specified attribute value has been derived during the consultation.

EXAMPLE 6.4

The following Horn clause represents a fact:

```
fact(patient,diagnosis,atherosclerosis,diag_1).
```

It has been indicated that the value `atherosclerosis` of the attribute `diagnosis` has been obtained by application of the production rule with the name `diag_1`.

In a similar way to that used in this example, it is recorded that an attribute's value has been entered by the user, or that a value has neither been entered by the user nor derived from the rule base.

The user may enter a command at the end of a consultation as well as during the consultation, but in the latter case only when a question is being asked. The interpretation of a command leads to a temporary interruption of the inference process; after the execution of the command has been completed, the inference process is resumed precisely at the point where it was suspended. We shall see that adding a more extensive user interface to the PROLOG top-down inference program discussed in Section 3.2.2 does not require radical changes to the basic inference method.

The main procedure of the program is given by the following `consultation` clause:

```
consultation(Object,Goal_attribute) :-
     trace_values(Object,Goal_attribute),
     print_output(Object,Goal_attribute).
```

which calls the procedure `trace_values`, the kernel of the inference engine, for a given object–attribute pair. The clauses of the procedures `trace_values`, `infer` and `select_rule` are modified only with regard to the new representations of production rules and facts:

```
trace_values(Object,Attribute) :-
     fact(Object,Attribute,_,_),!.
trace_values(Object,Attribute) :-
     infer(Object,Attribute),!,
     ask(Object,Attribute).

infer(Object,Attribute) :-
     select_rule(Object,Attribute),
     fail.
infer(_,_).

select_rule(Object,Attribute) :-
     add(Object,Attribute,Value,Rulename),
     asserta(fact(Object,Attribute,Value,Rulename)).
```

Note that, after the selection and evaluation of a production rule in `select_rule` has been completed, a new fact is added to the fact set, including the name of the rule from which the fact has been derived. We shall use this information in the explanation facilities which will be discussed in the following sections.

6.2.1 The command interpreter

Consider the `trace_values` clauses for top-down inference as shown above once more. After the selection and evaluation of the selected production rules has been completed, the procedure `ask` investigates whether this process has yielded an attribute value. If no values have been inferred from the production rules, the user is prompted to enter values for the attribute. However, instead of entering only a list of values, the user may also enter commands. An important part of every interactive expert system (in fact of every interactive computer program) is a *command interpreter*, which interprets commands entered by the user. The procedure ask should therefore be able to distinguish between answers and commands, and, if a command has been entered, to interpret the command. We have the following ask clauses:

```
ask(Object,Attribute) :-
     fact(Object,Attribute,_,_),!.
ask(Object,Attribute) :-
     objattr_prompt(Object,Attribute),
     read(Answer),!,
     interpret_command(Object,Attribute,Answer).
ask(Object,Attribute) :-
     asserta(fact(Object,Attribute,unknown,not_asked)).
```

Let us first examine the first and the third ask clause. The first ask clause has the same meaning as in Section 3.2.2; it determines whether or not a fact concerning the object–attribute pair occurs in the fact set. The third ask clause will be executed only if the derivation of values for the given attribute has failed and the attribute is not askable. Recall that for a non-askable attribute no prompt has been specified; the second clause therefore always fails in the case of a non-askable attribute. The third clause inserts a fact in the fact set in which it has been indicated, by means of the keyword not_asked, that no values have been derived from the rule base, and that the user has not been asked for further information. Note that thereby an explicit distinction is made between the value unknown entered by the user and the value unknown assigned to the attribute by the system in the above-mentioned situation of a non-askable attribute.

When the second ask clause is called for an askable attribute, a prompt is written to the screen and the user is allowed to enter either some attribute values or a command. The following input is recognized:

- A list of values may be entered for the object–attribute pair concerned.
- The how facility may be invoked to inform the user how values of a given object–attribute pair have been derived. The how facility is activated by entering a term of the form

  ```
  how(Object,Attribute).
  ```

  where Object and Attribute are instantiated to suitable constants.
- The why-not facility may be applied for determining why a particular attribute value has not been derived for a given

object–attribute pair. The why-not facility is activated by entering a term of the form

```
why_not(Object,Attribute,Value).
```

where `Object`, `Attribute` and `Value` are instantiated to suitable constants.

- The user may also prompt the system to show a production rule. Thc facility is activated by entering a term of the form

```
show(Rulename).
```

where `Rulename` is instantiated to the name (or number) of the desired rule.

In the second `ask` clause, the response of the user is read in by means of the built-in predicate `read`. The user's response is subsequently processed by the command interpreter. In the present PROLOG program, the command interpreter is implemented by the procedure `interpret_command`. Four clauses corresponding to the four mentioned possible responses of the user together constitute the procedure `interpret_command`:

```
interpret_command(Object,Attribute,[Value|Rest]) :-
    add_facts(Object,Attribute,[Value|Rest]).
interpret_command(Object,Attribute,how(H_Object,H_Attribute)) :-
    process_how(H_Object,H_Attribute),!,
    ask(Object,Attribute).
interpret_command(Object,Attribute,
    why_not(W_Object,W_Attribute,W_Value)) :-
    process_why_not(W_Object,W_Attribute,W_Value),!,
    ask(Object,Attribute).
interpret_command(Object,Attribute,show(Rulename)) :-
    process_show(Rulename),!,
    ask(Object,Attribute).
```

The first clause deals with the situation in which the user has entered a list of attribute values. Each one of these values is successively added as a single fact to the fact set by means of the procedure `add_facts`; in each fact it is also recorded that the attribute value has been obtained from the user:

```
add_facts(_,_,[]) :- !.
add_facts(Object,Attribute,[Value|Rest]) :-
    asserta(fact(Object,Attribute,Value,from_user)),
    add_facts(Object,Attribute,Rest),!.
```

The other `interpret_command` clauses deal with the commands indicated in their heads, respectively. After a command has been processed by the system, the inference has to be resumed at the point where the inference process was suspended. Therefore, the last three `interpret_command` clauses specify the proper call to the procedure `ask` after having dealt with the command. In this way, the user is again offered the opportunity to enter a command or a list of attribute values.

Section 6.2.2 discusses the implementation of the how facility; Section 6.2.3 examines the why-not facility. The procedure for printing production rules is not described here; the reader is encouraged to experiment with the program by developing the missing `process_show` clauses (see Exercise 6.1).

6.2.2 The how facility

The how facility offers the user a valuable tool for determining how the values of a particular attribute have been obtained. We already know that all information required for the how facility is recorded in the fact set. The procedure `process_how` implements the how facility:

```
process_how(Object,Attribute) :-
     fact(Object,Attribute,_,_),!,
     show_how(Object,Attribute).
process_how(Object,Attribute) :-
     !,write('Object-attribute pair has not been traced yet.'),
     nl.
```

If at least one fact concerning the object–attribute pair is present in the fact set, then the attribute has already been traced and the system should next investigate how the values for the attribute have been derived. In this case, the first `process_how` clause invokes the procedure `show_how`. Recall that the required information is stored in the fourth argument in the PROLOG fact representation. The second `process_how` clause deals with the case where there is not a single fact concerning the object–attribute pair present in the fact set. It is obvious that in this case the object–attribute pair has not been traced as yet.

The `show_how` procedure

```
show_how(Object,Attribute) :-
     fact(Object,Attribute,Value,Derived),
     message(Value,Derived),
     fail.
show_how(_,_).
```

investigates how the attribute values have been derived. It depends on the information present in the fourth argument of a fact which one of the following messages is sent to the screen:

```
message(Value,from_user) :-
      write('Attribute value '),
      write(Value),
      write(' has been entered by the user.'),
      nl,!.
message(unknown,not_asked) :-
      write('An attribute value has neither been derived nor'),
      nl,
      write('asked from the user.'),
      nl,!.
message(Value,Rule) :-
      write('Attribute value '),
      write(Value),
      write(' has been derived using the rule named '),
      write(Rule),
      nl,!.
```

6.2.3 The why-not facility

The why-not facility is a valuable means for the user to determine why a particular value has not been established for a given object–attribute pair. The system reacts to an activation of this facility by first inspecting the fact set. A number of different situations may then be distinguished. The following procedure `process_why_not` implements the why-not facility:

```
process_why_not(Object,Attribute,Value) :-
      fact(Object,Attribute,Value,_),!,
      write('Attribute value has been derived.').
process_why_not(Object,Attribute,Value) :-
      fact(Object,Attribute,_,from_user),!,
      show_why_not(Object,Attribute,Value),
      write('Attribute value has not been entered by the user.').
process_why_not(Object,Attribute,Value) :-
      fact(Object,Attribute,_,_),!,
      show_why_not(Object,Attribute,Value).
process_why_not(_,_,_) :-
      !,write('Object-attribute pair has not been traced yet.'),
      nl.
```

The first `process_why_not` clause deals with the case where a fact concerning the specified object–attribute–value tuple is present in the fact set, indicating that the user is wrong: the specified value has been derived by the system. In case one or more facts concerning the given object–

attribute pair occur in the fact set, and none of them mentions the specified constant, then, in inferring values for the attribute, the specified value has not been derived from the rule base; or, where the object–attribute pair has been asked from the user, only values different from the given one have been entered. The second and third process_why_not clauses deal with this case by means of a call to show_why_not. The last clause handles the situation where not a single fact concerning the object–attribute pair is present in the fact set. Note that this indicates that the attribute has not been traced as yet.

The show_why_not procedure finds out why the specified constant has not been inferred from the rule base. This is accomplished by inspecting the rule base.

```
show_why_not(Object,Attribute,Value) :-
    clause(add(Object,Attribute,Value,_),_),!,
    evaluate_rules(Object,Attribute,Value).
show_why_not(_,_,_) :-
    write('No rules present concluding about the given value.'),
    nl,!.
```

The first show_why_not clause deals with the case in which there are one or more production rules present in the rule base having the specified object–attribute–value tuple in their conclusion. We already know that the given tuple does not occur in the fact set and, therefore, that each one of these rules must have failed. Why these rules have failed is examined by means of the evaluate_rules procedure. The second show_why_not clause deals with the case where there are no production rules present in the rule base concluding the specified object–attribute–value tuple.

If there do occur production rules in the rule base specifying the given object–attribute–value tuple in their conclusion, then each of these rules is examined to find out why it has failed during the consultation. For this purpose, the procedure evaluate_rules recursively scans the rule base for each of them:

```
evaluate_rules(Object,Attribute,Value) :-
    clause(add(Object,Attribute,Value,Rulename),Body),
    evaluate_body(Rulename,Body),
    fail.
evaluate_rules(_,_,_).
```

The call to the built-in predicate clause selects a production rule having the given object–attribute–value tuple in its conclusion. If such a rule is found, the variable Body will have been instantiated to its antecedent.

This antecedent is subsequently examined by means of the procedure `evaluate_body`:

```
evaluate_body(Rulename,Body) :-
     evaluate_conditions(Body,Failed_condition),!,
     write('Rule ').
     write(Rulename),
     write(' has failed due to condition '),
     write(Failed_condition),
     nl,!.
```

The procedure `evaluate_body` calls `evaluate_conditions` for determining the first failed condition in the antecedent of the production rule; it is this condition that caused the production rule to fail. Of course, more than one condition could have failed if evaluated, but only one of them has actually been evaluated. (Note that if the look-ahead facility was applied, all failed conditions should have been collected.) As soon as the condition that caused the production rule to fail has been determined, this information is presented to the user.

The following `evaluate_conditions` procedure examines the conditions in the antecedent of the production rule concerned one by one:

```
evaluate_conditions(Body,Body) :-
     not(functor(Body,',',_)),!,
     not(call(Body)).
evaluate_conditions(Body,Failed_condition) :-
     arg(1,Body,Condition),
     call(Condition),!,
     arg(2,Body,Restbody),
     evaluate_conditions(Restbody,Failed_condition).
evaluate_conditions(Body,Failed_condition) :-
     arg(1,Body,Failed_condition),!.
```

The first `evaluate_conditions` clause deals with the situation that `Body` comprises only a single condition; it defines the termination criterion of the recursion. Note that, if the antecedent of the production rule considered contains more than one condition, at the initial call to `evaluate_body` the variable `Body` will be instantiated to a term having the functor ',' and two arguments, the first argument of which is the first condition of the antecedent and the second argument of which is a term comprising the remaining conditions. If `Body` contains more than one condition, the second `evaluate_conditions` clause recursively evaluates the conditions in `Body` by means of the built-in predicate `call` until one is encountered that fails. The evaluation then terminates by failure, and the second `evaluate_conditions` clause fails as well. The third clause passes the failed condition to the calling procedure `evaluate_body`.

EXAMPLE 6.5

To conclude this section, we shall illustrate the usage of the explanation facilities that have been discussed. We use a small, slightly modified set of three production rules taken from the HEPAR system mentioned in Chapter 1. We shall not go into the details of this expert system. The knowledge base contains three askable attributes, for which therefore prompts have been specified:

```
objattr_prompt(patient,complaint) :-
    nl,
    write('Enter the complaints of the patient.'),
    nl.

objattr_prompt(pain,nature) :-
    nl,
    write('What is the nature of the pain?'),
    nl.

objattr_prompt(bile_system,ultrasound) :-
    nl,
    write('Enter ultrasound findings.'),
    nl.
```

The knowledge base furthermore specifies two non-askable attributes, named `cholestasis` and `diagnosis`. The three HEPAR production rules are represented in PROLOG by means of the following four Horn clauses, where the third and fourth clause have been obtained from translating a single production rule with two conclusions into two Horn clauses, as described in Chapter 3:

```
add(patient,cholestasis,extrahepatic,chol_1) :-
    same(patient,complaint,abdominal_pain),
    same(patient,complaint,fever),
    same(pain,nature,colicky).
add(patient,cholestasis,intrahepatic,chol_2) :-
    same(patient,complaint,fever),
    same(patient,complaint,purpura),
    same(patient,complaint,abdominal_pain),
    notsame(pain,nature,colicky).
add(patient,diagnosis,'common bile duct stone',diag_1) :-
    same(patient,cholestasis,extrahepatic),
    same(bile_system,ultrasound,dilated_intrahepatic_bile_ducts).
add(patient,diagnosis,'Mirizzi''s syndrome',diag_2) :-
    same(patient,cholestasis,extrahepatic),
    same(bile_system,ultrasound,dilated_intrahepatic_bile_ducts).
```

A consultation of this small knowledge base could for example proceed as follows:

```
| ?- consultation(patient,diagnosis).

Enter the complaints of the patient.
|: [fever,abdominal_pain].

What is the nature of the pain?
|: [colicky].

Enter ultrasound findings.
|: how(patient,diagnosis).
Object-attribute pair has not been traced yet.

Enter ultrasound findings.
|: how(patient,cholestasis).
Attribute value extrahepatic has been derived using
the rule named chol_1

Enter ultrasound findings.
|: why_not(patient,cholestasis,intrahepatic).
Rule chol_2 has failed due to condition
same(patient,complaint,purpura)

Enter ultrasound findings.
|: why_not(patient,complaint,purpura).
No rules present concluding about the given value.
Attribute value has not been entered by the user.

Enter ultrasound findings.
|: [dilated_intrahepatic_bile_ducts].

The possible diagnoses of the patient are:
Mirizzi's syndrome, common bile duct stone
```

6.3 A user interface in LISP

In this section we reconsider the LISP program for top-down inference discussed in Chapter 3. The incorporation of a more elaborate user interface can be accomplished more easily by using more advanced data structures. Therefore, we shall once more examine the implementation of top-down inference in LISP, but this time concentrating on the development of its user interface. The program has been inspired by the EMYCIN system. We shall only discuss parts of the entire program.

As usual, a knowledge base consists of a domain declaration part and a rule base. As before, problem-solving knowledge is assumed to be represented in production rules specifying object–attribute–value tuples.

An object with its associated attributes is defined in the domain declaration by means of a LISP expression. Such an expression, called an *object specification* below, has the following form:

```
(object <name>
  (trans <string>)
  (attributes
  { (attribute <name>
       (trans <string>)
       (prompt <string>)
       (constraint <type>)
       (class <trace-class>)
       (legal <value-list>)
       (rules <rule-name-list>)) }* ))
```

An object specification starts with the keyword `object` followed by the object name. The translation of the name of the object follows the keyword `trans`; it is to be used in the user interface. Furthermore, the declarations of the attributes belonging to the object are specified following the keyword `attributes`. Each attribute declaration is preceded by the keyword `attribute` and the name of the attribute. For each attribute, the following information is stored:

- The translation of the attribute, following the keyword `trans`, which is to be employed in the user interface.
- A string following the keyword `prompt`, which is to be used for asking the user to enter values for the attribute. If instead of a string the value `nil` is filled in, the attribute may not be asked from the user (that is, the attribute is non-askable).
- The type of the attribute is specified after the keyword `constraint`. An attribute type denotes which type of values an attribute may take. The available types are `symbol`, for an attribute that takes only symbolic values, and `number` for numerical attributes.
- The trace class of an attribute is specified following the keyword `class`. It indicates whether the attribute is a goal attribute, an initial attribute or an 'ordinary' attribute. The *initial attributes* of an object are traced before the *goal attributes* of the object, and are used for collecting data at the beginning of a consultation. In a medical expert system, one may think of the name, age and sex of a patient, for example. The order in which the initial attributes are specified is normally used to impose an order on the initial questions for input to the user. An initial attribute has trace class `initial`; a goal attribute is denoted by the keyword `goal`. For all other attributes, the trace class `nil` is specified, meaning that such

an attribute will be traced only if it becomes a subgoal during the top-down inference process.

- Following the keyword `legal`, a list of *legal attribute values* is specified. If instead of a list of constants the special constant `any` has been specified, then arbitrary values are allowed for the attribute in production rules as well as in the user's input.
- The keyword `rules` is followed by a list of production-rule names having the attribute in at least one of their conclusions. By means of the empty rule name `nil` it is indicated that the attribute concerned cannot be derived from the rule base.

Note that, as in Chapter 3, no distinction is made between single-valued and multi-valued attributes – in fact, all attributes will be treated as multi-valued attributes. The extension allowing for this distinction is left as an exercise (see Exercise 6.2). The following is an example of an object specification in accord with the informal grammar presented above.

EXAMPLE 6.6

Consider the following object specification:

```
(object patient
  (trans "the patient")
  (attributes
    (attribute age
      (trans "the age")
      (prompt "Enter the age of the patient.")
      (constraint number)
      (class initial)
      (legal (0 120))
      (rules nil))
    (attribute complaint
      (trans "the complaint")
      (prompt "Enter the complaints of the patient.")
      (constraint symbol)
      (class nil)
      (legal (anorexia fever jaundice vomiting))
      (rules nil))
    (attribute diagnosis
      (trans "the diagnosis")
      (prompt nil)
      (constraint symbol)
      (class goal)
      (legal (hepatitis-A hepatitis-B hepatitis-C))
      (rules (diag-1 diag-2 diag-3)))))
```

This specification declares an object `patient` having three attributes. The first attribute, `age`, is a numerical attribute of trace class `initial`, indicating that it will be traced at the beginning of a consultation. Any numerical value greater than or equal to 0 and less than or equal to 120 may be entered as an attribute value. The second attribute, `complaint`, is neither an initial nor a goal attribute; it is therefore traced only when it becomes a subgoal in the course of a consultation. The attribute may take any subset of values from the set {`anorexia`, `fever`, `jaundice`, `vomiting`} as is shown following the keyword `legal`. Finally, the third attribute, `diagnosis`, is a symbolic goal attribute. This attribute may take the values `hepatitis-A`, `hepatitis-B` and `hepatitis-C`. The `rules` subexpression of this attribute refers to three production rules, with the names `diag-1`, `diag-2` and `diag-3`, which upon application infer one or more values for the attribute.

Production rules have a syntax which is very much like the syntax of rules defined in Section 3.2.3. However, in the present rule formalism, a production rule definition includes a unique name.

EXAMPLE 6.7

Consider the following LISP expresssion which represents a production rule:

```
(rule diag-1
  (and (lessthan patient age 30)
       (same patient complaint fever)
       (same patient complaint jaundice))
  (add patient diagnosis hepatitis-A))
```

This rule, which has been named `diag-1`, contains three conditions in a conjunction and one conclusion.

6.3.1 The basic inference functions

So far in Section 6.3 we have discussed the representation of objects, attributes and production rules by means of LISP expressions. We start this section by showing how these representations are translated into internal LISP data structures. At the same time, we shall briefly review some of the implementation details of the inference engine.

All expressions present in the knowledge base are read in and subsequently parsed by the function `Parse`:

```
(defun Parse (expr)
  (case (first expr)
    (object    (ConstructObject (rest expr)))
    (attribute (ConstructAttribute (rest expr)))
    (rule      (ConstructRule (rest expr)))
    (otherwise (error "Unknown keyword: ~A" (first expr)))))
```

This function controls the further parsing of an expression by examining its first subexpression. It yields one of the keywords `object`, `attribute` or `rule`; otherwise an error is signalled. If the first element of the expression `expr` equals the keyword `object`, the function `ConstructObject` is called with the remainder of the expression after removal of the first element as an argument. This function translates an object specification into a fill-in for the following structure:

```
(defstruct (object)
  (used nil)
  (trans nil)
  (attributes nil))
```

The field `used` will be employed for storing the inference status of the object in the course of the inference, and is given the value `t` as soon as the object has been activated. The fields `trans` and `attributes` are filled in with the expressions corresponding to the data following the identically named keywords in the object specification. The implementation of the function `ConstructObject` is left as an exercise for the reader.

If the first element in the expression processed by the function `Parse` is the keyword `attribute`, the function `ConstructAttribute` will be called. This function translates the attribute expression into a fill-in for the following structure:

```
(defstruct (attribute)
  (trans nil)
  (prompt nil)
  (class nil)
  (constraint nil)
  (legal nil)
  (rules nil)
  (traced nil)
  (value nil))
```

This structure contains several fields, six of which have been named after the corresponding keywords in the object specification; these six fields are filled in by information taken from the object specification. The seventh field, `traced`, will be used for indicating whether or not an attribute has been traced. If the field contains the value `t`, the attribute has been traced; otherwise it contains the value `nil`. Finally, the field `value` is used for storing the attribute values which have actually been derived.

All objects with their associated attributes are stored in a global variable `*objects*`, which is made special at the beginning of the program as follows:

```
(defvar *objects*)
```

Since each object in `*objects*` specifies its own attributes, this variable is at the same time used to refer to the entire fact set.

We have now fully described the parsing of objects and attributes; let us continue by examining the parsing of production rules. Recall that the function `Parse` controls the parsing process by inspection of the first subexpression of its `expr` argument. If this first subexpression equals the keyword `rule`, the function `ConstructRule` is called for translating a LISP expression representing a production rule into a fill-in for the following structure:

```
(defstruct (rule)
  (name nil)
  (used nil)
  (antecedent nil)
  (consequent nil))
```

The field `name` is used to store the rule identifier. The field `used` contains the information whether or not the rule has been applied as yet. If the rule has been applied, the field contains the truth value `t`; otherwise, the value `nil` is specified. The fields `antecedent` and `consequent` contain the identically named parts of the rule expression. The function `ConstructRule`, which takes care of the creation of the relevant rule data structure, is defined as follows:

```
(defun ConstructRule (rule)
  (setq *rule-base*
        (cons (set (first rule)
                   (make-rule
                     :name       (first rule)
                     :antecedent (cdadr rule)
                     :consequent (cddr rule)))
              *rule-base*)))
```

The name, antecedent and consequent of the production rule are extracted from `rule` and translated into a structure by means of the function `make-rule`. This structure is subsequently assigned to the name of the rule; the assignment is done by means of a call to the function `set`. Then the newly created production-rule structure is added to the global variable `*rule-base*` by means of the function `cons`.

The inference engine for manipulating these data structures has the same global organization as the one described in Chapter 3. A consultation of an expert system is started by means of a call to the function `Consultation`:

```
(defun Consultation (objects)
  (TraceObject (first objects))
  (PrintGoals objects))
```

The function `TraceObject` starts an inference process for the attributes of the first object. When the inference for the first object has finished, the conclusions obtained are printed to the screen by means of the function `PrintGoals`. Note that the first object should always contain at least one goal attribute to start the inference process.

In the function `TraceObject` shown below, first the field `used` of `object` is set to `t`. The function `TraceObject` traces all initial attributes of the given object and then its goal attributes. This trace process has been implemented as two subsequent iterative processes by means of a `dolist` form, in which for each initial attribute and each goal attribute the function `TraceValues` is called:

```
(defun TraceObject (object)
  (setf (object-used object) t)
  (dolist (attribute (object-attributes object))
    (if (eq 'initial (attribute-class attribute))
        (TraceValues object attribute)))
  (dolist (attribute (object-attributes object))
    (if (eq 'goal (attribute-class attribute))
        (TraceValues object attribute))))
```

The function `TraceValues` is quite similar to the one discussed in Section 3.2.3:

```
(defun TraceValues (object attribute)
  (unless (attribute-traced attribute)
    (TraceInfo object attribute)
    (if (not (Infer object attribute))
        (Ask object attribute))
    (setf (attribute-traced attribute) t)))
```

The function call to `attribute-traced` investigates whether or not the attribute `attribute` has already been traced. If the attribute has not been traced as yet, the function `TraceInfo`, which prints information about the status of the inference, is called; whether or not trace information will actually be printed depends on the value of the global variable `*tracing*`, which has been declared as special at the beginning of the program. The function `TraceInfo` takes two or three arguments where the third argument is optional, as indicated by the keyword `&optional`. The function represents only a modest attempt in implementing a trace facility; however, it can easily be extended.

```
(defun TraceInfo (object attribute &optional selected-rules)
  (when *tracing*
    (terpri)
    (unless (null object)
      (princ "Tracing: ")
      (PrintObjectAttributeTranslation object attribute))
    (unless (null selected-rules)
      (princ "Selected rules: ")
      (dolist (rule selected-rules)
        (prin1 (rule-name rule))
        (princ " "))
      (terpri))))
```

The function prints some information about the object–attribute pair being processed and the production rules which have been selected.

If the attribute `attribute` has not been traced as yet, the function `TraceValues` tries to infer values for the attribute from the rule base, to which end the function `Infer` is called. If rule application has not been successful and the attribute concerned is askable, the user is prompted by the function `Ask` to enter some values for it. To conclude, the function `TraceValues` sets the field `traced` of the attribute to the value to indicate that the attribute has now been traced.

The following function `Infer` once more calls the function `TraceInfo`:

```
(defun Infer (object attribute)
  (let ((selected (SelectRules attribute)))
    (TraceInfo nil nil selected)
    (dolist (rule selected (attribute-value attribute))
      (setf (rule-used rule) t) ; rule used once
      (PushHistory object attribute rule)
      (ApplyRule rule)
      (PopHistory))))
```

The selection of applicable production rules from the rule base is done by means of a call to the function `SelectRules`. Each production rule selected is subsequently applied by means of the function `ApplyRule`. As soon as all production rules have been applied, the iterative loop terminates. To collect information concerning the inference status for the explanation facilities, the two functions `PushHistory` and `PopHistory` are called. We postpone the treatment of these functions until Section 6.3.3.

In the function `SelectRules`, production rules are selected from the rule base simply by calling the selection function `attribute-rules`, which returns the rules referred to in the field `rules` of the attribute. So, contrary to the program discussed in Section 3.2.3, rules are not selected here by sequentially scanning the entire rule base:

```
(defun SelectRules (attribute)
  (let ((selected nil))
    (dolist (rule (mapcar #'eval
                          (attribute-rules attribute)) selected)
      (unless (rule-used rule)
        (setf selected (append selected
                               (list rule)))))))
```

Before a selected production rule is actually applied, `SelectRules` investigates by means of the function call `(rule-used rule)` whether or not the rule has already been applied. A rule that has already been applied is not admitted to the conflict set for the second time.

Note that application of a production rule has to be implemented in a different way than in Section 3.2.3 because of the difference in the data representation for facts employed. In Section 3.2.3, facts were stored as values of global variables; here, facts are kept in the `value` field of the attribute data structure, and the values are therefore less directly accessible by the LISP interpreter than in Section 3.2.3. The implementation of the functions `Ask` and `ApplyRule` is left as an exercise to the reader (see Exercise 6.2).

6.3.2 The command interpreter

In the previous section we have briefly reviewed the implementation of top-down inference in LISP which constitutes the point of departure for this section. Here we shall deal with the development of a more extended user interface. As in the PROLOG program discussed in Section 6.3.1, the program contains a command interpreter for processing the user's input. In the following LISP program the function `InterpretCommand` may be viewed as such. This function is called from the function `Ask`.

```
(defun InterpretCommand (response object attribute)
  (case response
    (facts   (ShowFacts *objects*))
    (?       (PrintPrompt attribute))
    (legal   (ShowLegalValues attribute))
    (why     (ExplainWhy object attribute 'why *history*))
    (trace   (setq *tracing* t))
    (notrace (setq *tracing* nil))))
```

The various commands which may be entered by the user and the actions to be taken by the program are specified in the `case` form. The following commands and actions are distinguished:

- If the user has entered the command `facts`, the function `ShowFacts` will be called, which prints the entire current fact set to the screen. For this purpose, it examines every object in the variable `*objects*`. Information for an object is printed only if the field `used` has been set to `t`. Furthermore, the values of an attribute will be printed only if the field `traced` of the attribute has the value `t`.
- If the user enters a question mark, the function `PrintPrompt` will be invoked, which prints the prompt defined for the attribute currently being asked.
- If the user enters the command `legal`, the function `ShowLegalValues` shows the legal values of the given attribute.
- The command `why` activates the why facility of the program. This function call passes the current object and (sub)goal attribute as arguments to the function `ExplainWhy`, together with the value of the global variable `*history*`. This variable is employed for storing information concerning the inference search space. In the next section we shall return to this variable and the why facility.
- The commands `trace` and `notrace` change the truth value of the global variable `*tracing*`, thus switching the trace facility on and off, respectively.

6.3.3 The why facility

In Section 6.1 we examined a number of facilities for explaining the inference behaviour of a rule-based expert system to the user. In Sections 6.2.2 and 6.2.3 we have shown implementations of the how and why-not facility in PROLOG. In this section we shall focus on an implementation of the why facility in LISP.

At the beginning of this chapter we remarked that adding explanation facilities to an expert system entails the collection and maintenance of bookkeeping information concerning the inference status. For the purpose of the why facility, we must at every inference step at least collect information concerning the object–attribute pair that is being traced and the production rule which is being applied to infer values for the attribute. In the LISP program we record this information in the global variable `*history*`. This variable maintains a stack, implemented as a list, of which each element represents the status information with respect to a single inference step. We use the following structure for storing information concerning one inference step:

```
(defstruct (explain-step)
  (object nil)
  (attribute nil)
  (rule nil))
```

In the fields `object` and `attribute` we collect the object–attribute pair which currently acts as a (sub)goal of the inference process; the field `rule` contains a reference to the production rule that is being applied for inferring values for the given attribute.

At each inference step, the function `Infer` calls the function `PushHistory` as soon as a selected production rule is to be applied. `PushHistory` pushes a new explain-step structure on the `*history*` stack:

```
(defun PushHistory (object attribute rule)
  (setq *history* (cons (make-explain-step
                          :object object
                          :attribute attribute
                          :rule rule)
                        *history*)))
```

After the selected rule has been applied, the first element of `*history*` is again removed, that is, the stack is popped. The popping of the history stack is done by means of the function `PopHistory`:

```
(defun PopHistory ( )
  (setq *history* (rest *history*)))
```

Now, when the user enters the command `why`, the function `ExplainWhy` inspects the contents of the variable `*history*`.

```
(defun ExplainWhy (object attribute command history)
  (cond ((eq command 'why)
         (if history
             (PrintInferenceStep (first history))
             (TopExplanation object attribute))
         (ExplainWhy object attribute (PromptUser) (rest history)))
        (t command)))
```

After an explanation has been presented, by a call to either `PrintInferenceStep` or to the function `TopExplanation`, the user is again given the opportunity to inspect the history stack further by a recursive call to `ExplainWhy`. In this way the complete inference path from the last (sub)goal to the goal attribute that started the inference process may be inspected. The function `PromptUser` prints a system prompt and awaits the user's input; if the user enters input data different from the command `why`, the body of `ExplainWhy` terminates and the last entered input is returned to the callee.

In the body of `ExplainWhy`, the function `PrintInferenceStep` is called for the first element of the `history` stack provided it is not empty. This function prints information concerning one inference step:

```
(defun PrintInferenceStep (inf)
  (princ "The following rule is being applied to infer")
  (terpri)
  (PrintObjectAttributeTranslation (explain-step-object inf)
                                   (explain-step-attribute inf))
  (PrintRule (explain-step-rule inf)))
```

The function `PrintInferenceStep` retrieves the object–attribute pair of the specified inference step by means of the selector functions `explain-step-object` and `explain-step-attribute`. The function `PrintObjectAttributeTranslation` is invoked for printing a translation of the given object–attribute pair to the screen. The function `explain-step-rule` retrieves from the same explain-step structure the production rule which is being applied to infer values for the specified attribute. This rule is subsequently printed by means of the function `PrintRule`.

If all inference steps constituting the inference path for a particular initial or goal attribute have been walked through, the function `TopExplanation` is called. This function just prints the current (sub)goal attribute and the associated object:

```
(defun TopExplanation (object attribute)
  (princ "The current goal to be proved is")
  (PrintObjectAttributeTranslation object attribute)
  (terpri))
```

The function `PrintObjectAttributeTranslation` is part of the quasi-natural language interface of the program. This function prints the translation of the object–attribute pair to the screen, using the method discussed in Section 6.1.

```
(defun PrintObjectAttributeTranslation (object attribute)
  (PrintAttributeTrans attribute)
  (princ " of ")
  (PrintObjectTrans object))
```

We encourage the reader to develop the remaining functions of the inference engine, the why facility and the quasi-natural language interface not explicitly shown here, using the data structures discussed above as a point of departure (see again Exercise 6.2).

EXAMPLE 6.8

We now demonstrate the usage of the why facility discussed above by means of a tiny knowledge base comprising three object specifications and three production rules. These object specifications and production rules have been taken from the HEPAR system, as in the PROLOG example in Section 6.2.3. The three objects occurring in the production rules are defined as follows:

```
(object patient
  (trans "the patient")
  (attributes
    (attribute diagnosis
      (trans "the possible diagnosis")
      (prompt nil)
      (constraint symbol)
      (class goal)
      (legal ("common-bile-duct stone" "Mirizzi's syndrome"))
      (rules (diag-1)))
    (attribute cholestasis
      (trans "the cholestasis")
      (prompt nil)
      (constraint symbol)
      (class nil)
      (legal (intrahepatic extrahepatic))
      (rules (chol-1 chol-2)))
    (attribute complaint
      (trans "the complaint"
      (prompt "Enter complaints of the patient.")
      (constraint symbol)
      (class nil)
      (legal (none abdominal-pain anorexia fever nausea purpura))
      (rules nil))))
```

```
(object pain
  (trans "the pain")
  (attributes
    (attribute nature
      (trans "the nature")
      (prompt "What is the nature of the paint?")
      (constraint symbol)
      (class nil)
      (legal (colicky continuous))
      (rules nil))))

(object bile-system
  (trans "the biliary tract")
  (attributes
    (attribute ultrasound
      (trans "the ultrasound findings")
      (prompt "Enter ultrasound findings.")
      (constraint symbol)
      (class nil)
      (legal (none dilated-intrahepatic-bile-ducts
                   dilated-extrahepatic-bile-ducts))
      (rules nil))))
```

As can be seen, the attribute `diagnosis` is the goal attribute of the object `patient`. All other attributes are neither initial nor goal attributes, and will therefore be traced only if required for tracing the goal attribute. The medical rule base in this example consists of the following three production rules:

```
(rule chol-1
  (and (same patient complaint abdominal-pain)
       (same patient complaint fever)
       (same pain nature colicky))
  (add patient cholestasis extrahepatic))

(rule chol-2
  (and (same patient complaint fever)
       (same patient complaint purpura)
       (same patient complaint abdominal-pain)
       (notsame pain nature colicky))
  (add patient cholestasis intrahepatic))

(rule diag-1
  (and (same patient cholestasis extrahepatic)
       (same bile-system ultrasound
             dilated-intrahepatic-bile-ducts))
  (add patient diagnosis "common-bile-duct stone")
  (add patient diagnosis "Mirizzi's syndrome"))
```

The consultation of this tiny knowledge base may for example proceed as follows:

```
> (ConsultationSystem)
Enter the name of the knowledge base: hepar.kb
Enter complaints of the patient.
-> why
The following rule is being applied to infer
the cholestasis of the patient
If
the complaint of the patient is abdominal-pain, and
the nature of the pain is colicky, and
the complaint of the patient is fever
then
conclude that the cholestasis of the patient
is extrahepatic
-> why
The following rule is being applied to infer
the possible diagnosis of the patient
If
the cholestasis of the patient is extrahepatic, and
the ultrasound finding of the biliary tract is
dilated-intrahepatic-bile-ducts
then
conclude that the possible diagnosis of the patient
is common-bile-duct stone, and
conclude that the possible diagnosis of the patient
is Mirizzi's syndrome
-> ?
Enter the complaints of the patient.
-> legal
Legal values: (none abdominal-pain anorexia fever nausea purpura)
-> (fever abdominal-pain)
What is the nature of the pain?
-> (colicky)
Enter ultrasound findings.
-> (dilated-intrahepatic-bile-ducts)
Final conclusion:
Object: the patient
Attribute: the possible diagnosis
Value(s): ("Mirizzi's syndrome" "common-bile-duct stone")
```

6.4 Rule models

In the previous sections we concentrated mainly on explanation facilities for obtaining insight into the inference behaviour of an expert system; for generating explanations of the inference we used only information from the top-down inference search space constructed during a consultation. These facilities, however, offer rather limited support, for example, to finding out which production rules are still lacking in the knowledge base and which rules are incorrect. A major shortcoming of these facilities is that they do not provide the knowledge engineer with an appropriate global high-level view of the knowledge present in the knowledge base. Since imposing a suitable domain-dependent structure on the knowledge base is one of the major tasks of the knowledge engineer, the availability of tools for reviewing the high-level structure of the knowledge base is quite essential for carrying out the knowledge-engineering task in a proper way. In this section, we shall examine a technique that is able to provide such a high-level view of a knowledge base. The method discussed has been taken from TEIRESIAS, a system that has been developed at the end of the 1970s by R. Davis for supporting the process of knowledge acquisition. Many of the ideas incorporated into TEIRESIAS were motivated by an analysis of the problems encountered in the development of the MYCIN system.

During the development of large knowledge bases, containing several hundreds of production rules, it often turns out that some sort of regularity is introduced into the rule base. This regularity mainly arises from the presence of several rules rather than a single rule concluding on a particular hypothesis. When the knowledge engineer adds a new rule to such a set of co-concluding rules, one may expect that the new rule adheres to the same regularity, that is, one may expect that it contains certain conditional patterns also occurring in other rules in the knowledge base concluding on the same hypothesis.

EXAMPLE 6.9

Consider the knowledge base of a medical expert system containing, among other rules, ten production rules concluding the value *aortic-regurgitation* for the attribute *diagnosis* of the object *patient*. Suppose that all of these rules specify the condition

same(*patient*,*sign*,*diastolic-murmur*)

Now suppose that a new rule is added to the given set, also drawing the conclusion aortic regurgitation. We may expect that this new rule also contains the above-mentioned condition. However, we stress that this is only an expectation; there may be good reasons why, in contrast with all other rules concluding on *aortic-regurgitation*, the new rule lacks that specific condition.

By exploiting regularities in conditions and conclusions of production rules, it is possible to construct a high-level description of a subset of similarly looking production rules. A set of similar rules and a description of the most typical conditions and conclusions occurring in them is called a *rule model*. Note that a rule model may be viewed as a form of meta-knowledge; it is a description of other knowledge, here a set of production rules.

In an expert system employing top-down inference a rule base can be partitioned into subsets of rules such that each partition contains all rules having the same object–attribute pair in one of their conclusions. Note that a production rule having more than one conclusion may occur in more than one partition, so the partitions do not have to be disjoint. Each partition is now taken as the point of departure for the construction of a rule model. Each partition can then be further divided into smaller partitions containing rules all specifying the same object–attribute–value tuple in the conclusion concerned. So the rules in a rule model concerning a specific object–attribute–value tuple will be a subset of the rules in a rule model concerning the same object–attribute pair. In this way we arrive at a taxonomy of rule models based on the subset relation. Before we go into further detail, we fix a language for the specification of rule models.

Definition: A *rule model* is an expression of the following form:

<rule-model> ::= ***model*** <model-name> ***is***
  supermodel <super-model> ;
  submodel { <model-name> }* ;
  antecedent { <singlet> }$^+$
    { <correlation> }* ;
  consequent { <singlet> }$^+$
    { <correlation> }* ;
  based-on { (<rule-name> <cf>) }$^+$
end

<super-model> ::= *<model-name>* | ***nil***

<singlet> ::= (<object> <attribute>
  { <pred-act> }$^+$ <cf-sum>)

<correlation> ::= ({ (<object> <attribute> { <pred-act> }$^+$) }$^+$ <cf-sum>)

<pred-act> ::= <predict> | <action>

The supermodel and submodel specifications are used to indicate the position of the rule model in the tree-like taxonomy of rule models. The antecedent and consequent parts of a rule model provide a kind of summary of the information in the antecedents and consequents of the production rules contained in the model. In the based-on part, the names of the rules on which the rule model has been based are listed. For each of these rules the certainty factor <cf> associated with the conclusion is given.

We shall first restrict the discussion to the properties of rule models describing object–attribute pairs; however, similar properties hold for the other types of rule model. The antecedent part of a rule model specifies data with respect to the objects, attributes and predicates occurring in the conditions of the production rules listed in the rule model. Information concerning the occurrence of an object–attribute pair in the conditions of the rules is stored as a *singlet*. In TEIRESIAS, a singlet is created for an object–attribute pair if it occurs in the condition part of at least 30% of the rules present in the rule model. The predicates listed in such a singlet cover together at least 75% of the conditions of the production rules in which the object–attribute pair occurs; the predicates occurring with the highest frequency have been included first. Finally, a singlet specifies the sum of all the certainty factors in the conclusions of the rules from which the singlet has been constructed; this is used as a measure for the information content of the given object–attribute pair.

EXAMPLE 6.10

Consider the following singlet in a rule model:

(*patient sign same notsame* 2.5)

It expresses that the object–attribute pair *patient.sign* occurs in the condition part of at least 30% of the production rules concerned. In these rules, the pair *patient.sign* occurs with the predicate *same* or the predicate *notsame* in at least 75% of cases. The sum of the certainty factors mentioned in the rules from which the singlet has been constructed is equal to 2.5.

A *correlation* in the antecedent part of a rule model expresses information concerning the combined occurrence of object–attribute pairs in the condition parts of the rules described by the rule model. In TEIRESIAS, a correlation is created for an object–attribute pair if it occurs in at least 80% of the rules together with one or more specific other object–attribute pairs. Note that a correlation contains a sum of certainty factors just as a singlet does.

EXAMPLE 6.11

Consider the following correlation:

((*patient sign same*) (*patient complaint same*) 1.5)

This expresses that, in the antecedent parts of the production rules of the rule model, the object–attribute pair *patient.sign* occurs in at least 80% of the rules in combination with the object–attribute pair *patient.complaint*. In such cases, both object–attribute pairs occur with the predicate *same*. The sum of the certainty factors specified in the conclusions of the rules in which both conditions occur equals 1.5.

The consequent part of a rule model contains information concerning the object–attribute pairs the rules described by the rule model have in common in their conclusion parts. This information is expressed in much the same way we have seen for the antecedent part of the model.

We have now reviewed the various constituents of a rule model. Let us give an example of an entire rule model.

EXAMPLE 6.12

Consider the following rule model:

model *patient-diagnosis* ***is***
  supermodel nil;
  submodel *pos-diagnosis neg-diagnosis*;
  antecedent (*patient complaint same* −0.4)
    (*patient sign same notsame* 0.2)
    ((*patient complaint same*) (*patient sign same*) −0.4);
  consequent (*patient diagnosis add* 0.2);
  based-on (*diag*-1 −0.4) (*diag*-2 0.6)
end

This contains information concerning production rules specifying the object–attribute pair *patient.diagnosis* in their conclusion. The model expresses that at least 30% of the production rules concluding on the object *patient* and its attribute *diagnosis* specify the object–attribute pairs *patient.complaint* and *patient.sign* in their antecedent part. The object–attribute pair *patient.complaint*

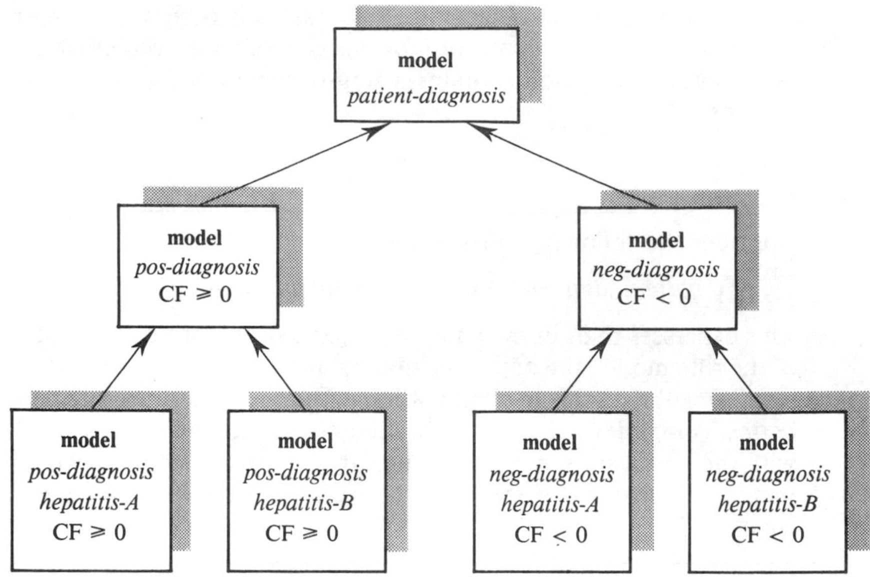

Figure 6.2 Example of a rule-model taxonomy.

occurs in at least 75% of cases with the predicate *same*, while for the object–attribute pair *patient.sign* we find in at least 75% of cases either the predicate *same* or the predicate *notsame*. Furthermore, the object–attribute pair *patient.complaint* occurs in at least 80% of the rules in combination with the object–attribute pair *patient.sign*. In these rules, both pairs occur with the predicate *same*. We see that the model has been based on two production rules, named *diag*-1 and *diag*-2, respectively, specifying the certainty factors −0.4 and 0.6. Note that, as the model has been based on two rules only, we have for example that at least one of them contains either of the two specified antecedent singlets in its condition part.

We have already mentioned that the rule models constructed from a knowledge base as sketched above are organized into a taxonomy. We shall now describe one of the possible ways to organize rule models in a taxonomy, once more based on TEIRESIAS. In general, this taxonomy constitutes a forest of tree structures, where the root of each tree contains information concerning production rules having a particular object–attribute pair in at least one of their conclusions. Figure 6.2 gives an example of such a rule-model taxonomy. The production rules described by these models contain the object *patient* and the attribute *diagnosis* in one of their conclusions. The root has two children, each of which is a specialization of the rule model in the root. One specialization contains information with respect to the subset of rules described by the root, having a certainty factor greater than or equal to zero in the conclusion specifying the object–attribute pair concerned; the other specialization concerns the subset of rules all having a certainty factor less than zero. Each of these specializations is further specialized by rule models for specific object–attribute–value tuples. For each object–attribute–value tuple the rule model again has two specializations; one for the positive-or-zero certainty factor case, and the other one for the case where the certainty factor is negative. Note that in a more general case not all possible rule models have to be present in the rule model taxonomy, since, for example, production rules having negative certainty factors in their conclusion might be missing from the rule base concerned.

EXAMPLE 6.13

The following rule model is a specialization of the rule model in Example 6.12:

> ***model*** *pos-diagnosis* ***is***
>   ***supermodel*** *patient-diagnosis*;
>   ***submodel*** *pos-diagnosis-hepatitis-A*;
>   ***antecedent*** (*patient sign same* 0.6);
>   ***consequent*** (*patient diagnosis add* 0.6);
>   ***based-on*** (*diag*-2 0.6)
> ***end***

This rule model is based on only a single production rule. Note that all the information provided by this model is also described in the rule model *patient-diagnosis* from Example 6.12. However, owing to the statistical nature of rule models, this will not always be the case.

Rule models can be of much help when extending or modifying a rule base which is already quite large, since they provide useful information on the typical patterns in production rules concluding on a certain subject. In TEIRESIAS, rule models have been used to control the knowledge input when building an expert system by informing the knowledge engineer about possibly missing conditions or conclusions in the rules entered. We must emphasize that only in large knowledge bases do rule models have enough predictive value to be of any help; for small knowledge bases, and in the initial implementation stage of an expert system, rule models generally will not be very useful.

Suggested reading

The papers by Weiner (1980) and Kass and Finin (1988) discuss the design of good explanation facilities for expert systems. The system XPLAIN is described in Swartout (1983). Buchanan and Shortliffe (1984) deals with various kinds of explanation which have been applied in MYCIN and the MYCIN derivatives EMYCIN, TEIRESIAS and GUIDON. This book also discusses various forms of dialogue between user and expert system. Hendler (1988) is a collection of papers dealing with the development of user interfaces for expert systems. Davis and Lenat (1982) discusses the characteristics of the system TEIRESIAS in much detail. A collection of papers on methodologies and tools for building expert systems is Guida and Tasso (1989).

EXERCISES

6.1 Consider the PROLOG program discussed in Section 6.2. This program provides only a how and a why-not facility. Extend this program by adding a why facility and a quasi-natural language interface for translating production rules into stylized English.

6.2 Consider the LISP program discussed in Section 6.3. Among other things, this program contains a why facility and a quasi-natural language interface.

(a) Develop the functions that are missing in the description and add a how and a why-not facility. Furthermore, make a distinction between single-valued and multi-valued attributes and extend both the user interface and the inference engine in such a way that they can cope with single-valuedness and multi-valuedness.

(b) Yes–no attributes are special single-valued attributes which can take only one of the values *yes* and *no* (or *true* and *false*, alternatively). The translation of this type of single-valued attribute in a quasi-natural language interface justifies special treatment. Consider for example the following condition:

same(patient,fever,yes)

A suitable translation of this condition is the sentence '*the patient has a fever*', which is obtained by associating the phrase '*the patient*' with the object *patient* and the phrase '*has a fever*' with the attribute *fever*. Note that the predicate and the constant specified in the condition are not included in the resulting sentence, but instead are used only for determining whether a positive or negative sentence is generated. Extend the knowledge base and the LISP functions for the user interface in such a way that the program translates yes–no attributes properly.

6.3 Consider the PROLOG program developed in Exercise 6.1 or the LISP program developed in Exercise 6.2, respectively.

(a) Develop a knowledge base for a problem domain you are familiar with. Pay particular attention to the structure of the knowledge base, particularly taking care that the top-down inference search tree will be more than one level deep during at least part of a consultation. Study the behaviour of the explanation facilities by applying the chosen program to your knowledge base.

(b) *Explanation by example* is a frequently used technique in tutoring: a subject is explained by presenting an example revealing its principles. Extend the PROLOG program by including a facility that supplements the system's response to why questions by typical examples. Extend your knowledge base developed in (a) so that you are able to demonstrate the applicability of this technique.

6.4 In Sections 6.1–6.3 we have mainly concentrated on the development of a user interface supporting a mixed-initiative dialogue. Try to modify one of the discussed programs in such a way that a user interface supporting a user-initiated dialogue is obtained. The user should be given the opportunity to start, interrupt and continue the inference process when desired; the user is never prompted for input by the system – all attributes are considered to be non-askable. Furthermore, the user should be permitted to add, modify, or remove facts freely.

6.5 Modern graphical user interfaces to an expert system have the advantage that the inference process of an expert system can be visualized much clearer than by using classical character-oriented user interfaces. Extend the PROLOG program from Exercise 6.1 or the LISP program from Exercise 6.2 in such a way that a graphical representation of the top-down inference search space is presented to the user. The representation has to provide information about which conditions in rules have failed, succeeded or not yet been evaluated; it also has to indicate which part of the rule base is currently being evaluated.

6.6 Providing meaningful explanations of the system's reasoning behaviour is not confined to rule-based systems only. Develop an explanation facility for a frame-based expert system that includes demons for passing control from one frame to another.

6.7 One of the major advantages of a typed knowledge-representation formalism, such as the production-rule formalism described in Section 6.3 where for attributes so-called legal values have been specified, is that many sources of errors in a knowledge base can be detected by simple type checks. The detection and handling of such errors at execution time, when an inference process operates on the knowledge base and fact set, is less straightforward and may even produce unpredictable results. Develop a type-checking program for the production-rule formalism discussed in Section 6.3. In particular, pay attention to the generation of meaningful error messages.

6.8 Consider two production rules such that, when one of them succeeds, the other rule succeeds as well, but by assigning a different value to the same single-valued attribute. Such production rules are called *conflicting*. Furthermore, we say that a production rule R_1 is *subsumed* by a rule R_2 if they have the same conclusions and rule R_1 has the same or more conditions than rule R_2. Finally, a production rule is called *unreachable* if none of the attributes in its conclusions will ever become a goal during top-down inference. In each of these three cases, it will be necessary to modify the knowledge base. A program that automatically finds such rules is therefore a convenient tool. Develop a PROLOG or LISP program that detects conflicting, subsumed and unreachable rules in a rule base of an expert system using production rules for knowledge representation and applying top-down inference as an inference method.

6.9 One of the problems with rule-based expert systems is that they become difficult to modify and maintain when the number of rules they contain surpasses a certain limit. Such systems are much easier to maintain when the rule base has been partitioned into several smaller modules each containing production rules that are related to each other in a given rule base. To find out which rules are related to each other, a *measure of relatedness* is required. A simple measure of relatedness is the number of object–attribute pairs two production rules have in common, in both conditions and conclusions, divided by half of the total number of object–attribute pairs occurring in the two rules. Only the production rules having the largest measure of relatedness greater than some threshold value $\alpha \in [0,1]$ are put in the same module. Every production rule is admitted in only one module. Develop a PROLOG or LISP program that transforms a given rule base into a collection of rule modules.

6.10 Most commercial expert system shells and expert system builder tools provide special editors for assisting in the interactive development of a knowledge base. Such editors are sometimes called *knowledge-base editors*. Typically, such editors offer special templates for object and attribute declarations, and production rules to ease the development of a knowledge base. Develop a flexible knowledge-base editor which assists the knowledge engineer in the development of a knowledge base.

6.11 The LISP program developed in Exercise 6.2 includes a set of functions performing a lexical and syntactical analysis of the knowledge base. Extract that particular part from the program and extend these functions in such a way that they generate a rule model taxonomy of a given knowledge base. Experiment with the thresholds of 30, 75 and 80% mentioned in Section 6.4 on the knowledge base you have developed for the expert system shell built in Exercise 6.3.

6.12 In Chapter 1 we have briefly discussed the process of knowledge engineering, the subject of a significant amount of active research. Most current methodologies for knowledge engineering suggest that the construction of an expert system should go through several distinct stages. In the initial stage, unstructured verbal and textual information is gathered from interviews with an expert, which will be transformed through a process of abstraction into a *conceptual model* of the problem domain. In such a conceptual model, a problem domain is described in terms of the relevant concepts and their interrelations. In the KEATS methodology, this abstraction process is supported by software tools. Read Motta *et al.* (1989) for a description of this methodology and the tools supporting it. Apply this methodology to a problem domain you are familiar with. Use an expert system shell or the LISP or PROLOG programs in this book to further elaborate the obtained conceptual model of the problem domain into an expert system.

OPS5, LOOPS and CENTAUR

In this chapter we shall study two typical examples of languages used for the development of expert systems, and a special-purpose expert system. In each of these, one or more of the principles of expert systems treated in the preceding chapters is employed in some special way. We start by considering OPS5, a language which has especially been designed for building production systems. The system supports the formalism of production rules for the representation of domain knowledge, and includes an algorithm for bottom-up inference. OPS5 bears stronger resemblance to a programming language than to an expert system shell; it provides no explanation facilities, and an extensive standard user interface is lacking. However, the language has been used with much success for building practical expert systems. The second system that will be dealt with in this chapter is LOOPS, an elaborate programming environment for symbolic processing, which has proved to be highly suitable for the development of expert systems. LOOPS supports a large number of different paradigms, not only with respect to knowledge representation but with respect to inference as well; the system may therefore be viewed as the prototypical expert-system builder tool. CENTAUR, the last system that will be discussed in this chapter, is a dedicated expert system in which production rules and frames are integrated. In addition to an algorithm for production rule inference, the system offers a complete inference engine for the manipulation of frames to which inheritance contributes only a small part. Although CENTAUR is not an expert system shell, many of the ideas realized in the system are believed to be applicable to a wider range of problem domains than the domain for which it was developed.

7.1 OPS5

During the last two decades, a significant amount of research has been carried out at the University of Carnegie-Mellon on the design and development of production systems, among others by C.L. Forgy, J. McDermott, A. Newell and M. Rychener. Some of the languages and systems that emerged from this long-term research effort are PSG, PSNLST and OPS. OPS underwent a number of changes, which eventually led to the *OPS5* language. The language is still a subject of further development; consequently, there currently exists an OPS family of several more or less related languages. The basic features these languages share are well presented in OPS5. The present section will be devoted to this member of the OPS family. The name OPS5 originates from the acronym 'Official Production System 5' in which the adjective 'official' should not be taken too seriously. The language is mainly used for building expert systems, and became increasingly popular in the AI community after its successful application in the development of the expert system XCON. The language, however, is suitable for developing other kinds of application in the field of symbolic processing as well. C.L. Forgy has developed a programming environment for OPS5 in MACLISP and Franz LISP; there are versions of the language available in Bliss and COMMON LISP as well. OPS-like languages are also part of more elaborate expert system builder tools, such as for example Knowledge Craft.

Section 7.1.1 describes how knowledge is represented in OPS5, and is followed by a discussion of the inference method employed by the OPS5 interpreter in Section 7.1.2. The OPS5 interpreter makes use of a form of bottom-up inference in an efficient implementation based on the rete algorithm mentioned in Chapter 3. This algorithm, which has been developed by C.L. Forgy, will be described in detail in Section 7.1.3.

7.1.1 Knowledge representation in OPS5

The major part of an *OPS5 program* is a set of production rules constituting the production section of the program. These production rules, or *productions* as they are called in OPS5 context, employ an object–attribute–value representation, similar to the one introduced in Section 3.1.3. In OPS5, the objects and attributes referred to in the production rules have to be declared in the *declaration section* of the program. An object declaration consists of the keyword `literalize`, followed by the name of the object declared and all its associated attributes. The name of an object is also called a *class name.*

EXAMPLE 7.1

Consider the following object declaration:

```
(literalize patient
  name
  age
  complaint
  sign)
```

It declares the object with the name `patient`, having the (single-valued) attributes `name`, `age`, `complaint` and `sign`.

An attribute is always taken to be single-valued unless explicitly declared as being multi-valued by means of a `vector-attribute` declaration. For ease of exposition, all attributes in this section are assumed to be single-valued.

During the execution of an OPS5 program, an object may become instantiated, that is, a copy or *instantiation* of an object may be created in which constants have been filled in for its attributes. The values assigned to the attributes are either constants or the special value `nil`, indicating that the value of the attribute is unknown. In OPS5 two different types of constants are distinguished: numerical constants, simply called *numbers*, and symbolic constants, called *atoms*. The created instantiation is subsequently inserted into the fact set, or the *working memory* as the fact set is called in OPS5. As soon as an instantiation of an object is in the working memory, it is called a *working-memory element.* Each working-memory element is provided with a positive integer, called a *time tag*, by means of which working-memory elements are uniquely identified. A newly created working-memory element is given as a time tag the successor of the time tag attached to the last-created working-memory element. Working-memory elements may be displayed in OPS5 by entering the command `(wm)`; `(wm)` shows only those attributes of an object that have already obtained a value.

EXAMPLE 7.2

Consider the following working-memory element concerning the object `patient` declared in the previous example:

```
10: (patient ^name John ^age 20 ^complaint fever)
```

It has been assigned the time tag 10. The first component of this working-memory element is the class name `patient`; all other components are attribute–value pairs. An attribute is distinguished from its value by being prefixed with the ^ sign. The working-memory element given above specifies the attributes `name`, `age` and `complaint`, and constants `John` (an atom), `20` (a number) and `fever` (an atom). Note that the `sign` attribute is not shown, which indicates that it has not been assigned a value as yet.

The declaration section of an OPS5 program is followed by a collection of productions in the *production section.* After it has been read in by the system, it constitutes the so-called *production memory.* The syntax of production rules in OPS5 differs from that introduced in Chapter 3. However, conceptually speaking, OPS5 productions closely resemble the production rules discussed before.

A production in OPS5 has the following form:

```
(p <name> <lhs> --> <rhs>)
```

The symbol `p` indicates that the expression represents a production; each production has a unique name <name>. Following the name of the production, we have the *left-hand side,* <lhs>, followed by the symbol --> , and finally the *right-hand side,* <rhs>. The left-hand side of the production is a collection of conditions to be interpreted as a conjunction; its right-hand side is a collection of conclusions.

EXAMPLE 7.3

Consider the following production rule represented in the formalism introduced in Chapter 3:

if
same(*patient*,*complaint*,*fever*) ***and***
same(*patient*,*sign*,*jaundice*) ***and***
greaterthan(*labdata*,*ASAT*, 100)
then
add(*patient*,*diagnosis*,*hepatitis-A*)
fi

This production rule can be represented in the OPS5 syntax as follows:

```
(p example
   (patient ^complaint = fever ^sign = jaundice)
   (labdata ^ASAT > 100)
   -->
   (make patient ^diagnosis hepatitis-A))
```

Note that the first two conditions concerning the object `patient` in the preceding production rule constitute only one (composite) condition in the corresponding OPS5 production.

The conditions in the left-hand side of a production are called *condition elements* in OPS5, instead of just conditions. A condition element consists of a class name followed by a number of attribute–predicate–value triples. A *predicate* expresses a test on an attribute value and a specified constant. The most frequently applied predicates are `<`, `<=`, `>=`, `>`, `<>` (not equal to) and `=`. If no predicate has been specified between an attribute and a value, the equality predicate `=` is assumed by default.

EXAMPLE 7.4

Consider the following condition element from the production dealt with in Example 7.3:

```
(patient ^complaint = fever ^sign = jaundice)
```

It specifies the class name `patient` and contains two tests on the attributes `complaint` and `sign`, respectively. The specified constants are `fever` and `jaundice`. Both attribute–predicate–value triples specify the equality predicate `=`.

Anticipating the discussion of the OPS5 interpreter, we mention here that the interpreter compares the class name and attribute–predicate–value triples present in a condition element on the one hand, with the attribute–value pairs in working-memory elements concerning the same object on the other hand, applying the test specified by the predicate. If the test succeeds for a given working-memory element, we say that the interpreter has found a *match.*

EXAMPLE 7.5

Consider the following condition element:

```
(patient ^age < 70)
```

and the following two working-memory elements concerning the same object `patient`:

```
1: (patient ^name John ^age 50)
2: (patient ^name Ann ^age 75)
```

We have that only the first working-memory element matches with the condition element, because for the first memory element the test `^age < 70` succeeds, while for the second one the test `^age < 70` fails. Note that in comparing the condition element with the working-memory elements the attribute `name` is disregarded because it is not referred to in the condition element.

The *negation* of a condition element in the left-hand side of a production is obtained by specifying a minus sign in front of the condition element concerned.

In addition to the specification of an isolated predicate, it is also possible to specify a conjunction or disjunction of tests. A conjunction is specified by placing the predicates and values of the conjunction between braces, as shown in the following example.

EXAMPLE 7.6

Consider the following condition element:

```
(person ^age { > 20 < 50 })
```

It expresses a conjunction involving the two predicates > and <. The OPS5 interpreter finds a match for this condition element only with working-memory elements specifying the attribute `age` for the class name `person` having a value greater than 20 and less than 50.

A disjunction of equality tests is expressed by specifying a collection of constants between the symbols << and >> at the value position. In case of a disjunction, it is not allowed to specify a predicate explicitly.

EXAMPLE 7.7

In the following condition element, we have expressed a disjunction of two equality tests:

```
(patient ^complaint << fever headache >>)
```

The OPS5 interpreter will find a match for this condition element with every working-memory element that specifies the attribute `complaint` for the class `patient` having one of the values `fever` and `headache`. So the following two working-memory elements match with the given condition element:

```
1: (patient ^complaint fever)
2: (patient ^complaint headache)
```

The right-hand side of a production consists of a number of conclusions, each comprising an action and a list of associated arguments. The actions are evaluated in the order of appearance. When evaluated, most actions will bring about certain changes to the working memory. Only the most frequently applied actions `make`, `remove` and `modify` will be discussed here in depth.

Execution of the action `make` creates a new working-memory element. In doing so, it assigns values to the attributes of the object as specified in the argument list of the `make` action. Attributes not explicitly referred to in the `make` action obtain the default value `nil`.

EXAMPLE 7.8

Suppose that we start with an empty working memory which has never been filled before. We enter the following declaration:

```
(literalize person
  name
  age)
```

Now, the action

```
(make person ^name John)
```

adds the following element to the working memory:

```
1: (person ^name John ^age nil)
```

Note that this working-memory element not only contains the attribute `name` with the value `John`, as indicated in the action, but the attribute `age` as well; since for the attribute `age` no value has been specified in the `make` action, it has been assigned the (default) value `nil`. It should be stressed that an attribute which has value `nil` will not be printed by the OPS5 interpreter; the output of the command `(wm)` will therefore differ from what has been shown here.

The action `remove` deletes an element from the working memory. This action takes one or more arguments called *element designators*. An element designator is either a variable bound to a working-memory element or an integer constant n referring to the working-memory element matching with the nth condition element of the production it is specified in. We shall return to the first possibility shortly; first we shall consider the numerical element designators. The OPS5 interpreter numbers the condition elements of a production starting by assigning the number 1 to the first condition element specified; each next condition element is assigned a number one greater than the last condition element encountered, with the exception of negated condition elements which are disregarded. For example, if we have a left-hand side comprising a negation enclosed between two non-negative condition elements, the element designator referring to working-memory elements matching with the third condition will be the number `2`. It is also possible to enter the action `remove` separate from a production. In this case, a numerical element designator is taken to be a time tag of a working-memory element. The effect of the action `remove` is that elements referred to by the element designators are removed from the working memory.

EXAMPLE 7.9

The execution of the action

```
(remove 10)
```

which has been specified separate from a production, results in the deletion of the element having a time tag equal to 10 from the working memory. The action `remove` also offers the dangerous possibility of deleting all elements from the working memory:

```
(remove *)
```

The action `modify` may be viewed as a combination of the earlier treated actions `remove` and `make`: it first removes a uniquely identified element from the working memory, and subsequently adds a new instantiation of the same object to it. Its argument list consists of an element designator followed by a collection of attribute–value pairs to be modified in the working-memory element referred to by the element designator. Only the values of attributes passed as arguments to the action `modify` will be altered by the execution of this action; the other attribute values remain the same. The time tag of the new working element is the previous maximal time tag incremented by two, reflecting the two-fold action of `modify`.

EXAMPLE 7.10

Consider the following declaration

```
(literalize person
  name)
```

and the following production expressing that from now on all anonymous persons will be called John:

```
(p example
   (person ^name = anonymous)
   -->
   (modify 1 ^name John))
```

Now suppose that the following action is carried out in an empty working memory:

```
(make person ^name anonymous)
```

After execution of this action, the working memory contains the following element:

```
1: (person ^name anonymous)
```

Subsequent application of the production defined above modifies the working memory as follows:

```
3: (person ^name John)
```

This is now the only element present in the working memory.

As we have discussed above, the actions `make` and `remove` may also be applied separate from productions. However, this is not the case for the action `modify`; its arguments should always refer to working-memory elements matching with condition elements in the production it is specified in.

OPS5 provides several other actions than those treated above; we shall only briefly mention some of these. There are actions available for input and output. For example, the action `openfile` opens a file. Files are closed by `closefile`. The action `accept` reads input from the keyboard. To conclude, the action `write` prints information on the screen.

Until now, we have considered only productions in which objects, attributes and constants were specified in the condition elements. However, OPS5 also permits local variables in productions, thus increasing their expressiveness. Variables may appear in the left-hand side of a production as well as in its right-hand side. A variable may occur in the left-hand side of a production in three different places:

- following a predicate, that is, at the position of a constant;
- in front of a condition element;
- following a condition element.

In the last two cases, the condition element and the variable are grouped together by means of a pair of braces; in these cases we speak of an *element variable*. Variables are distinguished syntactically from constants by the requirement that the name of a variable should begin with the < sign and end with the > sign.

EXAMPLE 7.11

The strings <X>, <1> and <a-very-long-variable-name> are examples of valid variable names.

If it is necessary to use a constant starting with the < sign or ending with the > sign, then the constant should be preceded by the \\ sequence (the *escape symbol*) indicating that the name stands for a constant instead of for a variable. Variables in condition elements may be *bound* to constants as illustrated in the following example.

EXAMPLE 7.12

Consider the following condition element:

```
(person ^name = <n> ^age = 20)
```

which contains the variable <n>. If the OPS5 interpreter is able to find a matching working-memory element for this condition element, the variable <n> will be bound to the constant value specified for the attribute name in the matching working-memory element (or possibly to nil).

In this example we have seen that variables in the position of a constant may be bound to an attribute value of a working-memory element. Element variables are more general; such a variable may be bound to an entire working-memory element as illustrated below.

EXAMPLE 7.13

Consider the following condition element:

```
{ (person ^name John) <pers> }
```

in which the element variable <pers> occurs. Suppose that the OPS5 interpreter finds a match for this condition element with the following working-memory element:

```
1: (person ^name John ^age 20)
```

Then, as a result, the variable <pers> will be bound to the entire matching working-memory element.

The following example demonstrates how an element variable may be used in the right-hand side of a production.

EXAMPLE 7.14

The production shown below specifies the same element variable in both its left-hand side and right-hand side, which is quite typical usage of element variables:

```
(p example)
   { (persons ^name John) <pers> }
   -->
   (remove <pers>))
```

Upon success, this production causes the deletion of all elements from working memory specifying the class name `person`, the attribute `name` and the constant value `John`. Note that, if we had specified the right-hand side `(remove 1)` instead of the one shown above, the same would have been achieved.

7.1.2 The OPS5 interpreter

OPS5 provides a bottom-up inference algorithm for the selection and application of production rules, which is very much like the bottom-up inference algorithm discussed in Chapter 3. Since, however, there are some differences, the principles of bottom-up inference will be briefly reviewed here, but this time from the perspective of OPS5.

During the selection phase of the inference algorithm, the OPS5 interpreter selects the productions from production memory having conditions all of which match with one or more elements from the working memory. It is said that there exists a *match* between a working-memory element and a condition element, if:

- The class names in the given working-memory element and condition element coincide.
- Every test expressed by means of a predicate in the condition element is satisfied for the specified constant and the attribute value in the working-memory element.

If a condition element contains a variable at the position of a constant, and if there already exists a binding for that variable, then after replacing the variable by its binding, the two conditions mentioned above should be met. If the variable is still unbound, the interpreter will attempt to create a binding for it by investigating for each working-memory element whether a match results after substituting the variable by the value of the corresponding attribute present in that working-memory element. To determine whether there exists a match of a condition element with a working-memory element, the interpreter examines only the attributes occurring in the condition element; all other attributes present in the working-memory element are simply ignored. If a variable that has been bound in a certain condition element occurs in some other condition element in the same production as well, and if its binding causes the condition element to match, we speak of a *consistent match.*

EXAMPLE 7.15

The following production contains a variable <n> appearing in two different condition elements:

```
(p small-arteries
   (artery ^name = <n> ^diameter < 2)
   (arm ^blood-vessel = <n>)
   -->
   (make small-arm-artery ^name <n>))
```

We suppose that the interpreter is able to find a match for the first condition element with some working-memory element with the class name artery that specifies a value for the attribute diameter less than the number 2. Then, as a result, the variable <n> will be bound to the value of the name attribute. The interpreter next searches the working memory for a working-memory element with the class name arm. If such a working-memory element is found then, to match, the value of its blood-vessel attribute must be equal to the previously created binding for the variable <n>. Now suppose that the production succeeds. Its conclusion is subsequently evaluated, resulting in the addition of a new instantiation of the object small-arm-artery to the working memory in which the value of the attribute name is equal to the constant that is the binding of the variable <n>.

We have now given a brief overview of the process of selecting applicable productions from the production memory in OPS5. We shall continue by considering some aspects of this selection process in further detail.

Instead of a set of productions, the selection process actually yields a set of *production instantiations*, similar to the rule instances introduced in Chapter 3. A production instantiation consists of a production together with a set of matching working-memory elements, one for each condition elements. A production may therefore appear more than once in the conflict set in different production instantiations. The time tags attached to working-memory elements do not play any role in the selection of applicable productions from the production memory. However, they become relevant in conflict resolution. Basically, two different conflict-resolution strategies are employed by OPS5 for choosing a production for evaluation. The first and most important conflict-resolution strategy employed is conflict resolution by recency. This form of conflict resolution has already been dealt with in Chapter 3. It will be reviewed only briefly. Recall from Chapter 3 that conflict resolution by recency will not always yield a unique production instantiation for evaluation. Therefore, OPS5 incorporates a second conflict-resolution strategy, namely conflict resolution by specificity. We have already mentioned in Chapter 3 that conflict resolution by specificity chooses those production instantiations having the largest number of tests in their left-hand side. If a unique production instantiation is still not obtained, an arbitrary one is chosen for evaluation. To summarize, a production instantiation is selected from the conflict set in OPS5 according to the following strategy:

(1) *Conflict resolution by recency.* To start with, the OPS5 interpreter takes the production instantiations from the conflict set with the maximal time tag. If this process yields more than one production instantiation, the process is repeated for the selected subset of instantiations, thereby disregarding the time tags previously applied in the selection process; instantiations for which all time tags are exhausted are removed from the conflict set. The entire process is repeated until a single instantiation is left, or until all time tags have been examined.

(2) *Conflict resolution by specificity.* If step 1 yields a set of more than one instantiation, then for each element in this set it is determined how many tests on constants and variables are specified in the left-hand side of the associated production. The instantiations with the maximal number of tests are selected.

(3) *Arbitrary selection.* If step 2 still yields a set of more than one instantiation, a single instantiation is chosen for evaluation on arbitrary grounds.

The conflict-resolution strategy in OPS5 described above is known as the *lex strategy*, since the most important criterion for selecting production instantiations is according to a *lex*icographical ordering of their time-tag sequences. In addition to this strategy, OPS5 also provides the so-called *mea strategy* (mea is an acronym for *means–ends analysis*). This strategy is usually applied to obtain a goal-driven inference behaviour using bottom-up inference. The mea strategy differs from the lex strategy by first choosing those instantiations from the conflict set having a maximal time tag for the working-memory element matching with their first condition element. The following steps are similar to the ones used in the lex strategy. The time tags of the working-memory elements matching with the first condition element are then disregarded.

The process of selection and application of productions from the production memory is called the *recognize–act cycle* of OPS5. The

Table 7.1 Data used in the ancestor problem.

Name	*Mother*	*Father*
Gaea	—	Chaos
Cronus	Gaea	Uranus
Rhea	Gaea	Uranus
Zeus	Rhea	Cronus
Hephaestus	Hera	Zeus
Leto	Phoebe	Coeus
Hera	Rhea	Cronus
Apollo	Leto	Zeus

recognize part of the cycle consists of the selection of applicable instantiations from the production memory as described above. The act part consists of the execution of the actions specified in the right-hand side of the instantiation chosen by conflict resolution.

We finish this section by giving an example demonstrating several of the features of the OPS5 language.

EXAMPLE 7.16

Consider a database specifying some information from Greek mythology, as shown in Table 7.1. We shall develop an OPS5 program that returns for a given character the names of her or his ancestors, using the data stored in this database; this problem is known as the *ancestor problem*. Although this is only a toy example, many practical problems characterized by a hierarchically structured search space closely resemble the ancestor problem. In general, the ancestors of any person included in the database can be retrieved as follows:

(1) Look up the name of the father of the given person, and search subsequently for his ancestors.

(2) Look up the name of the mother of the given person, and search for the ancestors of the mother as well.

The algorithm sketched above is a recursive one. However, OPS5 does not support recursion explicitly; it is therefore entirely left to the programmer to implement recursion using productions. We shall see that it is not difficult to implement recursion in OPS5. First we look at the various object declarations in the declaration section of our program.

The data concerning the characters specified in Table 7.1 can be represented by means of a single object. To this end we have declared an object with the class name `person` and the attributes `name`, `mother` and `father`:

```
(literalize person
  name
  mother
  father)
```

Furthermore, we need an object for temporary storage of the data concerning a given person while the program is engaged in searching the ancestors of another person. To this end, we define an object with the name `kept` which may be viewed as part of an implementation of a stack data structure. The object contains only a single attribute, `name`, for storing the name of a person to be processed at a later stage during the computation:

```
(literalize kept
  name)
```

To conclude, we need an additional third object for initiating the inference. This object with the class name `start` does not contain any attributes:

```
(literalize start)
```

The remaining and most important part of the program consists of two productions. By means of the first production, the inference is initiated as soon as an element with the class name `start` is inserted into the working memory. Among others things, execution of the actions of this production results in asking the user to enter the name of the person whose ancestors have to be looked up:

```
(p query
   { (start) <init> }
   -->
   (remove <init>)
   (write (crlf) |Enter name of person: |)
   (make kept ^name (accept)))
```

Recall that the actions in the right-hand side of the production are evaluated in the order of appearance. First, the working-memory element that started the inference and has been bound to the element variable `<init>` is removed. Next, the user is prompted to enter the name of a person. The name entered by the user is read by means of `(accept)`. By means of the action `make` a new working-memory element with the class name kept is added to the working memory. The attribute name of the new working-memory element is assigned the name entered by the user.

The second production constitutes the kernel of the program; it searches for the names of both parents of the given person. If the search succeeds, the names of the parents are pushed upon the stack as two kept working-memory elements, in order to be processed at a later stage.

```
(p ancestors
   { (kept ^name { <p-name> <> nil }) <wme> }
   (person ^name <p-name>
          ^mother <m-name>
          ^father <f-name>)
   -->
   (remove <wme>)
   (write (crlf) <m-name> and <f-name> are parents of <p-name>)
   (make kept ^name <m-name>)
   (make kept ^name <f-name>))
```

Examine this production closely. If the interpreter is able to find a matching working-memory element for its first condition element, the variable <p-name> will be bound to the value of the attribute name of some person working-memory element. Recall that after application of the first production one working-memory element with the class name kept is present, so initially the first condition succeeds. We have mentioned before that the kept instantiations may be viewed as simulating recursion by a stack. The first condition element of the production shown above may therefore be viewed as a means for inspecting the top element in the kept stack. Note that the condition succeeds only if the binding for the variable <p-name> is not equal to nil. The working-memory element matching the first condition element will be bound to the element variable <wme>. By means of the second condition element, the names of the father and the mother are looked up in the working memory, and will be bound to <m-name> and <f-name>, respectively. In the right-hand side of the production, the working-memory element matching with the first condition element is removed, thus simulating popping the stack. This working-memory element is no longer needed. The next action, write, prints the name of the person and the names of her or his father and mother to the screen. Finally, by means of two make actions two new kept working-memory elements are created specifying the names of the father and mother, respectively, of the given person. These new elements are added to the working memory, that is, pushed upon the `kept` stack of persons to be processed at a later stage. The names of these persons are used in one of the following inference steps to retrieve the other ancestors of the initially given person. The order in which these `make` actions are executed is important. Observe that the father working-memory element is always assigned a higher time tag than the mother working-memory element. Consequently, the program first looks for the male ancestors and, after having found all of them, returns to generate all female ancestors.

After the declarations and productions have been read in, the working memory is filled by executing the following `make` actions:

```
(make person ^name Gaea ^father Chaos)
(make person ^name Cronus ^mother Gaea ^father Uranus)
(make person ^name Rhea ^mother Gaea ^father Uranus)
(make person ^name Zeus ^mother Rhea ^father Cronus)
(make person ^name Hephaestus ^mother Hera ^father Zeus)
(make person ^name Leto ^mother Phoebe ^father Coeus)
(make person ^name Hera ^mother Rhea ^father Cronus)
(make person ^name Apollo ^mother Leto ^father Zeus)

(make start)
```

Below, we have reproduced the transcript of the interaction with OPS5 in solving the ancestor problem.

```
> (i-g-v)                    ; initialization
nil
> (load "ancestors.ops")     ; load program
**
> (run)                      ; execute program
Enter name of a person: Apollo

Leto and Zeus are parents of Apollo
Rhea and Cronus are parents of Zeus
Gaea and Uranus are parents of Cronus
nil and Chaos are parents of Gaea
Gaea and Uranus are parents of Rhea
nil and Chaos are parents of Gaea
Phoebe and Coeus are parents of Leto
end -- no production true
2 productions (9 // 9 nodes)
8 firings (33 rhs actions)
13 mean working memory size (17 maximum)
2 mean conflict set size (3 maximum)
12 mean token memory size (14 maximum)
```

7.1.3 The rete algorithm

We have mentioned before that OPS5 makes use of an inference algorithm much like the bottom-up inference algorithm discussed in Chapter 3. As we have argued in that chapter, a straightforward implementation of bottom-up inference may render a production system unacceptably inefficient, because at every inference step all facts in the fact set have to be matched against the left-hand sides of all productions. Now, it is a well-known fact that, when applying bottom-up inference, for many applications the inference state remains largely unchanged between successive inference steps; at every inference step only a few facts are added, modified or removed. The class of applications for which this statement is true are called *temporally redundant*. Of course, there are many applications which are characterized by significant changes in the working memory between successive inference steps; for example, in an expert system used as part of an on-line signal-processing application, the fact set generally is completely refreshed every time a fixed number of inference steps has been passed through. This class of applications is called *non-temporally redundant*.

Analysis of performance measurements of typical OPS5 programs has revealed that the part of the inference algorithm responsible for matching productions with facts may consume as much as 90% of the entire execution time of the program. So there seem to be ample reasons to look for optimizations of the matching part of the bottom-up inference algorithm. OPS5 provides such an optimized algorithm for bottom-up inference, called the *rete algorithm*. It has been developed by C.L. Forgy. The point of departure for this algorithm has been the assumption that the inference state is largely unaltered between successive inference steps. From the discussion above, it will be apparent that the rete algorithm has been especially designed for temporally redundant applications; it is less suitable for non-temporally redundant applications.

The algorithm operates on a kind of data-flow graph used for the representation of productions. This directed graph is called the *rete graph*. Later on we shall see that the working memory is incorporated in this graph. First we shall examine the way in which the rete graph is constructed. Any OPS5 program presented to the interpreter is compiled into a rete graph; the various parts of a production are translated into its vertices or arcs. The following example demonstrates how a simple condition element is translated into a graph representation.

EXAMPLE 7.17

Consider the following condition element:

```
(patient ^age < 40 ^complaint = fever)
```

For obtaining a match with this condition element the interpreter

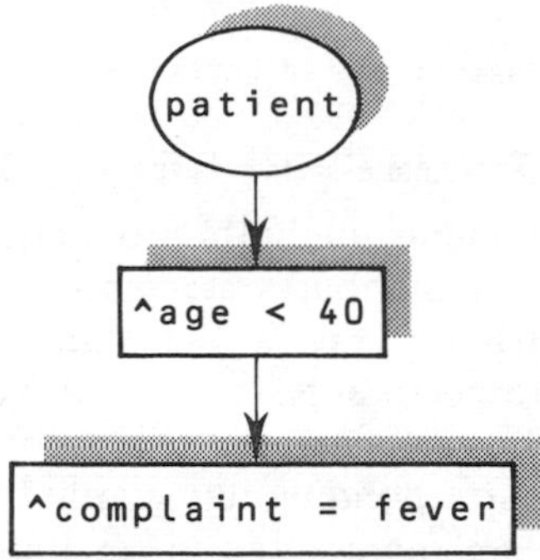

Figure 7.1 Rete graph for the condition element
(patient ^age < 40 ^complaint = fever).

has to perform three tests: a test concerning the class name `patient`, a test concerning the value of the attribute `age`, and a test with respect to the value of the attribute `complaint`. The rete graph into which this condition element is translated by OPS5 is shown in Figure 7.1.

Each test specified by a condition element is represented as a vertex in the corresponding rete graph. A test on the class name is indicated by means of an ellipse; each attribute–predicate–value triple occurring in a condition element is represented by means of a rectangle. Between the vertices representing the tests, arcs are drawn having directions indicating the order in which the tests have to be carried out. The entire right-hand side of a production is represented by a single vertex, called the *production vertex*. Production vertices are the leaves of the rete graph.

We have now dealt with the basic translation of a production into graph representation. One of the aims of the rete algorithm is to eliminate the redundancies in the representation of the productions. For example, if we have several productions containing similar condition elements, a number of these similar condition elements will be represented only once.

EXAMPLE 7.18

Consider the following two productions:

```
(p small
   (artery ^name = <n> ^diameter < 2)
   -->
   (make artery ^name = <n> ^type small))
```

```
(p large
   (artery ^name = <n> ^diameter > = 2)
   -->
   (make artery ^name = <n> ^type large))
```

The condition elements in both productions concern the class name `artery` and the attributes `name` and `diameter`. The test on the value of the attribute `name` is the same in both productions; however, their respective tests on the value of the attribute `diameter` differ. The test on the attribute `name` is now represented only once in the corresponding rete graph; the tests concerning the attribute `diameter` are represented in separate vertices, as depicted in Figure 7.2.

In the preceding examples, we have considered productions having one condition element only. All vertices in the resulting rete graphs had (at most) one incoming arc and one or more outgoing arcs. Such vertices are called *one-input vertices*. If a production contains more than one condition element in its left-hand side, then generally an extra vertex is required for linking these condition elements together. Such a vertex, which has two incoming arcs and one or more outgoing arcs, is called a *two-input vertex*. A two-input vertex will be indicated in the rete graph by means of a circle. If a given production contains n condition elements, then a total of $n - 1$ two-input vertices is required for the representation of the left-hand side of the production. In the following example, we shall see that a two-input vertex is also used for storing variable bindings and for specifying tests as to whether these variable bindings are consistent.

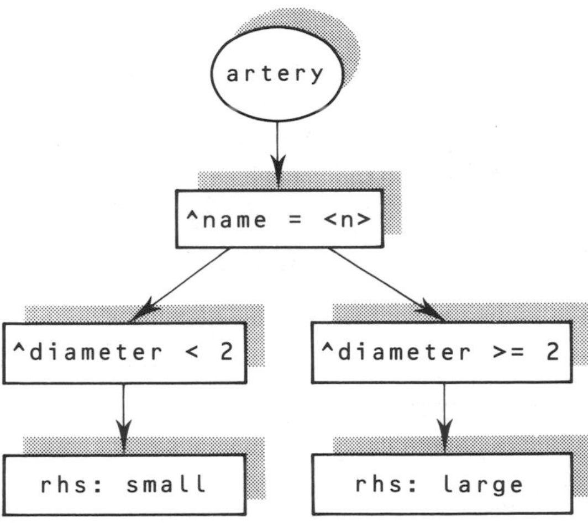

Figure 7.2 Two productions having the same condition element.

EXAMPLE 7.19

Each of the following two productions comprises two condition elements:

```
(p disjunction
   (expression ^type = boolean ^name = <e>)
   (operator ^name = <e> ^left = <x> ^right = <y> ^op = or)
   -->
   ...)
(p conjunction
   (expression ^type = boolean ^name = <e>)
   (operator ^name = <e> ^left = <x> ^right = <y> ^op = and)
   -->
   ...)
```

The two left-hand sides of these productions differ to only a slight extent; the attribute `op` in the second condition element of the first production concerns the constant `or` whereas the same attribute in the second condition element of the second production concerns the constant `and`. The similarity between the left-hand sides of these productions is again reflected in the rete graph shown in Figure 7.3. Note that the test on the attribute `name` is represented twice: once for the class name `expression`, and once for the class name `operator`. The two-input vertices in the graph specify a test on the bindings created for the variables.

For a collection of productions a rete graph is constructed in the manner described above. However, we have already remarked before that the rete graph is not only used for the compact representation of productions; it is further exploited for the storage of the working memory which once more improves the efficiency of the inference algorithm for temporally redundant applications. The working memory is distributed over the rete graph during the inference. Each new element to be added to the working memory occupies a location in the rete graph which is based on the tests it has passed. Informally speaking, a working-memory element travels through the graph along the specified arcs. After passing a collection of tests given by the one-input vertices, a working-memory element is finally stored in a two-input vertex, which for this purpose is provided with a local memory location. The one-input vertices have no local memory, because if the test specified by a one-input vertex succeeds, the working-memory element proceeds to the next one-input vertex for the next test, or to a two-input vertex to be stored. If, on the other hand, at least one of the tests on the working-memory element has failed, then the working-memory element may simply be ignored.

The way in which the working memory is processed in the rete

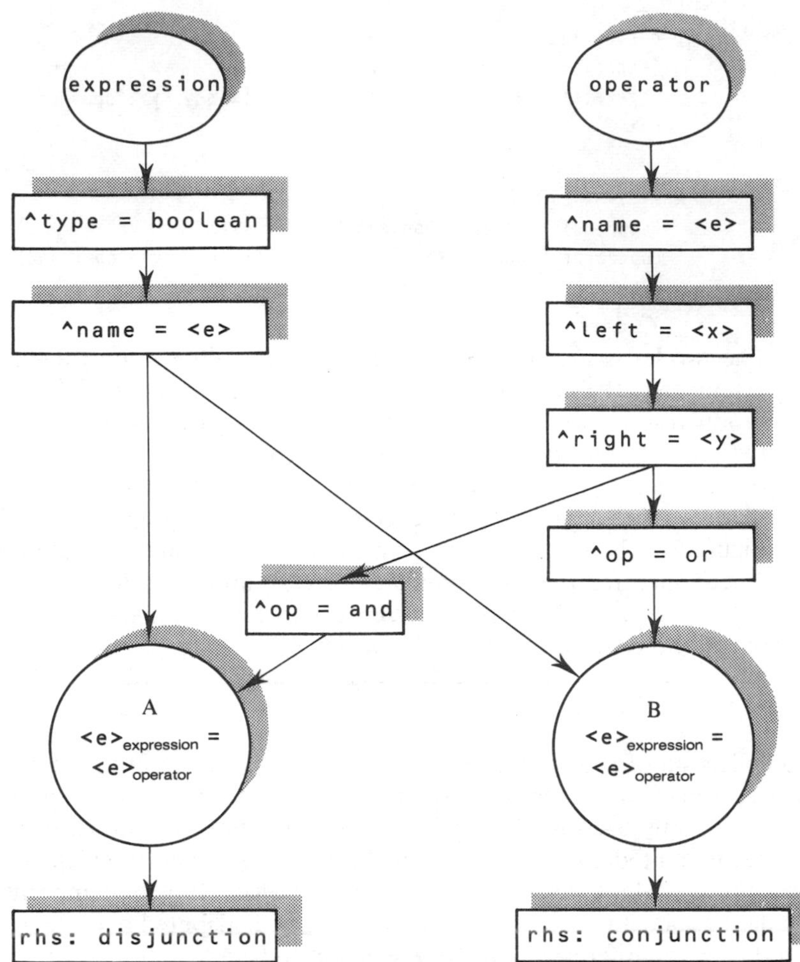

Figure 7.3 Rete graph of two productions.

graph may appropriately be viewed as the processing of a sequence of working-memory elements through the graph. Such a sequence of working-memory elements is called a *token*. A token consists of a collection of working-memory elements supplemented with a *tag* indicating whether the elements must be added to, or removed from the working memory. A token has the following form:

<token> ::= ⟨ <tag> { <working-memory-element> }$^+$ ⟩
<tag> ::= + | -

A token containing a plus sign as a tag indicates that its working-memory elements must be added to local memory by the interpreter. A token prefixed by a minus sign indicates that all working-memory elements which are present in local memory and correspond to the working-memory elements contained in the token must be removed.

EXAMPLE 7.20

Study Figure 7.3 once more and consider the following token:

```
(+ 1: (expression ^type boolean ^name ex10))
```

This token adds the working-memory element

```
(expression ^type boolean ^name ex10)
```

to the two-input vertices A and B depicted in the figure. The variable `<e>` in the condition element with class name `expression` will then be bound to the atom `ex10`.

Tokens are combined at two-input vertices by concatenating all elements stored into `+` or `-` tokens. If a two-input vertex contains a token of which the elements have successfully passed all its tests, the token will be moved on to the next vertex in the rete graph. In this way, the token may eventually reach the production vertex, where it will lead to the creation of a production instantiation which will be added to the conflict set. If at a certain stage of the inference all tokens in the rete graph have been processed, the conflict set will be constructed from the production vertices. All instantiations present in the conflict set then participate in the conflict resolution.

EXAMPLE 7.21

Consider once more the previous example, where the token

```
(+ 1: (expression ^type boolean ^name ex10))
```

was added to the two-input vertices shown in Figure 7.3. Now suppose that the vertex B already contained the token

```
(+ 3: (operator ^name ex10 ^left ex8 ^right ex9 ^op or))
```

Then, the local memory of B will be modified by storing the following new token:

```
(+ 1: (expression ^type boolean ^name ex10)
   3: (operator ^name ex10 ^left ex8 ^right ex9 ^op or))
```

Since the binding of the variable `<e>` results in a consistent match for the attribute `name`, the token is moved to the production vertex `disjunction`.

Until now, we have assumed that two-input vertices have only a single memory location. However, in OPS5 a separate memory is actually maintained both for the left and for the right incoming arc of a two-input vertex:

- The *left memory* (*lm*) contains tokens arriving from the left incoming arc together with possible variable bindings.
- The *right memory* (*rm*) contains tokens arriving from the right incoming arc of the two-input vertex and their possible variable bindings.

Figure 7.4 shows a rete graph where with each two-input vertex two local memory locations have been associated. If a positive token reaches a two-input vertex from its right incoming arc, it is possible that this token specifies some variable bindings. These will initially be stored in the right memory. Now, variable bindings stored in the right memory will be

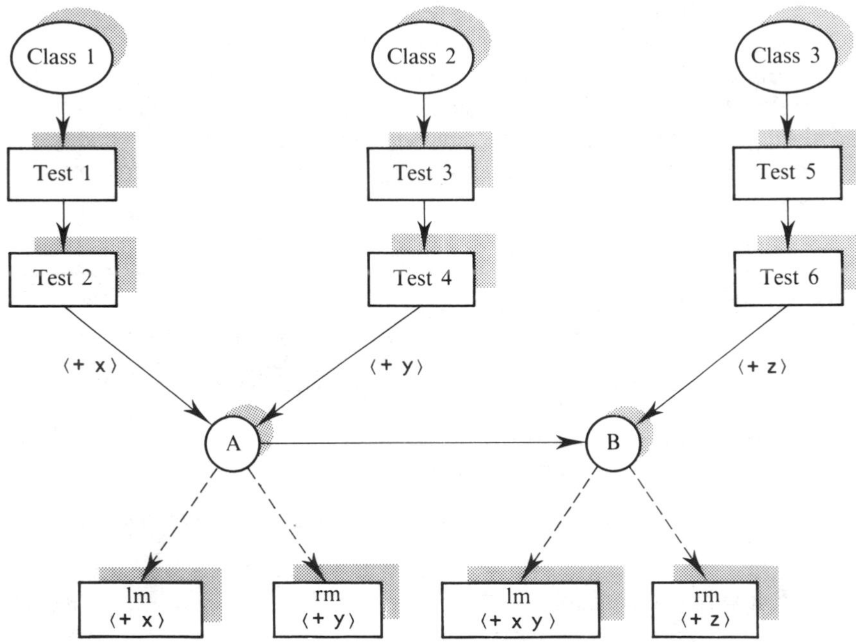

Figure 7.4 Rete graph with left and right memory.

compared to equally named variables present in the left memory. If these bindings turn out to be consistent, the token originating from the right memory is added to the left memory of the next two-input vertex or gives rise to the creation of an instantiation if a production vertex has been reached. If a negative token is sent through the graph and added to the right memory, the corresponding elements present in the right memory are removed from the tokens stored in both the right memory and the left memory of the next vertex.

7.1.4 Building expert systems using OPS5

We have presented the basic principles of OPS5 in the preceding sections. In this section we briefly touch on some strong and weak points of OPS5 viewed as a tool for building expert systems.

The OPS5 interpreter provides the knowledge engineer with an interactive programming environment, which is much like conventional programming environments for languages such as LISP and PROLOG. Interpreters for OPS-like languages usually include facilities for tracing the inference behaviour of the system at various levels of detail, and facilities for inspecting the stepwise execution of programs. These facilities are quite valuable for debugging OPS5 programs. Even more elaborate and flexible environments for production-system languages like OPS5 are available for special graphical workstations. For problems requiring more solving power for their solution than production rules only are able to provide, OPS5 offers an interface to LISP or BLISS, depending on the particular version of the OPS5 system employed.

Although OPS5 is a suitable language for building expert systems, it has several characteristics rendering it less flexible than is desirable. In many applications, for example, it appears to be necessary to model some domain-dependent control strategy using the standard inference method provided by the interpreter. For example, in a medical diagnostic expert system, it is desirable to have the various possible disorders considered as diagnoses for a given patient case examined in some specific order, starting with the disorders most likely to be present in the given patient and only then proceeding to more rare disorders if the disorders initially considered have been ruled out. However, it is no easy matter to adapt the standard inference behaviour of the interpreter to the need; this requires a thorough understanding of for example the conflict-resolution strategy employed in OPS5. Evidently, it makes no sense to put most of the effort of building an expert system into trying to adapt the standard inference strategies offered. This problem can be alleviated partly by making an explicit distinction between productions intended only to control the inference and productions used purely for representing the heuristic domain knowledge. Large OPS5 systems have usually been developed using this approach. However, there still is some danger that only the knowledge engineer who constructed the system will be sufficiently familiar with the domain-specific control strategy incorporated in the expert system. In such a case the expert system may be difficult to modify and maintain.

Another weakness of OPS5 closely related to the one mentioned above is that it offers only a single formalism for specifying knowledge. In large expert systems, it is usually advantageous to impose some kind of modularization on the knowledge base. A suitable modularization of a production system may for example be obtained by decomposing the knowledge base into several partitions, each of which concerns closely related pieces of knowledge. It will be evident that a modularized knowledge base is much easier to develop and maintain than one large collection of similar-looking production rules. Unfortunately, OPS5 does not offer any language constructs for modularization. The problems mentioned here are not restricted to OPS5 only, but apply to rule-based systems in general. We shall return to this observation in Section 7.3.

Most of the weaknesses mentioned above have been resolved in a more recent member of the OPS family: *OPS83*. To provide better control, OPS83 offers the knowledge engineer the possibility of developing her or his own conflict-resolution strategies to replace the standard recognize–act cycle as discussed above. Furthermore, OPS83 supports not only the production system concept but conventional imperative programming as well; the parts of a problem that are more readily solved using an algorithmic approach may now be handled accordingly. Finally, an OPS83 program may be subdivided into several modules, and each module can indicate which information from other modules must be made visible to it. The principal notions of OPS83 are, however, much like those of OPS5.

7.2 LOOPS

The next system we examine in this chapter is LOOPS, an extensive programming environment for knowledge-based systems. LOOPS was developed at the Xerox Palo Alto Research Center in the early 1980s, primarily by D.G. Bobrow and M.J. Stefik. LOOPS has grown out of research on languages for knowledge representation. This research was part of a large-scale project aiming at the construction of an expert assistant for designers of integrated digital circuits. Both developers of the LOOPS system had previously been involved in designing knowledge-representation languages; D.G. Bobrow had developed KRL in cooperation with T. Winograd, and M.J. Stefik had worked on UNITS. Facilities typically found in advanced expert-system builder tools are well represented in LOOPS, thereby justifying a treatment of this system here.

LOOPS is an acronym of Lisp Object Oriented Programming System. From this we may read the most important characteristic of the system: the support of object-oriented programming in a LISP environment. LOOPS has been embedded in the INTERLISP programming environment, thus providing the knowledge engineer with all the facilities from this LISP environment. Besides the paradigm of functional programming arising from the embedding in LISP, LOOPS supports several other programming styles as well, such as:

- *Object-oriented programming*, a style of programming in which programs are organized around autonomous objects, being entities for data and procedural abstraction and having local procedures and private data. All of the actions in object-oriented programming come from message passing between objects.
- *Data-oriented programming*, a style of programming in which a system's behaviour is determined by the activation of procedures on the examination of or a change in the data.
- *Rule-oriented programming*, a style of programming already introduced in Chapter 3, where a system's behaviour is determined by rule-based inference.

In the following sections each of the programming styles supported by LOOPS will be discussed. Within the context of this book, however, it is not possible to discuss all aspects of the LOOPS system in full detail; our aim is merely to give an impression of this comprehensive expert-system builder tool.

7.2.1 Object-oriented programming

When written in a procedural programming language like Pascal, a program is considered to be composed of a data-declaration part and a part specifying actions on data which have to be executed in sequential order. A program written in an object-oriented programming language comprises a number of autonomous parts called *objects*, each containing private data and local procedures called *methods*. Objects are able to communicate with each other by means of sending *messages*. This type of communication between objects is called *message passing*. Object-oriented programming provides a programmer with the principle of data abstraction; when a certain object wishes to inspect the state of another object, this can only be achieved by sending the latter object a request for this information, that is, by sending it a message. A system's behaviour is determined by the behaviour of the autonomous objects.

In LOOPS three types of object are discerned which are organized in a *taxonomy* of objects:

- A *class* is a description of one or more similar objects. The notion of a class in LOOPS is similar to the notion of a class frame introduced in Chapter 4.
- An *instance* is a unique object belonging to a particular class. The instances in LOOPS are similar in concept to the instances of frames discussed in Chapter 4.
- A *meta-class* is a class whose instances are classes themselves. A meta-class generally consists of a set of templates for frame-like data structures.

A class is composed of the following parts:

- a *class name*;
- a *meta-class part*, naming the meta-classes the class belongs to;
- a *superclass part*, indicating the position of the class in the taxonomy by specifying its superclasses;
- a number of *variables*;
- a number of *methods*.

In a class, variables may take values. A variable has a name, a value and a *property list*, a feature taken from LISP. The property list of a variable is used to store meta-information about both the variable and its value. A property list can for example be used for storing a *default value* for the variable, for setting *constraints* on values to be assigned to the variable, and for specifying relationships to other variables; these relationships are called *dependencies*. A property list attached to a variable may furthermore contain a *certainty factor* for the value the variable has adopted and the information that led to the current belief in the value, called the value's *support*.

In a class, two types of variables are discerned:

- *Class variables* are used for storing information shared by all instances of the class. A class variable is typically used for information about the class taken as a whole.
- *Instance variables* contain information specific to instances of the class separately. The instance variable part of a class definition specifies the names and default values of the variables to be created for instances of the class.

Besides a number of variables, a class definition generally also contains a number of methods. A *method* is a procedure describing how an instance of the class should react on receiving a certain message. In a class with each method a so-called *selector* is associated. For responding to a message, an instance uses these selectors for selecting and activating the proper method from the class it belongs to.

EXAMPLE 7.22

The following is an example of a class definition in LOOPS, where we have slightly modified the LISP-like syntax of classes in LOOPS to arrive at a syntax more like the one employed for frames in Chapter 4:

```
class truck is
  metaclass class;
  superclass (vehicle,cargoCarrier);
  class-variables
    tankCapacity = 79 (doc "gallons of diesel");
  instance-variables
    owner = ((default Pie)(doc "owner of truck"));
    highway = ((default 66)(doc "route number of the
                                  highway"));
    milePost = ((default 0)(doc "location on the
                                  highway"));
    direction = ((default east)(doc "north, south, east or
                                  west"));
    cargoList = ((default nil)(doc "list of cargo
                                  descriptions"));
    totalWeight = ((default 0)(doc "weight of cargo in
                                  tons"))
  methods
    drive = truck.drive (doc "moves the vehicle");
    park = truck.park (doc "parks the truck");
    display = truck.display (doc "draws the truck")
end
```

In the object taxonomy, the class with the name *truck* has two superclasses: the classes with the names *vehicle* and *cargoCarrier*, respectively. In the class only one class variable, *tankCapacity*, has been defined, with value 79. Several instance variables have been defined. Each instance variable has associated two properties: a property specifying a default value and a property containing an explanation of the meaning of the variable. Furthermore, three methods have been defined. The first of these has the name *drive* as a selector; *truck.drive* is the name of the procedure specifying the actual method. The remaining methods have as selectors the names *park* and *display*.

We have remarked above that all actions in an object-oriented program come from objects sending messages to each other. An object can activate another object by sending it a message expressing a commission to execute a certain method. The object that receives the message executes the specified method and returns the obtained result to the sender of the message. Message passing can therefore be viewed as indirect invocation of procedures (*remote procedure call*).

A message consists of an object name, a selector and a number of arguments. Messages are sent using the function ←, called the *send function*. In general, a message takes the following form:

(← <object> <selector> <argument$_1$> ··· <argument$_n$>)

On evaluation of the send function, the selector and the values that result from evaluating the n arguments are passed to the specified object. If in <object> the keyword `self` has been specified, the object sends the message to itself. A specification <object> starting with a dollar sign is taken to be an object name. If the specified object is a class, the selector corresponds to a specific method in that class or in one of its generalizations. If, on the other hand, the sender is an instance, the selector is used for selecting the proper method from the class the sender is an instance of. The selected method is executed with the arguments of the message substituted for its parameters.

Instances can be created dynamically from a class definition by sending a specific message to the corresponding class. A message for creating a new instance takes the following form:

(← <class> `new`)

The method handling this message creates a data structure containing the following information:

- A name to be used in referring to the newly created instance.
- A specification of the class the instance belongs to.
- A description of the instance variables and their properties. The definitions of instance variables and possibly their initial values are copied from the class the new instance belongs to. After the creation of the instance has been completed, the instance variables may locally be assigned new values.

EXAMPLE 7.23

The following is an example of an instance of the class with the name *truck* from the preceding example. The instance variables with the names *owner*, *highway*, *milePost* and *direction* have locally been assigned a new value. The remaining two instance variables, *cargoList* and *totalWeight*, defined in the class *truck* have not been given a value in the instance; we shall see that their values can be obtained by inheritance from the class *truck* the instance belongs to.

instance *truck*1 ***is***
  instance-of *truck*;
  instance-variables
    owner = *Sanjay*;
    highway = 66;
    milePost = 38;
    direction = *east*
end

Creating a new class is analogous to the creation of an instance. In this case, however, a message has to be sent to the meta-class that the new class has to be an instance of. Such a message takes the following general form:

```
(← <meta-class> new <class-name> <supers-list>)
```

The method `new` in the specified meta-class creates a data structure in which, among other things, variables and methods can be specified. The new class gets assigned the name <class-name> and is placed in the taxonomy dependent on the specification of its superclasses in <supers-list>.

The taxonomy in which the meta-classes, classes and instances are organized is the basis for inheritance where variables as well as methods may be inherited. An instance inherits all class variables and methods from the class it belongs to. In an instance definition, therefore, only the instance variables are specified. All instances of a specific class inherit the same methods; if the respective behaviour of two instances differs, this difference is due to different values of the instance variables in these instances only. When in a class only one superclass has been specified, the variables and methods of this superclass (and its generalizations) are inherited. Classes in LOOPS, however, can have more than one superclass in their superclass part. In that case, the class in principle inherits the union of variables and methods from all its generalizations. If, from two or more generalizations, different variables (or methods) having the same name can be inherited, the variable (or method) from the generalization specified left-most in the superclass part is actually inherited.

A class has the ability of modifying the information inherited from its superclasses in several ways:

- A new variable (or method) can be added to the inherited variables (or methods). This type of modification is called *addition*.

- A variable (or method) that has been inherited from a generalization may be overridden locally by a new variable (or method) having the same name as the inherited one. This way of modifying inherited information is called *substitution.*

LOOPS furthermore offers several ways for modifying inherited methods less drastically than substitution does: *incremental specialization* of a method is the ability to make a local addition to the inherited method. We discuss three types of incremental specialization:

- The function ←*super*, pronounced as 'send super', allows the extension of an inherited method with some local code. If a class inherits a certain method with an associated selector, a new method having the *same* selector may be defined in which the function `←super` is used to invoke the inherited method. In this way, local code can be inserted before and after the inherited method. Note that `←super` provides a way of specializing a method from a superclass without knowing exactly what is done in the higher method.
- The function ←*superFringe*, allows procedural combination of several inherited methods in cases where a class has multiple superclasses. `←superFringe` is similar in concept to `←super`, except that *all* methods with the same selector that occur in the superclasses of the class (instead of one) are invoked one after the other. When the function `←superFringe` has been specified, therefore, no choice is made in the case of multiple inheritance.
- The function *doMethod* allows the invocation of any method from any class of the taxonomy.

The object-oriented programming style of LOOPS provides an environment for building modularly structured expert systems. By exploiting the possibilities offered by the taxonomy of objects, we may arrive at a hierarchical partition of the problem domain. We shall show in Section 7.2.3 that objects can be used to modularize a collection of production rules into several smaller, and easier to handle, rule sets.

7.2.2 Data-oriented programming

If in an object-oriented program a specific object sends a message to another object, then the receiver of this message may as a side-effect modify its variables locally, thus changing its own status. In a data-oriented program, on the other hand, accessing a local variable may result in sending a message as a side-effect. In data-oriented programming the notion of *active values* is employed for this purpose. Any value or property (in a property list) of a variable may be defined as an active value. This means that a method is associated with the value that will be invoked as soon as the value of the variable is accessed, either by reading it or by assigning it a new value. Active values are similar in concept to the demons discussed in Chapter 4. An active value is attached to a variable by specifying an expression having the following form instead of an actual value:

```
#(<active-value-class> <local-state> <get> <put>)
```

Active values are objects just like the other objects in LOOPS, and are therefore organized in a taxonomy as well. In the specification of an active value, <active-value-class> indicates the object in which the invoked method can be found. The method <get> will be invoked when a value of the variable is requested; the method <put> will be invoked as soon as the variable is assigned a value. It is not necessary to specify both the <get> and <put> methods. When no <put> method has been specified, a new value for the variable will be stored in the <local-state> variable of the active value. When the <get> method has been omitted, upon a request for a value of the variable, the value of the <local-state> variable is returned by default.

7.2.3 Rule-oriented programming

Besides the functional, object-oriented and data-oriented programming styles, LOOPS supports yet another style of programming: *rule-oriented programming*. We have encountered this style of programming before in Chapter 3. In LOOPS rule-oriented programming is simply understood to mean inference with production rules. LOOPS offers many facilities for developing production systems.

In LOOPS production rules are organized in so-called *rule sets*. A rule set is an object, again like all other entities in LOOPS. Each rule set comprises a specification of how the production rules in this set should be selected for evaluation and of how the selected rules are to be applied. The rule-oriented style of programming can be integrated with the other programming styles supported by LOOPS; a rule set may be activated autonomously, but may also be specified as a method in a class object or may be installed as an active value. A rule set is created by means of sending a message of the following form to the meta-class `ruleSet`:

```
(← $ruleSet new)
```

The execution of the `new` method results in the creation of a new object having several components that may be filled in by the programmer:

- a name part to be filled in with a name used in referring to the newly created rule set;
- a part in which different types of variables may be defined;

- a part in which a *global control structure* may be specified;
- a part in which the actual production rules may be defined.

As we will discuss below, in the specification of a production rule several types of variables may be used. Some of these variables have to be declared explicitly in the rule set; those are the *temporary* (local) variables. Global INTERLISP variables may also be referred to in production rules.

In LOOPS, production rules have a form rather differing from the syntax we have seen in Chapter 3; LOOPS offers the programmer greater freedom in specifying conditions and conclusions. A production rule has the following form:

{ <md> } ***if*** { <condition> }* ***then*** { <conclusion> }* ;

<md> is a so-called *meta-description* in which information concerning the rule itself may be specified. A meta-description may for example be used to control the inference engine in evaluating that specific rule. The antecedent of the rule is a sequence of expressions to be taken in conjunction; no explicit logical connectives are used. When evaluating the rule, the conditions in the antecedent are evaluated one after the other in the order in which they have been specified. If the evaluation of a condition yields the value `nil`, the condition fails and the remaining ones will be ignored. If, on the other hand, evaluation of a condition yields a value different from `nil`, the condition is said to succeed and the following one will be examined. In the production rule formalism discussed in Chapter 3, conditions were taken to be tests specified by means of predicates. In a LOOPS rule several other types of expression may be specified as conditions, such as:

- An instance variable denoted by its name preceded by a colon ':'. Each rule set has a working memory; in general the object itself acts as such. The evaluation of a condition being merely an instance variable returns the value for that variable found in the working memory. Note that such a condition succeeds when the variable has a value different from `nil`.
- A class variable indicated by the '::' followed by the name of the variable.
- A method invocation, the returned value of which determines whether or not the condition succeeds.
- An arbitrary LISP form.
- A relational expression in which the relational infix operators such as `=`, `<` and `>` may be used.
- An assignment statement, the value of the right-hand side of which decides the success or failure of the condition.

A condition is negated by prefixing the symbol ~ to it. Conclusions in a LOOPS production rule in general are assignment statements and method invocations.

EXAMPLE 7.24

Consider the following LOOPS production rule:

if `:x ::y z ← 3` ***then*** `tried ← t (← $obj print);`

In this rule, three conditions and two conclusions have been specified. In the first condition the value of the instance variable `x` is examined; the second condition concerns the class variable `y`. The third condition is an assignment statement assigning the value `3` to the temporary variable `z`. Note that upon evaluation the last condition will always succeed. The first conclusion of the rule is an assignment statement as well, causing the truth value `t` to be assigned to the temporary variable `tried`. The second conclusion is a method invocation; on evaluation the method `print` specified in the object with the name `obj` will be executed.

The standard inference method employed in LOOPS is bottom-up inference, which may be refined by several special control structures. In the following example we demonstrate that a meta-description may be used explicitly to separate information that is primarily meant to control the inference locally from the object-level information.

EXAMPLE 7.25

Consider the following production rule:

if `~tried :v = 0` ***then*** `tried ← t (← self reset);`

On evaluation of the first condition, the value of the temporary variable `tried` is examined. Only if this variable has the value `nil` does the first condition succeed. Subsequently, the second condition is evaluated. If this condition succeeds, evaluation of the conclusion part of the rule results first in the assignment of the truth value `t` to the variable `tried` and secondly in the execution of the method `reset` of the object itself. If the value of the variable `tried` is not changed by the evaluation of other rules, this rule will not succeed a second time, since the first condition will always fail. In this example the temporary variable `tried` has been used to control the evaluation of this rule locally. In LOOPS this type of local control can be specified otherwise without the use of temporary variables. In the following production rule having the same meaning as the one shown above, a meta-description has been used to specify the local control:

```
{1} if :v = 0 then (← self reset);
```

The meta-description `{1}` indicates that the rule may be applied only once.

This example shows that meta-descriptions offer the possibility of specifying local control. It is often desirable to be able to specify global control information as well. For control knowledge global to an entire rule set, a so-called *global control structure* may be included in the rule set object. Several types of global control structures are discerned, such as:

- The control structure `do1`. If this structure has been specified in the rule set, only the conclusions of the first production rule that actually succeeds are evaluated. After this, the inference is terminated.
- The control structure `doAll`. This structure indicates that all successful production rules have to be applied one after the other. As soon as all rules have been evaluated once, the inference is terminated.
- The control structure `whileAll`. This control structure is a kind of iterative `doAll`; as long as a certain criterion is met, all production rules are applied repeatedly.

The following example shows how the `do1` control structure may be used.

EXAMPLE 7.26

Consider the following rule set:

```
rule-set example ;
temporary-vars a, b, c;
  if a b c then d1;
  if ~a b c then d2;
  if ~a ~b c then d3;
```

The production rules in this rule set are devised to exclude one another; at most one of the rules can succeed. Therefore, as soon as one of the rules has succeeded it is needless to evaluate the remaining rules. This control information can be represented more explicitly using the `do1` control structure. The following rule set is therefore equivalent to the one shown above; note that the order in which the rules have been specified has been exploited, producing rules with fewer conditions.

```
rule-set example₂;
control-structure do₁;
temporary-vars a, b, c;
  if a b c then d₁;
  if b c then d₂;
  if c then d₃;
```

7.2.4 LOOPS as an expert-system builder tool

In the preceding sections we have seen that LOOPS is a comprehensive programming environment, offering many facilities, mostly built around concepts from object-oriented programming. Evidently, LOOPS does not restrict the knowledge engineer in any respect in building specific applications, as expert system shells often do. However, it must be recognized that using an expert-system builder tool such as LOOPS requires a lot of training and experience on the part of the knowledge engineer before it is turned into a really productive tool. Moreover, there is always a danger that the expert system built will lack a clear conceptual structure, because there is no special support from LOOPS to help the knowledge engineer imposing a domain-dependent structure on the expert system.

The LISP community has now moved to COMMON LISP. As a consequence, several new extensions to COMMON LISP are currently under development, in particular object-oriented extensions in much the same way as the LOOPS system is an extension to the INTERLISP programming environment. One of these extensions is PORTABLE COMMON LOOPS (PCL) developed at the Xerox Palo Alto Research Center. The system provides similar facilities for object-oriented programming as discussed for LOOPS.

7.3 CENTAUR

In the late 1970s the rule-based expert system *PUFF* was developed by J.S. Aikins, J. Kunz and others at Stanford University, in collaboration with R.J. Fallat of the Pacific Medical Center in San Francisco, using the expert system shell EMYCIN. PUFF utilizes production rules for interpreting data which are obtained by performing certain pulmonary (lung) function tests on a patient to find out whether the patient shows any signs of pulmonary disease and to establish the severity of his or her condition.

In response to the specific problems encountered in developing PUFF, the hybrid expert system *CENTAUR* was developed by J.S. Aikins for the same purpose. One of the objectives in developing the CENTAUR system was the explicit separation of declarative knowledge concerning pulmonary disease and domain-specific knowledge used for controlling the inference. As we shall see shortly, such a separation yielded a system with simpler production rules than PUFF and with a more perspicuous inference behaviour. We shall first briefly review some of the problems that were encountered in the development of the diagnostic expert system PUFF using a rule-based approach. The knowledge representation scheme of CENTAUR is next described in Sections 7.3.2 and 7.3.3; Section 7.3.4 discusses the control structure in the system.

7.3.1 Limitations of production rules

The main reason for building a revised version of the PUFF system was the observation that a purely rule-based approach appeared to be too restrictive for building an expert system with a perspicuous structure and inference behaviour. The context in which production rules are applicable is given only locally by their conditions. Production systems therefore lack information concerning the broader context in which the problem solving takes place; the overall structure of the problem-solving process is only implicitly present in the knowledge base, hidden in the rule base, and is nowhere made explicit.

EXAMPLE 7.27

The disadvantage of the uniformity of production rules is illustrated by the following three production rules:

R_1: ***if*** *a* ***and*** *b* ***and*** *c* ***then*** *g* ***fi***
R_2: ***if*** *a* ***and*** *b* ***and*** *d* ***then*** *h* ***fi***
R_3: ***if*** *a* ***and*** *b* ***and*** *e* ***then*** *i* ***fi***

Each is applicable only in a context for which the conjunction of conditions *a* ***and*** *b* is satisfied. The represented knowledge would be much easier to grasp if this context was indicated more explicitly, for example in the following way:

context: *a* ***and*** *b* ***are satisfied***
  R_1: ***if*** *c* ***then*** *g* ***fi***
  R_2: ***if*** *d* ***then*** *h* ***fi***
  R_3: ***if*** *e* ***then*** *i* ***fi***
end

Another well-known problem arising from using merely production rules for representing a problem domain is that the domain-dependent problem-solving strategy has to be encoded in the same formalism as the heuristic domain knowledge. We have already mentioned this problem in connection with OPS5. When production rules are applied for representing procedural as well as declarative knowledge, it will not be possible to understand the meaning of the knowledge base separate from the inference methods employed. Moreover, it will often not be apparent to the user whether a certain production rule is employed to express heuristic domain knowledge or as part of the problem-solving strategy. Diagnostic rule-based expert systems like PUFF usually apply backward chaining as their main or even their only inference method. Since backward chaining is more like logical deduction than forward chaining in an OPS5-like manner, problem-solving knowledge cannot easily be recognized as such. The next example shows that production rules applied by backward chaining may indeed be used for representing problem-solving knowledge in an explicit manner; however, the result is not very satisfactory from a knowledge engineering point of view.

EXAMPLE 7.28

Suppose that we want to build a diagnostic medical expert system dealing with the domain of pulmonary disease. In most diagnostic expert systems, some kind of strategy to be followed in the process of diagnosis is incorporated. In this case, it may be necessary to consider the degree (moderate or severe) of the obstructive airways disease (OAD) the patient is suffering from, before establishing the subtype to which the patient's disorder belongs. Only then is the patient's disease elucidated. If we assume that the expert system uses backward chaining as its inference method, the following production rule expresses what has been stated informally above:

if
same(*patient,disease-type,oad*) ***and***
known(*disorder,degree*) ***and***
known(*disorder,subtype*) ***and***
known(*patient,diagnosis*)
then
add(*patient,disease,established*)
fi

Note that we have used the predicate *known* in three of the four conditions. This predicate is used in the rule to find out whether any value has been inferred for its attribute argument, that is, the predicate is used as a meta-predicate. Note that this rule only has the proper meaning by virtue of the order in which its conditions are evaluated by the interpreter. The following informally stated algorithm expresses much more explicitly the algorithmic nature of the production rule shown above:

> **if** *disease-type* = *oad* **then**
>   **determine** the *degree* of the disorder;
>   **determine** the *subtype* of the disorder suspected;
>   **if** *degree* and *subtype* have been confirmed
>   **then determine** the *diagnosis* of the patient **fi**
> **fi**

This type of explicit control specification is evidently to be preferred to the preceding rule.

Another frequently mentioned limitation of using production rules for building expert systems is that the typical findings, in the case of PUFF concerning particular pulmonary diseases, are distributed over many production rules. It is therefore not possible to retrieve knowledge concerning the typical characteristics of, for example, a disease in a straightforward way.

7.3.2 Prototypes

In CENTAUR domain knowledge is represented in two different formalisms: production rules and frame-like structures called *prototypes.* The prototypes in CENTAUR represent typical pulmonary disease patterns described in terms of the results to be expected from tests administered to patients suffering from a particular pulmonary disease. The most important test to which a patient is subjected is spirometry, by means of which various lung volumes and air flows can be determined. As will be discussed in Section 7.3.4, during consultation of the system the actual patient data is matched against the information described in these prototypes. The production rules, capturing the knowledge necessary for interpreting the test results obtained from a patient, are grouped in the prototypes in a kind of attributes indicating the function of that specific group of rules in the consultation process. In this way, knowledge meant to control the reasoning process is separated from the highly specialized domain knowledge. As we have seen in the preceding section, such an explicit separation cannot be readily achieved in a purely rule-based system. The specialized declarative domain knowledge not directly controlling the reasoning process is often called *object knowledge.* Knowledge for controlling reasoning about the object knowledge at a higher level of abstraction, and knowledge about the prototypes themselves, is called *meta-knowledge.* The prototype to which a production rule belongs explicitly states the context in which the rule is applicable.

From this we have that the production rules in the CENTAUR system have fewer conditions than the corresponding rules in PUFF; in the latter system each production rule implicitly states in its rule antecedent the context in which it is applicable.

In CENTAUR there are 22 prototypes containing knowledge about pulmonary disease. The prototypes are organized in a tree-like taxonomy. A part of this taxonomy is shown in Figure 7.5. A prototype comprises several *slots* for storing different types of information relevant to the CENTAUR system. In CENTAUR the term slot is used to denote a kind of field as in a COMMON LISP structure or a Pascal record. Essentially, there are two types of slot:

- Slots that are used to represent characteristic features of the pulmonary disease described in the prototype they are associated with, such as signs generally found in patients suffering from the disease. These slots are called *component slots* and contain the object knowledge of the CENTAUR system. The components are similar in nature to the frame attributes introduced in Chapter 4.
- Slots that are used to represent meta-knowledge. These slots contain general information, information about the relationships between the prototypes and information to control the inference process.

We shall turn to slots for the representation of meta-knowledge shortly. We shall first discuss the component slots in detail.

A component slot may contain one or more *facets*:

- A *name facet*, specifying the name of the characteristic feature described by the component.
- An *actual value facet*, filled in during the consultation process with the actual values that have been found in the patient for this feature.
- A *possible error values facet*, specifying data values for the feature that are inconsistent with the prototype the component is associated with, or that may be measurement errors. CENTAUR has the possibility of performing some action when a possible error value has been found; each data value in this facet is represented as a condition–action pair. Generally, the action associated with a possible error value directs the control flow to another prototype or prints a statement informing the user of the error value.
- A *plausible values facet*, specifying data values for the characteristic feature that are consistent with the situation described by the prototype. Similar to possible error values, plausible values are represented as condition–action pairs. All those values that are neither plausible values nor possible error values are called *surprise*

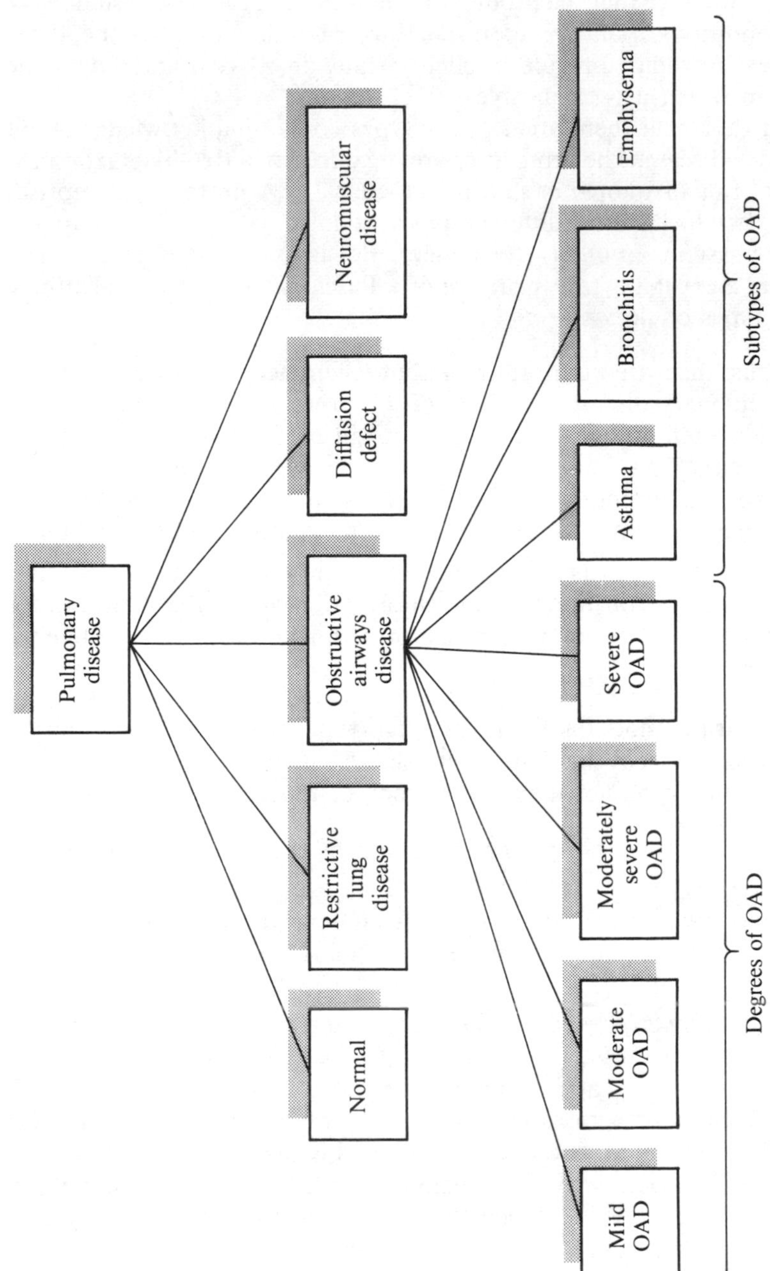

Figure 7.5 A part of the pulmonary disease taxonomy.

values. Surprise values cannot be accounted for by the situation represented by the given prototype.

- An *inference rules facet*, whose value is a list of production rules. These production rules represent highly specialized domain knowledge only, and are used to infer a value for the component when a value is needed but not known as yet. The inference rules facet therefore behaves like an if-needed demon.
- A *default value facet*, containing a default value for the component, independent of other values. All the components in a prototype with their default values form a picture of a typical patient suffering from the pulmonary disease described by the prototype.
- An *importance measure facet*, specifying a measure (from 0 to 5) that indicates the relative importance of the component in characterizing the situation described by the prototype. The importance measures are mainly used to determine whether the prototype matches the actual case data. An importance measure equal to 0 is used to indicate components whose values are not considered in the matching process.

EXAMPLE 7.29

An example of a component in CENTAUR is the following component having the name 'fev1' (forced expired volume in 1 second). It describes the volume of air that can be expelled by a person in 1 second by a forced expiration following a maximal inspiration; it is expressed as a percentage of the volume of air that can be expired irrespective of time (the so-called vital capacity, vc).

name: fev1
plausible values:
  if
    the value is less than 80
  then
    no action indicated
  importance measure: 5
  actual value: nil

In this component only four of the seven possible facets have been specified. The actual values slot contains the value nil, indicating that an actual value has not yet been established.

In the component with the name 'reversibility' an actual valuc has been entered. This component describes whether or not the effects of a particular pulmonary disease are reversible.

name: reversibility
plausible values: anyvalue
importance measure: 0
inference rules: (RULE019 RULE020 RULE022 RULE025)
actual value: 43

Notice that in the 'reversibility' component the inference rules slot does not contain actual production rules but only their names. These names serve as pointers to actual production rules stored in a global rule base. We will turn to this shortly.

In addition to a number of component slots, a prototype has several meta-knowledge slots. The *general information slots* give static general information about the prototype itself, such as book-keeping information, information used in communicating with the user, and information relating the prototype to other prototypes. These slots do not have any facets. The general information slots are:

- The *name slot*, specifying the unique name of the prototype. In general, the name of the pulmonary disease that is represented in the prototype is taken to be the name of the prototype.
- The *author slot*, containing the names of the experts that created the prototype.
- The *date slot*, the value of which is the date the prototype was created, or the date of the last update of the prototype.
- The *source slot*, describing the source that inspired the creation of the prototype.
- The *explanation slot*, containing English phrases explaining the contents of the prototype. These phrases are used in answering a user's request to explain the system's lines of reasoning.
- The *hypothesis slot*, containing an English description of the hypothesis that the system is investigating when the control is directed to this specific prototype.
- The *moregeneral slot*, containing a set of references to the more general prototypes in the prototype taxonomy. The moregeneral slot is equivalent to the is-a link discussed in Chapter 4. It is noted that the problems arising from multiple inheritance do not occur in CENTAUR because the taxonomy is merely a tree.
- The *morespecific slot*, containing a set of references to the more specific prototypes in the taxonomy. In this slot the inverse relation of the is-a link is specified.
- The *alternate slot*, specifying a set of pointers to alternative prototypes in the taxonomy.

Furthermore, within each prototype, context-specific control knowledge for controlling the inference locally is specified in *control slots*. These control slots contain LISP expressions that are executed by the system at specific times during the consultation. The slot name of a control slot indicates the moment during the consultation the control has to be applied. Essentially, four control slots may be associated with a prototype:

- The *to-fill-in slot*. The procedures that have been specified in this slot express actions to be taken by the system as soon as the prototype is selected to be contemplated as a plausible explanation for the patient's complaints and clinical signs. The information in this slot indicates which components of the prototype should have values and in what order they should be determined.
- The *if-confirmed slot*. Once a prototype has been filled in, the system decides whether the prototype should be confirmed as matching the actual patient data. Upon confirmation of a prototype, the actions described in the if-confirmed slot are executed.
- The *if-disconfirmed slot*. The if-disconfirmed slot specifies actions to be performed in the event that the prototype is disconfirmed. Generally, the if-confirmed and if-disconfirmed slots specify sets of prototypes to be explored next.
- The *action slot*. In the action slot some concluding statements in English are specified to be printed for the prototype after final conclusions have been derived.

A prototype has another three slots associated with it containing sets of production rules. These rules are to be used after the system has formulated sets of confirmed and disconfirmed prototypes. These slots are called *rule slots*:

- The *summary rules slot*, containing rules whose actions make summary statements about the intermediate results that have been derived in examining the prototype.
- The *fact-residual rules slot*, specifying rules that are to be applied when the set of confirmed prototypes does not account for all the facts known in the actual case. Residual facts can be an indication that the diagnosis is not complete, or that the patient's disease pattern is exceptional. The fact-residual rules attempt to make conclusions about these residual facts.
- The *refinement rules slot*, in which a set of production rules is specified which are to be used to refine a tentative diagnosis, producing a final diagnosis about the pulmonary disease the patient is likely to be suffering from. Refinement rules may also recommend that additional laboratory tests should be performed.

EXAMPLE 7.30

The following production rule, RULE050, is an example of a summary rule specified in the summary rules slot of the prototype describing the normal pulmonary function of a patient. From now on, production rules will be shown using a quasi-natural language interface.

> **RULE050**
> **if**
> the degree of obstructive airways disease as indicated by overinflation is greater than or equal to mild
> **then**
> it is definite (1.0) that the following is one of the summary statements about this interpretation: pulmonary function is within wide limits of normal.

The production rule RULE157 is an example of a fact-residual rule specified in the fact-residual rules slot of the prototype that describes the characteristics of a patient suffering from obstructive airways disease:

> **RULE157**
> **if**
> there is not sufficient evidence for restrictive lung disease, and the degree of obstructive airways disease of the patient is greater than or equal to moderately severe, and the tlc/tlc-predicted ratio of the patient is between 90 and 100
> **then**
> mark the tlc as being accounted for by restrictive lung disease, and it is definite (1.0) that the following is one of the conclusion statements about this interpretation: the reduced total lung capacity in the presence of obstruction indicates a restrictive component.

Finally, the following production rule, named RULE040, is specified in the refinement rules slot associated with the obstructive airways disease prototype. The tentative diagnosis that the patient is suffering from an obstructive airways disease is refined; the rule attributes the cause of the patient's airway obstruction to smoking.

> **RULE040**
> **if**
> the number of pack-years smoked is greater than 0, and the number of years ago that the patient quit smoking is 0, and the degree of smoking of the patient is greater

than or equal to the degree of obstructive airways disease of the patient

then

it is definite (1.0) that the following is one of the conclusion statements about this interpretation: the patient's airway obstruction may be caused by smoking.

The different types of production rules, that is, inference rules, summary rules, fact-residual rules and triggering rules that are still to be discussed, are part of a global set of production rules. This set of rules is subdivided by means of pointers to specific rules represented as rule names in the prototypes. When examining a prototype, only those rules referred to in the prototype are applied. We shall focus on the respective functions of the different types of rules during a consultation of the system in Section 7.3.4 when discussing the CENTAUR control structure.

To conclude with, each prototype has a number of slots that are filled in with values as the consultation proceeds:

- A *match measure slot*, containing a match measure dependent on the present consultation. This measure indicates how closely the data values of the actual case match the expected data values described in the prototype. The match measure is computed dynamically during the consultation as the components of the prototype are filled in, using the former match measure, the importance measures of the filled components and whether the actual values are classified as plausible values or not. After the actions specified in the to-fill-in slot of the prototype have been executed, the match measure is compared with a certain numerical threshold to determine whether the prototype should be confirmed or disconfirmed as matching the actual case data.
- A *certainty measure slot*, specifying a certainty measure which indicates how certain the system is that the actual data values in the case match the expected data values in the prototype. These certainty measures are similar in concept to the certainty factors introduced in Chapter 5. Certainty measures may initially be set by applying a *triggering rule*. A triggering rule is a rule that refers to values of components in its condition part and suggests prototypes as possible hypotheses by setting certainty measures in their conclusion part. RULE093 is an example of such a triggering rule:

RULE093

if

the dlco/dlco-predicted ratio of the patient is less than 80

then

suggest diffusion-defect with a certainty measure of 900,
suggest emphysema with a certainty measure of 800,
suggest restrictive lung disease with a certainty measure of 800

Because of the actual value of the dlco/dlco-predicted ratio of the patient, that is, the ratio of the measured and the predicted diffusing capacity of carbon monoxide (dclo), this triggering rule suggests the exploration of the 'diffusion defect' prototype, the 'emphysema' prototype and the 'restrictive lung disease' prototype, by assigning to the certainty measures of these prototypes a value greater than zero.

- An *intriggers slot* specifying the component values that triggered the initialization of the certainty measure of the prototype. For example, if the prototype describing obstructive airways disease is triggered by the value 126 of the 'tlc', that is, the total lung capacity, component, the intriggers slot will contain the pair `(tlc 126)`.
- An *origin slot* recording the invocation of one prototype by another during the consultation.

We will turn to these slots shortly.

EXAMPLE 7.31

The prototype describing obstructive airways disease serves as an example of the notions discussed above. Part of this prototype is shown in Figure 7.6. This prototype has the name 'oad' for obstructive airways disease. The moregeneral slot specifies an is-a link to a more general prototype in the taxonomy, in this case the prototype with the name 'pulmonary disease'. The keyword DOMAIN is used to indicate a certain type of is-a link. In the morespecific slot, pointers to prototypes containing more specific information have been specified. The keywords SUBTYPE and DEGREE may be used in controlling the inference; the control slots may direct the reasoning control to a specific set of prototypes, for instance the prototypes which have been labelled with the keyword DEGREE in the morespecific slot. In fact, this option has been used in the if-confirmed slot. If the pulmonary disease pattern represented in the 'oad' prototype matches the actual patient data, first the control is directed to the more specific prototypes that are indicated by the keyword DEGREE; these are the prototypes having the names 'mild-oad',

PROTOTYPE
name: oad
hypothesis: "there is obstructive airways disease"
explanation: "obstructive airways disease"
author: Aikins
date: "27-OCT-78 17:13:29"
source: Fallat
moregeneral: (DOMAIN pulmonary-disease)
morespecific:
(SUBTYPE asthma) (SUBTYPE bronchitis)
(SUBTYPE emphysema)
(DEGREE mild-oad) (DEGREE moderate-oad)
(DEGREE moderately-severe-oad)
(DEGREE severe-oad)
intriggers: nil
origin: nil
certainty measure: 0
match measure: 0
to-fill-in: nil
if-confirmed:
determine the degree of oad,
determine the subtype of oad
if-disconfirmed: nil
action:
An attempt has been made to deduce the findings about the diagnosis of obstructive airways disease. Display the findings about the diagnosis:
"There is evidence that the following is one of the summary statements about this interpretation:
<deg – oad> obstructive airways disease".
refinement-rules: (RULE036 RULE038 RULE039 RULE040 · · ·)
summary-rules: (RULE053 RULE054 RULE055 · · ·)
fact-residual-rules: (RULE157 RULE158 RULE159)

COMPONENTS
cname: reversibility
plausible values: any value
importance measure: 0
inference rules: (RULE019 RULE020 RULE022 RULE025)
actual value: nil

Figure 7.6 The prototype describing obstructive airways disease.

'moderate-oad', 'moderately-severe-oad' and 'severe-oad'. Subsequently, the subtype of the obstructive airways disease is determined by directing the control to the prototypes labelled with the SUBTYPE keyword, that is the prototypes with the names 'asthma', 'bronchitis' and 'emphysema'. In the if-disconfirmed slot no actions have been specified. The 'oad' prototype furthermore has several components, only one of which is shown in Figure 7.6: the 'reversibility' component.

7.3.3 Facts

In the implementation of the CENTAUR system, the actual component values that have been acquired are not only included in the prototypes themselves but in separate *facts* as well. Each fact corresponds to a component and represents either a pulmonary function test result or a value that has been established during the consultation process. These facts are visible for every prototype of the taxonomy; the fact set is therefore a kind of global working memory. Each fact is represented in a record-like data structure. In such a data structure several fields are discerned, each containing a specific property of the represented component value. In CENTAUR these fields are called slots as well. However, to avoid misconception we will adhere to the term field. A fact has six fields:

- An *fname field*, specifying the name of the fact. This name corresponds to the name of a component and should appear at least once in the taxonomy.
- A *fact value field*, containing the actual value of the component.
- A *certainty factor field*, indicating the certainty with which the component value has been established.
- A *where from field*, indicating from whence the component value has been obtained: from the user, from applying the inference rules, or from the default value slot associated with the component.
- A *classification field* indicating for each prototype containing the component whether the component value is a plausible value (PV), a possible error value (PEV) or a surprise value (SV) in the given prototype.
- An *accounted for field*, indicating which (confirmed) prototypes account for the given fact value. When a prototype is confirmed, all the facts that correspond to the components in the prototype and whose values are classified as plausible values for the component are said to be accounted for by that prototype. Information in this slot is used to determine which facts remain to be accounted for.

EXAMPLE 7.32

We consider the fact with the name 'tlc':

fname: tlc
fact value: 126
certainty factor: 0.8
where from: USER
classification: ((PV oad) (SV normal))
accounted for: oad

The name 'tlc' corresponds to a component occurring in the 'oad' and 'normal' prototypes. For this component the value 126 has been obtained from the user, who has associated the certainty factor 0.8 with this value. The value 126 has been classified as a plausible value for the component in the prototype describing obstructive airways disease and as a surprise value in the normal pulmonary function prototype. Since the value is plausible in a patient suffering from obstructive airways disease, the 'oad' prototype accounts for this value.

7.3.4 Reasoning in CENTAUR

In Sections 7.3.2 and 7.3.3, we have considered the knowledge-representation schemes in CENTAUR. In this section we focus on the manipulation of the represented information. The approach to reasoning with frames used in CENTAUR is called *hypothesize and match*. This reasoning strategy roughly amounts to the following: take a hypothesis, represented in a prototype, as being the diagnosis for the patient's disease, and try to match this hypothesis against the test results and patient data in the actual case. This strategy is part of the overall domain-independent control of the system. This overall control information is described in a prototype as well. This prototype represents the consultation task itself and is called the *consultation prototype*. The hypothesis-dependent control information is represented in the prototype control slots, as described in Section 7.3.2.

The basic control structure in CENTAUR is an *agenda-driven control*. An *agenda* is a sequence of *tasks*, each representing an action to be taken by the system. Tasks can be added to or deleted from the agenda. Figure 7.7 shows the general structure of an agenda. Connected with the agenda is an *interpreter*. The interpreter at every turn removes the top task from the agenda and executes it. When this task is finished, the process is repeated until the agenda is empty.

In CENTAUR there are two ways of adding tasks to the agenda:

- We recall that in the prototype control slots several tasks may be specified. When such a control slot is activated during the

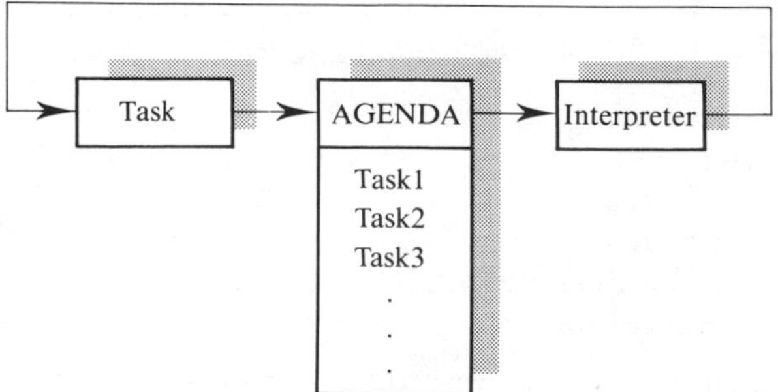

Figure 7.7 Agenda-driven control.

consultation of the system, the tasks specified in the slot are added to the agenda.

- The execution of one task may cause other tasks to be placed on the agenda.

Tasks are always inserted *in front of* the tasks already present on the agenda. The set of tasks from a prototype control slot is added to the agenda as a group, thus preserving the order in which the tasks have been specified. The agenda operates as a stack; the tasks on the agenda are executed in a last-in, first-out order. Note that operating the agenda as a stack has the effect of moving depth-first through the prototype taxonomy of CENTAUR as more specific pulmonary diseases are explored.

Figure 7.8 shows the control flow during a consultation of the CENTAUR system. At any time during the consultation, there is a single prototype on which the system focuses: this prototype is called the *current prototype*. Processing of the current prototype involves two steps:

(1) Filling in the prototype component slots with values. Filling in the component slots is guided by the tasks specified in the to-fill-in slot of the current prototype. If there are rules associated with a component they will be applied to infer component values. Only when these rules fail to yield a value, or when there are no rules associated with the component, is the user asked for a value.

(2) Evaluating whether there is a match between the actual data values obtained from the patient and the prototype's set of plausible values. Following the execution of the tasks in the to-fill-in slot, the interpreter connected with the agenda determines whether or not the prototype should be confirmed as matching the actual patient data. For this purpose the interpreter compares the dynamically computed match measure of the prototype with a preset numerical threshold. Depending on this comparison, the tasks from the

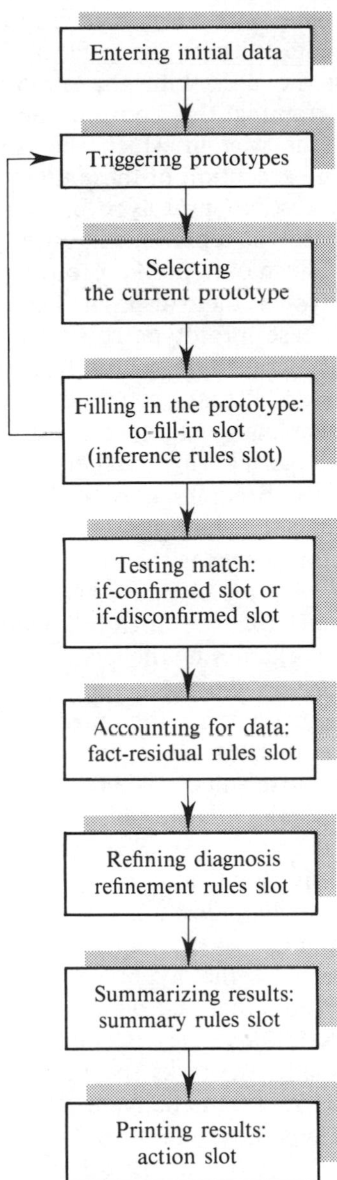

Figure 7.8 The control flow during a consultation.

if-confirmed slot or the tasks from the if-disconfirmed slot are placed on the agenda. These tasks specify how the consultation should proceed.

When starting with a consultation, the consultation prototype becomes the first current prototype. As has been mentioned before, this prototype represents the consultation task itself. The to-fill-in slot of this prototype contains tasks providing the user with the opportunity to set some options to be used in running the consultation. The tasks in the if-confirmed slot control the way in which the consultation develops through various stages. The execution of these tasks among other things results in the 'pulmonary disease' prototype being selected as the next current prototype. This prototype represents knowledge common to all of the pulmonary diseases. The more specific prototypes have the knowledge present in this prototype at their disposal. The tasks in the to-fill-in slot of the 'pulmonary disease' prototype control the acquisition of an initial set of pulmonary function test results from the user. Filling in these initial data has as a result that prototypes are suggested as being likely matches to the given data values as a result of their certainty measures being set by triggering rules. When a prototype has been suggested by data values, it becomes a *potentially relevant prototype.* From this set of potentially relevant prototypes those prototypes are selected that are relevant for executing the top task on the agenda. These prototypes are called *relevant prototypes.* The relevant prototypes are filled in with the data values that are already known in the case, using single inheritance merely by examining the fact set. When data values are classified as plausible values in the prototype, the certainty measure is raised by an amount dependent on the importance measure of the component slot. The certainty measure is lowered when data values are possible error values or surprise values. The relevant prototypes are then placed on a *hypotheses list*, which is subsequently ordered according to the certainty measures of the prototypes. So the first prototype represents the system's best hypothesis about how to match the actual case data. The first prototype on the hypotheses list subsequently becomes the current prototype.

When all hypotheses on the hypotheses list are confirmed or disconfirmed as matching the actual case data, the fact-residual rules, the refinement rules and the summary rules associated with each confirmed prototype are applied. Finally, the tasks specified in the action slots of the confirmed prototypes are executed. Note that instead of routinely considering all possible hypotheses in turn, as in a fully rule-based system, only prototypes that are triggered by data values are considered; prototypes that are not suggested by the triggering rules as likely explanations for the patient's signs will not be considered unless they are suggested later in the consultation as new facts are derived. Considering only those prototypes that are suggested by actual data values prevents many needless rule invocations and questions.

7.3.5 What has been achieved by CENTAUR?

We have now discussed the organization of the CENTAUR system in some detail. The question now arises of what has actually been achieved by redesigning the PUFF into the CENTAUR system. To answer questions such as these, J.S. Aikins has experimentally compared the consultations of the CENTAUR and PUFF systems, by presenting to both systems a representative sample of 20 cases. It turned out that PUFF always posed the questions to the user in more or less the same order, while the questioning order in CENTAUR was more dynamic in nature, dependent on the actual case at hand. Furthermore, the ability to focus on knowledge relevant for the present case to be solved, measured by the number of questions asked, was also better for CENTAUR than for PUFF. Finally, in 100 cases the judgements of two expert physicians were compared with the diagnostic conclusions of both PUFF and CENTAUR. It was shown that judgements of the physicians more often agreed with the conclusions drawn by CENTAUR than with the conclusions drawn by PUFF.

The main conclusion of J.S. Aikins was that the CENTAUR system is particularly strong as a tool for experimenting with control schemes in domains in which prototypical knowledge can be used to guide the problem solving. It will be evident that, although CENTAUR is a special-purpose system, its structure may be used for other problem domains as well. The system has given a major impetus to the building of expert systems with a better controlled inference behaviour. In our opinion, the CENTAUR approach has several strong points, all arising from the explicit separation of object and control knowledge. For example, the system has a clear and easy-to-grasp structure. Another pleasant consequence is that systems constructed using this approach are applicable not only for solving diagnostic problems, but for tutoring purposes as well.

Suggested reading

For further information on OPS5, the reader is referred to the book *Programming Expert Systems in OPS5* (Brownston *et al.*, 1985), the book *Rule-based Programming with OPS5* (Cooper and Wogrin, 1988) and the *OPS5 User's Manual* (Forgy, 1981). Those interested in experimenting with the OPS5 system should note that the Franz and COMMON LISP versions of OPS5 are in the public domain. The rete algorithm is described in Forgy (1982). The language OPS83 is described in Forgy (1985). The expert-system builder tool Knowledge Craft, which incorporates an OPS5-like language called CRL-OPS, is reviewed in Kahn and Bauer (1989).

LOOPS is fully described in the user's manual (Bobrow and Stefik, 1983). Further detailed information on LOOPS can be found in Stefik and Bobrow (1984), which discusses the object-oriented style of programming supported by LOOPS, and Stefik *et al.* (1986), which deals with the data-oriented programming style. In fact, our discussion of LOOPS has been based on these two papers. In Section 7.2 we remarked that D.G. Bobrow started his experiments with knowledge-representation languages with the development of KRL; information about this knowledge-representation language can be found in Bobrow and Winograd (1977). The UNITS system, developed by M.J. Stefik, is discussed in Stefik (1979).

The discussion of the CENTAUR system presented in this chapter has been based to a large extent on Aikins (1980). This report has been published in a shorter form as Aikins (1983). The rule-based expert system PUFF that motivated the development of CENTAUR is discussed in Aikins *et al.* (1984).

EXERCISES

7.1 Suppose that we have three boxes at different positions *a*, *b* and *c*, respectively, placed in a room. In addition, there is a robot in the room at position *d*, differing from the positions of the boxes. Develop an OPS5 program that transforms the initial state as described above into a state in which the three boxes are stacked on top of each other. Assume that the boxes can be moved by push actions of the robot and that no special action is required for stacking the boxes. The robot is allowed to move freely around the room.

7.2 Consider the following OPS5 program:

```
(literalize person
  name
  age

(literalize output name age)

(p names
   (person ^age = <x>)
   (person ^name = <y> ^age > <x> ^age = <z>)
   -->
   (make output ^name <y> ^age <z>))

(make person ^name john ^age 20)
(make person ^name john ^age 10)
(make person ^name anna ^age 50)
```

(a) Briefly describe the operations performed by this program on the working memory. What are the contents of the working memory after execution?

(b) Why is the production given above not acceptable to OPS5 if the first condition element is removed?

(c) When instead of the lex strategy the mea strategy is employed in the program above, what will the contents of the working memory be after execution?

7.3 Consider the following OPS5 program, of which only the productions are given:

```
(p one
   (o ^a = 6 ^c < 10)
   (p ^b = <x>)
   -->
   (make g ^c <x>))

(p two
   (o ^a = <x> ^c = 10)
   (p ^b = <x>)
   -->
   (make g ^d <x>))
```

Draw the schematic representation of the rete graph constructed by OPS5 for these two productions. Distinguish between class, one-input, two-input and production vertices.

7.4 Why is the rete algorithm not suitable for real-time applications in which at certain time intervals the working memory is refreshed? Design an algorithm that would be more suitable for such an application.

7.5 In which way does the algorithm of multiple inheritance of attribute values in LOOPS differ from the multiple inheritance algorithm described in Section 4.3? Which of the two algorithms do you consider to be the most natural one?

7.6 Consider the following class definition in LOOPS:

class *artery* ***is***
  metaclass *class*;
  superclass *blood-vessel*;
  class-variables
    wall = *muscular*
  instance-variables
    blood = (***default*** *oxygen-rich*);
    diameter = (***default*** 1)
end

and the following instance definition:

> ***instance*** *pulmonary-artery* ***is***
> ***instance-of*** *artery*;
> ***instance-variables***
> *blood* = *oxygen-poor*
> ***end***

(a) Explain the difference between class variables and instance variables in a class.

(b) Which attribute values do we have for the instance *pulmonary-artery*? Which attribute values do we have for any other instance of the class *artery* for which no attribute values are explicitly specified? Explain your answer.

7.7 OPS5 incorporates a method for bottom-up inference in which most of the control strategy is provided by the standard inference algorithm. On the other hand, LOOPS offers the knowledge engineer several control strategies to adapt the bottom-up inference method to the need. Why is it nevertheless difficult to model the conflict-resolution method incorporated in OPS5 using the language constructs provided in LOOPS?

7.8 Give a brief, informal description of the way in which prototypes control the inference in CENTAUR.

7.9 What is the main function of the default-value facets in the components of the prototypes in CENTAUR?

7.10 What is the purpose of the fact-residual rules in CENTAUR? Which information is stored in the fact set to be able to apply these rules?

7.11 Give a description of the agenda-controlled inference method applied in CENTAUR.

APPENDIX A

Introduction to PROLOG

PROLOG is a simple, yet powerful programming language, based on the principles of first-order predicate logic. The name of the language is an acronym for the French 'PROgrammation en LOGique'. About 1970, PROLOG was designed by A. Colmerauer and P. Roussel at the University of Marseille, influenced by the ideas of R.A. Kowalski concerning programming in the Horn clause subset of first-order predicate logic. The name of PROLOG has since then been connected with a new programming style, known as *logic programming*.

Until the end of the 1970s, the use of PROLOG was limited to the academic world. Only after the development of an efficient PROLOG interpreter and compiler by D.H.D. Warren and F.C.N. Pereira did the language enter the world outside the educational institutes. Interest in the language has increased steadily, and PROLOG seems still to be gaining in importance. There is a growing number of fields in which PROLOG is applied successfully. The main applications of the language can be found in the area of artificial intelligence, but PROLOG is being used in other areas in which symbol manipulation is of prime importance as well. Some application areas are:

- Natural-language processing
- Compiler construction
- Development of expert systems
- Work in the area of computer algebra
- Development of (parallel) computer architectures
- Database systems

PROLOG is particularly strong in solving problems characterized by requiring complex symbolic computations. As conventional imperative programs for solving this type of problem tend to be large and impenetrable, equivalent PROLOG programs are often much shorter and easier to grasp. The language in principle enables a programmer to give a formal specification of a program; the result is then almost directly suitable for execution on the computer. Moreover, PROLOG supports stepwise refinement in developing programs because of its modular nature. These characteristics render PROLOG a suitable language for the development of prototype systems.

There are several dialects of PROLOG in use, such as for example C-PROLOG, Micro-PROLOG and TurboPROLOG. C-PROLOG, also called Edinburgh PROLOG, is generally accepted as the de facto PROLOG standard. The language definition of C-PROLOG is derived from an interpreter developed by D.H.D. Warren, D.L. Bowen, L. Byrd, F.C.N. Pereira and L.M. Pereira, written in the C programming language for the UNIX operating system. Most dialects have only minor syntactical and semantic differences from the standard language. However, there is a small number of dialects which change the character of the language in a significant way, for example by the necessity of adding data-type information to a program. In recent versions of PROLOG, several features have been added to the C-PROLOG standard. For example, modern PROLOG versions provide a module concept and extensive interfaces to the operating system.

A.1 Logic programming

In more conventional, procedural languages such as Pascal, a program is a specification of a sequence of instructions to be executed one after the other by a target machine, to solve the problem concerned. The description of the problem is incorporated implicitly in this specification, and usually it is not possible to distinguish clearly between the description of the problem and the method used for its solution. In logic programming, the description of the problem and the method for solving it are explicitly separated from each other. This separation has been expressed by R.A. Kowalski in the following equation:

algorithm = logic + control

The term 'logic' in this equation indicates the descriptive component of the algorithm, that is, the description of the problem; the term 'control' indicates the component that tries to find a solution, taking the description of the problem as a point of departure. So the logic component defines *what* the algorithm is supposed to do; the control component indicates *how* it should be done.

A specific problem is described in terms of relevant objects and relations between objects, which are then represented in the clausal form of logic, a restricted form of first-order predicate logic. The logic component for a specific problem is generally called a *logic program*. The control component employs logical inference for deriving new facts from the logic program, thus solving the given problem; one speaks of the *inference method*. The inference method is assumed to be quite general, in the sense that it is capable of dealing with any logic program using the clausal form syntax.

The splitting of an algorithm into a logic component and a control component has a number of advantages:

- The two components may be developed separately from each other. For example, when describing thc problem we do not have to be familiar with how the control component operates on the resulting description; knowledge of the declarative reading of the problem specification suffices.
- A logic component may be developed using a method of stepwise refinement; we have only to watch over the correctness of the specification.
- Changes to the control component affect (under certain conditions) only the efficiency of the algorithm; they do not influence the solutions produced.

An environment for logic programming offers the programmer an inference method, so that only the logic program has to be developed for the problem at hand.

A.2 Programming in PROLOG

The programming language PROLOG can be considered to be a first step towards the practical realization of logic programming; as we will see below, however, the separation between logic and control has not been completely realized in this language. Figure A.1 shows the relation between PROLOG and the idea of logic programming discussed above.

A PROLOG system consists of two components: a *PROLOG database* and a *PROLOG interpreter*. A PROLOG program, essentially being a logic program consisting of *Horn clauses* (which however may contain some directives for controlling the inference method), is entered into the PROLOG database by the programmer. The PROLOG interpreter constitutes the inference method, which is based on *SLD resolution*. SLD resolution is discussed in considerable detail in Chapter 2.

Solving a problem in PROLOG starts with discerning the objects that are relevant to the particular problem, and the relationships that exist between them.

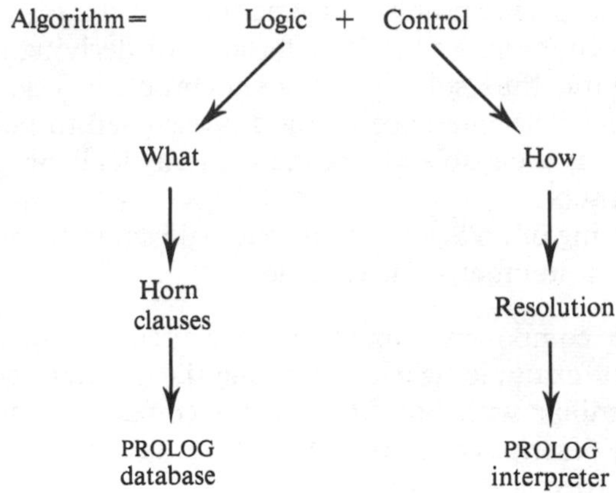

Figure A.1 The relationship between PROLOG and logic programming.

EXAMPLE A.1

In a problem concerning sets, for instance, we take constants as separate objects and the set as a whole as another object; a relevant relation between constants and sets is the membership relation.

When we have identified all relevant objects and relations, it must be specified which *facts* and *rules* hold for the objects and their interrelationships.

EXAMPLE A.2

Suppose that we are given a problem concerning sets. We may for example have the fact that a certain constant a is a member of a specific set S. The statement 'the set X is a subset of the set Y, if each member of X is a member of Y' is a rule that generally holds in set theory.

When all facts and rules have been identified, a specific problem may be looked upon as a query concerning the objects and their interrelationships. To summarize, specifying a logic program amounts to:

- specifying the *facts* concerning the objects and relations between objects relevant to the problem at hand;
- specifying the *rules* concerning the objects and their interrelationships;
- posing *queries* concerning the objects and relations.

A.2.1 Declarative semantics

Information (facts, rules and queries) is represented in PROLOG using the formalism of *Horn clause logic*. Chapter 2 discusses the Horn clause format in some detail; here we merely describe it briefly. A *Horn clause* takes the following form:

$$B \leftarrow A_1, \ldots, A_n$$

where $B, A_1, \ldots, A_n$, $n \geqslant 0$, are atomic formulas. Instead of the (reverse) implication symbol, in PROLOG usually the symbol :- is used, and clauses are terminated by a dot. An *atomic formula* is an expression of the form:

$$P(t_1, \ldots, t_m)$$

where P is a *predicate* (*symbol*) having m arguments, $m \geqslant 0$, and $t_1, \ldots, t_m$ are terms. A *term* is either a constant, a variable or a function of terms. In PROLOG two types of constant are distinguished: numeric constants, called *numbers*, and symbolic constants, called *atoms*. (Note that the word atom is used here in a meaning differing from that of atomic formula, thus deviating from the standard terminology of predicate logic.) Because of the syntactic similarity of predicates and functions, both are called *functors* in PROLOG. The terms of a functor are called its *arguments*. The arguments of a functor are enclosed in parentheses and separated by commas.

Seen in the light of the discussion from Section A.1, the predicate P in the atomic formula $P(t_1, \ldots, t_m)$ is interpreted as the name of the relationship that holds between the objects $t_1, \ldots, t_m$ which occur as the arguments of P. So, in a Horn clause B :– $A_1, \ldots, A_n$, the atomic formulas $B, A_1, \ldots, A_n$ denote relations between objects. A Horn clause is now interpreted as stating:

'B (is true) if A_1 and A_2 and $\cdots$ and A_n (are true)'

$A_1, \ldots, A_n$ are called the *conditions* of the clause, and B its *conclusion*. The commas between the conditions are interpreted as the logical $\wedge$, and the :- symbol as the (reverse) logical implication.

If $n = 0$, that is, if conditions A_i are lacking in the clause, then there are no conditions for the conclusion being satisfied, and the clause is said to be a *fact*. In case the clause is a fact, the :- sign is replaced by a dot.

Both terminology and notation in PROLOG differ slightly from those employed in logic programming. Table A.1 summarizes the differences and similarities. The use of the various syntactic forms of Horn clauses in PROLOG will now be introduced by means of examples.

Table A.1 Horn clauses and PROLOG.

Formal	*Name*	*In PROLOG*	*Name*
$A \leftarrow$	Unit clause	*A*.	Fact
$\leftarrow B_1,\ldots,B_n$	Goal clause	`?-` $B_1,\ldots,B_n$.	Query
$A \leftarrow B_1,\ldots,B_n$	Clause	A `:-` $B_1,\ldots,B_n$.	Rule

EXAMPLE A.3

The PROLOG clause

```
/*1*/  member(X,[X|_]).
```

is an example of a fact concerning the relation with the name `member`. This relation concerns the objects `X` and `[X|_]` (their meaning will be discussed shortly). The clause is preceded by a comment; in PROLOG, comments have to be specified between the delimiters `/*` and `*/`.

If a clause contains one or more conditions as well as a conclusion, it is called a *rule.*

EXAMPLE A.4

Consider the PROLOG clause

```
/*2*/  member(X,[_|Y]) :- member(X,Y).
```

which is a rule concerning the relation with the name `member`. The conclusion `member(X,[_|Y])` is subject to only one condition: `member(X,Y)`.

If the conclusion is missing from a clause, the clause is considered to be a query to the logic program. If a clause is a query, the sign :- is usually replaced by the sign `?-`.

EXAMPLE A.5

The PROLOG clause

```
/*3*/  ?- member(a,[a,b,c]).
```

is a typical example of a query.

A symbolic constant is denoted in PROLOG by a name starting with a lower-case letter. Names starting with an upper-case letter, or an underscore sign, _, indicate *variables* in PROLOG. A relation between objects is denoted by means of a functor having a name starting with a lower-case letter (or a special character, such as &, not having a predefined meaning in PROLOG), followed by a number of arguments, that is, the objects between which the relation holds. Recall that arguments are terms, that is, they may be either constants, variables or function symbols followed by terms.

EXAMPLE A.6

Consider the three clauses from the preceding examples once more. `member` is a functor having two arguments. The names `a`, `b` and `c` in clause 3 denote symbolic constants; `X` and `Y` are variables.

In PROLOG, a collection of elements enclosed in square brackets denotes a *list*. It is possible explicitly to decompose a list into its first element, the *head* of the list, and the remaining elements, the *tail* of the list. In the notation `[X|Y]`, the part in front of the bar is the head of the list; `X` is a single element. The part following the bar denotes its tail; `Y` is itself a list.

EXAMPLE A.7

Consider the list `[a,b,c]`. Now, `[a|[b,c]]` is another notation for the same list; in this notation, the head and tail of the list are distinguished explicitly. Note that the tail is again a list.

Each clause represents a separate piece of knowledge. So, in theory, the meaning of a set of clauses can be specified in terms of the meanings of each of the separate clauses. The meaning of a clause is called the *declarative semantics* of the clause. In Chapter 2 the declarative semantics of first-order predicate logic has been treated in considerable detail. Broadly speaking, PROLOG adheres to the semantics of first-order logic. However, there are some differences, such as the use of negation as finite failure, which has also been discussed in Chapter 2.

EXAMPLE A.8

Consider clauses 1, 2 and 3 from the preceding examples once more. Clause 1 states that the relation with the name `member` holds between a term and a list of terms if the head of the list equals the given term. Clause 1 is not a statement concerning specific terms, but is a general statement; this can be seen from the use of the variable `X`, which may be substituted with any term. Clause 2 represents the other possibility – that the constant occurs in the tail of the list. The last clause specifies the query whether or not the constant `a` belongs to the list of constants `a`, `b` and `c`.

A.2.2 Procedural semantics and the interpreter

In the preceding section we have viewed the formalism of Horn clause logic merely as a formal language for representing knowledge. However, the Horn clause formalism can also be looked upon as a programming language. This view of Horn clause logic is called its *procedural semantics.*

In the procedural semantics, a set of clauses is viewed as a program. Each clause in the program is seen as a *procedure* (*entry*). In the clause

$$B \text{ :- } A_1, \ldots, A_n.$$

we look upon the conclusion B as the *procedure heading*, composed of a procedure name and a number of formal parameters; $A_1, \ldots, A_n$ is then taken as the *body* of the procedure, consisting of a sequence of *procedure calls.* In a program all clauses having the same predicate in their conclusion are viewed as various entries to the same procedure. A clause without any conclusion, that is, a query, acts as the *main program.* In this book, no strict distinction is made between both types of semantics; it will depend on the subject dealt with, whether the terminology of the declarative semantics is used, or the terminology of procedural semantics is preferred. In the remainder of this section we shall discuss the PROLOG interpreter.

When a PROLOG program has been entered into the PROLOG database, the main program is executed by the PROLOG interpreter. The way the given PROLOG clauses are manipulated will be demonstrated by means of some examples.

EXAMPLE A.9

The three clauses introduced in Section A.2.1 together constitute a complete PROLOG program:

```
/*1*/  member(X,[X|_]).
/*2*/  member(X,[_|Y]) :-
             member(X,Y).
/*3*/  ?- member(a,[a,b,c]).
```

Clauses 1 and 2 are entries to the same `member` procedure. The body of clause 2 consists of just one procedure call. Clause 3 fulfils the role of the main program.

Let us suppose that the PROLOG database initially contains the first two clauses, and that clause 3 is entered by the user as a query to the PROLOG system. The PROLOG interpreter tries to derive an answer to the query using the information stored in the database. To this end, the interpreter employs two fundamental techniques: matching and backtracking.

Matching of clauses

To answer a query, the PROLOG interpreter starts with the first condition in the query clause, taking it as a procedure call. The PROLOG database is subsequently searched for a suitable entry to the called procedure; the search starts with the first clause in the database, and continues until a clause has been found which has a conclusion that can be matched with the procedure call. A *match* between a conclusion and a procedure call is obtained if there exists a substitution for the variables occurring both in the conclusion and in the procedure call such that the two become (syntactically) equal after the substitution has been applied to them. Such a match exists

- if the conclusion and the procedure call contain the same predicate, and
- if the terms in corresponding argument positions after substitution of the variables are equal; we then speak of a match for argument positions.

Applying a substitution to a variable is called *instantiating* the variable to a term. The most general substitution making the selected conclusion and the procedure call syntactically equal is called the *most general unifier* (*mgu*) of the two. For a more elaborate treatment of substitutions and unifiers, the reader is referred to Chapter 2.

If we have obtained a match for a procedure call, the conditions of the matching clause will be executed. If the matching clause has no conditions, the next condition from the calling clause is executed. The process of matching (and instantiation) can be examined by means of the special infix predicate `=`, which tries to match the terms at its left-hand and right-hand side and subsequently investigates whether the terms have become syntactically equal.

EXAMPLE A.10

Consider the following example of the use of the matching predicate `=`. The first line representing a query has been entered by the user; the next line is the system's output.

```
?- f(X) = f(a).
X = a
```

As can be seen, the variable `X` is instantiated to `a`, which leads to a match of the left-hand and right-hand side of `=`.

On first thoughts, instantiation seems similar to the assignment statement in conventional programming languages. However, these two notions differ considerably. An instantiation is a binding of a variable to a value which cannot be changed, that is, it is not possible to overwrite the value of an instantiated variable by some other value. (We will see, however, that under certain conditions it is possible to create a new instantiation.) So it is not possible to express by instantiation a statement like

$$X := X + 1$$

which is a typical assignment statement in a language like Pascal. In fact, the 'ordinary' assignment, which is usually viewed as a change of the state of a variable, cannot be expressed in standard logics.

A variable in PROLOG has for a lexical scope the clause in which it occurs. Outside that clause, the variable and the instantiations to the variable have no influence. PROLOG does not have global variables. We shall see later that PROLOG actually does provide some special predicates which have a global effect on the database; the meanings of such predicates, however, cannot be accounted for in first-order logic. Variables having a name consisting of only a single underscore character have a special meaning in PROLOG. These variables, called *don't-care variables*, match any possible term. However, such a match does not lead to an instantiation to the variable, that is, past the argument position of the match a don't care variable loses its 'binding'. A don't care variable is usually employed at argument positions which are not referred to later on at some other position in the clause.

EXAMPLE A.11

In our `member` example, the interpreter tries to obtain a match for the following query:

```
/*3*/  ?- member(a,[a,b,c]).
```

The first clause in the database specifying the predicate `member` in its conclusion is clause 1:

```
/*1*/  member(X,[X|_]).
```

The query contains at its first argument position the constant a. In clause 1 the variable X occurs at the same argument position. If the constant a is substituted for the variable X, we have obtained a match for the first argument positions. So X will be instantiated to the constant a. As a consequence, the variable X at the second argument position of the conclusion of clause 1 has the value a as well, since this X is the same variable as at the first argument position of the same clause. We now have to investigate the respective second argument positions, that is, we have to compare the lists [a,b,c] and [a|_]. Note that the list [a,b,c] can be written as [a|[b,c]]; it can easily be seen that we will succeed in finding a match for the second argument positions, because the don't care variable will match with the list [b,c]. So we have obtained a match with respect to the predicate name as well as to all argument positions. Since clause 1 does not contain any conditions, the interpreter answers the original query by printing yes:

```
/*3*/  ?- member(a,[a,b,c]).
yes
```

EXAMPLE A.12

Consider again clauses 1 and 2 from the preceding example. Suppose that, instead of the previous query, the following query is entered:

```
/*3*/  ?- member(a,[b,a,c]).
```

Then, again, the interpreter first tries to find a match with clause 1:

```
/*1*/  member(X,[X|_]).
```

Again we have that the variable X will be instantiated to the constant a. In the second argument position of clause 1, the variable X also has the value a. We therefore have to compare the lists [b,a,c] and [a|_]; this time, we are not able to find a match for the second argument positions. Since the only possible instantiation of X is to a, we will never find a match for the query with clause 1. The interpreter now turns its attention to the following entry of the member procedure, which is clause 2:

```
/*2*/  member(X,[_|Y]) :-
           member(X,Y).
```

When comparing the first argument positions of the query and the conclusion of clause 2, respectively, we infer that the variable X will again be instantiated to the constant a. For the second argument positions we have to compare the lists [b,a,c] and [_|Y]. We obtain a match for the second argument positions by instantiating the variable Y to the list [a,c]. We have now obtained a complete match for the query with the conclusion of clause 2. Note that all occurrences of the variables X and Y within the scope of clause 2 will have been instantiated to a and [a,c], respectively. So, after instantiation we have

```
member(a,[_|[a,c]]) :-
    member(a,[a,c]).
```

Since clause 2 contains a condition, its conclusion may be drawn only if the specified condition is fulfilled. The interpreter treats this condition as a new query:

```
?- member(a,[a,c]).
```

This query matches with clause 1 in the same way as has been described in Example A.11; the interpreter returns success. Subsequently, the conclusion of clause 2 is drawn, and the interpreter prints the answer yes to the original query.

Backtracking

When, after the creation of a number of instantiations and matches, the system does not succeed in obtaining the next match, it systematically tries alternatives for the instantiations and matches arrived at so far. This process of finding alternatives by undoing previous work is called *backtracking*. The following example demonstrates the process of backtracking.

EXAMPLE A.13

Consider the following PROLOG program:

```
/*1*/ branch(a,b).
/*2*/ branch(a,c).
/*3*/ branch(c,d).
/*4*/ branch(c,e).
/*5*/ path(X,X).
/*6*/ path(X,Y) :-
          branch(X,Z),
          path(Z,Y).
```

Clauses 1–4 represent a specific binary tree by means of the predicate branch; the tree is depicted in Figure A.2. The

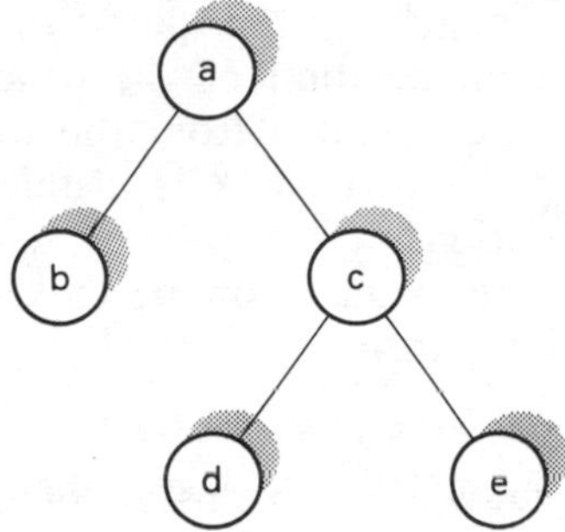

Figure A.2 A binary tree.

symbolic constants `a`, `b`, `c`, `d` and `e` denote the vertices of the tree. The predicate `branch` in `branch(a,b)` has the intended meaning 'there exists a branch from vertex `a` to vertex `b`'.

Clauses 5 and 6 for `path` specify under which conditions there exists a path between two vertices. The notion of a path has been defined recursively; the definition of a path makes use of the notion of a path again.

A *recursive definition* of a relation generally consists of two parts: one or more *termination criteria*, usually defining the basic states for which the relation holds, and the actual recursion describing how to proceed from a state in which the relation holds to a new, simpler state concerning the relation.

The termination criterion of the recursive definition of the `path` relation is expressed above in clause 5; the actual recursion is defined in clause 6. Note that the definition of the `member` relation in the preceding examples is also a recursive definition.

Now, suppose that after the above program is entered into the PROLOG database, we enter the following query:

```
/*7*/  ?- path(a,d).
```

The interpreter first tries to obtain a match with clause 5, the first clause in the database specifying the predicate `path` in its conclusion:

```
/*5*/  path(X,X).
```

For a match for the respective first argument positions, the variable `X` will be instantiated to the constant `a`. Matching the second argument positions fails because `a`, the instantiation of `X`, and the constant `d` are different from each other. The interpreter therefore tries the next clause for `path`, which is clause 6:

```
/*6*/ path(X,Y) :- branch(X,Z),path(Z,Y).
```

It will now find a match for the query; the variable X occurring in the first argument position of the conclusion of clause 6 is instantiated to the constant a from the first argument position of the query, and the variable Y is instantiated to the constant d. These instantiations again pertain to the entire matching clause; in fact, clause 6 may now be looked upon as having the following instantiated form:

```
path(a,d) :- branch(a,Z),path(Z,d).
```

Before we may draw the conclusion of clause 6, we have to fulfil the two conditions branch(a,Z) and path(Z,d). The interpreter deals with these new queries from left to right. For the query

```
?- branch(a,Z).
```

the interpreter finds a match with clause 1:

```
/*1*/ branch(a,b).
```

by instantiating the variable Z to b. Again, this instantiation affects all occurrences of the variable Z in the entire clause containing the query, so we have:

```
path(a,d) :- branch(a,b),path(b,d).
```

The next procedure call to be handled by the interpreter is therefore

```
?- path(b,d).
```

No match is found for this query with clause 5. The query however matches with the conclusion of clause 6:

```
/*6*/ path(X,Y) :- branch(X,Z),path(Z,Y).
```

The interpreter instantiates the variable X to b, and the variable Y to d, yielding the following instance of clause 6:

```
path(b,d) :- branch(b,Z),path(Z,d).
```

Note that these instantiations for the variables X and Y are allowed; the earlier instantiations for variables X and Y concerned *different* variables since they occurred in a different clause and therefore within a different scope. Again, before the query path(b,d) may be answered in the affirmative, we have to check the two conditions of the instance of clause 6 obtained. Unfortunately, the first condition

```
?- branch(b,Z).
```

does not match with any clause in the PROLOG program. (As can be seen in Figure A.2, there is no outgoing branch from the vertex b.)

The PROLOG interpreter now cancels the last match and its corresponding instantiations, and tries to find a new match for the originating query. The match of the query `path(b,d)` with the conclusion of clause 6 was the last match found, so the corresponding instantiations to `X` and `Y` in clause 6 are cancelled. The interpreter now has to try to find a new match for the query `path(b,d)`. However, since clause 6 is the last clause in the program having the predicate `path` in its conclusion, there is no alternative match possible. The interpreter therefore goes yet another step further back.

The match of `branch(a,Z)` with clause 1 will now be undone by cancelling the instantiation of the variable `Z` to `b`. For the query

```
?- branch(a,Z).
```

the interpreter is able to find an alternative match, namely with clause 2:

```
/*2*/ branch(a,c).
```

It instantiates the variable `Z` to `c`. Recall that the query `branch(a,Z)` came from the match of the query `path(a,d)` with clause 6:

```
path(a,d) :- branch(a,Z),path(Z,d).
```

The undoing of the instantiation to `Z` and the subsequent creation of a new instantiation again influences the entire calling clause:

```
path(a,d) :- branch(a,c),path(c,d).
```

Instead of the condition `path(b,d)` we therefore have to consider the condition `path(c,d)`. By means of successive matches with the clauses 6, 3 and 5, the interpreter derives the answer `yes` to the query `path(c,d)`. Both conditions to the match with the original query `path(a,d)` are now fulfilled. The interpreter therefore answers the original query in the affirmative.

This example illustrates the modus operandi of the PROLOG interpreter, and, among other things, it demonstrates that the PROLOG interpreter examines clauses in the order in which they have been specified in the database. According to the principles of logic programming, a logic program is viewed as a set of clauses, so their respective order is of no consequence to the derived results. As can be seen from this example, however, the order in which clauses have been specified in the PROLOG database may be important. This is a substantial difference between a logic program and a PROLOG program; whereas logic programs are purely declarative in nature, PROLOG programs tend to be much more procedural. As a consequence, the programmer must bear in mind properties of the PROLOG interpreter when developing a PROLOG program. For example, when imposing some order on the clauses in the database, it is usually necessary that the clauses acting as a termination criterion for a recursive definition, or having some other special function, are specified before the clauses expressing the general rule.

A.3 Overview of the PROLOG language

Until now, all predicates discussed in the examples have been defined on purpose. However, every PROLOG system offers a number of predefined predicates, which the programmer may utilize in programs as desired. Such predicates are usually called *standard predicates* or *built-in predicates* to distinguish them from the predicates defined by the programmer.

In this section, we shall discuss several standard predicates and their use. Only the predicates which have been used throughout this book and a small number of other frequently applied predicates will be dealt with here. A complete overview is usually included in the documentation concerning the particular PROLOG system. This discussion is based on C-PROLOG, Release 1.5.

A.3.1 Reading in programs

By means of the predicate `consult`, programs can be read from file and inserted into the PROLOG database. The predicate `consult` takes one argument, which has to be instantiated to the name of a file before execution.

EXAMPLE A.14

The query

```
?- consult(file).
```

instructs the interpreter to read a PROLOG program from the file with the name `file`.

It is also possible to insert into the database several programs from different files. This may be achieved by entering the following clause:

```
?- consult(file_1),...,consult(file_n).
```

PROLOG offers an abbreviation for such a clause; the required file names may be specified in a list:

```
?- [file_1,...,file_n].
```

A.3.2 Input and output

Printing text on the screen can be done by means of the predicate `write`, which takes a single argument. Before execution of the procedure call `write(X)`, the variable `X` must be instantiated to the term to be printed.

EXAMPLE A.15

The clause

```
?- write(output).
```

prints the term `output` on the screen. Execution of the call

```
?- write('This is output.').
```

results in

```
This is output.
```

When the clause

```
?- create(Output),write(Output).
```

is executed, the value to which `Output` is instantiated by a call to some user-defined predicate `create` will be printed on the screen. If the variable `Output` is instantiated to a term containing uninstantiated variables (the internal representation of) the variables will be shown as part of the output.

The predicate `nl` just indicates a new line, causing output to start at the beginning of the next line. `nl` takes no arguments.

We also have some means for input. The predicate `read` reads terms entered from the keyboard. The predicate `read` takes only one argument. Before executing the call `read(X)`, the variable `X` has to be uninstantiated; after execution of the `read` predicate, `X` will be instantiated to the term that has been entered. A term entered from the keyboard has to end with a dot followed by a carriage return.

A.3.3 Arithmetical predicates

PROLOG provides a number of arithmetical predicates. These predicates take as arguments arithmetical expressions; arithmetical expressions are constructed as in usual mathematical practice, that is, by means of infix operators, such as `+`, `-`, `*` and `/`, for addition, subtraction, multiplication and division, respectively. Generally, before executing an arithmetical predicate all variables in the expressions in its left-hand and right-hand side have to be instantiated to terms containing only numbers and operators; the arguments will be evaluated before the test specified by means of the predicate is performed. For example, in a condition `X < Y` both `X` and `Y` have to be instantiated to terms which on evaluation yield numeric constants, before the comparison is carried out. The following arithmetical predicates are the ones most frequently used:

```
X > Y.
X < Y.
X >= Y.
X =< Y.
X =:= Y.
X =\= Y.
```

The last two predicates express equality and inequality, respectively. Note that the matching predicate `=` is not an arithmetical predicate; it is a more general predicate the use of which is not restricted to arithmetical expressions. Furthermore, the predicate `=` does not force evaluation of its arguments.

Besides the six arithmetical predicates shown above, we also have in PROLOG an infix predicate with the name `is`. Before executing

```
?- X is Y.
```

only the right-hand side `Y` has to be instantiated to an arithmetical expression. Note that the `is` predicate differs from `=:=` as well as from the matching predicate `=`; in the case of `=:=` both `X` and `Y` have to be instantiated to arithmetical expressions, and in the case of the matching predicate neither `X` nor `Y` has to be instantiated. If in the query shown above `X` is an uninstantiated variable, after execution of the query it will be instantiated to the value of `Y`. The values of both the left-hand and the right-hand side are subsequently examined for equality; it is obvious that this test will always succeed. If, on the other hand, the variable `X` is instantiated to a number (or the left-hand side itself is a number), the condition will succeed if the result of evaluating the right-hand side of `is` equals the left-hand side, and fail otherwise. All other uses of the predicate `is` lead to a syntax error.

EXAMPLE A.16

Consider the following queries and answers, which illustrate the differences and similarities between the predicates `=`, `=:=` and `is`:

```
?- 3 = 2+1.
no

?- 3 is 2+1.
yes

?- 3 =:= 2+1.
yes

?- 3+1 = 3+1.
yes

?- 3+1 =:= 3+1.
yes

?- 3+1 is 3+1.
no

?- 1+3 = 3+1.
no

?- 1+3 =:= 3+1.
yes
```

The following examples illustrate the behaviour of these predicates when the left-hand side is an uninstantiated variable. PROLOG returns the computed instantiation:

```
?- X is 2+1.
X = 3

?- X = 2+1.
X = 2+1
```

We have left out the example `?- X =:= 2+1`, because it is not permitted to have an uninstantiated variable as an argument to `=:=`.

The predicates `=:=` and `is` may be applied only to arithmetical arguments. The predicate `=`, however, also applies to non-arithmetical arguments, as has been shown in Section A.2.2.

EXAMPLE A.17

Execution of the query

```
?- X = [a,b].
```

leads to the instantiation of the variable `X` to the list `[a,b]`. If the predicate `=:=` or the predicate `is` had been used, the PROLOG interpreter would have signalled an error.

A.3.4 Examining instantiations

A number of predicates is provided which can be used to examine a variable and its possible instantiation. The predicate `var`, taking one argument, investigates whether or not its argument has been instantiated. The condition `var(X)` is fulfilled if `X` at the time of execution is uninstantiated; otherwise, the condition fails. The predicate `nonvar` has a complementary meaning.

By means of the predicate `atom`, also taking one argument, it can be checked whether the argument is instantiated to a symbolic constant. The predicate `atomic`, which also takes a single argument, investigates whether its argument is instantiated to a symbolic or numeric constant. The one-argument predicate `integer` tests whether its argument is instantiated to an integer.

EXAMPLE A.18

Consider the following queries specifying the predicates mentioned above, and answers of the PROLOG interpreter:

```
?- atomic([a]).
no

?- atomic(3).
yes

?- atom(3).
no

?- atom(a).
yes

?- integer(a).
no
```

A.3.5 Controlling backtracking

PROLOG offers the programmer a number of predicates for explicitly controlling the backtracking behaviour of the interpreter. Note that here PROLOG deviates from the logic programming idea.

The predicate `call` takes one argument, which before execution has to be instantiated to a procedure call; `call` takes care of its argument being handled like a procedure call by the PROLOG interpreter in the usual way. Note that use of the `call` predicate allows for 'filling in' the program during run-time.

The predicate `true` takes no arguments; the condition `true` always succeeds. The predicate `fail` also has no arguments; the condition `fail` never succeeds. The general application of the predicate `fail` is to enforce backtracking, as shown in the following example.

EXAMPLE A.19

Consider the following clause:

```
a(X) :- b(X),fail.
```

When the query `a(X)` is entered, the PROLOG interpreter first tries to find a match for `b(X)`. Let us suppose that such a match is found, and that the variable `X` is instantiated to some term. Then, in the next step, as a consequence of its failure, `fail` enforces the interpreter to look for an alternative instantiation to `X`. If it succeeds in finding another instantiation for `X`, then again `fail` will be executed. This entire process is repeated until no further instantiations can be found. In this way all possible instantiations for `X` will be found. Note that, if no side-effects are employed to record the instantiations of `X` in some way, the successive instantiations leave no trace. It will be evident that in the end the query `a(X)` will be answered by `no`.

The predicate `not` takes a procedure call as its argument. The condition `not(P)` succeeds if the procedure call to which `P` is instantiated fails, and vice versa. Contrary to what one would expect in the case of ordinary logical negation, PROLOG does not look for facts `not(P)` in the database (these are not even allowed in PROLOG). Instead, negation is handled by confirming failed procedure calls. This form of negation is known as *negation as (finite) failure*; for a more detailed discussion of this notion the reader is referred to Chapter 2.

The *cut*, denoted by !, is a predicate without any arguments. It is used as a condition which can be confirmed only once by the PROLOG interpreter; on backtracking it is not possible to confirm a cut for the second time. Moreover, the cut has a significant side-effect on the remainder of the backtracking process; it forces the interpreter to reject the clause containing the cut, and also to ignore all other alternatives for the procedure call that led to the execution of the particular clause.

EXAMPLE A.20

Consider the following clauses:

```
/*1*/  a :- b,c,d.
/*2*/  c :- p,q,!,r,s.
/*3*/  c.
```

Suppose that on executing the call `a`, the successive procedure calls `b`, `p`, `q`, the cut and `r` have succeeded (the cut by definition always succeeds on first encounter). Furthermore, assume that no match can be found for the procedure call `s`. Then, as usual, the interpreter tries to find an alternative match for the procedure call `r`. For each alternative match for `r` it again tries to find a match for condition `s`. If no alternatives for `r` can be found, or similarly if all alternative matches have been tried, the interpreter would normally try to find an alternative match for `q`. However, since we have specified a cut between the procedure calls `q` and `r`, the interpreter will not look for alternative matches for the procedure calls preceding `r` in the specific clause. In addition, the interpreter will not try any alternatives for the procedure call `c`, so clause 3 is ignored. Its first action after encountering the cut during backtracking is to look for alternative matches for the condition preceding the call `c`, that is, for `b`.

There are several circumstances in which specification of the cut is useful for efficiency or even necessary for correctness. In the first place, the cut may be used to indicate that the selected clause is the only one that can be applied to solve the (sub)problem at hand, that is, it may be used to indicate 'mutually exclusive' clauses.

EXAMPLE A.21

Suppose that the condition `b` in the following clause has been confirmed:

```
a :- b,c.
```

and that we know that this clause is the only one in the collection of clauses having `a` as a conclusion, which is applicable in the situation in which `b` has been confirmed. When the condition `c` cannot be confirmed, there is no reason to try any other clause concerning `a`; we already know that `a` will never succeed. This unnecessary searching can be prevented by specifying the cut following the critical condition:

```
a :- b,!,c.
```

Furthermore, the cut is used to indicate that a particular procedure call may never lead to success if some condition has been fulfilled, that is, it is used to identify exceptional cases to a general rule. In this case, the cut is used in combination with the earlier mentioned predicate `fail`.

EXAMPLE A.22

Suppose that the conclusion a definitely may not be drawn if condition b succeeds. In the clause

```
a :- b,!,fail.
```

we have used the cut in conjunction with fail to prevent the interpreter looking for alternative matches for b or trying any other clause concerning a.

We have already remarked that the PROLOG programmer has to be familiar with the working of the PROLOG interpreter. Since the cut has a strong influence on the backtracking process, it should be applied with great care. The following example from Clocksin and Mellish (1981) illustrates errors to which a careless use of the cut may lead.

EXAMPLE A.23

Consider the following three clauses, specifying the number of parents of a person; everybody has two of them, except Adam and Eve, who have none:

```
/*1*/  number_of_parents(adam,0) :- !.
/*2*/  number_of_parents(eve,0) :- !.
/*3*/  number_of_parents(X,2).
```

Now, the query

```
?- number_of_parents(eve,2).
```

is answered by the interpreter in the affirmative. Although this is somewhat unexpected, after due consideration the reader will be able to figure out why yes instead of no has been derived.

For convenience, we summarize the side-effects of the cut:

(1) If a cut has been specified in a clause, we have normal backtracking over the conditions preceding the cut.

(2) As soon as the cut has been 'used', the interpreter has committed itself to the choice for that particular clause, and for everything done after calling that clause; the interpreter will not reconsider these choices.

(3) Normal backtracking occurs over the conditions following the cut.

(4) When on backtracking a cut is met, the interpreter 'remembers' its commitments and traces back to the originating query containing the call that led to a match with the clause concerned.

We have seen that all procedure calls in a PROLOG clause will be executed successively until backtracking emerges. The procedure calls, that is, the conditions are connected by commas, which have the declarative semantics of the logical $\wedge$. However, it is also allowed to specify a logical $\vee$ in a clause. This is done by a semicolon, `;`, indicating a choice between conditions. All conditions connected by `;` are evaluated from left to right until one is found that succeeds. The remaining conditions will then be ignored. The semicolon `;` has higher precedence than the comma `,`.

A.3.6 Manipulation of the database

Any PROLOG system offers the programmer means for modifying the contents of the database during run-time. It is possible to add clauses to the database by means of the predicates `asserta` and `assertz`. Both predicates take one argument. If this argument has been instantiated to a term before the procedure call is executed, `asserta` adds its argument as a clause to the database before all (possibly) present clauses that specify the same functor in their conclusions. On the other hand, `assertz` adds its argument as a clause to the database just after all other clauses concerning the functor.

EXAMPLE A.24

Consider the PROLOG database containing the following clauses:

```
fact(a).
fact(b).
yet_another_fact(c).
and_another_fact(d).
```

If we enter the following query to the system:

```
?- asserta(yet_another_fact(e)).
```

The database will have been modified after execution of the query as follows:

```
fact(a).
fact(b).
yet_another_fact(e).
yet_another_fact(c).
and_another_fact(d).
```

Execution of the procedure call

```
?- assertz(fact(f)).
```

modifies the contents of the database as follows:

```
fact(a).
fact(b).
fact(f).
yet_another_fact(e).
yet_another_fact(c).
and_another_fact(d).
```

By means of the one-placed predicate retract, the first clause having both conclusion and conditions matching with the argument is removed from the database.

A.3.7 Manipulation of terms

Terms are used in PROLOG in much the same way as records are in Pascal, and structures in COMMON LISP. In these languages, various operations are available to a programmer for the selection and modification of parts of these data structures. PROLOG provides similar facilities for manipulating terms. The predicates arg, functor and =.. (pronounced as 'univ') define such operations.

The predicate arg can be applied for selecting a specific argument of a functor. It takes three arguments:

```
arg(I,T,A).
```

Before execution, the variable I has to be instantiated to an integer, and the variable T must be instantiated to a term. The interpreter will instantiate the variable A to the value of the Ith argument of the term T.

EXAMPLE A.25

The procedure call:

```
arg(2,diagnosis(hepatitis_A,0.5,_),A).
```

leads to instantiation of the variable A to the value 0.5.

The predicate functor can be used for selecting the left-most functor in a given term. The predicate functor takes three arguments:

```
functor(T,F,N).
```

If the variable T is instantiated to a term, then the variable F will be instantiated to the functor of the term, and the variable N to the number of arguments of the functor.

EXAMPLE A.26

The procedure call

```
functor(patient(diagnosis(hepatitis_A,0.5,_)),F,N).
```

leads to instantiation of the variable `F` to the constant `patient`. The variable `N` will be instantiated to the integer `1`.

The predicate `functor` may also be applied in a 'reverse mode'; it can be employed for constructing a term with a given functor `F` and a prespecified number of arguments `N`. All arguments of the constructed term will be variables.

The predicate `=..` also has a dual function. It may be applied for selecting information from a term, or for constructing a new term. If in the procedure call

```
X =.. L.
```

`X` has been instantiated to a term, then after execution the variable `L` will be instantiated to a list, the first element of which is the functor of `X`; the remaining elements are the successive arguments of the functor.

EXAMPLE A.27

Consider the following procedure call:

```
diagnosis(hepatitis_A,0.5,[1]) =.. L.
```

This call leads to instantiation of the variable `L` to the list `[diagnosis,hepatitis_A,0.5,[1]]`.

The predicate `=..` may also be used to organize information into a term. This is achieved by instantiating the variable `L` to a list. Upon execution of the call `X =.. L`, the variable `X` will be instantiated to a term having a functor which is the first element from the list; the remaining elements of the list will be taken as the arguments of the functor.

EXAMPLE A.28

The procedure call

```
X =.. [diagnosis,hepatitis_B,0.8,[0.5,0.6]].
```

leads to instantiation of the variable `X` to the term `diagnosis(hepatitis_B,0.8,[0.5,0.6])`.

Nóte that, contrary to the case of the predicate `functor`, in case of the predicate `=..` prespecified arguments may be inserted into the new term.

To conclude this section, we will consider the predicate `clause`, which can be used for inspecting the contents of the database. The predicate `clause` takes two arguments:

```
clause(Head,Body).
```

The first argument, `Head`, must be sufficiently instantiated for the interpreter to be able to find a match with the conclusion of a clause; the second argument, `Body`, will then be instantiated to the conditions of the selected clause. If the selected clause is a fact, `Body` will be instantiated to `true`.

Suggested reading

Readers interested in the theoretical foundation of PROLOG and logic programming should consult Kowalski's *Logic for Problem Solving* (1979) and Lloyd's *Foundations of Logic Programming* (1987). However, it is not necessary for developing PROLOG programs to be familiar with these theoretical aspects.

For an introduction to the PROLOG language readers are referred to Clocksin and Mellish (1981). An excellent introductory book to programming in PROLOG, with an emphasis on artificial intelligence applications, is Bratko (1990). More experienced programmers interested in the more technical aspects of PROLOG may find Sterling and Shapiro (1986), Kluźniak and Szpakowicz (1985) and Campbell (1984) valuable sources of information.

APPENDIX B

Introduction to LISP

The programming language LISP was designed by J. McCarthy between 1956 and 1958 at the Massachusetts Institute of Technology (MIT) as a language for the construction of 'intelligent' computer systems. The name of the language, which is an acronym for 'LISt Processing', readily indicates the most important and strongest feature of the language, namely list manipulation. LISP was the origin of a new programming style known as *functional programming*. The language furthermore has relations with *lambda calculus* and *term rewriting systems*, important fields of research in theoretical computer science.

The first LISP interpreters became available at the beginning of the 1960s, which makes the language one of the oldest still used programming languages. Although in the course of time LISP underwent many changes, most of these were not fundamental in nature; many were caused by the incorporation of concepts from other types of programming languages into LISP. The language provides a terse notation. A pleasant consequence is that algorithms having a lengthy formulation in a more conventional procedural programming language can often be expressed in LISP in a short and elegant way. Furthermore, it is possible in LISP to modify a program dynamically during its execution by interpreting data as program parts, a feature that is particularly important for the development of interpreters for formal languages.

Right from its inception LISP was applied in the burgeoning field of artificial intelligence, then led by J. McCarthy, A. Newell and H.A. Simon. McCarthy used the language for the development of a general problem solver named 'Advice Taker'. At present, LISP is still mainly used for applications in which symbol manipulation predominates, such as in artificial intelligence in general and for the development of expert systems in particular. For more than a decade, LISP was the only language commonly employed in artificial intelligence, a circumstance which was only recently changed by the introduction of PROLOG. Some application areas in which LISP is frequently applied are:

- Symbolic computer algebra (MACSYMA)
- Theorem proving (Boyer–Moore theorem prover)
- Natural-language processing (SHRDLU)
- Expert systems (INTERNIST–I, MYCIN)
- Expert system builder tools (ART, KEE, Knowledge Craft, OPS5)

LISP has also been employed with success outside the area of artificial intelligence, for example for the construction of compilers and interpreters for formal languages such as the algebraic specification language OBJ.

Until some years ago there were many different dialects of LISP in use, of which the most familiar are MACLISP, INTERLISP, LELISP, ZETALISP and SCHEME. This multiplicity of dialects was a result of the lack of a standard language definition. In 1983 a number of eminent LISP researchers proposed COMMON LISP in an effort to enforce a LISP standard, which largely has succeeded. COMMON LISP shows many characteristics taken from older LISP dialects, in particular from MACLISP, ZETALISP, and SCHEME. In addition, many concepts from other types of programming languages have been incorporated.

B.1 Fundamental principles of LISP

In this section we shall discuss the basic principles of LISP by means of a general introduction to the representation and manipulation of data in LISP. In Section B.2, a selected number of specific features of the language will be discussed. In both sections, the LISP of our choice is COMMON LISP.

B.1.1 The LISP expression

Data are represented in LISP by means of *expressions* (previously also called *s-expressions*). An expression is either an *atom* or a *list* of expressions. An atom may be numeric or symbolic. A numeric atom is also called a *number*; a symbolic atom is simply called a *symbol*. In this book, names of symbols are denoted by lower-case letters; in COMMON LISP, however, the internal representation of all alphabetic letters is in upper-case by default. A list may be an empty list, which is indicated by the symbol `nil` or by `( )`, or alternatively a finite sequence of expressions enclosed by a pair of parentheses. Figure B.1 illustrates this subdivision of expressions schematically.

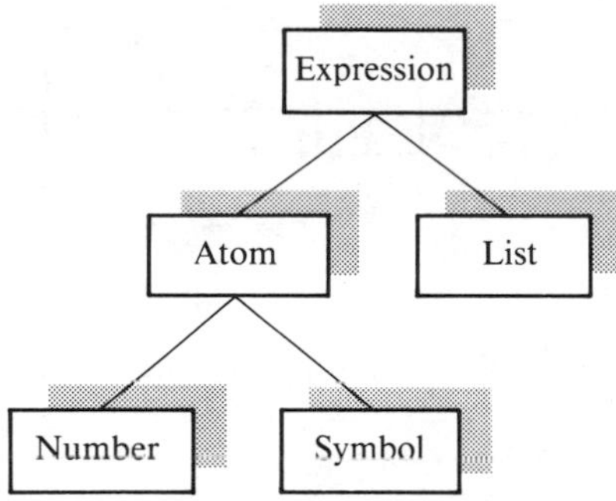

Figure B.1 LISP expressions.

EXAMPLE B.1

The following three expressions are all atoms: `a`, `3`, `a-long-atom`. The first and the last atom are symbols; the second is a number. Examples of lists are:

```
(a b c)
(a (b c d))
((1 a) (2 b))
```

The first list contains three atoms: `a`, `b` and `c`. The second list contains two expressions: the atom `a` and the list `(b c d)`. The third list comprises two expressions, both lists.

A list containing expressions which are also lists is called a *nested list*.

An important property of lists is that the removal of the first expression from a list again yields a list. Actually, a list is built from a more basic data structure, the so-called *cons* or *dotted pair*. A dotted pair is a data structure consisting of two elements; its first element is called the *car* and its second element is called the *cdr* (pronounced 'cudder'). The syntax of a cons is as follows:

$$(e_1 \, . \, e_2)$$

where e_1 and e_2 are expressions. A list can therefore be viewed as being either the empty list or syntactic sugar for a special kind of dotted pair in which the second element is again either a dotted pair or the empty list. The dotted pair occurring at the deepest nesting in a list always specifies as its second element the empty list.

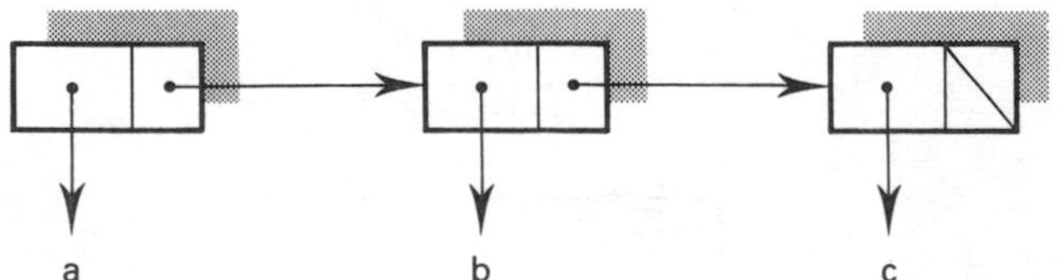

Figure B.2 Representation of the list `(a b c)`.

EXAMPLE B.2

The list

```
(a b c)
```

can be expressed as a dotted pair as follows:

```
(a . (b . (c . nil)))
```

The list may be represented graphically as shown in Figure B.2.

Since the dotted-pair notation of lists turns out to be rather cumbersome, generally the earlier discussed list notation is preferred.

Beside dotted pairs, lists and atoms, COMMON LISP also offers the programmer a large number of other more conventional data types, such as *arrays*, *structures* (records), *strings* and *streams*. Furthermore, the language offers an information-hiding mechanism, by means of *packages*, which has much in common with the notion of packages as employed in Ada. In this book we shall not go into the details of all these different data types.

B.1.2 The form

With the introduction of expressions, the basic syntax of the LISP language has been described completely. A LISP program is just a collection of expressions which are to be evaluated by a LISP interpreter (the LISP *evaluator*). To distinguish these expressions from expressions representing data, the former expressions are often called *forms*. The LISP interpreter may be viewed as a system that reads in a form, evaluates it, and then prints the result of the evaluation. This sequence of steps is called the *read–eval–print loop* of LISP.

In a form, the first element is taken to be a *function name* and the remaining elements are taken as the *arguments* to the specified function. Evaluation of a form by the LISP interpreter yields a *function value* as a result. In COMMON LISP, evaluation of a form starts with the evaluation of the arguments to the function specified in the form; the values returned by the LISP evaluator are substituted for the corresponding *formal parameters* of the definition of the function concerned. Then the function will be *applied* to its arguments. This method of evaluation is called evaluation according to the *substitution model*. The mechanism of parameter transfer is known as *call by value*. The substitution model is all that is needed to describe the meaning of programs from a functional programming point of view.

EXAMPLE B.3

The function with the name `car` takes a dotted pair or a list as an argument. Upon evaluation it returns as a function value the first element of the specified argument. On evaluation of the form

```
(car (quote (a . b)))
```

first the expression `(quote (a . b))`, the argument to `car`, is evaluated. The function `quote` switches off the LISP interpreter temporarily; as a consequence, the argument is returned unmodified. In this example, we have that evaluation of the expression `(quote (a . b))` yields the dotted pair `(a . b)`. There also exists an abbreviation for this frequently used function in LISP, namely the apostrophe. Hence, the following two LISP forms are equivalent:

```
(quote (a . b))
'(a . b)
```

Further evaluation of the form `(car (quote (a . b)))` results in the substitution of the dotted pair `(a . b)` for the formal parameter of the function `car`. Application of the function `car` to this argument yields the function value `a`.

Evaluating a form may have side-effects, which are then the real purpose of the evaluation of the form. An often used side-effect is the *assignment* of an expression to a symbol, which is then viewed as a *variable*. This side-effect occurs as a result of evaluation of the functions `set`, `setq` and `setf`.

EXAMPLE B.4

The result of evaluating the form

```
(setq x 'a)
```

is that the variable `x` is assigned the value `a`. Note that `x` is not preceded by an apostrophe.

Another function which is also used for its side-effect is the function `print`. The value of any argument to `print` is written to the screen or to a stream given as the second argument to `print`. The function value yielded by `print` is usually not relevant. In general, all input/output functions produce side-effects.

Side-effects are required in most realistic programs, for example to gain in efficiency; furthermore, there are situations in which the use of side-effects results in a more natural solution to the problem concerned. However, it must be stressed that the use of side-effects, in particular assignment, conflicts with the basic idea of functional programming, and that unwieldy use of side-effects may lead to programs that are difficult to comprehend. A problem with side-effects is that their meaning is not captured by the simple substitution model of evaluation discussed above, since this model presupposes that the state of a LISP system is unchanged after the completion of the evaluation of a form. Hence, the substitution model does not fully describe the semantics of forms in general. A complete description of the semantics of forms is provided by the *environment model*, which subsumes the substitution model. In this model, evaluation of a form is described with respect to an environment of variables with associated values. Each element in a given environment is a *frame* of variable–value pairs, and an environment is defined as an ordered collection of such frames. During the evaluation of a form, the values of variables are looked up in the environment. Note that side-effects may modify the values variables have in the environment.

LISP offers the programmer a large number of predefined functions; some of these will be discussed in Section B.2. For some of the available predefined functions, the evaluation is somewhat different from the standard evaluation. In these cases one speaks of *special forms*. The way special forms are treated depends on the particular predefined function employed. Finally, there are several forms available in LISP which on evaluation just return themselves. These forms are called *self-evaluating forms*; all numbers and the symbols `nil` and `t` are examples of self-evaluating forms. Note that self-evaluating forms never have to be prefixed by the `quote` function when employed in some enclosing form.

B.1.3 Procedural abstraction in LISP

LISP provides the programmer with a large number of predefined or *primitive* functions, such as the functions `car` and `cdr` from the previous examples. However, like most modern programming languages LISP also offers a means for *procedural abstraction*; it is possible to combine a collection of forms into a larger composite form having an effect equivalent to the combined effects of the individual forms after parameter substitution. Such a composite form is created and given a name by means of *function definition* by employing the special form with the function name `defun`. The first argument to `defun` is the *name* of the function to be defined, the second argument is taken to be the *formal parameter list*, and the remaining arguments together constitute the *body* of the function describing its behaviour. Function definition will be illustrated by means of the following example.

EXAMPLE B.5

We shall define a LISP function *element* for checking whether or not a given element belongs to a set of elements. If the element belongs to the set, the function has to return the truth value *true*; otherwise it has to return the truth value *false*. We shall represent the set of elements as a list. In LISP the truth value *true* is represented by the symbol `t`; the truth value *false* is represented by the symbol `nil`. Note the dual meaning of the symbol `nil`. The function `element` will now be defined in a recursive manner, which is quite typical for functional programming. If the list representing the given set is empty, the given element cannot be an element of the set, and the function value `nil` is returned. If, on the other hand, the list is not empty, the element occurs in the set either if it is equal to the first expression in the list or if it occurs in the remainder of the list after removal of the first element. We obtain the following function definition:

```
(defun element (x s)
  (cond ((null s) nil)
        (t (or (equal x (first s))
               (element x (rest s))))))
```

As can be seen, the name of the function is `element`. The formal parameter list consists of two parameters `x` and `s` representing the given element and the set, respectively; the remaining forms constitute the body of the function. The primitive function `cond`, the so-called *conditional form*, in the body of the function is used to express a choice. Each argument to `cond` comprises a *test* followed by the form to be evaluated if the test succeeds. In our case the first argument to `cond` is the form `((null s) nil)` specifying the test `(null s)`. The primitive function `null` is used for investigating whether or not the list `s` is empty. If the test `(null s)` yields the truth value `t` then the next form in the first argument to `cond` is evaluated, that is, the self-evaluating form `nil`. This value `nil` will then be returned by the function, and the remaining subforms of `cond` will be ignored. However, if the test `(null s)` fails, the next argument to `cond` is evaluated; in the present case this is the form `(t (or (equal x (first s)) (element x (rest s))))`. The test in this second argument, t, always succeeds. As a consequence, the form with the function name `or` will be evaluated next. First, it is checked whether the element `x` equals the first element of `s` using the primitive function `equal`. If they are not equal, a recursive call to `element` examines whether the element `x` occurs in the remainder of the list `s`. If, on the other hand, `x` equals the first element of `s`, the test `(equal x (first s))` succeeds, and the function value `t` is returned. We shall discuss the functions `null`, `or` and `equal` in further detail in Section B.2.

In this example, we employed the primitive function `first`. This function is equivalent to the function `car` mentioned earlier. For several frequently used functions, COMMON LISP provides function names which better indicate the effect of their application than the names in the older LISP dialects do. In a small number of cases in which these older names have more or less become established in the LISP community, COMMON LISP offers the programmer both the old name of the function and the new one.

EXAMPLE B.6

The following *function calls* with associated function values indicate how the function `element` just defined may be used. The function value returned is shown following the `=>` sign.

```
(element 'a '(d e f g s a))
=> t

(element 'e '(d f g))
=> nil
```

Note that in each call both arguments to `element` have been quoted to prevent evaluation by the LISP interpreter.

B.1.4 Variables and their scopes

We have mentioned before that a LISP program is just a collection of forms. The majority of the forms in a typical LISP program are function definitions in which variables have been specified. Variables are indicated by symbols which are taken as their names. There are two ways for a variable to obtain a value. It can be *assigned* a LISP expression, which is achieved by means of one of the functions `set`, `setq` and `setf`, or it can be *bound* to a value then called its *binding*. When a new binding is created for a variable the old binding is saved in the new, expanded environment. The old binding and the corresponding environment are restored as soon as the new binding has been released. On the other hand, when a new value is assigned to a variable no new environment is created; the old value is simply overwritten by the new one (if the variable is unbound at the time of assignment, the variable–value pair is simply added to the environment). So, in the case of assignment, an old value is lost forever.

Two types of variables are distinguished: *lexical* and *special variables*. A lexical variable can be referred to only within the LISP construct in which it has been defined; only within this construct may it obtain a binding. It is said that such variables have a *lexical scope*. Lexical variables may be viewed as a kind of local variable. The notion of a lexical variable has been taken from the Algol-like programming languages. All variables occurring in a COMMON LISP program have a lexical scope by default; a special variable has to be declared as such explicitly. Special variables differ from lexical variables by the fact that one can refer to a special variable as long as the evaluation of the form in which the variable has been bound has not yet terminated. Special variables may therefore be considered as a kind of global variable. Although the scope of a lexical variable is statically determined by the program text, the scope of a special variable is determined dynamically during the execution of the program. It is therefore said that special variables have a *dynamic scope*.

EXAMPLE B.7

Consider the following two function definitions:

```
(defun Example (x y)
  (Print-Both y))

(defun Print-Both (y)
  (print x)
  (print y))
```

The function call `(Example 2 3)` yields an error message as soon as the interpreter tries to evaluate the form `(print x)`, because in the function `Print-Both` the lexical variable `x` is unbound. However, if the variable `x` has been declared as a special variable, `x` will stay bound to `2` as long as the evaluation of the body of `Example` has not been completed. In this case the function `Example` will successively return the values `2` and `3`.

The primitive function `defvar` may be applied to declare a variable as being special. This function always associates an initial value with the newly declared variable.

EXAMPLE B.8

After evaluation of the form:

```
(defvar x)
```

the variable `x` will be considered by the LISP interpreter as being special. Optionally, a second argument may be specified to the function `defvar`, which will be assigned to the variable. If no second argument is specified, as in this example, the variable will obtain the initial value `nil`.

B.2 Overview of the language LISP

As has been mentioned in the introduction, LISP is particularly strong in symbol manipulation. To this end, LISP offers a large number of language facilities. However, a complete enumeration, let alone a full description of the language facilities provided by COMMON LISP, would go far beyond the intention of this appendix. In this section we merely consider the most important features of COMMON LISP. Many of the language constructs described here have one or more options for handling special cases. Since in this book few of the options are actually used, we will describe them only in exceptional cases.

B.2.1 Symbol manipulation

The primitive LISP functions most widely known, even among non-LISP programmers, are those for list processing. It is from the emphasis on the manipulation of lists and symbols that LISP is commonly known as a language for symbol manipulation. In this section, a selected number of symbol-manipulation functions will be discussed.

Some primitive functions for list processing

In Section B.1 we encountered the functions `first` and `rest`. The function `first`, also called `car`, takes a list (or dotted pair) as an argument, and returns the first element of its argument as a function value. The function `rest`, also called `cdr`, equally takes a list (or dotted pair) as an argument, but returns the list that results after removal of the first element of the original list.

EXAMPLE B.9

Consider the following calls to the functions `first` and `rest` and the function values returned by the LISP interpreter:

```
(first '(a b c d))
=> a

(rest '(a b c d e))
=> (b c d e)

(rest '(a))
=> nil
```

Note that the last call upon evaluation returns the empty list `nil` in accord with the discussion of the relationship between dotted pairs and lists in Section B.1.1.

The functions `car` and `cdr` select the first and the remaining elements from a list, respectively. The other elements of a list may be selected by means of a composite call to these functions.

EXAMPLE B.10

The second element in the list `(a b c)` is obtained as follows:

```
(car (cdr '(a b c)))
=> b
```

For composite combinations of calls to `car` and `cdr`, LISP offers a convenient abbreviation. The following abbreviated function calls and their meanings illustrate the general idea:

```
(cadr  <list>) ≡ (car (cdr <list>))
(caadr <list>) ≡ (car (car (cdr <list>)))
(caddr <list>) ≡ (car (cdr (cdr <list>)))
(cdadr <list>) ≡ (cdr (car (cdr <list>)))
```

In addition, LISP offers the function `nth` for selecting the $(n + 1)$th subexpression from a list.

EXAMPLE B.11

The following function call and its returned function value illustrate the use of the primitive function `nth`:

```
(nth 2 '(a b c d))
=> c
```

Functions for retrieving data such as the ones discussed above are often called *selector functions*. Besides these selector functions, LISP also provides a number of primitive functions for constructing new lists. Such functions are called *constructor functions*. An important constructor function is the function `list`, which builds a new list from the values of its arguments. The function `append` takes zero or more lists as its arguments and concatenates them. The function `cons` is used for combining two expressions by taking them as the car and the cdr of a newly created dotted pair. Note that the functions `list` and `append` may take an arbitrary number of arguments, whereas the function `cons` takes precisely two arguments. If possible, the LISP interpreter presents the results after evaluation of a form specifying a constructor function to the user in list notation instead of as a dotted pair. The following example demonstrates the use of these constructor functions.

EXAMPLE B.12

Consider the following function calls and the return function values:

```
(list)
=> nil

(list 'a '(b c))
=> (a (b c))

(list '(a b) '(c d))
=> ((a b) (c d))

(append '(a b) '(c d))
=> (a b c d)

(cons 'a 'b)
=> (a . b)

(cons '(a b) '(c d))
=> ((a b) c d)
```

Note the differences in the results obtained by these functions when applied to the same arguments.

In addition to the selector and constructor functions discussed above, LISP further provides a number of *mutator functions*. A mutator function modifies its list argument by means of a side-effect. These functions are dangerous because they have an effect that goes far beyond the form in which they are applied, and they must therefore be used with great care. Typical examples of mutator functions are the functions `rplaca` and `rplacd`, and the function `setf`. The first two functions replace the car and the cdr, respectively, of their first argument by the second argument.

EXAMPLE B.13

Consider the following function calls to the primitive functions `rplaca` and `rplacd` and the returned function values:

```
(rplaca '(a b c) 'd)
=> (d b c)

(rplacd '(a b c) 'd)
=> (a . d)
```

As can be seen, the values returned by these functions are their modified first arguments.

In a function call to `rplaca` or `rplacd`, a variable may be specified as a first argument to the function. In that case the value of the variable will be modified by the function as a side-effect.

The function `setf`, whose name stands for *set field*, is the generalized version of the assignment function `setq`. The `setq` function just evaluates its second argument and assigns the result to its first argument. The `setf` function, however, first evaluates its first argument yielding a memory address, a so-called *place*, and then assigns the value of the second argument to that place.

EXAMPLE B.14

Let us demonstrate the side-effects of applying the functions `rplaca` and `setf` on the value of a given variable:

```
(setq x '(a b))
=> (a b)

(rplaca x 'b)
=> (b b)

x
=> (b b)

(setf (cadr 'x) 'a)
=> a

x
=> (b a)
```

Note that `setq` and `setf` return the value of their last argument, whereas `rplaca` returns its modified first argument.

The property list

In the preceding section we have mentioned that LISP symbols may be used as variables, which can then be assigned certain values or bound to values. Data, however, can also be stored in a so-called *property list* or *p-list* of a symbol. In LISP, each symbol has an associated p-list, which is initially empty. A p-list is a sequence of pairs, in which each pair consists of a symbol and an expression. The first element of a pair is called the *indicator* or the *property name*; the second element is called the *property value* or simply the *value*.

The indicator is used in retrieving a property value. A value is extracted from the p-list by means of the primitive function `get`. This function takes two arguments; the first argument is a LISP symbol, and the second argument is an indicator. On evaluation of a call to the function `get`, the value associated with the indicator in the p-list of the specified symbol is returned.

EXAMPLE B.15

Consider the symbol `patient` having the following p-list:

```
(age 20 disorder jaundice)
```

which consists of two pairs: `(age . 20)` and `(disorder . jaundice)`. The following function calls yield the following results:

```
(get 'patient 'disorder)
=> jaundice

(get 'patient 'age)
=> 20

(get 'patient 'name)
=> nil
```

A p-list is constructed by means of a call to the function `get` in combination with a call to the function `setf`. A pair can be removed from a given p-list by means of the function `remprop` by providing the indicator of the pair that must be removed as an argument. Upon evaluation the function `remprop` returns the pair that has been removed; the rest of the p-list remains unchanged.

EXAMPLE B.16

Consider again the symbol `patient` with its associated p-list from the preceding example. Suppose that we want to add the property `complaints` to the symbol `patient`. This can be accomplished as shown below:

```
(setf (get 'patient 'complaints) '(anorexia nausea))
=> (anorexia nausea)
```

The resulting p-list is now as follows:

```
(complaints (anorexia nausea) age 20 disorder jaundice)
```

The following call to the primitive function `remprop`:

```
(remprop 'patient 'age)
=> (age 20)
```

results in the removal of the pair with the indicator `age` from the p-list. After this deletion we have:

```
(get 'patient 'age)
=> nil
```

The association list

By means of a p-list we can store data with a symbol; accessing the thus stored data is straightforward. Another, similar means for storage and retrieval of data is offered by the so-called *association list* or *a-list* for short. Unlike p-lists, association lists are not associated with symbols; an a-list is an ordinary list having dotted pairs as elements. The first element of a dotted pair in an a-list is used as the *key* for retrieval of the second element. For selecting data from an a-list, LISP offers a primitive function called `assoc`. This function takes two arguments; the first argument is a key and the second is the a-list to be searched for the key. The function `assoc` returns the dotted pair in which the key occurs or `nil` if the key does not occur in the specified a-list. In addition to the function `assoc` LISP provides the function `rassoc`, which differs from `assoc` by taking the second element of a dotted pair in an a-list as the key.

EXAMPLE B.17

Consider the following function calls and returned function values:

```
(assoc 'age '((age . 20) (disorder . jaundice)))
=> (age . 20)

(rassoc 'jaundice '((age . 20) (disorder . jaundice)))
=> (disorder . jaundice)

(assoc 'x '((y . z)))
=> nil
```

B.2.2 Predicates

In Section B.1.3, we encountered the function `null`, which specified a test. This function is called a *predicate*. A predicate is a function that performs a test on its arguments. If the test fails, the value `nil`, representing the truth value *false*, is returned; otherwise a value not equal to `nil` is returned. Generally the value `t` is returned; however, sometimes a more informative value is yielded.

Data-type predicates

LISP provides the programmer with a large variety of predicates for investigating the data type of a particular LISP expression, for example for finding out whether it is a list, an atom, a number, an array or a function.

The predicate `atom` investigates whether or not its argument is an atom. If this turns out to be the case, the value `t` is returned; otherwise it returns the value `nil`.

EXAMPLE B.18

Consider the following function calls:

```
(atom 'a)
=> t

(atom 2)
=> t

(atom '(a b))
=> nil
```

So non-empty lists are not atoms but numbers are.

For finding out whether a LISP expression is a symbol or a number, we have the predicates `symbolp` and `numberp` at our disposal. The predicate `listp` tests whether its argument is a list.

EXAMPLE B.19

The following function calls and the function values returned show the behaviour of the predicates mentioned above:

```
(symbolp 'a)
=> t

(symbolp 2)
=> nil
```

```
(numberp 2)
=> t

(numberp 'a)
=> nil

(symbolp '(a b))
=> nil

(listp '(a b))
=> nil

(listp '(a . b))
=> nil

(listp 'a)
=> nil
```

Now let us look at the following example concerning the empty list.

EXAMPLE B.20

Consider the following four forms:

```
(atom nil)
=> t

(atom '( ))
=> t

(listp nil)
=> t

(listp '( ))
=> t
```

This example shows that the empty list, `nil`, is an exception to the general rule that an expression is either an atom or a list; it is both. Furthermore, it shows that it makes no difference whether the notation `nil` or `( )` is used for the representation of the empty list.

This explains why the special predicate `null` is required to test whether its argument is of the type 'empty list'.

EXAMPLE B.21

The use of the predicate `null` is illustrated by means of the following function calls:

```
(null nil)
=> t

(null '(a))
=> nil

(null 'a)
=> nil
```

Relational predicates

The predicate `equal` takes two arguments and tests whether its two arguments represent the same expression. It examines numbers as well as atoms and lists on equality. To be equal, numbers must be of the same type, such as integer or float. The predicate `equal` checks the equality of arguments without restricting to information with regard to their internal representation. In contrast, the predicate `eq` investigates whether its arguments are stored at the same memory location, that is, have the same memory address. If two arguments are equal according to `eq`, they are equal according to `equal` as well. However, the reverse does not hold. When specifying the predicate `eq` instead of `equal`, the programmer has to be sure which data will and which data will not have been stored at the same memory location. This is partly system dependent; in every LISP system, however, symbols with the same name are equal according to `eq`.

EXAMPLE B.22

Consider the following LISP forms demonstrating the behaviour of the two equality predicates:

```
(equal 'a 'a)
=> t

(eq 'a 'a)
=> t

(equal '(a b) '(a b))
=> t

(eq '(a b) '(a b))
=> nil

(equal 'a '(a b))
=> nil

(equal 3 2)
=> nil
```

Table B.1 Meaning of numeric predicates.

Predicate	*Meaning*
=	All arguments are equal
/=	Not all arguments are equal
<	Arguments are monotonically increasing
>	Arguments are monotonically decreasing
<=	Arguments are monotonically non-decreasing
>=	Arguments are monotonically non-increasing

```
(equal 2 2)
=> t

(equal 2 2.0)
=> nil
```

Numbers are usually tested on equality using the special predicate =, which automatically converts its arguments to the same data type. The predicate = takes one or more numeric arguments. For comparing numbers, several other numeric relational predicates are available as well. These predicates are described in Table B.1.

EXAMPLE B.23

The following examples demonstrate the use of the numeric predicates:

```
(= 2 2.0 2e+0)
=> t

(= 2 3 2)
=> nil

(= 2 2 2 2 2)
=> t

(< 0 1 2 3 4 5)
=> t

(> 5 3 2 1 1 0)
=> nil

(>= 5 3 2 1 1 0)
=> t
```

The predefined predicate `member` takes two arguments: an expression (often a symbol) and a list. The predicate investigates whether or not the expression is equal, according to `eq`, to one of the elements in the list. If the given expression occurs in the list, the function returns as its function value the part of the list from, and including, the given expression until the end of the list; otherwise it returns `nil`.

EXAMPLE B.24

Consider the following two function calls:

```
(member 'b '(a b c d))
=> (b c d)

(member 'f '(a b c d))
=> nil
```

As can be seen, the first call to the function `member` succeeds and returns the sublist starting with the element `b` instead of just `t`. The second `member` call fails since `f` does not occur in the given list, and therefore the value `nil` is returned.

Because `member` uses the predicate `eq` to check on equality, it actually examines whether a given expression occupies the same memory location as one of the elements in the given list. Therefore, this version of the member predicate is generally not applicable to finding out whether a given list occurs in a nested list. However, by means of a special `:test` keyword option, we may indicate which equality predicate must be used internally as a test. The same applies to the predicates `assoc` and `rassoc`, which also use the predicate `eq` by default. The following example demonstrates the practical consequence of this option.

EXAMPLE B.25

Consider the following function calls to `member`. In the second function call we have indicated that the predicate `equal` must be used internally for comparison instead of the predicate `eq`:

```
(member '(b c) '(a (b c) (d e)))
=> nil

(member '(b c) '(a (b c) (d e)) :test #'equal)
=> ((b c) (d e))
```

Logic predicates

To conclude this section, a number of logic predicates is discussed. The predicate `not` yields the function value `t` if its argument is the empty list; otherwise it returns the value of its argument unmodified. In fact, the predicate has the same effect as the function `null` discussed earlier.

EXAMPLE B.26

We know that evaluation of the form `(= 2 3)` yields the value `nil`; the function value returned from prefixing this form by the predicate `not` therefore yields the value `t`:

```
(not (= 2 3))
=> t
```

The predicate `and` evaluates its zero or more arguments from left to right, until an argument is encountered which on evaluation returns the value `nil`; then the evaluation stops and the value `nil` is returned. If none of the arguments yields the value `nil` on evaluation, the value of the last evaluated argument is returned. The predicate `or` also takes zero or more arguments and equally evaluates them from left to right, but this time until some argument is met yielding a value not equal to `nil`. This value is then the function value of `or`; otherwise the value `nil` is returned.

EXAMPLE B.27

The behaviour of the predicates `and` and `or` is illustrated by means of the following function calls:

```
(and (> 3 2)
     (equal 'a 'a))
=> t

(or (null 'a)
    (member 'a '(b a c)))
=> (a c)
```

B.2.3 Control structures

COMMON LISP offers the programmer a rich variety of modern control structures. In this section, we shall discuss the conditional and iterative control structures. Furthermore, we shall examine a special type of control structure for extending an environment by creating new bindings for variables.

Conditional control structures

In the older dialects of LISP, the main conditional control structure provided for formulating a choice between alternatives was the function `cond`. This function is still available in COMMON LISP, but in addition a number of simpler conditional control structures is provided. We start our exposition with these functions.

The function `if` takes two or three arguments. Its first argument is a *test*; the second argument is called the *then part* and will be evaluated if the specified test succeeds. The optional third argument is called the *else part* and will be evaluated if the test fails.

EXAMPLE B.28

In the following function call to `if` the previously discussed predicate `=` is applied:

```
(if (= 2 3)      ; test
    'equal       ; then part
    'not-equal) ; else part
=> not-equal
```

The `if` form is usually applied in situations in which a choice has to be made between two distinct function calls both yielding relevant function values. An alternative for using the `if` form with only the then part is to use the `when` form. The function `when` takes one or more arguments. Its first argument specifies a test; if evaluation of this test yields a value not equal to `nil`, all subsequent forms, called the body of `when`, are evaluated. Note that contrary to the `if` form the body of `when` may comprise more than one form. The value returned by the function `when` is `nil` if the specified test fails, and the value of the last form in the body otherwise. The function `when` is normally used for conditionally producing side-effects; its function value is then irrelevant. The function `unless` is similar to the function `when`, except that its body is evaluated if the test specified in its first argument fails.

EXAMPLE B.29

Consider the following function call to `when`:

```
(when (member 'a '(a b c ))
  (setq x 2)
  (* x 3))
=> 6
```

The body of `when` contains two forms. The first form is an assignment to the variable `x`, which is subsequently used in the second form.

The function `cond` is more complicated than the control structures we have treated so far. The use of this function has already been discussed briefly in Section B.1.3. The function takes zero or more arguments, each of which is a list, generally called a *clause*. The first expression in each clause denotes a *test*. The clauses of `cond` are evaluated in the order of their specification. The first clause of which the test succeeds will be further executed; of this clause only the remaining forms, called the *consequents*, are evaluated. The `cond` form returns as its function value the value of the last evaluated consequent. The remaining clauses are skipped.

EXAMPLE B.30

Consider again the `cond` form introduced in Section B.1.3:

```
(cond ((null s) nil)
      (t (or (equal x (first s))
             (element x (rest s)))))
```

This form comprises two clauses. The test in the second clause, `t`, always succeeds. However, the first clause is always evaluated before the second one; if the test in the first clause `(null s)` succeeds, the second clause is skipped.

Iterative control structures

The formulation of an algorithm in LISP is often carried out in a recursive manner, which generally results in a function that is both more perspicuous and elegant than a similar iterative specification would have been. However, there are algorithms which can be better expressed using an iterative control structure. Fortunately, COMMON LISP offers a number of iterative control structures for this purpose.

The most general iterative function provided in COMMON LISP is the function `do`. The syntax of the `do` form is:

```
(do ( {(<var> <init-form> <step-form>)}*)
    (<test-form> . <result-form>)
  <body>)
```

On evaluation of a `do` form, first all function values of the initialization forms specified in <init-form> are determined. These values are subsequently bound to the corresponding variables given in <var>. If an <init-form> is lacking, the corresponding variable in <var> is initialized with the value `nil`. The evaluation of the forms in <init-form> is carried out in a non-deterministic order and can best be considered as being done in parallel. The scope of each of the variables in <var> is the body of the `do` form. So these variables are lexical. After this initialization has been completed, the test form specified in <test-form> is evaluated. If the test succeeds, that is, if it yields a value different from `nil`, the iteration terminates and the forms in the <result-form> are evaluated. The function value of `do` is the value of the last evaluated form from the <result-form>. If, on the other hand, the test fails, then the forms in the <body> are evaluated next. Following the evaluation of the body, each of the forms specified in the <step-form> is evaluated, again in some non-deterministic order. The values yielded by these forms are subsequently taken as the new bindings of the variables in <var>. If no <step-form> has been specified for a variable, its binding is left unchanged.

EXAMPLE B.31

Consider the following form for adding up the first hundred elements of an array `x`:

```
(do ((i 0 (+ i 1))
     (sum 0))
    ((= i 100) sum)
  (setq sum (+ sum (aref x i))))
```

In this form, we have two subexpressions of the form (<var> <init-form> <step-form>): the subform `(i 0 (+ i 1))` which increments the variable by one at each iteration step, and the subform `(sum 0)`. In the latter subform a <step-form> is lacking; hence, the value of `sum` is not modified when the next iteration step starts. The variable `sum`, however, is changed as a result of evaluation of the body of the `do` form. The value of the variable `sum` is returned as soon as the variable `i` has attained the value 100. The form `(aref x i)` extracts the `i`th element from the array `x`. The first element in the array has index 0.

The `do` form just discussed is sometimes called the *parallel do form*. There also exists a *sequential do form*, the `do*` form, which differs from the parallel `do` form by its init and step forms being evaluated one by one in the order in which they have been specified. Each value resulting from the evaluation of an init or step form is bound to the associated variable immediately after the value has been obtained. In this way it becomes possible to refer in an init or step form to a variable which has obtained a binding in some earlier evaluated init or step form. The syntax of the `do*` form is, with the obvious exception of the function name, the same as for `do`.

For many common situations the `do` form is too general. Therefore, some simpler iterative control structures are also available. Here, we discuss only one of the most frequently used iterative forms: the `dolist` form. The syntax of the `dolist` form is:

```
(dolist (<var> <list-form> <result-form>)
  <body>)
```

In this form, <list-form> has to be a list of expressions, which are bound successively to the variable <var>; after each binding the <body> is evaluated. As soon as all elements in the <list-form> have been processed, the value of <result-form> is returned as a function value of `dolist`.

EXAMPLE B.32

Consider the following form:

```
(dolist (x '(a b c d))
  (prin1 x))
abcd
=> nil
```

First, the variable `x` is bound to the symbol `a` and the body of `dolist` prints the value of `x`. Next, the variable `x` is bound to `b`, and so on. In this way, the symbols `a` up to `d` inclusive are printed successively. Since we have not specified a <result-form> in the example, the function returns the value `nil`.

Local bindings of variables

For creating a new binding for a variable in a new environment, generally the `let` form is employed. The syntax of this form is as follows:

```
(let ( { (<var> <init-form>) }*)
  <body>)
```

Upon evaluation of the `let` form, first the values of the forms in the <init-form> are determined. These values are then bound to the corresponding variables in <var>. Evaluation of the init forms is done in a non-deterministic order just as in the parallel `do` form. After this initialization, the body of the `let` form is evaluated. The function value returned by `let` is obtained from the evaluation of the last form present in the body. The `let` form is usually applied for introducing local, lexical variables; the scope of these variables is the body of the form. After the evaluation of the `let` form has been terminated, the old environment of variable bindings will be re-established.

EXAMPLE B.33

Consider the following function definition:

```
(defun Example (x)
  (print x)
  (let ((x 2))
    (print x))
  (print x))
```

When the function `Example` is called with the argument `1`, the values `1`, `2` and `1` are printed successively.

Since the ordinary `let` form evaluates all forms in <init-form> in some non-deterministic order, it is called the *parallel let form.* LISP also offers a *sequential let form*, called the `let*` form, which evaluates its init forms in the order of specification; immediately after a value for an init form has been determined, it binds this value to the associated variable.

EXAMPLE B.34

In the form below we have to use two `let` forms for computing (a finite approximation to) sin($\frac{1}{2}\pi$):

```
(let ((pi 3.1415926))
  (let ((x (* pi 0.5)))
    (sin x)))
```

In the first `let` form we bind the variable `pi` to the appropriate value. For binding the variable `x` to the value $\frac{1}{2}\pi$, we need to access the value the variable `pi` has obtained. For this purpose we have to introduce into the enclosing `let` form another `let` form with the init form `(* pi 0.5)`. The same, however, can be accomplished with one `let*` form only:

```
(let* ((pi 3.1415926)
       (x (* pi 0.5)))
  (sin x))
```

B.2.4 The lambda expression

In Section B.1.3 we described how a new function may be defined using the `defun` form. A major disadvantage of the discussed function definition is that we have to specify a function name for a new function in cases in which we need it only once in the program. For this purpose of function definition without naming, the so-called *lambda expression*, is available. A lambda expression is specified by means of a `lambda` form as follows:

((lambda <parameter-list> <body>) <arg-list>)

where <parameter-list> is the list of formal parameters and <arg-list> is the argument list. Upon evaluation of a `lambda` form, first the arguments are substituted one by one for the corresponding parameters, before the body is evaluated. The following example illustrates the application of the `lambda` expression.

EXAMPLE B.35

Consider the following function definition:

```
(defun Hypotenuse (a b)
  (sqrt (+ (* a a) (* b b))))
```

This function may be called as follows:

```
(Hypotenuse 3 4)
=> 5
```

If the function `Hypotenuse` is called only once in the entire program, there is no need to introduce a new function name. In this case we might use the following lambda expression instead:

```
((lambda (a b) (sqrt (+ (* a a) (* b b)))) 3 4)
=> 5
```

which returns the same result. The list `(a b)` following the symbol `lambda` is the list of formal parameters of the lambda expression. The numbers `3` and `4` are the arguments to the nameless function; their values are substituted for the formal parameters `a` and `b`, respectively, before the body of the `lambda` form is evaluated.

The lambda expression is normally applied in conjunction with the function `funcall`, which will be discussed in the next section.

B.2.5 Enforcing evaluation by the LISP interpreter

At the beginning of this appendix we mentioned that in LISP it is possible to interpret data as programs. To this end LISP offers several primitive functions, the most frequently applied of which are `eval`, `apply` and `funcall`.

The function `eval` may be considered as a kind of interface to the LISP interpreter. In fact, any form presented to LISP is evaluated using `eval` implicitly; it is this function that defines the standard evaluation rule. If we enter an explicit call to `eval` to LISP, its argument is evaluated twice: once by the standard evaluation rule, which then passes the resulting value of the argument to the function `eval`, where it is evaluated for the second time. The function value returned by the function `eval` is the result of this second evaluation.

EXAMPLE B.36

Consider the following call to `eval`:

```
(eval (list '+ '(first '(2 3)) 4))
=> 6
```

The LISP evaluator first evaluates the argument to `eval`. It returns the following form: `(+ (first '(2 3)) 4)`. Subsequent evaluation of this form by `eval` yields the value `6`.

The function `apply` takes a form specifying a function name or lambda expression as its first argument; its remaining one or more arguments are LISP expressions to which the function or lambda expression has to be applied. These expressions are concatenated and then passed as an argument list to the specified function or lambda expression. The function name or the lambda expression must be specified in the special `function` form. The effect of `function` is similar to `quote`; it inhibits evaluation.

EXAMPLE B.37

Consider the following call to `apply`:

```
(apply (function element) 'a '((b a c)))
=> t
```

It specifies the function `element` defined in Section B.1.3. Upon evaluation of the `apply` form, this function is applied to the symbol `a` and the list `(b a c)`. Note that we have to specify `'((b a c))` since the expressions `'a` and `'((b a c))` are concatenated before they are passed to `element`.

Instead of `function` we may also use the symbol `#'`, which is an abbreviation for the function `function`, in a similar way as `'` is an abbreviation for the function `quote`. In the previous example, the first argument to `apply` may therefore be specified as `#'element`. The main difference between `quote` and `function` is that the latter takes the bindings of the lexical variables into account when the given function `element` is evaluated. It is said that `function` handles the symbol `element` as a *lexical closure*.

The function `funcall` has much in common with the function `apply`. Just like the function `apply`, the function `funcall` takes a function name or a lambda expression as its first argument, but in contrast to `apply` it takes *zero* or more further arguments. Furthermore the function `funcall` just applies the specified function or lambda expression to its remaining arguments.

EXAMPLE B.38

Consider the following function call:

```
(funcall #'+ 1 2 3 4 5 6)
=> 21
```

It yields the sum of the six specified numbers by applying the function `+` to them.

Until now, we have demonstrated in our examples the use of `apply` and `funcall` only in conjunction with a function. The functions `apply` and `funcall`, however, may also be used together with a lambda expression.

EXAMPLE B.39

Evaluation of the form:

```
(funcall #'(lambda (a b) (sqrt (+ (* a a) (* b b)))) 3 4)
```

yields the same result as the evaluation of the lambda expression given in the previous section.

A compact notation for repeated application of a function or lambda expression to successive arguments is offered by the function `mapc`. This function applies its first argument, which has to be a function or a lambda expression, to all elements of the second argument which has to be a list. The function `mapc` is often employed in conjunction with a function having side-effects.

EXAMPLE B.40

In this example, we use the function `mapc` for successively printing the elements of a list:

```
(mapc #'print '(a b c))
a
b
c
=> nil
```

B.2.6 Macro definition and the backquote

Besides the function definition, COMMON LISP provides yet another method for dynamically extending the language: *macro definition.* A macro is invoked in a way similar to a function. However, the arguments to a macro call are *not* evaluated before the call is actually executed. In evaluating a macro call the arguments are immediately substituted for the corresponding formal parameters which also occur in the body of the macro. This process of substitution is known as *macro expansion.* The form resulting from macro expansion is evaluated.

A macro is defined by means of `defmacro`. The following example illustrates the principal idea. In this example the body of the macro definition contains the *backquote function*: `. The main effect of this function is similar to that of the `quote` function; it switches off evaluation temporarily. However, there is a difference. In contrast with the `quote` function, when the backquote function is used it is possible to switch on the evaluation selectively by means of the specification of a comma; if some formal parameter is preceded by a comma, it will be substituted by the corresponding argument.

EXAMPLE B.41

In Section B.2.2 we discussed a number of conditional control structures. Now, suppose that the `if` function was no part of the COMMON LISP language; then we might think of adding this special form to the LISP system by means of the following function definition:

```
(defun other-if (condition then-part else-part) ; bugged!
  (cond ((condition) then-part)
        (t else-part)))
```

Now look at the following function call:

```
(other-if (equal 'a 'a) (print 'equal) (print 'not-equal))
```

Upon evaluation the values `equal` and `not-equal` are printed successively, and then an error is signalled. This is explained as follows. Before the function other-if is applied, its three arguments are evaluated first, so the test, the then part and the else part are evaluated, which results in the values equal and not-equal being printed. This clearly was not our intention. The problem can be solved by preceding each argument to other-if by quote, and then applying the function eval in the body of the given function. This solution is not very satisfactory since prefixing each argument in every call to other-if by a quote is undesirable. The best solution to this problem is obtained by using a macro definition. We may obtain the following macro definition for the special other-if form:

```
(defmacro other-if (condition then-part else-part)
  '(cond (,condition ,then-part)
         (t ,else-part)))
```

Upon evaluation of the macro other-if, first its actual arguments are substituted for the corresponding parameters, which are preceded by a comma. The form that results is subsequently evaluated. Readers should convince themselves that the call to other-if shown above has the required effect when employing the defined macro.

B.2.7 The structure

We have seen before that LISP supports *data abstraction* in a flexible way by offering a rich variety of data structures and possibilities for function and macro definition. So it is a relatively straightforward task to implement in LISP various data types with associated constructor and selector functions. However, most conventional data types are already built in. This is the case for a data type similar to the record data type in Pascal-like languages, namely the *structure*, which consists of a number of components called *fields* or *slots*, each having a unique name. A structure type is defined by means of the function defstruct. The arguments to this function are the name of the new structure type and its successive fields, possibly provided with initial values. If no initial values have been specified for a field, it is initialized with the value nil by default.

EXAMPLE B.42

The following function call defines a new structure type with the name person:

```
(defstruct person
  (name)
  (age 30)
  (married 'no))
```

The new structure type has three fields: `name`, `age` and `married`. These fields initially have the values `nil`, `30` and `no`, respectively.

For each structure type we have a so-called *constructor function* at our disposal for creating a new structure of the given structure type. The name of the constructor function is composed of the name of the structure type preceded by the symbol `make-`. In creating a new structure, it is possible to specify new initial values for the fields. Each field is referred to by means of a keyword which is composed of the name of the field prefixed by a colon.

EXAMPLE B.43

The following form assigns a structure of type `person` to the variable with the name `a-person`:

```
(setq a-person (make-person :name 'john :age 20))
```

By means of the keyword `:name` the value `john` is filled in for the field `name`; similarly the field `age` is assigned the initial value `20`. The field `married` has not been specified explicitly; its value is therefore copied unchanged from the original structure.

As soon as a structure type is defined, a number of so-called *selector functions* is also created, one for each field, for accessing the values of the fields. The name of a selector function is composed of the name of the structure type followed by a minus sign, which in turn is followed by the required field name.

EXAMPLE B.44

Consider once more the variable `a-person`, which has been assigned a structure of type `person`. When we apply the selector function `person-name` to `a-person`, we obtain the value of the field `name`:

```
(person-name a-person)
=> john
```

With the definition of a structure type, a *copier function* is also created for making copies of structures. The name of the copier function is `copy-` followed by the name of the structure to be copied.

B.2.8 Input and output

To conclude this brief introduction to LISP, a number of input and output functions will be described.

The primitive function `load` reads LISP forms from a data file, the name of which is specified as an argument to `load`. Upon evaluation, `load` dynamically adds the declarations, functions and macros present in the file to the LISP environment.

EXAMPLE B.45

The following function call:

```
(load "example")
```

results in reading in the forms present in the file with the name `example`.

Using `load` the forms read from file are evaluated. It is also possible to read expressions from a file without evaluation. This can be done using the function `read`, which reads one LISP expression at a time; to read a single line from the file, which need not be an entire LISP expression, the function `read-line` may be used. Both `read` and `read-line` assume by default that the input is entered from the keyboard. However, by opening a file by means of a call to the primitive function `open`, an input stream is created which redirects the input to a file which can then be read.

EXAMPLE B.46

Suppose that the file `example` contains the single expression `(a b c)`. This expression can be read in as follows:

```
(let ((file (open "example")))
  (read file))
=> (a b c)
```

The function value returned by the function `open` is either an *input* or an *output stream*. The function `close` can be used for closing an input or output stream. A frequently applied form for processing data from a file is:

```
(let ((file (open "example")))
  (Process file)
  (close file))
```

The most often used function for printing an expression is the function `print`. This function creates a new line, then prints the expression which is the value of its argument and pads it by one blank. Printing is a side-effect; the value of `print` is equal to the function value of its argument but is usually ignored in the program.

EXAMPLE B.47

The following function call illustrates the behaviour of the function `print`:

```
(print 'a)
a
=> a
```

In addition to the function `print`, LISP offers three other functions for producing output. The function `prin1` prints its argument, just as `print` does, but does not start the output on a new line and does not add a blank. The function `princ` is especially designed for producing user-friendly output. The behaviour of these functions is demonstrated in the following example.

EXAMPLE B.48

Consider the following three function calls to the output functions discussed above. Note the difference in the output of these functions when applied to the same argument:

```
(print "Enter value:")
"Enter value:"
=> "Enter value:"

(prin1 "Enter value:")"Enter value:"
=> "Enter value:"

(princ "Enter value:")Enter value:
=> "Enter value:"
```

LISP also offers a so-called *pretty print function*, called `pprint`. This function is less frequently applied than the print functions described above. The advantage of this function is that it produces its output in a formatted way.

The function `terpri` is used for directing future output to a new line.

EXAMPLE B.49

By combining the functions `terpri` and `prin1` the output is printed on a new line. Without the call to the function `terpri` the output would immediately follow the specification of the `let` form:

```
(let ((x 2))
  (terpri)
  (prin1 x))
2
=> 2
```

It should be noted that no blank is added at the end of the output line, so the result still differs from that produced by `print`.

An output function with a large number of options is the function `format`. This function is a powerful tool for producing nice-looking formatted output. In this book, it suffices to give a small number of examples covering the most frequent applications of `format`.

EXAMPLE B.50

Consider the following function calls and their associated side-effects and function values:

```
(setq x '(a b c))
=> (a b c)

(format t "~%Value: ~A" x)
Value: (a b c)
=> Value: (a b c)

(format t "~%The list ~A contains three elements" x)
The list (a b c) contains three elements
=> The list (a b c) contains three elements
```

The first argument to `format` in the two function calls given above is `t`, indicating that the output should be sent to the screen. The second argument to `format` is a format string which may contain some control characters. The effect of the control character `~%` in the above examples is that the output starts on a new line; the character `~A` specifies the location in the format string where the value of the third argument should be substituted.

To conclude, the function `y-or-n-p` takes an optional format string as an argument. Upon evaluation, this format string is printed, after which the LISP evaluator awaits input from the user. As input only one of 'y' and 'n' is accepted. The function `y-or-n-p` returns as function value `t` if 'y' has been entered, and `nil` if 'n' has been entered.

EXAMPLE B.51

The following function call to `y-or-n-p` demonstrates the behaviour of the function:

```
(y-or-n-p "~%Are you ill? ")
Are you ill? y
=> t
```

Suggested reading

The history of LISP has been discussed by J. McCarthy (1978b). Sammet (1969) also pays attention to the history of LISP. The basic principles of the language have been treated by J. McCarthy (1978a); this paper includes a full listing of a LISP evaluator. Information on OBJ can be found in Futatsugi *et al.* (1985), MACSYMA is discussed in Moses (1978), and the Boyer–Moore theorem prover is covered in Boyer and Moore (1988). Most large LISP programs, including the ones mentioned above, are now available in COMMON LISP.

The COMMON LISP standard is defined in the book of G.L. Steele (1984), which every COMMON LISP programmer should possess. Introductory books on the language containing a lot of useful programming examples include Winston and Horn (1989) and Brooks (1985). An interesting book which discusses various sorts of data abstraction and procedural abstraction in the LISP dialect SCHEME is Abelson *et al.* (1985). This book also deals with programming style, and discusses several useful implementation techniques.

There is currently much work going on to extend COMMON LISP by an object-oriented subsystem called COMMON LISP OBJECT SYSTEM, or CLOS for short. A preliminary definition of CLOS is given in Bobrow *et al.* (1988). PORTABLE COMMON LOOPS (PCL) is an experimental CLOS-like object-oriented extension to COMMON LISP which is available from the Xerox Corporation, Palo Alto.

References

Abelson, H., Sussman, G.J., and Sussman, J. (1985). *Structure and Interpretation of Computer Programs*. Cambridge, MA: MIT Press

Aikins, J.S. (1980). *Prototypes and Production Rules: a Knowledge Representation for Computer Consultations*. Report no. STAN-CS-80-814, Computer Science Department, Stanford University, Stanford, CA

Aikins, J.S. (1983). Prototypical knowledge for expert systems. *Artificial Intelligence*, **20**, 163–210

Aikins, J.S., Kunz, J.C., Shortliffe, E.H. and Fallat, R.J. (1984). PUFF: an expert system for interpretation of pulmonary function data. In *Readings in Medical Artificial Intelligence: The First Decade* (Clancey, B.C. and Shortliffe, E.H., eds.). Reading, MA: Addison-Wesley

Aït-Kaci, H. and Nasr, R. (1986). LOGIN: a logic programming language with built-in inheritance. *Journal of Logic Programming*, **3**, 185–215

Bankavitz, R.A., McNeil, M.A., Challinor, S.M. *et al.* (1989). A computer-assisted medical diagnostic consultation services implementation and prospective evaluation of a prototype. *Annals of Internal Medicine*, **110**, 824–32

Barr, A. and Davidson, J. (1980). *Representation of Knowledge, a Section of the Handbook of Artificial Intelligence*. Report no. STAN-CS-80-793, Computer Science Department, Stanford University, Stanford, CA

Bennett, J.S., Creary, L., Englemore, R. and Melosh, R. (1978). *SACON: A Knowledge-Based Consultant for Structural Analysis*. Report no. STAN-CS-78-699, Computer Science Department, Stanford University, Stanford, CA

Bibel, W. and Jorrand, P. (eds.) (1986). *Fundamentals of Artificial Intelligence*. Lecture Notes in Computer Science 232. Berlin: Springer-Verlag

Black, P.K. and Eddy, W.F. (1985). *Models of Inexact Reasoning*. Technical Report no. 351, Department of Statistics, Carnegie-Mellon University, Pittsburgh, PA

Bobrow, D.G. and Stefik, M.J. (1983). *The LOOPS Manual*. Palo Alto, CA: Xerox Corporation

Bobrow, D.G. and Winograd, T. (1977). An overview of KRL, a knowledge representation language. *Cognitive Science*, **1**(1), 3–46

Bobrow, D.G., DeMichiel, L.G., Gabriel, R.P. *et al.* (1988). *COMMON LISP OBJECT SYSTEM Specification*. Palo Alto, CA: Xerox Corporation

Bonnet, A. (1985). *Artificial Intelligence, Promise and Performance*. Englewood Cliffs, NJ: Prentice-Hall

Boyer, R.S. and Moore, J. (1972). The sharing of structure in theorem-proving programs. In *Machine Intelligence 7* (Meltzer, B. and Michie, D., eds.). Edinburgh: Edinburgh University Press

Boyer, R.S. and Moore, J. (1988). *A Computational Logic-Handbook*. Boston, MA: Academic Press

Brachman, R.J. (1983). What IS-A is and isn't: an analysis of taxonomic links in semantic networks. *IEEE Computer,* **16** (10), 30–6

Brachman, R.J. and Levesque, H.J. (eds.) (1985). *Readings in Knowledge Representation*. Los Altos, CA: Morgan Kaufmann

Brachman, R.J. and Schmolze, J.G. (1985). An overview of the KL-ONE knowledge representation system. *Cognitive Science*, **9**(2), 171–216

Bratko, I. (1990). *PROLOG Programming for Artificial Intelligence* 2nd edn. Reading, MA: Addison-Wesley

Brooks, R.A. (1985). *Programming in COMMON LISP*. New York: John Wiley & Sons

Brough, D.R. and Alexander, I.F. (1986). The fossil expert system. *Expert Systems*, **3**, 76–83

Brownston, L., Farrell, R., Kant, E. and Martin, N. (1985). *Programming Expert Systems in OPS5: An Introduction to Rule-Based Programming*. Reading, MA: Addison-Wesley

Buchanan, B.G. and Duda, R.O. (1983). Principles of rule-based expert systems. *Advances in Computers*, **22**, 163–216

Buchanan, B.G. and Feigenbaum, E.A. (1978). DENDRAL and METADENDRAL: their applications dimension. *Artificial Intelligence*, **11**, 5–24

Buchanan, B.G. and Shortliffe, E.H. (1984). *Rule-Based Expert Systems: The MYCIN Experiments of the Stanford Heuristic Programming Project*. Reading, MA: Addison-Wesley

Buchanan, B.G., Sutherland, G.L. and Feigenbaum, E.A. (1969). HEURISTIC DENDRAL: a program for generating explanatory hypotheses in organic chemistry. In *Machine Intelligence 4* (Meltzer, B. and Michie, D., eds.). Edinburgh: Edinburgh University Press

Burks, A.W. (1960). *Collected Papers of Charles Sanders Peirce*. Cambridge, MA: Harvard University Press

Campbell, J.A. (1984). *Implementations of PROLOG*. Chichester: Ellis Horwood

Chang, C.L. and Lee, R.C.T. (1973). *Symbolic Logic and Mechanical Theorem Proving*. New York: Academic Press

Charniak, E. and McDermott, D. (1986). *Introduction to Artificial Intelligence*. Reading, MA: Addison-Wesley

Clancey, B.C. and Shortliffe, E.H. (eds.) (1984). *Readings in Medical Artificial Intelligence: The First Decade*. Reading, MA: Addison-Wesley

Clocksin, W.F. and Mellish, C.S. (1981). *Programming in PROLOG*. Berlin: Springer-Verlag

Cohen, P.R. (1985). *Heuristic Reasoning about Uncertainty: An Artificial Intelligence Approach*. London: Pitman

Cooper, G.F. (1984). *NESTOR*. Report HPP-84-48, Stanford University, Stanford, CA

Cooper, T.A. and Wogrin, N. (1988). *Rule-Based Programming with OPS5*. San Mateo, CA: Morgan Kaufmann

Dalen, D. van (1983). *Logic and Structure* 2nd edn. Berlin: Springer-Verlag

Davis, M. (1957). A computer program for Presburger's procedure. In *Summaries of Talks Presented at the Summer Institute for Symbolic Logic* 2nd edn. Institute for Defense Analysis

Davis, R. and Lenat, D.B. (1982). *Knowledge-Based Systems in Artificial Intelligence*. New York: McGraw-Hill

Deliyanni, A. and Kowalski, R.A. (1979). Logic and semantic networks. *Communications of the ACM*, **22**(3), 184–92

Dempster, A.P. (1967). Upper and lower probabilities induced by a multivalued mapping. *Annals of Mathematical Statistics*, **38**, 325–39

Dombal, F.T. de, Leaper, D.J., Staniland, J.R., McCann, A.P. and Horrocks, J.C. (1972). Computer-aided diagnosis of acute abdominal pain. *British Medical Journal*, **ii**, 9–13

Duda, R.O., Hart, P.E. and Nilsson, N.J. (1976). Subjective Bayesian methods for rule-based inference systems. *AFIPS Conference Proceedings of the 1976 National Computer Conference*, **45**, 1075–82

Duda, R.O., Gaschnig, J. and Hart, P.E. (1979). Model design in the PROSPECTOR consultant program for mineral exploration. In *Expert Systems in the Microelectronic Age* (Michie, D., ed.). Edinburgh: Edinburgh University Press

Eddy, W.F. and Pei, G.P. (1986). Structures of rule-based belief functions. *IBM Journal on Research and Development,* **30**(1), 93–101

Enderton, H.B. (1972). *A Mathematical*

Introduction to Logic. London: Academic Press

Ernst, G. and Newell, A. (1969). *GPS: A Case Study in Generality and Problem Solving*. New York: Academic Press

Fagan, L.M. (1980). *VM: Representing Time-Dependent Relations in a Clinical Setting*. PhD Thesis, Heuristic Programming Project, Stanford University, Stanford, CA

Fikes, R. and Kehler, T. (1985). The role of frame-based representation in reasoning. *Communications of the ACM*, **28**(9), 904–20

Findler, N.V. (ed.) (1979). *Associative Networks*. New York: Academic Press

Forgy, C.L. (1981). *OPS5 User's Manual*. Report no. CMU-CS-81-135, Department of Computer Science, Carnegie-Mellon University, Pittsburgh, PA

Forgy, C.L. (1982). Rete: a fast algorithm for the many pattern/many object matching problem. *Artificial Intelligence*, **19**, 17–37

Forgy, C.L. (1985). *The OPS83 User's Manual*. Pittsburgh, PA: Production System Technology

Froidevaux, C. and Kayser, D. (1988). Inheritance in semantic networks and default logic. In *Non-Standard Logics for Automated Reasoning* (Smets, P., Mamdani, E.H., Dubois, D. and Prade, H., eds.), pp. 179–212. London: Academic Press

Frost, R.A. (1986). *Introduction to Knowledge Base Systems*. London: Collins

Futatsugi, K., Goguen, J.A., Jouannaud, J.P. and Meseguer, J. (1985). Principles of OBJ2. In *Proceedings of the Symposium on Principles of Programming Languages*, pp. 52–66. New York: ACM

Gaag, L.C. van der (1988). *The Certainty Factor Model and Its Basis in Probability Theory*. Report no. CS-R8816, Centre for Mathematics and Computer Science, Amsterdam

Gaag, L.C. van der (1989). A conceptual model for inexact reasoning in rule-based systems. *International Journal of Approximate Reasoning*, **3**(3), 239–58

Gaag, L.C. van der (1990). *Probability-Based Models for Plausible Reasoning*, Dissertation, University of Amsterdam

Gallier, J.H. (1987). *Logic for Computer Science: Foundations of Automatic Theorem Proving*. New York: John Wiley & Sons

Genesereth, M.R. and Nilsson, N.J. (1987). *Logical Foundations of Artificial Intelligence*. Los Altos, CA: Morgan Kaufmann

Giarrantano, J. and Riley, G. (1989). *Expert Systems: Principles and Programming*. Boston, MA: PWS-Kent

Gordon, J. and Shortliffe, E.H. (1984). The Dempster–Shafer theory of evidence. In *Rule-Based Expert Systems: The MYCIN Experiments of the Stanford Heuristic Programming Project* (Buchanan, B.G. and Shortliffe, E.H., eds.). Reading, MA: Addison-Wesley

Gorry, G.A. and Barnett, G.O. (1968). Experience with a model of sequential diagnosis. *Computers and Biomedical Research*, **1**, 490–507

Green, C.C. (1969). Theorem proving by resolution as a basis for question-answering systems. In *Machine Intelligence 4* (Meltzer, B. and Michie, D., eds.). Edinburgh: Edinburgh University Press

Green, C.C. and Raphael, B. (1968). The use of theorem proving techniques in question-answering systems. *Proceedings of the 23rd National Conference of the ACM*, pp. 169–81

Guida, G. and Tasso, C. (1989). *Topics in Expert System Design*. Amsterdam: North-Holland

Guyton, A.C. (1976). *Textbook of Medical Physiology*. Philadelphia, PA: W.B. Saunders

Harmon, P. and King, D. (1985). *Expert Systems, Artificial Intelligence in Business*. New York: John Wiley & Sons

Hayes-Roth F., Waterman D.A. and Lenat, D.B. (1983). *Building Expert Systems*. Reading, MA: Addison-Wesley

Hendler, J.A. (ed.) (1988). *Expert Systems: the User Interface*. Norwood, NJ: Ablex Publishing Corporation

Ishizuka, H. (1983). Inference methods based on extended Dempster & Shafer's theory for problems with uncertainty/fuzziness. *New Generation Computing*, **1**, 159–68

Jackson, P. (1990). *Introduction to Expert Systems* 2nd edn. Wokingham: Addison-Wesley

Jensen, F.V., Andersen, S.K., Kjaerulff, U. and Andreassen, S. (1987). MUNIN — on the case for probabilities in medical expert systems: a practical exercise. In *AIME 87, Lecture Notes in Medical Informatics 33* (Fox, J., Fieschi, M. and Engelbrecht, R., eds.), pp. 149–60. Berlin: Springer-Verlag

Kahn, G.S. and Bauer, M. (1989). Prototyping: tools and motivations. In *Topics in Expert System Design* (Guida, G. and Tasso, C. eds.). Amsterdam: North-Holland

Kanal, L.N. and Lemmer, J.F. (eds.) (1986). *Uncertainty in Artificial Intelligence.* Amsterdam: North-Holland

Kanal, L.N., Levitt, T.S. and Lemmer, J.F. (1989). *Uncertainty in Artificial Intelligence 3.* Amsterdam: North-Holland

Kass, R. and Finin, T. (1988). The need for user models in generating expert systems explanations. *International Journal of Expert Systems*, **1**(4), 345–75

Kim, J.H. and Pearl, J. (1983). A computational model for causal and diagnostic reasoning in inference systems. *Proceedings of the 8th International Joint Conference on Artificial Intelligence*, pp. 190–93.

Kluźniak, F. and Szpakowicz, S. (1985). *PROLOG for Programmers*. New York: Academic Press

Kowalski, R. (1979). *Logic for Problem Solving*. New York: North-Holland

Kraft, A. (1984). XCON: an expert configuration system at Digital Equipment Corporation. In *The AI Business: The Commercial Uses of Artificial Intelligence* (Winston, P.H. and Prendergast, K.A., eds.). Cambridge, MA: MIT Press

Lauritzen, S.L. and Spiegelhalter, D.J. (1987). Local computations with probabilities on graphical structures and their application to expert systems (with discussion). *Journal of the Royal Statistical Society (Series B)*, **50**(2), 157–224

Lecot, K.G. (1986). *Inexact Reasoning in PROLOG-Based Expert Systems*. Report no. CSD-860053, University of California, Los Angeles, CA

Lemmer, J.F. and Kanal, L.N. (1988). *Uncertainty in Artificial Intelligence 2.* Amsterdam: North-Holland

Levesque, H.J. and Brachman, R.J. (1985). A fundamental tradeoff in knowledge representation and reasoning. In *Readings in Knowledge Representation* (Brachman, R.J. and Levesque, H.J., eds.). Los Altos, CA: Morgan Kaufmann

Lindsay, R.K., Buchanan, B.G., Feigenbaum, E.A. and Lederberg, J. (1980). *Applications of Artificial Intelligence in Organic Chemistry: The DENDRAL Project*. New York: McGraw-Hill

Lloyd, J.W. (1987). *Foundations of Logic Programming* 2nd edn. Berlin: Springer-Verlag

Loveland, D.W. (1978). *Automated Theorem Proving: A Logical Basis*. New York: North-Holland

Lucas, P.J.F. (1989). *Multiple Inheritance and Exceptions in Frame Systems*. Report no. CS-R8931, Centre for Mathematics and Computer Science, Amsterdam

Lucas, P.J.F., Segaar, R.W. and Janssens, A.R. (1989). HEPAR: an expert system for the diagnosis of disorders of the liver and biliary tract. *Liver*, **9**, 266–75

Luger, G.F. and Stubblefield, W.A. (1989). *Artificial Intelligence and the Design of Expert Systems*. Redwood City, CA: Benjamin/Cummings

McCarthy, J. (1978a). A micro-manual for LISP – not the whole truth. *ACM SIGPLAN Notices*, **13**(8), 215–16

McCarthy, J. (1978b). History of LISP. *ACM SIGPLAN Notices*, **13**(8), 217–23

McCune, W.W. (1989). *OTTER 1.0 Users' Guide*. Report ANN-88/44, Mathematics and Computer Science Division, Argonne National Laboratory, Argonne, IL

McDermott, D. (1982a). Non-monotonic logic II: non-monotonic modal theories. *Journal of the ACM*, **29**, 33–57

McDermott, D. and Doyle, J. (1980). Non-monotonic logic I. *Artificial Intelligence*, **13**, 41–72

McDermott, J. (1982b). R1: a rule-based configurer of computer systems. *Artificial Intelligence*, **19**, 39–88

McKeown, D.M., Harvey, W.A. and McDermott, J. (1985). Rule-based interpretation of aerial imagery. *IEEE Transactions on Pattern Analysis and Machine Intelligence*, **7**(5), 570–85

Melle, W. van (1979). A domain-independent production rule system for consultation programs. *Proceedings of the 6th International Joint Conference on Artificial Intelligence*, pp. 923–5

Melle, W. van (1980). *A Domain*

Independent System that Aids in Constructing Knowledge-based Consultation Programs. PhD dissertation. Report no. STAN-CS-80-820, Computer Science Department, Stanford University, Stanford, CA

Melle, W. van, Scott, A.C., Bennett, J.S. and Peairs, M. (1981). *The EMYCIN Manual*. Report no. STAN-CS-81-16, Computer Science Department, Stanford University, Stanford, CA

Miller, R.A., McNeil, M.A., Challinor, S.M. *et al.* (1986). The INTERNIST-I/Quick Medical Reference report. *West. Journal of Medicine*, **145**, 16–22

Miller, R.A., Pople, H.E. and Myers, J.D. (1982). INTERNIST-I, an experimental computer-based diagnostic consultant for general internal medicine. *New England Journal of Medicine*, **307**, 468–76

Minsky, M. (1975). A framework for representing knowledge. In *The Psychology of Computer Vision* (Winston, P.H., ed.). New York: McGraw-Hill

Moses, J. (1978). *The MACSYMA Primer*. Cambridge, MA: MathLab Group, Laboratory of Computer Science, Massachusetts Institute of Technology

Motta, E., Rajan, T. and Eisenstadt, M. (1989). A methodology and tools for knowledge acquisition in KEATS-2. In *Topics in Expert System Design* (Guida, G. and Tasso, C., eds.). Amsterdam: North-Holland

Neapolitan, R.E. (1990). *Probabilistic Reasoning in Expert Systems: Theory and Algorithms*. New York: John Wiley & Sons

Newell, A. (1973). Production systems: models for control structures. In *Visual Information Processing* (Chase, W.G., ed.). New York: Academic Press

Newell, A. and Simon, H.A. (1963). GPS, a program that simulates human thought. In *Computers and Thought* (Feigenbaum, E.A. and Feldman, J., eds.). New York: McGraw-Hill

Newell, A. and Simon, H.A. (1972). *Human Problem Solving*. Englewood Cliffs, NJ: Prentice-Hall

Newell, A., Shaw, J.C. and Simon, H.A. (1957). Empirical explorations with the Logic Theory Machine. *Proceedings of the Western Joint Computer Conference*, **15**, 218–39

Nilsson, M. (1984). The world's shortest PROLOG interpreter? In *Implementations of PROLOG* (Campbell, J.A., ed.). Chichester: Ellis Horwood

Nilsson, N.J. (1982). *Principles of Artificial Intelligence*. Berlin: Springer-Verlag

Patil, R., Szolovits, P. and Schwartz, W.B. (1982). Modeling knowledge of the patient in acid–base and electrolyte disorders. In *Artificial Intelligence in Medicine* (Szolovits, P., ed.). Boulder, CO: Westview Press

Pauker, S.G., Gorry, G.A., Kassirer, J. and Schwartz, W.B. (1976). Towards the simulation of clinical cognition . . . Taking a present illness by computer. *American Journal of Medicine*, **60**, 981–96

Pearl, J. (1988). *Probabilistic Reasoning in Intelligent Systems: Networks of Plausible Inference*. Palo Alto, CA: Morgan Kaufmann

Quillian, M.R. (1968). Semantic memory. In *Semantic Information Processing* (Minsky, M., ed.). Cambridge, MA: MIT Press

Reboh, R. (1981). *Knowledge Engineering Techniques and Tools in the PROSPECTOR Environment*. Technical Note 243, SRI International, Menlo Park, CA

Reiter, R. (1980). A logic for default reasoning. *Artificial Intelligence*, **13**, 81–132

Robinson, J.A. (1965). A machine-oriented logic based on the resolution principle. *Journal of the ACM*, **12**, 23–41

Robinson, J.A. (1979). *Logic: Form and Function. The Mechanization of Deductive Reasoning*. New York: North-Holland

Sammet, J.E. (1969). LISP 1.5. In *Programming Languages: History and Fundamentals* (Sammet, J.E., ed.). Englewood Cliffs, NJ: Prentice-Hall

Sauers, R. (1988). Controlling Expert Systems. In *Expert System Applications* (Bolc, L. and Coombs, M.J., eds.). Berlin: Springer-Verlag

Selz, O. (1922). *Zur Psychologie des produktiven Denkens und des Irrtums*. Bonn: Friedrich Cohen

Shafer, G. (1976). *A Mathematical Theory of Evidence*. Princeton, NJ: Princeton University Press

Shortliffe, E.H. (1976). *Computer-Based Medical Consultations: MYCIN*. New York: Elsevier

Shortliffe, E.H. and Buchanan, B.G. (1975).

A model of inexact reasoning in medicine. *Mathematical Biosciences*, **23**, 351–79

Siekmann, J. and Wrightson, G. (eds.) (1983a). *Automation of Reasoning 1. Classical Papers on Computational Logic 1957–1966*. Berlin: Springer-Verlag

Siekmann, J. and Wrightson, G. (eds.) (1983b). *Automation of Reasoning 2. Classical Papers on Computational Logic 1967–1970*. Berlin: Springer-Verlag

Slagle, J.R. (1965). Experiments with a deductive question-answering program. *Communications of the ACM*, **8**, 792–8

Smets, P., Mamdani, E.H., Dubois, D. and Prade, H. (1988). *Non-Standard Logics for Automated Reasoning*. London: Academic Press

Smith, R.G. and Baker, J.D. (1983). The DIPMETER ADVISOR system: a case study in commercial expert system development. *Proceedings of the 8th International Joint Conference on Artificial Intelligence*, pp. 122–9

Sowa, J.F. (1984). *Conceptual Structures: Information Processing in Mind and Machine*. Reading MA: Addison-Wesley

Steele, G.L. (1984). *COMMON LISP: The Language*. Burlington, MA: Digital Press

Stefik, M.J. (1979). An examination of a frame-structured representation system. *Proceedings of the 6th International Joint Conference on Artificial Intelligence*, pp. 845–52

Stefik, M.J. and Bobrow, D.G. (1984). Object-oriented programming: themes and variations. *The AI Magazine*, **2**(4), 40–62

Stefik, M.J., Bobrow, D.G. and Kahn, K.M. (1986). Integrating access-oriented programming into a multi-paradigm environment. *IEEE Software*, **3**(1), 10–18

Sterling, L. and Shapiro, E. (1986). *The Art of PROLOG: Advanced Programming Techniques*. Cambridge, MA: MIT Press

Swartout, W.R. (1983). XPLAIN: a system for creating and explaining expert system consulting programs. *Artificial Intelligence*, **21**, 285–325

Szolovits, P. (ed.) (1982). *Artificial Intelligence in Medicine*. Boulder, CO: Westview Press

Szolovits, P. and Pauker, S.G. (1978). Categorical and probabilistic reasoning in medical diagnosis. *Artificial Intelligence*, **11**, 115–44

Thayse, A. (1988). *From Standard Logic to Logic Programming*. Chichester: John Wiley & Sons

Touretzky, D.S. (1986). *The Mathematics of Inheritance Systems*. London: Pitman

Touretzky, D.S., Horty, J.F. and Thomason, R.H. (1987). A clash of intuitions: the current state of non-monotonic multiple inheritance systems. *Proceedings of the 10th International Joint Conference on Artificial Intelligence*, pp. 476–82

Vesonder, G.T., Stolfo, S.J., Zielinski, J.E., Miller, F.D. and Copp, D.H. (1983). ACE: an expert system for telephone cable maintenance. *Proceedings of the 8th International Joint Conference on Artificial Intelligence*, pp. 116–21

Waterman, D.A. and Hayes-Roth, F. (1978). *Pattern-directed Inference Systems*. New York: Academic Press

Weiner, J.L. (1980). Blah, a system which explains its reasoning. *Artificial Intelligence*, **15**, 19–48

Weiss, S., Kulikowski, C. and Safir, A. (1978). A model-based method for computer-aided medical decision making. *Artificial Intelligence*, **11**, 145–72

Winston, P.H. (1984). *Artificial Intelligence*. Reading, MA: Addison-Wesley

Winston, P.H. and Horn, B.K.P. (1989). *LISP* 3rd edn. Reading MA: Addison-Wesley

Wos, L., Overbeek, R., Lusk, E. and Boyle, J. (1984). *Automatic Reasoning: Introduction and Applications*. Englewood Cliffs, NJ: Prentice-Hall

Zadeh, L.A. (1975). Fuzzy logic and approximate reasoning. *Synthese*, **30**, 407–28

Zadeh, L.A. (1983). The role of fuzzy logic in the management of uncertainty in expert systems. *Fuzzy Sets & Systems*, **11**(3), 199–228

Zarri, G.P. (1984). Expert systems and information retrieval: an experiment in the domain of biographical data management. *International Journal of Man–Machine Studies*, **20**, 87–106

Index